THE ROUGH GUIDE TO

Southwest China

written and researched by

David Leffman

www.roughguides.com

Contents

Introduction to
Southwest China

Cut off by mountains from the eastern Chinese heartlands and the national capital in Beijing, Southwest China – the provinces of Sichuan, Chongqing, Yunnan, Guizhou and Guangxi – has always stood alone. With half of its borders butting up against neighbouring nations and its landmass reaching from a tropical coastline to the frosted peaks of the Tibetan Plateau, the Southwest's isolation has long preserved great stretches of wilderness and fostered unique cultures, from Dong with their drum towers and indigo jackets to yak-herding, plateau-dwelling Khampa Tibetans. Civilizations rose and fell here for over two thousand years before the thirteenth-century Mongol armies made the first serious attempts to bring the entire Southwest under centralized control. Initial resistance and revolts over the centuries that followed cemented the region's rugged image in the Chinese mind, with the Southwest as a romanticized frontier whose archaic customs, grand landscapes and wooden villages have somehow survived the frenetic modernizations sweeping the rest of the country.

Yet whether you're arriving from elsewhere in China or crossing one of the many international borders direct into the Southwest, the pace of change here is tangible. Modern skylines dominate the provincial capitals, motorbikes and tractors are replacing horses and buffalo, satellite dishes decorate remote homesteads, and youngsters are leaving the countryside to find work and wealth in the cities. New roads, rail lines and airports are bringing formerly remote outposts within relatively easy reach, encouraging visitors and heralding change. Travelling can still be an exhausting business, but it's an exciting time to explore: little-known backwaters can become much-hyped tourist stops almost overnight, while adventurous travellers can still get away from it all on epic bus rides to giant sinkholes, riotous festivals and national parks that weren't even mapped a decade ago.

ABOVE YANZIGOU, BELOW GONGGA SHAN, SICHUAN **OPPOSITE** RED-HAT SECT LAMA PLAYING A SHAWM

Where to go

There are dozens of entry points into Southwest China. You might overland from Laos or Vietnam, take a backroads route from Hunan or fly to one of the regional centres, with **Chengdu**, the enjoyable capital of vast **Sichuan** province, a popular first port of call, with its mellow teahouses and locally bred pandas. East are a string of low-key temples and a whole district of historic buildings at **Langzhong**, while quirky **Zigong** boasts salt mines and a dinosaur museum. Save energy for **Leshan**'s renowned Big Buddha, the largest such sculpture in the world, and the magnificent scenery and temples at the holy Buddhist mountain of **Emei Shan**.

In contrast, western Sichuan occupies the edge of the arid, mountainous Tibetan plateau, a region of yak pastures, backbreaking bus journeys, dusty monastery towns and the reek of butter tea. There are abundant opportunities for horse trekking at **Songpan**, **Langmusi** and **Tagong** – and stunning scenery at **Jiuzhaigou** – but the real attraction here is in simply hanging out among Khampa cowboys and monks. Don't miss hamlets around **Danba**, the incredible printing hall at **Dêgê**, or **Litang**'s August horse races – or the exhilarating bus ride from here into Yunnan.

To the east lies thin and largely rural **Chongqing**. Its capital, **Chongqing City**, is hot, polluted and overcrowded, but – for a few days at least – a strangely likeable place whose position on the Yangzi makes it a terminus for cruises east through the **Three Gorges** into the rest of China. Outside the city, the gem-like Buddhist rock art at **Dazu** provides glimpses of daily life in medieval China, while newly accessible sites along the

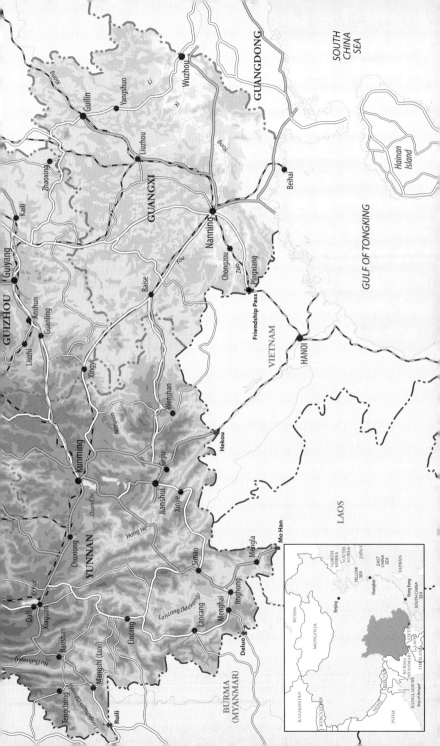

FACT FILE

• Covering 1.4 million square kilometres (equivalent to Germany, France and Italy combined), Southwest China occupies around 15% of China's **area**, with a **population** of over 246 million – about a fifth of the national total. Almost three-quarters are Han, with the remainder comprising over fifty minorities including Yi, Zhuang, Tibetans and Hui.

• China's **media** is tightly controlled: Facebook, YouTube and Twitter are often blocked, and in 2011 the government banned films and TV series featuring time travel, probably because they didn't want people imagining alternate – and possibly better – versions of history.

• China's main **religions** are Buddhism and Taoism, overlaid – especially in the Southwest – with local folk beliefs, alongside fair numbers of Christians and Muslims. The moral code of Confucianism is less a religion than part of the Chinese psyche.

• Southwest China's **geography** includes karst landforms, deep river valleys, high plateaus, mountain ranges and a few flat, fertile basins. The longest river is the Yangzi (6275km), and the highest peak is Gongga Shan (7556m) in western Sichuan.

• People plot all sorts of strategies to claim the honour of **paying restaurant bills** in China – pretending to nip off to the toilet while others are still eating is a good ruse.

Yangzi include massive limestone "bridges" at **Wulong** and an exciting whitewater ride on public ferries down the Little Three Gorges.

Jammed up against the borders with Tibet, Burma, Laos and Vietnam, **Yunnan** enjoys the Southwest's biggest mix of landscapes and peoples, and the most streamlined tourist industry. The easy-going capital, **Kunming**, has temples, parks, pagodas and the renowned Stone Forest; southeast, via classical Chinese gardens at **Jianshui**, are spectacular rice terraces around **Yuanyang**. For most, though, Yunnan's northwest exerts the greatest pull: there are the picturesque, heavily touristed towns of **Dali**, **Lijiang** and **Shangri-La** to explore, each with its own ethnic groups and cultures; forgotten old tea-horse-road staging posts like **Shaxi**; and superlative trekking through **Tiger Leaping Gorge**. There's less obvious appeal to Yunnan's far west – though the Burmese border town of **Ruili** has its surreal moments – but southerly **Xishuangbanna** offers more trekking and contact with ethnic minorities, this time in the jungles abutting Laos.

Guizhou is the southwest's poor cousin, full of ugly mining towns and rugged limestone landscapes. Central **Guiyang** is a hub for wider exploration, though there's an interesting route north into Sichuan from here via **Zunyi**'s Communist history and remote bamboo forests at **Chishui**. Southeast, you can hop on local buses through the **Qiandongnan** region via wooden Miao and Dong villages, lively markets and wild festivals; near the Hunan border, the beautiful old town of **Zhenyuan** sits below the cryptic Southern Great Wall, only recently discovered. Western Guizhou's highlights include incredible caves at **Longgong** and **Zhijin**, plus stone Bouyei villages around **Anshun**.

Less than a day by train from Hong Kong, **Guangxi** still feels undeveloped, though the fabled karst pinnacles flanking the **Li River** between **Guilin** and **Yangshuo** have been pulling in tourists for centuries, and there's easy access north from here to more rice

terracing at **Longji Titian** and Dong hamlets such as **Chengyang** along the Hunan-Guizhou border. The provincial capital, **Nanning**, sits far to the southwest near the Vietnamese border, where a string of unusual attractions includes rare monkeys, 2000-year-old cliff art and the enormous limestone sinkhole of **Dashiwei Tiankeng**.

When to go

Stretching from the coastal tropics to the Himalayan plateau, Southwest China's climate (see p.45) is extremely diverse. **Summers** (June–Aug) are stiflingly humid with torrential rains, especially in southern Guangxi, Xishuangbanna and Chongqing City (rated as one of China's "three summer furnaces"). Wet weather also causes landslides, leading to road closures in rural areas. Southern **winters** are moderate – it's the best time to appreciate Xishuangbanna's tropical climate – though Yunnan and Sichuan's Tibetan regions will likely be under snow between December and March. In bad years, snow can spread right through Guizhou (otherwise better known for its rain) as far south as Guangxi.

Broadly speaking, **spring** (April–May) and **autumn** (Sept–Nov) are the best times for a visit, when the weather is generally warm and dry throughout the region and the landscape looks its best. Note that for political reasons, Tibetan areas of Sichuan and Yunnan are **closed** through March (see p.64).

RARE WILDLIFE

Southwest China's wealth of habitats are the last refuge for some frighteningly rare **animals**. The most famous is the **giant panda**, which survives in pockets of high-altitude bamboo forests in western Sichuan. The world's highest-living primate, the golden or snub-nosed monkey, feeds on lichen and leaves in alpine forests through Yunnan and Guizhou, while the white-headed langur lives among Guangxi's tropical karst formations. Less-endangered species include **black-necked cranes**, mandarin ducks, lammergeyers and blue eared pheasants.

SPICY RIBS, RABBIT AND POTATOES, SICHUAN-STYLE

Author picks

In six months crisscrossing Southwest China, our author wore out two pairs of hiking shoes, learned to love butter tea and enjoyed his first sight of snub-nosed monkeys in the wild. He also found these out-of-the-way favourites.

Best ancient towns For an atmospheric overnight stay, try Langzhong (p.90) or less-touristed Zhongshan (p.160) or Nuodeng (p.206).

Heaviest night out Chengdu's *Music House* (p.76) is the place to indulge in – or observe – record-breaking whisky consumption.

Killer views Tolkienesque peaks from the top of Moon Hill (p.334) and Gongga Shan's distant snows from Emei Shan's summit (p.105).

Spiciest meal There are plenty to try, including Guizhou's *lazi ji* (with an equal volume of meat and chillies) and the infamous Sichuan hotpot, a bubbling broth into which you dip meat or veg.

Historic remains Ponder the soulful remnants of the Southern Great Wall (p.300), the forgotten city of Jinsha (p.69), and the Wulong Temple in Guizhou (p.306).

Oldest hotel The *Dujia Kezhan* in Langzhong (p.92), claims to have been in business since the tenth-century Tang dynasty.

Toughest trek The fifteen-day Kora Circuit around 6700m-high Kawa Karpo (Meili Xue Shan), Yunnan (p.244).

Our author recommendations don't end here. We've flagged up our favourite places – a perfectly sited hotel, an atmospheric café, a special restaurant – throughout the guide with the ★ symbol.

21

things not to miss

It's not possible to see everything that Southwest China has to offer in one trip – and we don't suggest you try. What follows, in no particular order, is a selective taste of the region's highlights, including beautiful beaches, outstanding national parks, fascinating wildlife encounters and unforgettable urban experiences. All highlights have a page reference to take you straight into the guide, where you can find out more.

1 JIUZHAIGOU AND HUANGLONG

Pages 117 & 118

These reserves in northern Sichuan hold dazzling strings of kingfisher-blue lakes, ponds and calcified waterfalls and stunning alpine peaks.

2 MARKET DAY

Page 290

Rural markets in Yunnan and Guizhou are great places to buy local handmade textiles and meet some of the southwest's many ethnic groups.

3 DALI

Page 206

The capital of the Bai ethnic group swarms with Chinese tour groups and Western backpackers, unwinding among the mountain and lake backdrops.

16 SICHUANESE FOOD
Page 61

Spike your tastebuds on this famously spicy cuisine, laced with a mouth-tingling combination of chillies and Sichuan peppercorns.

17 CRUISE DOWN THE YANGZI
Page 163

Encounter awesome scenery and a wealth of historic sights along the world's third-longest river.

18 TIBETAN MONASTERIES
Page 136, 134 & 238

The rambling monasteries at Dêgê, Ganzi and Shangri-La rear up like fortresses, their golden prayer wheels and russet walls stark against the blue Tibetan skies.

19 HORSE-TREKKING
Page 133

Spend a few days in the saddle among northern Sichuan's gorgeous alpine scenery at Songpan, Tagong or Langmusi.

20 BIG BUDDHA (DAFO) AT LESHAN
Page 99

Feel dwarfed by the world's largest Buddha carving, which gazes peacefully over a vicious stretch of rapids in Sichuan.

21 MEILI XUE SHAN
Page 243

Holy to Tibetans and a magnet for hikers, this snowcapped mountain sits astride one of the region's last great wilderness areas.

Itineraries

The following itineraries will take you right across the region, taking in less-visited sights as well as classic attractions, from small ethnic villages on the Guangxi border to Sichuan's busy historic towns and the heights of the Tibetan plateau. Given the scale of the region, don't worry if you can't complete the list – clocking up a handful will give you a feel for the themes.

PEOPLES

Half of China's 56 **ethnic groups** live in the Southwest, where they sometimes outnumber mainstream (Han) Chinese. You'd need a month to visit all these.

❶ Miao, Kaili Centred around Kaili in Guizhou, and famed for their spectacular, riotous festivals where women dress in splendid silver and embroidery assemblages. **See p.284**

❷ Dong, Chengyang Spend the night in wooden Dong villages on the Guangxi-Guizhou border, dotted with distinctive drum towers and shady wind-and-rain bridges. **See p.341**

❸ Dai, Jinghong Southern Yunnan's main ethnic group, similar to the Thais and especially known for their fun water-splashing festivities. **See p.256**

❹ Bai, Dali Their kingdom once stretched from Tibet to Cambodia, and still contains attractive, tourist-friendly Dali town and the villages surrounding the shores of nearby Er Hai. **See p.207**

❺ Naxi, Lijiang A once-powerful group who ruled half of northern Yunnan for 400 years from their rustic capital, home to one of China's most famous old towns. **See p.220**

❻ Yi, Xichang Nomadic, clannish and much feared hill-dwellers who used to raid their neighbours for slaves; they're now pacified and

settled around this prosperous city in Sichuan's remote south. **See p.106**

❼ Tibetans, Danba Hardy people whose dusty monastery towns, full of red-robed clergy and wild-eyed cowboys, are spread through western Sichuan and northern Yunnan. Danba is a good base for exploring pretty local hamlets. **See p.128**

EPIC EATING EXPERIENCES

Southwest China's cuisines tend to feature heavy doses of **chilli**: give yourself three weeks to track down the following – and a week on plain rice to recover afterwards.

❶ Qiguo in Jianshui Another local speciality: chicken slow-simmered with astringent medicinal herbs in a uniquely shaped casserole dish to keep in the flavours. **See p.197**

❷ Rice wine in Langde Shang Watch out for this potent firewater when visiting Miao homes – it's obligatory to down a few bowlfuls during local festivals. **See p.292**

❸ Gege in Wanzhou Break a Yangzi cruise to try this street snack of meat covered in chilli, Sichuan pepper and ground rice and steamed in a little bamboo basket. **See p.167**

❹ Hotpot in Chongqing Order plenty of cooling beer when tackling Southwest China's signature dish: meat, vegetables and noodles cooked fondue-style in boiling chilli stock. **See p.155**

❺ Mapo doufu in Chengdu Try this appetizingly spicy Sichuanese staple – tofu in chilli sauce – in the restaurant which claims to have invented it in the 1880s. **See p.73**

❻ Teahouse in Huanglong Relax in a riverside teahouse at this charming temple village, sipping a cup of local *zhu ye qing* tea. **See p.77**

❼ Butter tea in Songpan A staple of Tibetan life many find hard to stomach: industrial quantities of tea leaves, boiling water and yak butter with a little salt, churned until frothy. **See p.114**

SMALL TOWNS, BIG HISTORIES

China often seems all about **history**, and these now-unassuming places have unusually big pasts. Allow a month to tie them all together.

❶ Zunyi See the building where Mao ousted his Russian advisers in 1936 and began his forty-year grip on the country. **See p.279**

❷ Zigong Salt mines, dinosaurs and magnificent nineteenth-century guildhalls colour this once-important trading town. **See p.93**

❸ Langzhong Roam a cobbled maze of ancient wooden shops, hotels and restaurants surrounding the tomb of the famed third-century warrior Zhang Fei. **See p.90**

❹ Sanxingdui Visit the museum where remains of a previously unknown, 3000-year-old bronze-working civilization was discovered in the 1980s. **See p.78**

❺ Dêgê Gritty monastery town whose extraordinary scripture printing hall is one of the cornerstones of Tibetan culture. **See p.136**

❻ Yuhu Quiet village below magnificent, snowcapped Yulong Xue Shan, where botanist Joseph Rock lived in the 1930s. **See p.226**

❼ Shaxi Catch the lively Friday market at this picturesque Bai township, a staging post on the ancient tea-horse trail between China and Tibet. **See p.216**

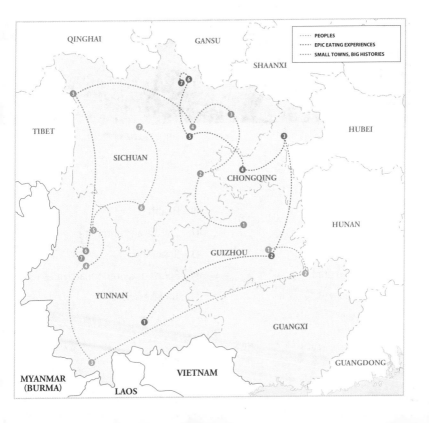

TRAFFIC INTERSECTION, CHENGDU

Basics

Getting there

China's busiest international gateways are **Beijing, Shanghai and Hong Kong**, from where it's easy to catch connecting flights, trains or even buses into Southwest China. It's also possible to fly from adjacent Southeast Asian countries direct to Chengdu and Kunming, and there are well-established overland routes into Southwest China from Vietnam, Laos, Thailand and – with restrictions – Burma (Myanmar).

Airfares are at their highest during the fortnight before Christmas, the fortnight before Chinese New Year (see p.39) and from mid-June to early October. The cheapest times to fly are in February (after Chinese New Year), May and November.

Stock operators such as STA, Trailfinders and Flight Centres are good places to get a feel for fares, before checking discount websites such as ⓦlastminute .com, and even airline websites themselves for special deals – and, often, a lot more flexibility with refunds and changing dates.

Flights from the UK and Ireland

You can fly direct from **London Heathrow** to Beijing (10hr), Shanghai (11hr) or Hong Kong (12hr) with Air China, Virgin Atlantic, British Airways, China Eastern and Cathay Pacific. Other airlines flying via a change of planes in a hub city include Aeroflot, Air France, BMI, Emirates, KLM, Lufthansa, Malaysian, Singapore and Thai. Flying to China from other UK airports or from the Republic of Ireland involves either catching a connecting flight to London or flying via the airline's hub city.

From the UK, the lowest available return **fares** to Beijing, or Shanghai start from £500 in low season or £800 in high season; flights to Hong Kong are slightly cheaper. The best deals are likely to be by finding a discount fare to Beijing or Shanghai, and a separate internal flight to the Southwest (see p.24); the same applies to travel via Hong Kong, as long as you don't fly into China from Hong Kong itself, but fly out of Shenzhen (see p.25).

Flights from the US and Canada

Hong Kong, Beijing and Shanghai are well served from the **US** and **Canada**, with Air Canada, Air China, Cathay Pacific, Continental, United, Northwest Airlines and China Eastern all offering direct flights. You can also fly with Japan Airlines and Korean Airlines via a change of planes in Tokyo or Seoul. It takes around thirteen hours' flying time to reach Beijing from the West Coast; add seven hours or more to this if you start from the East Coast.

Return **fares** to Hong Kong, Beijing and Shanghai are broadly comparable: in low season, expect to pay US$1400/CAN$1600 from the West Coast (Los Angeles, San Francisco, Vancouver), or US$1600/ CAN$1900 from the East Coast (New York, Montréal, Toronto). Expect to pay at least 25 percent more during high season.

Flights from Australia, New Zealand and South Africa

The closest entry point into China from **Australia** and **New Zealand** is Hong Kong, though from Australia you can also fly direct to Shanghai and Beijing. High-season **prices** for Australia and New Zealand are 30 percent higher than the minimum fares quoted below.

From eastern Australia, Air New Zealand, Cathay Pacific, China Eastern, Emirates, Qantas and Virgin Atlantic fly direct to Hong Kong or Shanghai (8hr; A$1200), or Beijing (10hr; A$1000). Again, Malaysian, Korean, Thai and Cathay can get you into China via stopovers. From Perth, fares to the above destinations are A$100 or so more expensive.

Flights from New Zealand are limited; the only direct flights are the Air New Zealand routes from Auckland to Shanghai and Hong Kong, which cost around NZ$1200, and the Air Singapore, Air New Zealand and Malaysian Airlines flights to Hong Kong (around NZ$1800).

From **South Africa**, South African Airlines have direct flights to Hong Kong (14hr), which cost around ZAR9000–11000 depending on the season.

Flights from Southeast Asia

Aside from the following direct services into Southwest China from **Southeast Asia**, you can also fly to Chengdu, Nanning and Guilin with other regional airlines, via stopovers inside China – though you might have to wait eight hours or more for connections.

From **Thailand**, Thai Airways flies from Bangkok to Chengdu (3hr 10min; THB14,000) and Kunming (2hr 15min; THB10,500). From **Laos**, Lao Airlines fly from Vientiane to Kunming (1hr 50min; US$290); there's also talk of a flight between Luang Prabang and Jinghong in the near future. From **Vietnam**, you can travel with Vietnam Airlines from Hanoi to

A BETTER KIND OF TRAVEL

At Rough Guides we are passionately committed to travel. We feel that travelling is the best way to understand the world we live in and the people we share it with – plus **tourism** has brought a great deal of benefit to developing economies around the world over the last few decades. But the growth in tourism has also damaged some places irreparably, and **climate change** is exacerbated by most forms of transport, especially flying. All Rough Guides' trips are carbon-offset, and every year we donate money to a variety of charities devoted to combating the effects of climate change.

Kunming (2hr; US$300); and from **Malaysia** with Malaysia Airlines, again to Kunming (3hr 30min; MYR850). Finally, Air China fly from **Yangon** in Burma to Kunming (3hr 30min; US$211).

Round-the-World tickets

If China is only one stop on a much longer journey, a Round-the-World ticket put together by an agent can have you touching down at a handful of cities around the globe. Southeast Asian capitals usually feature, as does Hong Kong, so you can arrange to land, for instance, in Vietnam and make your own way overland through Southwest China to pick up your next flight from Hong Kong. Off-the-shelf RTW tickets begin at around £800/US$1800; tailor-made versions will be more expensive.

AGENTS AND OPERATORS

Absolute Asia South Africa ☎ 076 802 1640, US ☎ 800 736 8187, ⓦ absoluteasia.com. Numerous 6- to 16-day luxury tours of China, including a "Yunnan Highlights", and trips to Guilin, Yangshuo and the Yangzi.

Adventure Center US ☎ 800 228 8747 or 510 654 1879, ⓦ adventure-center.com. Dozens of tours in China, including Southwest and Yunnan-specific trips, from a week-long whizz around highlights to extended hiking and biking expeditions.

Adventures Abroad US ☎ 800 665 3998 or 360 775 9926, ⓦ adventures-abroad.com. Small-group specialist "for the mature traveller", whose China-wide tours often touch on Yunnan; also offers 16- to 32-day packages roaming the Southwest.

Asian Pacific Adventures US ☎ 800 825 1680 or 818 886 5190, ⓦ asianpacificadventures.com. Tours focusing on Southwest China's often-overlooked rural corners and ethnic groups, especially in Guizhou and Yunnan.

Bike Asia China ☎ 0773 882 6521, ⓦ bikeasia.com. Long-standing, reliable operator based in Yangshuo in Southwest China, and offering 8- to 15-day bike expeditions through rural Guangxi, Guizhou and Yunnan.

Bike China China ☎ 1388 226 6575, ⓦ bikechina.com. Another experienced China-based company, with 5- to 14-day trips, mostly in Yunnan; some are extremely challenging.

Birdfinders UK ☎ 01258 839 066, ⓦ birdfinders.co.uk. Regular trips to find rare and endemic species, mostly in remote corners of Sichuan.

China Holidays UK ☎ 020 7487 2999, ⓦ chinaholidays.co.uk. Aside from mainstream packages to the Three Gorges and Guilin, they also offer ethnic tours in Guizhou, martial art study tours, and birdwatching trips in Sichuan.

CTS Horizons UK ☎ 020 7836 9911, ⓦ ctshorizons.com. The China Travel Service's UK branch, offering an extensive range of tours including Yangzi cruises and Yunnan-specific packages.

Exodus UK ☎ 020 8675 5550, ⓦ exodus.co.uk. Well-regarded overland package trips across China, including Guilin and the Yangzi.

Explore Worldwide UK ☎ 01252 760 000, ⓦ explore.co.uk. Big range of small-group tours and treks, including Tibet tours and trips along the Yangzi.

Focused Tours US ☎ 303 632 9255, ⓦ focusedtours.com. Regular small-group tours of Southwest China's karst landscapes, including colossal sinkholes in Guangxi and Chongqing.

Geographic Expeditions US ☎ 800 777 8183 or 415 922 0448, ⓦ geoex.com. Comfortable travel among the ethnic groups of Guizhou, Tibet, Yunnan and western Sichuan.

Imaginative Traveller UK ☎ 0845 287 2822, ⓦ imaginative -traveller.com. An emphasis on the unusual, with cycling tours, a panda trek in Sichuan and a Kunming–Kathmandu overland trip.

Intrepid Travel Australia ☎ 1300 364 512, UK ☎ 020 3147 7777, ⓦ intrepidtravel.com. Highly recommended, small-group tours with the emphasis on low-impact, cross-cultural contact; visits some fairly out-of-the-way corners of Southwest China.

Khampa Caravan China ☎ 0887 828 8648, ⓦ khampacaravan. com. Excellent operation specializing in overland trips in northwestern Yunnan (see p.238).

Mountain Travel Sobek US ☎ 888 831 7526, ⓦ mtsobek. com. Hiking and cultural tours in the Kham region of northwestern Yunnan.

North South Travel UK ☎ 01245 608 291, ⓦ northsouthtravel. co.uk. Friendly, competitive travel agency, offering discounted fares to Beijing and Hong Kong. Profits are used to support projects in the developing world, especially the promotion of sustainable tourism.

On the Go Tours UK ☎ 020 7371 1113, ⓦ onthegotours.com. Runs group and tailor-made tours to China, with a heavy emphasis on Guangxi's Guilin and Longsheng areas.

Pacific Delight Tours US ☎ 800 221 7179, ⓦ pacificdelighttours.com. City breaks, cruises along the Li and Yangzi

TRANSPORT FROM WITHIN CHINA

Flying from **Beijing** or **Shanghai** to one of the southwest's provincial capitals takes around three hours and costs ¥1500, much less through a Chinese online agent like ⓦelong.com (see p.29).

Flights into China from **Hong Kong** are extremely expensive; it's far cheaper to take a bus over the border to Shenzhen Airport (2hr; HK$100) and fly from there instead. Fares from Shenzhen to Guilin, Nanning or Guiyang (1hr; under ¥1000) are cheaper than those to Chongqing, Chengdu or Kunming (2hr 30min; ¥1500). Hong Kong agents such as CTS (ⓦctshk.com) can arrange everything for you, including China visas (see p.47).

Taking the **train** from arrival points is slower but also feasible. From **Beijing** or **Shanghai**, you're looking at from 28 hours to Guilin or Chengdu (¥250–800 depending on seat and train type) to two days to reach Kunming (¥320–900). From **Hong Kong**, you again need to first cross into China; catch the express to Guangzhou East train station (2hr 30min; HK$300), from where you can reach Nanning (12hr; ¥95–285), Kunming and Guiyang (24hr; ¥175–530), and Chengdu or Chongqing (35hr; ¥250–790).

Hong Kong is about the only place close enough to consider catching a **bus** into Southwest China; once more, you need to get to Shenzhen first. Your best bet here is to catch Hong Kong's MTR commuter train to **Lok Ma Chau** (HK$45), cross the Chinese border on foot, then catch a taxi (¥15–20) to Shenzhen's huge **Futian bus station** (深圳福田汽车站, **shēnzhèn fútián qìchēzhàn**). Buses run all over China from here, but the most useful destinations for those travelling in Southwest China are Guilin or Nanning (12hr; ¥180).

There is more information on transport in "Getting around" (see p.26).

rivers and a range of tours to western Yunnan.

Pepper Mountains China ⓦ peppermountains.com. Tailored treks and tours through the untouristed backblocks of Sichuan, looking for rare wildlife and ethnic groups.

STA Travel Australia ☎ 134 782, NZ ☎ 0800 474 400, South Africa ☎ 0861 781 781, UK ☎ 0871 2300 040, US ☎ 800 781 4040; ⓦ statravel.co.uk. Worldwide specialists in independent travel; also student IDs, and good discounts for students and under-26s. China options include 8- to 21-day tours, covering Beijing, Shanghai and the Yangzi and Li rivers, among others.

Trailfinders Australia ☎ 1300 780 212, Ireland ☎ 021 464 8800, UK ☎ 0845 054 6060; ⓦ trailfinders.com. Well-informed agent for independent travellers. Numerous China options on offer.

Travel CUTS Canada ☎ 800 667 2887, US ☎ 800 592 2887, ⓦ travelcuts.com. Canadian youth and student travel firm.

Travel Indochina Australia ☎ 1300 138 755, NZ ☎ 0800 750 507, UK ☎ 01865 268 940, US ☎ 866 892 9216; ⓦ travelindochina. com.au. Covers the obvious Southwest China sights, but goes a bit beyond them, too; also arranges cross-border visas for Thailand, Laos, Vietnam and Cambodia.

USIT Ireland ☎ 01 602 1906, Northern Ireland ☎ 028 9032 7111, ⓦ usit.ie. Ireland's main student and youth travel specialists.

Wild China US ☎ 888 902 8808, ⓦ wildchina.com. Small group tours to out-of-the-way places, such as minority villages in Guizhou and Yunnan, as well as hiking after pandas in Sichuan and footstepping nineteenth-century explorers in remote Yunnan.

World Expeditions Australia ☎ 02 8270 8400, Canada ☎ 613 241 2700, NZ ☎ 09 8545 9030, UK ☎ 020 8545 9030; ⓦ worldexpeditions.com. Offers cycling and hiking tours in rural areas, including Guangxi and Yunnan treks.

Overland into Southwest China

China has two open borders with **Vietnam**. Travelling via the **Friendship Pass** into Guangxi, you can catch **buses** direct to Nanning from Hanoi, Haiphong or Yalong Bay (8hr; $US23–26), or the twice-weekly Hanoi–Nanning **train** (12hr; US$30–40). You could also, of course, simply walk across and catch a bus to Nanning (p.356); this is also possible at **Hekou** in Yunnan, where onwards transport is available to Jianshui, Kunming and Xinjie (see p.200). Note that Chinese border officials at these crossings have been known to **confiscate** guidebooks to China, as they colour in Taiwan differently from the mainland, which is taken to indicate support for Taiwan's separatist cause – keep this book disguised and buried in your bags.

The crossing from **Laos** is via **Mo Han**, south of Jinghong in Yunnan's Xishuangbanna region. There's a daily **bus** all the way through from Luang Namtha to Jinghong (8hr; US$12), or you can do the same route on local buses, crossing the border on foot. Formalities are very relaxed and unlikely to cause any problems, though take some hard cash as there are no banking facilities at the border. A Kunming–Laos **train line** via Mo Han – due, eventually, to reach **Singapore** – is also in the pipeline, though the project keeps getting bogged down in politics; 2016 seems a likely completion date at present.

Another interesting overland route is by **boat** up the Mekong from **Chiang Saen in Thailand** to

THE TRANS-SIBERIAN

One of the most romantic ways to reach China is on the **Trans-Siberian Express** train from Moscow to Beijing. There are actually two routes: the **Trans-Manchurian** (6 days), which runs almost as far as the Sea of Japan before turning south through Dongbei (Manchuria) to Beijing; and the more scenic **Trans-Mongolian** (5 days), which passes Lake Baikal, Mongolian grasslands, northwestern China's desert and the Great Wall.

Trains are comfortable and clean: second-class compartments contain four berths, while first-class have two and a private shower. Meals are included while the train is in China. In Mongolia, the dining car accepts payment in Chinese and Mongolian currency; in Russia, US dollars or Russian roubles can be used. US dollars can be changed on the train throughout the journey. Bring backup snacks and that long novel you've always wanted to read.

With the trains' popularity (especially in summer) and the complexities involved organizing the necessary multiple visas, it's best to make bookings through a specialist agent. These also offer package tours, which can work out a fair deal too. For Moscow to Beijing, expect to pay around US$1300 for first class, or US$900 for second. **Recommended agents** include: Real Russia (ⓦrealrussia.co.uk), Monkey Business (ⓦmonkeyshrine.com), All Russia Travel Service (ⓦrusrailtravel.ru), Mircorp (ⓦmircorp.com), Regent Holidays (ⓦregent-holidays.co.uk) and Sundowners (ⓦsundownersoverland.com).

Finally, for detailed, up-to-date information on all ways to get tickets, check ⓦseat61.com/trans-siberian.htm.

Jinghong (7hr; $US100), which travels along the border with Laos. The only land border with **Burma** (Myanmar) open to Westerners is at Jiegao, near **Ruili** in Yunnan, but this crossing has to be organized through a specialist agent. At present the only open overland route from **Tibet** (see p.64) is aboard the **train** from Lhasa to Chengdu in Sichuan (45hr; ¥330–1100).

Note that you will need to have a **Chinese visa** before attempting to enter the country overland; these are not available at borders (see p.47).

Getting around

Southwest China's public transport is extensive and good value: you can fly to all provincial capitals and many cities, the rail network is useful, if not tremendously comprehensive, and you can reach the remotest corners on local buses. Sichuan and Yunnan's Tibetan regions are the sole areas where there are frequent restrictions on independent travel (see p.64).

However, **getting around** such a large, rugged region requires planning, patience and stamina. In particular, **public holidays** are rotten times to travel, as half China is on the move between family and workplace. The **Spring Festival** is notoriously bad: ticket prices rise (legally, by no more than fifteen percent, though often by up to fifty), bus- and train-

station crowds swell insanely, and even flights become scarce.

By rail

Southwest China's **rail network** is efficient and reliable, linking the regional capitals and often providing easy routes into otherwise remote regions. The Chinese government invests billions of yuan annually on the network, considering a healthy transport infrastructure essential to economic growth – and political cohesion. Recent years have seen some impressive developments: a rail line over the mountains to **Tibet**; the country's first ultra-fast **bullet trains**, which have cut travel times between Chengdu and Chongqing by two-thirds; and a new **high-speed** network linking Beijing and Shanghai to Chengdu and Kunming, due for completion around 2014.

Food, though expensive and ordinary, is always available on trains, either as polystyrene boxes of rice and stir-fries wheeled around along with snacks, or in a restaurant car. You can also buy snacks from vendors at train stations during the longer station stops.

Timetables and booking

Booths outside train stations sell **national train timetables** in book form and single sheets covering local services, which are often also printed on the back of city maps. These are all in Chinese only, and can be very complex (even

Chinese people have trouble with the books); it's much easier to check **online train schedules** in English at @travelchinaguide.com/china-trains.

Station ticket offices are almost all computerized, and while queues can tie you up for an hour or more of jostling, you'll generally get what you're after if you have some flexibility. At the counter, state your destination, the train number if possible, the day you'd like to travel, and the class you want, and have some alternatives handy. If you can't speak Chinese, get someone to write things down for you before setting out, as staff rarely speak English.

In cities, you'll also find downtown **advance purchase offices**, where you pay a small commission (around ¥5/ticket); it makes sense to try these places first as train stations are often located far from city centres.

Agents, such as hotel or hostel travel services, can book tickets for a commission of ¥40 or more each. You can also **book tickets online**, and have them delivered to your hotel door in major Chinese cities, through @travelchinaguide.com or @china highlights.com; you'll pay a surcharge of about 25 percent for this, though China Highlights **waives** this fee if you write an article for their website.

If you've bought a ticket but decide not to travel, you can get eighty percent of the fare **refunded** by returning the ticket to a ticket office at least six hours before departure. The process is called tuipiao (退票, **tuìpiào**) and there's sometimes a window especially for this at stations.

Once on the train, you can **upgrade any ticket** at the controller's booth, in the hard-seat carriage next to the restaurant car (usually #8), where you can sign up for beds or seats as they become available.

Tickets and classes

Tickets – always one way – show the date of travel and destination, along with the train number, carriage and seat or berth number. They become **available** up to twenty days in advance, though it can be as little as four. There are **four ticket classes**: soft sleeper, hard sleeper, soft seat and hard seat, not all necessarily available on each train. You can also buy an **unreserved ticket** (无座, **wúzuò**; literally "no seat"), which lets you board the hard-seat section of the train – though you might have to stand for the entire journey if you can't upgrade on board.

Sleepers

Soft sleeper (软卧, **ruǎnwò**) costs around the same as flying, and gets you a berth in a four-

person compartment with a soft mattress, fan, optional radio and a choice of Western- or Chinese-style toilets. You also get the first sitting in the dining car.

Hard sleeper (硬卧, **yìngwò**), about two-thirds the price of ruǎnwo, is the best value. Carriages are divided into twenty sets of three-tiered bunks; the lowest bunk is the largest, but costs more and gets used as communal seating during the day; the upper bunk is cheapest but headroom is minimal. Each set of six bunks has its own vacuum flask of **boiled water** (topped up from the urn at the end of each carriage) – bring your own mugs and tea. Every carriage also has a toilet and washbasin, which can become unsavoury. There are fairly spacious luggage racks, though make sure you chain your bags securely while you sleep.

In either sleeper class, on boarding the carriage you will have your ticket exchanged for a **metal tag** by the attendant. You'll be woken by the attendant and have the tag swapped back for your ticket (so you'll be able to get through the barrier at the station) half an hour before you arrive at your destination, whatever hour of the day or night this happens to be.

Seats

Soft seat (软座, **ruǎnzuò**) is widespread on services whose complete route takes less than a day. The prices compare with an express-bus fare, and the seats have plenty of legroom and are well padded. More common is **hard seat** (硬座, **yìngzuò**), which costs around half the soft-seat fare but is only recommended for relatively short journeys, as you'll be sitting on a padded three-person bench, with every available inch of floor space crammed with travellers who were unable to book a seat. You'll often be the focus of intense and unabashed speculation from peasants and labourers who can't afford to travel in better style.

Classes of train

Different **classes of train** each have their own code letters on timetables. **High-speed** services include the G-class, which travel up to 380km/h; then the 250km/h D-class; followed by Z-, T- and K-class trains, which can still reach 150–200km/h. These all have modern fittings with text tickers at the carriages' end scrolling through the temperature, arrival time at the next station and speed.

Ordinary trains (普通车, **pǔtōng chē**) have a number only and range from those with clean carriages and able to top 100km/h to ancient plodders with cigarette-burned linoleum floors and

SAMPLE TRAIN FARES

As there can be up to four prices for any one train, depending on seat or berth type, **rail fares** are not given through the guide. The fares below, for one-way travel, illustrate costs between Southwest China's provincial capitals, and should help to give an idea of the prices involved within the region. Note, however, that high-speed services will be more expensive.

	Hard seat	Hard sleeper	Soft sleeper
From Chengdu			
Chongqing	¥120	–	–
Nanning	¥215	¥595	¥925
Kunming	¥125	¥420	¥615
Guiyang	¥75	¥365	¥500
From Chongqing			
Nanning	¥145	¥440	¥750
Kunming	¥145	¥430	¥745
Guiyang	¥62	¥195	¥330
From Nanning			
Kunming	¥95	¥305	¥525
Guiyang	¥115	¥325	¥530
From Kunming			
Guiyang	¥95	¥265	¥530

grimy windows. A few busy, short-haul express services, such as the Nanning–Beihai train, have **double-decker carriages**.

Boarding the train

Get to the station with time to spare before departure. All luggage has to be **X-rayed** at the station entrance to check for dangerous goods such as firecrackers. You then need to work out **which platform** your train leaves from – most stations have electronic departure boards in Chinese, or you can show your ticket to station staff who will point you in the right direction. Passengers are not allowed onto the platform until the train is in and ready to leave, which leads to some mighty stampedes out of the crowded waiting rooms when the gates open. Carriages are **numbered** on the outside, and your ticket is checked by a guard as you board.

By bus and minibus

Buses and minibuses go everywhere that trains go, and well beyond, usually more frequently and occasionally faster. Finding the departure point isn't always easy though; even small places can have multiple bus stations, generally located on the side of town in which traffic is heading.

Bus stations open around 6am; in cities, the last departures might be at midnight; smaller rural depots tend to wind down mid-afternoon. **Timetables** – except electronic ones – can be ignored; ask station staff about schedules and frequencies, though they generally can't speak English; just point to the Chinese place-name characters given in the guide. Note that where we haven't given bus frequency for destinations in the guide, services are around every thirty minutes. **Tickets** are easy to buy: main station ticket offices are often computerized, queues are seldom bad, and – with the exception of backroad routes, which might only run every other day – you don't need to book in advance. In country towns, you sometimes buy tickets on board the bus. **Destinations** are displayed in Chinese characters on the vehicle windscreen. Take some **food** along, although buses usually pull up at inexpensive roadhouses at mealtimes. Only the most upmarket coaches have **toilets**; drivers stop every few hours or if asked to do so by passengers – although roadhouse toilets are some of the worst in the country.

Downsides to bus travel include drivers who spend the journey chatting on their mobile phone; frequent unscheduled stops and detours for food, fuel and passengers; and the fact that vehicles are obliged to use the horn before overtaking anything – **earplugs** are recommended. **Roadworks** are a near-certainty too, as highways are continually being repaired, upgraded or replaced; in 2010, a 100km-long jam on the Tibet–Beijing highway, blamed on roadworks, took nine days to clear. And it has to be said that some of the Southwest's roads are simply **terrifying**, negotiating hairpin bends high up on icy mountainsides; what makes these epics worth the ride are the landscapes and your fellow passengers – rugged Tibetan cowboys, monks and wind-scoured farmers.

Types of buses

There are various **types of buses**, though there's not always a choice available for particular routes and if there is, station staff will assume that as a foreigner you'll want the fastest, most comfortable and most expensive service.

Ordinary buses (普通车, pǔtōng chē) are cheap and basic, with lightly padded seats; they're never heated or air-conditioned, so dress accordingly. Seats can be cramped and luggage racks tiny; you'll have to put anything bulkier than a satchel on the roof or your lap, or beside the driver. They tend to stop off frequently, so don't count on an average speed of more than 30km/h.

Express buses (快车, kuài chē) are the most expensive and have good legroom, comfy seats that recline, air conditioning and video. Bulky luggage gets locked away in the belly of the bus, a fairly safe option.

Sleeper buses (卧铺车, wòpù chē) have cramped, basic bunks instead of seats, minimal luggage space – you'll need to chain your packs securely – and a poor safety record. Don't take them if anything else is available.

The final option is **minibuses** (小车, xiǎochē; or 包车, bāochē) seating up to twenty people, common on routes of less than 100km or so. They cost a little more than the same journey by ordinary bus, can be extremely cramped, and often circuit the departure point for ages until they have filled up. You usually pay the drivers directly for these, rather than buying a ticket from an office at the bus station, even If they use the bus station as a terminal.

Renting a vehicle

Driving a car across China is an appealing idea, but currently forbidden to foreign tourists (though foreign residents can take a driving test). The alternative is to **rent a taxi or minibus**, complete with driver, which averages ¥400 a day, negotiated in advance according to distance and your bargaining skills. You'll also be expected to provide meals and, if an overnight trip, accommodation for the driver. It's cheapest to approach drivers directly, though if you can't speak Chinese your accommodation should be able to help, and some tour operators run vehicles, too – and might include the services of an interpreter.

By plane

The main **Chinese airlines** are Air China (Ⓦairchina .com.cn), China Southern (Ⓦcs-air.com) and China Eastern (Ⓦce-air.com), which are overseen by **CAAC**, the Civil Aviation Administration of China. Flying is worth considering for long distances as prices compare with soft-sleeper train travel; planes are modern and well maintained and service is good.

Fares are based on one-way travel (so a return ticket is the price of two one-way tickets) and include all taxes. **Buying tickets** from local airlines offices or hotel desk tour agents is easy, and there seem to be enough flights to cope with demand. Agents shouldn't charge booking fees, and frequently give **substantial discounts** on advertised fares, especially if you book a day or two in advance. Competitive fares are also available **online** at Ⓦelong.net and Ⓦenglish.ctrip.com. You'll need to provide a phone number to confirm the booking and to book more than 24 hours in advance if using an overseas credit card.

Timetables are displayed at airline offices and agent desks, and often on the back of city maps; there's a handy **online schedule** at Ⓦfeeyo.com /enflight.htm.

ROAD RULES

The Chinese theoretically drive on the right although, like everything in China, **road rules** seem subject to negotiation and it's common to see vehicles running red lights, using pavements as short cuts, or simply driving on the left. **Size** is important: there's a pecking order, with lorries and buses at the top, cars in the middle, and cyclists and pedestrians below, terrorized by all. Driving licences are notoriously easy to obtain without passing a test, and drink-driving is a big problem; over 200 people a day are killed nationwide in traffic accidents. Be extremely careful when **crossing the road**, even at designated places with traffic lights.

Airlines frequently provide an **airport bus** running to and from the airport. As these can be 30km or more from city centres, it's worth finding out if a bus is available, if not already mentioned in this guide. Check-in time for all flights is two hours before departure, and though delays are routine it's advisable to arrive on time.

By ferry

There are a few opportunities to ride **public ferries** in Southwest China, including the exciting trip down the **Daning River** to the Yangzi (see p.170), and along the mighty **Yangzi** itself from Chongqing City, through the Three Gorges to Yichang (see p.162–174). You can also make a day-cruise down the **Li River** between Guilin and Yangshuo in Guangxi province, past a forest of pointy mountains (see p.325). If you're heading for the beaches of Hainan Island in the South China Sea, meanwhile, you can travel by boat from Beihai in Guangxi (see p.359).

By bicycle

China has the highest number of **bicycles** (自行车, zìxíngchē) of any country in the world, despite a rising trend towards mopeds, motorbikes and cars. Few cities have any hills and some have bike lanes; bikes are also extremely useful for exploring the countryside around places like Yangshuo, Dali and Lijiang. Dedicated individuals have even made long-distance trips right across Southwest China; agents offering **specialized bike tours** include Bike China (ⓦ bikechina.com), Bike Asia (ⓦ bikeasia.com) and Cycle China (ⓦ www.cyclechina.com).

Renting a bicycle

Bikes can be **rented** through hostels, touts in popular tourist areas or from city rental shops (often near train stations) for ¥5–15 a day, plus a **deposit** (¥200–400) and/or some form of ID. Most rentals are bog-standard black rattletraps – the really deluxe models feature working bells and brakes – though you can sometimes even find half-decent mountain bikes.

You are fully **liable** for anything that happens to the bike while it's in your care, so check brakes, tyre pressure and gears before renting. There are **repair shops** all over the place should you need a tyre patched or a chain fixed up (around ¥2). If the bike sustains any serious damage, it's up to the parties involved to sort out responsibility and payment on the spot. Always use a **bicycle chain or lock** – they're available everywhere – and in cities, leave your vehicle in one of the ubiquitous designated **parking areas**, where it will be guarded by an attendant for a small fee.

Buying and transporting a bike

Buying a bike is a sensible option if you're going to be based anywhere for a while. All department stores sell them: a heavy, unsophisticated machine will only set you back about ¥250; whereas a mountain bike will be upwards of ¥500. A **folding bike** (around ¥350) is a great idea, as you can cycle around all day and when you're tired, put it in the boot of a taxi; plus, you can take it from one destination to another on the bus.

You can also bring **your own bike** into China; international airlines usually insist that the front wheel is removed, deflated and strapped to the back, and that everything is thoroughly packaged. Chinese domestic airlines, trains and ferries all charge to carry bikes, and the ticketing and accompanying paperwork can be baffling. Where possible, it's easier to stick to long-distance buses and stow it for free on the roof or in the hold, no questions asked.

Tours

Local tour operators are listed through the guide, and offer excursions from city coach tours to river cruises and multi-day cross-country hikes or horse treks. These tours can be good value: travel, accommodation and food – usually plentiful and excellent – are generally included, as might be the services of an interpreter and guide. And in some cases, tours are the most practical way to see something worthwhile, saving endless bother organizing local transport and accommodation. In general, **foreign-owned operations** tend to give better service – or at least to understand better what Westerners want when they take a tour.

On the **downside**, there are disreputable companies who'll overcharge for mediocre services, foist unhelpful guides on you and spend three days on what could better be done in an afternoon. Bear in mind that many Chinese tour guides are badly paid, so supplement their income by taking tourists to souvenir shops where they'll receive commissions. Always make exhaustive advance enquiries about the tour, such as exactly what the price includes and the departure/return times, before handing any money over. **Tipping** tour guides is not expected in China.

City transport

All Chinese cities have some form of **public transit system**. Chongqing, Chengdu, Kunming and Nanning have (or are building) **light-rail** systems and underground **metros**; elsewhere, the **city bus** is the transport focus. These are cheap and run from around 6am to 9pm or later, and are usually slow and crowded.

Taxis are always available in larger towns and cities; main roads, transit points and tourist hotels are good places to find them. They either cost a fixed rate within certain limits – ¥6 seems normal – or about ¥8 to hire and then ¥1–3 per kilometre. You'll also find (motorized- or cycle-) **rickshaws** and **motorbike taxis** outside just about every bus and train station, whose highly erratic rates are set by advance bargaining.

Accommodation

Chinese hotel rooms generally follow the same functional design, irrespective of age or expense: a rectangular space with a bed, TV and bedside phone, and an en suite to the left or right of the entrance. But the range of establishments is increasing, from foreigner-friendly hostels to guesthouses in antique buildings, budget business accommodation, upmarket international chains and even trendy boutique-style hotels.
Price is a poor indicator of quality, with a good deal of overlap between the various places. The Chinese hospitality industry is on a steep learning curve, so new places are often vastly better than old ones.

Security in accommodation is reasonably good; if you lock valuables inside your bag before going out, you are unlikely to have problems (though passports and bank/credit cards are best kept with you at all times in a money belt).

ACCOMMODATION PRICES

Prices given in the guide are official, **rack rate figures**. Except in hostels (see p.33) these prices, and those displayed at hotel receptions, will usually be reduced after haggling, and most staff will expect some negotiation. You'll often get a third off, sometimes even more in low season. The prices given by booking websites (see below) usually include a significant discount.

Finding a room

Increasingly, **booking ahead** is a routine procedure, by phone, through accommodation websites, or by using a **dedicated booking website** such as eLong (Ⓦelong.net) or China Trip (Ⓦenglish.ctrip.com), both of which have English-language content and offer massive discounts on mid-range to upmarket hotel rates. These two don't require pre-payment for rooms, you simply reserve through the website and pay on arrival. Budget travellers should check out **hostel websites** such as Hostel Bookers (Ⓦhostel-bookers.com), or hostel organization websites (see p.33). Sometimes, the local CITS (see p.52) can also wrangle good discounts for you.

If you haven't booked ahead, time things so that you reach your destination in broad daylight, then deposit your bag at a left-luggage office at the train or bus station and check out possible accommodation options. New arrivals at city bus and train stations are often besieged by **touts** wanting to lead them to a hotel where they'll receive a commission for bringing guests in; these people are generally OK, but you do need to be very clear about how much you're willing to pay before being dragged all over town.

Be aware that **room rates** displayed at hotel receptions – and as printed in this guide – are almost always just the starting point in negotiations. Staff are generally open to bargaining and it's normal to get thirty percent off the advertised price, even more perhaps in low season or where there's plenty of competition. Always ask to **see the room** first. Rooms usually have either **twin beds** (双人房, **shuāngrén fáng**) or **single beds** (单人房, **dānrén fáng**), which often means "one double bed", rather than a small bed; some places also have triples or even quads.

If you find yourself being **turned away** by hotels, they probably haven't obtained **police permission**

临时住宿登记表
REGISTRATION FORM FOR TEMPORARY RESIDENCE
请用正楷填写 Please write in block letters

英文姓 Surname	英文名 First name	性别 Sex
中文姓名 Name in Chinese	国籍 Nationality	出生日期 Date of birth
证件种类 Type of certificate (eg "Passport")	证件号码 Certificate no.	签证种类 Type of visa
签证有效期 Valid date of visa	抵店日期 Date of arrival	离店日期 Date of departure
由何处来 From	交通工具 Carrier	往何处 To
永久地址 Permanent address		停留事由 Object of stay
职业 Occupation		
接待单位 Received by		房号 Room no.

to take foreigners, and would face substantial fines for doing so. The situation is dependent on the local authorities: foreigners are technically allowed to stay anywhere in Yunnan; but it's almost impossible to find an amenable hotel in parts of rural Guizhou. Being able to speak Chinese greatly improves your chances, as does being able to write your name in Chinese on the register (or having it printed out so the receptionist can do this for you) – in which case the authorities need never know that a foreigner stayed.

Checking in and out

Checking in involves filling in a form giving details of your name, age, date of birth, sex and address, places where you are coming from and going to, how many days you intend staying and your visa and passport numbers. Upmarket hotels have English versions, and might fill them in for you, but hotels unaccustomed to foreigners usually have them in Chinese only, and might never have seen a foreign passport before – which explains why hotel receptionists can panic when they see a foreigner walk in the door. We've included an example of this form in English and Chinese (see box, above) to help smooth difficulties.

You always **pay in advance**, including a **deposit**, which may amount to twice the price of the room. Assuming you haven't broken anything – make sure everything works properly when you check in – deposits are refunded; just don't lose the receipt.

In really cheap places, you won't get a **key** from reception; instead, you'll get a piece of paper that you take to the appropriate floor attendant who will give you a room card and open the door for you whenever you come in. If your room has a **telephone**, disconnect it to avoid being woken by prostitutes calling up through the night.

Check-out time is noon, though you can ask to keep the room until later for a proportion of the daily rate. Make sure you arrange this before check-out time, however, as staff may otherwise refuse to refund room deposits, claiming that you have overstayed. Conversely, if you have to leave very early in the morning (to catch transport, for instance), you may be unable to find staff to refund your deposit, and might also encounter locked front doors or compound gates. This is most of a problem in rural areas; often the receptionist sleeps behind the desk and can be woken up if you make enough noise.

Hotels

The different Chinese words for hotel are vague indicators of the status of the place. Sure signs of upmarket pretensions are **dajiudian** (大酒店, dà jiǔdiàn) which translates as "big wine shop" or, in the countryside, **shan zhuang** (山庄, shān zhuāng) or "mountain resort". **Binguan** (宾馆, bīnguǎn) and **fandian** (饭店, fàndiàn) are more general terms for hotel, covering everything from downmarket lodgings to smart new establishments; **guesthouses** (客栈, kèzhàn), **hostels** (招待所, zhāodàisuǒ) and **inns** (旅馆, lǚguǎn; or 旅舍, lǚshè) are reliably basic. Sometimes you'll simply see a sign for "**accommodation**"(住宿, zhùsù).

Whatever type of hotel you are staying in, there are two things you can rely on: one is a pair of plastic or paper **slippers**, which you use for walking to the bathroom, and the other is a **vacuum flask** of drinkable hot water that can be refilled any time by the floor attendant – though upmarket places tend to provide **electric kettles** instead. **Breakfast** is sometimes included in the price; nearly all hotels, even fairly grotty ones, will have a restaurant where at least a Chinese breakfast of buns, pickles and *congee* is served between 7 and 9am.

Upmarket

The provincial capitals and many popular tourist resorts have international-standard **upmarket** four- or five-star hotels. All the usual facilities are on offer – swimming pools, gyms and business centres – though the finer nuances of service will sometimes be lacking. **Rack rates** for standard doubles in these places are upwards of ¥900, with a fifteen-percent service charge on top; the use of credit cards is routine.

Even if you cannot afford to stay in one, upmarket hotels can be pleasant places to escape from the hubbub, and nobody in China blinks at the sight of a stray foreigner roaming around the foyer of a smart hotel. As well as air conditioning and clean toilets, you'll find cafés and bars (sometimes showing satellite TV), telephone and fax facilities and seven-days-a-week money changing (though this is usually only for guests).

Mid-range

Every town in China has at least one **mid-range** hotel. The quality of mid-range places is the hardest to predict from the price: an old establishment with cigarette-burned carpets, leaking bathrooms and grey bedsheets might charge the same as a sparkling new hotel next door; newer places are generally better. In remote parts, you should get a twin in a mid-range place for ¥150, but expect to pay at least ¥300 in any sizeable city.

There's been a recent explosion in **urban budget hotels** aimed at money-conscious businessmen, which offer small, clean double en suites with wi-fi or internet jacks right in city centres. Some places like Kunming and Chengdu have local brands, but **nationwide chains** include *7 Days Inn* (Ⓦ7daysinn. cn), *Home Inn* (Ⓦhomeinns.com) and *Motel 168* (Ⓦmotel168.com). At around ¥200 a double, they're a very good deal and need to be **booked in advance**

both because of their popularity and because you'll only get the cheapest rooms this way – prices are otherwise fixed. The English-language pages on their websites are rarely up to date, but staff at reception usually speak a little English if you call ahead.

Cheap hotels

Cheap hotels, with doubles costing less than ¥150, vary in quality from the dilapidated to the perfectly comfortable. In many cities, they're commonly located near the train or bus stations, though they may need persuading to take foreigners. Where they do, you'll notice that the Chinese routinely rent **beds** rather than rooms – doubling up with one or more strangers – as a means of saving money. Foreigners are seldom allowed to share rooms with Chinese people, but if there are three or four foreigners together it's often possible for them to share one big room; otherwise you might have to negotiate a price for the whole room.

Hostels and guesthouses

There's a rapidly expanding network of **youth hostels** (青年旅舍, qīngnián lǚshè) in Southwest China, many affiliated with the International Youth Hostel Association (IYHA). Contact details for individual hostels are given through the guide, and booking ahead is always advisable. Note that hostel **rates** are usually not negotiable, though you will sometimes get a discount if booking through an agency like Ⓦhostelbookers.com, or staying for a week or more.

Privately run **guesthouses** offer anything from hostel-style facilities in rural homes right up to moderate luxury inside restored antique mansions; you don't find them everywhere but they provide a welcome variety to the cookie-cutter uniformity of other accommodation choices. Prices for double rooms in these guesthouses are generally cheaper than in an equivalent hotel.

Youth hostel associations

The YHA China **website** isn't always up to speed, and there's sometimes better info and easier booking available through the international IYHA site or Ⓦhostelbookers.com. IYHA members get a ¥10 discount, and you can join at any hostel in China for ¥60.

CHINA AND INTERNATIONAL

YHA China Ⓦyhachina.com.
International Youth Hostel Association (IYHA) Ⓦhihostels. com.

US AND CANADA

Hostelling International–American Youth Hostels US
☎ 301 495 1240, W hiusa.org.
Hostelling International Canada Canada ☎ 800 663 5777,
W hihostels.ca.

UK AND IRELAND

Youth Hostel Association (YHA) UK ☎ 0800 019 1700, W yha.
org.uk.
Scottish Youth Hostel Association UK ☎ 0845 293 7373,
W syha.org.uk.
Irish Youth Hostel Association Ireland ☎ 01 830 4555,
W anoige.ie.
Hostelling International Northern Ireland Northern
Ireland ☎ 028 9032 4733, W hini.org.uk.

AUSTRALIA, NEW ZEALAND AND SOUTH AFRICA

Australian Youth Hostels Association Australia ☎ 02 9565
1699, W yha.com.au.
Youth Hostelling Association New Zealand New Zealand
☎ 0800 278 299 or 03 379 9970, W yha.co.nz.
Hostelling International South Africa South Africa ☎ 021
424 2511, W hisa.org.za.

Camping

Though there are no proper facilities for **camping** in Southwest China, you might get the opportunity to pitch a tent while hiking, biking or horse-trekking around remoter corners. It's becoming an accepted part of a "Wilderness Experience" among younger Chinese too, and major cities such as Chengdu and Kunming have **outdoor stores** selling designer fleeces, tents, backpacks, boots and other necessities.

If looking for a pitch yourself, you want to choose a spot far away from the prying eyes of thousands of local villagers. Don't bother trying to get **permission** for camping: this is the kind of activity that the Chinese authorities have no clear idea about, so if asked they will certainly answer "no".

Food and drink

While there are places in Southwestern China where food seemingly revolves around chillies and rice noodles, there are in fact a wide variety of local cooking styles, including regional Chinese, Tibetan, Thai and even Burmese. Western food is available too, at least in big cities and popular tourist destinations, and fresh ingredients are sold at every market

stall – though unless you're living long term in the country, there are few opportunities to cook for yourself. You'll need a comprehensive menu reader and useful phrases for ordering food and drink (see p.407).

Breakfast, snacks and street food

Breakfast is not usually a big event by Chinese standards: a bowl of *zhou* rice porridge (also known as *congee*) flavoured with pickles and eaten with plain buns, or *doujiang* (sweetened soya milk) accompanied by a fried dough stick. The one exception is in Guangxi, where you can sometimes find the **traditional Cantonese breakfast** of dim sum (also known as *yum cha*), involving a selection of tiny buns, dumplings and dishes served with tea.

Other **snacks and street food** are available through the day from stalls located around markets, train and bus stations. These serve **kebabs**, **spiced noodles**, baked **yams and potatoes**, boiled eggs, various steamed or stewed dishes dished up in earthenware **sandpots**, grilled corn and – especially in Sichuan – countless local treats known as *xiaochi*. Also common are steamed **buns**, which are either stuffed with meat or vegetables (**baozi**) or plain (**mantou**, literally "bald heads"). The buns originated in northern China but are now eaten everywhere, as are ravioli-like **jiaozi**, stuffed with a meat or vegetable filling and either fried or steamed; **shuijiao** are boiled *jiaozi* served in soup. Some restaurants specialize in *jiaozi*, offering a bewildering range of fillings and selling their wares by weight.

Eating out

The cheapest hole-in-the-wall **canteens** serve basic, filling food that costs a few yuan a plate and is often much better than you'd expect from the furnishings. Proper **restaurants** are usually bright, busy places whose preferred atmosphere is **renao**, or "hot and noisy", rather than the often quiet norm in the West. **Prices** at these places obviously vary a lot, but even expensive-looking establishments charge only ¥15–50 for a main dish, and servings tend to be generous. Restaurants are often divided up by floor, with the cheapest, most public area on the ground floor and more expensive private booths with waitress service upstairs.

While the cheaper places might have long hours, **restaurant opening times** are early and short: breakfast lasts from around 6–9am; lunch

SOUTHWESTERN COOKING

Southwestern cooking is one of China's four major regional styles. Although divided itself – local cuisines and specialities are described throughout the guide – its characteristic taste is **spicy and sour**, with pungent, constructed flavours favoured over natural ones.

Rice is the staple through most of the Southwest, eaten either plain boiled or as noodles – flat and wide in Guizhou, or in thin strands in Yunnan. It's replaced on the Tibetan Plateau by **wheat** buns or noodles and **barley**, ground to meal and mixed with tea as *tsampa*.

Chillies are perhaps the most important ingredient in regional cooking – a popular saying goes "No Chillies, No Food". Local varieties are short and, individually, not particularly hot; it's the quantity used in dishes such as Chongqing's *lazi ji* or the ubiquitous, fondue-like **hotpot** that makes food so spicy.

While **pork** is the default meat in much of China, Southwesterners consume an unusual quantity of **beef** and **mutton** as well, thanks partly to a substantial regional Muslim population. Muslims – or the Mongol armies they arrived with – also introduced **roast meats**; duck-roasting ovens can be seen outside restaurants throughout eastern Yunnan. You'll also encounter **game meats** – anything from deer to wild pheasant, rabbit and cane rats – in Guilin and, especially in Guizhou, **dog**.

Very unusually for China, **goat's cheese** and **yoghurt** are eaten in parts of Yunnan, mostly around Dali – again, the habit was probably imported by the Mongols.

Vegetables accompany every Chinese meal, used to balance tastes and textures of meat. There's usually a wide range on offer, from leafy greens to beans, crisp water chestnuts, mountain mushrooms, crunchy bamboo shoots, sweet potatoes and yams, and long white radishes.

Soya beans are a useful source of protein in a country where meat has often been a luxury. Beans are salted as a relish, fermented to produce **soy sauce**, or boiled and pressed to make white cakes of **tofu** (bean curd). Soft and flavourless fresh tofu is served with a chilli relish as a popular snack; it can be pressed further to create a firmer texture, fermented to create cheese-like **stinking tofu**, deep-fried until crisp or cooked in stock as a meat substitute. The **skin** that forms on top of the liquid while tofu is being made is itself skimmed off, dried, and used as a wrapping for spring rolls and the like.

The huge variety of **dried**, **salted** and **pickled** vegetables provides the region's characteristically sour flavours, but is also a useful way of preserving agricultural surplus in what is largely a poor rural region. Cool, high-altitude plateaus are especially good for **wind-drying** meats; **yak** jerky is sold in western Sichuan, while Yunnan **ham** is the finest in all China.

11am–2pm; and dinner from around 5–9pm, after which the staff will be yawning and sweeping the debris off the tables around your ankles.

Ordering and dining

Pointing is all that's required at street stalls and small restaurants, where the ingredients are displayed out front in buckets, bundles and cages; canteens usually have the fare laid out or will have the selection scrawled illegibly on strips of paper or a board hung on the wall. You either tell the cook directly what you want or buy **chits** from a cashier, which you exchange at the kitchen hatch for your food and sit down at large communal tables or benches.

When you enter a proper restaurant you'll be escorted to a chair and promptly given a pot of tea, along with pickles and nuts in upmarket places. The only **tableware** provided is a spoon, a bowl and a pair of chopsticks. Unless you're in a big tourist destination, **menus** will be Chinese-only and the restaurant staff are unlikely to speak English, though fortunately there's a growing trend in **photo-menus** – some regional Chinese dishes have such obscure names that even non-local Chinese have no idea what they are. Alternatively, have a look at what other diners are eating – the Chinese are often delighted that a foreigner wants to eat Chinese food, and will indicate the best food on their table.

If this fails, you might be escorted through to the kitchen to make your choice by **pointing** at the raw ingredients. You need to get the idea across if you want different items cooked together, otherwise you might end up with separate plates of nuts, meat and vegetables when you thought you'd ordered a single dish of chicken with cashews and green peppers. Unless you're specific about how you want your food prepared, it inevitably arrives stir-fried.

MEDICINAL COOKING

There's no boundary in Chinese cooking between food and **medicine**, as in Traditional Chinese Medicine (TCM) everything you eat or drink is believed to affect your health. This means that even ordinary dishes can be looked at in a medicinal way: chicken and beef, for example, are "warming" – they add yang energy to your system – while seafood such as crab is yin or "cooling". Along with specific **medicinal herbs**, culinary spices such as ginger, cinnamon, garlic, chillies and tangerine peel all have medicinal uses, too, which means that – if you know what your ailment is in TCM terms – you can actually create dishes to restore your health. Sadly, however, while there are abundant cookbooks based around medicinal cookery, there are few restaurants in China specializing in the idea.

When **ordering**, unless eating a one-dish meal like Beijing duck or a hotpot, try to select items with a range of tastes and textures; it's also usual to include a soup. In cheap places, servings of noodles or rice are huge, but as they are considered basic stomach fillers, quantities decline the more upmarket you go. Note that dishes such as *jiaozi* and some seafood are sold by **weight**: a liang (两, **liǎng**) is 50g, a banjin (半斤, **bàn jīn**) 250g, a jin (斤, **jīn**) 500g, and a gongjin (公斤, **gōngjīn**) 1kg.

Dishes are all **served** at once, placed in the middle of the table for diners to share. With some poultry dishes you can crunch up the smaller bones, but anything else is spat out onto the tablecloth or floor, more or less discreetly depending on the establishment – watch what others are doing. **Soups** tend to be bland and are consumed last to wash the meal down, the liquid slurped from a spoon or the bowl once the noodles, vegetables or meat in it have been picked out and eaten. **Desserts** aren't a regular feature in China, though sweet soups and buns are eaten (the latter not confined to main meals), particularly at festive occasions.

Resting your chopsticks together across the top of your bowl means that you've finished eating. After a meal, the Chinese don't hang around to talk over drinks as in the West, but get up straight away and leave. In canteens, you'll **pay** up front, while at restaurants you ask for the **bill** and pay either the waiter or at the front till. **Tipping** is not expected.

Western food

Western food is most readily available in cities with large expat populations, such as Chengdu and Kunming, and popular tourist destinations like Dali, Lijiang and Yangshuo. Here you'll find foreign-owned **cafés and bars** serving pub-style pasta, steak and pizza dishes, along with generic Chinese food, coffee and cakes, at relatively steep prices. Elsewhere, all cities have a Chinese-brand **Western-style café** or two, often in upmarket hotels; coffee at these places is usually freshly brewed and good, but the food is variable. Some hotel restaurants also offer expensive but huge **buffet breakfasts** of scrambled egg, bacon, toast, cereal and coffee. You'll find Western **fast-food chains** such as *McDonald's*, *KFC* and *Pizza Hut*, alongside domestic versions like *Dicos*, in all provincial capitals and many larger towns.

Self-catering

Self catering for tourists is feasible to a point; some youth hostels have **kitchens** you can use, but normally things are more limited. **Instant noodles** are a favourite travel food with the Chinese, available anywhere – just add boiling water, leave for five minutes, then stir in the flavourings supplied. **Fresh fruit and veg** from markets needs to be washed and peeled before eating raw; you can supplement things with **dried fruit**, nuts and seeds, roast and cured **meats**, **biscuits** and all manner of **snacks**.

In cities, these things are also sold in more hygienic situations in **supermarkets**, usually located in the basements of major shopping centres; some provincial capitals also have branches of the international chain **Carrefour** (家乐福, **jiālèfú**), where you can find small caches of Western foods.

Do-it-yourself **barbecues** are becoming popular at suitable outdoor venues and tourist sights; outdoor shops and supermarkets sell one-use barbecue sets complete with tray, charcoal and tongs – just buy meat, veg and matches.

Drink

Water is easily available in China, but never drink what comes out of the tap. **Boiled water** is always on hand in hotels and trains, either provided in large vacuum flasks or an urn, and you can buy **bottled spring water** at station stalls and supermarkets.

VEGETARIAN FOOD

Though Chinese meals anyway tend to feature a far greater quantity of vegetables than meat, **vegetarianism** has been practised for almost two thousand years in China for both health and philosophical reasons. The cooking takes several forms: **plain vegetable dishes**, served at home or in ordinary restaurants; **imitation meat dishes** which use gluten, bean curd and potato to mimic the natural attributes of meat, fowl and fish, and are still called by their usual name, such as honey pork; and **Buddhist cooking**, which often avoids onions, ginger, garlic and other spices considered stimulating.

Having said this, vegetarians visiting China will find their options limited. The Chinese believe that vegetables lack any physically fortifying properties, and strict vegetarian diets are unusual; cooking fat and stocks in the average dining room will also be of animal origins. In addition, there's a stigma of poverty attached to not eating meat, and as a foreigner no one will understand why you don't want meat when you could clearly afford to gorge yourself on a regular basis. Major temples – such as Chengdu's Wenshu Yuan (see p.66) – often have vegetarian restaurants attached; elsewhere, to be sure that you aren't being served anything of animal origin, tell your waiter that you are a **Buddhist** (see p.408).

Tea

Tea has been drunk in China since antiquity; over the centuries a whole social culture has sprung up around this beverage, spawning **teahouses** that once held the same place in Chinese society that the local pub or bar does in the West (see p.66). Plantations of neat rows of dark tea bushes adorn hillsides across Southwestern China, while the brew is enthusiastically consumed, from the highlands of Tibet – where it's mixed with barley meal and butter – to every restaurant and household between Hong Kong and Beijing.

Often the first thing you'll be asked in a restaurant is *he shenme cha* – "what sort of tea would you like?" Chinese tea comes in red, green and flower-scented **varieties**, depending on how it's processed. Some, such as *pu'er* from Yunnan, Fujian's *tie guanyin*, Zhejiang's *longjing* or Sichuan's *zhuye qing*, are highly sought after; indeed, after locals in Yunnan decided that banks weren't paying enough interest, they started investing in *pu'er* tea stocks, causing prices to soar.

The manner in which it's **served** also varies from place to place: sometimes it comes in huge mugs with a lid, elsewhere in glass tumblers or dainty cups served from a miniature pot. When drinking in company, it's polite to top up others' cups before your own; if someone does this for you, lightly tap your first two fingers on the table to show your thanks. If you've had enough, leave your cup full; in a restaurant take the lid off or turn it over if you want the pot refilled during the meal.

Recently, **Taiwanese bubble tea** – with milk, sugar and sago balls, and usually called simply "**milk tea**" (奶茶, **nǎi chá**) – has become popular, especially served cold in the summer. It's also worth trying some Muslim **Eight Treasures Tea** (八宝茶, **bābǎo chá**) which involves dried fruit, nuts, seeds and crystallized sugar heaped into a cup with the remaining space filled with hot water, poured with panache from an immensely long-spouted copper kettle.

Alcohol

The popularity of **beer** in China rivals that of tea, and, for men, is the preferred mealtime beverage (drinking alcohol in public is considered improper for Chinese women, though not for foreigners). Germans set up China's first brewery in the northeastern port of **Qingdao** during the nineteenth century, and now almost every city produces a local brand of four-percent Pilsner. Sold in litre bottles, it's always drinkable, often pretty good, and is cheaper than bottled water. **Draught beer** is becoming available across the country.

Watch out for the term "**wine**" on English menus, which usually denotes **spirits**, made from rice, sorghum or millet. Serving spirits to guests is a sign of hospitality, and they're always used for toasting at banquets. Home-brewed **rice wine** is on hand in much of rural Guizhou and Guangxi, and can be surprisingly drinkable (and potent); mainstream **grain spirits** – especially the expensive, nationally famous Moutai and Wuliangye – are extremely strong and pretty vile to the Western palate. **Imported** spirits are sold in large department stores and in city bars, but are always expensive.

China does have several commercial **vineyards**, the best of which is Changyu from Yantai in Shandong province, whose product you'll find across China. There are ongoing efforts to launch wine as a stylish niche product, with limited success so far.

Western-style bars are found in provincial capitals and tourist destinations. They serve local and imported beers and spirits, and are popular with China's middle class as well as foreigners. Mostly, though, the Chinese drink alcohol only with their meals – all restaurants serve at least local beer and spirits.

Soft drinks

Canned drinks, usually sold unchilled, include various lemonades and colas. **Fruit juices** can be unusual and refreshing, flavoured with chunks of lychee, lotus and water chestnuts; southern Yunnan is especially good for freshly squeezed juice bars. **Coffee** is grown and drunk in Yunnan, and instant coffee powder can be found in any supermarket. **Milk** is sold in powder form as baby food, and increasingly in bottles for adult consumption as its benefits for invalids and the elderly become accepted wisdom – though a recent spate of child deaths traced to melamine-contaminated milk have seen sales plummet since 2010.

The media

Xinhua is the state-run news agency that supplies the national print and TV media. All content is Party-controlled and censored, though there is a limited openness about social issues and natural disasters as long as the government is portrayed as successfully combating the problem. Stories about corrupt local officials, armed uprisings by peasants being forced off their land, or the appalling conditions of coal-mine workers do occasionally get through the net, though both journalists and editors take a risk reporting such things: several doing so have been jailed for "revealing state secrets", or even beaten to death by the thugs they were trying to expose.

Newspapers and magazines

The national Chinese-language newspaper is the **People's Daily** (with an online English edition at ⓦ english.peopledaily.com.cn), though all provincial capitals and many major cities produce their own dailies with a local slant. The only national English-language newspaper is the **China Daily** (ⓦ chinadaily .com.cn), which is scarce outside big cities; full of Party-approved success stories, it also features interesting cultural and social articles too.

Kunming, Chengdu and Chongqing have much livelier free **English-language magazines** aimed at

expats – listed through the guide – containing listings of local venues and events, plus classifieds and feature articles; they're monitored by the authorities, though this doesn't stop them sailing quite close to the wind at times.

Television

Chinese television comprises a dozen or more channels run by the state television company, **CCTV**, plus a host of regional stations; not all channels are available across the country. The content features news, flirty game shows, travel and wildlife documentaries, soaps and historical dramas, and bizarre song-and-dance extravaganzas; it's all extremely repetitive and after a night or two you've probably experienced everything it has to offer. Tune in to **CCTV 1** for news; **CCTV 5** is dedicated to sport; **CCTV 6** shows films (with at least one war feature a day, in which the Japanese get mightily beaten); **CCTV News** broadcasts an English-language mix of news, documentaries and travel shows; while **CCTV 11** concentrates on Chinese opera. The regional stations are sometimes more adventurous, with a current trend for frank dating games, which draw much criticism from conservative-minded government factions for the rampant materialism displayed by the contestants.

Radio

Radio isn't a big part of Chinese life, and has a tough time competing with TV and the net. There are plenty of **stations** though, where you can pick up everything from Western and Chinese classical music to soft pop ballads, punk and chat shows.

For **news from home**, you'll need to bring a shortwave radio with you or listen online to the **BBC World Service** (ⓦ bbc.co.uk/worldservice), **Radio Canada** (ⓦ rcinet.ca), the **Voice of America** (ⓦ voa.gov) and **Radio Australia** (ⓦ abc.net.au/ra). None of these are currently censored, though there might be occasional clampdowns depending on internal events in China.

Festivals

China celebrates many secular and religious festivals, three of which – the Spring Festival (Chinese New Year), the May 1 Labour Day and National Day on October 1 – involve nationwide holidays.

SPRING FESTIVAL (CHINESE NEW YEAR)

The **Spring Festival** is two weeks of festivities marking the beginning of the lunar New Year, usually in late January or early February. In Chinese astrology, each year is associated with one of **twelve zodiac animals**, and the passing into a new phase is a momentous occasion. The festival sees China at its most colourful, with shops and houses decorated with good-luck messages.

The first day of the festival is marked by a **family feast** at which *jiaozi* (dumplings) are eaten, sometimes with coins hidden inside. To bring luck, people **dress in red clothes** (red being a lucky colour) and eat **fish**, since the Chinese script for fish resembles the script for "surplus", something everyone wishes to enjoy during the year. **Firecrackers** are let off almost constantly to scare ghosts away and, on the fifth day, to honour Cai Shen, god of wealth. Another ghost-scaring tradition is the pasting up of images of door gods at the threshold.

Outside the home, New Year is celebrated at **temple fairs**, which feature acrobats and clouds of smoke as the Chinese light incense sticks to placate the gods. The celebrations end with the **lantern festival**, when the streets are filled with multicoloured paper lanterns; many places also have flower festivals and street processions with paper dragons and other animals parading through the town. It's customary at this time to eat **tang yuan**, glutinous rice balls stuffed with sweet sesame paste.

Avoid travel during these times, as the country's transport network becomes severely overloaded.

Most festival dates are set by the **Chinese lunar calendar**, in which the first day of the month is the time when the moon is at its thinnest, with the full moon marking the middle of the month. By the West's Gregorian calendar, such festivals fall on a **different day** every year – check online for the latest dates. Most festivals celebrate the turning of the seasons or auspicious dates, such as the eighth day of the eighth month (eight is a lucky number in China), and are times for gift giving, family reunions, feasting and setting of firecrackers. It's always worth visiting temples on festival days, when the air is thick with incense, and people queue up to kowtow to altars and play games that bring good fortune, such as trying to hit the temple bell by throwing coins.

Aside from the following national festivals, Southwest China's **ethnic groups** punctuate the year with their own ritual observances, which are described in the relevant chapters of the guide – they're also listed under "festivals" in our index.

A HOLIDAYS AND FESTIVALS CALENDAR

January/February: Spring Festival Everything shuts down for a national holiday during the first three days of this two-week festival (see box, above).

February: Tiancang Festival On the twentieth day of the first lunar month, Chinese peasants celebrate Tiancang, or Granary Filling Day, in the hope of ensuring a good harvest later in the year.

March: Guanyin's Birthday Guanyin, the Bodhisattva of Mercy, and probably China's most popular deity, is celebrated on the nineteenth day of the second lunar month.

April 5: Qingming Festival Also referred to as Tomb Sweeping Day, this is the time to visit the graves of ancestors and burn ghost money in honour of the departed.

May 1: Labour Day A national holiday when everyone has a break, taking a few days off work either side.

May 4: Youth Day Commemorating the student demonstrators in Tian'anmen Square in 1919, which gave rise to the Nationalist "May Fourth Movement". It's marked in most cities with flower displays.

June 1: Children's Day Most schools go on field trips, so if you're visiting a popular tourist site, be prepared for mobs of kids in yellow baseball caps.

June/July: Dragonboat Festival On the fifth day of the fifth lunar month, dragonboat races are held in memory of the poet Qu Yuan, who drowned himself in 280 BC. The traditional food to accompany the celebrations is *zongzi* (lotus-wrapped rice packets). Another national holiday.

August/September: Ghost Festival The Chinese equivalent of Halloween, when ghosts from hell are supposed to walk the earth. It's not celebrated so much as observed; it's regarded as an inauspicious time to travel, move house or get married.

September/October: Moon Festival On the fifteenth day of the eighth month of the lunar calendar, the Chinese celebrate what's also known as the Mid-Autumn Festival. Moon cakes, containing a rich filling of sugar, lotus-seed paste and walnuts, are eaten, and plenty of spirits consumed. The public get a further day off.

September/October: Double Ninth Festival Nine is a number associated with yang, or male energy, and on the ninth day of the ninth lunar month such qualities as assertiveness and strength are celebrated. It's believed to be a good time for the distillation (and consumption) of spirits.

September 28: Confucius Festival The birthday of Confucius is marked by celebrations at all Confucian temples.

October 1: National Day Another three-day holiday when everyone celebrates the founding of the People's Republic. TV is even more dire than usual as it's full of programmes celebrating Party achievements.

December 25: Christmas This is marked as a religious event only by the faithful, but for everyone else it's an excuse for a feast and a party.

Health

No vaccinations are required to visit China, except for yellow fever if you're coming from an area where the disease is endemic. It's worth taking a first-aid kit with you, particularly if you will be travelling extensively outside the cities, where getting hold of the appropriate medicines might be difficult. Include bandages, plasters, painkillers, oral rehydration solution, medication to counter diarrhoea, vitamin pills and antiseptic cream. A sterile set of hypodermics may be advisable, as re-use of hypodermics does occur in China. Note there is general ignorance of sexual health issues, and AIDS and STDs are widespread – always practise safe sex.

The most common health hazard in China is the **cold and flu infections** that strike down a large proportion of the population in the winter months. **Diarrhoea** is also common, usually in a mild form while your stomach gets used to unfamiliar food, but also sometimes with a sudden onset accompanied by stomach cramps and vomiting, which indicates food poisoning. In both instances, get plenty of rest, drink lots of water, and in serious cases replace lost salts with oral rehydration solution (ORS); this is especially important with young children. Take a few sachets with you, or make your own by adding half a teaspoon of salt and three of sugar to a litre of cool, previously boiled water. While down with diarrhoea, avoid milk, greasy or spicy foods, coffee and most fruit, in favour of bland foodstuffs such as rice, plain noodles and soup. If symptoms persist, or if you notice blood or mucus in your stools, consult a doctor as you may have dysentery.

To avoid stomach complaints, eat at places that look busy and clean and stick to fresh, thoroughly cooked food. Don't drink **untreated tap water** – boiled or bottled water is widely available.

Hepatitis A is a viral infection spread by contaminated food and water, which causes an inflammation of the liver. The less common **hepatitis B** virus can be passed on through unprotected sexual contact, transfusions of unscreened blood, and dirty needles. Hepatitis symptoms include yellowing of the eyes and skin, preceded by lethargy, fever and pains in the upper right abdomen.

Typhoid and cholera are spread by contaminated food or water, generally in localized epidemics; both are serious conditions and require immediate medical help. Symptoms of typhoid include headaches, high fever and constipation, followed by diarrhoea in the later stages. The disease is infectious. Cholera begins with a sudden but painless onset of watery diarrhoea, later combined with vomiting, nausea and muscle cramps. **Rapid, severe dehydration** rather than the infection itself is the main danger, and should be treated with constant oral rehydration solutions.

Summer outbreaks of **malaria and dengue fever** occur across southern China, usually in localized areas. Symptoms are similar – severe headaches, joint pains, fever and shaking – though a rash might also appear with dengue. There's no cure for dengue fever, whereas malaria can be prevented and controlled with medication; both require immediate medical attention to ensure that there are no complications. You can minimize your chances of being bitten by mosquitoes in the first place by wearing light-coloured, full-length clothing and insect repellent in the evenings when mosquitoes are active.

Temperature and humidity

In tropical China, the **temperature and humidity** can take a couple of weeks to adjust to. High humidity can cause heat rashes, prickly heat and fungal infections. Prevention and cure are the same: wear loose clothes made of natural fibres, wash frequently and dry off thoroughly afterwards. Talcum or anti-fungal powder and the use of mild antiseptic soap help, too.

Don't underestimate the strength of the **sun** in the tropics or high up on the Tibetan Plateau. Sunscreen is hard to find, except in foreign-owned department stores such as Carrefour. Signs of dehydration and **heatstroke** include a high temperature, lack of sweating, a fast pulse and red skin. Reducing your body temperature with a lukewarm shower will provide initial relief.

Conversely, Northern Yunnan and western Sichuan also get very cold. Watch out here for **hypothermia**, where the core body temperature drops to a point that can be fatal. Symptoms are a weak pulse, disorientation, numbness, slurred speech and exhaustion. To prevent the condition, wear lots of layers and a hat, eat plenty of carbohydrates, and stay dry and out of the wind. To treat hypothermia, get the victim into shelter, away from wind and rain, give them hot drinks – but not alcohol – and easily digestible food, and keep them warm. Serious cases require immediate hospitalization.

Altitude

High altitude prevents the blood from absorbing oxygen efficiently, and can lead to altitude sickness, also known as **AMS** (acute mountain sickness). Most people feel some symptoms above 3000m, including becoming easily exhausted, headaches, shortness of breath, sleeping disorders and nausea; they're intensified if you ascend to altitude rapidly, for instance by flying direct from lowland cities to Jiuzhaigou or Deqing. Relaxing for the first few days, drinking plenty of water and taking painkillers will ease symptoms. Having acclimatized at one altitude you should still ascend slowly, or you can expect the symptoms to return.

If for any reason the body fails to acclimatize to altitude, serious conditions can develop including **pulmonary oedema** (characterized by severe breathing trouble, a cough and frothy white or pink sputum), and **cerebral oedema** (causing severe headaches, loss of balance, other neurological symptoms and eventually coma). The only treatment for these is rapid descent without delay; you also need to see a doctor as soon as possible.

Hospitals, clinics and pharmacies

Medical facilities in China are best in major cities with large expat populations, where there are often high-standard clinics, and the hotels may even have resident doctors. Elsewhere, larger cities and towns have hospitals, and for minor complaints there are plenty of pharmacies that can suggest remedies, though don't expect English to be spoken.

Chinese **hospitals** use a mix of Western and traditional Chinese medicine approaches, and sometimes charge high prices for simple drugs and use procedures that aren't necessary – they'll put you on a drip just to administer antibiotics – so always ask for a second opinion from a Western-trained doctor if you're worried (your embassy should be able to recommend one if none is suggested in the guide). In an **emergency**, you're better off taking a cab than waiting for an ambulance – it's quicker and will work out much cheaper. There's virtually **no health care** in China even for its citizens; expect to pay around ¥500 as a consultation fee.

Pharmacies are marked by a green cross, and if you can describe your ailment or required medication, you'll find many drugs which would be restricted and expensive in the West are easily available over the counter for very little money. Be wary of **counterfeit drugs**, however; check for spelling mistakes in the packaging or instructions.

MEDICAL RESOURCES FOR TRAVELLERS

Canadian Society for International Health Ⓦ csih.org. Extensive list of travel health centres.
CDC Ⓦ cdc.gov/travel. Official US government travel health site.
International Society for Travel Medicine Ⓦ istm.org. Has a full list of travel health clinics.
Hospital for Tropical Diseases Travel Clinic UK Ⓦ thehtd.org.
MASTA (Medical Advisory Service for Travellers Abroad) UK Ⓦ masta.org for the nearest clinic.
The Travel Doctor – TMVC Ⓦ tmvc.com.au. Lists travel clinics in Australia, New Zealand and South Africa.
Tropical Medical Bureau Ireland Ⓦ tmb.ie.

Insurance

China is a relatively **safe** place to travel, though traffic accidents, respiratory infections, petty theft and transport delays are all fairly common occurrences – it's sensible to ensure you've arranged some form of **travel insurance** before leaving home.

ROUGH GUIDES TRAVEL INSURANCE

Rough Guides has teamed up with WorldNomads.com to offer great **travel insurance** deals. Policies are available to residents of over 150 countries, with cover for a wide range of adventure sports, 24hr emergency assistance, high levels of medical and evacuation cover and a stream of travel safety information. Roughguides.com users can take advantage of their policies online 24/7, from anywhere in the world – even if you're already travelling. And since plans often change when you're on the road, you can extend your policy and even claim online. Roughguides.com users who buy travel insurance with WorldNomads.com can also leave a positive footprint and donate to a community development project. For more information go to Ⓦ roughguides.com/shop.

Culture and etiquette

The Chinese are, on the whole, pragmatic, materialistic and garrulous. The sniggers and the unhelpful service experienced by foreigners are almost always due to nervousness and the language barrier, rather than rudeness. Visitors who speak Chinese will generally encounter a delighted (and sometimes amazed) audience wherever they go, with people invariably asking about their country of origin, their job and the reason they are in China.

If you're invited to someone's **home**, take along a **gift** – a bottle of spirits, some tea or an ornamental trinket are good choices (anything too utilitarian could be considered patronizing) – though your hosts won't impolitely open this in front of you. **Restaurant bills** are not shared out between the guests but instead people will go to great lengths to pay the whole amount themselves. Normally this honour will fall to the person perceived as the most senior, and as a foreigner dining with Chinese you should make some effort to stake your claim, though it is probable that someone else will grab the bill before you do.

Privacy

There's almost no concept of **privacy** in China – even public toilets are built with partitions so low that you can chat with your neighbour while squatting. Loneliness and darkness are associated with death, so all leisure activities – including restaurant meals and visits to natural beauty spots or holy sites – are done in large, bright, noisy groups. The desire of some Western tourists to be "left alone" in these circumstances is variously interpreted by locals as eccentric, arrogant, or even sinister.

Exotic foreigners also can become targets for **blatant curiosity**. People stare and point, voices on the street shout out "helloooo" twenty times a day, or – in rural areas like the backroads of Yunnan or Guizhou – even run up and jostle for a better look, exclaiming loudly to each other, *laowai, laowai* ("foreigner"). This is not usually intended to be aggressive or insulting, though the cumulative effects of such treatment can be annoying and alienating.

Spitting and smoking

Various other forms of behaviour perceived as antisocial in the West are considered perfectly normal in China. **Spitting**, for example, is done with casual disregard on buses, trains, restaurants and even inside people's homes. Outside the company of urban sophisticates, it would not occur to people that there was anything disrespectful in delivering a powerful spit while in conversation with a stranger.

Despite an erratically enforced **ban** in some public places, **smoking** is almost universal among men, and any attempt to stop others from lighting up is met with incomprehension. **Handing out cigarettes** is a basic way of establishing goodwill, and non-smokers should take them "for later"; foreigners refusing cigarettes are usually believed to be doing so because they consider Chinese brands too downmarket – it seldom occurs to anyone that you might not smoke at all.

Clothing

Chinese **clothing** styles lean towards the casual, and summertime skimpy clothing is common in urban areas (less so in the countryside), particularly among women. Although Chinese men commonly wear shorts and expose their midriffs in hot weather, Western men who do the same should note that the sight of **body hair** – chest or legs – will instantly become the focus of giggly gossip. The generally relaxed approach to clothing applies equally when visiting temples, though in **mosques** men and women alike should cover their bodies above the wrists and ankles. As for **beachwear**, bikinis and briefs are in, but nudity has yet to make its debut.

Casual clothing is one thing, but **scruffy clothing** is quite another. While the average Chinese peasant might reasonably be expected to have wild hair and wear dirty clothes, the sight of a comparatively rich foreigner doing so will arouse a degree of contempt.

Meeting people

When **meeting people** it's useful to have a name or **business card** to flash around – Chinese with business aspirations hand them out at every opportunity, and are a little crestfallen if you can't produce one in return. It's polite to take the proffered card with both hands and to have a good look at it before putting it away – though not in your back pocket. If you don't speak Chinese but have your name in Chinese printed on them, they also become useful when checking in to hotels that are reluctant to take foreigners, as the staff can then copy your name into the register.

Shaking hands is not a Chinese tradition, though it is fairly common between men. **Bodily contact** in the form of embraces or back-slapping can be observed between same-sex friends, and these days, in cities, a boy and a girl can walk round arm in arm and even kiss without raising an eyebrow. **Voice level** in China seems to be pitched several decibels louder than in most other countries, though this should not necessarily be interpreted as a sign of belligerence.

Sex and gender issues

Women travellers in China usually find incidence of **sexual harassment** less of a problem than in other Asian countries. Chinese men are, on the whole, deferential and respectful. A more likely complaint is being ignored, as the Chinese will generally assume that any man accompanying a woman will be doing all the talking. **Women on their own** visiting remote temples or sights need to be on their guard – don't assume that all monks and caretakers have impeccable morals.

Prostitution, though illegal, is everywhere in China. Single foreign men are likely to be approached inside hotels; it's common practice for prostitutes to phone around hotel rooms at all hours of the night. Bear in mind that the consequence of a Westerner being caught with a prostitute may be unpleasant, and that AIDS is on the increase.

Homosexuality is increasingly tolerated by the authorities and people in general, though public displays may get you in trouble. **Dating** a local won't raise many eyebrows in these relaxed times, though displays of mixed-race public affection certainly will.

Shopping

China is a good place to shop for souvenirs, folk art, clothes, household goods and fake designer labels – but not for real designer brands or electronic goods, which are cheaper at home or online (and also more likely to be the genuine article). Every settlement has a market, while larger cities will also have big department stores, shopping malls and even international supermarket chains.

Prices in stores are fixed, but **discounts** (折扣, zhékòu) are common: they're marked by a number between one and nine and the character "折", indicating the percentage of the original price you have to pay – "8折", for example, means that the item is on sale at eighty percent of its original price. At **markets** – especially blatant tourist affairs – you're expected to **bargain** for goods unless prices are displayed. Chinese shoppers usually state the price they're willing to pay, rather than beginning low and working up to it after haggling. If you can speak Chinese, hang around for a while to get an idea what others are paying, or just ask at a few stalls selling the same things. Don't become obsessed about saving every last yuan; being charged more than locals and getting ripped off from time to time is inevitable.

Souvenirs

Souvenirs popular with foreign tourists include "chops" (stone seals with your name engraved in characters on the base); all manner of reproduction antiques, from porcelain to furniture; mementoes of Mao and the Cultural Revolution – Little Red Books and cigarette lighters that chime "The East is Red"; T-shirts and "old-style" Chinese clothes; scroll paintings; and ethnic jewellery and textiles. Chinese tourists also look for things like local teas, "purple sand" teapots and bright tack. Pretty much the same selection is sold at all tourist sites, irrespective of relevancy. For **real antiques**, you need specialist stores or markets – some are listed in the guide – where anything genuine is meant to be marked with a wax seal and requires an export licence to take out of the country. The Chinese are clued-up, avid collectors and value their culture highly, so don't expect to find any bargains.

Clothes

Clothes are a very good deal in China, with brand stores such as Giordano, Baleno, Meters/Bonwe and Yishion selling high-quality smart-casual wear. All major cities have specialist stores stocking **outdoors and hiking gear**, though quality can vary. **Sizes** bear no relationship to what it says on the label, so always try things on before buying them. **Silk** and other fabrics are also good value, if you're into making your own clothes. **Shoes** are inexpensive too, though anything larger than size 8/42 is rare.

Books and maps

The state media organization, Xinhua, runs multi-floor **bookshops** in most cities; there are also a few independent stores in Chengdu, Dali and Kunming. They're useful for Chinese-language **maps**, **travel guides**, **dictionaries** and language study materials, all sorts of specialist cultural tomes from acupuncture to martial arts, architecture and calligraphy, and usually carry a limited stock of books in English – Victorian potboilers, Chinese classics in translation, cookery books and the like. One of the nicest aspects of bookstores is that the majority of customers blatantly have no intention of buying anything, and are simply there to read novels or text books for free – nobody seems to mind.

CDs, DVDs and Western goods

All bookstores and many market stalls in China sell **music CDs** of everything from Beijing punk to Beethoven, plus **DVDs** of all manner of domestic and international movies (often subtitled – check on the back). While extremely cheap at ¥5–35, many of these are **pirated**. Genuine DVD films may be **region-coded** for Asia, so check the label and whether your player at home will handle them; there are no such problems with CDs.

Your best bet for any sort of **Western goods** is to head to provincial capitals, many of which have a branch of **Carrefour** (家乐福, jiālèfú) or **Wal-Mart** (沃尔玛, wòěrmǎ).

Sports and outdoor activities

Since 2008, when China hosted the Olympics, athletic passion has become almost a patriotic duty. But the most visible forms of exercise are fairly timeless; head to any public space in the morning and you'll see citizens going through all sorts of martial arts routines, playing ping pong and street badminton, even ballroom dancing. Sadly though, facilities for organized sport are fairly limited.

The Chinese are good at **"small ball" games** such as squash and badminton, and, of course, table tennis, at which they are world champions, but admit room for improvement in the "big ball" games, such as **football**. Nevertheless, Chinese men follow foreign football avidly, with games from the European leagues shown on CCTV5. There's also a national obsession among students for **basketball**, which has been played in China since the early twentieth century; the country has produced NBA star **Yao Ming**, who plies his trade for the Houston Rockets.

If China has an indigenous "sport", however, it's the **martial arts** – not surprising, perhaps, in a country whose history is littered with long periods of civil conflict. Today, there are hundreds of Chinese martial arts styles, usually taught for exercise rather than for fighting.

Outdoor activities

Though it's not really in the Chinese nature to romantically pit themselves against the elements, there's an increasing interest in the Great Outdoors and, with it, a growing popularity for **outdoor activities.** Exploring the wilds of Yunnan and Sichuan is beginning to appeal to adventurous young city-born Chinese – always dressed in the latest outdoor gear – along with hiking, mountaineering and four-wheel-drive expeditions.

Yangshuo's karst peaks have been a focus for **rock climbing** for over a decade (see p.330), with growing interest around Dali (see p.209). Ⓦ karstclimber.com and Ⓦ chinaclimb.com have more information

Tibetans have been known for their horses since the Yuan dynasty, and there's organized **horse trekking** in the alpine meadows of Western Sichuan at Songpan (see p.114), Langmusi (see p.122) and Tagong (see p.133). There's a good deal of adventurous **hiking** in Southwest China too: the ascent of Emei Shan (see p.101); jungle trekking in Xishuangbanna (see p.256); following the Yangzi through Tiger Leaping Gorge near Lijiang (see p.233); the *kora* circuit around Meili Xue Shan (see p.243); or valley-hopping across the mountains separating the Lancang and Nu rivers (see p.245).

Almost all of these require you to be fit, carrying suitable gear and self-sufficient; you might also need to hire **guides** – details are given through the guide.

Travel essentials

Addresses and street names

Even in the countryside, **street names** – if given at all – are usually labelled both in Chinese characters and Romanized *pinyin*. Roads are often **divided** into north (北, běi), south (南, nán), east (东, dōng), west (西, xī) or middle (中, zhōng) sections; so

AVERAGE TEMPERATURES AND RAINFALL

CHENGDU

	Jan	Feb	Mar	Apr	May	Jun	Jul	Aug	Sep	Oct	Nov	Dec
Max/min (°C)	10/5	14/7	19/10	24/16	27/18	29/20	30/22	30/22	27/17	23/12	18/6	14/5
Max/min (°F)	50/41	57/45	66/50	75/61	81/64	84/68	86/72	86/72	81/63	74/54	64/43	57/41
Precipitation (mm)	10	12	26	42	58	108	179	205	84	32	13	14

CHONGQING

	Jan	Feb	Mar	Apr	May	Jun	Jul	Aug	Sep	Oct	Nov	Dec
Max/min (°C)	9/5	13/7	18/11	23/16	27/19	29/22	34/24	35/25	28/22	22/16	16/12	3/-8
Max/min (°F)	48/41	55/45	64/52	73/61	81/66	84/72	93/75	95/77	82/72	72/61	61/54	37/18
Precipitation (mm)	26	28	49	99	165	224	182	122	114	92	53	26

GUIYANG

	Jan	Feb	Mar	Apr	May	Jun	Jul	Aug	Sep	Oct	Nov	Dec
Max/min (°C)	8/2	11/4	15/7	21/12	24/15	26/18	28/20	28/20	25/17	20/13	16/8	11/4
Max/min (°F)	46/36	52/40	59/45	70/54	75/59	79/64	82/68	82/68	77/63	68/55	61/46	52/39
Precipitation (mm)	24	24	41	78	172	202	202	141	77	95	43	23

JINGHONG

	Jan	Feb	Mar	Apr	May	Jun	Jul	Aug	Sep	Oct	Nov	Dec
Max/min (°C)	26/12	29/12	32/15	33/18	32/21	32/23	31/23	31/23	31/22	29/20	27/16	25/13
Max/min (°F)	79/54	84/54	90/59	91/64	90/70	90/73	88/73	88/73	88/72	84/68	81/61	77/55
Precipitation (mm)	15	14	37	62	154	161	249	213	146	98	45	35

KUNMING

	Jan	Feb	Mar	Apr	May	Jun	Jul	Aug	Sep	Oct	Nov	Dec
Max/min (°C)	20/8	22/9	25/12	28/16	29/18	29/19	28/19	28/19	28/18	24/15	22/12	20/8
Max/min (°F)	68/46	72/48	77/54	82/61	84/64	84/66	82/66	82/66	82/64	75/59	72/54	68/46
Precipitation (mm)	8	18	28	41	127	132	196	198	97	51	56	15

NANNING

	Jan	Feb	Mar	Apr	May	Jun	Jul	Aug	Sep	Oct	Nov	Dec
Max/min (°C)	18/10	20/11	24/13	28/17	32/20	35/23	35/25	33/23	32/22	30/17	27/15	22/10
Max/min (°F)	65/50	68/52	75/55	82/63	90/68	95/73	95/77	91/73	90/72	86/63	81/59	72/50
Precipitation (mm)	48	43	71	77	171	230	283	209	116	53	41	30

"Tengyue Dong Lu", "Tengyue Zhong Lu", and "Tengyue Xi Lu" are all parts of the same "Tengyue Road". However, **numbering** can be seemingly random: we've given them where possible, but they can't always be used to quickly locate an address.

Costs

China is not a **cheap** destination in Asian terms, but prices are lower than in Europe and the US, and Southwest China is one of the least costly regions in the country. Food and transport are inexpensive, and accommodation is largely fair value, though **entry fees** for temples, scenic areas and historic monuments are becoming expensive even by inter-national standards – so much so, that the central government is trying to get local authorities to reduce them (with little effect so far).

It used to be government policy to **surcharge** foreigners for public transport and admission fees for sights. Though the practice is officially banned, you might still be sold the most **expensive option** for these things, without being informed of less costly alternatives; take comfort in the fact that Chinese tourists suffer the same treatment. **Discount rates** for pensioners and students are available for many entry fees; students generally need a Chinese student card, though ISIC cards sometimes work, while pensioners can often just use their passports to prove they are over 60 (women) or 65 (men).

By doing everything cheaply and sticking mostly to the less expensive interior provinces, you can survive on £29/US$45/¥300 a day; travel a bit more widely and in better comfort and you're looking at £58/US$90/¥600 a day; while travelling in style and visiting only key places along the east coast, you could run up daily expenses of £145/US$225/¥1500 and above.

Crime and personal safety

While the worst that happens to most visitors to Southwest China is that they have their **pocket picked** on a bus or get **scammed** (see below), you do need to take care. Carry passports and money in a concealed **money belt**, and keep some foreign notes – perhaps around US$200 – separately from the rest of your cash, together with any travellers'-cheque receipts, your insurance policy details, a spare bank card If you have one and photocopies of your passport and visa. Be wary on buses, the favoured haunt of pickpockets, and trains, particularly in hard-seat class and on overnight journeys.

One of the most dangerous things you can do in China is **cross a road**: marked pedestrian crossings might as well not be there for all the attention shown them by motorists; and even when traffic lights flash green to show it's safe to cross, you'll find that vehicles are still permitted to turn in to or out of the road. **Hotel rooms** are on the whole secure, dormitories much less so, though often it's your fellow travellers who are the problem here. Most hotels should have a safe, but it's not unusual for things to go missing from these. Be cautious in cities **late at night**; similarly, **walking alone** across the countryside is ill-advised, particularly in remote regions. If anyone does try to rob you, run away or, if this isn't possible, stay calm and don't resist.

You may see stress-induced **street confrontations**, though these rarely result in violence, just a lot of shouting. Another occasional hazard are gangs of **child beggars**, organized by a nearby adult. They target foreigners and can be very hard to shake off; handing over money usually results in increased harassment.

The police

The police, known as the **Public Security Bureau** or **PSB**, are recognizable by their dark blue uniforms and caps, though there are a lot more around than you might at first think, as plenty are undercover. They have much wider powers than most Western police forces, including establishing the guilt of criminals – trials are used only for deciding the sentence of the

SCAMS

A good number of **professional con artists** target tourists with variations on the following scam. A sweet-looking young couple, a pair of girls or perhaps a kindly old man, will ask to practise their English or offer to show you round. Having befriended you – which may take hours – they will suggest some refreshment, and lead you to a teahouse, art gallery or restaurant. After eating or drinking, you will be presented with a bill for thousands of yuan, your new "friends" will vanish or pretend to be shocked, and some large gentlemen will appear. It's hard to believe just how convincing these people can be – never eat or drink with a stranger unless you know how much you're expected to pay.

accused, though this is changing and China now has the beginnings of an independent judiciary. If the culprit is deemed to show proper remorse, this will result in a more lenient sentence.

The PSB also have the job of looking after foreigners, and you'll most likely have to seek them out for **visa extensions**, reporting theft or losses, and obtaining **permits** for Tibet. On occasion, they might seek you out; it's common for the police to call round to your hotel room if you're staying in a remote place – they usually just look at your passport and then move on.

While individual police can often go out of their way to help foreigners, the PSB itself has all the problems of any police force in a country where corruption is widespread, and it's best to minimize contact with them.

Offences to avoid

With adjacent opium-growing areas in Burma and Laos, Southwest China (and the rest of the country) has a massive **drug problem**. Heroin use has become fairly widespread, particularly in depressed rural areas, and ecstasy is used in clubs and discos. In

EMERGENCY NUMBERS

Police ☎110
Fire ☎119
Ambulance ☎120
Though it's generally quicker and cheaper taking a taxi to the nearest hospital than calling for an ambulance.

the past, the police have turned a blind eye to foreigners with drugs, as long as no Chinese are involved, but you don't want to test this out. In 2010, China executed a British national for drug trafficking, and annually holds mass executions of convicted drug offenders on the UN anti-drugs day in June.

Visitors are not likely to be accused of **political crimes**, but foreign residents, including teachers or students, may be expelled from the country for talking about politics or religion. The Chinese they talk to will be treated less leniently. In **Tibetan areas**, and around **international borders**, censorship is taken much more seriously; photographing military installations (which can include major road bridges), instances of police brutality or gulags is not a good idea.

Electricity

The **electricity supply** runs on 220 volts, with the most common type of **plug** a dual flat prong. Some hotels, though, have universal sockets, and adaptors are widely available from neighbourhood hardware stores.

Entry requirements

All foreign nationals require a **visa** to enter China, available worldwide from some Chinese embassies and consulates, specialist tour operators and **visa agents**, and online. Your best first port of call is usually the website for your nearest Chinese embassy (see below), which will have information on how to apply online; if this isn't convenient then it will also have the latest on how and where to apply in person or by mail. Visas are also easy to obtain in **Hong Kong**, often without the documentation insisted on by overseas agents, if you're planning to come that way – see ⓦfmcoprc.gov.hk/eng/. Visas are **not available on arrival**.

IMPORT REGULATIONS

You're allowed to **import into China** up to 400 cigarettes and 1.5l of alcohol and up to ¥20,000 cash. Foreign currency in excess of US$5000 or the equivalent must be declared. It's **illegal** to import printed or filmed matter critical of the country, but this is currently only a problem with Chinese border guards at crossings from Vietnam, who have confiscated guidebooks; keep them buried in the bottom of your bags.

Visas must be **used** within three months of issue, and **cost** US$30–100 depending on the visa type, the length of stay, the number of entries allowed and your nationality. Visa offices may levy **additional processing costs**. Your passport must be valid for at least another six months from your planned date of entry into China, and have at least one blank page for visas. You'll be asked your **occupation**; don't admit to being a journalist, photographer or writer. At times of political sensitivity, you may be asked for a copy of onwards air tickets, proof of funds, and hotel bookings in your name. **Don't overstay your visa**: the fine is ¥500 a day, along with the possibility that you may be deported and banned from entering China for five years.

Tourist visas (L) and **business visas** (F) are valid for three, six or twelve months, and can be single or multiple entry – though multiple entry visas usually require you to leave China every thirty days. Three-month tourist visas are easy to obtain, but the others usually need supporting documentation from host organizations within China. Twelve-month **work visas** (Z) again require an invitation, plus a health certificate.

Students intending to study in China for less than six months need an invitation or letter of acceptance from a college there and they'll be given an F visa. If you're intending to study for longer than six months, there is an additional form, available from Chinese embassies and online, and you will also need a health certificate; then you'll be issued with an X visa, which allows you to stay and study for up to a year.

CHINESE EMBASSIES AND CONSULATES

A fairly up-to-date list of Chinese embassies worldwide can be found at ⓦ china-embassy.info.
Australia 15 Coronation Drive, Yarralumla, Canberra, ACT 2600, ⓦ au.china-embassy.org.
Burma 1 Pyidaungsu Yeiktha Rd, Yangon ☎ 009 522 1926.
Canada 515 St Patrick St, Ottawa, Ontario, K1N 5H3 ⓦ ca. chineseembassy.org.
Ireland 40 Ailesbury Rd, Dublin 4 ⓦ ie.chineseembassy.org.
Laos Wat Nak Rd, Sisattanak, Vientiane ☎ 856 21 315100.
New Zealand 2–6 Glenmore St, Wellington ⓦ chinaembassy.org. nz.
South Africa 972 Pretorius St, Arcadia, Pretoria ⓦ chinese-embassy.org.za.
Thailand 57 Ratchadapisake Rd, Bangkok ⓦ chinaembassy.or.th/ eng.
UK 49–51 Portland Place, London W1B 1JL ⓦ www. chinese-embassy.org.uk.
USA 2300 Connecticut Ave, Washington DC 20008 ⓦ china-embassy.org.
Vietnam 46 Hoang Dieu Rd, Hanoi ⓦ vn.china-embassy.org.

Visa extensions

Once inside China, **visa extensions** are handled by the **Public Security Bureau** (**PSB**), so you can apply for one in any reasonably sized town – the department will be called something like "Aliens' Entry Exit Section". The cost and amount of hassle involved varies depending on where you are and your nationality. In particular, many places want to see a **receipt from your accommodation**, proving that you're staying in the town in which you're applying.

A **first extension**, valid for a month, is easy to obtain and costs ¥160 (US citizens pay more). However, the particular PSB office may decide to levy extra charges on top, or even waive the fee completely. In some small towns, the process takes ten minutes; in cities, it can take up to a week. One of the most amenable, straightforward offices is at Xiaguan (**Dali**), if you're heading there.

A **second or third extension** is harder to get, and impossible if your visa was originally issued in Hong Kong. In major cities, you will probably be turned away, though you'd be unlucky to come away without some kind of extension from PSB offices in small towns. You will be asked your reasons for wanting an extension – simply saying you want to spend more time in this wonderful country usually goes down well, or you could cite illness or transport delays. Don't admit to being low on funds.

Fourth or even fifth extensions are possible, but you'll need to foster connections with a PSB office. Ask advice from a local independent travel agent – they often have the right sort of contacts.

Internet

Internet bars (网吧, **wǎngbā**) with high-speed connections are everywhere in China, from big cities – where some seat hundreds of people – to rural villages. They're invariably full of network-gaming teenagers, and are usually hidden away off main roads, rarely on ground floors, and only ever signed in Chinese. They're generally **open** 24hr and cost ¥2–5/hr, though you may have to pay a ¥10 deposit and each bar has its own setup: sometimes you're given a card with a password to use on any available machine, sometimes the staff log you in at a particular terminal. You might also be asked to show your **passport**, or even **Chinese ID card**, or risk being turned away.

All large hotels have **business centres** where you can get online, but this is expensive, especially in the classier places (around ¥30/hr). Better value are the backpacker hostels, where getting online costs around ¥5 per hour or is free. But the best deal is to tote a **laptop** or similar – cities such as Chengdu and Kunming have cafés with free **wi-fi**, and many hotels and even youth hostels have **ADSL sockets** in their rooms.

In an attempt to keep control of news and current affairs, China's **internet censors** have set up the dryly named "Great Firewall" or Net Nanny, which blocks access to any websites deemed undesirable by the state – currently including Twitter, YouTube and Facebook. Foreign online news services such as the BBC have also been blocked in the past, though nowadays you're only likely to experience problems if, for example, there are riots in Tibet. To get around it, you need to use a **web proxy or VPN** (Virtual Private Network) such as Wltopia, Hotshot Shield or Ultrasurf, all of which cost a few dollars a month and offer a free limited period trial. Technically this is illegal, but the government pays no attention to foreigners who do this – just about every foreign business in China runs a VPN. For Chinese nationals, it's a different matter, and you will never find a public computer, such as in a hotel or business centre, running one.

Laundry

Laundromats are virtually unknown in China. Big city hotels, and youth hostels all over, offer a **laundry service** for anything between ¥10 and ¥100; alternatively, some hostels have self-service facilities or you can use your room sink (every corner store in China sells washing powder). Otherwise, ask at accommodation either for the staff to wash your clothes or for the nearest laundry, where they usually **charge** by dry weight.

Left luggage

Most train stations and main bus station, have **left-luggage offices** (行李寄存处, **xíngli jìcúnchù**) open about 6am–5pm or later; they charge ¥2–10 per item. You're not meant to leave things overnight, and they tend to lock up pretty promptly, so confirm times when you leave your bags. Accommodation will often look after luggage too, but you want to check how secure their storage room is; the cost is anything from free to ¥5 a day.

Living in China

It is fairly easy for foreigners to **live in Southwest China** full time, whether as a student, a teacher or for work. Anyone planning to stay more than six months is required to pass a **medical** (from approved clinics) proving that they don't have any venereal disease – if you do have a VD, expect to be deported and your passport endorsed with your ailment.

Large cities such as Kunming and Chengdu have no restrictions on where foreigners can reside, though either you or your landlord must register with the local PSB. **Property rental** is inexpensive if you avoid purpose-built foreign enclaves – two-bedroom flats cost upwards of ¥1500 a month, though ¥10,000 and above is more likely for a modern city-centre apartment. The easiest way to find accommodation is to go through an **agent**, who will generally charge one month's rent as a fee. There are plenty who advertise in expat magazines and online.

Various blogs (see p.52) also have more information on living in China, from the practical to the very eccentric and specialist.

Teaching

Various schemes place **foreign teachers** in Chinese educational institutions – contact your nearest Chinese embassy (see p.47 for addresses) for details. Some employers ask for a TEFL qualification, though a degree, or simply the ability to speak the language as a native, is usually enough.

The standard **teaching salary** for a foreigner is ¥3500 per month for a bachelor's degree, ¥4000 for a master's degree and ¥5000 for a doctorate. This isn't enough to put much away, but you should also get **subsidized on-campus accommodation**, plus a fare to your home country, one way for a single semester and a return for a year's work. The **workload** is usually fourteen hours a week and if you work a year you get paid through the winter holiday. Most teachers find their students keen, hard-working, curious and obedient, and report that it was the contact with them that made the experience worthwhile. That said, avoid talking about religion or politics in the classroom as this can get them into trouble. You'll earn more – up to ¥12,000 a month – in a **private school**, though be aware of the risk of being ripped off by a commercial agency (you might be given more classes to teach than you'd signed up for, for example). Check out the institution thoroughly before committing yourself.

Studying

Universities in Chengdu and Kunming now host substantial populations of Western **students**. Most study **Mandarin**, though there are many additional options available – from martial arts to traditional opera or classical literature – once you break the language barrier. Courses **cost** from the equivalent of US$2400 a year, or US$800 a semester. Hotel-style **campus accommodation** costs around US$10 a day; most people move out as soon as they speak enough Chinese to rent a flat.

Your first **resource** is the nearest Chinese embassy, which can provide a list of contact details for Chinese universities offering the courses you are interested in; most universities also have English-language websites. Be aware, however, that promotional material may have little bearing on what is actually provided; though teaching standards are good, university administration departments are often a shambles. Ideally, visit the campus first and be wary of paying course fees up front until you've spoken to a few students.

Working

There is plenty of **work** available for foreigners in major Chinese cities, where a whole section of expat society get by as actors, cocktail barmen, Chinglish correctors, models, freelance writers and so on. This sort of work is likely to come from people you know, or via adverts in expat magazines (see p.52); if you're being employed above board, rather than cash-in-hand, you'll need to open a Chinese bank account. To really make any money here, however, you need to either be employed by a foreign company or start your own business.

Mail

The **Chinese mail service** is fast and efficient, with letters taking a day to reach destinations in the same city, two or more days to other destinations in China, and up to several weeks to destinations abroad. **Overseas postage rates** are fairly expensive and vary depending on weight, destination and where you are in the country. The **International Express Mail Service** (EMS), however, is unreliable, with items often lost in transit or arriving in pieces, despite registered delivery and online tracking. **DHL** (ⓦdhl.com), available in a few major cities, is a safer bet.

Main post offices are open daily between about 8am and 8pm; smaller offices may keep shorter hours or close at weekends. As well as at post offices, you can post letters in green postboxes, though these are rare outside big cities.

To **send parcels**, turn up with the goods you want to send and the staff will sell you a box and pack them in for ¥15 or so. Once packed, but before the parcel is sealed, it must be checked at the customs window and you'll have to complete masses of paperwork (instructions are in French and Chinese, but straightforward enough), so don't be in a hurry. If you are sending valuable goods bought in China, put the receipt or a photocopy of it in with the parcel, as it may be opened for customs inspection farther down the line.

Poste restante services are available in any city. Mail is kept for several months, and you'll need to present ID when picking it up. Have letters addressed to you c/o Poste Restante, GPO, street, town or city, province. Check under both your surname and given names, as mail can easily be misfiled.

Maps

English-language maps focusing on Southwest China are limited. The *Nelles* 1:1,500,000 series covers the region in two sheets, Southern China and Central China, which also include generous portions of neighbouring provinces and countries. Similar all-China maps include the excellent 1:4,000,000 map from *GeoCenter*, which shows relief and useful sections of all neighbouring countries, and the *Collins* 1:5,000,000 map. The newest road and rail networks are likely to be missing from all of these, but they're good for general use; you'll need to buy them **before leaving home**.

Once in China, **street maps** are available from street kiosks, hotel shops and bookshops for almost every town and city. Most are in Chinese only, showing bus routes, hotels, restaurants and tourist attractions; local bus, train and flight timetables are often printed on the back as well. The same vendors also sell pocket-sized **provincial road atlases**, again in Chinese only.

Provincial capitals and tourist destinations such as Dali, Lijiang and Shangri-La also produce maps **in English**, available at upmarket hotels, principal tourist sights or tour operators' offices.

Money

The mainland Chinese currency is formally called **yuan** (¥), more colloquially known as **renminbi** (RMB, literally "the people's money") or **kuai**. One yuan breaks down into ten **jiao**, also known as **mao**.

Paper money was invented in China and is still the main form of exchange, available in ¥100, ¥50, ¥20, ¥10, ¥5 and ¥1 notes, with a similar selection of mao. One mao, five mao, and ¥1 coins are increasingly common, though people in rural areas may never have seen them before and refuse to take

them. China suffers regular outbreaks of **counterfeiting** – everyone checks their change for watermarks, metal threads and the feel of the paper.

The yuan floats within a narrow range set by a basket of currencies, keeping Chinese exports cheap (much to the annoyance of the US). At the time of writing, the **exchange rate** was approximately ¥6.5 to US$1, ¥10.5 to £1, ¥9 to €1, ¥6.5 to CAN$1, ¥6.5 to A$1, ¥5 to NZ$1 and ¥1 to ZAR1. Check **current rates** at ⓦxe.com.

Banks and ATMs

Banks in major Chinese cities are sometimes open seven days a week, though **foreign exchange** is usually only available Monday to Friday, approximately 9am–noon and 2–5pm. All banks are **closed** for the first three days of the Chinese New Year, with reduced hours for the following eleven days, and at other holiday times.

Visa, Plus, Mastercard and Cirrus **cards** can be used to make cash withdrawals from **ATMs** operated by the Bank of China, the Industrial and Commercial Bank of China, China Construction Bank and Agricultural Bank of China, as long as they display the relevant logo. In major cities, almost every one of these banks' ATMs will work with foreign cards, but elsewhere it's likely that only the main branch of the Bank of China will have a suitable machine. Note that some ATMs are inside banks or shopping centres, so close when they do, though many are accessible 24 hours a day. The maximum for each withdrawal is ¥2500; your bank back home will **charge a fee** on each withdrawal, either a fixed rate or a percentage of the transaction. Keep your exchange **receipts** and when you leave you can change your yuan into dollars or sterling at any branch of the Bank of China.

Foreign currency and cheques

Travellers' cheques can be replaced if lost or stolen (keep a list of the serial numbers separate from the cheques) and attract a slightly better rate of exchange than cash. The **downsides** include having to pay a fee when you buy them, and that they can be cashed only at branches of the Bank of China and at tourist hotels.

It's worth taking along a small quantity of **foreign currency** (US, Canadian or Australian dollars, British pounds or euros) as cash is more widely exchangeable than travellers' cheques. Don't try to change money on the **black market** – profits are tiny and you'll almost certainly get ripped off.

Credit cards and wiring money

China is basically a cash economy, and **credit cards** (Visa has the largest presence, followed by Mastercard and American Express) are only accepted at big tourist hotels and the fanciest restaurants, and by some tourist-oriented shops; there is usually a **four percent handling charge**. It's straightforward to obtain **cash advances** on a Mastercard or Visa card at many Chinese banks and ATMs (look for the Plus logo – the commission is three percent), and book hotels and the like online.

It's possible to **wire money** to China through Western Union (**W** westernunion.cn); funds can be collected from one of their agencies or nominated branches of the Agricultural Bank, Postal Savings Bank and others.

Opening hours

China officially has a **five-day week**, though this only really applies to government offices, which open Monday to Friday approximately 8am–noon and 1–5pm. Generalization is difficult, though: post offices open daily, as do many shops, often keeping long, late hours, especially in big cities. Although banks *usually* close on Sundays – or for the whole weekend – even this is not always the case.

Opening hours for tourist sights are usually daily, 8am–5pm with no lunch break. Most **public parks** open from about 6am. **Museums** often close one day a week. If you arrive at an out-of-the-way place that seems to be closed, however, don't despair – knocking or poking around will often turn up a drowsy doorkeeper. Conversely, you may find other places locked and deserted when they are supposed to be open.

For dates of **public holidays**, see p.39.

Phones

Everywhere in China has an **area code**, which must be used when phoning from outside that locality; these are given for all telephone numbers throughout the guide. **Local calls** are free from land lines, and **long-distance** China-wide calls are ¥0.3 a minute. **International calls** cost from ¥3.5 a minute (much cheaper if you use an IP internet phonecard – see below).

Card phones, widely available in major cities, are the cheapest way to make domestic long-distance calls (¥0.2 for 3min), and can also be used for international calls (under ¥10 for 3min). They take **IC Cards** (IC卡, IC **kǎ**) which come in units of ¥20, ¥50 and ¥100. There's a fifty percent discount after 6pm and

on weekends. You will be cut off when your card value drops below the amount needed for the next minute. A cheaper option is the **IP card** (IP卡, IP **kǎ**), which can be used with any phone, and comes in ¥100 units. You dial a local number, then a PIN, then the number you're calling. Rates are as low as ¥2.4 per minute to the US and Canada, ¥3.2 to Europe. These cards can only be used in the places you buy them – move to another city and you'll have to buy a new card.

Skype usually works fine if you run it off your own machine, but you may have problems using it at an internet café.

Mobile phones

Mobile coverage in China uses the **GSM** system, and is excellent and comprehensive; phones seem to work just about everywhere, except the very remotest corners of the Tibetan Plateau. Assuming your phone is unlocked and compatible, buy a **Chinese SIM card** (SIM卡, SIM **kǎ**) from any phone shop or street kiosk; the best brand is China Telecom's **shenzhouxing** (神州行, **shénzhōuxíng**). SIM cards **cost** upwards of ¥80 depending on how "lucky" the number is – favoured sixes and eights bump up the cost, unlucky fours make it cheaper. They come with ¥50 of time, which you extend with prepaid top-up cards (充值卡, **chōngzhí kǎ**). Making and receiving domestic calls this way costs ¥0.6 per minute; an international call will cost around ¥8 a minute, though often you can only send texts overseas.

IC, IP and SIM cards are sold from corner stores, warehouse-sized mobile-phone emporiums, and by street hawkers (usually outside the mobile-phone emporiums) – look for long printed sheets of available phone numbers pasted up outside stores.

CALLING HOME FROM ABROAD

Note that the initial zero is omitted from the area code when dialling the UK, Ireland, Australia and New Zealand from abroad.
Australia international access code + 61
Ireland international access code + 353
New Zealand international access code + 64
South Africa international access code + 27
UK international access code + 44
US and Canada international access code + 1

You can also **buy new mobile phones** from the phone emporiums; failing that, many supermarkets have whole floors dedicated to them. International brands are more expensive than at home, but Chinese versions are often good value for money; the very cheapest cost around ¥200. Make sure the staff change the operating language into English for you. Stalls outside will have far cheaper **second-hand mobiles** (二手手机, èrshǒu shǒujī), but you're taking a risk with these.

Photography

Photography is a popular pastime among the Chinese, and all big towns and cities have **photo stores** selling the latest cameras, where you can also download your images onto disk for around ¥30. Camera batteries, memory cards and film are fairly easy to obtain in city department stores. **Film processing** is harder to arrange; it's probably best to take it home with you.

Chinese people are often only too pleased to have their picture taken, though many temples **prohibit photography** inside buildings, and you should avoid taking pictures of anything to do with the military, or that could be construed as having strategic value, including ordinary structures such as bridges in sensitive areas along borders, or in the Tibetan regions.

Time

All China occupies a **single time zone**, eight hours ahead of GMT, thirteen hours ahead of US Eastern Standard Time, sixteen hours ahead of US Pacific Time and two hours behind Australian Eastern Standard Time. There is no daylight saving.

Tourist information

The **internet** is your best source of information before you travel, as Chinese tourist offices overseas mostly sell packages and have little to offer individual travellers.

Once here, you'll find the **CITS** (China International Travel Service; 中国国际旅行社, zhōngguó guójì lǚxíngshè) and alternatives such as the **CTS** (China Travel Service; 中国旅行社, zhōngguó lǚxíngshè) everywhere from large cities to obscure hamlets. While they all book flight and train tickets, local tours and accommodation, their value to independent travellers varies – some offices are clued-up and helpful, others indifferent and uninformed. Don't take it for granted that anyone will speak English.

Other sources of information on the ground include **accommodation** staff and tour desks – especially at youth hostels – and **backpacker cafés** in destinations such as Dali, Lijiang and Yangshuo that see heavy numbers of foreign tourists.

With their large expat populations, Chengdu and Kunming have **weekly English-language magazines** with bar, restaurant and other listings. These are usually distributed free in bars and upmarket hotels, and have accompanying websites, listed in the guide.

CHINESE TOURIST OFFICES ABROAD
Australia and New Zealand Ⓦ cnto.org.au.
Canada Ⓦ tourismchina.org.
UK Ⓦ cnto.org.uk.
USA Ⓦ cnto.org.

GOVERNMENT WEBSITES
Australian Department of Foreign Affairs Ⓦ dfat.gov.au.
British Foreign & Commonwealth Office Ⓦ fco.gov.uk.
Canadian Department of Foreign Affairs Ⓦ international.gc.ca.
Irish Department of Foreign Affairs Ⓦ foreignaffairs.gov.ie.
New Zealand Ministry of Foreign Affairs Ⓦ mfat.govt.nz.
South African Department of Foreign Affairs Ⓦ dfa.gov.za.
US State Department Ⓦ state.gov.

CHINA ONLINE
There's a confusing abundance of English-language **websites and blogs** covering all aspects of China; the following is a selection of favourites. You'll need a proxy to access some of these from inside China.

China Backpacker Ⓦ chinabackpacker.info. Heaps of trekking information for both well-known and very off-the-beaten-path destinations in Southwest China. Dated in parts but elsewhere well ahead of the curve; a great resource.

China Bloglist Ⓦ chinabloglist.org. Directory with links to over 500 blogs about China, most of whose eccentric and obsessive writers claim unique insights into the country, its people and culture.

China Daily Ⓦ chinadaily.com.cn. The official, state-approved version of the news. Not as stodgy as you'd expect, but don't look for in-depth analysis, or controversial subject matter.

China Digital Times Ⓦ chinadigitaltimes.net. The broad brush-strokes behind China's social, political and economic development, plus background to regional news and trends.

China Expat Ⓦ chinaexpat.com. Aimed at foreign residents, but a generally useful English-language resource, with a wide range of China-related articles and plenty of links.

China From Inside Ⓦ chinafrominside.com. Glimpses into China's traditional martial arts, with dozens of English-language articles and interviews with famous masters.

China Hush Ⓦ chinahush.com. Translations of what Chinese net forums are saying about popular national press stories – but not the sort of stories that would ever surface in the *China Daily*.

chinaSMACK Ⓦ chinasmack.com. Similar to China Hush, but with a cruel tabloid slant. Gives a rare insight into the underbelly of contemporary Chinese life.

China Trekking Ⓦ chinatrekking.com. More inspiring trekking background; plenty of maps and firsthand details you won't find elsewhere.

Ethnic China Ⓦ ethnic-china.com. Thumbnail sketches and interesting, wildly uneven articles about China's ethnic minority groups.

Keke Xili / Land of Snows Ⓦ kekexili.typepad.com or Ⓦ landofsnows.com/los/Home.html. Invaluable firsthand, up-to-date coverage of events inside the Kham Tibetan areas of western Sichuan and Northern Yunnan.

Managing the Dragon Ⓦ managingthedragon.com. Blog commentary on Chinese economic subjects from investor-who-lost-millions Jack Perkowski (who has since bounced back).

Middle Kingdom Life Ⓦ middlekingdomlife.com. Online manual for foreigners planning to live and work in China, providing a sane sketch of the personal and professional difficulties they're likely to face.

Travel China Ⓦ travelchinaguide.com. Unusual in covering obscure places and small-group tours, as well as the normal run of popular sites and booking links.

Youku Ⓦ youku.com. One of the many YouTube clones in China, with a similar range of content (all in Chinese).

Zhongwen Ⓦ zhongwen.com. A handy online Chinese/English dictionary.

Travelling with children

Children in China are usually indulged and pampered, and foreigners travelling with children can expect to receive lots of attention from curious locals – and the occasional admonition that the little one should be wrapped up warmer.

While **formula and nappies** might be available in modern, big-city supermarkets, elsewhere you'll need to bring a supply (and any medication if required) with you – local kids don't use nappies, just pants with a slit at the back, and when baby wants to go, mummy points him at the gutter. Similarly, **changing facilities** and **baby-minding services** are virtually unknown outside high-end international hotels.

While there are few places in Southwest China designed specifically for children, the way that most tourist sites are decked up like fairground rides makes them attractive for youngsters in any case. Things to watch for include China's poor levels of **hygiene** (keeping infants' and toddlers' hands clean can be a full-time occupation), spicy or just unusual **food**, plus the **stress levels** caused by the ambient crowds, pollution and noise found in much of the country – though it often seems to affect parents worse than children.

Travellers with disabilities

In China the **disabled** are generally hidden away, so attitudes are not very sympathetic and little special provision is made. As the country undergoes an economic boom, much of the country resembles a building site, with intense crowds and traffic, few access ramps and no effort to make public transport accessible. **Ribbed paving** down every city street is intended to help blind people navigate, but in reality Chinese pavements are unevenly surfaced obstacle courses of trees and power poles, parked vehicles, market stalls and random holes – the last thing anyone designs them for is unobstructed passage. Only a few International hotel chains, such as *Holiday Inn*, have experience in assisting disabled visitors.

Given the situation, it may be worth considering an **organized tour**. Take spares of any specialist clothing or equipment, extra supplies of drugs (carried with you if you fly), and a prescription including the generic name (in English and Chinese characters) in case of emergency. If there's an association representing people with your disability, contact them early on in the planning.

Sichuan

WANNIAN TEMPLE, EMEI SHAN

1

Sichuan

According to the Tang poet Li Bai, the journey to his populous homeland of Sichuan (四川, sìchuān) was "harder than the road to heaven". Mountains ring the province and until recently the only way here was to make the dangerous trip up the Yangzi via the Three Gorges or follow bandit-ridden roads through gaps in the ranges to the north and south. Westwards – well, westwards was Tibet, which, despite centuries of trade in tea, horses and wool, China only had nominal control of until the 1950s. Remote, though cosmopolitan and never entirely isolated, Sichuan developed its own food, politics and lifestyle, inaccessible enough to ignore central authority and to provide sanctuary for those fleeing it.

Sichuan splits into very different halves, cut by a diagonal range of hills that slant southwest across the province – and which, as the terrible **2008 earthquake** proved, follow a tectonic fault. **East** of this line, the subtropical Red Basin is one of China's most densely settled areas, an engaging mosaic of unusual historic sites, lively cities and rural scenery whose fertile soil produces three harvests a year; hit the region in spring, and hills are covered in a sea of brilliant yellow rape flowers. Among all this bounty sits **Chengdu**, Sichuan's relaxed but overcrowded capital, whose teahouse culture and panda breeding centre make for an enjoyable few days' stopover. Packed with antique buildings and cobbled lanes, attractive **Pingle** and larger **Langzhong** are the pick of the old towns nearby, though quirky **Zigong** not only sports impressive architecture, but also salt mines and a dinosaur museum. Imperial patronage of Buddhism saw religious sites flourish over a thousand years ago during the Tang dynasty, best experienced at the hulking, aptly named Big Buddha at **Leshan**, and **Emei Shan**, a forested holy mountain with over 65km of hiking tracks linking dozens of temples, in which visitors and pilgrims can stay overnight.

In contrast, **western Sichuan** is, geographically and culturally, part of Tibet; a wild, thinly populated land of snowcapped peaks, where yaks roam the tree line and roads traverse 5000m-high mountain ranges along hair-raising gradients. Most of the people here are **Khampa Tibetans**, tough, nomadic, yak-herding cowboys tearing around the scenery on horseback or, more likely nowadays, motorbikes. Indeed, monastery towns such as **Litang**, **Ganzi**, **Langmusi** and **Dêgê** have a rugged Wild West feel, full of red-robed monks, dust and cattle, and surrounded by open prairies dotted with

Highlights

❶ **Teahouses** Participate in a great Sichuanese institution by kicking back in a bamboo chair with a bottomless cup of tea at your side to watch the world go by. **See p.66**

❷ **Pandas** Enjoy great views of these charismatic beasts chewing through mountains of bamboo at Chengdu's breeding centre, or chance your luck at seeing one in the wild at remote Wanglang Reserve. **See p.70 & 111**

❸ **Zigong** An enjoyably quirky city with historic salt mines, extensive dinosaur remains and atmospheric, antique guildhalls. **See p.93**

❹ **Dafo** At 71m tall, the world's largest Buddha sculpture humbles visitors to insignificant specks – six people can stand on his toenail. **See p.99**

❺ **Emei Shan** Follow an ancient pilgrim trail through thick forests atop this famous Buddhist mountain, overnighting at monasteries along the way. **See p.101**

❻ **Songpan** Saddle up and ride into the mountains, meadows and forests surrounding this bustling and historic walled town. **See p.114**

❼ **Jiuzhaigou** An expensive but gorgeous scenic reserve, where a string of brilliantly blue lakes and waterfalls cascade down a long alpine valley. **See p.118**

❽ **Litang** Share the pavements with yaks and Tibetan cowboys at this gritty monastery town, which hosts electrifying horse races each August. **See p.137**

HIGHLIGHTS ARE MARKED ON THE MAP ON P.58–59

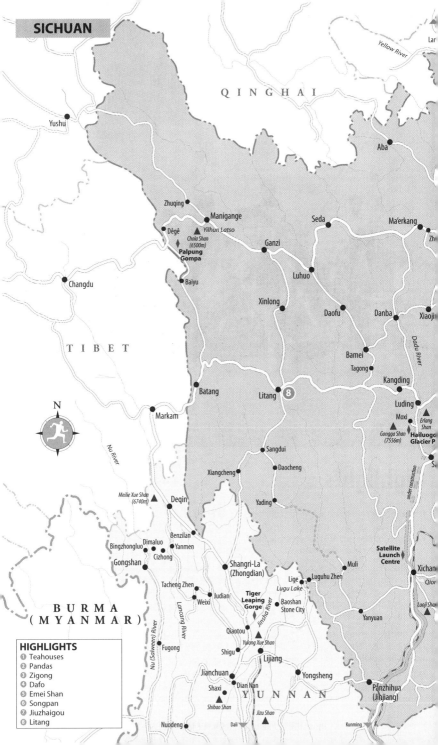

SICHUAN

QINGHAI

Yellow River

Lar

Yushu

Zhuqing

Manigange

Dêgê   Yilhun Latso

Chola Shan
(6500m)
Palpung
Gompa

Baiyu

Changdu

TIBET

Markam

Nu River

N

Batang

Litang

8

Sangdui

Xiangcheng   Daocheng

Yading

Deqin

Benzilan

Bingzhongluo Dimaluo Yanmen

Cizhong

Gongshan

Shangri-La
(Zhongdian)

Tacheng Zhen

Weixi   Judian

BURMA
(MYANMAR)

Lancang River

Nu (Salween) River

Fugong

Tiger
Leaping
Gorge

Qiaotou

Yulong Xue Shan

Shigu

Jianchuan

Dian Nan

Shaxi

Shibao Shan

Nuodeng

Seda

Ganzi

Luhuo

Xinlong   Daofu

Bamei

Tagong

Kangding

Ma'erkang

Zh

Danba

Xiaoji

Dadu River

Luding

Moxi   Erlang
Shan

Gongga Shan Hailuogo
(7556m)   Glacier P

S

under construction

Satellite
Launch
Centre

Muli

Lige
Lugu Lake

Luguhu Zhen

Baoshan
Stone City

Yanyuan

Lijiang

Yongsheng

YUNNAN

Jizu Shan

Dali

Xichan

Qior

Luoji Shan

Panzhihua
(Jinjiang)

Kunming

HIGHLIGHTS
1. Teahouses
2. Pandas
3. Zigong
4. Dafo
5. Emei Shan
6. Songpan
7. Jiuzhaigou
8. Litang

Meilie Xue Shan
(6740m)

Jinsha River

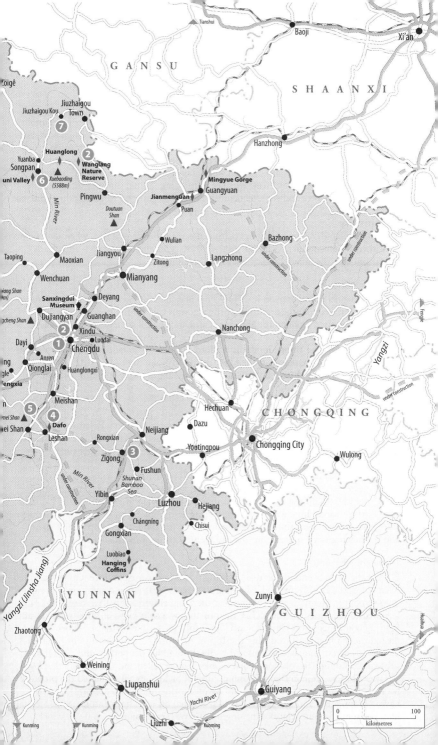

1

wildflowers and yak-felt tents. At **Songpan** and **Tagong** you can go horse-trekking, heavily touristed **Jiuzhaigou** and **Huanglong** feature startlingly blue alpine lakes, there's wildlife at **Wanglang** and beautiful Tibetan hamlets around **Danba**. If you're lucky you'll catch one of the many regional **horse races**, where Tibetans show off their considerable equestrian skills.

Sichuan's **road and bus** infrastructure is comprehensive, though almost always bogged down in roadworks. Distances make travel through western Sichuan – and beyond into Yunnan – time-consuming at best; winter snows cause further setbacks. Western Sichuan is also periodically **closed to foreigners**, so it's essential to check on the latest situation before heading out (see the box, p.64). The province is crossed by the Xi'an–Kunming **rail line**, with another route connecting Chengdu with Chongqing, so train is of most use for travel beyond Sichuan's borders. Sichuan's **weather** features hot, humid summers and cold winters, with the north and west frequently buried under snow for three months of the year.

Brief history

Eastern Sichuan developed a distinct culture as early as the Bronze Age, when settlements flourished at **Sanxingdui** and **Jinsha** 1600–800 BC, contemporary with – and clearly influenced by – the Shang dynasty elsewhere in China.

Early conquests

Irrigation works at **Dujiangyan** in 256 BC opened up the Chengdu plains to intensive farming, soon drawing the attention of the vigorous Qin armies from easterly Shaanxi province, who used Sichuan (or **Shu**, as the province is still sometimes known) as a strategic base to conquer all of China in 221 BC. Their example was repeated four centuries later by the **Three Kingdoms** warlord Liu Bei – who failed, however, to reunify the country after the collapse of the Han (see p.69) – and around 617 AD by the peasant general Li Shimin, who became the great Tang-dynasty emperor **Taizong**.

From Tang to Qing

Sichuan blossomed under the **Tang**, when the province produced Wu Zetian, the country's only empress, and numerous famous scholars and poets. Relations were also established with the Tibetan Kham states in what is now western Sichuan, which saw the Tang princess Wencheng wedded to the Tibetan king – a union later used as justification that Tibet was part of China.

Prosperity continued through the subsequent **Song** dynasty, when the world's first paper money was printed in Chengdu in 1024, but by the late **Ming** some six hundred years later, the Kham states had been conquered by the aggressive Fifth Dalai Lama in Lhasa. At the same time, war was depopulating eastern Sichuan, though transmigrants from eastern China got things going again during the **Qing**, setting up as merchants and revitalizing trade routes from the eighteenth century onwards.

The twentieth century

During the early twentieth century, fighting flared across the province. **China** reclaimed Kham after the British invaded Tibet in 1904 (see p.370); but a dispute over foreign involvement in Sichuan's railways toppled the Qing empire soon afterwards, and Tibet regained the territory. By the 1930s, the province was split between rival warlords, and fighting continued until China's new Communist government annexed Tibet and ousted the feuding factions during the 1950s. As centres of popular dissent, western Sichuan's Tibetan monasteries suffered badly throughout the period, and during the subsequent **Cultural Revolution**, when monks were expelled and the temples destroyed.

It was Chinese premier **Deng Xiaoping**, himself Sichuanese, who pulled the province back from destitution after Mao's death by promoting free-market reforms. Despite having Chongqing and the Yangzi corridor sheared off its eastern end in 1997, Sichuan has been a major beneficiary of the ongoing **Go West campaign** (see p.375), which

HOT STUFF: SICHUANESE COOKING

Sichuanese cooking usually involves heavy use of **chilli** (辣椒, làjiāo), which arrived in China via the Portuguese in the sixteenth century. Combined with **Sichuan pepper** (花椒, huājiāo), a dried berry with soapy perfume and mouth-tingling afterbuzz, it creates the classic **mala** effect, literally "hot and numb". Worried restaurant staff in Sichuan usually ask foreign diners "*chi lajiao, huajiao ma?*" ("can you eat chillies and Sichuan pepper"?); they'll point out milder dishes if you say no, but don't expect to be spared if you answer in the affirmative. Locals cram them in until their faces turn crimson, explaining addiction on medical grounds (chillies warm you in winter and help you sweat in summer), but once conditioned, you'll find flavours are far more complex than they appear at the initial, eye-watering, mouthful – and infinitely tastier than the tabasco-laden stir-fries served up as Sichuanese food overseas.

Classic *mala* dishes include **mapo doufu** (麻婆豆腐, mápó dòufu), a simple but satisfying mix of bean curd and minced pork; **strange-flavoured chicken** (怪味鸡, guài wèi jī), a cold dish dressed in a mouthwateringly aromatic sauce of sesame paste, soy sauce, sugar and green onions mixed in with the chillies and Sichuan pepper; and the innocently named **boiled beef slices** (水煮牛片, shuǐzhǔ niúpiàn), which packs more chillies per spoonful than almost any one Sichuanese dish.

Other dishes are nowhere near as spicy. There's the popular family meal of **twice-cooked pork** (回锅肉, huíguō ròu), where a piece of fatty meat is boiled, sliced thinly and then stir-fried with green chillies (it ends up looking and tasting a bit like bacon); **fish-flavoured pork** (海鲜肉, hǎixiān ròu), whose "seafood" sauce is made from vinegar, soy sauce, sugar and ginger; enduringly popular **gongbao chicken** (宫保鸡丁, gōngbǎo jīdīng), the local version of stir-fried chicken and peanuts; **tea-smoked duck** (樟茶鸭, zhāngchá yā), served cold, aromatic and juicy; and **crackling rice** (锅巴肉片, guōbā ròupiàn), a meat soup poured over a sizzling bed of crisp, deep-fried rice crusts – as much a performance piece as a meal.

Some restaurants also specialize in **snacks**: cucumber with chilli-oil and sesame seeds; **carry-pole noodles** (担担面, dāndān miàn), named after how street vendors once carted the noodles and spicy sauce in wooden buckets on the ends of a shoulder pole; deliciously smoky **tiger-skin peppers** (虎皮青椒, hǔpí qīngjiāo), scorched then fried with salt and dark vinegar; **gege** (格格, gégé), a snack of spicy meat steamed in ground rice, served in a tiny bamboo basket; and a huge variety of fun dumplings, including sweet **tangyuan rice balls** (汤圆, tāngyuán) and savoury **chaoshou** (抄手, chāoshǒu), the local version of wuntun soup dumplings.

One Sichuanese meal now found China-wide is **hotpot** (火锅, huǒguō), eaten everywhere from streetside canteens to specialist restaurants. You get skewers of raw meat or vegetables – hence the local name of "**fragrant kebabs**" (串串香, chuànchuàn xiāng) – cooked by you at the table in a bubbling pot of **stock**, either clear and unspiced (白汤卤, báitāng lǔ) or, more usually, blood-red with chillies (麻辣烫, málà tàng).

encourages Chinese industry from the wealthy eastern provinces to relocate inland, and today eastern Sichuan is booming.

The situation in western Sichuan remains less rosy. Though the monasteries have been reactivated and modern infrastructure laid down since the 1990s, the Tibetan majority remains disenfranchised. There's great resentment over the Chinese tourist industry's unsympathetic development of Tibetan holy sites, of meddling in religion, and of heavy-handed military crackdowns during recent uprisings over the border in Tibet. It's also obvious that the monasteries today house a fraction of the number of monks that they once did, and that – despite superficial improvements – life for many remains desperately poor.

Chengdu

成都, chéngdū

CHENGDU is a determinedly modern city, full of traffic, high-rise department stores, ever-increasing numbers of ring roads and mushrooming residential development. But

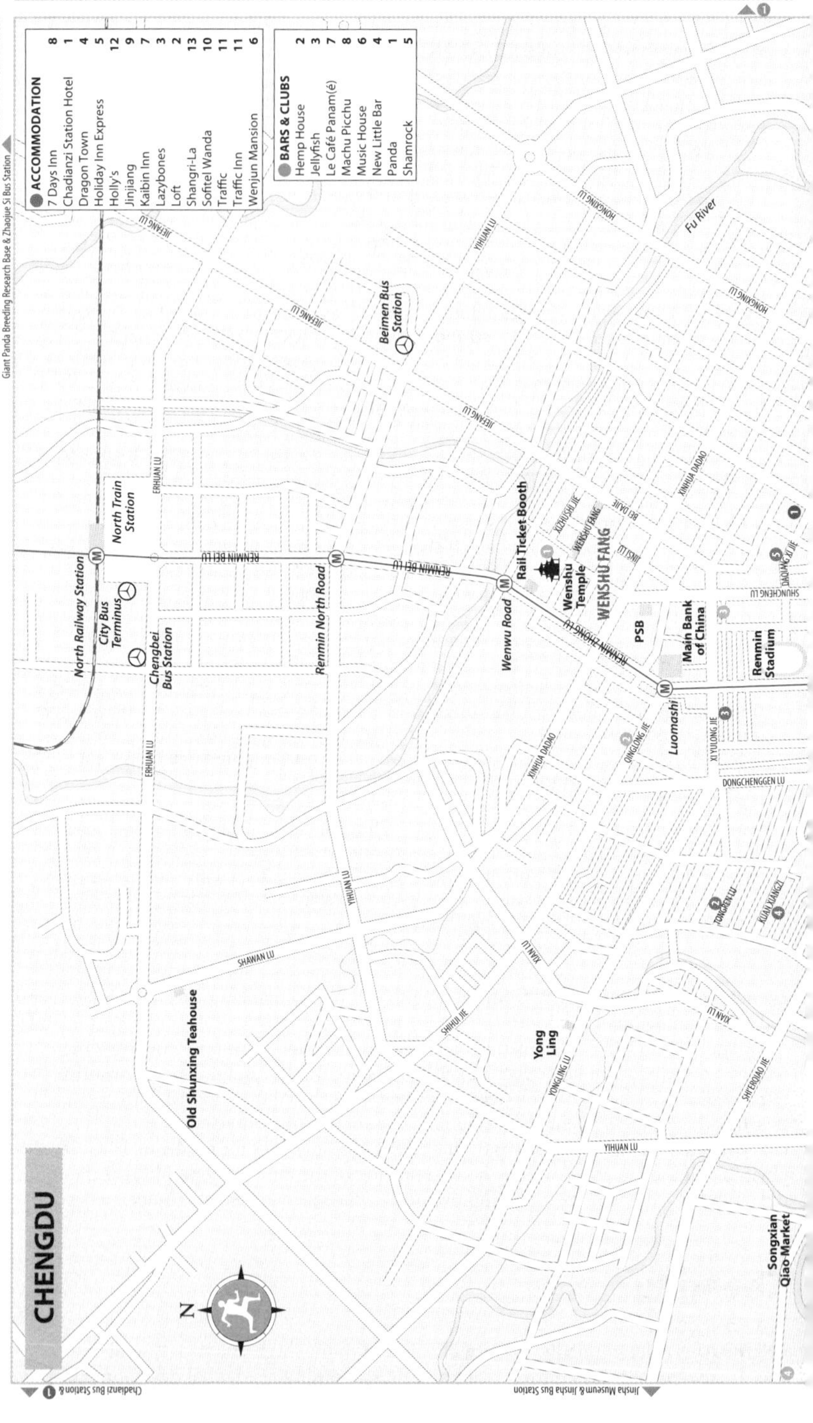

1
CHENGDU
ACCOMMODATION
7 Days Inn 8
Chadianzi Station Hotel 1
Dragon Town 4
Holiday Inn Express 5
Holly's 12
Jinjiang 9
Kaibin Inn 7
Lazybones 3
Loft 2
Shangri-La 13
Sofitel Wanda 10
Traffic 11
Traffic Inn 11
Wenjun Mansion 6
BARS & CLUBS
Hemp House 2
Jellyfish 3
Le Café Panam(é) 7
Machu Picchu 8
Music House 6
New Little Bar 4
Panda 1
Shamrock 5
Giant Panda Breeding Research Base & Zhaojue Si Bus Station
Chadianzi Bus Station & 1
Jinsha Museum & Jinsha Bus Station
N
North Railway Station
City Bus Terminus
North Train Station
Chengbei Bus Station
Beimen Bus Station
Renmin North Road
Wenwu Road
Rail Ticket Booth
Wenshu Temple
WENSHU FANG
PSB
Main Bank of China
Renmin Stadium
Luomashi
Fu River
Old Shunxing Teahouse
Yong Ling
Songxian Qiao Market
JIEFANG LU
ERHUAN LU
RENMIN BEI LU
RENMIN ZHONG LU
YIHUAN LU
HONGXING LU
XINHUA DADAO
BEI DAJIE
XIZHUSHI JIE
WENSHU FANG
JINSI JIE
SHUNCHENG LU
DAQIANG XI JIE
QINGLONG JIE
XI YULONG JIE
DONGCHENGGEN LU
TONGREN LU
KUAN XIANGZI
SHAWAN LU
XIAN LU
SHIHUI JIE
YONGLING LU
SHIERQIAO JIE

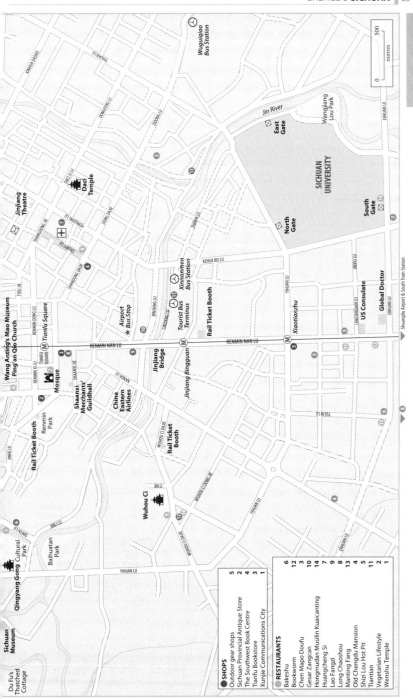

1

SHOPS

Outdoor gear shops	5
Sichuan Provincial Antique Store	2
The Southwest Book Centre	4
Tianfu Bookstore	3
Xunjie Communications City	1

RESTAURANTS

Bakeshu	6
Bookworm	12
Chen Mapo Doufu	3
Gesar Zangcan	10
Hongmudan Musilin Kuaicanting	14
Huangcheng Si	7
Lao Fangzi	9
Long Chaoshou	8
Manting Fang	13
Old Chengdu Mansion	4
Shizi Lou Hot Pit	5
Tiantian	11
Vegetarian Lifestyle	2
Wenshu Temple	1

Du Fu's Thatched Cottage

Sichuan Museum

Qingyang Gong Cultural Park

Wang Antirig's Mao Museum
Ping'an Qio Church

Jinjiang Theatre

Wuguiqiao Bus Station

Daci Temple

Jin River

East Gate

Wangjiang Lou Park

SICHUAN UNIVERSITY

North Gate

South Gate

Mosque

Shaanxi Merchants' Guildhall

China Eastern Airlines

Renmin Park

Tianfu Square

Airport Bus Stop

Xinnanmen Bus Station

Xinnanmen Bus Terminus

Tourist Bus Terminus

Rail Ticket Booth

Rail Ticket Booth

Jinjiang Bridge

Jinjiang Binguuan

Xiaotianzhu

US Consulate

Global Doctor

Wuhou Ci

Balhuatan Park

RENMIN NAN LU

Shuangliu Airport & South Train Station

Jin River

1

it's also a cheerful place; seasonal floral displays and ubiquitous ginkgo trees lend colour to its many excellent **parks**, and the population is self-consciously laidback, enjoying its **teahouse culture** at every opportunity and unfazed by this being interpreted as laziness by other Chinese.

There are downsides too – the city's traffic congestion and smog are atrocious – but get past these and Chengdu is Southwest China's most culturally rewarding city, whose elegant Buddhist and Daoist **temples**, busy monuments to warlords and poets, Bronze-Age relics at the **Jinsha Museum** and local opera style are rich testament to three thousand years of history. There's also one of China's most outstanding cuisines to spike your taste buds on, and the chance to get close-up views of locally bred **pandas**. Most visitors spend at least a few days here, enjoying the sights and exploiting its role at the centre of Sichuan's **transport network** to plan trips through western Sichan to Yunnan or Tibet.

Brief history

Eastern Sichuan had already been settled by the Neolithic **Baodun culture** as early as 2700 BC, though its first flowering came over a thousand years later at **Jinsha** (see p.69). Chengdu itself became a regional capital during the fourth century BC, and by Han times it was known as **Brocade City**, its silk travelling as far as imperial Rome. Two Tang-dynasty emperors sought sanctuary here after fleeing down the "Sichuan Road" from neighbouring Shanxi province, as did the great eighth-century poet **Du Fu** (see p.68).

Sacked in 1279 by the Mongols, who slaughtered the entire population, Chengdu had somehow recovered enough within the next decade to impress **Marco Polo** with its handsome bridges (and profitable customs duties), though the surrounding countryside was still devastated. The Ming and Qing eras saw Chengdu suffer similar cycles of destruction and restoration: after a massacre by Zhang Xianzhong during the 1640s (see p.151), migrants from central China were deliberately settled here to repopulate the city.

TO WESTERN SICHUAN AND TIBET

Tibet, along with northern and western Sichuan – including everywhere west of Ya'an, and also towns like Zöigê and Langmusi – is periodically **closed to foreigners**, usually because of unrest, or fears of unrest, among the population. At present, the whole region is off-limits every **March**, when tempers run high during the anniversary of the Dalai Lama fleeing Tibet in 1959; violent anti-Chinese riots in Lhasa during March 2008 spilled across into Sichuan, where trouble flared again in 2011.

At other times, western Sichuan is largely open to independent exploration, and visitors can travel by bus right through the region into northern Yunnan. However, foreigners **cannot enter Tibet** overland on public transport; expect to be turfed off the bus and booted back the way you came should you try.

At the time of writing, all travellers to Tibet must be on an **organized tour** (upwards of ¥1000) arranged through an agent and following a pre-arranged schedule; you cannot travel independently, nor stay on in Tibet once your tour is finished. Agents have off-the-rack itineraries covering popular sights in and around Lhasa, or you can help piece together more elaborate schedules. Agents can also arrange essential **permits for Tibet** (¥400), and transport to Lhasa – either **train** (44hr; ¥700 hard sleeper, ¥1000 soft sleeper) or by **flying** (2hr; ¥1200). Note that train tickets are in great demand from June until October. It might also be possible to **rent a jeep** and driver for an overland trip; expect the journey from Chengdu to Lhasa to take ten days and cost ¥16,000–20,000.

Every year, a few intrepid travellers dodge around the regulations, but if caught in Tibet without a permit you can expect a fine, a lengthy lecture and possible deportation from China. More information about Tibet, and routes in from Yunnan, can be found in relevant sections of the guide (see p.238) and at ⓦlandofsnows.com.

There were less serious uprisings during the **nineteenth century**, though in 1911 a strike in Chengdu over rail construction sparked nationwide riots that contributed to the fall of the Qing dynasty. Held by the Nationalists through **World War II**, the city profited from its proximity to China's wartime capital at Chongqing, becoming a major industrial, educational and business centre. Despite setbacks through the 1960s – when the Cultural Revolution saw the ancient city walls finally pulled down – Chengdu has bounced back yet again, and is now home to three million people.

Tianfu Square

天府广场, tiānfǔ guǎngchǎng

Tianfu Square, at Chengdu's centre, is a granite plaza with a subterranean metro stop, prettied up at night by dancing fountains illuminated by coloured lights. To the north, a beatific **statue of Chairman Mao**, his raised arm seemingly hailing a cab, was built over the site of the former governor's palace, demolished in the 1950s. West is Chengdu's main **mosque** (皇城清真寺, huángchéng qīngzhēn sì), last survivor of the city's old Islamic quarter; Muslims first appeared in Sichuan during the Tang dynasty, though – as in much of Southwest China – most arrived with the Mongols during the thirteenth century. Tianfu Square is due for a major facelift in the near future; the new **Chengdu Museum** is already under construction near to the mosque.

Northwest of Tianfu

Northwest of Tianfu at 25 Xihuamen Jie, there's a taste of 1920s architecture at **Ping'an Qiao Church** (平安桥天主教堂, píng'ān qiáo tiānzhǔ jiàotáng), featuring a spacious complex of grey-brick cloisters and barrel-vaulted ceilings, notably plain and short of statuary for a Catholic establishment.

Directly behind Ping'an Qiao Church – walk west along Ping'an Xiang, then turn north 150m along tiny Wuhu Jie – is **Wang Anting's Mao Museum** (王安廷小小展览馆, wáng āntíng xiǎoxiǎo zhǎnlǎnguǎn; donation) whose elderly, rather deaf curator has spent fifty years amassing an eccentric collection of Maomorabilia. The newspaper cuttings, posters, statues and 64,000 badges are all the worse for wear and displayed inside his squalid, lean-to home.

Daci temple

大慈寺, dàcí sì • Daci Si Lu • ¥3

A kilometre east of Tianfu Square, past the pedestrianized shopping precinct of **Chunxi Lu** (see p.76), **Daci temple** is a small nunnery dedicated to the Tang-dynasty monk **Xuanzang**, who was inducted into the priesthood here before beginning a seventeen-year journey to India to study Buddhism at its source. He returned to China in 645 AD with a massive trove of holy scriptures, and spent the rest of his life translating them under the emperor's patronage. Today, unfairly, he's best known as the witless pilgrim **Tripitaka** in the classic *Journey to the West* (see p.397), upstaged continuously by his mischievous disciple, Monkey.

Daci Temple illustrates the persistence of belief in China: founded during the seventh century, it was renovated in the Tang, totally destroyed during the Ming, rebuilt in the 1860s, used as a factory during the Cultural Revolution, and again restored during the 1990s. Of most interest is a side-wing **museum**, which houses a few pieces of Tang masonry and accounts of Xuanzang's journeys, along with a portrait of him carrying a bamboo backpack. There's also a small vegetarian restaurant serving basic noodle dishes here, open at lunchtime.

Wenshu temple

文殊院, wénshū yuàn • Daily 8am–5pm • ¥5 • Wenwu Lu metro

Wenshu temple, a sizeable Chan (Zen) monastery between Tianfu Square and the north train station, is dedicated to **Wenshu**, the Buddhist incarnation of Wisdom. He's usually portrayed riding a **blue lion**, images of which are scattered around the temple. The Ming-style halls themselves are unpretentious, open-plan wooden buildings with high, raked ceilings, and the pleasantly spacious courtyards and surrounding gardens all convey an air of tranquillity, despite the temple's burgeoning popularity. Plenty of visitors are here to pray, planting pink incense sticks and candles in the huge iron burners, though even more invade the **teahouse area** on the east side, a sea of bamboo chairs, stone tables, teacups and chattering crowds, covered with a crust of discarded peanut husks and sunflower seeds. The adjacent vegetarian restaurant is popular too – see p.74. Take time to check out the tall, narrow **pagoda** near the entrance; according to locals it contains **Xuanzang's skull** (see p.65), though other places in China also lay claim to his remains.

Wenshu Fang

文殊坊, wénshū fāng

East of Wenshu temple, **Wenshu Fang** is the largest of Chengdu's reconstructed "antique" quarters, an open area of old shops, houses, restaurants and flagstoned roads, all bustling with tourists. There are some genuine period pieces here – the elaborate **Aidao Tang** nunnery, and a stone gateway leading to a courtyard with a **relief map** of Chengdu carved on one wall – but really you're here to stroll, snack, pick up a souvenir and generally soak up the enjoyably dated atmosphere.

Renmin Park

人民公园, rénmín gōngyuán • Free except during local festivals • Tianfu Square metro

A ten-minute walk west of Tianfu Square, **Renmin Park** houses a few acres of trees, paved paths, ponds, lawns and bright ornamental gardens, providing an introduction to Chengdu's relatively mellow pace of life. Just inside the north entrance, the ever-busy **Heming teahouse** (鹤鸣茶馆, hèmíng cháguǎn) is shaded by wisteria and

TEAHOUSES

The Sichuanese have a reputation for being garrulous, and their enthusiasm for a natter is most obvious in the province's many **teahouses**. From downtown Chengdu to the back lanes of Litang, these hold much the same place in Sichuanese life as a local bar or pub does in the West; some are formal establishments with illuminated signs spelling out *chadian*, *chaguan* or *dachadian* (all meaning "teahouse"); others are just a spread of bamboo or plastic chairs in the corner of a park, a temple or any available public space.

Whatever the setting, just sit down and a waiter will approach to ask what sort of tea you'd like – the default jasmine-scented variety costs around ¥5 a cup, up to ¥40 or more for a really fine brew. Most are served in the three-piece Sichuanese **gaiwancha**, a squat, handleless cup with lid and saucer. **Refills** are unlimited – either the waiter will give you a top-up on passing your table, or you'll be left with a flask of boiling water. In a country where it's unusual to find somewhere to relax in public, teahouses are very welcome: idlers can spend the whole day chatting, playing mahjong, reading or just staring into space, without anyone interrupting – except cruising **masseurs** and **ear-wax removers**.

Renmin Park's *Heming* teahouse (see above) is a good introduction, and is popular with Chinese and foreigners alike. The oldest teahouse in town is probably at the *Rongcheng* hotel (容城宾馆, róngchéng bīnguǎn), south of Tianfu Square on Shaanxi Jie, which is built around the former Shaanxi Merchants' Guildhall; Qingyang Gong (see opposite) is where to mix with chatty locals; while if you like your tea with Sichuan opera, try the antique decor of Jin Li's theatre (see p.70).

1

marked by a large bronze teapot at the gate; it overlooks a pond and the surrounding vines attract plenty of wild birds. Nearby, the tall **Monument to the Martyrs** is an obelisk commemorating the 1911 rail disputes that marked the beginning of the end for China's Qing dynasty. Otherwise, the park is a good place to stroll or watch martial artists training at dawn; look for vendors with little burners and a slab of marble along the paths who "draw" skilful designs of Chinese zodiac animals with molten **toffee**. There's a **food festival** here in spring, and a **canteen** next to the teahouse serving Sichuanese snacks.

Kuan Xiangzi

宽巷子, kuān xiàngzi

After an uprising in Chengdu in 1789, a Manchu garrison was stationed in the city and built themselves a miniature version of Beijing's *hutong* alleyways in the area north of Renmin Park along **Kuan Xiangzi** and two adjacent lanes. These old streets have now been renovated and turned into a busy entertainment district, full of antique grey-brick houses in various period styles, snack stalls, restaurants and street performers. It's another good place to lounge in a teahouse and immerse yourself in a celluloid version of old China, especially at night, when red lanterns are hung up along the lanes and competing coloured lights add to the mix.

Yong Ling

永陵博物馆, yǒng líng bówùguǎn • Daily 9am–5pm • ¥20 • Bus #48 from Xinnanmen bus station via Xi Yu Long Jie, near the Luo Ma Shi metro station

Yong Ling is the tomb of Wang Jian, a Tang-dynasty general who seized power in Sichuan in 907 AD and set himself up as Emperor of Shu. He was succeeded in 918 by his inept son Wang Yan, who lost the kingdom to a resurrected Tang in 925, but not before he'd concealed his father's tomb under a 15m-high conical hill, which was discovered and excavated in 1942. The three barrel-vaulted brick chambers had been robbed in antiquity, but a jade belt, gold seal and a small, placid **statue** – believed to be the only contemporary sculpture of an emperor – remained, as did the immoveable **sarcophagus platform**, a 6m-long stone plinth beautifully carved in relief with flowers and female musicians. The platform is supported by twelve life-sized warrior busts sunk up to their waists in the floor; with their curly hair, big noses and generous beards, these pall-bearers are clearly not Chinese – the Tang dynasty was known for its close links with central Asia.

Qingyang Gong

青羊宫, qīngyáng gōng • Daily 8am–5pm • ¥10 • Tourist bus #901 or bus #82 from Binjiang Lu

Qingyang Gong is Chengdu's largest Taoist monastery, whose odd name – it means "Green Goat Temple" – relates to the cryptic last words of the Taoist sage **Laozi** as he rode his buffalo off into the sunset: "Look for a green ram once you have practised Taoism for a thousand days". His disciple Yinxi followed these instructions and duly encountered the goat on the spot that Qingyang Gong was later founded.

The legend is echoed at the 20m-high **Bagua Pavilion**, an octagonal structure wrapped in gold dragons, where a life-sized statue of Laozi sits astride his buffalo. There's more outside the **Three Purities Hall**, where worshippers rub two oversized **bronze goats** for luck – though on closer inspection, the right-hand "goat" turns out to be the simultaneous incarnation of all twelve Chinese zodiac animals, with deer's antlers, lion's paws and so on. The open-fronted hall itself was built in 1669 and contains giant gilded statues of the Three Purities along with smaller representations of Taoist Immortals and sacred animals.

1

The rest of the complex is full of little halls, gingko trees and the inevitable noisy teahouse, and at weekends you might find **professional storytellers** recounting folk tales to crowds. Don't miss the courtyard behind the **Duomu Hall**, where a wall has been painted with the three auspicious characters for Luck (福, fú), Longevity (寿, shòu) and Wealth (禄, lù); people stumble towards them with their eyes closed, hoping to make contact, while their friends stand around laughing.

Songxian Qiao curio market

送仙桥古玩艺术城, sòngxiānqiáo gǔwán yìshù chéng • Tourist bus #901 or bus #82 from Binjiang Lu to Songxian Qiao stop

About 700m west of Qingyang Gong on Qingyang Shang Jie, **Songxian Qiao curio market** is a large spread of stalls and permanent shops dealing in all manner of antiques, and it's easy to spend an hour browsing. It's busiest at weekends, but there's always a good spread of books, paintings, carvings, embroidery, wooden furniture latticework and window screens, porcelain, temple statues and monumental granite troughs. Some of this is pure tourist tack, some is genuinely old, but most is good-quality reproduction and prices are reasonable (you'll need to haggle).

Sichuan Museum

四川省博物馆, sìchuān shěng bówùguǎn • Tues–Sun 9am–5pm • Free • Tourist bus #901 or bus #82 from Binjiang Lu to Songxian Qiao stop

Diagonally across the road from the curio market, **Sichuan Museum** offers a snapshot of provincial history over three floors. Downstairs is packed with **Han pottery** and sculptures, so fantastically animated and full of life you wonder how Chinese art became so heavy and formal; there are musicians, acrobats, animals and a statue of the fierce Qin-dynasty general Ruan Wenzhong. Upstairs, local **Bronze Age cultures** are sketched out in animal-headed urns and ornamental weapons, and there's a thorough pottery display, with mock-ups of antique kilns found in the Chengdu area. The top floor is of most interest for its collection of **ethnic textiles** and the **Tibetan Buddhist Gallery**, full of intricate **thangkas** (see p.240) and multi-armed statuettes – including a few politely described as "double-bodied figures".

Du Fu's Thatched Cottage

杜甫草堂, dù fǔ cǎotáng • Daily 8am–6pm • ¥60 • Tourist bus #901 or bus #82 from Binjiang Lu

Out past the museum, some 3km from central Chengdu, **Du Fu's Thatched Cottage** is an evocative memorial to the eighth-century Tang-dynasty poet **Du Fu** (see below). These gardens were founded two centuries later by fellow-poet **Wei Zhuang**, reaching their current layout of artfully arranged bamboos, pools, bridges and flowerbeds around 1800. There's nothing dramatic to see, but it's a pleasant place to ponder statues of a sadly emaciated Du Fu and check out the small museum illustrating his life.

PALACES, HUTS AND COMPASSION: DU FU

Du Fu's works, which often focused on war and the life of ordinary Chinese citizens, were tinged with compassion and sorrow, complementing the more romantic imagery of his contemporary **Li Bai** (see p.84). Born in 712, Du Fu struggled for years to obtain a position at the imperial court in Chang'an (modern Xi'an), succeeding in 755 only after one of his sons had died of starvation and as the empire was beginning to disintegrate. Fleeing the war-ravaged capital for Chengdu in 759, he spent the next five years in a grass-roofed hut outside the city's west wall, where he wrote some 240 of his 1400 surviving poems. After his patron Yan Wu died in 764, Du Fu left Chengdu and to wander central China "like a lonely gull between the earth and the sky", dying on a boat in Hunan six years later.

Jinsha Museum

金沙遗址博物馆, jīnshā yízhǐ bówùguǎn • 5km west from the centre at 227 Qingyang Dadao • Daily 8am–6pm • ¥80 •
Tourist bus #901 to the entrance, or bus #47 from Renmin Xi Lu to Jinsha bus station, then walk 500m up Qingyang Dadao to the museum

In 2000, developers excavating a building site west of Chengdu at Jinsha uncovered remains of previously unknown **prehistoric settlement** dating back to Sichuan's enigmatic **Ba-Shu** culture. Covering five square kilometres, **Jinsha** blossomed from 1200 to 600 BC and has yielded house remains, tools and artefacts, thousands of graves, and scores of **sacrificial pits** filled with ornaments and animal bones.

Jinsha Museum comprises gardens and two well-planned, modern exhibition halls built right over these fascinating finds. The **Site Exhibit Hall** covers a grid of sacrificial pits, which were dug a couple of metres deep into the brown soil; 3000-year-old tree roots excavated here suggest that the area was forested when the pits were dug. The glass-sided building is well lit, and wooden boardwalks allow a close look, though the elephant tusks, animal bones and jade artefacts found here have all been removed. A separate **Exhibition Hall**, on three levels, houses realistically imagined dioramas of the site, plus the pick of the finds, including hundreds of beautifully coloured, translucent jades, small statues of tigers and kneeling slaves with bound hands, and a thin, serrated **gold disc** depicting a "sunbird".

Wuhou Ci

武侯祠, wǔhóu cí • Daily 8am–6pm • ¥60 • Tourist bus #901 or bus #82 from Binjiang Lu

Just southwest of the centre, **Wuhou Ci** – the "Shrine to the Minister of War" – is named after the famous third-century strategist Zhuge Liang; though as his emperor, Liu Bei, is also buried here, the whole site is really a big monument to the **Three Kingdoms** period (see below). Nicely planted gardens with big trees surround a temple-like complex, whose halls and open-air galleries are full of oversized **painted statues** of famous characters who fought for the Kingdom of Shu (Sichuan), including a grey-faced, fierce Zhang Fei (see p.92), a pale Liu Bei robed in gold, and an atypically relaxed-looking Guan Yu, now enshrined in the Chinese pantheon as the god of war. Zhuge Liang gets his own hall, where he sits between his son and grandson holding a characteristic ostrich-feather fan – there's also a large **bronze drum** (see p.350) hanging up on the wall.

THE THREE KINGDOMS

The empire, long divided, must unite; long united, must divide. Thus it has ever been.

So, rather cynically, begins one of China's best-known stories, the fourteenth-century historical novel *Romance of the Three Kingdoms*. Well founded in fact, the tale recounts events of the **Three Kingdoms**, when warlords split China into competing states at the end of the Han dynasty.

The main action began in 189 AD. On the one side was the crafty **Cao Cao**, chancellor to the Han throne, whose motto was "Better to wrong the world than have it wrong me". Facing him was the virtuous **Liu Bei**, a distant relative of the imperial house, whose watery character was compensated for by his spirited sworn brothers **Zhang Fei** and **Guan Yu**. Having joined forces to put down a rebellion by the Yellow Turbans, Cao and Liu fell out and began fighting; after years of subtle strategy, guerilla sniping and all-out warfare, Liu engaged the aid of the wily **Zhuge Liang** and a third warlord, **Sun Quan**, and in 208 AD defeated Cao in a naval engagement on the Yangzi known as the **Battle of the Red Cliffs**.

Despite success at the Red Cliffs, no one victor had a large enough force to unify the country. Instead, each retreated to form a private kingdom: Cao Cao withdrew north to the Yellow River basin where he established the state of **Wei**; Sun Quan set up **Wu** farther south along the lower Yangzi; while Liu Bei built a power base in the riverlands of Sichuan, the state of **Shu**. Following Guan Yu's death, Liu marched against Wu but his troops mutinied, killing Zhang Fei. Humiliated, Liu died of shame at Baidicheng (see p.169) and the war smouldered on until the original players were all dead. A coup in Wei against Cao's successor saw the Sima clan emerge victorious; they founded a new dynasty, the **Jin**, and finally united China – albeit briefly – in 280 AD.

Out the back and reached along a wavy path, **Liu Bei's Tomb** is a walled mound planted with pine trees, an essential pilgrimage site for any Chinese named "Liu", who want to claim connection to one of China's emperors. The tomb has never been excavated so you can't go inside, but it's generally believed that, after his death in 223 AD at Baidicheng on the Yangzi (see p.169), only Liu's head was buried here. Elsewhere, there's a small **Three Kingdoms Culture Hall** containing period pottery and weapons, a modern sculpture of the "Oath in the Peach Garden", where Liu, Zhang Fei and Guan Yu swore brotherhood, and some expensive teahouses – go elsewhere for a cup.

Jin Li

锦里, jǐn lǐ • Tourist bus #901 or bus #82 from Binjiang Lu

Running along the east side of Wuhou Ci, **Jin Li** is a narrow, twisting, flagstoned lane done up in generic Song style, with teahouses, souvenir shops and plenty of stalls selling a range of Chengdu's famous **snacks**; cold spiced noodles, grilled skewers of lamb and "Three Blasts" (三大炮, sān dàpào), where rice-flour balls are bounced rapidly off a drum into a tray of roasted flour, then served in a sweet syrup – more a performance than a meal. It's a fun place to mill with weekend crowds, and at the rear is an antique, open-air **theatre**, showing nightly performances of Sichuan opera (8pm and 9pm; ¥120).

The Tibetan Quarter

Chengdu's **Tibetan quarter** lies south of Wuhou Ci along Wuhouci Dong Jie, full of shops stocked to their roofs with heavy clothes, leather cowboy boots, chunky amber and turquoise jewellery, knives and prayer wheels, conches and other temple accessories – not to mention heavy-duty blenders capable of whipping up a gallon of butter tea in one go. None of this is for tourists; most customers are Tibetan women with braided hair, monks and cowboys, all looking decidedly tall and robust next to the local Chinese.

The Giant Panda Breeding Research Base

大熊猫繁育研究基地, dàxióngmāo fányù yánjiū jīdì • 10km northeast of Chengdu • Daily 8am–6pm • ¥58 • ⓦ panda. org.cn • Tourist bus #902 from outside the Traffic hotel (¥2); hostel minibus tours are ¥98/person, including entry

Chengdu's **Giant Panda Breeding Research Base** is a pleasant, well-managed zoo whose giant and red pandas (see p.112) are clearly healthy and occupy spacious, well-vegetated enclosures where they can hide if they feel like it. Most of the time they're all too happy to lounge around in full view, however – though red pandas are shyer – devouring piles of bamboo left around for their pleasure, and you can get some excellent photos. There are shady paths and lawns for visitors to stroll around, so give yourself a couple of hours here, and bring a picnic lunch.

Everything in China is a growth industry nowadays and pandas are no exception; the base's **breeding programme** has become so successful – reputedly by showing the notoriously indifferent bears "panda porn" to get them in the mood – that they're talking about setting up a business to sell them to foreign zoos. This means that there are often younger animals about, which you can sometimes be photographed holding in the cub enclosure (¥1000).

Despite what you'll hear, the pandas don't spend the whole day sleeping, though they're more active before their mid-morning feed. The base is heaving on summer weekends and holidays, but on quiet afternoons the bored staff spend their time teaching the pandas tricks.

ARRIVAL AND DEPARTURE   CHENGDU

Chengdu has multiple **train** and **bus** stations, the most important of which are covered below. There's also a **second airport** under construction 55km east, due to open in 2012, which will be linked to the city by a light railway. If travelling through western Sichuan or to **Tibet**, read the box on p.64 first. For adventurous trips to **Yunnan**, you can reach Lugu Hu

Note that in Chengdu's listings and throughout the guide, where buses are **frequent** throughout the day (every 30min or more), we have not flagged departure frequencies.

and Lijiang via Xichang (p.109) and – assuming the region is open – Shangri-la via Litang (p.140). Heading east, **Chongqing City** is best reached in just two hours aboard the high-speed, D-class train.

BY PLANE

Shuangliu airport (双流机场, shuāngliú jīchǎng) is 16km southwest of town, connected by an airport bus (approx every 30min; 30min; ¥10) to Yandao Lu, off Renmin Nan Lu opposite the *Jinjiang* hotel; a taxi costs around ¥50. Buy plane tickets through accommodation or at China Eastern, corner of Jinli Dong Lu and Xia Nan Dajie ☎ 028 8615 5233, ✆ ce-air.com.

Destinations Beijing (6 daily; 2hr 30min); Chongqing City (1 daily; 45min); Guangzhou (4 daily; 2hr); Guilin (2 daily; 1hr 30min); Guiyang (5 daily; 1hr 10min); Jinghong (2 daily; 1hr 45min); Jiuzhaigou (5 daily; 55min); Kunming (5 daily; 1hr 20min); Lhasa (6 daily; 2hr); Lijiang (5 daily; 1hr 25min); Nanning (4 daily; 2hr 55min); Shanghai (6 daily; 2hr 30min); Shenzhen (6 daily; 2hr 20min); Tengchong (2 daily; 1hr 40min); Xichang (6 daily; 1hr).

BY BUS

Buses from Chengdu's long-distance stations overlap, so it's not always necessary to travel to the city outskirts to find a bus: check central Xinnanmen station first, and if there's nothing there, look for a station located in the direction you're headed (for example, Chadianzi station for western or northern Sichuan; Zhaojue Si or Beimen stations for northeastern destinations). Note that buses from Chadianzi start very early, so consider spending the night before at the station hostel (see p.72).

Beimen (北门汽车站, běimén qìchēzhàn), northeast of the centre on Yihuan Lu. Bus #27 orbits the city along Yihuan Lu, or it's a 10min walk to Renmin Lu and the metro.

Destinations Langzhong (hourly; 5hr; ¥92); Xindu (40min; ¥5); Yibin (hourly; 5hr; ¥101); Zigong (hourly; 4hr; ¥98).

Chadianzi (茶店子客运站, chádiànzǐ kèyùn zhàn), 8km northwest of the city. Bus #82 travels to Binjiang Lu via Du Fu's Cottage and Qingyang Gong.

Destinations Danba (1 daily; 12hr; ¥160); Jiuzhaigou (1 daily; 9–11hr; ¥175); Kangding (3 daily; 8hr; ¥120); Ma'erkang (1 daily; 16hr; ¥180); Songpan (1 daily; 8–12hr; ¥160); Zöigê (1 daily; 14hr; ¥175).

Jinsha (金沙汽车站, jīnshā qìchēzhàn), 5km west of the centre; bus #47 from Renmin Xi Lu, near Tianfu Square metro.

Destinations Anren (5 daily; 2hr; ¥10); Dayi (2hr; ¥10); Qionglai (every 15min; ¥20).

Xinnanmen (新南门汽车站, xīnnánmén qìchēzhàn), just southeast of the centre.

Destinations Daocheng (1 daily; 20hr); Dujiangyan (7am–2pm; 1hr 30min; ¥15); Emei Shan (4hr; ¥45); Hailuogou (1 daily; 9hr; ¥110); Huanglongxi (1hr 30min; ¥12); Jiuzhaigou (1 daily; 8–12hr; ¥175); Kangding (8am–2pm; 8hr; ¥120); Leshan (3hr; ¥40); Luodai (1hr; ¥5.50); Pingle (5 daily; 2hr 30min; ¥24); Qingcheng Shan (2hr; ¥20); Ya'an (5 daily; 2hr; ¥44).

Zhaojue Si (照觉寺汽车站, zhàojué sì qìchēzhàn), 5km northeast of the centre on bus #1 or #45 from Renmin Nan Lu.

Destinations Guanghan (1hr 10min; ¥12); Guangyuan (4hr; ¥80); Jiangyou (2hr; ¥30); Jianmen Guan (5 daily; 4hr; ¥62).

BY TRAIN

Buy train tickets at the stations, through hostels and agents (with at least a ¥30 booking fee) or at the downtown rail ticket offices shown on our map (see p.62); there are more at Xinnanmen and Beimen bus stations.

North train station (成都火车站, chéngdū huǒchēzhàn), about 5km north of the centre at the top of Renmin Lu. Catch the metro down Renmin Lu, or walk through the station square, turn left and it's 200m to the city bus terminus: #16 runs down Renmin Lu to the south train station, #52 and #27 circuit Yihuan Lu, and #55 passes near the *Traffic* hotel and Xinnanmen bus station.

Destinations Beijing (4 daily; 16–30hr); Chongqing City (15 daily; 2hr 15min); Dujiangyan (9 daily; 45min); Guangyuan (20 daily; 4–6hr); Guangzhou (4 daily; 30–40hr); Guilin (1 daily; 25hr); Guiyang (7 daily; 12–20hr); Jiangyou (21 daily; 2hr 30min); Lhasa (1 daily; 44hr); Nanning (1 daily; 32hr); Qingcheng Shan (9 daily; 50min); Shanghai (5 daily; 36hr); Shenzhen (1 daily; 37hr); Xi'an (9 daily; 16hr).

South train station (火车南站, huǒchē nán zhàn), about 6km south of the centre; take the metro or bus #16 into town.

Destinations Emei (8 daily; 2hr 30min); Kunming (5 daily; 22hr); Panzhihua (7 daily; 13hr); Xichang (10 daily; 10hr).

GETTING AROUND

Chengdu's streets are approaching gridlock, despite the construction of a new **metro line** through the city centre, and roads are so clogged that bikes – and even cars – often short-cut along pavements. Use the metro where possible and allow time to get around.

1

By bike All the hostels rent out bicycles at ¥20 a day plus ¥300 deposit.

By bus City buses operate daily from about 6am until 9pm or later and cost ¥1, or ¥2 if a/c.

By metro Chengdu's metro line (daily 7am–9pm; ¥2–4) runs south through the city between the two train stations, with stops at Tianfu Square and along Renmin Lu. An east–west branch is due for completion around 2015.

By minibus Hiring a minibus for the day through a hostel costs a steep ¥500 and up.

By taxi ¥6 to hire, then ¥1.5/km.

By tourist bus These (¥2) depart from a stop right outside the *Traffic* hotel. Bus #901 (irregular; alternatives are given in the text): Chunxi Lu, Wuhou Ci, Qingyang Gong, Sichuan Museum, Du Fu's Thatched Cottage, Jinsha Museum. Bus #902 (daily 8am–4.30pm, at least hourly): Giant Panda Breeding Research Base.

INFORMATION

Tourist information For current information on every aspect of the city, plus background articles about Chengdu, Sichuan and China, log on to ⓦ gochengdoo.com. Chengdu's hostels, with their English-speaking staff, internet access and travellers' notice boards are useful on the ground; you can also chat to foreign residents at the *Bookworm* (see p.74) or the backpacker-oriented *Dave's Oasis* on Binjiang Lu (ⓦ davesoasis.com).

Dragon Expeditions Near Wuhou Ci at 9, Gao Sheng Qiao Lu ☎ 028 8508 2770, ⓦ dragonexpeditions.com. Have been organizing climbing and hiking tours and handing out advice about the region since 2007, and are highly recommended.

Western Sichuan Tours Yulin Nan Lu ☎ 139 8003 5421, ⓦ wstourix.com. Regular guided mountain treks (on foot and horseback) and birdwatching expeditions.

ACCOMMODATION

HOSTELS

Chadianzi Bus Station Hostel 茶店子客运站住宿, chádiànzǐ kèyùnzhàn zhùsù ☎ 028 8750 6615. Clean, basic rooms above the bus station; worth considering if you have an early-morning departure. **¥60**

Dragon Town 龙城宽巷子青年旅馆, lóngchéng kuānxiàngzi qīngnián lǚguǎn. 26 Kuan Xiangzi ☎ 028 8664 8408. Atmospherically set behind a stone gateway in a reproduction antique building, this hostel perfectly fits the mood of Chengdu's busiest old quarter. Rooms are slightly tatty around the edges – some bathrooms need refitting – but otherwise this is a good budget choice. Dorms **¥35**, doubles **¥110**

Holly's 九龙鼎青年客栈, jiǔlóngdǐng qīngnián kèzhàn. 246 Wuhou Ci Dajie ☎ 028 8554 8131. Set among Tibetan shops and martial art supply stores (there's a sports college nearby), this long-running hostel with slightly threadbare rooms and extremely helpful staff has a

book exchange, a roof-garden café and a Tibetan restaurant next door. Dorms **¥30**, doubles **¥100**

Lazybones 懒骨头青年旅馆, lǎngǔtóu qīngnián lǚguǎn. 16 Yangshi Jie ☎ 028 6537 7889, ⓦ chengduhostel.com. Bus #16 or metro to "Luomashi" stop. Clean hostel in a renovated building just north of Tianfu Square, well located for Wenshu Temple and Kuan Xiangzi. Dorms **¥35**, doubles **¥120**

★ **Loft** 四号虎工厂青年旅馆, sìhào hǔgōngchǎng qīngnián lǚguǎn. 4 Tongren Lu, aka Xiangtong Xiang ☎ 028 8626 5770, ⓦ lofthostel.com. Industrial-chic operation inside a converted factory with exposed concrete pillars, wooden floors and a glassed-in courtyard garden. The quiet residential location is a plus. Dorms **¥40**, doubles **¥180**

★ **Traffic Inn** 交通饭店, jiāotōng fàndiàn. Behind the Traffic Hotel at 77 Linjiang Lu, near Xinnanmen bus station ☎ 028 8545 0470, ⓦ redcliffinn.cn. Simple, clean modern doubles and twins with or without bathroom, plus

---

TOURS FROM CHENGDU

As well as booking plane and train tickets (for a fee), Chengdu's youth hostels (see above) can set up **tours** to the Panda Breeding Base (¥98, including entry), Sichuan opera (¥120), Qingcheng Shan (¥98) and Tibet (¥1000, not including flights/train or permits), plus Yangzi cruises (from ¥500) and Songpan horse treks (¥600).

The best independent **guide** in Chengdu is Tray Lee (☎ 0139 0803 5353, ✉ lee@rt98.com or ✉ leevisit@qq.com), who can sometimes be found in Renmin Park. He speaks perfect English, knows Sichuan backwards, and has been guiding foreigners around for over twenty years. Northern and western Sichuan's **mountains** – including Siguniang Shan (p.130) and Gongga Shan (p.129) – are attracting increasing numbers of trekkers, climbers and mountaineers. We've listed local contacts in relevant parts of the guide; there are also two established Chengdu operators, best contacted online in advance.

dorms (in the main hotel building). The *Highfly Café* here serves Western and Chinese staples. Dorms ¥25, doubles ¥85

HOTELS

7 Days Inn 7天连锁酒店 / 陕西街店, qītiān liánsuǒ jiǔdiàn / shǎnxī jiē diàn. 106 Shaanxi Jie ☎ 028 8168 9988. Budget hotel right in the city centre, within walking distance of Renmin Park and Tianfu Square. Staff here keep the place in great order; rooms are small but spotless and comfortable, and it's likely to be booked out – call in advance. ¥190

★ **Holiday Inn Express** 鼓楼快捷假日酒店, gǔlóu kuàijié jiàrì jiǔdiàn. 72 Daqiang Xi Jie ☎ 028 8678 5666, ⊛ holidayinnexpress.com.cn. Comfortable, modern and efficient – what you'd expect from this budget international chain. Prices rise considerably if there's a conference on in town. ¥390

Jinjiang 锦江宾馆, jǐnjiāng bīnguǎn. 80 Renmin Nan Lu ☎ 028 8550 6666, ⊛ jjhotel.com. 1950s, Soviet-style tourist hotel, now revamped with some panache to make the international grade and featuring luxurious rooms, bilingual staff and a host of restaurants – plus a fully uniformed Sikh guard on the front door. ¥1200

Kaibin Inn 凯宾酒店盐市口店, kǎibīn jiǔdiàn yánshìkǒu diàn. 1 Xiao Kejia Xiang ☎ 028 8667 2888, ⊜ kaibinhotel@yahoo.com.cn. It's hard to find the entrance – it's in a walkthrough between Chunxi Lu and Hongxing Lu – but this well-priced budget hotel is pretty

central. The rooms compare well to those at *7 Days Inn*, although the staff could be more helpful. ¥190

Shangri-La 香格里拉大酒店, xiānggélǐlā dàjiǔdiàn. 9 Binjiang Dong Lu ☎ 028 8888 9999, ⊛ shangri-la.com. International chain occupying a thirty-storey tower block on the riverside southeast of the city centre, with a spa, indoor swimming pool and probably the best views in Chengdu. ¥1200

Sofitel Wanda 索菲特万达大饭店, suǒfēitè wàndá dàfàndiàn. 15 Binjiang Zhong Lu ☎ 028 6666 9999, ⊛ sofitel.com. It's hard not to be impressed by the full-sized fan palms and acres of marble in the lobby of this smart hotel. Restaurants, bars and a swimming pool are part of the package. ¥1000

★ **Traffic** 交通饭店, jiāotōng fàndiàn. 77 Linjiang Lu, near Xinnanmen bus station ☎ 028 8545 1017. Don't be discouraged by the slightly spartan atmosphere; this well-maintained older hotel features spotless modern doubles with TV and shared or private bathroom, and is excellent value for money. Staff are deadpan but helpful. The attached *Traffic Inn* (see opposite) is their backpackers' wing. ¥180

Wenjun Mansion 文君楼宾馆, wénjūnlóu bīnguǎn. 180 Qintai Lu ☎ 028 8613 8884. In a street done up like a "Chinatown" in the West, complete with gaudy restaurants and antique-style buildings, this tidy, multi-floored place imitates a traditional courtyard design, though the functional rooms lack character. Beds ¥60, doubles ¥240

EATING

Chengdu's three antique quarters are also **food streets**: Wenshu Fang and Jin Li are good for the city's famous snacks – such as *dandan mian*, *san dapao* and dumplings – while Kuan Xiangzi is awash with hotpot restaurants. Indeed, inexpensive **hotpot** places are common throughout the city, and your accommodation can point you to the nearest. **Vegetarians** should visit Wenshu temple or *Vegetarian Lifestyle* (see p.74). Sichuanese food tastes especially good with **beer** – try locally brewed "Snow" (雪花啤酒, xuěhuā píjiǔ).

SICHUANESE

★ **Chen Mapo Doufu** 陈麻婆豆腐, chén mápó dòufu. Upstairs at 197 Xi Yulong Jie. Founded in 1862, this is the home of Grandma Chen's bean curd, where ¥20 buys a large bowl of tofu glowing with minced meat and *mala* sauce. They also do a good range of Sichuanese favourites.

Lao Fangzi 老方子, lǎo fāngzǐ. 243 Wuhou Ci Dajie ☎ 028 8509 8822. The original restaurant of what is now a China-wide chain, serving Sichuanese classics in a fairly laid-back environment. Try the house-style cold chicken (very spicy), shredded dry-fried yak meat, black-bean rabbit cubes, shredded pork in "cut" buns and a host of vegetable dishes. Most mains ¥35 or less.

Long Chaoshou 龙抄手饭店, lóng chāoshǒu fàndiàn. East off Chunxi Lu. A big, busy dumpling house with fast-food ambience and plastic chairs, renowned for its local snacks. A big bowl of *chaoshou* in soup costs ¥12, or

try carrypole noodles (¥5), rabbit cubes with orange peel (¥16), lamb kebabs (¥16) or *zhong* dumplings (¥5).

★ **Manting Fang** 满庭芳, mǎntíng fāng. Erhuan Lu, at Yulin Lu ☎ 028 8517 7958. Classic Sichuanese dishes served in smart surroundings; try the mouthwatering chicken (口水鸡, kǒushuǐ jī), rice-coated spareribs, dry-fried beans, tiger-skin peppers and *mapo* tofu. Fine flavours prove that Sichuanese cuisine can be about more than just chillies and oil. Count on ¥80/person in a group.

Old Chengdu Mansion 老成都公馆菜, lǎo chéngdū gōngguǎn cài. 37–41 Qinghua Lu, just outside Du Fu's Thatched Cottage ☎ 028 8732 0016, ⊛ sichuanfood.cn. Upmarket Sichuanese theatre restaurant requiring "proper dress" – smart casual is fine – you dine in a central atrium and watch opera performances on the stage. It's touristy and expensive, but fun as a one-time experience. Mains ¥60 and up.

Shizi Lou Hotpot 狮子楼火锅琴台店, shīzi lóu huǒguō qíntái diàn. 101 Qintai Lu, a "Chinatown"

1

street between Renmin Park and Qingyang Gong. Glitzy hotpot establishment named after a bloodbath-in-a-teahouse episode in *Outlaws of the Marsh* (see p.397). Choose white stock, red stock, or a divided pot with both, then pay from ¥15–30/plate for straightforward veg and meat up to several hundred yuan for rare fungi and game.

Tiantian 天添饭店, tiāntiān fàndiàn. 16 Yulin Dong Jie. Excellent home-style Sichuanese cooking at this inexpensive gem; try the roast duck in soup, greens with gingko nuts, garlic cucumber and a spicy-hot salad known as "tiger food" (老虎菜, lǎohǔ cài). Around ¥30 a head.

REGIONAL CHINESE AND VEGETARIAN

Gesar Zangcan Ximianqiao Heng Jie. One of many nearby Tibetan restaurants, authentic down to the DVDs of Tibetan pop, a cowboy clientele and begging acolytes going round the tables. Expect butter tea in metal teapots, dumplings, fresh yoghurt and fried, boiled or chopped yak; don't count on vegetables. Around ¥20/person.

Hongmudan Musilin Kuaicanting 红牡丹穆斯林快餐厅, hóng mǔdān mùsīlín kuàicāntīng. Kehua Jie, off Erhuan Lu, Sichuan University south gate. You'd be hard-pressed to find a more authentic Uighur Muslim restaurant outside of their northwestern Chinese homeland; lashings of greasy pilau rice, mutton stews, spicy chicken and freshly made *lamian* ("pulled noodles"). Lamb kebabs and flat Turkish bread are sold outside. Not hygienic, but nothing costs more than ¥20 or so.

Huangcheng Si 皇城寺大饭店, huángchéng sì

dàfàndiàn. 108 Xiyu Jie, just west of Tianfu Square. Halal restaurant inside the mosque, popular and not expensive. They serve mostly northwestern Chinese food, much of it very spicy; use the Chinese photo-menu as the English menu is limited. ¥35/head.

Vegetarian Lifestyle 枣子树铂金店, zǎozishù bójīn diàn. 3/F Bojingcheng Building, 27 Qinglong Jie, just west of the Bank of China ☎ 028 8628 2848. Local branch of a nationwide chain with fresh, light Chinese vegetarian dishes – the crispy "eel", mixed dumplings, pumpkin soup and dry-fried green beans are excellent.

Wenshu temple The long-running vegetarian restaurant here is open from mid-morning until around 2pm, serving informal, ¥15 set meals in the courtyard, or more sophisticated dishes inside (from ¥18 each).

WESTERN

Bakeshu 八棵树, bākēshù. 9 Ping'an Xiang ☎ 028 8669 9060. Next to the church and of similar vintage, this Singaporean-run restaurant features dark wooden interiors, veranda seating and an eclectic, colonial menu encompassing French wine, T-bone steak and Malaysian curries. A smart place for a coffee too. Mains ¥160.

Bookworm 老书虫, lǎo shūchóng. 2–7 Yujie Dong Lu ⓦ chengdubookworm.com. Difficult to know how to classify this Western expat hangout: it's part bar, part restaurant-café and part bookshop hosting regular music and literary events. A good place to chill over a coffee (¥15), or fill up on burgers or stews (from around ¥45).

NIGHTLIFE

Chengdu's combination of outgoing locals and expat students and professionals means its **nightlife**, unusually for China, has a real buzz. Check ⓦ gochengdoo.com for the latest, but the following are good places to start; most lie off Renmin Lu in the south of town, not too far from the university campus. The three-day **Zebra Music Festival** in May, originally held as a benefit gig for victims of the 2008 earthquake, is where to find up-and-coming rock bands from Chengdu and beyond.

Hemp House 麻糖, mā táng. 3rd Floor, Oriental Times Plaza, Dongmen Daqiao. DJs or live bands – anything from

folk to mainstream rock and Beijing punk – served up to a good mix of local Chinese and Western residents.

SICHUAN OPERA

Sichuan opera (川戏, chuānxì) is a rustic variant on Beijing's, but as well as sharing Beijing's bright costumes, stylized action and glass-cracking vocals, *chuanxi* has two specialities: fire-breathing and rapid face-changing, where the performers – apparently simply by turning around or waving their arms across their faces – completely change their make-up.

Nightly **variety shows** catering to tourists are held around town, featuring short opera scenes, fire-breathing and face-changing, comedy skits, puppetry, shadow-lantern play and storytelling. These are pretty enjoyable and you might even catch occasional full-length operas. Venues include **Shufeng Yayun** (蜀风雅韵, shǔfēng yǎyùn) in the Cultural Park (enter off Qintai Lu); the Ming-style open-air theatre at the end of Jin Li, near **Wuhou Ci** (武侯祠古戏台, wǔhóu cí gǔxìtái); the **Old Shunxing Teahouse** (顺兴老茶馆, shùnxīng lǎo cháguǎn), northwest of the centre at Floor 3, Chengdu International Convention Centre, 258 Shawan; and the downtown **Jinjiang Theatre** (锦江川戏馆, jǐnjiāng chuānxìguǎn) at 54 Huaxing Zheng Jie, a lane north of Shangdong Jie. Seats cost ¥120–220, depending on the venue and row.

Jellyfish 水母酒吧, shuǐmǔ jiǔbā. 143 Kehua Bei Lu, ⓦ jelly-jelly.com. Industrial space, its every inch now painted black (there's even all-black furniture) and converted to a cocktail bar. Pool table and lounge upstairs, small outdoor terrace, bar with excellent, inexpensive cocktails, and the rest for DJ-driven dancing.

Le Café Panam(é) 巴黎咖啡, bālí kāfēi. 143 Kehua Bei Lu ⓦ cafepaname.com. French expat hangout with laidback atmosphere, inexpensive beer and regular bands and events.

Machu Picchu 马丘比丘咖啡馆, mǎqiū bǐqiū kāfēiguǎn. 14 Fanghua Heng Jie. Friendly, laidback café with mainly Chinese customers, hosting weekend folk sessions and open jams – often just Western-style guitar, sometimes regional Chinese folk sounds.

Music House 音乐房子, yīnyuè fángzi. Yulin Shenghuo Plaza, Yulin Nan Lu. Local celebrity/media hangout, pretty cramped inside, with bands and DJs relayed through a third-rate sound system. Most of the crowd couldn't care less; the main point here is the insane sale and consumption of whisky – apparently they're going for a world record.

New Little Bar 小酒馆芳沁店, xiǎojiǔguǎn fāngqìn diàn. 87 Fangqin Jie. Small place ever popular for a quick drink or two, but also by far the best live rock and pop venue in Chengdu, occasionally attracting international acts.

Panda 熊猫俱乐部, xióngmāo jùlèbù. Jianshe Nan Lu, east of the city centre. Warehouse-sized, electronica-driven venue, the brainchild of local serial nightclub owner Tan Zhong. It's a bit far from the centre, but the only place you'll hear dance music in town.

Shamrock 三叶草爱尔兰西餐酒吧, sānyècǎo àiěrlán xīcān jiǔbā. 15 Renmin Nan Lu Section 4 ⓦ shamrockinchengdu.com. Irish sports bar that's been around forever, with live music or DJ most nights and a happy hour 4–9pm on Fri.

SHOPPING

Chengdu's main **shopping district** lies east of Tianfu Square around pedestrianized **Chunxi Lu** (春熙路, chūnxī lù), where you'll find boutiques and department stores such as Taiping, Ito Yokado and Isetan, and high-density crowds.

Antiques Aside from the Songxian Qiao curio market (see p.64), the Sichuan Provincial Antique Store, at the corner of Dongchenggen Lu and Renmin Xi Lu, has a dusty but varied collection of genuine antique porcelain, wooden screens and collectables.

Books The Southwest Book Centre, opposite the south end of Chunxi Lu, and the Tianfu Bookstore, at the southwest corner of Tianfu Square, both stock a huge range of maps, guidebooks in Chinese, DVDs and English-language novels on multiple floors.

Clothes There are brand-name clothing stores along Chunxi Lu, the area east of Renmin Bei Lu, near the north train station, is a massive wholesale clothing market; look out too for fluffy panda earmuffs, hats, slippers and bags.

Mobile phones Everything you need is in or around Xunjie Communications City, cnr of Taisheng Lu and Daqiang Dong Jie, west of the GPO.

Outdoor gear Dragon Expeditions (see p.72) have the best selection of serious outdoor gear in Chengdu. For decent Chinese-brand waterproofs, fleeces, sleeping bags, tents, boots, stoves and accessories, try the generic outdoor stores opposite Wuhou Ci, and also at the Renmin Nan Lu–Yihuan Lu intersection.

DIRECTORY

Banks The main Bank of China (Mon–Fri 8.30am–5.30pm) is on Renmin Zhong Lu. Many other branches and banks around town have ATMs accepting foreign cards.

Consulates Thailand, Floor 2, *Kempinski Hotel*, 42 Renmin Nan Lu Section 4 ☎ 028 8519 2266; US, 4 Lingshiguan Lu, Renmin Nan Lu ☎ 028 8558 3992, ⓦ chengdu.usembassy-china.org.cn.

Internet All hostels and most hotels have terminals and wi-fi; there's also wi-fi at the *Bookworm* and *Café Panam(e)*. The huge net bar above Xinnanmen bus station charges ¥3/hr; you might need a passport to log on.

Medical centre English-speaking Global Doctor, Floor 2, Lippo Tower, 62 Kehua Bei Lu ☎ 028 8528 3638; 24hr emergency number ☎ 01398 225 6966, ⓦ globaldoctor.com.au.

Post office The GPO is in a 1920s building at the corner of Shuwa Bei Yi Jie and Xinglong Jie, daily 8am–6pm. There's an EMS centre opposite.

PSB 391 Shuncheng Da Jie, near Wenshu temple; visa section on the second floor, open Mon–Fri 9am–noon and 1–5pm.

Central Sichuan

Lured away by more spectacular attractions elsewhere, not so many people linger in **central Sichuan**, the area immediately surrounding Chengdu. If you're just after a day-trip, however, there are plenty of rewarding excursions: **Qingcheng Shan** is an easier, more accessible version of Emei Shan (see p.80); the old towns of **Huanglongxi** and **Luodai**, though prone to serious tourist overload during weekends and festivals, are fun for a feed and a couple of hours' wander around antique lanes; while **Sanxingdui**, **Dujiangyan**, **Liu's Manor** and Xindu's **Baoguang Temple** round out local history. More distant places – the tea-horse town of **Pingle**, and Ya'an's pandas and tea terraces – could each conceivably be fitted into a single day, though an overnight trip would be more relaxed. All are covered by local **buses**, though it can take a while to escape Chengdu's traffic; Dujiangyan and Qingcheng Shan are also best reached by **train** from the north train station.

Huanglongxi

黄龙溪古镇, huánglóngxī gǔzhèn

HUANGLONGXI is a rustic riverside village 40km south of Chengdu whose half-dozen **Qing-dynasty streets** – narrow, flagstoned and lined with rickety wooden shops – featured in the martial arts epic. Once an important marketplace, it's now selling *Crouching Tiger, Hidden Dragon* itself to tourists, full of souvenir stalls, restaurants and shops displaying **grindstones** for making **soft bean curd** (豆花, dòu huā).

Once on the 500m-long main street, turn right for the large and slightly shabby **Gulong Temple** (古龙寺, gǔlóng sì), whose courtyard contains a large, sagging fig tree propped up by crutches designed to look like dragons. A hall here once served as the town **Yamen**, or courthouse, and restorations emphasize the punishments meted out in former times: poles for beating suspects until they confessed; a heavy *cangue*, a wooden yoke worn about the neck; and a dog-headed guillotine for executing common criminals (those for officials were tiger-headed).

There are plenty of teahouses and places for lunch, after which you might check out Huanglongxi's other sights – tiny **Chaoyin Temple** (潮音寺, cháoyīn sì), guarded by a whiskered statue of Nanwu, a dragon spirit in human form; and **Zhenjiang Temple** (镇江寺, zhènjiāng sì) with its ancient, beribboned banyan.

ARRIVAL AND DEPARTURE | HUANGLONGXI

By bus Huanglongxi buses depart Chengdu's Xinnanmen bus station every 30min until mid-afternoon (1hr 30min; ¥12). The last bus leaves Huanglongxi by 4pm.

EATING AND DRINKING

Huanglongxi's main street is lined with open-fronted, family-owned **restaurants** serving fried shrimps, catfish and eels, along with twice-cooked pork and other home-style dishes. Afterwards, take the steps down to the river from Zhenjiang Temple and lounge on bamboo chairs under the willows at any of the open-air teahouses.

Luodai

洛带古镇, luòdài gǔzhèn

LUODAI, 20km east of Chengdu, was once a prosperous base for China's **salt trade**. Ethnic **Kejia** (Hakka) merchants from Guangdong and central China were especially drawn to Luodai, as their relatives had been settled here in transmigration programmes during the early Qing dynasty (see p.367). By the 1700s, these migrants had become wealthy enough to build themselves imposing **guildhalls**, three of which survive.

You arrive in Luodai's functional modern quarter: turn right out of the station to the end of the road, then left up 250m-long **Luodai Zhen Jie**, the last old street in town. A brightly painted statue of the Taoist spirit of Longevity adorns the front of the **Hubei-Hunan Guildhall** (湖广会馆, húguǎng huìguǎn; ¥5) here, whose arched gateways enter into a series of pretty but lifeless courtyards. The nearby **Jiangxi Guildhall** (江西会馆, jiāngxī huìguǎn; ¥5) is similar, but the **Guangdong Guildhall** (广东会馆, guǎngdōng huìguǎn) – built in 1747 and recognizable by its yellow-tiled roof and southern-style

1

wavy eaves – is much more animated, thanks to its teahouse-restaurant (see below) – a meal here pretty well justifies the excursion.

ARRIVAL AND DEPARTURE	LUODAI

By bus Minibuses to Luodai (8am–6pm; 1hr; ¥5.50) leave frequently from a depot behind Chengdu's Xinnanmen station. Buses back to Chengdu run until late afternoon.

EATING AND DRINKING

★ **Guangdong Guildhall Restaurant** 广东会馆川餐厅, guǎngdōng huìguǎn chuān cāntīng. A whole side-wing of this old stone-and-beam building is given over to eating. Their (heavily Sichuanese-influenced) Kejia-style cooking is excellent: a plate of smoked goose with three vegetable dishes and soup comes in around ¥60.

Xindu

新都, xīndū

Some 16km northeast of Chengdu, the market town of **XINDU** sits at the start of the ancient "Road to Sichuan" (see p.84), to which the cheerful and tranquil **Baoguang Temple** (宝光寺, bǎoguāng sì; ¥15) here owes its fame. Hidden away behind a bright-red spirit wall at the rear of a large square, Baoguang Temple had its moment of glory when the Tang emperor **Xizong** fled to Sichuan during a rebellion in 880 AD and found sanctuary for a night at this Buddhist monastery. He later funded rebuilding, but the temple was razed during Ming-dynasty turmoils, and was only restored during the 1830s. Tang traces survive in the layered, thirteen-storey **Sheli Pagoda**, and some column supports decorated with imperial dragons at the **Qinfo Hall**. Baoguang's highlight, however, is its **luohan hall**, which houses 518 colourful, surreal statues of Buddhist saints, along with 59 Buddhas and Boddhidarma, founder of the Chan (Zen) sect.

ARRIVAL AND DEPARTURE	XINDU

By bus Bus #650 to Xindu (40min; ¥5) departs from the rear of Chengdu's Beimen station. Once at Xindu, take local bus #1 or #8 for a kilometre to the temple.

EATING AND DRINKING

Baoguang Temple Vegetarian Restaurant 宝光寺素菜馆, bǎoguāng sì sùcài guǎn. inside the temple, to the right; open daily 10am–2pm. Classic Buddhist food, concentrating on simple mixed vegetable stir-fries such as "Monks' Food" (罗汉菜, luóhàn cài). Also does more complex dishes like *gongbao* chicken, using imitation meat; and excellent sweet white fungus soup. There's an English menu with pictures. Mains from ¥15.

Sanxingdui Museum

三星堆博物馆, sānxīngduī bówùguǎn • 25km northeast of Chengdu • Daily 8.30am–5pm • ¥80 • Buses to Guanghan, 8km short of the site, depart from Chengdu's Zhaojue Si bus station (1hr 10min; ¥12). From Guanghan's bus station, catch local bus #6 (¥1) to the museum. Returning to Chengdu, flag down long-distance buses outside the museum, or retrace your steps

---

SAINTS, SOOTHSAYERS AND LUOHAN HALLS

Buddhism's eighteen original **luohans** – also known as **arhats**, or saints – have, since the religion's arrival in China 1900 years ago, grown to include over five hundred famous monks, emperors, folk heroes and even the occasional foreigner (look for big noses, curly hair and full beards). This has spawned **luohan halls**, where statues of the five hundred, often grotesquely caricatured, are arranged in a cross-shaped maze, with an isolated statue of Guanyin at the centre.

For an idea of what fate has in store for you, choose a luohan at random as your starting point, count your years of age to a new luohan (moving left for men, right for women), then note the luohan's number. Give this number to the attendant monk at the luohan hall's entrance, and you'll receive a card with obscure advice on how to make the most of your future.

In 1986 an archeological team investigating the site of a Shang-dynasty town outside Guanghan (广汉, guǎnghàn), discovered an extraordinary set of rectangular **sacrificial pits** containing a trove of jade, ivory, gold and **bronze** artefacts, all of which had been deliberately broken up before burial. Excavation revealed a settlement that from 1600 BC was a centre for the **Ba-Shu culture**, until it was upstaged by Jinsha (see p.69) and abandoned around 800 BC.

All this is covered at the excellent **Sanxingdui Museum**, with two main halls and English captions. The thousands of artefacts on display are both startling and nightmarish, the products of a very alien view of the world: a 2m-high bronze figure with a hook nose and oversized, grasping hands standing atop four elephants; metre-wide masks with obscene grins and eyes popping out on stalks; a 4m-high "spirit tree" entwined by a dragon with knives and human hands instead of limbs; and finely detailed bronzes, jade tools and pottery pieces.

Dujiangyan

都江堰, dūjiāngyàn

For over two thousand years **DUJIANGYAN**, an otherwise unremarkable junction town 60km northwest of Chengdu at the edge of the Chengdu plains, has played a pivotal role in Sichuanese history. It was here in 256 BC that the provincial governor **Li Bing** and his son **Erlang** harnessed the capricious Min River with a complex of dams, artificial islands and channels, opening up 32,000 square kilometres of eastern Sichuan to intensive agriculture. Their **Dujiangyan Irrigation Scheme** remains fully functional – even though the modern Zipingpu Dam, 9km upstream, has made the project's flood-control aspects redundant.

The irrigation scheme

About 1km north of Dujiangyan's crowded, functional centre, you can spend a good half-day exploring the heart of the Lis' project at **Lidui Park** (离堆公园, líduī gōngyuán; daily 8am–6pm; ¥90). Looking like a giant chesspiece, an ancient stone statue of Li Bing found on the riverbed in 1974 graces **Fulong Temple** (伏龙观, fúlóng guàn), which sits at the tip of the first channel. From here the path crosses the Min via artificial islands and the **Anlan Suspension Bridge**, one of the major landmarks on the old trade routes into western Sichuan, whose foothills rise abruptly on Dujiangyan's outskirts.

Across the bridge, steps ascend to **Erwang Miao** (二王庙, èrwáng miào), a stone memorial hall with hugely flared eaves dedicated to the Lis, recently rebuilt after suffering severe damage in the 2008 quake. Look for an old fresco showing a bird's-eye view of the irrigation scheme, and an alcove bust of **Ding Baozhen**, the nineteenth-century governor after whom the Sichuanese dish *gongbao jiding* ("Governor's Chicken Cubes") is named. Ding was an able official who renovated Dujiangyan's irrigation scheme, supported China's modernization, executed the powerful and corrupt palace eunuch An Dehai and reformed Sichuan's salt trade (see p.93).

Heading back, follow signs for the wooded **Songmao Road**, another fragment of the ancient route into western Sichuan, which passes through two stone gateways and the old **Town God's Temple** on the way to the exit.

ARRIVAL AND DEPARTURE	**DUJIANGYAN**

By train Dujiangyan is best reached by high-speed train from Chengdu's north train station (9 daily 7.15am–7.25pm; 50min; ¥15). The last train back departs Dujiangyan around 8.35pm.

EATING

The outflowing canal between the town's centre and the park is lined with inexpensive alfresco **restaurants**, all with bundles of fresh vegetables, piles of mushrooms and tofu, and buckets of freshwater crayfish, snails, eels and frogs laid out in front. They cook any combination to order, but make sure you fix prices in advance.

1

Qingcheng Shan

青城山, qīngchéng shān

Feeling amazingly fresh after Chengdu's smog, **Qingcheng Shan** sits at the point where western Sichuan's densely forested foothills rise abruptly from the Chengdu plains, 15km from Dujiangyan and 75km northwest of Chengdu. The mountain has been a Taoist site since Zhang Ling, founder of the important Tianshi sect, died here in 157 AD, and its many shrines are set in courtyards with open-fronted halls, at the back of which are ornate, glassed-in cases containing brightly painted statues. They're all pretty similar; none gives much protection from the weather and so reflect the seasons, dripping wet and mossy on a rainy summer day, coated by winter snows, or carpeted in yellow ginkgo leaves in early November. Most people concentrate on Qingcheng's more accessible **front section**, but there's also a wilder **rear section**; you can't walk directly between the two.

Qingcheng front section

青城前山, qīngchéng qián shān · ¥90

Stone-flagged steps from the gates ascend to the 1200m-high summit of Qingcheng's **front section** in a couple of hours; it's an easy, pleasant hike but there's also a cable car (¥35 each way). The pick of shrines along the way are **Cihang Dian** (慈航殿, cíháng diàn), dedicated to the Taoist goddess of compassion; **Tianshi Cave** (天师洞, tiānshī dòng), a small hollow where Zhang Ling lived before his death at the age of 122; and **Shangqing Gong** (上青宫, shàngqīng gōng), whose attractions include gateway calligraphy by the Guomindang leader Chiang Kaishek (see p.371). At the top is a modern, six-storey **tower** containing a 12m-high golden statue of Laozi and his buffalo, with views off the balconies of backsloping ridges and lower temples poking out of the forest.

Qingcheng rear section

青城后山, qīngchéng hòu shān · ¥90

About 5km from the front section, Qingcheng's rear section is accessed via the antique-style tourist township of **Qingcheng Shan Zhen** (青城山镇, qīngchéng shān zhèn). It's an enjoyable, if tiring, six-hour round-trip hike from here up through thick forest to atop of **Yinghua Shan**, Qingcheng's 2128m apex; along the way are more pavilions, a plank road – the wooden slats morticed straight into the cliffside – several waterfalls and, below the peak, the atmospheric and aptly named **White Cloud Temple** (白云宫, báiyún gōng).

ARRIVAL AND DEPARTURE   QINGCHENG SHAN

By train Qingcheng Shan is reached via Dujiangyan on high-speed train from Chengdu's north train station (9 daily, 7.15am–7.25pm; 50min; ¥15). The last train back departs Qingcheng Shan at 8.30pm. From Qingcheng Shan station, minibuses shuttle to the mountain's two trailheads (20–40min; ¥5–10).

ACCOMMODATION AND EATING

Qingcheng Shan Zhen was a big building site at the time of writing, but there was plenty of **accommodation** here before the earthquake – the temples are your best bet. Temples can also provide bowls of **noodles** and stir-fried vegetables, along with fragrant, locally grown green tea.

Shangqing Gong Offers accommodation in basic dorms or doubles with a/c and bathrooms. Don't expect too much; you are halfway up a mountain here. Beds **¥15**, doubles **¥80**

Liu's Manor

刘氏庄园, liúshì zhuāngyuán · Daily 8am–4pm · ¥60

During the early 1930s, Sichuan was split between feuding warlords and Tibetan armies, all fighting each other for control of the shadow-province of **Xikang** – a region

1

now encompassing all of western Sichuan. Two of the major players were **Liu Wenhui**, who eventually drove the Tibetans out of Xikang with the help of Muslim troops from neighbouring Qinghai; and his nephew **Liu Xiang**, who ousted his battle-weary uncle in 1935 but then returned Xikang to him as a peace offering.

Liu's Manor, 50km west of Chengdu at the county town of **Anren** (安仁镇, ānrén zhèn), is a sprawling 1930s grey-brick complex of interlocking courtyards, gardens and single-storey wooden halls. Once the elegant home of Liu Wenhui's elder brother, **Liu Wencai**, it's well worth a visit to see how the Communists villified the landlord class after they took power in 1949 – you'll need the best part of a day for the return trip and a couple of hours on site. Nothing escapes being used as evidence of Liu Wencai's crimes: his parlour for entertaining "landlords, local tyrants, and bandit chieftains"; rooms for smoking opium; and the showpiece **Rent Collection Courtyard**, where 114 anguished, life-sized sculptures depict families beggared by crushing rents, babies murdered by henchmen and parents imprisoned for debt. Liu Wencai's descendants are campaigning to have his name cleared, now that property no longer equates with theft in China.

ARRIVAL AND DEPARTURE   **LIU'S MANOR**

By bus There are direct buses from Chengdu's Jinsha bus station to Anren, or aim first for the county town of Dayi (大邑, dàyì), 10km northwest of Anren, and look for Anren buses there.

Anren destinations Chengdu (several daily; 2hr; ¥10); Dayi (20min; ¥5).

Dayi destinations Anren (20min; ¥5); Chengdu (2hr; ¥12); Qionglai (30min; ¥7).

Pingle

平乐古镇, pínglè gǔzhèn

As a stage on the Chengdu–Ya'an–Kangding **tea-horse road** (see box, below), **PINGLE** was once a riverside marketplace dealing in oil, salt and cloth. Today this small country town, 90km west of Chengdu, consists of low-key concrete buildings surrounding a core of a dozen largely unreconstructed old lanes, whose names – Straw Sandal Street, Eight Shop Street, Hay Market Street – recall the old days. Ancient trees are strung with votive red ribbons and paper lanterns, shops sell local snacks and chilli-tofu paste, there's a working **smithy** and wooden **theatre stage**, and evening flotillas of candles are floated downstream on little paper boats. The town is just far enough from Chengdu not to be overrun by tourists, at least midweek, when it makes for a mellow overnight trip.

Pingle's only real sight is the red sandstone **Leshan Bridge** (乐山大桥, lèshān dàqiáo) spanning the shallow Baimo River, which dates to the early Qing dynasty. Over the

THE TEA-HORSE ROADS

Southwest China's old **tea-horse roads** (茶马古道, chámǎ gǔdào) form a web of trade routes threading between Yunnan, Sichuan and Tibet, along which goods have been traded for hundreds, if not thousands, of years. **Tea** was particularly important, especially **pu'er** from southern Yunnan, which was compressed into dense "bricks" and portered, in massively heavy loads, over the mountains into Tibet. Here they were exchanged for wool and **horses**, needed by the Chinese military. Staging posts and marketplaces along the way blossomed: some, such as **Pingle** (see above) in Sichuan and **Shaxi** in Yunnan (see p.216), faded as modern roads and trains took away business; others – like **Kangding** (see p.124) in western Sichuan – became major administrative hubs. In many areas Muslim **Hui** ran the original horse caravans, and now own the trucking companies that have replaced them – one reason that you'll find mosques and Muslim communities scattered through the Tibetan fringes of Yunnan and Sichuan.

There's been a recent **revival** of interest in the tea-horse roads, and it's rare to find an old town in the region failing to mention the role they've played in local history. Much of this is exaggerated (not least in heavily touristed towns), but there are places – notably the markets at Shaxi and **Weishan** (see p.205) – where you can still experience scenes from the horse-road days.

1

river, the banks are lined with the requisite open-air **teahouses** where locals sprawl in the summer heat, playing cards or mahjong; it's worth dropping into the nearby *Jianxian Lou* restaurant and *Pinglou Tang* winehall (see below) for a look at their antique-style fittings.

ARRIVAL AND DEPARTURE   PINGLE

By bus Pingle's bus station is in the new part of town; turn left out of the station then first right and you're on 100m-long Yuwang Xin Jie, which leads down to the old town. Direct buses to Pingle run from Chengdu's Xinnanmen station; from elsewhere, head first for Qionglai (邛崃, qiónglái), 20km from Pingle. Qionglai also has

connections to Ya'an and Dayi.
Pingle destinations Chengdu (5 daily, last at 4.50pm; 2hr 30min; ¥24); Qionglai (20min; ¥5).
Qionglai destinations Chengdu (every 15min; 2hr; ¥20); Dayi (30min; ¥7); Pingle (20min; ¥5); Ya'an (1hr; ¥15).

ACCOMMODATION AND EATING

Family-run guesthouses in the old town offer simple rooms for around ¥60; they hang flags outside with the characters for "accommodation" (住宿, zhùsù). Mosquitoes can be a problem in summer; check netting. Numerous **canteens** around town serve noodles, stir-fries and juicy beggar's chicken (叫花鸡, jiàohuā jī – a whole bird baked in a clay casing). Watch out for curiously addictive candied chilli peppers – you're definitely in Sichuan.

Dahe 大河客栈, dàhé kèzhàn. Changqing Jie ☎028 8878 2830. Straightforward guesthouse along main road in the old town; it can get a little noisy on busy days. **¥60**
Jianxian Lou 剑仙楼饭店, jiànxiān lóu fàndiàn. Near Leshan Bridge, on the far side of the river ☎028 8920 2606. Renovated two-storey teahouse with central atrium, where storytellers used to entertain crowds with martial arts tales; with the period furnishings, it's not hard to imagine yourself in a kung fu film, waiting for a fight to start. Tea and Sichuanese home-style meals around ¥30 a head.

Pingle Youth Hostel 平乐国际青年旅舍, pínglè guójì qīngnián lǚshè. 32 Taizi Jie ☎028 8878 3331. Two modern buildings with antique frills on the outside but functional, user-friendly rooms inside. Dorm **¥35**, doubles **¥100**
Pingluo Tang 平落堂酒道馆, píngluò táng jiǔdào guǎn. Over the river and left along the bank for 150m ☎028 8878 1666. Old courtyard mansion and distillery guarded by stone lions and an ornate gateway, now up and running as a restaurant and hotel with antique-style doubles. **¥288**

Ya'an and around

Some 120km southwest of Chengdu, the ugly transport hub of **YA'AN** (雅安, yǎ'ān) sits on the green foothills of 3000m-high **Erlang Shan**, the steep ranges marking the border with western Sichuan. The town has long been associated with **tea**: China's earliest tea trees were planted thousands of years ago on nearby **Mengding Shan**, and from the Song dynasty Ya'an became a major marketplace on Sichuan's **tea-horse road** (see box, p.81). A few small-scale processing factories survive, though the once-esteemed quality has dropped over the centuries in favour of harvesting the coarse, strongly flavoured leaves preferred by Tibetans. It was near Ya'an too that Frenchman **Père David** became the first European to set eyes on a **panda skin**, and there's the opportunity to see pandas (albeit captive ones) outside town at **Bifengxia**.

Ya'an itself is an underwhelming few streets lined with cheap concrete buildings; if you don't stop here, you'll pass through en route to Kangding (see p.124) – or possibly to a little-used back road to Siguniang Shan (see p.130). The highway through town, **Tingjin Lu**, follows the **Qingyi River** west for a couple of kilometres to the junction with the Kangding road; there's a life-sized **bronze sculpture** of porters and mules here, both weighed down under their loads, a monument to the tea-horse days.

ARRIVAL AND DEPARTURE   YA'AN

By bus The bus station is at the eastern end of Tingjin Lu; minibuses from outside run to Bifengxia (30min; ¥5) and Mengding Shan (45min; ¥8) through the day. Aside from routes west to Kangding, you can also try to reach

Siguniang Shan from Ya'an by hopping there in stages via Baoxing and Qiaoqi (see opposite).
Destinations Baoxing (2hr; ¥22); Chengdu (5 daily; 3hr; ¥44); Kangding (every hour; 5hr; ¥75).

ACCOMMODATION AND EATING

A night in Ya'an won't rank among your most memorable in China, though the following places are decent enough. There are **snack stalls** around the bus station; otherwise eat at **accommodation**.

Ibis 宜必思酒店, yíbìsī jiǔdiàn. 36 Yanjiang Zhong Lu ☎083 5222 5555, ☵ibishotel.com. Clean and tidy budget hotel east of the centre, part of an international chain. You don't get much space or trimmings, but it's all modern and everything works. **¥170**

Merry 美客美家酒店, měikè měijiā jiǔdiàn. 266 Tingjin Lu ☎083 5263 5178. Fairly central option on the eastern side of town near the bus stations. The plain, modern rooms have computers and internet access. It's nothing special, but a fair choice. **¥170**

Yudu 雨都饭店, yǔdū fàndiàn. 157 Tingjin Lu ☎083 5260 1958. Another central hotel, inside a huge tower west of the bus station. Most of the rooms have good views, and the worn furnishings were getting a thorough upgrade at the time of writing. **¥210**

Mengding Shan

蒙顶山, měngdǐng shān • ¥75 • Bus from Ya'an (45min; ¥10) or Chengdu's Xinnanmen station (3hr 45min; ¥30)

In 53 BC, **Wu Lizhen** planted seven tea trees on **Mengding Shan**, a pretty mountain about 10km northeast of Ya'an, establishing the first known Chinese tea plantation. From the Song dynasty onwards, Mengding Shan's tea formed part of the region's annual "tribute" of local produce to the emperor, and today the misty mountain is covered in little shrines, restaurants and **tea houses**, linked by flagstoned footpaths through the forest. Local transport terminates at the gates, some two-thirds up the mountain, from where you can hike (or take a cable car; ¥40) to the summit in a couple of hours.

Bifengxia

碧峰峡, bìfēngxiá • Minibuses shuttle between Ya'an bus station and Bifengxia through the day (30min; ¥5)

After the 2008 earthquake (see p.111) closed Sichuan's major panda study base at **Wolong Nature Reserve**, the survivors were relocated to a sister centre at **Bifengxia**, a deep, forested gorge 15km north of Ya'an. At Wolong you could see captive pandas surrounded by their native habitat, but Bifengxia sits well below the altitude at which these animals naturally occur. The centre does offer opportunities for **volunteer work** (check availability and costs at ☵chinagiantpanda.com) – but otherwise it's a long way to come to see a more rural version of Chengdu's panda breeding base.

From the gates, tour buses run through the park to the **panda base** (¥118), where various buildings and large, open-air pens are linked by walking trails through the forest. The enclosures have a little bit too much concrete but the dozen or so bears are well supplied with food and seem to enjoy a good rapport with park staff. You'll have to be here quite early to see much of the **baby pandas**, if any; though despite signs asking you to keep quiet so they can sleep, they are often hauled out into the sun for photo-shoots with tourists.

> ### PÈRE DAVID AND THE BLACK-AND-WHITE BEAR
>
> On 11 March 1869, the French priest and naturalist **Père Armand David** was exploring the mountains north of Ya'an, when a hunter showed him the skin of a black-and-white bear: the **first panda** ever seen by a European. David had arrived in China aged 36 in 1862, and spent most of the next twelve years traversing the country's remoter corners discovering scores of new plant and animal species, including the giant panda and **snub-nosed monkey** (see p.231). Both the rare **dove tree** (*Davidia involucrata*) and **Père David's deer** are named after him, the latter saved from extinction after a few animals were shipped to Europe shortly before the rest were slaughtered during the Boxer Rebellion in 1900.
>
> **Père David's church** (邓池沟天主教堂, dèngchígōu tiānzhǔ jiàotáng) still stands at **Heping village** (和平村, hépíng cūn), around 90km north of Ya'an via the town of **Baoxing** (宝兴, bǎoxīng). From Baoxing, you need to hire a minibus to reach Heping, which sits at the edge of the totally undeveloped **Fengtong Zhai nature reserve** (蜂桶寨自然保护区, fēngtǒng zhài zìrán bǎohùqū), said to be packed with dove trees.

1

Northeast Sichuan

Northeast of Chengdu, **Shudao** – the "Sichuan Road" to the former imperial capital at Xi'an – follows fertile river valleys for 400km to the border with Shaanxi. It's a region rich in culture and personality: friendly **Jiangyou** was home to Li Bai, one of China's greatest poets; **Jianmenguan**, the narrow Sword Pass where the road breaks through a mountainous barrier, played a vital strategic role during the Three Kingdoms period; and the country's only empress was born at **Guangyuan**. **Doutuan Shan**, with its death-defying martial monks, is the pick of local holy sites; while at **Cuiyun Lang** you can still travel along flagstoned sections of the original road. Sadly, the region suffered badly during the **2008 earthquake** (see p.111), and many sites were still being patched up at the time of writing.

A fair way east of Shudao, the pleasant riverside town of **Langzhong** is an interesting place to spend a night or two. Its large grid of Qing-dynasty streets are soaked in local lore, while its truly ancient family-run hotels are unique in China.

An expressway and rail line links Chengdu to Guangyuan, just 60km short of the Shaanxi border, but many of the sights lie further east along the old road between Jiangyou and Jianmenguan, for which you'll need local buses. Note that Shudao is also the start of routes to the national park at **Jiuzhaigou**: either from Jiangyou, via Pingwu and Wanglang (see p.111); or from Guangyuan direct to Jiuzhaigou town (p.118). Langzhong is easily reached directly from Chengdu or Guangyuan. Jiangyou, Guangyuan and Langzhong are the only places with **banks** capable of dealing with foreign currency.

Jiangyou

江油, jiāngyóu

JIANGYOU is a friendly, quiet town on the Fu River about 170km northeast of Chengdu, pricipally known for its connections with the brilliant Tang poet **Li Bai** – though it's also the access point for quirky **Doutuan Shan**. The town is compact, barely 1500m wide, with main street **Fujiang Lu** running north–south, crossed by Jinianbei Jie and Shixian Lu.

Narrow **Tai Bai Park** (太白公园, tàibái gōngyuán) flanks the Changming stream, which flows south through town into the river, with willows and placid teahouses, bright flower-beds and sandstone memorial arches. On the Changming's west bank, the **Li Bai Memorial Hall** (李白纪念馆, lǐ bái jìniàn guǎn; daily 8am–5pm; ¥30) fails to capture the great man's spirit: there's a statue of the poet inside attractive Ming-style halls, along with Chinese accounts of his life and a worn, eleventh-century tablet mentioning Li by name.

There's far more sense of place 8km south of town at **Li Bai's Former Home** (李白故居, lǐ bái gùjū; daily 8am–5pm; ¥50; catch city bus #9 from near the bus stations on Taiping Lu), a quiet complex of old courtyards surrounded by whispering pine trees. There's also a shrine to his ancestor, the Han-dynasty general Li Xin, steles carved with his many poems, and the **tomb** of his sister, Li Yueyuan.

LI BAI

Born in China's far northwest – there are theories that he may not even have been Chinese – **Li Bai** (701–762) grew up in Jiangyou, becoming famous first as a swordsman and then for his evocative, spontaneous poetry. Like the Romantic movement in the West a millennium later, Li Bai linked atmosphere and landscape with human emotions, his work closest to Coleridge in its vivid, sometimes incomprehensible, imagery. Unusually for a man of his talents, he never took the civil service exams, though he did become a favourite of the emperor Xuanzong until being ousted by palace intrigues. Also known as **Tai Bai**, Li Bai was also notorious for his many, many verses celebrating **alcohol**, and he allegedly drowned in the Yangzi after drunkenly trying to embrace the moon's reflection.

Doutuan Shan

窦团山, dòutuán shān • 25km northwest of Jiangyou • ¥67 • Buses (1hr; ¥18.50 return) run from the Hongfei depot via Wudu (武都, wǔdū), where you might have to change vehicles

Doutuan Shan is a small twin-peaked ridge whose handful of eccentric temples were totally demolished by the 2008 earthquake. The quake even twisted the stone staircases up the mountain into corkscrew shapes, and the very peaks needed to be shored up with scaffolding afterwards to prevent their collapse. Repairs were well under way at the time of writing, hopefully returning the mountain to its former glory.

The ornate entrance is at **Yunyan Temple** (云岩寺, yúnyán sì), whose eighteenth-century halls are filled with cheerfully cohabiting Taoist and Buddhist statuary, with Doutuan Shan's two sheer-sided pinnacles rising behind. Following the path behind Yunyan Temple, you'll find racks of spiky weapons and a forest of 3m-high **wooden posts**, atop which kung fu monks practise high-speed boxing routines five times daily. The reason for this balancing practice becomes clear if you continue uphill – a surprisingly short, easy ascent on stone steps – to the mountain's main summit, which forms a small terrace outside **Dongyue Hall** (东岳殿, dōngyuè diàn), dedicated to Taoism's supreme deity, the Yellow Emperor. Every twenty minutes, Taoist monks cross from here to a tiny pavilion on the adjacent peak, using a **chain bridge** slung over the 50m-deep chasm and performing acrobatics as they go – you won't begrudge them their safety rope. The original bridge was built by the Tang-dynasty governor **Dou Zhiming**, who became a recluse here and after whom the mountain is named.

ARRIVAL AND DEPARTURE   JIANGYOU

The **train station** is about 3km northeast of town; the **south bus station** (汽车南站, qìchē nán zhàn) and adjacent **79 bus station** (79队车站, qīshíjiǔ duì chēzhàn) are just south of the centre on Taiping Lu. City bus #2 connects all stations with central Fujiang Lu. Buses to Pingwu and Jiuzhaigou depart the 79 bus station; use the south bus station for elsewhere.

By bus Chengdu (2hr; ¥22); Guangyuan (4 daily; 4hr; ¥35); Huanglong (2 daily; 8hr; ¥108); Jiuzhaigou (hourly; 6hr; ¥75); Pingwu (6am–3pm, every 30min; 3hr 30min; ¥29); Songpan (2 daily; 8hr; ¥110); Zitong (1hr 30min; ¥15).

By train Chengdu (21 daily; 2hr 30min); Guangyuan (18 daily; 2hr 40min); Xi'an (8 daily; 14hr).

GETTING AROUND

By bus City buses cost ¥1. #2 runs from the train station, via Fujiang Lu, to the bus stations. Doutuan Shan buses depart the Hongfei station (鸿飞车站, hóngfēi chēzhàn), diagonally across from the 79 bus station on Taiping Lu.

ACCOMMODATION

Jindu 金都宾馆, jīndū bīnguǎn. Opposite the south bus station, Taiping Lu ☎081 6325 8133. Friendly, extremely basic guesthouse, convenient for early-morning departures. **¥60**

Jinxin 金鑫酒店, jīnxīn jiǔdiàn. Between the two bus stations on Taiping Lu ☎081 6327 7222. Smart, shining budget hotel with attentive staff, though in a slightly downbeat location; decent restaurant too. **¥130**

Taibai 太白大酒店, tàibái dàjiǔdiàn. Just north of the centre at 49 Shicheng Zhong Lu ☎081 6322 2888. Modern business hotel, well maintained with good service and surprisingly low rates. **¥160**

EATING

Hotpot **restaurants** line Changming stream outside Taibai Park; the lanes north from the bus stations are also full of inexpensive restaurants.

Jinxin hotel restaurant Accomplished kitchen turning out light Sichuanese dishes such as Zhangfei beef (see p.91), spicy *mu'er* salad, stir-fried bitter gourd and steamed dumplings stuffed with egg yolk. ¥25 a head.

★ **Xiaoxue Jia** 小雪家, xiǎo xuě jiā. In the lane next to the Jinxin hotel. A whole run of inexpensive Sichuanese food, and northern dishes given a Sichuanese twist – the *fangxian paigu*, roasted, aromatic and meltingly soft spareribs – are deservedly popular. Two can eat well for under ¥70.

DIRECTORY

Banks The main Bank of China, with ATM, is on the central Jinianbei Jie–Jiefang Lu crossroads.

Zitong

梓潼, zǐtóng

Some 40km east of Jiangyou, **ZITONG** is a dishevelled market town on the Zitong River, where the Chengdu plains cede to more rugged country. A couple of antique pieces survive from earlier times – a multi-arched **stone bridge** not quite spanning the river, and a needle-sharp **pagoda** in the fields south of town – but the main point of interest is 10km north at **Qiqu Shan Grand Temple** (七曲山大庙, qīqū shān dàmiào; daily 8am–5pm; ¥35), an imposing red-walled complex shrouded in pine forests.

The temple was originally a shrine to the fourth-century Sichuanese minister **Zhang Yazi**, later deified as **Wencheng**, the god of literature. Considerably expanded during the Ming dynasty, the two-dozen well-proportioned halls are ranged up the hilltop in the Taoist manner, all full of heavy cedar beams, painted statuary and an atmosphere of authenticity rarely experienced in modern Chinese temples. It takes two hours to have a good look around, so you might find yourself spending the night at Zitong between buses.

ARRIVAL AND GETTING AROUND — ZITONG

By bus Despite its small size, Zitong has two bus stations, about 500m apart, on Wuding Lu, the main road through town. There's regular transport through the day north as far as Puan; for Chengdu, catch a bus to Mianyang (绵阳, miányáng) and change there. Around town, bus #1(¥3) and minibuses (¥15) run to Qiqu Shan Grand Temple in around 15min; flag them down along the main road through town.
Destinations Chengdu (via Mianyang; 3hr; ¥30); Jiangyou (1hr 30min; ¥15); Mianyang (1hr; ¥8); Puan (2hr; ¥18); Wulian (40min; ¥15).

ACCOMMODATION

Xishu 西蜀宾馆, xīshǔ bīnguǎn. Wuding Lu ☏081 6822 1221. Zitong's most convenient place to stay, near the bus stations and pretty well maintained. ¥120

Wulian and Jueyuan Temple

North of Zitong the road winds up into the hills, its verges frequently flanked by venerable rows of cypress trees. At times these arboreal corridors diverge cross-country, following a much earlier version of the "Sichuan Road", which in places is still paved with flat riverstones and cobbles.

Around 45km from Zitong, a few shops mark the junction to **WULIAN** (武连, wǔlián), a single-street town 3km away, just beyond which is **Jueyuan Temple** (觉苑寺, juéyuàn sì; ¥18). This genuine Ming-dynasty temple, complete with amazing contemporary **frescoes** depicting the life of Buddha, was another earthquake victim and it's not yet clear how much – or any – of the frescoes survived, though even earlier stone statues and tablets escaped destruction. The three small wooden halls were due to be completely restored by late 2012; if the frescoes survived, they're some of the oldest in Sichuan and well worth the detour.

ARRIVAL AND DEPARTURE — WULIAN

By bus Transport between Zitong and Puan drops you off at the main-road intersection, from where motorbike-taxis can run you up to Wulian (¥3). The last buses along the main road pass after 4pm.
Destinations Puan (1hr; ¥8); Zitong (40min; ¥15).

Puan

普安, pǔān – also known as Jian'ge (剑阁, jiàngé)

Fifty kilometres north from Wulian, via more cypresses and pretty views of hills undulating off into the distance, **PUAN** is a mostly modern, scruffy place, of most use for its bus station. The town sits on a J-shaped bend in the highway, and if you've an hour or so to spare it's worth poking around in the backstreets, where there's a fourteenth-century **gate-tower** and an old street, **Yan Jie** (烟街, yān jiē), lined with rickety old stores.

ARRIVAL AND DEPARTURE   PUAN

By bus Puan's bus station is just off the main road through town, slightly north of the centre.
Destinations Cuiyun Lang (15min; ¥5); Guangyuan (2hr; ¥38); Jianmenguan (1hr; ¥9); Wulian junction (1hr; ¥8); Zitong (2hr; ¥18).

Cuiyun Lang

翠云廊, cuìyún láng • ¥50 • Passing buses on the Puan–Jianmenguan–Guangyuan road will drop off and pick up

Just 7km north up the Jianmenguan road from Puan, **Cuiyun Lang**, the "Green Cloud Corridor", is where 500m of the old Sichuan Road – huge trees, flagstones and all – has been tidied up and preserved. You only need about half an hour here to wander the old avenue, along which at least two emperors once trod; the trees have been given fanciful names and spurious histories. It's a beautiful spot, though the entry fee is steep for what is, essentially, a Chinese park.

Jianmenguan

剑门关, jiànménguān • ¥100

Jianmenguan, the Sword Pass, forms a slash in the barrier of 500m-high cliffs which cut across the Sichuan Road about 20km north of Cuiyun Lang and 50km south of Guangyuan. The Three Kingdoms general **Jiang Wei** successfully defended Shu (Sichuan) here against the Kingdom of Wei's vastly superior armies; they eventually managed to circle south over the mountains and captured Chengdu in 263 AD despite his efforts. Jiang Wei later plotted an uprising but was discovered and killed; his **tomb** (姜维幕, jiāng wéi mù) still stands at Jianmenguan.

The site was given a thorough makeover recently, and the bus drops you at the gates among a new village of antique-style shops and canteens flanking a flagstoned road, all very well built. Once through a memorial arch, paths run to Jiang Wei's tomb, or through the pass itself, where a heavy stone **gateway** and watchtower half-blocks the gap; families queue up here to have their photos taken next to a rock inscribed "Jianmenguan" in Chinese. Then comes a steep, slippery and dangerously narrow path, which follows Shudao's original route for 2km along the base of a cliff, after which you'll appreciate the sentiment behind Li Bai's poem, *Hard is the Road to Shu*. You arrive on a terrace halfway up the cliff, with great views back to the narrow pass; you can rest up at one of the teahouses here, or catch a **cable car** back to ground level. If you're just beginning to enjoy the slightly hair-raising hike, however, you can continue up broad steps hacked in the cliff-face to the forested ridge above, where a much easier, forty-minute trail continues through the trees to tiny, unremarkable **Liangshan Temple** (凉山寺, liángshān sì).

ARRIVAL AND DEPARTURE   JIANMENGUAN

By bus Jianmenguan township – a newly built "old town", but nicely done – sits on the main Puan–Guangyuan road, right by the pass. Through traffic will drop you off; there's transport all day to Puan (1hr; ¥9) and Guangyuan (1hr 30min; ¥17.50). If you're travelling along the direct Jiangyou Guangyuan expressway, get out at Jiange (剑阁, jiàngé) and catch a minibus (¥10) for the final 10km to Jianmenguan.

EATING

There are dozens of inexpensive **restaurants** in Jianmenguan township; everyone serves local-style tofu (剑门老豆腐 干, jiànmén lǎo dòufu gān), smoked, pressed and thinly sliced.

1

WU ZETIAN, EMPRESS OF CHINA

China's only acknowledged empress, the Tang-dynasty ruler **Wu Zetian**, was born near Guangyuan in 624. Taken as a concubine by Emperor Taizong, she wormed her way into the affections of Crown Prince Li Zhi, who took her as a second wife when he became Emperor Gaozong in 649. She used charm, diplomacy and sheer ruthlessness to eliminate rivals – including an empress, several concubines and members of her own family – and long before Gaozong died in 683 had become the real power behind the throne. In 690 she deposed her own son and founded a new dynasty, ruling as **Empress Wu of Zhou**. Though not shy of using violence and favouritism if she felt it necessary, as empress Wu Zetian generally chose able ministers, accepted criticism and became a great patron of Buddhism. Her later years were marred by palace intrigue and a **coup** restored the Tang dynasty under her son, Zhongzhong, shortly before her death in 705.

Guangyuan

广元, guǎngyuán

GUANGYUAN is a shambolic manufacturing city, close to the border with Shaanxi province and halfway between Chengdu and Xi'an by road or rail. It's a jumping-off

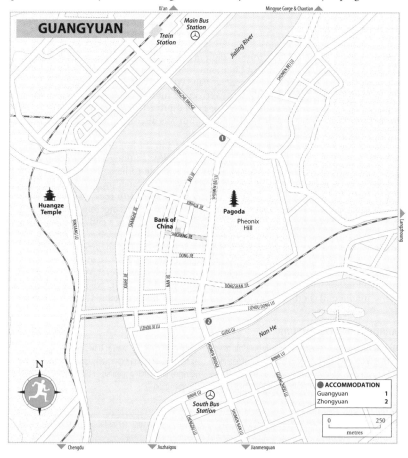

point for **Jiuzhaigou buses**, though a couple of historical anchors are worth a look in their own right: the important **Huangzhe Temple**, commemorating the Tang empress Wu Zetian, and stretches of the old road north to the border on the way to **Chaotian town**.

Guangyuan surrounds a 2km-long strip of the south-flowing **Jialing River**, at the junction of the much smaller Nan He. East of the Jialing, **Shumen Bei Lu** is the main road south through town; it's lined with old brick and tile buildings and the only real sight in the vicinity is **Phoenix Hill Park** (凤凰山公园, fènghuáng shān gōngyuán), a rocky bump crowned by a futuristic, concertina-shaped **pagoda**. There are also foreign-friendly **ATMs** in the tangle of shopping streets between Shumen Bei Lu and the river – the first for a while if you've come up along Shudao.

Huangze Temple

皇泽寺, huángzé sì • South of the train station on Binjiang Lu • ¥25 • Bus #6 terminates outside

Huangze Temple is the only one in China honouring the empress **Wu Zetian** (see box, opposite), recently rebuilt after centuries of neglect caused by her overturning of Confucian values, in which women had little status. There's a unique carving of a **phoenix** at the entrance steps, a sign of female imperial power – normally this would be of a dragon, representing an emperor. The cliffside behind was carved into a series of grottoes in Tang times, the lower one containing a gilded, life-sized **statue** of a fashionably portly Wu Zetian. Above are a 4m-high trinity of Amidah Buddha flanked by disciples and a very feminine **Guanyin**, whose curvy, languid form shows a definite Indian influence. Most other sculptures at the site have been sadly weathered, but look for Ming panels depicting the stages of **sericulture**, from picking mulberry leaves to unravelling the silkworms' cocoons.

Mingyue Gorge

明月峡, míngyuè xiá • ¥50 • Buses to Chaotian (朝天, cháotiān; 45min; ¥15) can drop you off

It's 30km north from Guangyuan to **Mingyue Gorge** and a 500m-long reconstructed section of an **old plank road** (明月峡古栈道, míngyuè xiá gǔ zhàndào). Once used extensively to shift goods and armies through China's mountainous regions, these were made by chiselling horizontal post-holes into a cliff-face, inserting stone beams, and then laying wooden decking across them. They often ran hundreds of metres above the ground, and some stretches were over 20km long; you can still see the original gallery holes through the headwaters of the Little Three Gorges near Ningchang (see p.171). In use as early as the Qin dynasty but now long redundant, this fragment allows you to experience what it was like to travel one – luckily, it's in sound condition, and not too high off the ground.

ARRIVAL AND DEPARTURE   GUANGYUAN

The **train station** and adjacent main **bus station** are a kilometre northwest across the Jialing, while the south bus station is south of the centre over the Nan He. City bus #6 (¥1) runs between the two via Shumen Bei Lu; a taxi costs ¥8.

By bus Note that buses to Jiuzhaigou don't travel via Pingwu (see p.111). There's also a good, though fairly slow, direct road to Langzhong.
Main bus station destinations (广元市客运中心, guǎngyuán shì kèyùn zhōngxīn): Chengdu (6hr; ¥95); Jiuzhaigou (1 daily; 8hr; ¥120); Langzhong (4hr; ¥47).

South bus station destinations (南河汽车站, nán hé qìchēzhàn): Chengdu (6hr; ¥95); Jiangyou (4hr; ¥35); Jianmenguan (1hr 30min; ¥17.50); Puan (2hr; ¥28).
By train Chengdu (20 daily; 5hr 30min); Jiangyou (18 daily; 2hr 30min); Kunming (1 daily; 24hr); Xi'an (9 daily; 10hr).

ACCOMMODATION AND EATING

Any foreigner appearing at the north bus station or the train station square will be grabbed by touts for **hostels** charging around ¥35 a bed. For **meals**, hotpot stalls and inexpensive restaurants fill the town's backstreets.

Guangyuan 广元宾馆, guǎngyuán bīnguǎn. In the north of town at 466 Shumen Bei Lu ☎083 9333 0999. One of the smarter options in town, a well-maintained older operation with recently refurbished rooms and good restaurant. ¥200

Zhongyuan 中源快捷88酒店, zhōngyuán kuàijié bāshíbā jiǔdiàn. 2 Shunen Nan Lu ☎083 9327 7888. At the southern end of Shumen Bei Lu, just before it crosses the Nan He and a few minutes' walk from the south bus station, this is one of several cheap hotels in the vicinity. Some rooms are shabby – bootprints on the walls, broken windows, dripping taps – others perfectly sound and comfortable. ¥110

DIRECTORY

Banks There's a useful Bank of China with an ATM west off Shumen Bei Lu at the corner of pedestrianized Shichang Jie.

Langzhong

阆中, làngzhōng

The small city of **LANGZHONG** is located about 225km northeast of Chengdu, occupying a broad thumb of land around which the Jialing River loops on three sides. With water in front and hills to the north, Langzhong is said to enjoy perfect *feng shui* (see p.381) and once played a pivotal role in provincial history, becoming the **Sichuanese capital** for seventeen years at the start of the Qing dynasty. Notable people associated with Langzhong include the Three Kingdoms general Zhang Fei, who is buried here, and Luo Xiahong, the Han-dynasty inventor of the Chinese calendar. In addition, about a quarter of Langzhong comprises a protected **old town**, Sichuan's largest by far: there are atmospheric hotels, heaps of antique architecture and low-key sights, and quiet cobbled lanes lit at night by paper lanterns. It's somewhere to spend a pleasant day strolling around.

> ### OLD TOWN TICKETS
>
> It's free to enter Langzhong's old town, but to visit its buildings you must either pay per sight or buy a **combined entry ticket**, sold at sight ticket desks, which save a few yuan. An **¥80 ticket** covers entry to the Zhang Fei Temple, Huaguang Lou, Gongyuan, Zhongtian Lou and assorted old buildings, with similar ¥70 and ¥30 tickets for fewer sights.

The old town

Grafted onto the modern city, Langzhong's **old town** covers about a square kilometre north of the river, a neat grid of flagstoned streets flanked by wooden buildings. Many of these are classical **courtyard houses** (四合院, sìhéyuàn), whose central halls, divided up by wooden screens, open into a series of courtyards, decorated with potted flower gardens; the Chinese describe this strung-out design as *chuan* (串, chuàn), also the character for "kebab".

Many of these are open to the public as museums, such as the **Museum of Water Culture** (华夏水博物馆, huáxià shuǐ bówùguǎn; daily 8am–6pm; ¥20), and the **Fengshui Museum** (风水博物馆, fēngshuǐ bówùguǎn; daily 8am–6pm; ¥20). As the buildings themselves are of most interest, however, you'll see just as much at the old hotels, which only charge visitors ¥2 or so to look around; check the map for locations. Langzhong is also full of **traditional businesses** beavering away inside open-fronted stores, where you can watch mattresses being stuffed with kapok, old-style barbers and tailors, stonemasons and coffin-makers turning out their wares, and gift shops loaded with locally produced Zhangfei beef (a sort of spicy silverside) and Baoning vinegar. One place worth checking out is the **Zhuoshang Silk Workshop** (卓尚蚕丝坊, zhuóshàng cánsīfāng; free), at the corner of Neidong Jie and Zhuangyuan Jie; founded in 1926, you can still see the whole process, from raw silk being unravelled from boiled moth cocoons through to carpets being woven on a hand-loom. The shop here – and others in the vicinity – sell the finished product.

Huaguang Lou and around

华光楼, huáguāng lóu • Daily 8am–6pm • ¥15

Orient yourself near the river at **Huaguang Lou**, a three-storey, 36m-high Tang-style gate tower on Dadong Jie, last reconstructed in 1867. Views from the upper storeys take in the old town's spread of grey-tiled roofs and die-straight Dadong Jie, lined with rickety shops.

A short walk west, **Huoshen Lou** (火神楼, huǒshén lóu) is an ornate, nineteenth-century wooden gallery dedicated to the fire god, who doubtless needs to be kept happy in such a combustible town. Lanes wind south from here to riverside **Binjiang Lu**, a paved promenade lined with small **bars**, whose open-air tables make it a pleasant place to sit in the evening over a beer.

Zhongtian Lou

中天楼, zhōngtiān lóu • Daily 8am–6pm • ¥10

Up in the north of the old town, **Zhongtian Lou** is an elegant wooden pavilion built over the Wu Miao Jie–Bei Jie junction, which once marked Langzhong's centre; it's a modern reconstruction after the earlier version was dismantled in 1916 to widen the road. You can climb up from the south side of Wumiao Jie for more views.

The Examination Hall

贡院, gòng yuàn • Daily 8.30am–5pm • ¥35

There's an unusual target for history buffs northeast on Xuedao Jie, where the seventeenth-century **Gongyuan** is one of only two surviving **imperial examination halls** in China. You can see the cells and long courtyard where candidates lived and were

1

tested on their knowledge of the Confucian classics, on which the country was (in principle) governed. Scholars who passed the exams could look forward to a position at court – not to mention an escape from the life of genteel poverty that was otherwise their lot.

Zhang Fei Temple

张飞庙, zhāngfēi miào • Daily 8.30am–5pm • ¥40

Langzhong's most popular sight is the **Zhang Fei Temple** on Xi Jie, a shrine to the ferocious Three Kingdoms general Zhang Fei, oath brother to Guan Yu and Lu Bei (see box, p.69). The three balanced each other: Liu Bei was morally upright, but lacked vigour; Guan Yu was the ideal of martial virtue, powerful and just; while Zhang Fei was loyal and determined, but untameably fierce. After Guan Yu's capture and execution by the armies of Wu, Zhang Fei went wild, driving his troops so hard that they finally mutinied and murdered him in 221 AD while campaigning at Langzhong.

Like the town, the temple is pleasantly rough around the edges, with uneven cobbles, vegetated roofs and walls at all angles. Side-wings house dioramas of Zhang Fei's life, many of them violent; there's also reproduction armour and the halberd and spears that Zhang Fei was known for. A huge, realistically painted statue of the general scowls down at you beneath the **main hall**'s interlocking roof brackets; behind is the grassy mound of his **tomb**, where a finally triumphant Zhang Fei sits between two demons who are holding his cringing assassins **Zhang Da** and **Fan Qiang** by the hair. Walk either side to circuit his tomb mound, which is planted with trees; his head was passed around as a war trophy, finally laid to rest at Yunyang on the Yangzi (see p.168), but his body is buried here.

ARRIVAL AND DEPARTURE   LANGZHONG

By bus Langzhong's main bus station (南部客运站, nánbù kèyùn zhàn) is 5km southeast of town; city buses (¥1) can drop you on Zhang Fei Dadao within walking distance of the old town. Taxis (¥10) are not allowed into the old town but will take you to the gates. Transport to

Guangyuan departs the downbeat Baba Si bus station (巴巴寺客运站, bābā sì kèyùn zhàn) in the north of town.

Destinations Chengdu (5hr; ¥92); Chongqing City (5hr; ¥110); Guangyuan (4hr; ¥47).

ACCOMMODATION

Langzhong's old town specializes in attractive **antique-style hotels**, their wooden, open-sided halls arranged around little courtyards decked out with carved screens, bonsai and stone water tubs. They're great fun to spend the night at, though rooms tend to be fairly ordinary, and soundproofing clearly wasn't a priority when these places were built – you might need earplugs for your neighbour's TV. You'll only pay the prices quoted during national holidays. Smaller **guesthouses** offer basic rooms for ¥60 or so; look for flags outside with the characters for "accommodation" (住宿, zhùsù).

Dujia Kezhan 杜家客栈, dùjiā kèzhàn. 63 Xiaxin Jie ☎ 081 7622 4436, ⓦ djkz.com.cn. An atmospheric old mansion which claims to have been in business long enough to have housed the Tang poet Du Fu; the building is beautiful but some of the rooms need a refit. **¥480**

★ **Earth-to-Gold Inn** 土生金钱庄客栈, tǔshēngjīn qiánzhuāng kèzhàn. 50 Dadong Jie ☎ 081 7622 1880, ⓦ lztsj.cn. Originally a bank founded by a businessman from Anhui province, hence the elegant, eastern Chinese "Huizhou" layout of galleried rooms around a central courtyard. There's an impregnable grey-brick storeroom at the back, and the reception desk is like a bank-teller window. Extremely friendly management and tidy, well-aired rooms give this place the edge. **¥360**

Lijia Dayuan 李家大院, lǐjiā dàyuàn. 47 Wumiao Jie ☎ 081 7623 6500, ⓔ langzhonglijia@163.com. Grand old building dating back in part to the Ming dynasty, when it was a pharmacy; it has especially beautiful carved window screens and courtyards full of decorative plants. Doubles here are larger and better furnished than at *Dujia Kezhan*, despite the lower price. **¥168**

Qinjia Dayuan 秦家大院, qínjiā dàyuàn. 67 Nan Jie ☎ 081 7622 8967. Another venerable courtyard mansion full of low beams and creaky stairs, distinctive for being commandeered in 1935 as a Red Army HQ – staff dress in period costume and hold song-and-dance nights featuring Red Army ditties. There's a popular restaurant too. **¥380**

Tianyi Youth Hostel 天一青年旅舍, tiānyī qīngnián lǚshè. 100 Dadong Jie ☎ 081 7622 5501.

Nice rooms in a cosy modern place with antique touches right next to the Fengshui Museum. Staff are clueless if you need local information but it's extremely clean and tidy. Doubles with shared bathroom ¥80, en suite ¥188

★ **Zhuangyuan Ge** 状元阁古客栈, zhuàngyuán gé gǔ kèzhàn. 36 Zhuangyuan Jie ☎081 7623 9909. Small but exquisite courtyard hotel whose best doubles feature ornate, canopied beds and carvings illustrating the Confucian virtues; there's also a calligraphy writing hall and a tearoom. ¥336

EATING AND DRINKING

The many rustic-looking **canteens** around town all sell much the same run of Sichuanese snacks, buns and noodles. **Hotels** such as *Qinjia Dayuan* have the best restaurants, but they may well be closed Oct–March, when there are fewer tourists about. In the evening, the score of tiny bars and teahouses along **Binjiang Lu** are a good place to sit out for a drink overlooking the river.

Bashu Tese 巴蜀特色, bāshǔ tèsè. 48 Wumiao Jie. Local snacks and home-style cooking, including "Five Tigers" beef, spring rolls and eye-wateringly spicy cold jelly noodles.

Cheng Shifa Canting 城实发餐厅, chéng shífā càntīng. Dongtan Jing Jie, a narrow street just outside the old town. Great Sichuanese place with all the favourites including "chilli-fragrant spareribs", crisp-fried with lashings of spices. There's no English spoken, or menu, but a generous meal for two costs under ¥70.

Southeast Sichuan

Southeast of Chengdu, the Yangzi and Min rivers converge and Sichuan bumps up against several of its neighbours. There's a pocket of fairly esoteric attractions here: **Zigong** is a treat, with well-preserved architecture, dinosaurs and salt mines, plus an unusually revealing statue of Confucius at nearby **Fushun**. The port city of **Yibin** has less to recommend it, though it's a useful stepping stone to the eerie **Shunan Bamboo Sea** and a remote cliff decorated with ancient **hanging coffins**. You could spend a week roaming the region, or just stop off at key sights for the night, perhaps en route to **Chongqing**, or Chishui in **Guizhou** province (see p.282).

Zigong

自贡, zìgòng

Some 250km southeast of Chengdu, the industrial city of **ZIGONG** has long been an important source of **salt**, tapped as brine welling up from subterranean artesian basins. In the fourth century, the Sichuanese were sinking 300m-deep boreholes here using bamboo-fibre cables attached to massive stone bits; by the 1600s, bamboo buckets were drawing brine from wells bored almost a kilometre beneath Zigong centuries before European technology (which borrowed Chinese techniques) could reach this deep. The nineteenth century saw Zigong's skyline studded with bamboo drilling rigs and the ornate roof-ridges of merchants' **guildhalls**, many of which have survived among less distinguished modern architecture. **Natural gas**, a by-product of drilling, was used from the earliest times to boil brine in evaporation tanks, and now also powers Zigong's buses and taxis.

Zigong's compact, hilly centre lies on the north side of the narrow **Fuxi River**. There's no main street in town; all the central roads are equally busy with markets, shops and facilities. Zigong is unusual in having three excellent local **museums**, all fully captioned in English, covering salt history and **dinosaurs**; two of Sichuan's most atmospheric **teahouses**, both over a century old; and for having resisted the urge to overdevelop its attractions – there are tourist sights here, but this is not a tourist town. A busy day here is enough to pack in the main attractions, half of it spent in town, the rest touring a couple of sights northeast of the centre on the **#3 bus** route.

Xiqin Guildhall

西亲会馆, xīqīn huìguǎn • Daily 8.30am–5pm • ¥20

Begin a city tour at the splendid **Xiqin Guildhall** on central Jiefang Lu, built in the Qing dynasty by merchants from Shaanxi and now an absorbing **salt museum**. Photos and

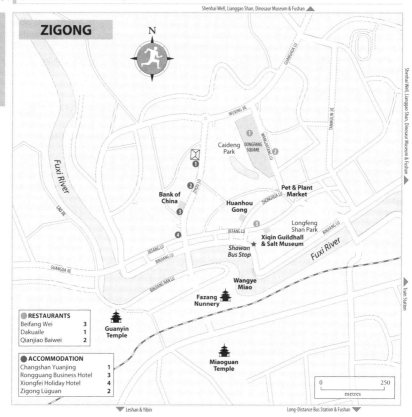

relics chart Zigong's mining history, from pictorial Han-dynasty tomb bricks, carved with cartoon-like panels showing salt panning, to the bamboo piping, frightening metal drills and wooden derricks used until the 1980s. All this is overshadowed by the building itself, whose curled roof corners, flagstone-and-beam halls and gilded woodwork – illustrating Confucian moral tales – were renovated in 1872 by master craftsman Yang Xuesan.

Some teahouses

Several similar contemporary buildings survive near Xiqin Guildhall, notably **Wangye Miao** (王爷庙, wángyé miào), jutting out over the river on Binjiang Lu; and **Huanhou Gong** (桓侯宫, huánhóu gōng), a former butchers' guildhall built in 1875 whose beautifully carved stone gateway overlooks the junction of Jiefang Lu and Zhonghua Lu. Both are now highly atmospheric **teahouses**, where you can join locals playing cards or chatting in the central courtyards.

Caideng Park

彩灯公园, cǎidēng gōngyuán

Right in the centre of the old town, **Caideng Park** is a focus for the city's spectacular new year **Lantern Festival**, and has a beautiful **covered arched bridge** spanning the small lake. There are a couple of entrances: either at the park's northwest corner off Wuxing Jie; or southeast through a small **pet and plant market** on the edge of **Dongfang Square** (东方广场, dōngfāng guǎngchǎng), a pedestrianized shopping district.

1

Shenhai Well

燊海井, shēnhǎi jǐng • Daily 9am–5pm • ¥20 • Bus #3 from the Shawan stop, near Wangye Miao

About 4km northeast of the centre on the #3 bus route, **Shenhai Well** was the deepest ever drilled using traditional methods, and in 1835 reached a fraction over 1000m. Operational until 1966, the 20m-high wooden tripod derrick still overlooks the site, where you can inspect bamboo-fibre cables, stone engravings on the wall detailing the well's development (much of it using buffalo power), and the tiny well shaft itself, corked and reeking of gas. The wooden-beamed warehouse behind is now a small-scale **salt factory**, where you can see the muddy brine being purified by boiling it with **soy milk**; the resultant scum is skimmed off as it rises, leaving a crust of pure white salt in the evaporation trays.

The Dinosaur Museum

恐龙博物馆, kǒnglóng bówùguǎn • Daily 9am–5pm • ¥42 • Bus #3 from the Shawan stop, near Wangye Miao

Bus #3 terminates among pleasantly shambolic street markets at **Dashanpu** (大山铺, dàshānpù), from where it's 250m to Zigong's excellent **dinosaur museum**, built over the site of excavations carried out during the 1980s. Near-perfect skeletal remains of dozens of Jurassic fish, amphibians and dinosaurs – including monumental thighbones, and Sichuan's own **Yangchuanosaurus**, a toothy, lightweight velociraptor – have been left partially excavated *in situ*, while others have been fully assembled for easy viewing, posed dramatically against painted backgrounds.

ARRIVAL AND DEPARTURE   ZIGONG

If you're heading to the **Shunan Bamboo Sea** (see p.97) and want to skip Yibin, it's just two hours from Zigong down the expressway – contact the *Xiongfei Holiday Hotel* about renting a minibus with a driver for the day. Note too that Zigong is relatively close to Dazu's stunning **Buddhist carvings** (p.157), and **Chongqing City** (p.144).

By bus The long-distance bus station is about 2km south of town on Dangui Dajie; turn right out of the station and it's 100m to the city bus stop (#33 will drop you near the Wangye Miao on Binjiang Lu) – cabs charge about ¥7.
Destinations Chengdu (5hr; ¥82); Chongqing City (4hr; ¥68); Dazu (4hr; ¥60); Emei (3hr; ¥58); Fushun (1hr 20min; ¥25); Leshan (3hr; ¥55); Neijiang (2hr; ¥35); Yibin (1hr; ¥25).

By train Zigong's train station is east of the centre on Jiaotong Lu, from where bus #34 heads into town.
Destinations Chengdu (6 daily; 5hr); Chongqing City (2 daily; 7hr); Guiyang (4 daily; 14hr); Kunming (3 daily; 17hr); Yibin (10 daily; 1hr 45min).

ACCOMMODATION

Changshan Yuanjing 长山远景宾馆, chángshān yuǎnjǐng bīnguǎn. 133 Ziyou Lu ☎081 3539 0666. Alternative to the similar *Rongguang*, though not as welcoming. **¥160**
Rongguang Business Hotel 荣光商务酒店, róngguāng shāngwù jiǔdiàn. 25 Ziyou Lu ☎081 3211 7777. This budget hotel doesn't look much from the street, but it's spotless inside and some rooms come with computers and extra-large beds. Staff are attentive rather than friendly. **¥140**

Xiongfei Holiday Hotel 雄飞假日酒店, xióngfēi jiàrì jiǔdiàn. 193 Jiefang Lu ☎081 3211 8899. Comfortable, smart hotel overlooking the river with clean, spacious rooms, all recently refurbished; it's the most upmarket choice in the town centre. Good restaurant and café too. **¥720**
Zigong Lüguan 自贡旅馆, zìgòng lǚguǎn. 55 Ziyou Lu ☎081 3210 2614. Bedrock accommodation in two adjacent buildings; it's an old place in poor condition and its doubles are only recommended if you're on a tight budget. **¥60**

EATING AND DRINKING

Zigong's **food** is reputedly the spiciest in Sichuan, a claim best explored at *Qianjiao Baiwei*. For a quick snack, outdoor wonton and noodle vendors surround the southern end of Dongfang Square. The city also has an extraordinary density of **teahouses**, even for Sichuan; don't miss a session at central *Wangye Miao* or *Huanhou Gong*, with their century-old wood and intricate stonework decor, where tea plus unlimited hot water costs from ¥4 a cup.

1

Beifang Wei 北方味, běifāng wèi. *Diagonally across from the salt museum.* A no-frills canteen with heavy communal benches, surly staff and tasty, inexpensive northern Chinese snacks. Steamed *jiaozi* are their speciality, served with cold side-dishes. Fill up for ¥10.

Dakuaile 大快乐西餐咖啡厅, dàkuàilè xīcān kāfēitīng. *Dongfang Guangchang.* Restaurant chain serving slightly overpriced Western-style fast food (pasta, pizza etc) in a mellow, café-style environment. Coffee ¥65 a

pot; meals from ¥40.

★**Qianjiao Baiwei** 千椒百味火锅馆, qiānjiāo bǎiwèi huǒguō guǎn. *Wangjiatang Lu.* So you know what you're letting yourself in for, the name of this popular, bright and noisy hotpot restaurant means "A Thousand Chillies, A Hundred Flavours". A decent selection of meats and vegetables for two, cooked by yourself in the delicious crimson stock, costs ¥80.

Fushun

富顺, fùshùn • Buses (1hr 20min; ¥25) from Zigong station

Fushun is a small town 40km southeast of Zigong on the Tuo River, worth a half-day trip to see its unusual **Confucian Temple** (文庙, wén miào; ¥15) on Jiefang Jie. This was founded in 1044 as a college for scholars hoping to sit the imperial exams, a plan that paid off during the Ming dynasty, when ten percent of all Sichuan's examination candidates came from Fushun. It's an imposing complex, with a wall of red sandstone memorial arches at the entrance and a strange stone bridge over the pond out front, elaborately carved with zodiac animals, but what really makes this temple unique is the **nude statue of Confucius** stuck up on the roof ridge, for reasons nobody seems willing to discuss.

While you're in town, **Qianfo Temple** (千佛寺, qiānfó sì; ¥15), 1km away on Fuda Lu, is a recent complex built below a group of Tang-dynasty Buddha carvings; the temple's vegetarian restaurant has a good reputation.

Yibin

宜宾, yíbīn

A crowded, grubby port with a modern veneer, the city of **YIBIN** sits 80km south of Zigong where the Jinsha and Min rivers combine to form the **Chang Jiang**, the main body of the Yangzi. Yibin produces three substances known for wreaking havoc: enriched plutonium; Wuliangye *bai jiu*, China's second-favourite spirit; and *ranmian*, "burning noodles", whose chilli content has stripped many a stomach lining. The central backstreets are full of busy market stalls, and a few old mementoes survive in the solid **Daguan Lou** (大观楼, dàguān lóu) bell tower and ponderous stone **Shui Dong gateway** (水东门, shuǐ dōngmén) down by the old docks, but in truth there's little to do here in between organizing transport to the border, the highly atmospheric **Shunan Bamboo Sea** or the remote, enigmatic **hanging coffins**.

ARRIVAL AND DEPARTURE   YIBIN

BY BUS

Note that if you're heading to Chishui, just over the border in Guizhou (see p.282), aim first for Luzhou (泸州, lúzhōu), then change buses. The trip takes 5hr 30min in total; if you end up at Jiuzhi, just walk across the bridge into Chishui.

Chuan Gao bus station (川高客运站, chuān gāo kèyùn zhàn), 5km northwest of town, handles fast long-distance services. Catch city bus #4 from Bei Da Jie.

Destinations Chengdu (5hr; ¥90); Chongqing City (5 daily; 6hr; ¥98); Leshan (4hr; ¥65); Luzhou (2hr; ¥30); Zigong (1hr; ¥25).

Beimen station (北门汽车客运站, běimén qìchē kèyùn zhàn), in the backstreets just north of the city centre, deals with rattletrap country buses to the same destinations as Chuan Gao station; services are cheaper but journey times are longer.

Nan'an bus station (南岸汽车客运站, nánàn qìchē kèyùn zhàn), 5km south of the river on the #4 bus from Bei Da Jie, has departures to the Bamboo Sea and the hanging coffins.

Destinations Changning (for the Bamboo Sea; 1hr 30min; ¥18); Gongxian (for the hanging coffins; 2hr 30min; ¥28); Shunan Bamboo Sea (3 daily; 2hr; ¥28).

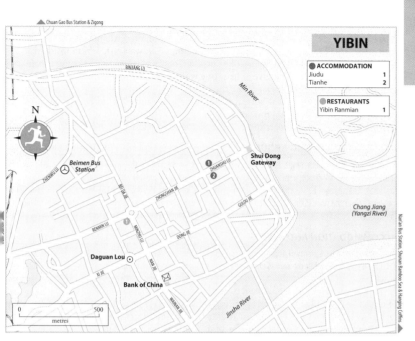

BY TRAIN

Yibin's train station is 3km southwest of the city centre; a taxi into town costs ¥9.

Destinations Chengdu (6 daily; 6hr 30min); Chongqing City (2 daily; 8hr 15min); Guiyang (4 daily; 12hr 30min); Kunming (3 daily; 15hr); Zigong (9 daily; 1hr 30min).

ACCOMMODATION AND EATING

Yibin's cheapest **hotels** won't take foreigners, and most places that will are overpriced. There's further accommodation at the Bamboo Sea (p.98). Yibin isn't a great place for a blow out **meal**, though the backstreets are full of noodle and stir-fry places – head to the *Jiudu* for something more substantial.

Jiudu 酒都饭店, jiǔdū fàndiàn. 50 Zhuanshu Jie ☎083 1818 8588. You'll find a decent quality of service at this business hotel, with spa, gym and several restaurants; rooms are a little faded for the price. The location, in a relatively quiet street in an older part of town, is a plus. **¥420**
Tianhe 天和宾馆, tiānhé bīnguǎn. Zhuanshu Jie, opposite the Jiudu ☎083 1516 6333. A basic budget

hotel with clean and tidy rooms; they're startled to see a foreign face, but there are no problems staying here. **¥120**
Yibin Ranmian 宜宾燃面, yíbīn ránmiàn. Next to the crossroads on Renmin Lu. Famous hole in the wall, recently smartened up, whose raft of cold snacks includes *ranmian* noodles dressed in chopped nuts, coriander, vinegar and chillies. Their most expensive dish is ¥10.

The Shunan Bamboo Sea

蜀南竹海国家公园, shǔnán zhúhǎi guójiā gōngyuán · 80km southeast of Yibin · ¥85

The **Shunan Bamboo Sea** covers more than forty square kilometres of mountain slopes with feathery green tufts, making for a refreshing few days' rural escape. It's a relatively expensive one, though, and if you want to see similar scenery at budget rates you might consider heading to Chishui in Guizhou province (see p.282). The main problem is

1

simply **getting around** within the park; there are roads throughout but bus services are unpredictable and you'll probably end up having to charter taxis.

Having said this, Shunan is a beautiful spot, its graceful 10m-high stems eerily repeating into the distant, dark green gloom. The two main settlements – both little more than small groupings of hotels – are **Wanling** (万岭, wànlǐng), 1.5km inside the west gate, and **Wanli** (万里, wànlǐ), 20km inside. There's pleasure in just being driven around, but make sure you have at least one **walk** along any of the numerous paths and get a look down over the forest to see the bowed tips of bamboo ripple in waves as breezes sweep the slopes. The surreal atmosphere is enhanced by it being a favourite **film location** for martial arts movies and TV series, so don't be too surprised if you encounter Song-dynasty warriors galloping along the roads.

ARRIVAL AND GETTING AROUND SHUNAN BAMBOO SEA

By bus Direct buses from Yibin's Nan'an bus station to Shunan's West Gate are erratic; if they don't materialize aim for small Changning (长宁, chángníng), from where minibuses cover the final 15km. Once inside, buses round the park (¥10) operate on their own schedule – they're most frequent in the mornings and afternoons. A taxi or minibus for the day will cost ¥200–250.

Changning destinations Chengdu (5hr; ¥95); Luzhou (5 daily; 3hr; ¥45); Shunan West Gate (20min; ¥10); Yibin (1hr 30min; ¥18).

ACCOMMODATION AND EATING

Wanling and Wanli have plenty of **accommodation**; the cheapest ask around ¥50 a bed though most charge upwards of ¥200 for a double. **Food** in the park is universally good and not too expensive, with lots of fresh bamboo shoots and mushrooms.

Feicui 翡翠宾馆, fěicuì bīnguǎn. Right at the park's centre ☎083 1498 0104. Old-style wood and concrete two-star complex set among vegetation; prone to damp but heaters keep the rooms warm. There's a good restaurant. **¥250**

Shunan 蜀南宾馆, shǔnán bīnguǎn. Near the Western Gate ☎083 1498 0555. Huge pile, very comfortable but not taking advantage of the local scenery; you could be anywhere. **¥300**

Zhuhai 竹海饭店, zhúhǎi fàndiàn. Wanli ☎083 1273 9096. Large and well-furnished holiday hotel complex surrounded by its own bamboo garden. **¥300**

The Bo hanging coffins

僰人悬棺, bórén xuánguān • ¥35 • If you can't find direct transport from Yibin's Nan'an bus station, aim first for ugly Gongxian (珙县, gǒngxiàn), then change to a nearby depot for Luobiao buses. It's a very long day-trip – you'll have to leave Luobiao by mid-afternoon to catch connecting services all the way back

Scores of enigmatic wooden **hanging coffins** cover a rural cliffside 90km south of Yibin, out in the broad **Dengjia river valley**. They're believed to have been left by the enigmatic **Bo people**, who once ranged east from here through the Three Gorges area (see p.169), before being dispersed by imperial troops after their leader rashly declared himself emperor during a sixteenth-century uprising. Similar coffins dating back over two thousand years have been found through the region, and the **Tujia** ethnic group, who live on the Chongqing–Hubei border, claim the Bo as their ancestors; little else is known about them.

From where the bus terminates at the dispiriting hilltop settlement of **LUOBIAO** (洛表, luòbiǎo), it's a pleasant 3km walk downhill into the valley to where the coffins first appear up on the rock faces. They're simple boxes in themselves, mortised into cliffs on wooden frames, or placed in shallow caves, with the surrounding rocks daubed in simple ochre designs depicting the sun, people and horses. There's no interpretation offered on site, but the remote setting and mystery surrounding how an entire culture could be reduced to such intangible remains might well make it worth the long excursion from Yibin.

Southern Sichuan

1

Some 150km southwest of Chengdu lies the edge of the Red Basin and the foothills of mountain ranges that sprawl into Tibet and Yunnan. Fast-flowing rivers converge here at **Leshan**, where more than a thousand years ago sculptors created **Dafo**, a giant Buddha overlooking the waters, one of the world's most imposing religious monuments. An hour away, **Emei Shan** rises to more than 3000m, its forested slopes rich in scenery and temples. You could day-trip to either from Chengdu, though Emei Shan really deserves an overnight stay plus a day on the mountain. Just avoid both during holidays, when crowds are so awful that the army is sometimes called in to sort out the chaos.

Way south of Emei Shan on the way to the Yunnan border, **Xichang** is a remote but engaging town with a dusty old quarter and busy markets. The nearby **Liang Shan** range is central to Sichuan's **Yi minority**, though with few tourist facilities here, you'll need some determination to explore the area. Xichang is also a staging post for some bumpy back-roads trips; either via **Muli** into western **Sichuan**, or over into **Yunnan** at Lijiang or Lugu Lake.

There's no train station at Leshan, but Emei Shan and Xichang are both on the **Chengdu–Kunming railway**; almost everywhere else is served by regular buses, though you might have to hire a minibus on remoter roads.

Leshan and Dafo

The town of **LESHAN** (乐山, lèshān) sits 180km south of Chengdu and 50km from Emei Shan, at the convergence of the Qingyi, Min and Dadu rivers. The reason to head here is to spend half a day at the incredible **Big Buddha**, better known as **Dafo**, whose hulking form was carved into the cliffside opposite Leshan over a thousand years ago.

Leshan itself is a humdrum, spread-out place on the west side of the Min with very little to hold your attention – despite his size, Dafo is sunk into a niche and actually invisible from town – unless you're planning to catch a ferry to the Buddha from the **docks** on Binjiang Lu. There are plenty of restaurants, but Leshan isn't somewhere to stay overnight unless you get stuck – most hotels won't take foreigners, and Emei Shan's atmospheric temple accommodation is just over an hour away (see p.101).

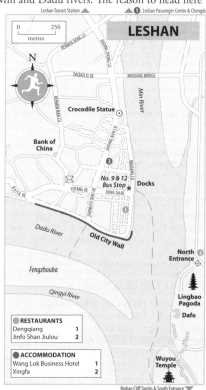

Dafo

大佛, dàfó • April–Sept daily 7.30am–6.30pm; Oct–March daily 8am–5.30pm • ¥90 • See p.100 for bus information

Impassive and gargantuan, **Dafo** peers out from under half-lidded eyes, oblivious to the swarms of sightseers trying to photograph his bulk. At 71m tall, this is the world's largest Buddhist sculpture – Dafo's ears are 7m long, his eyes 10m wide, and around six people

1

> ## GETTING TO DAFO
>
> Two **buses from Leshan** can drop you at Dafo's north entrance; allow 40min for either. **Bus #3** (¥1) runs from the Passenger Centre via Jiading Zhong Lu and the Minjiang Bridge; **bus #13** (¥1) runs up Zhongfu Qiao Jie, near the docks, and then also crosses the Minjiang Bridge before heading to Dafo.
>
> A full-frontal of the Buddha seen from the water really brings home Dafo's mighty scale, complementing close-up views on site. **Ferries to Wuyou Temple** (¥70) depart the **docks** (乐山港, lèshān gǎng) opposite Dafo on Binjiang Lu, pausing as they pass below the Buddha; note that they don't depart until they have a certain number of passengers. Cheapskates after similar views can catch a **public ferry** (¥1) from under the old gate tower at the bottom of Zhongfu Qiao Jie to midstream **Fengzhouba**, then walk down this long shingle island to face the Buddha.

at once can stand on his big toenail – though statistics can't convey the initial sight of this squat icon, comfortably seated with his hands on his knees, looming over you. What with the Buddha, associated temples and even older tombs, you'll need a good couple of hours to take everything in.

Work began on Dafo in 713, after a Buddhist monk named **Haitong** decided that carving a **giant Buddha** image into the cliffs here would calm Leshan's hazardous rapids and protect shipping navigating between Chengdu and the Yangzi. The government provided funding to get the project under way, but when a local official demanded a kickback, Haitong gouged out his own eyes in protest. Others then continued his work, and the Buddha was completed in 803 after the regional governor **Wei Gao** donated his salary. Dafo's calming influence worked too: rubble from the project filled in the rapids and made the rivers safe.

Along the cliffs

Once through Dafo's main **north entrance** (大佛北门, dàfó běimén), an easy flight of stone steps rises to the wooded clifftop and the crowded terrace around Dafo's ears, with views down onto the still-turbulent river. There's also a modern statue of Haitong up here, fumbling a rosary and looking slightly insane. Descending the one-way **staircase of nine turns** from here brings you down to the water by the Buddha's toes, staring up at his now-distant head; return to the top via the 500m-long **cliff road** cut into the rocks, dating in part to the eighth century. The path continues through woodland, past minor sights and clifftop galleries offering more river views, until you reach **Wuyou Temple** (乌优寺, wūyōu sì), a warm, pink-walled monastery occupying the top of Wuyou Shan – don't miss the grotesque gallery of saints in the luohan hall.

Beyond the temple is a covered bridge and then a side-path to the **Mahao cliff tombs** (麻浩崖墓, máhào yá mù), stone chambers chiselled deep into the rocks during the Han dynasty, 500 years before work began on Dafo. A small museum displays characteristically cheerful clay figurines and detailed models of contemporary houses, complete with farm animals. From here, either descend to the river and pick up a boat back to Leshan's docks, or catch bus #3 or #13 back to town from the **south entrance** (大佛南门, dàfó nánmén).

ARRIVAL AND DEPARTURE   LESHAN AND DAFO

By bus Leshan has two bus stations 5km out in the suburbs; both handle the same destinations. The larger Leshan Passenger Centre (乐山客运中心站, lèshān kèyùn zhōngxīn zhàn) is northwest on Baiyang Xi Lu; catch bus #9 or #12 to the docks, or bus #3 to Dafo. Leshan Transit Station (乐山联运车站, lèshān liányùn

chēzhàn) is north on Longyou Lu; bus #1 can get you to Zhongtu Qiao Jie, near the dock.

Destinations Chengdu (2hr 30min; ¥45); Chongqing City (6hr; ¥98); Dazu (1 daily; 5hr 30min; ¥72); Emei Shan Town (40min; ¥8); Kangding (1 daily; 6hr; ¥90); Ya'an (5 daily; 3hr; ¥52); Yibin (4hr; ¥65); Zigong (3hr; ¥40).

ACCOMMODATION AND EATING

Leshan claims fame for its **soft tofu** (豆花, dòu huā), served at all local restaurants. Another tasty street snack is spicy steamed meat served in a "cut" bun like a sandwich, with generous quantities of coriander leaf.

Dengqiang 邓强饭店, dèngqiáng fàndiàn. 158 Binjiang Lu. The best of several Sichuanese restaurants near the docks, with smart, antique-style furnishings and generally low prices (though some fish dishes are very expensive). A large fish and tofu casserole, enough for two, costs ¥35.

Jinfo Shan Jiulou 金佛山酒楼, jīnfó shān jiŭlóu. Across the road from Dafo's north entrance. Handy place to grab a filling stir-fry lunch before or after visiting the Buddha; they have an English menu and the food is tasty.

Wang Lok Business Hotel 宏乐商务酒店, hónglè shāngwù jiŭdiàn. 117 Baiyang Xi Lu ☎083 3245 0020. Budget hotel with the usual bed-TV-desk arrangement right next to the Passenger Centre; useful if you rock into town late at night. **¥100**

Xingfa 兴发酒店, xīngfā jiŭdiàn. 105 Jiading Nan Lu ☎083 3227 1888. Small, modern, friendly hotel in the older part of town down near the docks, whose manageress speaks a little English. **¥130**

Emei Shan

峨眉山, éméi shān

The holy mountain of **EMEI SHAN**, 60km west of Leshan, has been pulling in pilgrims – and more recently, tourists – for over two thousand years. Originally a Taoist retreat, Emei became a Buddhist site following the sixth-century visit of **Boddhisatva Puxian** and his six-tusked elephant – images of whom you'll see everywhere – and extensive Ming-dynasty rebuilding on the mountain converted almost all of Emei's temples to Buddhism. Aside from dozens of highly atmospheric **temples** – where you can stay overnight – the main draw is the **hike** up endless stone steps to Emei's summit, through a pristine natural environment of thick forests, which change markedly through the year – lush, green and wet in the summer; brilliant with reds and yellows in autumn; or white and very cold in winter.

The access point is **Emei Shan Town** (峨眉山市, éméi shān shì), a purely functional transit hub with **train and bus stations** 7km short of the mountain's trailhead at **Baoguo**. There are a few sights and temples around Baoguo, beyond which you'll have to pay Emei's entry fee. It's possible to conquer the mountain in a single day from Baoguo using buses and cable cars, but three would allow you to hike up at a reasonable pace – it's tough going – spend a night or two in a temple, and perhaps assault the 3000m-high summit area. Don't feel you have to climb this high, however, particularly if the weather is bad; there's plenty to keep you occupied lower down.

EMEI SHAN HIKING PRACTICALITIES

Bring a **torch** in case you unexpectedly find yourself on a path after dark. **Footwear** needs to have a firm grip; in winter, when stone steps become dangerously icy, straw sandals and even iron cleats – both sold for a few yuan and tied onto your soles – are an absolute necessity. Don't forget **warm clothing** for the top, which is around 15°C cooler than the plains and liable to be below freezing between October and April; lower paths are very humid during the summer. You'll also want some protection against the near certainty of **rain**. Leave any heavy gear with accommodation at the bottom of the mountain or in Chengdu if you're contemplating a round trip. Fairly useful **maps** of the mountain (¥5) are sold in Baoguo.

There are some **hotels** on the mountain, but Emei Shan is one of the few places in Southwest China you can stay in **temples** (see p.105) – don't miss out on the experience. **Food** on the mountain, however, is overpriced and ordinary. Stir-fries and noodle soups are available either at roadside stalls – where you can also buy **bottled water** – or at vegetarian temple restaurants, where you can sometimes eat with the monks.

If you need **information** or a **guide**, contact Patrick Yang (☎0137 0813 1210, ✉patrickyanglong@yahoo.com.cn), who speaks good English and has been taking foreign tour groups up Emei Shan for years. He also arranges day-long "culture tours" for about ¥100/person, touring a kung fu school, noodle factory and kindergarten, with lunch in a farmer's house.

1

Baoguo
报国, bàoguó

BAOGUO is one straight kilometre of hotels and restaurants running up past a **bus station** and an ornamental **waterfall** to a gilded pavilion. It's somewhere to grab a meal and a good night's sleep – even if you don't plan to hike up the mountain, the splendid **Baoguo** and **Fuhu temples** are amazing places to stay. Uphill and second left from the bus station, **Lingxiu Hot Springs** (灵秀温泉, língxiù wēnquán; daily 2pm–midnight; ¥168) is a modern spa complex with landscaped outdoor pools, best saved for a post-hike soak to unkink trail-weary muscles.

Bear left at the pavilion for the **Cultural Corridor**, a set of halls outlining how Confucianism, Taoism and Buddhism have always peacefully coexisted at Emei – reflecting current government guidelines rather than historical accuracy. Indeed, outdoor bronze statues of kung fu practitioners are a reminder that Emei Shan has a reputation for **martial arts**, developed by the Song-dynasty "White Ape Master" Situ Xuankong – although, wishing to avoid commercializing their skills, monks here don't teach openly.

Baoguo Temple
报国寺, bàoguó sì • Daily 7am–7pm • ¥8

Walk through the gardens behind the waterfall and you'll emerge in front of the large and serene **Baoguo Temple**, founded in 1615 and featuring flagstoned courtyards and

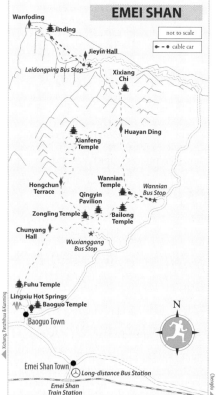

high-roofed halls, decorated with potted magnolias and cycads. Statues of Puxian and Guanyin, the Bodhissatva of Compassion, pin this down as an obviously Buddhist establishment, though the figures of the **eight immortals** carved into the rear hall's stone balustrades betray Baoguo's Taoist origins. In its own pavilion on a hill opposite Baoguo's entrance, the Ming-dynasty **Shengji Evening Bell** (圣积晚钟, shèngjī wǎnzhōng), encrusted with characters, can be heard 15km away – it's rung on special occasions.

Fuhu Temple

If you follow the vehicle road uphill past the waterfall and then bear left, it's 1km to the charming Fuhu Temple, which sits surrounded by ancient ginkgo trees. Emei's largest place of worship, the current maze of beautifully proportioned stone halls and courtyards dates to 1661, though extensive renovations around 2002 added a new luohan hall (see p.78). Today it's a nunnery dedicated to Guanyin, whose treasures include the bronze sixteenth-century **Huayan Pagoda**, 7m high and engraved with 4700 Buddha images.

1

Up the mountain

Trails open daily 7am–6pm • Ticket ¥150, valid three days

Emei Shan can be hiked via two routes from Baoguo, both of which scale relentless flights of stone steps: the 60km **long route** and the 40km **short route**. Most people knock 15km or so off these by catching **buses** (see opposite) from Baoguo to alternative starting points near **Qingyin Pavilion** (Wuxianggang bus stop) or **Wannian Temple**; leaving early enough, you could make it to the top in one day from either of these via the short route, descending the next day – though your legs will be like jelly afterwards. If you're really pushed for time, you could get up and down in a single day by catching a minibus between Baoguo Temple and **Jieyin Hall** (Leidongping bus stop), located a cable-car ride from the summit, but this way you'll miss out on what makes Emei Shan such a special place. **Temples** along the way offer accommodation and food (see opposite).

The long route

Following the **long route**, it's 5km from Fuhu Temple to **Chunyang Hall** (纯阳殿, chúnyáng diàn), a nunnery founded in honour of the Taoist immortal Lü Dongbin, spookily surrounded by mossy pine trees. A further 5km lands you at **Qingyin Pavilion** (清音阁, qīngyīn gé), built deep in the forest where two streams converge and tumble through a small gorge down the **Ox-heart Rock** (牛心石, niúxīn shí). It's a charming spot with a small **temple** (en-suite doubles ¥140, dorms ¥15), although it can get busy – the **Wuxianggang bus stop**, where some walkers start their trip, is just 3km from here.

To continue the long route, follow the path up past the left side of Qingyin; this takes you along a riverbed and past a **monkey-watching area**, before starting to climb steeply through a series of gorges. About 6km further on, **Hongchun Terrace** (洪椿坪, hóngchūn píng; beds ¥40) is an eighteenth-century temple named after surrounding *hongchun* (toona) trees, and is about as far as you'd make it on the first day.

After this it's a very tough 15km of seemingly unending narrow stairs to **Xianfeng Temple** (仙峰寺, xiānfēng sì; beds ¥40), a strangely unfriendly place, though well forested with pine and dove trees and planted with camellias and rhododendrons. The following 12.5km are slightly easier, heading partly downhill to a dragon-headed bridge, then up again to where the trail joins the north route near **Xixiang Chi** (see below), around 43km from Fuhu Temple and two-thirds of the way to the summit.

The short route

Emei's **short route** begins at the **Wannian bus stop**. From here a 3km path or cable car (¥50) ascends to the elegant and venerable **Wannian Temple** (万年寺, wànnián sì; entry ¥6; dorms ¥20, doubles ¥140), though most of the original halls perished in a fire during the 1940s. Wannian is also known as *Baishui* (White Water) after a temple **pond**; seeing autumn leaves reflected in it is one of the mountain's famous sights, celebrated by the Tang poet **Li Bai** (p.84). Out back a squat brick **pavilion**, built in 1601, houses a stunning, life-sized enamelled bronze **sculpture of Puxian**, riding a gilt lotus flower astride his great six-tusked white elephant. Weighing 62 tonnes and standing over 7m high, this masterwork was commissioned by the Song emperor Taizu and brought from Chengdu in pieces – note the golden spots on the elephant's knees, which people rub for good luck.

From Wannian, a steady 14km hike through bamboo and pine groves – pausing every now and then to let **mule trains** ferrying temple supplies past – should see you where the short and long routes converge just south of **Xixiang Chi** (洗象池, xǐxiàng chí), the Elephant Bathing Pool, where Puxian's elephant stopped for a wash. The eighteenth-century **monastery** here (beds ¥20, doubles with/without a/c ¥200/80) sits on a ridge, and on cloudy days – being more or less open to the elements and prowled by monkeys – it's amazingly atmospheric, though somewhat run-down and frigid in winter. It's a popular place to rest up, so get in early to be sure of a bed.

On to the top

Beyond Xixiang Chi the path gets easier, but you'll encounter gangs of aggressive **monkeys** who threaten you for food with teeth bared; you'll probably feel safer with a stick in your hand and need to keep a good grip on your bags. The path continues for 9km past some ancient, gnarled rhododendrons to **Jieyin Hall** (接引殿, jiēyǐn diàn) where the 50km-long road from Baoguo, which has snaked its way round the back of the mountain, ends at **Leidongping bus stop** and a **cable car** to the summit (¥40 up, ¥30 down). The area is thick with minibus tour parties fired up for their one-day crack at the peak, and is also where to find buses back to Baoguo. **Hotels** around Jieyin are badly maintained and very expensive – they have been known to charge ¥200 for a mat on the floor – and you shouldn't plan to stay here.

The summit

Whether you take the cable car or spend the next couple of hours hoofing it, 3077m-high **Jinding** (金顶, jīndǐng), the Golden Summit, is the highest accessible point on the mountain. There are two temples: the friendly **Woyun Nunnery** (卧云庵, wòyún ān; dorms ¥30, doubles ¥200) and the oversized **Huazang Temple** (华藏寺, huázàng sì; doubles ¥220), crowned by a massive gilded statue of a multi-faced Puxian on four elephants. Huazang is believed to have been founded in the Han dynasty and once contained a bronze hall, which was totally destroyed by a lightning strike during the nineteenth century.

If you've made it this far, it's worth catching the **sunrise**, which on good days lights up the sea of clouds below the peak. In the afternoon, these clouds sometimes catch rainbow-like rings known as **Buddha's Halo**, which surround and move with your shadow, while in clear conditions you can even make out the snowcapped spike of Gongga Shan (see p.127), 150km to the west.

ARRIVAL AND DEPARTURE   EMEI SHAN

Emei's **train station** and **main bus station** are close to each other 3.5km outside Emei Shan Town; catch blue city bus #1 (¥1) from either until you reach a roundabout with a golden statue in the middle; cross the roundabout and catch green city bus #5 (¥1.5) for the final 6km to Baoguo. Some long-distance buses terminate at **Baoguo bus station**, from where all transport up the mountain originates.

EMEI SHAN TOWN
By bus Chengdu (2hr 30min; ¥45); Leshan (40min; ¥8).
By train The *Teddy Bear Hotel* (see p.106) can book train tickets from Emei along the Chengdu–Kunming line for a fee. The last train to Chengdu leaves around 9pm.
Destinations Chengdu (7 daily; 2hr 30min); Kunming (3

daily; 17hr); Panzhihua (6 daily; 11hr); Xichang (8 daily; 8hr).

BAOGUO
By bus Chengdu (on the hour, daily 8am–6pm; 2hr 30min; ¥45); Leshan (40min; ¥12).

GETTING AROUND

By mountain bus These depart Baoguo bus station every 30min, daily 6am–5pm: Leidongping (雷洞坪车站, léidòngpíng chēzhàn; for Jieyin Hall and the summit;

¥40 up, ¥30 down); Wannian Temple (万年寺车站, wànnián sì chēzhàn; ¥20); Wuxianggang (五显岗车站, wǔxiǎngǎng chēzhàn; for Qingyin Pavilion; ¥20).

ACCOMMODATION AND EATING

Almost all **temples** offer basic dorm beds (from ¥15), and most have doubles with shared bathrooms (¥80) or en suites (¥150); you book at reception desks, usually signed in English near temple entrances. Try to get in by 4pm between spring and autumn, when there are a fair number of people on the trails and beds can become scarce. There are temples both in Baoguo (see p.102) and up the mountain (noted in the text). There are also dozens of inexpensive **hotels** back off the main road in Baoguo, signed in English as "inns", where you should be able to wrangle a comfortable double for ¥120. Prices for all accommodation can double during holidays.

Anywhere in Baoguo that isn't a hotel or selling souvenirs is probably a **restaurant**; many have English menus. Aside from the usual stir-fries and Sichuanese home cooking, some places serve pheasant and other game. Up the mountain, temples and **stalls** offer simple dishes.

3077 Hostel 峨嵋山青年旅社，éméi shān qīngnián lǔshè. Left out of the bus station, then second left (the hot springs road) ☎083 3559 1698, ⓦ57ems.com. This is a pleasant, modern hostel with large outdoor area and all facilities. Dorms ¥40, doubles ¥120

★ **Baoguo Temple** 报国寺，bàoguó sì. The real deal, with misty halls, chanting monks, stone courtyards and ancient fittings. Accommodation is well maintained and very popular. Beds ¥15, doubles ¥80, with en suite ¥150

★ **Fuhu Temple** 伏虎寺，fúhǔ sì. At least as good as Baoguo Temple, for the same reasons. Dorms ¥15, doubles ¥80, en suite ¥150

Teddy Bear 玩具熊酒店，wánjùxióng jiǔdiàn. Down a side-street downhill from the bus station ☎083 3559 0135, ⓦteddybear.com.cn. A sound backpacker staple with English-speaking management, stuffy dorms, better doubles, internet and a restaurant. Dorms ¥30, doubles ¥180

DIRECTORY

Banks The last building in Baoguo is an Agricultural Bank of China, with ATM.

Shopping There are several open-air markets near the bus station in Baoguo, specializing in local tea – including the mountain's famous *zhuye qing* (竹叶青，zhúyèqīng) – medicinal herbs, walking sticks and trinkets.

Xichang
西昌，xīchāng

Given its remote location in the otherwise undernourished, mountainous countryside of Sichuan's far south, **XICHANG** is a surprisingly active, prosperous city. The focus for Sichuan's **Yi** community, who occupy the surrounding **Liang Shan** ranges, Xichang is also a **launch site** for China's Long March Space Programme, and a staging post for some back-roads trips **to Yunnan**.

Downtown Xichang is a kilometre-broad block laid out between the often dry Dong He and Xi He rivers, with arrival points out in the suburbs. You could happily poke around the markets and old town for an hour or two, though with longer you should definitely concentrate on the scenery and sights at nearby **Qiong Hai** and **Lu Shan**. If possible, visit during the **Yi torch festival**, held opposite the south bus station outside the Liangshan Cultural Centre (凉山民族文化中心，liángshān mínzú wénhuà zhōngxīn); the Yi worship fire and you can expect to see a scary amount of it about, alongside mass singing, drinking and dancing.

Yuecheng Square
月城广场，yuèchéng guǎngchǎng

Xichang's public focus is **Yuecheng Square**, best in the evening when crowds gather for mass dances. A blocky sandstone **statue** on the road here, showing the Yi chieftain

---

THE YI

China's seven million **Yi** are concentrated through Sichuan's Liang Shan region, though their shamanistic religion, language and unique, **wavy script** – seen on signs all around Xichang – suggest an origin closer to the western limit of their territory, near Dali in Yunnan. Though men dress in anonymous clothing, Yi women favour finely embroidered jackets and sometimes twist their hair into bizarre horned shapes; married women also wear wide, flat black bonnets.

The Yi were originally a **matriarchal slave society** divided into an aristocratic "black" caste, headed by chieftains or **tusi**, and tenants and labourers who comprised four "white" castes. The caste system was dismantled by the Communist government in 1956 – an event charted by British journalist Alan Winnington in his *Slaves of the Cool Mountains* (see p.394) – though decandants of black and white Yi still don't intermarry. Shamans, or **bimo**, have survived however, and there's a chance of at least a superficial view of the old ways during occasional festivals. These are riotous occasions with heavy drinking sessions, bullfights and wrestling matches interspersed with music and archery displays.

Best is the **Torch Festival** on the 24th of the sixth lunar month, commemorating both an ancient victory over a heavenly insect plague, and the wife of Tang-dynasty chieftain Deng Shan, who starved to death rather than marry the warlord who had incinerated her husband. The **Yi New Year** arrives early, in the tenth lunar month.

Yuedan swearing brotherhood with a Red Army commander during the Long March in 1935, makes a useful landmark. Streets northeast of the square are choked by daily **markets** where you'll see Yi women from the hills wearing embroidered capes and black, flat bonnets half a metre wide.

Datong Gate
大通门, dàtōng mén • Daily 9am–9.30pm • ¥1

Just northeast of the markets, **Datong Gate** is a reconstructed section of Xichang's city walls dating to 1387. Steps climb the crenellated tower, where there's a tea terrace and balustrade carvings of lewd lionesses. The cross of streets behind mark out Xichang's **old town**, full of grimy old teahouses, noodle shops and businesses selling everything from silverwork to flowers, farm gear, charcoal, food and clothing. Other antique structures nearby include the unrestored **North Gate** (北门, běimén) on Bei Jie, and an inaccessible mosque, church and pagoda.

Qiong Hai
邛海, qióng hǎi • City bus #106 from Sanchakou Lu and the south bus station circuits the lake in 2hr via access roads to the Slave Museum and Lu Shan

Just southeast of Xichang, 12km-long **Qiong Hai** is one of Sichuan's largest lakes. Its attractive scenery is linked by a circuit road from town – though the best views and sights are in fact at Lu Shan, the range of hills immediately to the south. Right at the

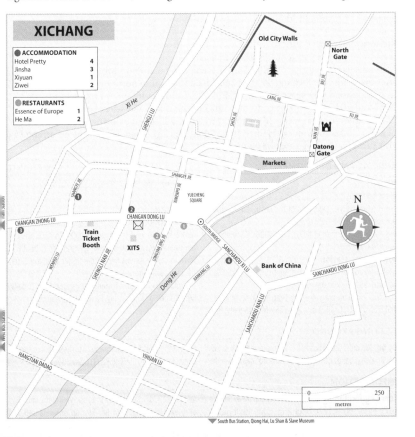

1

far end of the lake, flamboyant **Lingying Temple** (灵鹰寺, líng yīng sì; ¥5), whose brightly painted halls are shared by Taoist and Buddhist deities, is a good place to get off the bus for a walk; the lake's calm waters often beautifully reflect the surrounding mountains. If you're just after a picturesque setting with a local meal thrown in, aim for **Xiaoyu Village** (小渔村, xiǎoyú cūn), reached directly from town on **bus #111** from South Bridge, which has traditional houses and restaurants specializing in lake fish.

Lu Shan

泸山, lú shān • City bus #14, #22 or #106 from Sanchakou Lu to the museum access road or cable-car station

Lu Shan, a slanted range of dry hills partially covered in green pine forests, hems in Qiong Hai's south shore, with some excellent views from temples and lookout points that dot the heights. Routes up begin about 4km from Xichang off the lakeshore road, either on a direct **cable car** (索滑道, suǒ huá dào; ¥20 up, ¥30 return), or by catching bus #202 (¥1) up the winding 3km road. The road – but not the cable car – passes the **Yi Slave Museum** (黎族奴隶社会博物馆, lízú núlì shèhuì bówùguǎn; daily 9am-4pm; free), with a fabulous lake panorama from the museum forecourt. Inside, dioramas of fortified villages, festival clothing, woodcarvings and books written in Yi script throw considerable light on Yi culture, even if it is laced with glib propaganda contrasting the misery of former times with the Yi's cheerful integration into Chinese society. Bus #202 and the cable car wind up at a clutch of monasteries; monkey-infested **Guangfu Temple** (光福寺, guāngfú sì; ¥3) is the oldest and most opulent, with a fine **vegetarian restaurant**. There's a walking track – including around 4000 steps – from here up to Lu Shan's 2317m **summit**, though it's disappointingly crowned by a radio tower.

Xichang Satellite Launch Centre

西昌卫星发射中心, xīchāng wèixīng fāshè zhōngxīn

Mao once lamented that "China cannot even get a potato into orbit", but a decade after his death, the **Xichang Satellite Launch Centre**, 55km north of Xichang, propelled its first payload into space atop of a Long March Rocket in 1984. Probes launched in 2007 and 2010 were designed to map areas of the moon and select landing sites for future exploration. It seems likely that the centre will soon be downgraded in favour of newer facilities on tropical Hainan Island. For the time being, it's possible to **arrange a visit** through the XITS (see below).

ARRIVAL AND DEPARTURE   XICHANG

BY BUS

West bus station (旅游服务集散中心, lǚyóu fúwù jísàn zhōngxīn), 2km west of the centre on Hangtian Dadao; catch bus #14 into town.
Destinations Chengdu (1 daily; 12hr; ¥120); Kangding (2 daily; 9hr; ¥98).
South bus station (旅游汽车客运中心, lǚyóu qìchē kèyùn zhōngxīn), 1km south on Sanchakou Nan Lu; catch bus #14 into town.
Destinations Kunming (1 daily; 14hr; ¥123); Lugu Hu (2 daily; 8hr; ¥73); Luoji Shan (2hr; ¥35); Muli (5 daily; 8hr;

¥67); Panzhihua (3hr; ¥48); Yanyuan (4hr; ¥48).

BY TRAIN

Xichang's **train station** is a few kilometres west of the centre; city bus #6 (¥1) runs to Chang'an Dong Lu. You can buy train tickets at the bus stations, and also from booths in town; it can be almost impossible to get anything better than hard seats, however.
Destinations Chengdu (10 daily; 10hr); Emei Shan (7 daily; 8hr); Kunming (4 daily; 9hr); Panzhihua (9 daily; 3hr).

GETTING AROUND

By bus Xichang's useful bus #14 (¥1) runs from the West bus station along Chang'an Dong Lu, past Yucheng Square, over the

South Bridge and down Sanchakou Lu to the South bus station. It then continues to the foothills of Lu Shan (see above).

INFORMATION

Tourist information Xichang International Travel Service (XITS; 西昌国际旅行社, xīchāng guójì lǚxíngshè)

☏ 083 4322 3061, are hidden in a courtyard at the end of an alley east of Shengli Nan Jie. Turn up unannounced and you'd be lucky to find anyone in. For Satellite Launch Site visits, contact them as far in advance as possible, perhaps via accommodation tour desks in Chengdu: they'll need photographs, copies of your passport and a fee.

ACCOMMODATION

Hotel Pretty 美丽华大酒店, měilìhuá dàjiǔdiàn. 79 Sanchakou Xi Lu ☎ 083 4223 7777, ⊚ pretty-hotel.com. New boutique-hotel affair; fairly smart with comfortable bedrooms, conference facilities, several restaurants and a sauna. ¥200

Jinsha 金沙宾馆, jīnshā bīnguǎn. 57 Chang'an Zhong Lu ☎ 083 4322 8169. Quiet, older hotel amenable to haggling over room rates; rooms are a little musty and could do with redecorating, but everything works. ¥130

Xiyuan 西苑宾馆, xīyuàn bīnguǎn. 70 Ximen Po Jie ☎ 083 4323 5111. Friendly, basic hotel, about the cheapest deal in town; solo travellers can usually wrangle a half-price room. ¥90

Ziwei 紫薇酒店, zǐwēi jiǔdiàn. 60 Chang'an Dong Lu ☎ 083 4328 5888. Small, clean, modern rooms with glassed-in bathrooms and optional computers. Best in town for the price. ¥120

EATING

A clutch of inexpensive **food stalls** on the west side of Yuecheng Square delivers huge portions of fried rice, fried greens, beef noodle soup and the like for under ¥10. The *Hotel Pretty* has a decent Chinese restaurant.

Essence of Europe 欧洲字居, ōuzhōu zìjū. Floor 3, Dada Shopping Centre, near the statue on Chang'an Dong Lu. Western-style café-restaurant with windows over the street and cute, white-picket trim to booths. Good for a caffeine fix at ¥35 a pot.

He Ma 何妈私家菜, hé mā sījiā cài. Longyanjing Jie. The best of several family-run restaurants in this street, serving medicinal soups (¥30) and a heap of Sichuanese favourites: cold jelly noodles, spicy cucumber and chicken, dry-fried beef shreds, big soups and a corn, prawn and celery stir-fry. Dishes ¥15–35.

DIRECTORY

Banks The main Bank of China, with ATMs, is over the bridge on Sanchakou Xi Lu.
Post Office Opposite the *Ziwei* hotel on Chang'an Dong Lu.
Shopping Numerous gift shops around town sell locally made plates and goblets lacquered with Yi-inspired designs in black, red and yellow, Long March Rocket models, buckwheat tea and dried mushrooms. There's a good one just outside the South bus station. The markets overflow with pomegranates in spring.

Liang Shan

凉山, liáng shān
Liang Shan, the "Cool Mountains", spread west from Xichang in a series of ranges and plateaus. These dry, eroded uplands are the real Yi homelands, and well into the twentieth century the various Yi castes and clans waged war on each other, raiding their

TRAVEL OPTIONS FROM XICHANG

Xichang is quite a transport nexus: aside from direct trains south to Kunming or north to Emei Shan and Chengdu, there are direct buses to **Kangding** (see p.124) in western Sichuan, and some interesting back-roads trips to try.

Right on the Sichuan–Yunnan border 250km west from Xichang, **Lugu Lake** (p.229) is another straightforward but bumpy bus ride away through dry, dramatic, mountain scenery; there's regular transport south from here to **Lijiang** (p.218).

A more usual route to Lijiang is to catch the train or ride a bus down the expressway 230km south to the sprawling industrial city of **Panzhihua** (攀枝花, pānzhīhuā), then change buses for Lijiang – it's probably quicker than going via Lugu Lake, but there's nothing to break the journey. In Panzhihua, local bus #64 runs between the train and bus stations (30min); or catch faster taxis and minibuses. An early-morning bus to Lijiang (8hr) travels via an incredible mountainside road. There are also buses from Xichang to **Muli** (p.110) from where, with some initiative, it's possible to make your way through remote Tibetan regions to Yading and Daocheng.

1

neighbours for valuables and slaves. Outsiders fared better – the Austrian botanist **Heinrich Handel-Mazzetti** (see p.227) explored up here without being molested during World War I – though the slightest social gaffe could lead to slaughter; the British adventurer **John Brooke** was killed after unintentionally offending a *tusi* in 1908.

Though people today are friendly enough, it's still not especially easy to explore Liang Shan. Tourist facilities are nonexistent and you'll need some Chinese and motivation to get much out of the region. One suggested target is **Luoji Shan** (螺髻山, luójì shān), a 4359m-high mountain range about 40km south of Xichang with thick forests, high-altitude lakes ringed by peaks and traditional Yi villages whose houses are guarded by animals carved in the wooden eaves over the doorways. Base yourself at one-street **Luoji Shan town** (螺髻山镇, luójì shān zhèn), where there are several simple guesthouses.

Muli and beyond

The reason to visit **Muli**, a dusty little roadhead town 270km west of Xichang, is for the chance to tackle an unreliable **route to Yading** in western Sichuan (see p.140) – you'll need some spoken Chinese to be able to organize things.

The bus to Muli initially follows the Xichang–Lugu Lake road, over stark, eroded mountains dotted with pine and eucalyptus, to the fertile plateau surrounding single-street **Yanyuan** (盐源, yányuán). Leaving the Xichang–Lugu Lake road here, the road makes a long, slow climb north out of the valley, then the scenery repeats until the final, winding ascent to Muli.

Muli

木里, mùlǐ

MULI is a tiny concrete-and-tile town in a beautiful mountain setting, high on a hillside overlooking a gorge. The botanist **Joseph Rock** (see p.227) visited in 1923; aside from Yi, local ethnic groups include **Tibetans** and Naxi. Wandering the kilometre-long street which circuits town from the bus station turns up a couple of places to stay and eat, a line of **silversmiths** hammering out Tibetan jewellery – coral rings, turquoise earrings, silver bracelets – and stores selling essentials, such as portable churns for making **butter tea** (see p.126).

There's a rough 300km-long road to Yading via **Muli Dasi** (木里大寺, mùlǐ dàsì), a Tibetan monastery 3000m up the side of the Litang valley. No buses make the journey, but you can hire **minibuses** for the two-day trip or, if your Chinese is up to it, horses and guides.

ARRIVAL AND DEPARTURE　　　　　　　　　　　　　　MULI AND BEYOND

By bus Buy tickets out from Muli the day before as most buses leave by 8am and tickets sell out quickly. For Lugu Lake and Yunnan, catch a bus to Yanyuan, from where minibuses run on demand (¥160 for the vehicle, split between the number of passengers). For Yading minibuses, ask at the bus station or the *Kazhuo* hotel, and be prepared

for disappointment; expect to pay ¥300/day for the vehicle, including the driver's return journey.

Destinations Yanyuan (3 daily; 3hr 30min; ¥28); Xichang (5 daily; 8hr; ¥67).

Yanyuan bus station destinations Lugu Lake (1 daily; 3hr; ¥30); Muli (3 daily; 3hr 30min; ¥28); Xichang (5hr; ¥48).

ACCOMMODATION AND EATING

Baixing Chufang 百姓厨房, bǎixìng chúfáng. In front of the *Kazhuo* hotel. Sichuanese stir-fries and soups are served at this friendly, spacious canteen.

Bus Station Hotel 车站宾馆, chēzhàn bīnguǎn. At the bus station. Typical of Muli's clean, ordinary, inexpensive hostels. **¥60**

Kazhuo 卡卓大酒店, kǎzhuó dàjiǔdiàn. 75 Longqin Jie ⊙ 083 4652 2888. Look for the large stone lions outside, then walk around to the rear. Large, airy doubles with heavy wooden furniture and modern bathrooms; easily the best place in town and usually almost deserted. **¥120**

DIRECTORY

Banks There's an Agricultural Bank here, but no foreign-friendly ATM; bring as much money as you'll need.

Northern Sichuan

Eastern Sichuan's plains end abruptly north of Chengdu, and the 500km-broad spread of icy mountains, moist pine forest and grassland between here and the border with Gansu province offers an accessible taster of **Tibetan culture**, especially if you haven't the time to explore western Sichuan. Most people cut through the region in about a week, stopping at the old garrison town of **Songpan**, a popular base for horse-trekking, en route to spectacular alpine scenery and vivid blue lakes at **Jiuzhaigou** – one of China's most heavily touristed sights, despite its relative isolation. **Muni** and **Huanglong** offer slightly less visited alternatives.

Beyond Songpan, the grassland town of **Zöigê** and Tibetan monasteries at **Langmusi** offer horseriding and the region's most important Lamaseries; **Tibetan New Year**, *losar*, is held in February or March and is celebrated especially enthusiastically here, with dances and temple fairs. Slightly to the east of all this, you'll need at least an extra three days for **Wanglang Nature Reserve**, an undeveloped pocket of rugged high-altitude terrain known for its **wild pandas**; you've almost no chance of seeing one, but there's plenty of other wildlife and it's a fantastic place to experience their true habitat.

Travel through northern Sichuan greatly improved after the 2008 earthquake (see below) destroyed the notoriously dangerous stretch of **Highway 213** from Chengdu via Wenchuan and Songpan – known as the "Tiger's Mouth" after the risk you took by using it. This has been rebuilt as a fast, reliable road: you can reach Songpan from Chengdu in six hours, and Jiuzhaigou in nine. A parallel **rail line** is also under construction, with the first trains scheduled for 2014. Alternatively, you can get direct to Jiuzhaigou by bus from Guangyuan (p.89), which is on the Chengdu–Xi'an train line. For Wanglang, however, you need the longer, more easterly road via Jiangyou and Pingwu (see p.112).

Wanglang Nature Reserve

王朗自然保护区, **wánglǎng zìrán bǎohùqū** • Free • Book accommodation and check access conditions in advance on ☎ 081 6882 5312, ✉ scwlnrt@my-public.sc.cninfo.net

Surrounded by the remote summits of northern Sichuan's Min Shan range, some way west of the Jiangyou–Jiuzhaigou road, **Wanglang Nature Reserve**'s alpine forest, boggy meadows, scree-flanked peaks and dense thickets of bamboo are perfect **giant panda** habitat. Although you'd have to be extraordinarily fortunate to see one of these rare bears, other animals – including takin, musk deer and goat-like serow – are less elusive; if nothing else, experiencing the tough local conditions will make you realize why pandas are so scarce in their natural state (and what wildlife cameramen go through to film them). At over 2800m, it can snow throughout the year, and will almost certainly be cut off between November and March. Bring **binoculars**.

THE 2008 EARTHQUAKE

In May 2008, a magnitude 7.9 **earthquake** struck in the mountains 100km north of Chengdu, killing 80,000 people. **Beichuan**, at the quake's epicentre, and nearby Wenchuan were literally reduced to rubble; hillsides and mountain ranges collapsed, and new lakes formed as rivers were dammed by landslides. The quake followed a diagonal fault running southwest across Sichuan, so relatively distant towns along Shudao (see p.84) were seriously damaged while Chengdu, though fairly close, escaped virtually unscathed.

Reconstruction is ongoing, involving the rebuilding of towns and villages, historic sites and stretches of the Chengdu–Songpan–Gansu highway. One unusual victim of the quake was **Wolong panda reserve**, a breeding centre west of Dujiangyan; surviving animals were shifted to Bifengxia (see p.83), though there are plans to build a new breeding centre at Wolong. Beichuan itself has been left partly demolished as a memorial, with the new town of **Yongquan** now housing former residents.

1

PANDAS

Two animals share the name panda: the **giant panda** (大熊猫, dà xióngmāo), the black-eyed bear which has become the worldwide symbol for endangered species; and the unrelated, racoon-like **red panda** (小熊猫, xiǎo xióngmāo). There's no traditional mythology about them in China, but during the 1950s the giant panda was adopted as a national symbol by the Communist government because it was uniquely Chinese, was coveted by the West and (unlike the dragon) had no associations with the country's imperial past.

News of giant pandas first reached Europe in the nineteenth century through **Père Armand David** (see p.83). Though once widespread in southwestern China, their endangered status is a result of human encroachment combined with the vagaries of their preferred food – **fountain bamboo** – which periodically flowers and dies over huge areas. Half of Sichuan's panda habitat was lost to logging between 1974 and 1989, which, coupled with a bamboo die-off during the 1980s, reduced the total population to an estimated 1590 animals, scattered through mountainous **reserves** in Sichuan, Yunnan, Shaanxi and Guizhou.

You've virtually no chance of seeing pandas in the wild – even researchers can spend years looking for them – but if you want to experience their habitat, head to **Wanglang Reserve** (see below) in northern Sichuan. Otherwise, be content with close-up views at **Chengdu's breeding centre** (p.70) or **Bifengxia** (p.83).

From Pingwu to the reserve

The nearest town to Wanglang is **PINGWU** (平武, píngwǔ), 110km north of Jiangyou; from here it's a further 60km along the Jiuzhaigou road to **Luotongba** (罗通坝, luótōngbà), a string of souvenir stalls on the roadside run by Baima Tibetans. At Luotongba, an increasingly rough, 40km-long road runs west into the mountains, terminating in a low valley at the **national park headquarters**. Surrounded by birch and larch woodland, the local area is good for birds, especially wallcreepers and **blue eared pheasants**, which strut around the meadows in the morning. Two vehicle tracks head further out to **Baisha Gou** and **Baixiong Gou**; they're walkable, but you'll need a full day to make the return hike along either, or to ask park staff about hitching a ride one way.

Baisha Gou

白沙沟, báishā gōu

The 12km-long **Baisha Gou** track initially climbs uphill through old-growth forest of ancient pines, with a tangled bamboo and willow understorey. At **Dacaoping boardwalk**, there's an hour's circuit around boggy moorland ringed by iced-up conifers thick with old man's beard and orchids, and a deep, total silence in between pheasants' booming squawks. At the end of the road, Baisha Gou itself is an open shale slope with fawn-coloured outcrops rising above, circled by eagles; it's a natural rock garden coloured by bilberries, primulas and rhododendrons of all sizes, with a summertime "flower sea" in adjacent valleys.

Baixiong Gou

白熊沟, báixióng gōu

Baixiong Gou's 9km-long access road, below steep, open valley slopes, gives the best chance of seeing serow and Wanglang's forty-odd takin – you'll need good eyesight to spot them up on ridges and binoculars to know what you're looking at. Baixiong Gou is a valley thick with spruce, firs and junipers; a **boardwalk** follows a stream through short, dense thickets of **arrow bamboo**, the panda's favourite food – though there's said to be just one on this side of the reserve.

ARRIVAL AND DEPARTURE	WANGLANG NATURE RESERVE

By bus Wanglang can only be reached by hiring a minibus in Pingwu (2hr 30min; ¥300 single); they park opposite

Pingwu's bus station, or call ☎ 159 0822 6927. Returning, you could try to hitch out to the Pingwu–Jiuzhaigou road and flag down passing buses, though they are usually full; failing this, you'll have to arrange things with the driver who brought you in. Also note that Jiuzhaigou buses don't originate in Pingwu; passing Chengdu–Jiuzhaigou buses stop for lunch next to Pingwu's Baosi Temple (报恩寺,

bàosī sì), where you can ask about available seats.
Pingwu destinations Chengdu (2 daily; 5hr 30min; ¥59); Jiangyou (every 30min; 3hr 30min; ¥29); Jiuzhaigou (2 daily passing through; 3hr 30min; ¥70).

GETTING AROUND

On foot The national park staff might provide lifts around Wanglang, otherwise you'll be walking. You should wear or carry warm, fully weatherproof kit at all times, along with hiking food and a torch. Under no circumstances leave the roads or marked circuit walks – there's little chance of being found should something go wrong.

ACCOMMODATION AND EATING

Forest Lodge ☎081 6882 5312, ✉scwlnrt@my-public. sc.cninfo.net. Wanglang's sole accommodation – you must book in advance – in a row of comfortable wooden chalets with heating and hot water at the national park headquarters. Breakfast and supper are included but servings are bland and small, so bring plenty of snacks. **¥200**

Wenchuan

汶川, wènchuān

Around 130km north of Chengdu, **WENCHUAN** (汶川, wènchuān) was substantially rebuilt post-quake and doesn't offer much reason in itself to stop unless you want to buy fresh **Sichuan pepper**, which grows on spiky bushes around here. The area is key, however, to northern Sichuan's **Qiang** ethnic group, who wear black turbans and tend the apple and walnut groves lining the roadside. The Qiang – also known as **Erma** – number around 300,000 and once formed a powerful kingdom across north and western Sichuan, though they were gradually overwhelmed by Chinese and Tibetan expansion and retreated to fortified villages in the hills, their flat-roofed, rectangular split-stone houses and 20m-high **watchtowers** dotting the slopes above town.

Taoping

桃坪乡, táopíng xiāng

For a look at Qiang culture, **Taoping**, a picturesque village of narrow stone lanes 20km west of Wenchuan, makes a good base. Locals claim Taoping was founded in 111 BC; there's a small museum and several square-sided watchtowers here, each decorated with yak skulls, along with plenty of traditional stone houses – **Yang's Courtyard** (杨家大院, yángjiā dàyuàn) has been lived in by the same family for over fifty generations. Good, stiff **hikes** from Taoping head up into the mountains to villages such as **Jiashan** (佳山, jiāshān), via some spectacular views – take a stick to fend off dogs along the way.

ARRIVAL AND DEPARTURE   TAOPING

By bus Buses travelling the Wenchuan–Ma'erkang road can drop you at Taoping; Wenchuan–Taoping minibuses depart when they have enough customers.

Destinations Wenchuan to: Chengdu (8 daily; 4hr; ¥65); Ma'erkang (2 daily; 6hr; ¥90); Songpan (2 daily; 2hr 30min; ¥40); Taoping (1hr; ¥2).

ACCOMMODATION AND EATING

With buses throughout the day, you shouldn't need to stay in Wenchuan. If Taoping's *Erma* guesthouse is full, many local homes take in guests. There's a small store selling biscuits and basics in Taoping.

Erma 尔玛人家, ěrmǎ rénjiā. Taoping village. Homestay accommodation in a friendly Qiang household in this pretty, historic village. The rate includes meals. **¥45**

Songpan

松潘, sōngpān

Set on a 2200m-high plateau 320km north of Chengdu, **SONGPAN** was founded in Qing times as a garrison town straddling the Min River. Strategically, it guards the neck of a valley along the **road to Gansu**, built up against a stony ridge to the west and surrounded on the remaining three sides by 8m-high stone **walls**. As the gateway to northern Sichuan, Songpan feels very much like a frontier town, dusty and full of Tibetan and Qiang villagers in from the hills to go shopping, an interesting place to poke around in for the day while arranging **horse-trekking** around the mountains nearby.

Inside the walls

Downtown Songpan forms an elongated, easily navigated rectangle inside the 6m-high **old city walls**, which can be climbed in various places for views over the town. The partially pedestrianized main road runs south for 750m from the **north gate**, a mighty stone construction topped with a brightly painted wooden pavilion. Around two-thirds of the way down, **Gusong Qiao** (古松桥, gǔsōng qiáo) is a covered bridge over the river whose roof, its corners drawn out into long points, is embellished with painted dragon, bear and flower carvings.

Side-roads head off to the monumental **east gate** and west into a small grid of **market lanes** – look for people selling huge slabs of yak butter – surrounding the town's **main mosque** (there's another north of town), an antique wooden affair painted in subdued yellows and greens, catering to Songpan's substantial **Muslim population**, men in white caps, women wearing large straw hats and headscarves. **Shops** are stocked with handmade woollen blankets (¥800–1200), fur-lined jackets (¥320), ornate knives, saddles, stirrups, bridles and all sorts of silver, amber and coral **jewellery**, catering primarily to local Tibetans and Qiang. Early on in the year, you'll also see furtive groups of men dealing in **caterpillar fungus** (see box, p.116).

Just outside the **south gate** is a **second gateway**, with what would originally have been a walled courtyard between the two, where caravans were inspected for dangerous goods before entering the city proper. You can ascend the walls here, and walk partway round the town.

To the west gate

For a decent two-hour return walk and fantastic view of the area, head up to Songpan's **west gate**, which sits high on a ridge above town. From the *Shunjiang* motel, cross the road and follow a water channel to the foot of the hills. Take the path on the **left** here

---

HORSE-TREKKING FROM SONGPAN

One reason to stop in Songpan is to spend a few days **horse-trekking**, exploring grassland plateaus, the hot springs and waterfalls of **Muni Valley** (see p.117) and the icy **Xuebaoding** mountains. The pace is slow and steady – you won't need any prior experience in the saddle – but it's a fun way to experience the local landscapes, and gives you a taster of what travel through the region might once have been like.

Shunjiang Horse Treks 顺江马队, shùnjiāng mǎduì. Between the north gate and the bus station ☎ 083 7723 1161. From their office next to the motel of the same name, this small company charges ¥220 a day/person, excluding entry fees to reserves, environment protection fees (¥10–20) and grazing for the horses (¥20). Accommodation is in tents, and the guides are attentive, though prepare for extreme cold,

excruciating saddles and tasteless food; some groups have bought and slaughtered a goat (¥400) to bolster rations. Note that Shunjiang's staff can be awkward if crossed, so talk to others about their experiences first, and be sure to agree beforehand on exactly what your money is buying. If you don't like their attitude, consider saving the experience for Langmusi's more amenable operators (see p.122).

as it zigzags up the slippery, gravelly slope; look for crow-like **choughs** and plants including gentians, violets and spiky **shouji trees**, whose yellow fruit is used to make a non-alcoholic drink. After half an hour you'll see remains of the crumbling **old city wall**, which gamely rises steeply towards a small village. Just before you reach it, bear left again along the top of the ridge, and it's a few minutes to the west gate. Songpan stretches below; northeast are the snowcapped Xuebaoding mountains.

For the **descent**, simply follow paths straight down towards town, via a cemetery and the bright **Chenghuang Temple** (城隍庙, chénghuáng miào), emerging in the back lanes near the north gate.

ARRIVAL AND DEPARTURE   SONGPAN

The next few years should also see a **train line** snaking north from Chengdu to Songpan.

BY PLANE
Jiuzhai airport is 30km north of Songpan at Chuanzhusi town (川主寺, chuānzhǔsì), with taxis waiting for Songpan (40min; ¥50) and Jiuzhaigou (2hr 30min; ¥200). Your accommodation can arrange tickets but flights are extortionately expensive for the distance involved.
Destinations Beijing (1 daily; 4hr); Chengdu (6 daily; 50min); Chongqing City (1 daily; 1hr 10min).

BY BUS
Songpan bus station is 250m outside the north gate, with most traffic heading south to Chengdu or north to Jiuzhaigou. For Huanglong or the Muni Valley, your best bet is to get a group together and charter a minibus for the day (¥300–400 for an eight-seater); they hang around outside the south gate, or ask at *Emma's Kitchen*. For Langmusi, buses heading to Hezuo in Gansu might drop you off on the highway junction, 5km short of town; otherwise, catch the first bus to Zöigê at 10am and you should make the 2pm connection to Langmusi.

1

CATERPILLAR FUNGUS

In spring, every town in western Sichuan becomes a marketplace for the bizarre **caterpillar fungus** that grows in the mountains and is prized for use in both Tibetan and Chinese medicine. The growth infects moth grubs, somehow coercing them into burrowing underground before turning their body into a fat, caterpillar-shaped fungus. In spring, a grass-like fruiting body sprouts from the former caterpillar's head, which pokes through the soil above – hence their Tibetan name *yartsa gumbu*, meaning "winter insect, summer grass" (shortened to "insect grass", 虫草, **chóngcǎo**, in Chinese). Depending on their size, they're worth between ¥10 and ¥80 each, and locals keep quiet about good places to find them; you'll see people in town with bags of the fungus, carefully rubbing earth off with toothbrushes before getting them weighed.

Destinations Chengdu (3 daily; 6hr; ¥135); Hezuo (1 daily; 8hr; ¥140); Jiuzhaigou park (3 daily; 2hr; ¥32); Jiuzhaigou town (3 daily; 3hr; ¥40); Ma'erkang (1 daily; 6hr; ¥98); Pingwu (1 daily; 4hr; ¥60); Wenchuan (2 daily; 2hr 30min; ¥40); Zöigê (2 daily; 4hr; ¥42).

INFORMATION

Tourist information English-speaking Emma at *Emma's Kitchen* (☎082 7723 1088, @ emmachina@hotmail.com) is your best source; she can advise on local hikes, how to plan a horseriding trip, and might be able to set up lifts in private vehicles heading your way.

ACCOMMODATION

Songpan can be **cold**, even in summer; ask about heating, electric blankets and hot water before booking a room.

Jiaotong Binguan 交通宾馆, jiāotōng bīnguǎn. At the bus station ☎083 1723 1818. Clean hostel which does the job without frills. **¥60**
★ **Old House** 古韵客栈, gǔyùn kèzhàn. Opposite the bus station ☎083 7723 1368. Nice galleried wooden house run by a Muslim family, the only place in town with real character. Rooms are carpeted, but there's no a/c.

Dorms **¥25**, doubles **¥80**
Shunjiang Guesthouse 顺江青年客栈, shùnjiāng qīngnián kèzhàn. Between the north gate and the bus station ☎083 7723 1201. Courtyard motel with plain, tiled dorms and en-suite doubles, run by the horse-trekking team. Dorms **¥25**, doubles **¥80**

EATING AND DRINKING

Songpan's cheapest **places to eat** are the noodle joints between the north gate and the bus station; Muslims also sell fresh bread and yak jerky (牦牛肉, máoniú ròu) in shops around town. You should also try sweet, thick and only mildly alcoholic Tibetan barley beer (青稞酒, qīngkē jiǔ). Open-air **teahouses** are everywhere through Songpan's backstreets, especially along the river past the western mosque.

★ **Emma's Kitchen** 小欧洲西餐厅, xiǎo ōuzhōu xīcāntīng. Between the north gate and the bus station. You'll find a helpful owner and a mix of Chinese, Western and Tibetan staples in this cheerful backpackers' restaurant. Good coffee and beer too. Meals around ¥35.
Shunfeng Feiniu 顺风肥牛, shùnfēng féiniú. Down little Dongtou Alley. Mongolian hotpot restaurant – where you cook thinly sliced meat and vegetables in a chilli-free stock – one of many places to eat along this street.

★ **Xingyue Lou** 星月楼, xīngyuè lóu. Main street. Muslim restaurant with superb roast duck and an English menu; even usually bland tofu and spinach soup tastes good here. Staff can be abrupt. Count on ¥35/head.
Xishan Yuan 西山苑, xīshān yuàn. In the back lanes west of the supermarkets. Small but pretty teahouse serving snacks too in their tiny rear courtyard. You'll walk past coming back from the west gate.

DIRECTORY

Banks The Agricultural Bank of China, about 100m inside the north gate, has an ATM accepting credit cards. This is the last ATM if you're heading to Zöigê and Langmusi.

Internet *Emma's Kitchen* has a couple of terminals; there's also a net bar down Dongtou Alley.
Massage There's a blind masseurs' clinic next to *Emma's Kitchen*, and you'll need their services if you've just spent a

1

few days in the saddle. ¥50/hr.
PSB Shuncheng Bei Lu, ☏ 083 7723 2735. A fairly routine place to apply for a visa extension, but give them five days.

Shopping Aside from the Tibetan stores through town, a few shops outside the north gate sell basic outdoor gear – fleeces, gloves and beanies.

The Muni Valley

牟尼沟, móuní gōu • ¥70 • Only accessible via eight-seater minibus (around ¥400 for the day) or on horseback – from Songpan, head 15km south along the Wenchuan highway to Anhong village (安宏乡, ānhóng xiāng), then 20km northwest to the park gates

The **Muni Valley** is a forested scenic reserve, shaped like a 50km-long reversed letter "C". Horse treks from Songpan head here; otherwise, it's a low-key alternative to Jiuzhaigou and Huanglong, appealing if you want to dodge the crowds though with less spectacular scenery. Muni's southern end focuses around **Zhaga waterfall**, a 104m-long calcified cascade, while the north is strung along **Erdao Hai**, a series of brilliantly blue lakes with a lukewarm **hot spring**, only accessible on horseback. There are also Tibetan **temples** and small villages around the edges of the reserve; bear in mind that most of Muni rises above 3000m, so is cold even in summer. Vehicle roads run through the park, along with hiking and horse trails.

Huanglong

黄龙, huánglóng • ¥200.
Huanglong covers over a thousand square kilometres of rough terrain below 5588m-high **Xuebaoding**, the Min Shan range's highest peak, a white triangle visible to the east on clear days. Most of Huanglong is inaccessible, and what everyone comes to see is a forested, 4km-long valley, carved out by a now-vanished glacier. Mineral-rich streams cascading down the valley have created yellow, calcified terraces in their wake, overflowing with hundreds of vivid **blue ponds**, and their scaly appearance gives Huanglong – "Yellow Dragon" – its name.

Around the reserve

A 10km circuit track – much of it on well-made **boardwalks** over the fragile formations – ascends east up the valley from the main-road **park gates**, through surprisingly thick deciduous woodland, pine forest and, finally, rhododendron thickets. There's also a **cable car** (¥80 up, ¥40 down) from the gate to a viewing platform high over the valley, from where it's an easy hour to the upper temple. Allow three or four hours on site.

The pick of Huanglong's scenery includes the broad **Golden Flying Waterfall** and the kilometre-long calcified **Golden Sand cascade**, where the shallow flow tinkles over innumerable ridges and pockmarks. Around 3km along, the small **Middle Temple** (the lower one has long gone) was once an important **Bon** shrine; today, it seems inactive – even if signs do ask you to circuit to the right in the Bon manner. At the head of the valley, **Huanglong Temple** (黄龙古寺, huánglóng gǔ sì) is a slightly grander Qing building, featuring an atrium and two small Taoist halls, dedicated to the local guardian deity **Huanglong Zhenren**. Behind here, there's a 300m-long stretch of multi-hued blue pools, contrasting brilliantly with the drab olive vegetation; the best views are from a small platform on the slopes above.

ARRIVAL AND DEPARTURE	HUANGLONG
By bus Huanglong is 60km northeast of Songpan. **From Songpan**, buses are erratic and you usually have to hire a minibus (¥300–400 for an eight-seater for the day). A daily	bus from **Jiuzhaigou** runs in summer (leaves Jiuzhaigou 7am, departs Huanglong 3pm; 3hr; ¥40).

ACCOMMODATION AND EATING

Hualong Shanzhuang 华龙山庄, huálóng shānzhuāng. At the park gates ☏ 083 7724 9333.

Nicely designed in a faux-Tibetan style, this upmarket option is the only place to stay in Huanglong. It looks good, though frequent power outages and offhand staff are drawbacks, given the price. Food is available here, and at a single canteen near the Middle Temple. **¥480**

Jiuzhaigou

九寨沟, jiǔzhàigōu

Around 100km from Songpan or Huanglong, **Jiuzhaigou** – Nine Stockades Gully – was settled centuries ago by **Amdo Tibetans**, whose fenced villages gave the area its name. Hemmed in by high, snowy peaks, Jiuzhaigou's valleys form a south-orientated Y shape, with stunning, peacock-blue **lakes** descending them in a series of broad steps fringed in thick forests. The colours are most spectacular in the autumn, brilliantly set off by red and gold leaves in the surrounding forests, and at the onset of winter in early December, when everything is dusted by snow. Now a **national park**, Jiuzhaigou gets incredibly busy – it clocks up over a million visitors annually – so don't come here expecting a quiet commune with nature; it is, however, efficiently run, with erosion-resistant boardwalks everywhere and a percentage of the pricey **entry fee** donated to the park's Tibetan residents.

Jiuzhaigou town and Jiuzhaigou Kou

You might find yourself 40km east of the national park at **JIUZHAIGOU TOWN** (九寨沟县, jiǔzhàigōu xiàn) if you came up via Pingwu or from Guangyuan (see p.88). There are banks, shops and a bus station here, and cruising shared taxis which leave whenever full for the half-hour run to Jiuzhaigou Kou.

JIUZHAIGOU KOU (九寨沟口, jiǔzhàigōu kǒu; also known as **Zhangzha**) is a 1500m-wide blob of services strung along the main road either side of the **national park gates**. The bus station, *Sheraton* hotel and a few of the restaurants are east of the entrance, back towards Jiuzhaigou town, with most of the cheaper places to stay and eat west of the gate, on the Songpan side – all are within walking distance.

Jiuzhaigou National Park

九寨沟景区, jiǔzhàigōu jǐngqū • Daily 7am–5.30pm • ¥220/day • Ⓦ jiuzhai.com

Shuzheng Valley stretches 14km south from the park gates, with a marshy complex of pools at the foot of imposing Dêgê Shan forming **Shuzheng lakes** (树正海, shùzhèng hǎi), the largest group in the reserve and cut partway along by the 20m-high **Shuzheng Falls**. Here there's a tourist **village** featuring rustic dwellings on the lakeshore where you can don Tibetan garb and pose on horseback for photos.

At the head of the Shuzheng Valley, **Nuorilang** (诺日朗, nuòrìlǎng) comprises a **tourist centre** with a canteen and toilets, close to **Nuorilang Falls** (诺日朗瀑布, nuòrìlǎng pùbù), Jiuzhaigou's most famous cascades. They look best from the road, framed by trees as water forks down over the strange, yellow crystalline rock faces.

The road forks at Nuorilang, split by the solid bulk of **Wonuosemo**, a mountain named after the Tibetan goddess whose shattered mirror is said to form Jiuzhaigou's lakes. The

---

GO ANTICLOCKWISE: BON

Bon is Tibet's native religion, a shamanist faith founded by **Tonpa Shenrab** in distant antiquity. It lost influence in Tibet after 755 AD, when the Tibetan royalty began to favour the more spiritual doctrines of Buddhism. As Yellow Hat Sect Lamaism (see p.414) developed and became the dominant faith, followers of Bon – **Bonpa** – were forced out to the fringes of the Tibetan world, where the religion survives today.

Though Bon is superficially similar to Lamaism the two religions are, in many respects, directly opposed. Bonpa circuit their stupas anticlockwise, use black where Lamas would use white, and still have rituals derived from animal sacrifice. Because of this last feature, both the Chinese government and Lamas tend to view Bon as a backward belief, and Bonpa are often not keen to be approached or identified as such.

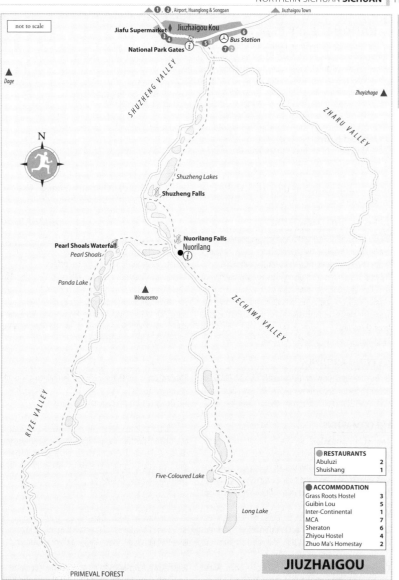

not to scale

Jiafu Supermarket　Jiuzhaigou Kou

National Park Gates

Bus Station

Dage

SHUZHENG VALLEY

Zhayizhaga

ZHARU VALLEY

N

Shuzheng Lakes

Shuzheng Falls

Nuorilang Falls
Nuorilang

Pearl Shoals Waterfall
Pearl Shoals

Panda Lake

Wonuosemo

ZECHAWA VALLEY

RIZE VALLEY

Five-Coloured Lake

Long Lake

RESTAURANTS
| Abuluzi | 2 |
| Shuishang | 1 |

ACCOMMODATION
Grass Roots Hostel	3
Guibin Lou	5
Inter-Continental	1
MCA	7
Sheraton	6
Zhiyou Hostel	4
Zhuo Ma's Homestay	2

JIUZHAIGOU

PRIMEVAL FOREST

western branch heads up 20km-long **Rize Valley**, first passing **Pearl Shoals Falls**, where a whole hillside has calcified into an ankle-deep cascade ending in a 10m waterfall similar to Nuorilang's. There are steep-sided flooded valleys beyond here; **Panda Lake** is the prettiest, with a waterfall and dense vegetation around the shore (a good place to use the boardwalks). At the end of the road is the **Primeval Forest**, a belt of truly ancient, eerie pines on the slopes of Mount Ganzigongai, with more marked circuit trails.

East from Nuorilang, there's less to see down 18km-long **Zechawa Valley**, though there are peaks everywhere and the **Five-coloured Lake**, which, for sheer intensity, if not

1

NATIONAL PARK PRACTICALITIES

As Jiuzhaigou national park **tickets** (¥220) are only valid for a day, and there's around 50km of trails to explore, you need to get in close to 7am, when the gates open. **Buses** run every few minutes; you hail them at regular stops within the park or wave them down as they pass. The best way to minimize being crowded out is to head straight for the far end of the park, then work back towards the gates; buses out this way dry up through the afternoon.

If you're after any sort of solitude, there's a network of **boardwalks** that parallel the roads, but on the far side of the lakes – very few people use them and you don't have to go far to find yourself alone among the scenery. Whatever you might see others doing, **stay on marked paths** at all times to avoid causing erosion.

Maps are posted everywhere, with free pocket versions available at the Visitor Centre.

scale, is unequalled in the park. At the road's end, the mundanely named **Long Lake** looks south into the mountains and, at 3103m, is Jiuzhaigou's highest body of water.

ARRIVAL AND DEPARTURE
JIUZHAIGOU

By plane Jiuzhaigou's airport is near Songpan; see p.115. You can buy plane tickets at the airline counter inside the Vistors' Centre at the park gates. A taxi to the airport costs ¥200.

By bus Some buses from Guangyuan or Jiangyou/Pingwu terminate at Jiuzhaigou town; catch a taxi to Jiuzhaigou Kou (30min; ¥10). Leaving, buses from Jiuzhaigou Kou cover the same destinations as Jiuzhaigou town, so you don't need to head there first. For Zöigê or the main-road drop-off to Langmusi, try to get aboard a Lanzhou bus; if they aren't

running or won't take you, you'll have to travel via Songpan. As almost all services depart before 8am (the sole afternoon bus is to Songpan), buy tickets the day before.

Jiuzhaigou Kou destinations Chengdu (2 daily; 9hr; ¥140); Guangyuan (1 daily; 8hr; ¥120); Huanglong (1 daily; 3hr; ¥40); Lanzhou (1 daily; 11hr; ¥230); Ma'erkang (1 daily; 7hr; ¥150); Mianyang (via Pingwu and Jiangyou; 2 daily; 7hr; ¥90); Songpan (2 daily; 2hr 30min; ¥30); Wenchuan (1 daily; 5hr 30min; ¥90).

GETTING AROUND

By bus Unlimited use within the national park costs ¥90. Some people dodge this and walk everywhere, but given Jiuzhaigou's scale – over 30km from end to end – this isn't really feasible.

Shared taxis These run between Jiuzhaigou town and Jiuzhaigou Kou (¥10/person, or ¥40 for the vehicle). There's a taxi rank outside the national park gates.

INFORMATION

Tourist information At the national park gates, Jiuzhaigou's Visitor Centre has general information on the park's scenery, wildlife and history, hands out maps and sells souvenir yak jerky and panda earmuffs. You can also find out about guided hikes in the Zharu Valley here (see

box, below). The Nuorilang Tourist Centre inside the park is similar, and has a canteen too. For information about hiking and horseriding outside the park, contact the helpful owner of *Zhuo Ma's Homestay*.

ACCOMMODATION

Unless otherwise stated, all **accommodation** is at Jiuzhaigou Kou. There's nowhere to stay within the park, unless you're on an eco-trek in the Zharu Valley. Unheated accommodation closes through winter (Nov–April), so check in advance.

Grass Roots Hostel 草根人家, cǎogēn rénjiā. About 500m west of the park entrance ☏ 083 7776 4922. White,

tiled rooms in Jiuzhaigou's tourist quarter; a functional place to sleep and use the laundry, internet and booking services. **¥80**

THE ZHARU VALLEY

East of Jiuzhaigou's crowds, the **Zharu Valley** has been set aside for low-volume **eco-tourism**, with **guided hikes** taking in high-altitude pasture, 4400m-high Zhayizhaga sacred mountain, and some tiny Tibetan settlements. You need to be fit as there's a fair amount of distance covered even on day-trips. All-inclusive trips – entry, English-speaking guides, camping gear, food and transport to the trailheads – cost ¥380 for one day, ¥760 for an overnight stay, and ¥1580 for a tough three-day trek. Contact ✉ ecotourism@jiuzhai.com for all information and bookings.

Guibin Lou 贵宾楼, guìbīn lóu. Down a path immediately east of the park gates ☎083 7773 9066. Located next to the entrance, this building is intended for VIPs, though they take anybody. The cheaper rooms are pretty threadbare, but it's a nice, warm building with a Tibetan-style atrium in the lobby, a good place to unwind with a cup of tea. Aim for a quarter of the absurd rack-rate, or go to the *Sheraton*. ¥780

★ **Inter-Continental** 九寨天堂洲际大饭店, jiǔzhài tiāntáng zhōujì dàfàndiàn. 20km from the park gates towards Songpan ☎021 5101 3030, ⓦ ichotelsgroup.com. Stylish hotel in a beautiful setting, backed by pine forests and serrated peaks; they've even built a giant glasshouse which you can sit warmly inside during winter. It's a long way from the park, but they arrange trasnport. ¥800

MCA MCA国际乡村客栈, MCA guójì xiāngcūn kèzhàn. On the stream behind the bus station ☎083 7773 9818. Well-managed and welcoming (if rather bare and institution-like) hostel. It can get lively with the bar

and restaurant downstairs. ¥80

Sheraton 喜来登国际大酒店, xǐláidēng guójì dàjiǔdiàn. 1km east of the park gates ☎083 7773 9988, ⓦ starwoodhotels.com. Bizarre, circular complex with large oval plaza at the front, on its own by the roadside. Well appointed inside with spacious rooms, a large pool, restaurants and everything else you'd expect from this international chain. ¥750

Zhiyou Hostel 自游国际青年旅舍, zìyóu guójì qīngnián lǚshè. About 500m west of the park entrance ☎083 7776 4617. Fairly plain, basic building but they've tried hard to brighten things up with Tibetan prayer flags, a wooden balcony and even carpets in a few rooms. ¥80

★ **Zhuo Ma's Homestay** 13km west of Jiuzhaigou Kou ☎0135 6878 3012, ⓦ abuluzi.com. Simple rooms with shared facilities in a Tibetan wood and stone house, courtesy of the incredibly hospitable Zhuo Ma. She seems to know everyone in the area and offers plenty of local information. Call ahead to arrange a pick-up from the bus station. Per person rate including meals ¥180

EATING

Jiuzhaigou Kou has dozens of mainstream Chinese **restaurants**, mostly west of the park entrance. None stand out – just look for somewhere busy. Prices are high – you'll generally have to pay ¥20 for a simple stir-fry and ¥45–100 for a restaurant dish. Near the *Sheraton*, look for tents with goats hanging up and signs reading "藏家乐"(zàngjiālè); these offer a touristy, noisy and fun evening, with food, dancing and an outdoor fire for ¥100. **Inside the park**, Nuorilang's Tourist Centre has set lunches at ¥60–80. There's a Jiafu **supermarket** on the main road west of the park entrance, towards Songpan.

★ **Abuluzi** 阿布镥孜风情藏餐吧, ābùluzī fēngqíng zàng cānba. Behind the bus station, east of the reserve gates ☎1356 878 3012. Scrumptious Tibetan food, served up in a comfortable, brightly decorated restaurant, run by the owners of *Zhuo Ma's Homestay*. Dishes range from simple vegetable stews to grilled meats, fried yak and goat, and even soups using Tibetan medicinal herbs, including

caterpillar fungus (see p.116). Excellent value and atmosphere; mains ¥15–80.

★ **Shuishang** 水上餐厅, shuǐshàng cāntīng. Streamside in front of the Guibin Lou hotel. Pleasant restaurant hidden away in a rustic wooden building; not many people seem to know about it so it feels empty at times. Their mushroom hotpot, featuring a variety of local fungi, is exceptional. ¥45/head.

DIRECTORY

Banks There are ATMs at the Visitor Centre and outside the *Sheraton* hotel.

Internet At the hostels.

The Aba grasslands

Songpan sits just east of the vast, marshy **Aba grasslands**, which sprawl over the Sichuan, Gansu and Qinghai borders. Resting at around 3500m and draining into the headwaters of China's mighty Yellow River, the grasslands are home to nomadic herders and lots of **birdlife**, including black-necked cranes and golden eagles. The district capital, **Aba town** (阿坝县, ābā xiàn; also known as **Ngawa**) has two important monasteries and a large population of monks, but is off-limits: there were serious **riots** here following the 2008 disturbances in Tibet, and the entire grasslands remains uneasy, with sporadic protests and police crackdowns which sometimes see the region closed to visitors. When it's accessible, you'll cross the edge of the grasslands at the quiet town of **Zöigê** if you're heading from Songpan to Langmusi.

Zöigê

About 160km from Songpan at the Aba grasslands' northernmost edge, **ZÖIGÊ** (诺尔盖, nuòěrgài; also known as **Nuo'ergai** or **Ruo'ergai**) is an orderly, torpid grid of markets and shops between Shuguang Lu and parallel Shangye Jie. Most people are here because they've missed the bus out, but things perk up during the June/July **horse races**, when nomads set up tents outside the town and show off their riding skills. The town's low-key **Daza monastery** (达扎寺, dázā sì) was founded in 1663 and is also worth a visit, especially for the small, spooky chapel ahead and around to the right – look for paintings of skeletons and flayed skins on the door, and a terrace hung with animal skulls and stuffed, blood-spattered wolves.

ARRIVAL AND DEPARTURE ZÖIGÊ

By bus Zöigê's bus station is on Shuguang Lu; most services leave at dawn, with afternoon buses to Langmusi and Songpan. There's no bus to Jiuzhaigou; you'll have to travel via Songpan.

Destinations Chengdu (1 daily; 12hr; ¥160); Hezuo (in Gansu; 1 daily; 4hr; ¥55); Langmusi (2 daily; 2hr; ¥25); Linxia (in Gansu; 1 daily; 6hr; ¥70); Ma'erkang (1 daily; 8hr; ¥90); Songpan (2 daily; 4hr; ¥45).

ACCOMMODATION AND EATING

There are plenty of places along Zöigê's main streets to grab a simple Chinese meal; or hang out at the brightly painted *A-Lang* **teahouse** (啊郎茶馆, ā láng cháguǎn), across from the post office on Shangye Jie.

Dazang 大藏阳光酒店, dàzàng yángguāng jiǔdiàn. 88 Jingpin Jie, near the town centre ☎083 7229 1998. Small but well-furnished hotel decked out with Tibetan paintings and unexpectedly cosy, modern rooms for such a backwater town. **¥250**

Ruoliang 若粮宾馆, ruòliáng bīnguǎn. Shangye Jie ☎083 7229 8081 or 7229 8360. A clean and quiet option with simple tiled rooms and constant, solar-powered hot water. **¥80**

Zangle 藏乐宾馆, zànglè bīnguǎn. Shangye Jie ☎083 7229 8685. Similar to the *Ruoliang*. **¥80**

Langmusi

郎木寺, lángmùsì

Just off the highway, 90km north of Zöigê, you'll find the scruffy monastery town of **LANGMUSI**, which balances on the southern edge of **Amdo**, one of the three groups of semi-independent kingdoms that once made up Tibet – the other two are U-Tsang, now greater Tibet, and Kham, which covers western Sichuan (see p.60). You're on the Sichuan–Gansu border here; apparently the line runs right through the town. Surrounding forests, mountain scenery and lamaseries are as grittily Tibetan as anything you'll find in western Sichuan and there's great **hiking** and **horse-trekking** in the vicinity, making it easy to spend a couple of days here.

The lamaseries

Langmusi is visibly poor, with many thatched houses and dirt lanes rich in animal smells, whose 250m-long main street runs westwards to two small, eighteenth-century

---

GO CLOCKWISE: VISITING MONASTERIES

Among the draws of Tibetan towns are their **Buddhist monasteries**, or Lamaseries, most of which belong to the Yellow-Hat Gelugpa sect. Monasteries form huge medieval-looking complexes sprawling over hillsides, with a central core of large, red-walled, gold-roofed temples surrounded by a maze of smaller buildings housing monks and staff. Monasteries are **free** to enter except where noted; if there are no signs to the contrary, assume that **photography is forbidden** inside temples. Monks are generally friendly, encouraging you to explore, steering you away from closed areas, and sometimes offering food and accommodation – though don't take these for granted. Most importantly, except at the region's few **Bon** temples (see p.118), remember to orbit **clockwise** around both individual temples and the complex as a whole.

lamaseries (entry ¥25). Bear right over a bridge, and the road leads uphill to **Saizu Gompa**, a relatively sturdy establishment with an orange, tiled roof whose main hall's walls are covered in pictures of meditating Buddhas. Monks use the front courtyard for **debating**, a ritualized activity where one man claps his hands while haranguing his colleague, who sits cross-legged on the ground.

For **Gaerdi Gompa**, bear left along the main road and then aim for the temple buildings in the back lanes; this is the larger complex with several sizeable, tin-roofed halls, but seems almost totally deserted.

ARRIVAL AND DEPARTURE
LANGMUSI

By bus Unless you're arriving on direct transport from Zöigê, you'll be dropped 5km short on the Sichuan–Gansu highway; motorbike-taxis charge ¥5 to town. Heading out, Zöigê buses depart from the main street (ask at your accommodation the night before for times; 2hr; ¥25). If enough people show, you might also score a minibus ride later in the day to Zöigê, which would save time there in limbo between connections. Accommodation can advise on catching traffic heading along the highway to Songpan, or Hezuo in Gansu, and can help charter minibuses to Jiuzhaigou and elsewhere (about ¥800 for a five-seater).

ACCOMMODATION AND EATING

You can't get lost in Langmusi – all the following are within a few metres of the main street. Trouble with getting **room deposits** refunded at checkout seems to be a recurring problem in town. There are several simple Muslim and Chinese **restaurants** along the main street.

Black Tent Café Most stylish of Langmusi's handful of travellers' hangouts, with stone and timber decor, Tibetan artwork, comfy sofa-benches, excellent coffee and Western breakfasts.

Dacang Langmu 达仓郎木宾馆, dácāng lángmù bīnguǎn ☎ 094 1667 1338. Relatively new place with dorms, normal doubles and suites, plus a Muslim restaurant. Beds ¥25, doubles ¥80

★ **Langmusi Binguan** 郎木寺宾馆, lángmùsì bīnguǎn ☎ 094 1667 1086. Plain but bright rooms, hot water in the evening, a rooftop terrace and a very helpful

manager. You need to bargain doubles down. Beds ¥25, doubles ¥80

Leisha's Café-restaurant serving huge, tasty portions of Chinese–Tibetan–Muslim dishes; the staff are a mine of information but don't speak much English. Mains ¥15–30.

Nomad's Youth Hostel 旅朋青年旅舍, lǚpéng qīngnián lǚshè ☎ 094 1667 1460. Cosy, dim old wooden building with bunk-bed dorms; pretty basic and can get noisy if there's a large, sociable group packing it out, but well run and friendly. Dorms ¥20

INFORMATION

Tours Langmusi Tibetan Horse Trekking (☎ 094 1667 1504, ⓦ langmusi.net), across from the *Langmusi Binguan*, is a thoroughly professional operation whose one- to four-day trips take in nomad camps and mountain scenery – the website has current schedules and costs. They can also advise on places **to hike**, but make sure you're equipped for dogs (see p.134) and changeable weather.

DIRECTORY

Banks There are no banks at Langmusi.

Internet There's a net bar opposite the *Langmusi Binguan*, full of young, network-gaming monks.

Western Sichuan

Western Sichuan, the immense region extending from Ya'an to the border with Tibet, is a thoroughly exciting place to travel. The landscapes couldn't be farther from Chengdu's mild plains: there are lowland valleys chequered green and gold with barley; flowery grasslands grazed by yaks and dotted with black felt tents; hamlets of square, fortress-like stone houses; ravens tumbling over snowbound gullies and stark mountain passes; and unforgettable views of mountain ranges rising up against crisp blue skies.

Larger towns through the west have significant Han and Hui (Muslim) populations, but historically the region was not part of Sichuan at all but formed a set of small eastern Tibetan states known as **Kham**. The Tibetans who live here, called the **Khampas**, speak their own dialect, and see themselves as distinct from their cousins further west – it wasn't until the seventeenth century, during the aggressive rule of the **Fifth Dalai Lama**, Lobsang Gyatso, that monasteries here were forcibly converted to the dominant **Gelugpa** (or Yellow Hat) sect. The Khampas fought the Nationalists during the 1930s and the Communists during the 1950s, and retain their tough, independent reputation – culturally the region remains emphatically Tibetan, containing not only some of China's most important lamaseries, but also an overwhelmingly Tibetan population. Towns here are alive with livestock, pilgrims, red-robed clergy and Khampa cowboys in slouch hats – though like horsemen worldwide, Tibetans are ditching their trusty steeds for motorbikes and four-wheel-drives as fast as they become available. Even so, the regional **horse races** are a blast – Litang's is best.

This region is accessed from the administrative capital **Kangding**, itself worth a stopover for easy access to the nearby **Hailuogou glacier** and **Tagong grasslands**, or as a springboard north to pretty **Danba** or the snowcapped peaks of **Siguniang Shan**. Alternatively, you can either weave northwest towards Tibet via the monastery towns of **Ganzi** and **Dêgê**, with a faith-inducing mountain pass and Dêgê's **Scripture Printing Hall** as the pick of the sights along the way; or head due west to the high-altitude monastic seat of **Litang**, from where you can continue down to more spellbinding mountain-and-pasture scenery at **Yading**, or make the bumpy journey to Shangri-La in **Yunnan**.

Kangding

康定, kāngdìng

KANGDING (Dardo in Tibetan) guards the gateway to western Sichuan and the Kham Tibetan world, 250km west of Chengdu. A crowded, artless collection of modern white-tiled blocks packed along the fast-flowing **Zheduo River**, this looks a very Chinese town. But Tibetans are a very visible presence, and the deep gorge that Kangding is set in is overlooked by chortens and the frosted peaks of **Daxue Shan** (the Great Snowy

TRAVELLING IN WESTERN SICHUAN

Travel in western Sichuan requires some stamina: journeys are long, roads twist interminably, breakdowns are common, and landslides, ice or heavy snow can block roads for days at a time. What makes it all worthwhile are your fellow passengers, mostly monks and wild-looking Khampa youths, who every time the bus crosses a mountain pass cheer wildly and throw handfuls of paper prayer flags out of the windows. Buying **bus tickets** is frustrating, however – expect unpredictable schedules and ticket offices, early departures and unhelpful station staff.

Almost all the region rises above 2500m – one pass exceeds 5000m – and you'll probably experience the effects of **altitude** (see p.41). You'll need to carry enough **cash** to see you through beyond Kangding, as there are few ATMs and no banks capable of foreign currency transactions. As for the seasons, the area looks fantastic from spring through to autumn – though warm, weatherproof clothing is essential all year. Be aware too that the region is **closed to foreigners** through March (see p.64) – the dates vary, but can extend into April.

INTO TIBET

Though routes west of Dêgê and Litang press right through to **Lhasa**, for now Westerners trying to cross the Tibetan border from Sichuan are almost certain to be pulled off the bus and booted back the way they came. Political considerations aside, these are some of the world's most dangerous roads, high, cut by gorges and permanently snowbound, and the Chinese government is not keen to have foreigners extend the list of people killed in bus crashes along the way. What might make the journey worth the risk is that it takes you within sight of the world's highest unclimbed mountain ranges, and even those hardened by stints in the Himalayas have reported the scenery as staggeringly beautiful.

Mountains) – whatever the maps might say, this is where Tibet really begins.

The town was once an important marketplace for **tea**, portered over the mountains **from Ya'an** (see p.82). Kangding has also long been an administrative centre, first under the Kham state of **Chakla**; then when Liu Wenhui used it as his base for governing **Xikang** during the 1930s (see p.80); and now as the capital of huge **Ganzi prefecture**, which spreads west from here to the Tibetan border. Bus schedules mean that a Kangding **stopover** is likely, but with a couple of temples, interesting back lanes and an unusually good regional museum, it's not the worst of fates.

Anjue Temple and around

Kangding's central **Anjue Temple** (安觉寺, ānjué sì) is a small affair just off Yanhe Xi Lu, built in 1654 at the prompting of the Fifth Dalai Lama. The main hall is unusual in being covered in miniature golden Buddha statues instead of the usual gory murals, and features some fine **butter sculptures** of animals and meditating sages. East along the river from here, the **town square** is a fun place at dusk, full of skateboarding children and a huge TV screen broadcasting Tibetan pop, with hundreds of people dancing in a ring below.

The mosque

清真寺, qīngzhēn sì

Muslims have settled in many Tibetan towns, where they work as muleteers, metalworkers and butchers, and over the river off Yanhe Dong Lu, Kangding's **mosque** sports a traditional gateway framed by little minarets. Nearby **markets** mostly sell clothing and household knick-knacks; there's also the old town spring nearby, where people still wash their clothes and mops in the clear blue water.

Paoma Shan

跑马山, pǎomǎ shān • ¥50

A lane opposite the mosque heads up to the entrance of **Paoma Shan**, the thickly forested mountain southeast of town, which hosts a **horse-race festival** in the middle of the fourth lunar month at a Roman-theatre-style racetrack up on the slopes. It's an easy half-hour walk up steps to lookouts over the town, from where level paths trail off between the pine trees; or you can catch a **cable car** (¥30) from near the museum (see below).

The Cultural Heritage Museum

非物质文化遗产博物馆, fēiwùzhì wénhuà yíchǎn bówùguǎn • Daily 8am–6.30pm • ¥30

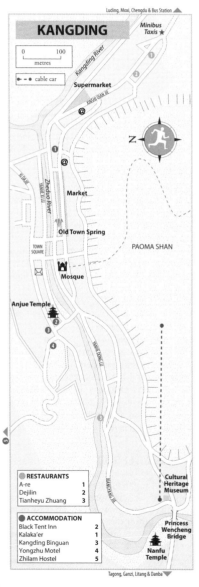

KANGDING

Luding, Moxi, Chengdu & Bus Station

Minibus Taxis ★

Kangding River

0   100
metres

cable car

Supermarket

XINSHI QUAN JIE

@

Zheduo River

YANHE XI LU

Market

XI LU JIE

Old Town Spring

TOWN SQUARE

PAOMA SHAN

Mosque

Anjue Temple

YANHE DONG LU

XIANGYANG JIE

Cultural Heritage Museum

Princess Wencheng Bridge

Nanfu Temple

● RESTAURANTS	
A-re	1
Dejilin	2
Tianheyu Zhuang	3

● ACCOMMODATION	
Black Tent Inn	2
Kalaka'er	1
Kangding Binguan	3
Yongzhu Motel	4
Zhilam Hostel	5

Tagong, Ganzi, Litang & Danba

1

Following the main road southwest out of town brings you to the short stone arch of the **Princess Wencheng Bridge** (文成公主桥, wénchéng gōngzhǔ qiáo), almost invisible under layers of colourful, fluttering **prayer flags**; these "speak" the prayers printed on them every time they move, so you'll find them hung up on high passes, temples and bridges throughout the Tibetan regions, anywhere the wind might catch them.

Turn sharp left before the bridge and it's 50m uphill to Kangding's informative **Cultural Heritage Museum**, where it takes about half an hour to tour the displays of domestic and agricultural tools, dioramas of yaks ploughing, butter churns and rugs. Pick of the exhibits are the **building** itself – a multistorey, fortress-like stone Tibetan house, of a sort you'll see throughout the west – and the colourful, minutely detailed **thankas** (devotional paintings). The museum's upper floor is devoted to **Tibetan medicine** which, like Chinese, uses an immense number of plants and minerals as drugs.

Nanfu Temple

南甫寺, nánfǔ sì

Once over Wencheng Bridge, a side-path runs uphill to **Nanfu Temple**, built here in 1639 after the original site was sacked by the Mongols. Present renovations have reached two side halls containing a large gilded statue of Tsongkhapa and murals of Buddha in all his incarnations – images that, with their typically Tibetan iconography of skulls, demons, flayed skins and fierce expressions, paint a far less forgiving picture of Buddhism than the mainstream Chinese brand.

ARRIVAL AND DEPARTURE   KANGDING

By bus Kangding's bus station is about 2km east of town; staff are brusque but helpful. Watch out for aggressive hotel touts outside, who try to grab your bags. A taxi into Kangding costs ¥5–7, or you can catch the single town bus, which stops outside and runs to Yanhe Dong Lu.
Destinations Batang (1 daily; 2 days; ¥150); Chengdu (hourly; 8hr; ¥127); Danba (2 daily; 4hr; ¥42.50); Daocheng (1 daily; 13hr; ¥130); Dêgê (1 daily; 2 days; ¥180); Ganzi (1

daily; 12hr; ¥130); Litang (9hr; ¥98); Manigange (1 daily; 15hr; ¥160); Tagong (1 daily; 3hr; ¥55); Xichang (1 daily; 8hr; ¥110).
By taxi Minibus taxis cluster outside the bus station and at the end of Xinshi Qian Jie, serving Chengdu, Tagong, Danba and Litang; prices are much the same as the bus but they won't go until they're full. For Luding, take a cab from the same places (1hr; ¥20).

ACCOMMODATION

Black Tent Inn 安觉寺黑包客栈, ānjué sì hēibāo kèzhàn. Anjue Temple ☎1580 836 6530. Extremely basic dormitories and common washroom, none too modern but clean enough and certainly inexpensive for town. Usually closed in winter. Beds ¥25
Kalaka'er 卡拉卡尔饭店, kǎlākǎěr fàndiàn. Yanhe Dong Lu ☎083 6282 8888. The best of Kangding's upmarket hotels; they try hard, rooms are fairly spacious and warm, and facilities are well maintained. ¥480
Kangding Binguan 康定宾馆, kāngdìng bīnguǎn.

Behind Anjue Temple ☎083 6283 2077. The town's original tourist hotel, now tired and overpriced though some of the rooms have been renovated and the restaurant does good Chinese food. Fairly typical of Kangding's mid-range options. ¥380
★**Yongzhu Motel** 拥珠驿栈, yōngzhū yìzhàn. Head uphill from Anjue Temple, turn left and the hotel is up a lane on the right ☎083 6283 2381. Clean and tiled, with a brightly painted atrium, maps of the region and all-important electric blankets. The owner won't

---

TIBETAN FOOD

If you're travelling from eastern Sichuan, Kangding is probably the first place you'll have a chance to try **Tibetan food**. Tibetans are not allowed to kill animals but, despite being Buddhist, even monks and Lamas eat **meat** – with no winter crops they'd starve to death otherwise.

The mainstay of the Tibetan diet are **momos**, steamed meat dumplings similar to Chinese *baozi*; **butter tea**, made from a blend of tea, salt and yak butter (nauseating if thought of as tea, but quite tasty as a soup); and **tsampa**, roasted barley meal kneaded with butter tea into a nutty-tasting dough. Yak and mutton **stews** also feature, but **vegetables** don't get much attention – the growing season is very short – and vegetarians will have a tough time of it.

1

bargain, but it's a good choice for the town centre. **¥120**

★ **Zhilam Hostel** 汇道客栈, huìdào kèzhàn. 10min uphill hike from town past the Yongzhu Motel, or catch a cab for ¥7 or so ☎083 6283 1100, ⊕zhilamhostel.com. Extremely friendly guesthouse

decked in Tibetan furnishings, with three dorms and two en-suite doubles. They also hand out heaps of information about climbing in western Sichuan. There's a café and restaurant, internet and you can get laundry done. Dorms **¥35**, doubles **¥260**

EATING

Xinshi Qian Jie has heaps of cheap noodle and stir-fry **restaurants**, with all ingredients laid out in front; food is pretty filling and tasty if nothing fancy.

A-re 阿热藏餐, ā-rè zàngcān. Xinshi Qian Jie. Splendidly decorated fake-Tibetan Chinese restaurant, with the menu revolving around yak meat. Mains ¥30–40.

Dejilin 德吉林藏餐, déjílín zàngcān. Xinshi Qian Jie. A crowded little room, one of several real Tibetan diners in the vicinity, with murals, butter tea, meat dumplings, beef rice, sour noodles, self-carve mutton and

communal bench tables. They have an English menu – the literal translations might chase you away – but it's not a tourist restaurant. Most dishes ¥15 or less.

Tianheyu Zhuang 天河鱼庄, tiānhéyú zhuāng. Yanhe Dong Lu. Chongqing-style spicy hotpot restaurant; popular in the evenings when they have to set up tables on the pavement outside. ¥25 a head.

DIRECTORY

Banks There are branches of the Agricultural and Construction banks, with ATMs, all through the centre, and outside the bus station.

Shopping Kangding's most interesting shopping street is Xinshi Qian Jie; there's a big supermarket here for general supplies; and a Tibetan outfitters near the *Dejilin* restaurant, with rugs, cowboy hats, knives and jewellery.

Luding

泸定, lúdìng · Taxis head between Kangding (1hr; ¥20), Moxi (1hr; ¥15) and Luding in daylight hours, picking up on the main road

The riverside market town of **LUDING** sits where the route to Moxi and Hailuogou glacier (see below) splits from the Chengdu–Kangding road, 40km south of Kangding. A few minutes here is enough to check out the attractive old **Luding Suspension Bridge** (泸定桥, lúdìng qiáo; ¥15), one of the great icons of the Long March (see p.280). In May 1935, the Red Army reached the Dadu River here to find that a nominal Nationalist force, baulking at destroying the only crossing for hundreds of kilometres, had pulled the decking off the bridge but left the chains intact. Under heavy fire, 22 Communist soldiers climbed hand-over-hand across the chains and took the west bank. Official accounts say that only three Long Marchers were killed.

Though substantial by local standards, the bridge is simply a 100m-long series of thirteen heavy-gauge chains spanned by wobbly planks. The Dadu flows roughly below, while temple-style gates and ornaments at either end lend the bridge an almost religious aspect; a pavilion on the far side houses a **museum** with period photos.

Hailuogou Glacier Park

海螺沟冰川公园, hǎiluógōu bīngchuān gōngyuán · ¥95 · Bus through park ¥60

Hailuogou Glacier Park encloses an alpine backdrop of deep valleys forested in pine and rhododendron, with the four **glaciers** in question descending **Gongga Shan** (贡嘎山, gònggā shān; Minya Konka in Tibetan). At 7556m, this is western China's highest mountain, a stunning sight on the rare mornings when the near-constant cloud cover and haze of wind-driven snow above the peak suddenly clear. The park is well organized for visitors and seeing the glaciers is easy enough – you can just about do it on a busy day-trip from Kangding. With proper equipment and preparation, it's also possible to make a tough but extremely rewarding **circuit** around Gongga Shan (see p.129). Weatherproof **clothing** is advisable whatever you're planning.

1

Moxi

磨西, móxī

The park entrance is at **MOXI**, a group of hotels, restaurants and souvenir stalls around 100km from Kangding. Downhill from the crossroads, it's 150m to Moxi's original single street of wooden shops and a small **Catholic church** built in the 1920s; the colourful bell tower overlooks a European, box-like main building, its eaves pinched as a concession to local aesthetics. After the action at Luding, Mao and the Red Army recouped here before heading off on a disastrous 56km trek north over the mountains to Xiaojin (see p.130), in which Mao nearly joined the hundreds of victims of exposure and altitude sickness.

Around the park

Buses carry you 25km from the gates at Moxi to the main glacier, via accommodation at the 8km, 15km and 22km marks. These were once humble campsites, but each now hosts a large hotel, with **hot springs** (¥65) on hand at the first two – **Camp 2**, near where the thicker pine forests begin, is the nicest spot to stay within the park. From **Camp 3**, it's 3.5km to the glacier, where you can reach a **viewing platform** by cable car (¥150 return) or by simply hiking up along a small path (allow two hours). From the platform, the glacier is revealed as a tongue of blue-white ice scattered with boulders and streaked in crevasses edged in black gravel, with – if you're lucky – Gongga Shan's peak rising in the distance.

ARRIVAL AND DEPARTURE   **HAILUOGOU GLACIER PARK**

By taxi Shared taxis run between Moxi and Luding whenever full (1hr; ¥15).

ACCOMMODATION AND EATING

Aside from budget beds in Moxi, there are lodge-style **hotels** at the three camps within the park. Eat either at your accommodation or at any of the scores of anonymous stir-fry **restaurants** nearby.

★ **Gongga Shan Glacier Spa Resort** 贡嘎山冰川温 泉度假村, gònggā shān bīngchuān wēnquán dùjiàcūn. Camp 2 ☎ 083 6326 6171. Beautifully located among landscaped, terraced spa pools, with icy peaks and forest as a backdrop. Better rooms are attractively wood-panelled but cheaper ones are fairly average. Non-residents get unlimited spa use for ¥100. Beds **¥180**, doubles **¥580**

★ **Hamu Hostel** 哈姆青年旅舍, hāmū qīngnián lǚshè. Moxi, where the road from Kangding enters town ☎ 1528 157 2918. Cosy and comfortable backpacker staple, and unusual in allowing guests use of its kitchen; they also have a laundry and free internet. They cater to

trekking parties and are very clued up about the area (see box, opposite). Dorms **¥30**, doubles **¥80**

Milan Youth Hostel 米兰青年旅舍, mǐlán qīngnián lǚshè. Moxi, down near the church ☎ 083 6326 6518, ☎ 1310 837 7771, ☎ hlgml.cn. Another clean, pleasant budget option outside the park, with bright, colour-coded rooms and hard beds. Dorms **¥30**, doubles **¥80**

Yinshan Dajiudian 银山大酒店, yínshān dàjiǔdiàn. Camp 3 ☎ 083 6326 6383. Pretty comfortable hotel, though not up to the *Spa Resort's* levels, and the closest accommodation to the glaciers. **¥480**

Danba and around

丹巴, dānbā

DANBA (also known as Rongzhag) forms a thin 2km stretch of shops along a deep river valley 125km north of Kangding. It's a crossroads town on routes to Siguniang Shan, Ma'erkang and the Ganzi–Tagong road that's worth a stopover to visit the beautiful **Tibetan hamlets** nearby. Coming up from Kangding, you pass the **Caihong Bridge** (彩虹 桥, cǎihóng qiáo) and drive through town to the bus station. In between, along pedestrianized **Jianshe Jie**, you'll find stores selling Tibetan rugs, pots, jackets, saddles, leather boots, jewellery and temple accessories, along with food and supplies.

Tibetan villages

The steep, mica-laden hillsides surrounding Danba are dotted with **Tibetan villages**, some dolled up for tourists, others less developed, but all startlingly attractive with their green fields, groves of fruit trees, solid stone houses banded in bright colours, dusty tracks full of livestock and swooping views over deep gorges to distant mountain peaks. You can wander around one or two in an afternoon, but staying the night will give you more time to get the most out of the scenery. Thanks to a **fee** of around ¥30 to enter each village, most homes can afford satellite TV dishes and solar hot water.

Only 7km from Danba, **Jiaju** (甲居, jiǎjū) is the most popular site, a spread-out hamlet with flagstoned paths that gets packed out with tourists during national holidays. At other times it seems a genuine-enough place, slow-paced and rural, pleasantly lacking souvenir stalls and fast-food canteens. Other targets include **Zhonglu** (中路, zhōnglù), 10km northeast along the Xiaojin road and famous for its Sichuan peppercorns and square-sided, centuries-old **watchtowers**; the riverside hamlet of **Buke** (布科, bùkē), 12km west; and more towers at **Suopo** (梭坡, suōpō), 10km southeast towards Kangding.

ARRIVAL AND DEPARTURE
DANBA AND AROUND

By bus Danba's bus station is at the north end of town, handling all long-distance transport.
Destinations Chengdu (2 daily; 10hr; ¥118); Ganzi (1 daily; 10hr; ¥90); Kangding (2 daily; 4hr; ¥42.50); Ma'erkang (1 daily; 4hr; ¥40).

By minibus These run whenever full and congregate at the south end of town near the Caihong Bridge. You can also hire a whole van for ¥200–400 depending on destination.
Destinations Bamei (2hr; ¥22); Kangding (3hr 30min; ¥45); Tagong (4–5hr; ¥45); Xiaojin (1hr 30min; ¥30).

GETTING AROUND

By bus A shared minibus to any of the Tibetan villages should cost around ¥20/person return, including waiting time. Either arrange through accommodation in Danba, or head to the bridges at either end of town and talk to drivers direct.

ACCOMMODATION

Danba Dajiudian 丹巴大酒店, dānbā dàjiǔdiàn. Sanche He Nan Lu, near the Caihong Bridge, Danba ☏ 083 6352 2869. One of several ordinary budget hotels down the south end of town. **¥120**

★ **Jiaju Tibetan Homestay** 甲居藏寨民居接待户, jiǎjū zàngzhài mínjū jiēdàihù. Jiaju village ☏ 1354 146 7365. Impossible to give directions to; phone from the gate and they'll send someone along. One of Jiaju's numerous local homestays – all charge a similar amount for supper, bed and breakfast. Amenities are basic but there should be hot water. Rates are per person. **¥50**

Qiche Lüguan 汽车旅馆, qìchē lǚguǎn. Above the bus station, Danba. Beds with shared facilites. Useful if you're catching an early bus, otherwise you can usually wrangle the same price for a better room at *Zaxi Zhoukang*. Beds **¥40**

★ **Zaxi Zhoukang** 扎西卓康游客之家, zāxī zhuókāng yóukè zhījiā. Sanche He Nan Lu, near the Caihong Bridge, Danba ☏ 083 6352 1806. Bus drivers usually drop foreigners off here, whether or not they want to get out, but rooms are tiled and clean and it's well run. Not much English is spoken but with Chinese you can get plenty of advice about exploring local villages, and arrange minibus rental. **¥80**

TREKKING AROUND GONGGA SHAN

Treks around Gongga Shan take in starkly beautiful scenery, exhausting gradients, yaks, terrible weather and the tough, hospitable Tibetans for whom all this is normal life. The best people to contact in advance about organizing are Dragon Expeditions (🌐 dragonexpeditions. com) and Western Sichuan Tours (🌐 wstourix.com) in Chengdu. On site, Moxi's *Hamu Hostel* can provide packhorses – essential, given the extreme altitude – equally vital **guides**, and advice. An all-inclusive package will cost around US$150/day, and treks take 3–14 days.

A popular route starts just south of Kangding at **Yulin** (榆林, yúlín), and crosses southwest over a series of 4000m-high passes to the **Moxi Gully** (confusingly, nowhere near Moxi village). This runs south to the solid stone **Konka Monastery** (贡嘎寺, gònggā sì), from where you can day-trip up to **Konka Base Camp**, used by summit assault groups, and adjacent **Gangba Glacier**. From here you continue to **Bawang Lake** before looping east over another high pass and down to the hot springs village of **Caoke** (草科乡, cǎokē xiāng), about an hour's drive south of Moxi.

1

Xiaojin

小金, xiǎojīn

About 60km east of Danba, **XIAOJIN** is a gritty, single-street place of tiled-box design, dramatically laid out along hairpin bends above a deep gorge; you'll need to change transport here for Siguniang Shan. If you get stuck in Xiaojin – as the Long Marchers did in 1935 after crossing Daxue Shan from Moxi (see p.128) – fill in time tracking down Xiaojin's mosque, defunct nineteenth-century church, ruined Buddhist monastery and the remains of two ancient **iron chain suspension bridges** (the latter 5km north of town on the Ma'erkang road).

ARRIVAL AND DEPARTURE   XIAOJIN

By bus Aside from the scheduled buses, **minibuses** to Danba or Rilong/Siguniang Shan (about 2hr; ¥30 to either) leave when full from a small minibus depot 150m right out of Xiaojin's bus station.

Destinations Chengdu (1 daily; 12hr; ¥110); Ma'erkang (1 daily; 4hr; ¥48).

ACCOMMODATION

Dianhua Binguan 电话宾馆, diànhuà bīnguǎn. Next to the bus station ☎083 7278 2888. No need to go further; this is one of the best deals in town – ordinary rooms, but in good repair. **¥80**

Rilong and Siguniang Shan

About 50km east of Xiaojin, **RILONG** (日隆, rìlóng) is a small, low-key tourist centre that hugs a bend in the road, with accommodation and a few stores strung along its length. You're here because quadruple-peaked, 6250m **Siguniang Shan** (四姑娘山, sìgūniang shān –"Four Girls Mountain") rears up behind the village. There's excellent **hiking and climbing** here, not to mention superb alpine scenery, but you need to come prepared for very changeable and cold weather, even in summer. Proper **hiking boots** are also pretty essential, as the mountain's lower reaches are almost always muddy.

Three valleys run up below the snow-etched peaks; lower down the countryside is open, but this develops into thick birch and pine forests draped in strings of "old man's beard", patches of meadow, and wildlife such as marmots, hares and plenty of birds.

Changping Gou

长坪沟, chángpíng gōu • ¥70, plus ¥20 to use the bus

The closest valley to town is **Changping Gou**, which starts 500m up along the river from the *Climbers and Travellers Hostel*. From the entrance, the road runs for 6.5km to the ruined **Lama Temple** (喇嘛寺, lāma sì), from where you continue on foot along a marked trail which follows a muddy stream; it's 4.5km from here, via **Kushu Tan** (枯树滩, kūshù tān), to the foothills of Siguniang Shan's four peaks, which stretch for a further 3km along the skyline.

Haizi Gou

海子沟, hǎizi gōu

Haizi Gou is a valley running parallel with Changping Gou, but behind the four peaks. It's known for its lakes (*haizi*) and alpine vegetation, especially rhododendrons; you really need **horses** to get in here, though this makes it less visited than the others.

Shuangqiao Gou

双桥沟, shuāngqiáo gōu • ¥80, plus ¥80 to use the bus

Shuangqiao Gou, off the Xiaojin road, is the most developed valley for tourism, with another bus service running you up to villages. There's good rock climbing here and a **guesthouse** – ask at Rilong's *Climbers and Travellers Hostel*.

By minibus Minibuses to and from Xiaojin (1hr 30min; ¥30) run when full; ask at accommodation about likely departure times. Access from Chengdu and Ya'an may also be possible (see box, below).

INFORMATION

Climbing information For advance advice, contact Dragon Expeditions (w dragonexpeditions.com) or Western Sichuan Tours (w wstourix.com) in Chengdu. On site, Mr Chen, the Chinese-speaking owner of the *Climbers and Travellers Hostel*, is a mountaineer with prolific experience of Siguniang Shan. He also rents out minibuses and can put you in touch with *Mr Wang's* guesthouse in Shuangqiao Gou. Be aware that rock climbers – though not hikers – require **permits** from the Sichuan Mountaineering Association at 10 Caotang Lu (near Du Fu's Thatched Cottage), Chengdu ☏ 028 8731 5555.

ACCOMMODATION AND EATING

All accommodation can organize **rental** of horses, camping and climbing gear, and guides if wanted. Aside from roadside stir-fry joints, there aren't many places to **eat** in Rilong; aside from *Sunny*, try the *Iced Rock Bar*, at the sharp bend in the road.

Climbers and Travellers Hostel 长坪山庄, chángpíng shānzhuāng. At the sharp bend ☏ 083 7279 1869 or ☏ 1368 439 2478. Long, low buildings around a half-courtyard; you get a bed, a pit toilet and a tap to wash under, but Chinese-speaking climbers will find the owner a mine of information about the mountains. Beds **¥30**
Longyun 龙云山庄, lóngyún shānzhuāng. Off the main road on the right as you're heading uphill ☏ 083 7279 1848. Chalet-like affair competing with the *Sunny Youth Hostel* opposite, though they don't have dorms. **¥160**
Sunny Youth Hostel 阳光熠国际青年旅舍, yángguāngyì guójì qīngnián lǚshě. Just down off the main road, close to Longyun ☏ 083 7279 1585, e sunnyhostel@yahoo.com.cn. Pleasant hostel with restaurant, laundry, 24hr hot water and luggage storage. Beds **¥25**, doubles **¥120**

Ma'erkang

马尔康, mǎěrkāng

If you're aiming for Songpan or Zöigê from Kangding or Danba, you'll be spending the night between buses in **MA'ERKANG** (aka Barkam), capital of Aba autonomous prefecture. This tidy government town of a dozen streets flanks the **Mosuo River**; pedestrianized **Tuanjie Jie** is the main shopping area, where there are also plenty of **teahouses**. If you get here early enough, Zhuokeji is an attractive Tibetan village to spend an hour walking around.

Zhuokeji

桌克基, zhuōkèjī • A taxi to Zhuokeji costs ¥18, or about ¥45 for the return trip including waiting time

The stone-built Tibetan village of **Zhuokeji** lies 7km east of Ma'erkang, where around twenty tightly packed houses with brightly coloured window frames and flower gardens overlook fields of barley and hemp – the village gates are guarded by a wooden cannon.

ALTERNATIVE ROUTES TO SIGUNIANG SHAN

Daily **buses** used to run to Rilong direct from Chengdu's Chadianzi and Xinnanmen stations in around 8hr via the **Wolong Panda Reserve**, but the reserve and road were badly damaged in the 2008 quake and buses don't currently use it. The route might be open to **minibuses**; ask in Chengdu.

There's also a route **from Ya'an** (see p.82), involving vehicle changes, stopovers and some luck, though it can be faster than travelling via Kangding and Xiaojin. Head first to **Baoxing** (宝兴, bǎoxīng), a Qiang town 70km north of Ya'an, where you'll need to spend the night; the *Yinyue Hotel* (银月宾馆, yínyuè bīnguǎn; ☏ 083 6682 6268; ¥80) is basic but clean. From here it's another 70km to the Tibetan tourist village of **Qiaoqi** (跷碛, qiāoqì), where wood-and-stone guesthouses charge ¥80 a night. You need to organize a **minibus** here for the final 210km to Rilong (6hr; ¥400), which crosses a high mountain pass.

On the hill opposite, the sheer, stark walls and watchtower of the unoccupied **Tusi Guanzhai** (土司官寨, tǔsī guānzhài; literally the "Landlord's Fortress") offer a bleak contrast, and sheltered Mao in 1935 during the Long March.

ARRIVAL AND DEPARTURE   MA'ERKANG

By bus Ma'erkang's bus station is about 3km east of town, connected by a local bus (¥1). Services leave early in the day.

Destinations Chengdu (2 daily; 12hr; ¥138); Danba (1 daily; 4hr; ¥40); Songpan (1 daily; 6hr; ¥98); Xiaojin (1 daily; 4hr; ¥48); Zöigê (1 daily; 8hr; ¥90).

ACCOMMODATION

Dazang Sunshine 大藏阳光酒店, dàzàng yángguāng jiǔdiàn. Over the river from the centre on Majiang Lu ☎083 7229 2999. Pricey and splendid in the Chinese hotel way, with rooms looking relatively unpretentious next to the heavily marbled lobby. Perhaps worth the expense after a tough bus journey. **¥460**

Minshan 岷山宾馆, mínshān bīnguǎn. 131 Binhe Lu ☎083 7282 2918. A bit more realistically priced than the *Dazang*, with pretty similar rooms. **¥220**
Yingbin 迎宾宾馆, yíngbīn bīnguǎn. Next to the bus station. Standard tiled rooms; convenient for early departures but it's a long way from town. **¥80**

Tagong and around

Around 110km northwest of Kangding, the long road to Ganzi and Dêgê winds up onto a 3700m-high plateau and reaches the tiny community of **Tagong**, which offers temples and access to mountains and the sprawling **Tagong Grasslands** and is a great place to pull up for a few days.

Tagong
塔公, tǎgōng

TAGONG (Lhagang in Tibetan) comprises a run of shops and accommodation lining a 500m-long stretch of the Kangding–Ganzi road. The township's focus is the modest **Lhagang Temple** (塔公寺, tǎgōng sì; ¥10), built to honour **Princess Wencheng**, who stopped here in 640 AD on her way to marry the Tibetan ruler Songtsen Gampo as part of a peace treaty between China and her western neighbour. The seventeenth-century **main hall**, busy with monks chatting on their mobile phones during morning prayers, houses a sculpture of Sakyamuni as a youth, said to have been brought here by the princess; while behind the monastery is **Fotalin**, a forest of a hundred 3m-high stupas, each built in memory of a monk.

Follow the road 500m past Lhagang Temple and you'll find the spectacular **golden stupa** (¥10), fully 20m tall and surrounded by a colonnade of **prayer wheels** – though according to the monks, this recent construction is less of a religious site than an excuse to collect tourist revenue. The imposingly jagged, snowy summit behind is 5820m-high **Yala Mountain**; contact Chyoger Treks (see p.134) for access and hiking information.

The Tagong Grasslands
塔公草原, tǎgōng cǎoyuán

Tagong sits at the edge of the **Tagong grasslands**, a string of flat-bottomed valleys surrounded by magnificent snowy peaks, whose vast swathe of pasture offers limitless scope for **horseriding** or **hiking**. Closest to town, **Shedra Gompa**'s monastery and Buddhist college is only a couple of kilometres away; **Shamalong** village is two hours along a track from the golden stupa; while **Ani Gompa** is a valley nunnery with a **sky-burial site** (see p.138) some two hours' hike cross-country. Get full directions for these routes from *Sally's* or the *Khampa Café* – and watch out for **dogs**.

ARRIVAL AND DEPARTURE   TAGONG AND AROUND

By bus Tagong has no bus station; transport stops along the main road, usually next to the temple square.

Accommodation can advise on times to flag down onwards long-distance buses to Ganzi, Kangding and beyond.

1

BEWARE OF THE DOGS

Western Sichuan's wild, open countryside makes for good hiking, but you need to watch out for **dogs**. Most of these are just the scrawny mongrels that roam around all Tibetan settlements, including monasteries; carry a pocketful of stones and a good stick, and you should be fine. Guard dogs, however, you need to keep well clear of: you don't want an encounter with a **Tibetan mastiff**. These huge, shaggy creatures have become sought-after pets in eastern China and fetch a lot of money – you'll see domesticated ones with red woollen collars paraded around Kangding and elsewhere – but in the Tibetan regions mastiffs are still kept for security purposes. Don't go near isolated houses or, especially, nomad tents without calling out so that people know you're there and will check that their dogs are chained up.

Destinations Bamei (1hr; ¥15); Danba (4hr; ¥45); Ganzi (1 daily; 9hr; ¥95); Kangding (3hr; ¥55).
By minibus Minibuses to Kangding and Danba run flexible schedules, and can always be chartered. If you're heading to Danba and can't find direct traffic, aim first for Bamei (see below).

INFORMATION

Tours and information *Angela's* offers plenty of helpful information about exploring the Tagong area on foot and horseback. For organized horse treks and cultural tours, contact long-established Chyoger Treks, based at *Sally's* (☎ 136 8449 3301 ⊛ definitelynomadic.com).

ACCOMMODATION AND EATING

Angela's Khampa Café Restaurant, information centre and cooperative run by an American who has been living in the area for years. Usually closed Nov–March.

★ **Jya Drolma & Gayla's Guesthouse** 甲志玛大姐家, jiǎzhìmǎ dàjiějiā. Facing the temple, it's the building behind you on the left ☎ 083 6286 6056. You'll probably be grabbed on arrival in Tagong by the owner, whose hospitality and traditional Tibetan home with brightly painted rooms – not to mention hot showers – are almost worth the trip in themselves. Dorms ¥25

Sally's Kham Restaurant Right on the square in front of the temple ☎ 139 9045 4752, ⊖ tagongsally@yahoo.com. Popular backpackers café with internet and Tibetan, Chinese and Western staples. Usually closed Nov–March.

Snowland Hostel 雪域旅社, xuěyù lǚshè Next to Sally's by the temple square ☎ 083 6286 6098. Good backpacker standby with bright, cosy rooms. Dorms ¥25

Tagong to Ganzi

Some 50km up the Ganzi road from Tagong, tiny **Bamei** (八美, bāměi) marks the junction with the Danba road; **minibuses to Danba** and Tagong await. A further 150km brings you to **Daofu** (道孚, dàofú), a fair-sized, orderly Tibetan settlement surrounded by hamlets. It's another 100km to **Luhuo** (炉霍, lúhuò) is where Kangding–Dêgê buses overnight, with well-stocked shops and the requisite gold-roofed monastery on the hill opposite. From here, Ganzi is just three more hours up the road.

ACCOMMODATION

Golden Sun Bamei. Hole up at this hospitable guesthouse if you get stuck between Tagong and Danba. Dorms ¥35
Kasa Dajiudian 卡萨大酒店, kǎsà dàjiǔdiàn. Next to the bus station, Luhuo ☎ 083 6732 2368. Tibetan-run hotel whose warm, large rooms – and hot showers – are most welcome if you've just spent ten hours on a bus. Dorms ¥35, doubles ¥80

Ganzi

甘孜, gānzī

GANZI (also known as **Garze**) sits at 3500m in a broad, flat-bottomed river valley, with the serrated Que'er Shan range rising to the south. You're well towards Tibet here, over 400km northwest of Kangding and just a day's bus ride short of the border, and even without Ganzi's important **Kandze Gompa**, it's well worth breaking the long journey to

Dêgê to soak up the atmosphere of this dusty, noisy town, with blue trucks rumbling through at all hours, wild crowds cruising the streets, and markets packing the back lanes. The highway runs east–west as main **Chuanzang Lu**, the crossroads with north-oriented **Jiefang Lu** marking the town centre, which is thick with workshops and stores selling knives, rugs, silverware, all sorts of jewellery, saddles, copper and tin kitchenware.

Kandze Gompa
甘孜寺庙, gānzī sìmiào

Ganzi owes its importance to the adjacent **Kandze Gompa**, a monastery founded by the Mongols after they invaded in 1642 and once the largest Gelugpa complex in the Kham region. A bit empty today, it remains an important cultural centre housing seven hundred monks, renowned for the teaching of religious dances and musical instruments. The **monastery** is 2km north of town – follow Jiefang Lu uphill from the bus station – and for such an obvious structure the entrance is not easy to find, hidden behind mud-brick homes among medieval backstreets. The recently renovated buildings are splendid, and just wandering around fills in time, though there's little specific to seek out aside from the **main hall** – covered in gold, murals and prayer flags, and with an incredible view of the valley and town from its roof. The large adobe walls below the monastery are remains of the Mazur and Khangsar **forts**, built by the Mongols after they took the region.

ARRIVAL AND DEPARTURE   GANZI

By bus Ganzi's bus station is right on the central crossroads. Staff here usually refuse to sell tickets; get them on the bus. Destinations Chengdu (1 daily; 2 days; ¥220); Dêgê (1 daily; 8hr; ¥95); Kangding (1 daily; 12hr; ¥130); Manigange (1 daily; 3hr 30min; ¥33); Xinlong (1 daily; 3hr; ¥28).

ACCOMMODATION AND EATING

Chengxin Binguan 诚信宾馆, chéngxìn bīnguǎn. Opposite the bus station ☎083 6752 5289. A typically functional, tiled place with shared bathrooms and toilets that would be so much better if it got cleaned out occasionally. Dorms **¥30**, doubles **¥80**
Golden Yak 金牦牛宾馆, jīn máoniú bīnguǎn. At the bus station ☎083 6752 5288. There's a variable collection of rooms at this dusty hotel; some of the doubles are surprisingly good, and there's 24hr hot water. Beds from **¥15**, doubles **¥80**
Himalaya 喜玛拉雅宾馆, xǐmǎlāyǎ bīnguǎn. Dong Dajie, just north off the main road ☎083 6752 1878 Better, brighter and livelier version of the Golden Yak. **¥120**

Manigange
马尼干戈, mǎnígàngē

Over a pass and out on the plains 95km northwest from Ganzi along the Dêgê road, the tiny, windswept township of **MANIGANGE** is a focus for Tibetan **horse races** in late August, similar to Litang's better-known affair. There's also good **hiking** 10km up the road – you'll have to hitch – around the holy lake of **Yilhun Lhatso** (心路海, xīnlù hǎi), a kilometre-wide pool at 4040m above sea level, fed by dusty-brown glaciers descending

> ## GANZI TO LITANG
> The most reliable way to travel between Ganzi and Litang is, unfortunately, by first backtracking to Kangding – meaning a two-day journey in all. To attempt a short cut (of sorts), catch the morning bus to **Xinlong** (新龙, xīnlóng), a quiet back-roads town 100km south of Ganzi; there's plenty of accommodation should you get stuck overnight. **Xinlong–Litang minibuses** run if they get enough people (160km; 8hr; ¥60–80 each, or about ¥300 for the whole van). Check first, however, with the Xinlong bus driver in Ganzi that the Xinlong–Litang stretch is open, as it's barely more than a walking track in places, subject to washouts and landslides. Most likely you won't save any time, but you'll at least see some fresh scenery.

1

the snow-tipped Que'er Shan. Scores of boulders in the vicinity carved with "*om mani padme hum*" in Tibetan characters testify to the lake's spiritual importance; the surrounding countryside is also a reserve for rare, broad-antlered **Thorold's deer**. Hikers need to be fully equipped for the altitude and cold climate, even in summer.

ARRIVAL AND DEPARTURE   MANIGANGE

By bus Dêgê (1 daily; 4hr; ¥40); Ganzi (1 daily; 3hr 30min; ¥33); Kangding (1 daily; 2 days; ¥135).

ACCOMMODATION AND EATING

Manigange Pani 马尼干戈帕尼饭店, mǎnígàngē pàní fàndiàn. Cheap beds and not much more – there's not even a toilet – though staff are friendly and welcoming. The usual stir-fries are on offer. Dorms **¥15**

Yulong Shenhai 玉龙神海宾馆, yùlóng shénhǎi

bīnguǎn. Surprisingly smart and tidy hotel; looks like a Tibetan mansion on the outside but rooms are the usual slightly spartan, clean affairs, some en suite. Simple food is available. Dorms **¥20**, doubles **¥35**

Cho-la

(雀儿山, què'ér shān)

The 100km-long **road from Manigange to Dêgê** is the most spectacular – and downright frightening – in the whole of Southwest China. It first follows a rounded valley below the toothy, snowbound **Cho-la** then, at the valley's head, it zigzags back on itself and climbs to just below the peaks. Crossing a razor-edged 5050m-high pass, the road kinks sharply to the right – miss the turning, and you'd drive straight over a vertical, kilometre-high cliff. As the road hairpins down the far side, monks on the bus don't help raise expectations of survival by their furious chanting, but with luck you'll be pulling up at Dêgê four hours after leaving Manigange.

Dêgê

德格, dégé

DÊGÊ, the last stop before the **Tibetan border**, just 25km away, initially appears to be no more than a small cluster of ageing concrete buildings squeezed into a narrow gorge. This was once, however, the most powerful Kham state, and the only one to resist Lhasa's seventeenth-century campaign of unification – hence the absence of Gelugpa-sect monasteries in the region. Instead, there's the stunning **Gongchen Gompa**, whose **printing hall** is one of the cornerstones of the Tibetan religous world.

Gongchen Gompa

筻庆寺庙, gàngqìng sìmiào

The red-walled **Gongchen Gompa** is one of Tibet's three cultural hubs (the other two are Lhasa and Xiahe, Gansu province), and this monastic complex is continually encircled by peregrinating pilgrims busy thumbing rosaries, who stick out their tongues in greeting if you join them. Inside, there always seem to be ceremonies going on at the half-dozen halls, which you may be allowed to observe; it's not hard to spend half a day here but, despite fantastic photo opportunities, cameras are absolutely forbidden inside any of the buildings.

Bakong Scripture Printing Hall

印经院, yìnjīng yuàn · ¥25

Gongchen Gompa's most important building is the four-storey **Bakong Scripture Printing Hall**, built in 1729. This houses 290,000 **woodblocks** of Tibetan texts, stored in racks on the second floor like books in a library, and covering everything from scriptures to scientific treatises – some seventy percent of all Tibetan literary works. You can watch the **printing process** on the third floor: two printers sit facing each other, with the block in between on a sloping board; one printer inks the block with a pad and lays a fresh page

THE AXU GRASSLANDS AND THE ROAD TO QINGHAI

The road northwest from Manigange runs 365km to adjacent **Qinghai** province, the stark, bleak plateau homeland of the **Amdo Tibetans** (see p.122). On the way, it crosses the **Axu grasslands**, held by some to be the birthplace of the legendary warrior-king **Gesar**, whose fame for slaughtering his enemies extends from Mongolia to Yunnan. Images of Gesar as a fiercely moustached horseman are found across western Sichuan, and he's the hero of *The Epic of King Gesar*, the world's longest literary work.

There's no scheduled traffic, but it's a well-used trucking road and accommodation in Manigange should be able to set you up with a lift (price by negotiation). One place to aim for on the grasslands is the **Dzogchen Gompa** (竹庆寺, zhúqìng sì), a Buddhist college and monastery 50km northwest of Manigange at tiny **Zhuqing** (竹庆, zhúqìng). The college is in poor condition but remains the region's major Nyingmapa ("old-sect") monastery, established in 1684 and famous for an opera version of the Gesar epic.

Assuming you make it through to Qinghai, the first town is **Yushu** (玉树, yùshù), devastated by a terrible earthquake in 2010. From here, regular bus services resume; it's takes at least a full day to reach Xining, Qinghai's capital, across the province's harsh interior.

over it; the other rubs a roller over the back of the page and then peels it off, placing it in a pile. Each page takes under six seconds to finish, and it's not unusual to watch ten pairs of printers going full pelt, turning out a hundred pages a minute between them.

ARRIVAL AND DEPARTURE   DÊGÊ

By bus Dêgê's bus stop is on the main road, with the adjacent ticket office open at 7am and again at 2.30pm; come prepared to fight for a place in the queue. There are also buses heading 305km west to Changdu (Chamdo), one of the largest towns in eastern Tibet – though foreigners have virtually no chance of getting past the border guards. Destinations Ganzi (1 daily; 8hr; ¥95); Kangding (1 daily; 2 days; ¥180); Manigange (1 daily; 4hr; ¥40).

ACCOMMODATION AND EATING

There's a small **supermarket** and dozens of stir-fry **restaurants** on the 500m road up to the monastery.

Dêgê 德格宾馆, dégé bīnguǎn. Uphill on the monastery road. Budget wing of the *Qiao'er Shan*, with basic, dingy rooms in an older wing. Dorms ¥35, doubles ¥100

Qiao'er Shan 雀儿山宾馆, què'ér shān bīnguǎn.

On the main road ☏ 083 6822 2167. Surly management and overpriced, but still the best option in town, with decent facilities and bright, smart doubles with heating. Their comfortable tearoom is a treat after the journey. ¥220

Litang

理瑭, lǐtáng

LITANG, 300km west of Kangding, is a lively, outwardly gruff place with a large Tibetan population and an obvious Han presence in its businesses and army barracks. Wild West comparisons are inevitable – you'll soon get used to sharing the pavement with livestock, and watching monks and Khampa toughs with braided hair and boots tearing around the windy, dusty streets on ribboned motorbikes. At 4014m above sea level, Litang is also inescapably **high**, so don't be surprised if you find even gentle slopes exhausting.

Litang's main street is a 1.5km-long section of the highway known as **Xingfu Lu**, with the town's grid of back lanes turned over to **market** activity. There's an interesting temple and a

LITANG

● ACCOMMODATION	
Crane Guesthouse	3
Gaocheng	1
Peace Guesthouse	5
Peace and Happy Hotel	4
Potala Inn	2

Ganden Thubchen Choekhorling Monastery

Gesar Statue

Market

Teahouse

Bus Station

not to scale

XINGFU LU

XINGFU LU

Batang

Kangding & Xining

Yunnan, Daocheng

Xiangcheng &

1

famous horse festival (see box, opposite) here, but it's fascinating just to people-watch: the shops are packed with Tibetans bargaining for clothes, solar-power systems for tents and practical paraphernalia for daily use, while Muslim blacksmiths turn out the town's renowned knives and jewellery. There are no **banks** useful to foreigners in Litang.

Ganden Thubchen Choekhorling monastery

理塘寺庙, lǐtáng sìmiào

Litang's enormous **Ganden Thubchen Choekhorling monastery** (also known as Chode Gompa) was founded in 1580 at the behest of the Third Dalai Lama. Today it's somewhat dilapidated – the complex was **shelled** in the 1950s after becoming a centre of resistance to the Chinese occupation of the Kham region – though still home to over a thousand monks. From the main crossroads in town, head north up Tuanjie Lu to the intersection, turn left, and follow the road – it's a fifteen-minute walk, or a ¥3 taxi ride. The complex is entirely encircled by a whitewashed stone wall, with the four main halls (two of them brand new) gleaming red and gold among an adobe township of monks' quarters.

At the **entrance** is a large stupa and pile of brightly painted mani stones left by pilgrims for good luck, whose inscriptions have been carved to resemble yaks. The **upper temple** (Tsengyi Zhatsang) is the most interesting, its portico flanked by aggressive statues of guardians of the four directions, along with a typical, finely executed mural of a three-eyed demon wearing tiger skins and skulls, holding the Wheel Of Transmigration. Inside are statues of Tsongkhapa and the Third Dalai Lama, along with photos of the current Dalai Lama and tenth Panchen Lama.

Side gates in the wall allow you to hike up onto the hills behind the monastery, sharing the flower-filled pasture with yaks, or join pilgrims circuiting the walls to the **sky-burial ground** to the right of the main gates. Sky burials are extremely graphic affairs, involving the corpse being dismembered by a Lama and the pieces put out for dogs and circling vultures to eat. Outsiders used to be banned from even entering a sky-burial ground, but nowadays Tibetans you meet in town might offer tours to see the ceremony.

ARRIVAL AND DEPARTURE   LITANG

By bus Litang's bus station is on the highway at the eastern end of town. Station staff are none too helpful and often don't know if seats are available until buses arrive – so buying tickets isn't easy.
Destinations Batang (1 daily; 4hr; ¥60); Daocheng (1 daily; 5hr; ¥43); Kangding (1 daily; 9hr; ¥98); Shangri-la/Zhongdian

(1 daily; 12hr; ¥110); Xiangcheng (1 daily; 4hr; ¥38).

By minibus and taxi Vehicles to Batang, Daocheng, Xinlong (for Ganzi) and anywhere else they can get enough customers for hang around outside the bus station in the mornings. They leave when full, or if you charter them; costs per person are the same or higher than by bus, journey times slightly faster.

ACCOMMODATION AND EATING

Most **accommodation** has internet, can give advice, rents motorbikes (¥120), provides meals and organizes local tours. Stir-fry **restaurants** run by Chengdu migrants line the main street, some of which have English menus and all pretty much the same Sichuanese food.

Crane Guesthouse 仙鸿宾馆, xiānhóng bīnguǎn. 500m west from the bus station on Xingfu Lu ☎083 6532 3850. The dorms and facilities in the older front building are verging on squalid; there are much better, newer doubles with solar hot water in the rear courtyard. Dorms ¥20, doubles ¥100

Gaocheng 高城宾馆, gāochéng bīnguǎn. Tuanjie Lu ☎083 6532 2706. The most upmarket Litang has to offer in accommodation, which means clean but elderly en-suite doubles above a noisy teahouse. ¥180

Peace Guesthouse Yajiang Lu ☎152 8360 5821, ☎jeegor-zero@yahoo.com. Not to be confused with the

hostel opposite the bus station, this is more of a backpackers venue, still simple but with better facilities. Dorms ¥25

Peace and Happy Hotel 平安涉外旅馆, píngān shèwài lǚguǎn. Across from the bus station on Xingfu Lu ☎083 6532 3861. A friendly, grubby place with tiny rooms and all shared facilities. Dorms ¥20

Potala Inn 布达拉大酒店, bùdálādà jiǔdiàn ☎083 6532 2533, ☎meiduo25@yahoo.com.cn. A Tibetan-run Chinese-style hotel with good-quality dorms and spectacular views from its two front bedrooms. Staff are slack unless the helpful, English-speaking owners are on hand. Dorms ¥35, doubles ¥160

LITANG'S HORSE FESTIVAL

Litang's week-long **horse festival** kicks off each August 1 on the plains outside town. Thousands of Tibetan horsemen from all over Kham descend to compete, decking their stocky steeds in bells and brightly decorated bridles and saddles. As well as the four daily **races**, the festival features amazing demonstrations of horsemanship, including acrobatics, plucking silk scarves off the ground and shooting – all performed at full tilt. In between, you'll see plenty of **dancing**, both religious (the dancers wearing grotesque wooden masks) and for fun, with both men and women gorgeously dressed in heavily embroidered long-sleeved smocks. Since protests in 2007, the festival has been the focus of a heavy military presence.

Batang

巴塘, bātáng

Some 180km west of Litang across the boggy **Haizi Shan** plateau, **BATANG** is a quiet, orderly little grid of shops, government offices and barracks in a wide valley just east of the Yangzi and the **Tibetan border** (though it's nearly 30km by road to the crossing). However, the border is closed to foreigners at present, and there's little to do here except enjoy the 2700m-high valley's warm microclimate and visit the **Chode Gaden Pendeling**, also known as the Kangning Temple (康宁寺, kāngníng sì), just outside town, which has a chapel dedicated to the Panchen Lama.

ARRIVAL AND DEPARTURE   BATANG

By bus The bus station is on the highway 500m east of the town centre, towards Kangding. Aside from the following, there are also daily buses to Lhasa, but you won't be allowed to buy tickets. Minibuses to Litang run when full.

Destinations Chengdu (several weekly; 3 days; ¥280); Kangding (1 daily; 2 days; ¥180); Litang (1 daily; 4hr; ¥60).

ACCOMMODATION

Jinlu Zhaodaisuo 金路招待所, jīnlù zhāodàisuǒ. Next to the bus station. Neat place with institution-like dorms and starched linen, which might or might not decide to take you. Dorms <u>¥25</u>

★ **W** W宾馆, W bīnguǎn. Left out of the bus station and 100m along Jinxianzi Dadao, the highway into town ☎ 083 6562 3132. By far the best deal in Batang; the building itself has the usual tiled en-suite doubles, but they're clean and spacious, and the owners are welcoming. <u>¥80</u>

DIRECTORY

Internet Available in the third floor of the main market, above the veggie stalls.

Post Office In Batang's central square, with a phone bar for international calls.

Litang to Daocheng

The main feature of the 140km-long Litang–Daocheng road is the bleak **Haizi Shan** (海子山, hǎizi shān), a former glacial cap and now a high, boulder-strewn moorland patterned by magenta flowers, small twisting streams and pale blue tarns. You descend off this past the **Benbo monastery** to the valley settlement of **Sangdui** (桑堆, sāngduī), a scattered hamlet of Tibetan homes 30km short of Daocheng at the junction of the Xiangcheng road.

Continuing to Daocheng, you follow the west side of a broad, long river valley; about 7km along, a bridge crosses to a track heading 5km over the valley to **Zhujie monastery**, famed for its meditating monks, and beautifully positioned halfway up the facing slope.

Daocheng

稻城, dàochéng

DAOCHENG (or **Dabpa**) is a small, touristy T-junction of low buildings and shops, of most use as a springboard to alpine scenery southeast at **Yading**. The main road runs in

1

past the bus station to the junction; turn left (north) and the road runs out into the countryside, degenerating into a track that winds up 5km later at the **Rapuchaka hot springs** (茹布查卡温泉, rúbùzhākǎ wēnquán), set among a tiny village at the head of a valley. **Bathhouses** here ask ¥3 for a soak, though some of the facilities are pretty verminous; you could also skirt around the boggy valley (look for orchids along the way) and hike cross-country along a ridge back into town – tiring, given the 3500m altitude.

ARRIVAL AND DEPARTURE
DAOCHENG

By bus Daocheng's bus station is chaotic, with services frequently oversubscribed or cancelled at short notice; it can be especially hard to get a seat on the bus to Shangri-La/Zhongdian in Yunnan. Wherever you're headed, come to the ticket office the day before and be prepared to fight for a place in the queue. You can also negotiate with minibus drivers outside the bus station for rides to Litang

and Xiangcheng. With advance warning, they might be willing to undertake the two-day ride to Muli via Yading (see below). Heading to Yading is no problem: when you get off the bus in Daocheng you'll be besieged by offers to take you there from everyone in town with a free vehicle.
Destinations Litang (1 daily; 4hr; ¥38); Shangri-la/Zhongdian (1 daily; 12hr; ¥110); Yading (2hr 30min; ¥50).

ACCOMMODATION AND EATING

Daocheng's best places to stay are the several warmly hospitable **Tibetan guesthouses**, where your ability to consume vast amounts of dumplings and butter tea will be put to the test. Toilets here are basic and you shower at the public bathhouse (¥5) or, more enjoyably, at the hot springs.

Daocheng Youth Hostel-Your Inn 稻城国际青年旅舍, dàochéng guójì qīngnián lǚshè. A little out of town over the Xingfu bridge ☎083 6572 7772, ✉yourinn@gmail.com. Nice hostel sympathetically built in the local Tibetan style, with wi-fi, a brightly painted common room, restaurant and bar. Dorms ¥30, doubles ¥100

Mama's No. 2 妈妈旅馆二号店, māma lǚguǎn èrhào diàn. Yanzhuo Lu ☎1399 046 1577. Turn right out of the bus station, left at the intersection, and it's about 200m. Tibetan homestay with highly decorated dorms, doubles and tents in the garden; you can also arrange barbecues. Dorms ¥20, doubles ¥70

Plateau Inn-Here Café 高原客栈, gāoyuán kèzhàn. 78 Gongga Lu, not far from the bus station

☎083 6572 8667, ✉inoat.com. Looks dilapidated on the outside – or at least like a stone bunker or fortress – but is actually another good hostel option with restaurant, hot water and internet. Dorms ¥30, doubles ¥100
★ **Seaburay** 喜波热藏家庄, xǐbōrè zàngjiā zhuāng. Left out of the bus station and follow the English signs ☎083 6572 8668. Bright Tibetan homestay with a colourful garden, run by an extremely friendly family. Dorms ¥30, doubles ¥100
Snow Wolf Guesthouse 雪狼子客栈, xuělángzi kèzhàn. Desha Jie ☎1350 829 5808. Even by Tibetan standards, the family room here is completely over the top – shelves, cupboards and seats are all intricately painted in red, gold and blue. Rooms are modern if not luxurious. Dorms ¥40, doubles ¥120

Yading
亚丁, yàdīng • ¥150

Yading is a scenic reserve of alpine meadows, lakes and 6000m-high peaks, whose entrance is 76km south of Daocheng at **YADING VILLAGE** (亚丁村, yàdīng cūn; also called Xianggelila, or "Shangri-la" – don't confuse it with the better-known one in Yunnan). Set on a terrace, Yading village is the base for explorations, with accommodation; basic **maps** are available at the gates, from where you hike, catch a local bus or rent a **horse** to explore the park. Bring in extra food, water and sleeping bags if possible.

The reserve

Around 12km from Yading's gates, **Luorong Pasture** (洛绒牛场, luòróng niúchǎng), is an elevated valley with views of Yading's three **holy mountains**, all around 6000m: Chanadorje, Jampelyang and Chenresig. The fit and fearless can make a **kora circuit** around Chenresig's lower peak; some of the ascents are very tough and you'll need a guide and proper hiking gear. The circuit takes two days return from Luorong Pasture, though catching a bus to the nearest point means you should be able to make the trek in around eleven hours, perhaps overnighting on the way back at **Chonggu Temple** (冲古寺, chònggǔ sì), on Chenresig's lower slopes.

In the saddle between Chenresig and Jampelyang are the spectacularly beautiful **Milk Lake** (牛奶海, niúnǎi hǎi) and **Five-coloured Lake** (五色海, wǔsè hǎi), the two making a full day's circuit from Luorong Pasture, either on foot or by hiring a horse.

ARRIVAL AND GETTING AROUND   YADING

By bus Daocheng–Yading Village minibuses run on demand (2hr 30min; ¥50). Once inside, buses run between the park gates and Lurong Pasture (¥50 single, ¥80 return).

On horseback Horses are available for rent within the park; you're looking at about ¥30–300 depending on the time and distance involved.

ACCOMMODATION AND FOOD

There are several **accommodation** options at Yading Village; all offer meals but these can be erratic. You can also stay in the park at the very basic Chonggu Temple.

Kangba Hostel 登巴客栈, dēngbā kèzhàn. Yading Village ☎ 1354 840 5770. There's a bright and cheerful living room, but the rest of this hostel is pretty bare, if clean. **¥100**

Xiangcheng and beyond

XIANGCHENG (乡城, xiāngchéng), 200km from Litang or 160km from Daocheng along the road to Yunnan, is a scattered spread of Tibetan farmhouses and red mud-brick watchtowers set in a deep valley looking south to the border. Once romantically known as the **White Wolf State**, today the core of Xiangcheng town comprises a functional few streets with the flat atmosphere of some long-abandoned outpost, and it's hard to recommend getting off the bus here, as it can be very tough to buy a ticket out afterwards. If you do, however, make sure you visit **Chaktreng Gompa**, high up on the valley's slopes.

Chaktreng Gompa

桑披岭寺, sāngpīlíng sì · ¥10 · Photos allowed

Xiangcheng's small, seventeenth-century **Chaktreng Gompa monastery** is highly unusual and well worth the 2km uphill hike from town. The three-storey temple has extraordinary **decorations**, including a portico carved with animals, murals of warrior demons squashing European-looking figures and a sculpture of a multi-headed, many-limbed Samvara in primary blues and reds cavorting in Tantric postures. Among all this is an eerie seated statue of **Tsongkhapa**, founder of Lamaism's Gelugpa or Yellow Hat Sect, wreathed in gold filigree and draped in silk scarves.

ARRIVAL AND DEPARTURE   XIANGCHENG

By bus Xiangcheng's semi-derelict bus station is a walled compound dotted with rubble and excrement; the town's short main street stretches beyond. No buses originate here, so you're relying on through traffic having spare seats – and competing with everyone else in town who wants to

get out. If all else fails, try to find others to share costs for renting a minibus to Litang or Daocheng (around ¥300 to either for the whole vehicle).
Destinations Daocheng (1 daily; 4hr; ¥40); Litang (1 daily; 4hr; ¥38); Shangri-la/Zhongdian (1 daily; 8hr; ¥89).

ACCOMMODATION

★ **Bamu Tibetan Guesthouse** 巴姆藏家庄, bāmǔ zàngjiā zhuāng. If the owner doesn't meet you, take the small steps uphill from inside the bus station compound and it's 50m. Xiangcheng's highlight, a traditional three-storey Tibetan home decorated in murals, whose dormitory resembles the interior of a temple. The twin rooms are a bit poky, however. There are great views from the roof, and a

basic outdoor shower and toilet – a torch is useful. Dorms **¥30**, doubles **¥70**
Coffee Tea Hotel 象泉宾馆, xiàngquán bīnguǎn. Just outside the bus station gates on the left ☎ 083 6582 6136. Clean, simple rooms attached to a good teahouse and bathhouse. Dorms **¥30**, doubles **¥70**

Chongqing

BUDDHIST CARVINGS AT BAODING SHAN, DAZU

2

Chongqing

Carved off the eastern end of Sichuan in 1997, Chongqing (重庆, chóngqìng) is a municipality – a city-province – comprising heavily industrialized Chongqing City, an attractive rural mix of nearby mountains and historic sights, and a 400km-long stretch of China's mighty Yangzi. The city is full of vitality, but most visitors find the crowds and pollution overwhelming and disappear downstream as soon as possible aboard Yangzi cruises, exiting into neighbouring Hubei province two days later through the imposing Three Gorges. Some key sights outside Chongqing City make it worth delaying your departure: don't miss Dazu's tremendous Buddhist carvings, whose detail, humanity and humour have been pulling in pilgrims since the Song dynasty, or the ancient battlefield at Diaoyu Cheng, where the fate of medieval Europe was decided.

Further afield, giant limestone sinkholes drop into the landscape at **Wulong county**, and the Yangzi cruise itself – despite the **Three Gorges Dam**, which has submerged riverside scenery and history under rising water levels – puts you within range of some awesome sights: **Baidi Cheng**, the historic "White King Citadel" at the mouth of the stunning **Qutang Gorge**; another giant sinkhole – the world's largest – at **Xiaozhai Tiankeng**; and a thrilling ride down the **Daning River** from Wuxi to the **Little Three Gorges**.

Travelling around Chongqing is straightforward: there's almost no rail network – just a high-speed link to Chengdu and lines south into Guizhou and north into the rest of China – so most journeys not along the river are made by bus. The **weather** is subtropical, with oppressively hot, sticky summers along the Yangzi basin (especially in Chongqing City) and surprisingly chilly, damp winters throughout – it even snows up in southern Chongqing's mountains.

Chongqing City

重庆市, chóngqìng shì

CHONGQING CITY is the gateway to Southwest China, an ever-expanding **port** some 2500km upstream along the Yangzi from Shanghai at the junction of the Yangzi and Jialing rivers. Also known as the **Mountain City** – it's built on steep hillsides – this is Southwest China's urban powerhouse, a thriving metropolis fifteen kilometres across, home to ten million residents and a substantial "bangbang army" of **migrant workers** from the region's poorer backwaters, many employed as day-labourers hauling goods up and down the city slopes on their carry-poles (*bangbang*). Busy, shambolic, overcrowded, grubby and atrociously hot in summer, beauty is not one of Chongqing's assets but the city exudes energy and it's a fascinating place to spend a few days while arranging a Yangzi cruise. There are a few absorbing sights – the elegant **Huguang Guildhall**, massive **Tongyuan Gate** and **Three Gorges Museum** – plus an older district at

Eating in Chongqing p.154	**Spareribs and princesses** p.167
The siege that saved Europe p.156	**The Daning–Wushan ferry** p.170
Cruising the Yangzi p.163	**The Three Gorges Dam** p.173

YANGZI CRUISE BOAT IN THE WU GORGE, THE THREE GORGES

Highlights

❶ Chongqing City A huge, polluted and highly charismatic port with a real sense of history, Southwest China's largest, liveliest metropolis is the terminus for Yangzi cruises. **See p.144**

❷ Diaoyu Cheng World history was changed at this modest hilltop fortification, when the Mongol leader Mengge Khan was killed during a thirty-year battle with Chinese armies for control of the country. **See p.156**

❸ Dazu An incredible procession of lively Song-dynasty rock carvings, covering everything from domestic chores to religious enlightenment, illuminate the hills around this small country town. **See p.157**

❹ Wulong Explore some of the world's largest limestone sinkholes, which lie hidden among the rough terrain of this newly opened scenic reserve in Chongqing's south. **See p.160**

❺ The Three Gorges Rub shoulders with the masses on public ferries, or cruise in comfort on a floating hotel, as you follow the Yangzi into Hubei province through an awe-inspiring corridor of high, sheer-sided cliffs. **See p.163**

❻ Daning River Board a public ferry for an exhilarating taste of what river travel in China used to be like, shooting rapids down to the dramatic Little Three Gorges. **See p.171**

HIGHLIGHTS ARE MARKED ON THE MAP ON P.146–147

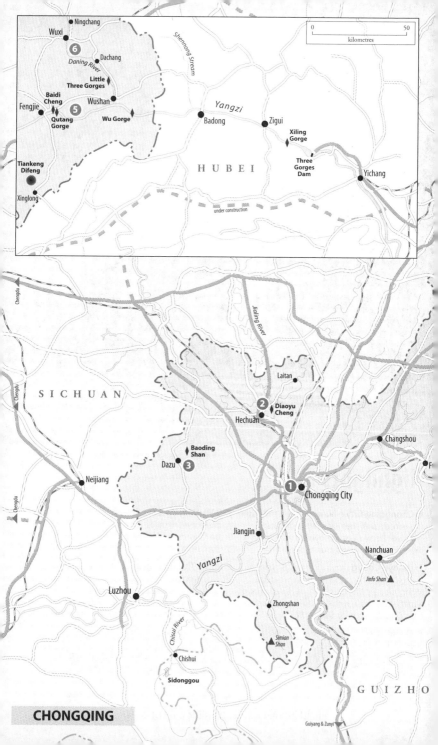

CHONGQING

Scale: 0 — 50 kilometres

Inset map (top)
- Ningchang
- Wuxi
- **6** Daning River
- Dachang
- Little Three Gorges
- Baidi Cheng
- Fengjie
- **5**
- Qutang Gorge
- Wushan
- Wu Gorge
- Shennong Stream
- Yangzi
- Badong
- Zigui
- Xiling Gorge
- Three Gorges Dam
- Yichang
- HUBEI
- Tiankeng Difeng
- Xinglong

Main map
- Chengdu
- Jialing River
- SICHUAN
- Laitan
- **2** Diaoyu Cheng
- Hechuan
- Changshou
- **3** Baoding Shan
- Dazu
- Neijiang
- Chengdu
- **1** Chongqing City
- Jiangjin
- Nanchuan
- Jinfo Shan
- Yangzi
- Luzhou
- Chishui River
- Zhongshan
- Simian Shan
- Chishui
- Sidonggou
- GUIZHO[U]
- Guiyang & Zunyi

HIGHLIGHTS
1. Chongqing City
2. Diaoyu Cheng
3. Dazu
4. Wulong
5. The Three Gorges
6. Daning River

SHAANXI

Daning River

Xi'an

Cheng Kou

SEE INSET LEFT FOR CONTINUATION EAST

Wuxi · Ningchang

Shennong Stream

⑥ *Daning River*

Dachang

Kaixian

Little Three Gorges

Baidi Cheng

Fengjie ⑤ Wushan

Yangzi

Badong

Qutang Gorge

Wu Gorge

Yunyang

◆ Zhang Fei Temple

Wanzhou

Tiankeng Difeng

Xinglong

Yangzi

Shibaozhai

Zhongxian

to Yichang

HUBEI

under construction

g Shan
Fengdu

Qianjiang

Wulong

Wu River

ng

Xiyang

HUNAN

to Zhangjiajie

N

Jishou

Dejiang

Guiyang & Zunyi   Huaihua   Huaihua & Sanjiang

0   50
kilometres

2

Ciqi Kou and, if it all gets unbearable, good transport connections out to sights at Dazu, Hechuan or the cooler mountain ranges south of town.

Brief history

Chongqing may have been capital of the shadowy **Ba kingdom** around 1000 BC, though the earliest records date the city to the conquest of Ba 700 years later by the emerging state of Qin, later rulers of all China. The Qin dispersed the Ba through eastern Sichuan and the Three Gorges where they remained right into the Ming dynasty, leaving their **hanging coffins** behind them (see p.98).

Chongqing gradually grew wealthy as a clearing house and marketplace for east-coast goods shipped up from eastern China through the treacherous Three Gorges, and where trade routes from as far afield as Tibet and Burma converged. Its name, meaning "Double Celebration", was bestowed by former resident **Zhaodun** in 1190, when he became emperor of the Song (though he was ignominiously deposed four years later by his grandmother). During the late Song dynasty, Chinese forces held Mongol invaders at bay for 36 years at nearby **Hechuan** (see p.156) before Chongqing City, by now enclosed by mighty stone walls, was ransacked; it fell again to rebel forces at the end of the Ming dynasty.

The city resumed its position as a defensive outpost in December 1937, after China's Nationalist–Communist alliance set up a **wartime capital** here, having been driven out of eastern China by the Japanese invasion that July. The US military also had a toehold in Chongqing under **General Stilwell**, until he fell out with the Nationalist leader, **Chiang Kaishek**, in 1944.

Though still showing a few historic scars, in recent years Chongqing has boomed thanks to the Chinese government's **Go West** policy (see p.375), and the efforts of local party chief **Bo Xilai**, one of China's rising political stars. Having taken on the organized crime that formerly plagued the city, jailing both gangsters and the corrupt government officials who supported them, Bo has also sponsored the restoration of Chongqing's historic monuments, so far unsuccessful attempts to make the city greener, and a drive to restore **Red Culture** – the civic-minded morals (if not the political rhetoric and disastrous economic policies) which defined China's early Communist era.

The peninsula

Chongqing City centres on a 4km-long, comma-shaped **peninsula** where the Yangzi and Jialing combine, and where you'll find many of the city's sights. The downtown area here surrounds the eastern **Jiefangbei** commercial district; **Chaotianmen docks**, where Yangzi ferries depart, are just a short walk away at the eastern tip of the peninsula. Once covered in rich public buildings, the peninsula was pretty well reduced to rubble by Japanese saturation bombing during World War II; reconstruction has been haphazard and largely unsympathetic but stretches of the **old city wall**, the elegant **Huguang Guildhall** and bizarre sculptures at the **Luohan Temple** have survived among the untidy jumble of modern skyscrapers and frenetic street markets. If you're heading down the Yangzi, don't miss the well-presented **Three Gorges Museum** at the peninsula's western end.

Jiefangbei

解放碑, jiěfàngbēi

Isolated by a broad, paved pedestrian square and glassy modern tower blocks, **Jiefangbei**, the Victory Monument, marks the peninsula's commercial heart, always packed to capacity with noisy, well-dressed crowds flitting between restaurants, cafés and nearby department stores. The monument itself was originally a memorial to **Sun Yatsen** (see p.370), before being appropriated by the Communists in 1949 to celebrate their liberation of the city from decades of right-wing occupation – though you'd expect them to have chosen something more inspiring than this drab, 20m-high clock tower.

2

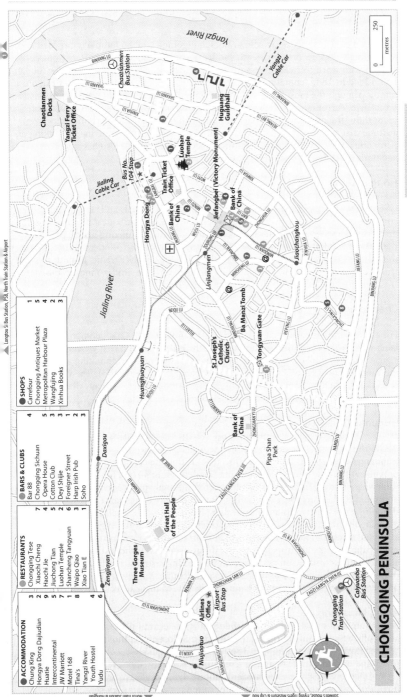

CHONGQING PENINSULA

● ACCOMMODATION

Chung King	3
Hongya Dong Dajiudian	2
Huatie	9
Intercontinental	5
JW Marriott	7
Motel 168	1
Tina's	8
Yangzi River Youth Hostel	4
Yudu	6

● RESTAURANTS

Chongqing Tese	3
Xiaochi Cheng	7
Haochi Jie	9
Jiuchong Tian	5
Luohan Temple	7
Shancheng Tangyuan	6
Waipo Qiao	1
Xiao Tian E	8

● BARS & CLUBS

Bar 88	4
Chongqing Sichuan Opera House	5
Cotton Club	3
Deyi Shijie	2
Foreigner Street	6
Harp Irish Pub	3
Soho	1

● SHOPS

Carrefour	1
Chongqing Antiques Market	5
Metropolitan Harbour Plaza	4
Wangfujing	2
Xinhua Books	3

Yangzi River

Chaotianmen Bus Station

Chaotianmen Docks

Yangzi Ferry Ticket Office

Yangzi Cable Car

Huguang Guildhall

Luohan Temple

Jialing Cable Car

Bus No. 104 Stop

Train Ticket Office

Jiefangbei (Victory Monument)

Bank of China

Bank of China

Hongya Dong

Jiaochangkou

Linjiangmen

Jialing River

Ba Manzi Tomb

Tongyuan Gate

St Joseph's Catholic Church

Huanghuayuan

Daxigou

Bank of China

Pipa Shan Park

Great Hall of the People

Three Gorges Museum

Zengjiayan

Airlines Office

Airport Bus Stop

Chongqing Train Station

Caiyuanba Bus Station

Niujiaotuo

Stilwell's House, Flying Tigers Museum & Ciqi Kou

North Train Station & Hongyan

Longtou Si Bus Station, P56, North Train Station & Airport

Luohan Temple

罗汉寺, luóhàn sì · Daily 8am–6pm · ¥10

Northeast of Jiefangbei along Minzu Lu, Chongqing's **Luohan Temple** is crowded in among high-rises, its ornate gateway hidden just off the street. The entrance passageway is lined with worn thirteenth-century sculptures, but the main sight here is the **luohan hall**, added in 1885, containing a maze of 524 disturbingly surreal statues of Buddhist saints – though the most lively, that of the Song-dynasty monk **Ji Gong**, stands outside on its own, surrounded by flowers and bottles of booze. Born in the eastern city of Hangzhou, Ji Gong caused so much trouble with his inebriated, authority-mocking attitude that no monastery would have him; instead he led a wandering life, taking on petty officials who were harassing ordinary people. The temple also has a good **vegetarian restaurant**, open at lunchtime.

Hongya Dong

洪崖洞, hóngyá dòng

Overlooking the Jialing River on Cangbai Lu, **Hongya Dong** is an entertainment complex sunk into the cliffside, full of snack stalls, restaurants and souvenir stores done up in antique style; at night it's ludicrously over-lit with competing neon signs. Across the road, the **Jialing cable car** (嘉陵江索道, jiālíng jiāng suǒdào; ¥3) offers rides high across the river to the city's northern suburbs, taking in views of river traffic, distant hills and trucks collecting landfill in low-season mud; you'll find the similar **Yangzi cable car** (长江索道, chángjiāng suǒdào; ¥3) southeast off Xinhua Lu.

Chaotianmen

朝天门, cháotiānmén

For a commanding panorama of waterfront activity, head to **Chaotianmen**, on a high bank right at the tip of the peninsula where the rivers mix. A paved **viewing area** makes a great perch to look down on **ferries** and barges along the river, honking as they go; the **Yangzi ferry ticket office** is just west on Chaoqian Lu (see p.163). The viewing area is also somewhere to appreciate Chongqing's **pollution** – there are days when you can barely make out the centre of the river, let alone the far bank.

Huguang Guildhall

湖广会馆, húguǎng huìguǎn · Changbin Lu · Daily 9am–6pm · ¥30 · Audio guide ¥10 plus ¥500 deposit

Above the Yangzi on the east side of the peninsula, the cheerful, yellow-walled **Huguang Guildhall** was built in 1759 so that visiting merchants from the Huguang provinces of central and southern China (modern Hunan and Hubei) would have somewhere to stay, entertain and hold meetings. Simply proportioned but skilfully decorated in close-up (even the drainpipes are carefully designed to look like bamboo), the complex of courtyards and interlocking halls shows a clever and fun use of space; there are theatre stages, meeting rooms, galleries, potted shrubs, high roofs with flared eaves and screens to keep the halls cool in summer. It also demonstrates how much money the traders had to spend, though ironically many of the intricately carved friezes are illustrations of the Confucian virtues, promoting restraint and limitation. A small **museum**, full of maps and old photos, also covers the Qing-dynasty resettlement projects that originally brought Huguang migrants to this part of China.

Along Minsheng Lu

Several unusual sights lie along **Minsheng Lu** in the central peninsula. Hidden down alleys off the north side of the road is the large **St Joseph's Catholic Church** (天主教若瑟堂, tiānzhǔ jiào ruòsè táng), built in 1860 in the European style, complete with square tower and arched windows, and covered in ivy. Roughly opposite, the **Ba Manzi Tomb** (巴曼子墓, bā mànzǐ mù) is even harder to locate, lying neglected in the basement of a furniture warehouse; plans are now afoot to renovate it. This grey-stone sarcophagus and mausoleum is the last resting place of the loyal Ba general **Manzi**, who killed himself after being forced to cede three cities to the rival state of Chu around 250 BC, in return for military aid against the Qin (who later conquered all China).

The Tongyuan Gate

通远门城墙公园, tōngyuánmén chéngqiáng gōngyuán

At Minsheng Lu's eastern end, the mighty **Tongyuan Gate** and attached short section of city wall is one of the last of the seventeen medieval entrances into Chongqing. You can climb the chunky fortification to the little public space on top, where there's a teahouse and a view down over life-sized bronze sculptures of Mongol hordes trying to scale the 10m-high stone battlements while defenders drop rocks on them. The Mongols finally broke through in 1277, as did the violent despot **"Yellow Tiger" Zhang Xianzhong** at the end of the Ming dynasty in 1644; he went on to briefly seize power in Sichuan, slaughtering tens of thousands of people, before being defeated by the rising Manchu armies.

The Great Hall of the People

人民大礼堂, rénmín dà lǐtáng • ¥5 • Light rail to Zengjiayan (曾家岩, zēngjiāyán) and follow the signs for 500m

At the peninsula's western end, the mighty **Great Hall of the People** rises 55m above **Renmin Plaza**'s acres of glaring granite paving. Completed in 1954, the hall's conical, green-glazed triple-tiered roof was modelled on Beijing's Temple of Heaven, but instead of being a shrine to the agricultural calendar, it now houses a concert hall. Aside from the grand scale, however, the interior is disappointingly plain.

Three Gorges Museum

三峡博物馆, sānxiá bówùguǎn • Daily 9am–5pm • Free • Light rail to Zengjiayan (曾家岩, zēngjiāyán) and follow the signs for 500m

Sat just across the plaza from the Great Hall of the People, the well-designed **Three Gorges Museum** is packed with historic artefacts – including entire cliff engravings and sculptures – removed from their original riverside locations before the Three Gorges Dam filled and submerged them for ever in 2008. There are four floors and some explanatory captioning in English; don't miss the **Han Dynasty Sculpture Hall**, which displays an amazing, 12m-long frieze of a court procession, showing acrobats and musicians, chariots and foot-soldiers, all performing for their king. The **Ancient Ba-Yu Hall** has some Neolithic grave site relics and Shang-era bronzes, including a tiger-topped storage jar; elsewhere are photos and dioramas of the Three Gorges region before it flooded. Appropriately enough, the museum building resembles a dam wall, the blue-green glassed-in lobby representing the mass of reservoir water.

West along the Jialing

A string of historic sights, mostly relating to Chongqing's position as China's wartime capital during the 1940s, lie along a 16km strip of the **Jialing River** west of the peninsula. **Stilwell's House** and adjacent **Flying Tigers Museum** have the greatest resonance for Westerners, though the former porcelain-making town of **Ciqi Kou** pulls in droves of Chinese tourists to its handful of nineteenth-century streets. You can tie them into a satisfying day-trip using buses and light rail, but allow enough time; it can take well over an hour to reach Ciqi Kou in heavy traffic.

Stilwell's House

史迪威将军博物馆, shǐdíwēi jiāngjūn bówùguǎn • Jialingxin Lu • Daily 9am–5pm • ¥5 • Light rail to Fotuguan (佛图关, fótúguān; ¥2), take Exit A and walk downhill for 100m – moving on to Hongyan and Ciqi Kou, buses leave from the Liziba stop (李子坝站, lǐzǐbà zhàn) on the main road below the house

Stilwell's House is a single-storey modernist building overlooking the river with hazy views of the city. From 1942 until 1944 it was home to General Joseph Stilwell, Chief

Commander of the US forces' China, Burma and India operations; his job was to coordinate the recapture of Burma and re-establish overland supply lines from India. He also tried to keep together the shaky Nationalist–Communist alliance, known as the **United Front** (see p.371), but his insistence that equal consideration be given to both the Guomindang and CCP caused him to fall out with Chiang Kaishek. The flat-roofed house has been decked out in period furniture, with informative photo displays in the basement charting Stilwell's career.

The Flying Tigers Museum

飞虎队展览馆, **fēihǔduì zhǎnlǎnguǎn** • Jialingxin Lu • March–Oct daily 9am–5pm • Free • Light rail to Fotuguan (佛图关, fótúguān; ¥2), take Exit A and walk downhill for 100m – moving on to Hongyan and Ciqi Kou, buses leave from the Liziba stop (李子坝站, lǐzǐbà zhàn) on the main road below Stilwell's House

Directly opposite Stilwell's House, the tiny **Flying Tigers Museum** is dedicated to a volunteer air force founded by Major General **Claire Chennault** in 1941 to defend the Burma Road and Chongqing from Japanese air raids. The force eventually accounted for 2600 Japanese aircraft, at the cost of 500 of their own. There are maps and photos here of the famous P-40 Tomahawk painted with a tiger's snarl, and portraits of the pilots, including US-trained Chinese. The original Tigers' logo, showing a winged, leaping cartoon jungle cat, was designed by Walt Disney.

Hongyan

红岩村, **hóngyán cūn** • Daily 8.30am–5pm • ¥30 • Bus #116 from Chaotianmen, or #808 from Caiyuanba, via Stilwell's House – moving on, bus #808 continues to Ciqi Kou

After the Japanese invaded eastern China in 1937, Chiang Kaishek set up his wartime government 8km west of Chongqing at the district of **Hongyan** – wisely distant from the easily targeted peninsula. The Communists were here too, the two opposing parties having temporarily allied to fight the Japanese, though Mao only visited under US auspices in August 1945, following Japan's defeat. Attempts to forge a postwar coalition foundered with Chiang's insistence that the Red Army disband, and nobody was surprised at the subsequent resumption of civil war.

Hongyan's scattering of European brick buildings are given only limited context: signs pick out the room used as the CCP propaganda department, the bed Mao slept in, buildings inhabited by Communist luminaries, without once mentioning the reasons behind their importance. As long as you're after atmosphere rather than information, it's interesting enough – and the heroic **waxworks** of Mao and Zhou Enlai (who spent far more time here than Mao) are worth the entrance fee.

Ciqi Kou

磁器口, **cíqì kǒu** • Bus #808 from the main road below Stilwell's house via Hongyan or #503 direct from Chaotianmen bus station

Once a thriving little port and pottery centre 16km west from Chongqing, **CIQI KOU** is now a quaint "old town" with a dozen cobbled lanes and timbered houses, something of a victim of its own popularity at weekends, when half of Chongqing seems to head here and the streets are barely negotiable with crowds. Outside these times Ciqi Kou is good for an hour's wander; shops sell touristy knick-knacks, idealized paintings of Ciqi Kou, and **food** – including Indian *roti*, candyfloss, hotpots and spicy fried pastry twists (陈麻花, chén máhuā).

Near the entrance, **Zhong's Courtyard** (钟家院, zhōngjiā yuàn; ¥4), founded by a nineteenth-century palace eunuch, is a bit worse for wear but has ornate wooden furniture and a roomful of contemporary photos of old Chongqing: travelling merchants with armed bodyguards, opium smokers, artisans and fortune tellers. A few streets back, **Baolun Temple** (宝轮寺, bǎolún sì; ¥5), though mostly modern concrete, is reputedly where the first Ming emperor retired as a monk. At the end of the village, stone steps descend to a sandy **beach** on the banks of the Jialing, where you can rent deckchairs and beach umbrellas.

ARRIVAL AND DEPARTURE

BY PLANE

Chongqing airport is 30km away, connected to the airlines office on Zhongshan San Lu by a 24hr shuttle (every 30min; ¥25). From the office, bus #103 runs to central Jiefangbei and Chaotianmen, close to most accommodation. A taxi from the airport to the peninsula costs about ¥70.

Destinations Beijing (6 daily; 2hr 10min); Chengdu (1 daily; 45min); Guangzhou (7 daily; 1hr 50min); Guilin (3 daily; 1hr 10min); Guiyang (3 daily; 45min); Jinghong (2 daily; 1hr 15min); Kunming (5 daily; 1hr 15min); Lhasa (3 daily; 2hr 30min); Lijiang (2 daily; 1hr 20min); Nanning (3 daily; 1hr 30min); Shanghai (12 daily; 2hr 5min); Shenzhen (7 daily; 1hr 45min); Wuhan (5 daily; 1hr 30min); Yichang (1 daily; 1hr).

BY BUS

The largest **bus station** in Chongqing is Caiyuanba, though you might well arrive at other long-distance **depots** scattered around the city. Leaving, Caiyuanba has departures to almost everywhere in the region, though check first with your accommodation in case you need one of the other depots – two are given below.

Caiyuanba bus station (菜园坝长途汽车站, càiyuánbà chángtú qìchēzhàn). Set among a nest of traffic overpasses at the western end of the peninsula, Caiyuanba is actually three adjacent bus stations with overlapping services. City buses pull up in the plaza out front; catch bus #503 along the waterfront to Chaotianmen via Binjiang Lu and the *Yangzi River Youth Hostel*, or #141 (or the forthcoming light rail) to the north train station.

Chaotianmen bus station (朝天门汽车站, cháotiānmén qìchēzhàn). At the northern tip of the peninsula within walking distance of Jiefangbei, a variety of long-distance buses end up here. It's also the terminus for city bus #141 from the north train station.

Longtou Si bus station (龙头寺长途汽车站, lóngtóu sì chángtú qìchēzhàn). By the north train station. Handles long-distance traffic from all over the Chongqing region, but you're most likely to arrive here from the Wanzhou hydrofoil port (see p.167). Bus #141 runs from the adjacent city bus terminus to Chaotianmen bus station; it's soon to have a light rail station too. A taxi costs ¥40.

Destinations from Chongqing City Chengdu (4hr 30min; ¥130); Dazu (2hr; ¥40); Hechuan (1hr 30min; ¥35); Jiangjin (1hr 30min; ¥25), Nanchuan (1hr 15min; ¥27); Wanzhou (3hr; ¥100); Wulong (3hr; ¥65).

BY TRAIN

Most trains use Chongqing's newer north train station, from where the high-speed D-class train is the quickest way to reach Chengdu. Fewer and fewer services depart from Chongqing station. Check with accommodation about which one to use. There's a train ticket booth on Minzu Lu in downtown Chongqing, and another at the Yangzi ferry ticket office at Chaotianmen.

Chongqing train station (重庆菜园坝火车站, chóngqìng càiyuánbà huǒchēzhàn). Near Caiyuanba bus station at the peninsula's western end. Bus #503 runs to Chaotianmen via riverside Binjiang Lu.

Chongqing north train station (重庆火车北站, chóngqìng huǒchē běizhàn). Bus #141 from adjacent city bus terminus to Chaotianmen bus station, in downtown Chongqing or bus #419 to Caiyuanba bus station; it's soon to have a light rail station. A taxi costs ¥40.

Destinations from Chonqing City Beijing (4 daily; 15–25hr); Chengdu (8 daily; 2hr 15min); Guilin (1 daily; 20hr); Guiyang (10 daily; 8–12hr); Kunming (3 daily; 19–24hr); Nanning (1 daily; 22hr); Shanghai (3 daily; 15–40hr); Shenzhen (1 daily; 32hr); Wuhan (7 daily; 10–19hr); Xi'an (5 daily; 12hr); Yichang (3 daily; 11hr 30min); Zigong (2 daily; 7hr 45min); Zunyi (11 daily; 5hr 30min–10hr).

BY BOAT

Detailed in our box on Yangzi cruises (see p.163).

GETTING AROUND

By bus City buses (¥1–2) are comprehensive if slow; you don't really need them around the peninsula, but they're useful for distant transit points or sights not yet covered by the light rail.

By light rail Chongqing's light rail system has one line at present, with eight more under construction or planned. The current line runs from the Jiefangbei area, along the north side of the peninsula and down to the city's southwest, and comes in handy for several sights; the second will connect the north train station with Caiyuanba bus station. Trains run every 6min from 6.30am to 10.30pm and cost under ¥3 a ride, depending on distance. Stations can be very hard to locate at street level – they're marked by green and yellow signs.

By taxis ¥7 to hire; a trip from the Caiyuanba bus station to Chaotianmen should cost around ¥20. Drivers have been know to take long detours if not watched, so it won't hurt to be seen studying a map along the way. Taxis are in short supply during frequent wet weather.

INFORMATION AND TOURS

Bookings Accommodation front desks can make all transport bookings, including Yangzi ferry tickets (see p.163).

Tourist information For an advance sketch of the city, both Chongqing Expat Club (🐦 cqexpat.com) and

Chongqing Expat (⁣ⓦ chongqingexpat.com) have English-language listings, forums and reviews about what Chongqing offers, geared to foreign residents' needs. Once here, ask at accommodation; hostel front desks speak English if your hotel doesn't.

Tours Hostels can organize local tours, including day-trips

to Dazu (1 day; ¥260) or Wulong (2 days; ¥460); and can also book you aboard evening river cruises (8pm; 1hr 30min; ¥78–88) which depart Chaotianmen docks. Boats have bars, are lit with fluorescent trim and no expense is spared to make their interiors appear opulent; it's a fun way to see the city looking its best at night.

ACCOMMODATION

Chung King 重庆饭店, chóngqìng fàndiàn. 41–43 Xinhua Lu ☎023 6391 6666, ⓦ chungkinghotel.cn. Pleasant mid-market hotel, its Art Deco exterior with period decor extending to the lobby; rooms are ordinary Chinese but nicely done and there's certainly some character drifting about. **¥458**

Hongya Dong Dajiudian 洪崖洞大酒店, hóngyá dòng dàjiǔdiàn. 56 Cangbai Lu ☎023 6399 2888. Occupying the upper level of this amusement-and-restaurant complex, this comfortable hotel has a bit too much glitz but the rooms are well appointed and most have river views. **¥400**

Huatie 华铁楼宾馆, huátiě lóu bīnguǎn. Outside Caiyuanba bus station ☎023 6160 3518. Clean, well-run basic hotel in a noisy, frenetic area; only really recommended if you have an early bus out. **¥120**

★ **Intercontinental** 重庆洲际酒店, chóngqìng zhōujì jiǔdiàn. 101 Minzu Lu ☎023 8906 6888, ⓦ ichotelsgroup.com. Coolly professional, modern business-class hotel in the city centre, with gym, spa, sauna and swimming pool. **¥900**

JW Marriott 77 Qingnian Lu ☎023 6388 8888, ⓦ marriott.com/ckgcn. Bit of a gloomy venue, though up to international business hotel standards. Their *Manhattan Steakhouse* on Floor 39 has city views; the lobby café offers ¥200/person Friday night seafood buffets. **¥900**

Motel 168 莫泰168解放碑店, mòtàiyī liùshíbā jiěfàngbēi diàn. 52 Cangbai Lu ☎023 6384 9999. Local branch of an urban hotel chain, built into a hillside overlooking the Jialing River; the cheaper rooms are large but windowless. Always full; book in advance or turn up early. **¥198**

★ **Tina's** 老街客栈, lǎojiē kèzhàn. 230 Zhongxing Lu ☎023 8621 9188, ⓦ cqhostel.com. Friendly hostel in an old-style building with a helpful, well-informed manager. It's fairly close to everything but hidden down an alley near the Chongqing Antiques Market; check their website for directions from arrival points. Dorms **¥30**, doubles **¥120**

Yangzi River Youth Hostel 重庆玺院国际青年旅舍, chóngqìng xǐyuàn guójì qīngnián lǚshè. 80 Changbin Lu ☎023 6310 4270, ⓦ chongqinghostels .com. Wood and grey-brick building with poky standard rooms but much better "Chinese-style" doubles. The staff are bumbling but helpful and sort everything out in the end. On a major road, close to the guildhall and Chaotianmen; bus #141 from the north train and bus stations runs past. Dorms **¥30**, doubles **¥120**

Yudu 渝都大酒店, yúdū dàjiǔdiàn. 168 Bayi Lu ☎023 6382 8888, ⓦ cqyuduhotel.com. Standard urban Chinese hotel, but central, well maintained, popular and good value if you put up a struggle at reception. There's a top-floor revolving restaurant, *Jiuchong Tian*. **¥598**

EATING

To sample Chongqing's *xiaochi*, or snacks, head to **Bayi Lu** or **Hongya Dong**, both designated "food streets" with numerous small, rapid-turnover canteens. Formal restaurants are getting scarce around the centre, with the bigger hotels or *Waipo Qiao* the best bets.

Chongqing Tese Xiaochi Cheng 重庆特色小吃城, chóngqìng tèsè xiǎochī chéng. Bayi Lu. Basement restaurant serving small plates of local snacks, with the emphasis on steamed buns and dumplings. A cheap way to fill up, though don't bother eating here unless they're busy, as the food gets a bit stale.

★ **Haochi Jie** 好吃街小排档, hǎochī jiē xiǎo páidàng. Bayi Lu. Tasty Chongqing street snacks – steamed spicy spareribs, cold jelly noodles, fried bitter gourd – all served inside one restaurant; point to steamers or plates of food out front or use the photo-menu. Bright, noisy and inexpensive – most dishes are ¥10 or so – but

EATING IN CHONGQING

Chongqing's **food** is essentially Sichuanese (see box, p.61), but generally more pungent – it uses a lot of raw garlic and spring onions. Famous dishes include chopped chicken fried with an equal weight of chillies (辣子鸡, làzi jī), pork hock stewed with sugar and, more than anything, hotpot. There's also a "Yangzi River" cooking style, a blend of eastern- and western-Chinese cooking which has travelled up the river.

they charge heavily for beer.

Jiuchong Tian 九重天, jiǔchóng tiān. Floor 29, Yudu hotel, 168 Bayi Lu. Revolving restaurant with cheesy music and well-presented, slightly pricey Sichuanese food; come at night to see Chongqing at her glittering best. Try steamed dumplings, cold-dressed bamboo shoots, rabbit shreds (served with cucumber slivers inside a pancake, Peking-duck style) and dry-fried mountain mushrooms. English photo-menu. Two can eat well for ¥150.

Luohan Temple 罗汉寺饭店, luóhàn sì fàndiàn. At Luohan Temple. Fairly smart but laidback vegetarian restaurant; the mouthwatering "chicken", bitter kale and pressed fresh bamboo are excellent. Cold snacks around ¥12, mains ¥30 or above.

Shancheng Tangyuan 山城汤圆, shānchéng tāngyuán. Bayi Lu. Locally famous hole in the wall

serving just one thing – boiled rice-flour balls filled with sweet sesame paste. A bowl costs just ¥3.

★ **Waipo Qiao** 外婆桥, wàipó qiáo. Floor 6 & 7, Metropolitan Plaza ☎023 6383 5988. Smart and fun hotpot place, with the ingredients floated past you in little boats; take what you want and get charged for the empties. There's also a separate canteen serving a big range of Chongqing's *xiaochi*, and more formal Sichuanese restaurant (with milder eastern Chinese options if you can't eat chillies). Snacks ¥10, hotpot or restaurant ¥35–75 a head.

Xiao Tian E 小天鹅, xiǎotiān'é. Hongya Dong, 58 Cangbai Lu. A branch of Chongqing's best-known hotpot restaurant, though they also do a good range of Sichuanese classics; it's fairly smart but still lively and loud inside. Mains ¥50.

DRINKING AND ENTERTAINMENT

Chongqing's most central knot of **bars and clubs** are in and around the hulking complex known as **Deyi Shijie** (得意世界, déyì shìjiè), diagonally across from the *Marriott*. Most places here feature DJ or live bands nightly after 9pm, and attract expats and young Chinese. Don't believe the label on bottles of local *Three Gorges* spirits – 好喝不上头 – "Good to Drink, No Hangover".

Bar 88 88 酒吧, bāshíbā jiǔbā. Mianquan Lu. Local branch of national bar chain, once famous as a gangster hangout, with nightly rock sessions as the backdrop to a general *Jack Daniel's* frenzy.

Cotton Club 棉花俱乐部, , miánhuā jùlèbù. Deyi Shijie. Foreign-owned disco-bar with eclectic musical tastes, from hard rock to R&B and ancient pop (Chinese and Western). Good party atmosphere, with a DJ on Sun.

Foreigner Street 洋人街, yángrén jiē. Across the river and northeast of the peninsula at Danzi Shi (弹子石, dànzǐ shí). Bizarre bar and restaurant district done up in various international styles, plus a strip of Great Wall and a Communist-era quarter daubed with Maoist slogans. Ask accommodation for the best buses to use – a cab should cost ¥30.

Harp Irish Pub 9F, Hongya Dong, Cangbai Lu (see p.150). Good place for a chat with expats and a break from China among English-speaking staff, draft Guinness and Kilkenny, plus a huge menu of ice-cold beers. Sports TV, comfy leather seats and free wi-fi too.

Soho 苏荷酒吧, sūhé jiǔbā. Deyi Shijie. Smart bar with massive dance space, always packed to bursting at weekends.

OPERA

Chongqing Sichuan Opera House 重庆川剧院, chóngqìng chuānjùyuàn. 75 Jintang Jie, not far from the Tongyuan Gate ☎023 6371 0153. Irregular performances of Sichuan opera (see p.74); ask accommodation to call ahead about the current programme.

SHOPPING

Antiques Chongqing Antiques Market (收藏品市场, shōucángpǐn shìchǎng), 75 Zhongxing Lu, fills four floors of what looks like a derelict department store. There are wooden screens, stone basins, statues, Mao-era relics, books, comics, pottery and ceramics; most is reproduction but it's an absorbing place to browse.

Bookshops Xinhua Books, at the Jiefangbei crossroads, is well supplied with English-language classics on Floor 4,

and maps, road atlases and Chinese-language travel guides, plus books about Chongqing, on the ground floor.

Department stores Carrefour is good for daily needs, Wangfujing or the Metropolitan Harbour Plaza for more upmarket shops; the latter has international brand stores (Hilfiger, Aquascutum, Armani), an HSBC bank, ice-rink, cinema and several restaurants.

DIRECTORY

Banks The main Bank of China is in the middle of the peninsula at 218 Zhongshan Yi Lu. Other banks with foreign-friendly ATMs are clustered around Carrefour at Jiefangbei.

Embassies and Consulates Canada, Suite 1705, Metropolitan Tower, 68 Zourong Lu (☎023 6373 8007); UK, Suite 2801 Metropolitan Tower, 68 Zourong Lu (☎023 6369 1500).

Medical Global Doctor, Room 701, Business Tower, *Hilton* hotel, 139 Zhongshan San Lu, 24hr ☎ 023 8903 8837 ✉ chongqing@globaldoctor.com.au. Mon–Fri 9am–6pm.
Post Office Located behind all the mobile-phone sellers at 5 Minquan Lu, Jiefangbei (daily 8.30am–9.30pm).
PSB In northern Chongqing at 555 Huanglong Lu, Yubei District ☎ 023 6396 1916. Their reputation for visa extensions is not good – go elsewhere if possible.

Around Chongqing City

If you can shake off the urge to flee Chongqing City for the Yangzi, a number of excellent rural sights are close enough for day-trips or a quick overnight stay. To the north, **Hechuan** town is the springboard to a Song-dynasty battlefield at **Diaoyu Cheng**, and the old hamlet of **Laitan**, where a giant Buddha has been sculpted into a cave. There's more Buddhist art west of the city at **Dazu**, where stunningly detailed and varied Song-dynasty rock carvings demand your attention for a day, perhaps as a stopover on the journey into Sichuan. Heading south, **Jinfo Shan**'s upper reaches provide a cool escape from Chongqing's summer inferno, as does the ancient village of **Zhongshan**, on Simian Shan's lower slopes. Finally, rugged limestone landscapes southeast of town at **Wulong** have only recently become accessible, from where it's possible to continue to the Yangzi at Fengdu (see p.165).

Diaoyu Cheng

钓鱼城, diàoyú chéng • Daily 9am–5.30pm • ¥40 • Bus #508 from outside Chongqing's Caiyuanba bus station runs to Hechuan (1hr 30min; ¥35); Hechuan–Diaoyu Cheng minibuses charge ¥5 – buses back to Chongqing depart until 5pm

In 1242, invading Mongol forces (see box, below) were brought up short by Song defences at **Diaoyu Cheng**, a fortified hilltop 70km north of Chonqing near the large town of **Hechuan** (合川, héchuān). Despite the site's huge historic significance – and not just for the Chinese – Diaoyu Cheng draws relatively few visitors, though it's an easy day-trip from Chongqing and there's a tangible atmosphere to soak up.

The fortifications and battlefield

Set in pretty, rural surrounds, Diaoyu Cheng's fortifications and battlefield are still visible, though you need some imagination to bring the site's momentous events to life. Minibuses from Hechuan deliver to a short flight of steps ascending **the sheer-sided hilltop**; once there, take the right-hand path and bear right again past some weather-beaten Buddhist carvings to a natural stone terrace, once a Song observation post known as the "**Fishing Terrace**" (钓鱼台, diàoyú tái). Opposite is **Huguo Temple (**护国寺, hùguó sì), now a museum featuring period stonework, paintings and maps illustrating key campaigns, and a useful diorama of the citadel – from which you'll realize that one of the reasons for Diaoyu Cheng's strength was the amount of water available up here in ponds.

THE SIEGE THAT SAVED EUROPE

Under Genghis Khan and his successors, **Mongol armies** swept through Eurasia, creating the largest contiguous empire in history. They laid siege to Diaoyu Cheng in 1242 but, harried by unexpectedly fierce resistance from Chinese forces under Wang Jian and Zhang Yu, the Mongols needed 36 years and two hundred battles to capture the fort – and lost a leader along the way when **Mengge Khan** died on the battlefield in 1259, killed by an arrow, artillery fire or dysentery, depending on which source you believe. Either way, his death changed world history as the eastern Mongol armies, poised at that moment to invade Europe, were instead recalled to elect a new khan. They chose his younger brother Kublai, who subsequently abandoned the European campaign to concentrate on conquering the rest of China.

Follow the escarpment from here and you'll come to crenellated **battlements**: immediately right is the solid **Huguo Gate** (护国门, hùguó mén), from where a long flight of steps descends to the plain below; turning left, it's around 1.5km along the hilltop to the **Cannon Emplacements** (炮台, pàotái), below which is the 1259 battlefield, now a set of terraced fields hemmed in by cliffs.

Laitan

涞滩古镇, láitān gǔzhèn • Free to enter town; combined Confucian Hall and Erfo ticket ¥30

The pleasant old town of **LAITAN**, with its rural setting, old walls and imposing giant Buddha sculpture, provides a low-key escape from Chongqing City's crowds and smog. Around 100km north of the city via **Hechuan** (合川, héchuān), the need to wait for connecting bus schedules makes this a full day-trip from Chongqing, though there's accommodation if you get stuck here for the night. You only need a couple of hours to look around; foreigners are unusual and you might get stared at, but people are friendly.

The old town

Unlike more cosmetic old Chinese towns, Laitan is atmospherically ramshackle; once under the double-arched stone gate, the rickety buildings, uneven flagstones and street hawkers selling eggs, incense and rice wine give the 200m-long main street a definite medieval character.

Despite its diminutive size, Laitan has its share of historical scars: the 5m-high stone walls, built in the early nineteenth century, repelled the Taiping armies (see p.344), and you might spend a few minutes at the unrestored courtyards of the **Confucian Hall** (文昌宫, wénchāng gōng; ¥20), whose statues were all decapitated during the cultural chaos of the 1960s. But the town's real draw is its red-walled **Erfo Temple** (二佛寺, èrfó sì; ¥10), founded in 881 AD – or rather, the **cave** behind. Among clouds of incense smoke, Song-dynasty sculptures of luohans and tiny Buddha images surround a splendid, 12.5m-high **Buddha** with an impossibly tranquil expression, covered in peeling gold leaf, all carved out of the looming sandstone cliff; wooden scaffolding allows an eye-to-eye perspective. The name "Erfo" – meaning "Buddha Number Two" – was bestowed in the sixteenth century, when Laitan's was the second-largest Buddha in Sichuan, after Leshan's Dafo (p.99).

ARRIVAL AND DEPARTURE
LAITAN

By bus Bus #508 from outside Chongqing's Caiyuanba bus station runs through the day to Hechuan (1hr 30min; ¥35). From Hechuan, catch a bus to single-street Longshi (龙市, lóngshì; 40min; ¥9.5), then a minibus to Laitan (10min; ¥2).

ACCOMMODATION AND EATING

Laitan has several guesthouses, though it's very quiet after dark and probably not worth a deliberate stay. Open-fronted **restaurants** along the main street display rough wooden benches and serve up inexpensive helpings of *gege* pork (see p.167), cured meat, stir-fries and, very unusually for China, **mint tea**. Around ¥15 a dish.

Huilong 回龙客栈, huílóng kèzhàn ☎023 4256 1999. A surprisingly substantial hotel given Laitan's size, with imitation Ming architecture, spacious rooms and nice gardens. **¥128**

Dazu and around

大足, dàzú

About 100km west of Chongqing, the small riverside town of **DAZU** is the base for viewing Tang- and Song-dynasty **Buddhist cliff sculptures** carved into caves and overhangs in the surrounding lush green hills. Monumental Buddhist carvings are hardly a rarity in this part of China, but Dazu's pack a real punch; nowhere else are

2

they executed with such gusto, cover such diverse themes, or are so well preserved. Some are small, others huge; many are brightly painted and form comic-strip-like narratives, their characters portraying religious, moral and historical tales.

Dazu town itself is a perfectly decent base, though you're just close enough to Chongqing to attempt a very full day-trip. The two main groups of sculptures are at **Bei Shan**, immediately outside Dazu, and **Baoding Shan**, 16km to the northeast; if you're pressed for time, head straight for Baoding, whose carvings are the most varied and entertaining.

Dazu town

Dazu town is a quiet grid of streets about 1.5km broad; central **Longgang Zhong Lu** is pedestrianized, but there's nothing to see besides a curious abundance of sword shops. There are plenty of places to eat and stay, however, and spending the night here makes sense if you don't want to rush your enjoyment of the carvings, or are stopping off in Dazu between Chongqing and eastern Sichuan.

ARRIVAL AND DEPARTURE DAZU TOWN

By bus Dazu's main bus station (大足汽车客运中心, dàzú qìchē kèyùn zhōngxīn), is in the south of town on Longzhong Lu, within walking distance of accommodation.

Destinations Chengdu (5 daily; 5hr; ¥92); Chongqing (2hr; ¥40); Zigong (3 daily; 4hr; ¥60).

ACCOMMODATION AND EATING

Aside from the hotel **restaurants**, Dazu is full of small, bright, nondescript places dealing in Sichuanese food. Don't expect to find English menus anywhere.

Dazu Binguan 大足宾馆, dàzú bīnguǎn. Near the bus station, Longzhong Lu ☏023 4372 1888. Once grand, now tired hotel with hard beds which is either packed with foreign tour groups or completely empty. Overlook this and rooms are clean and large, and the Sichuanese restaurant is decent. **¥180**

Jiaotong 大足交通宾馆, dàzú jiāotōng bīnguǎn. 260 Longzhong Lu ☏023 4377 5687. Fairly cheap and cheerful, recently renovated hotel. **¥120**

Jiayuan 家园商务酒店, jiāyuán shāngwù jiǔdiàn. 223 Longzhong Lu, about a 15min walk from the bus station ☏023 8522 2789. New, comfortable hotel with modern furnishings, wi-fi and relatively soft beds. **¥130**

Youzheng 邮政大酒店, yóuzhèng dàjiǔdiàn. 7 Hebin Lu ☏023 4372 4200. Downmarket budget hotel, with straightforward rooms and a good restaurant, run by the post office. **¥120**

Bei Shan

北山石刻, běishān shíkè • Daily 8.30am–5pm • ¥80, combined ticket with Baoding Shan ¥160 • 1km north of Dazu from the corner of Beishan Lu and Beihuan Zhong Lu, following stone steps ascending to the site entrance

Bei Shan's dignified, weighty sculptures are Dazu's oldest, guarded at their entrance by a brilliantly aggressive, full-scale rendition of the late Tang-dynasty general **Wei Junjing**, armour and all. Wei was campaigning against Sichuanese insurgents – or possibly founding his own breakaway kingdom – when he sponsored Dazu's first wave of art in 892 AD.

Around the corner, the rest of Bei Shan's carvings decorate a 500m-long overhang, set inside 264 numbered recesses. Completed in the twelfth century, they mostly feature the Bodhisattva **Guanyin** alongside portraits of the monks, nuns and private donors who helped fund the project. **Niche 130** shows an unusually fierce Guanyin as a demon-slayer, each of her many hands holding a weapon (and one severed head); next door in **niche 131**, she's in a more typical form, languidly gazing at the moon's reflection. **Niche 136** contains a 4.5m-high **prayer wheel**, looking like an octagonal merry-go-round mounted on a coiled dragon. The most impressive piece fills **niche 245** with a depiction of the Kingdom of Buddha, showing the trinity surrounded by clouds of Bodhisattvas, with heavenly palaces above and earthly toil below.

Baoding Shan

宝顶山石刻, bǎodǐng shān shíkè • 16km northeast of Dazu • Daily 8.30am–5pm • ¥100 – combined ticket with Baoding Shan ¥160 • Buses run from Dazu's bus station (every 30min; 30min; ¥2)

The ten thousand colourful and realistic carvings at **Baoding Shan** were the life work of the monk **Zhao Zhifeng**, who raised money, designed and oversaw the project between 1179 and 1245 – explaining the unusually cohesive nature of the images. The most impressive section here is **Dafowan**, whose 31 niches are naturally incorporated into the inner side of a broad, horseshoe-shaped gully, all packed with scenes from Buddhist scriptures and intercut with asides on daily life, and in an amazing condition given that most are unprotected from the weather.

2

Dafowan

大佛湾, dàfó wān

The bus drops you among a knot of souvenir stalls, where a kilometre-long path leads down to **Dafowan**'s entrance. Inside, Wenshu's lion (see p.66) guards the **Cave of Full Enlightenment**, a deep grotto where twelve life-sized luohans surround the Buddhist trinity, the roof carved with clouds and floating figures. Past here is a miniature pastoral of **buffalo and herders**, a peaceful parable on meditation, followed by a jutting rock shaped into a spirited **Fierce Tiger Descending a Mountain**. Demonic guardians painted blue, red and green greet you at the overhanging rock face beyond, which follows around to a 6m-high sculpture of a toothy, red-skinned giant with bushy eyebrows holding the segmented **wheel of predestination** (look for the delicately carved relief near his ankles of a cat stalking a mouse). Next comes a similarly scaled trinity of Amidhaba, Wenshu and Puxian, who balances a stone pagoda said to weigh half a ton on his palm; and then the **Dabei Pavilion**, housing a magnificent Guanyin gilded with peeling leaf, whose 1007 arms flicker up the wall behind her like flames.

By now you're midway around the site, and the cliff wall here is inset with a 20m-long **Reclining Buddha**, fronted by some realistic busts of important donors. The following two panels, depicting **Parental Kindness** and **Sakyamuni's Filial Piety**, unusually use Buddhist themes to illustrate Confucian morals, and feature a mix of monumental busts looming out of the cliff surrounded by miniature figures. Next comes the **Eighteen Layers of Hell**, a frightening scene of horse-headed demons knee-capping and boiling sinners, interspersed with amusing cameos such as the "Hen Wife" and the "Drunkard and his Mother". The final panel, portraying the **Life of Liu Benzun**, a Tang-dynasty ascetic from Leshan in Sichuan, is a complete break from the rest, with the hermit surrounded by multi-faced Tantric figures, showing a very Indian influence.

Jinfo Shan

金佛山, jīnfó shān • Entry ¥50, bus around scenic area ¥20, cable car ¥80

Peaking at 2251m, **Jinfo Shan** is a wild mountain area 120km southeast of Chongqing City, dotted with tiny hamlets and thick, primeval forests – including old-growth stands of ginkgo. There are several entrances; the 20km road from Nanchuan winds through pretty countryside to the **West Gate** (西大门, xī dàmén), where a new tourist centre greets arrivals. From here there's access up the mountain to a winter-only **ski area** (滑雪场, huáxuě chǎng) and a day-long **circuit trail** using bus, cable car and paved walking tracks to less seasonal viewing areas.

The pick of the sights includes **Bitan Yougu** (碧潭幽谷, bì tán yōugǔ), a 3.5km gully with forest, cliffs and waterfalls; the bizarrely named **Golden Turtle in Sunset** (金龟朝阳, jīnguī cháoyáng), a long, rounded summit area; and the violently jutting **Muzi Peak** (母子峰, mǔzǐ fēng) looming out of the clouds. You could probably make it back to Chongqing in one day, but that would be missing the point; there's accommodation at the entrance and also on the mountain.

2

By bus Jinfo Shan is accessed via the county town of Nanchuan (南川, nánchuān), 100km from Chongqing City. From Nanchuan's main bus station, catch city bus #101 to the old bus station, from where Jinfo Shan buses depart

(9am–4pm; every hr; 40min; ¥5).
Destinations from Nanchuan Chongqing City (1hr 15min; ¥27); Wulong (1hr 30min; ¥31).

Jinlin 金林宾馆, jīnlín bīnguǎn. Near Muzi Peak ☏ 136 5846 1118. Call ahead or ask at the gate to check if this place is open before heading up; it's a fairly basic guesthouse which can arrange meals. **¥100**

Tianxing 天星大酒店, tiānxīng dàjiǔdiàn. Jinfo Shan West Gate ☏ 023 7166 5555. Very stylish new establishment in wood and glass, offering comfortable rooms with broadband and cable TV, restaurants and even a conference centre. A good deal considering the location. **¥230**

Zhongshan

中山古镇, zhōngshān gǔzhèn

Way to the southwest of Chongqing City, **ZHONGSHAN** is a photogenic collection of rural wood-frame houses near the border with Sichuan and Guizhou, surrounded by bamboo groves and sunk into a small, rocky gorge. Founded around 860 AD as a port on inter-provincial trade routes, today damming has shrunk the river and the village has become a sleepy time capsule popular with art students, where old men gather to play cards and smoke cheroots, and the clack of mahjong tiles is about the only sign of life after dark. The single street, **Lao Jie**, is roofed over like a narrow, 500m-long barn, lined with **restaurants**, places to stay and stalls selling bamboo tubes and red-capped jars full of freshly brewed rice wine. After the city's hectic bustle, it's a relaxing spot to spend a night; there are no sights as such but you can sit out by the river and drink tea, cross the great stone slab of a bridge to a tiny pavilion on the far side, or go for a short walk to an abandoned temple downstream.

By bus Zhongshan is accessed via Jiangjin (江津, jiāngjīn), a tidy modern town on the Yangzi, 60km southwest of Chongqing; it's 56km south from here to

Zhongshan.
Destinations from Jiangjin Chongqing (1hr 30min; ¥25); Zhongshan (6 daily; 1hr; ¥13.50).

Most **restaurants** along Zhongshan's Lao Jie also offer **beds**; they hang signs outside for "guesthouse" (客栈, kèzhàn) or "accommodation" (住宿, zhùsù). Expect to pay ¥40/person for a tiny room with a basic shower and toilet. Restaurants display all the ingredients out front, so just point to what you want; check prices to avoid being overcharged.

Wulong County

武隆, wǔlóng

Wulong is a rugged county 150km southeast of Chongqing City, recently discovered to harbour enormous, spectacular **limestone** caves, gorges and sinkholes. Attractions are widely spaced among some very wild countryside, with roads, cable cars, visitor centres and accommodation still under construction. Highlights include **Three Natural Bridges**, 20km north of town (see p.162) – ask accommodation in Chongqing about the **Furong River** (芙蓉江, fúróng jiāng) and **Furong Cave** (芙蓉洞, fúróng dòng), 18km southeast, where you can cruise a 20km-long gorge; and **Fairy Mountain** (仙女山, xiānnǚ shān), 35km north, a broad area of rolling grassland, pine forest and rock formations.

Wulong town

The access point is the functional, industrial county town of **WULONG**, which is strung out for 3km along the Wu River, accessible from Chongqing, the Yangzi and Jinfo

Shan areas. There's nothing here apart from services, but you'll probably need to spend the night, especially if you plan to head up to the Yangzi afterwards.

ARRIVAL AND DEPARTURE   WULONG

Wulong town's bus and train **stations** are north of the Wu River off main **Wuxian Lu**, near roads into the scenic area.

By bus Wulong town is easily reached by bus from Chongqing, from Fengdu via Fuling (涪陵, fúlíng), and from Jinfo Shan via Nanchuan.
Destinations Chongqing (2hr 30min; ¥42); Fuling (2hr; ¥21); Nanchuan (1hr 30min; ¥31).

By train Wulong town is on the Chongqing–Huaihua rail line.
Destinations Chengdu (4 daily; 7–11hr); Chongqing (10 daily; 2–4hr); Guilin (1 daily; 18hr); Huaihua (for Fenghuang; 8 daily; 6–10hr).

GETTING AROUND

By bus Minibuses to Wulong's scenic sights leave from Wulong town's bus station whenever they have enough customers; destinations are signed in Chinese on their windscreens.
By taxi A taxi to anywhere in town costs around ¥5.

ACCOMMODATION

Touts for cheap **hotels** meet new arrivals at the bus station and should be able to find you a room nearby for ¥80.

Hongfu 宏福饭店, hóngfú fàndiàn. Cnr Wuxian Lu and Baiyang Lu ☎023 6450 1666. Around 150m from the bus station, with spacious but tired rooms, though renovations are in progress. Hard bargaining is needed to reduce the rate. **¥220**

★ **Luke Zhijia** 旅客之家, lǚkè zhījiā. Outside the train station at 2 Furong Dong Lu ☎023 7777 2888.

Surprisingly good, clean budget hotel; rooms even come with computers and internet access. **¥120**
Yuzhu Garden 瑜珠花园酒店, yúzhū huāyuán jiǔdiàn. 16 Wulong Lu, right on the river ☎023 7779 9888. Convincingly palatial, with acres of marble in the lobby, but the service and rooms are good too. **¥348**

Three Natural Bridges

天生三桥, tiānshēng sān qiáo • Daily 9am–6.30pm, last ticket 4pm • ¥95 including bus within park • Minibuses run from Wulong town (on demand; 45min; ¥9.50) and wait outside Three Natural Bridges' visitor centre for the return run

Three Natural Bridges comprises a massive system of collapsed caves and sinkholes, all overgrown with dense green vegetation but easily explored in three hours along a well-formed, 3km path. Transport from Wulong drops you at a **visitor centre**, where you buy a ticket and catch another bus up into the wet cloud forest on the plateau above the caverns. A **lift** descends into the first sinkhole, leaving you dwarfed below the awesome first "bridge", a cathedral-sized, open-ended cave of weather-stained rock streaked in white, yellow and orange. Steps descend through it to the valley floor, where sheer cliffs surround the incongruous grey-tiled wooden halls of the **Tianfu post-house**, a left-over set from Zhang Yimou's bodice-enhanced historical drama *Curse of the Golden Flower*.

From here, paths follow a stream across the floor of **Tianlong Tiankeng** (天龙天坑, tiānlóng tiānkēng), a 550m-wide, 270m-deep sinkhole; look up and it's like being at the bottom of a broad well. Exit Tianlong under the second "bridge", and continue along the stream through the third, the most narrow by far, where water jets out of a cliff-face. From here it's an uphill walk through more open country back to the bus.

The Yangzi and the Three Gorges

At 6400km, the **Yangzi** is China's longest river, and the third longest in the world. It rises high on western China's Qinghai Plateau, defines the borders between Tibet, Sichuan and Yunnan, passes through Chongqing into Hubei province, and finally empties into the East China Sea above Shanghai. Not surprisingly, one of the Yangzi's

names is "Long River" (长江, cháng jiāng), though above Yibin in Sichuan – for most of its journey through Southwest China, in fact – it's known as the "Golden Sand River" (金沙江, jīnshā jiāng). "Yangzi" is the name of a ferry crossing near the eastern Chinese city of Yangzhou, mistakenly applied by early European travellers to the whole river.

CRUISING THE YANGZI

Luxury cruise boats, public ferries and a hydrofoil through the Three Gorges run daily, year-round. The main **tourist season**, when you might have trouble getting tickets for next-day departures, is May–Oct. When **booking tickets**, make exhaustive enquiries about what is included in the price: there are a lot of con-artists about and if you don't like the way you're being treated, go elsewhere. Heading downriver, the hydrofoil leaves from **Wanzhou** (see p.167), while luxury and public vessels depart from **Chaotianmen** docks (see p.150) in Chongqing, where it can take some time to locate the specific dock – piers are numbered in Chinese only – and then reach it via the steps and rough pontoon boardwalks.

LUXURY CRUISERS

Luxury cruisers verge on five-star hotel standard, with comfortable cabins, glassed-in observation decks for watching the scenery go by, gyms, games rooms and restaurants. They cost upwards of ¥4000 and need to be **booked** through a reputable agent, preferably overseas, though you can also try out accommodation tour desks in Chongqing. Cruisers stop at specific sights as outlined in an **itinerary**, and usually include a side-trip to the Little Three Gorges or Shennong Stream. Cruisers are mainly patronized by wealthy Chinese and Western tour groups; English-speaking guides should be available. The trip from Chongqing to Yichang takes around 50hr; check current prices, facilities and vessels' history at ⓦyzcruises.com /english.

PUBLIC FERRIES

Public ferries linking towns along the Yangzi between Chongqing and Yichang are crowded and noisy with mainly local passengers; don't expect anything luxurious, as even private cabins are merely functional. You can book a berth for the whole route, or simply hop between towns on them; note, however, that tickets are not transferable between vessels, so if you get off you'll need to buy a new ticket to board another ferry. Ferries begin at Chaotianmen in Chongqing City and typically stop at Fengdu, Zhongxian, Fengjie, Wushan, Zigui and the Three Gorges Dam, though not all ferries pull in at all ports, so it's possible that you'll miss some key sights. At each stop, departure times are announced in Chinese, and you may or may not have long enough to get off and explore. **Meals** are cheap and basic, though there's plenty available onshore at stops. Bring snacks, and in winter, warm clothing.

Buy **tickets** either through accommodation (in Chongqing, Chengdu or elsewhere) or at the **Ferry Ticket Office** at Chaotianmen docks in Chongqing City (daily 8am–5pm), where electronic boards in Chinese show timetables and prices. As a guide, **fares** from Chongqing to Yichang cost ¥1700 per person for a double with bathroom, ¥860 for a double with a shared bathroom, ¥540 for a bed in a quad, down to ¥130 for a bunk in a sixteen-berth dorm. Be aware that, unless specifically stated in a tour package, ferry prices are purely for the cabin: food, entry fees to sights and even use of the ship's observation decks will cost extra. Agents offer packages for around ¥2800, including cabin, entry to all sights, meals and incidental transport. The journey from Chongqing to Yichang again takes around 50 hours, but you'll need to factor in extra time if you plan to visit more distant sights, such as Tiankeng Difeng or the upper reaches of the Daning River – each of which needs at least an overnight stay ashore.

HYDROFOIL

The **hydrofoil to Yichang** (5 daily; 6–7hr; ¥300) departs from Wanzhou (p.167); buses from Chongqing City's Longtou Si bus station run direct to the hydrofoil port (3hr; ¥100). The vessels go like torpedoes and your only look at the scenery is through spray-splattered, smoked perspex windows, so they're probably best avoided unless you need to return to your starting point after a cruise. Book everything at the Ferry Ticket Office in Chongqing, or via accommodation in Yichang (see p.175).

2

Brief history

Until the appearance of reliable roads and railways during the twentieth century, the Yangzi was a major **transport artery** linking eastern China to the remote southwestern provinces. The journey was monumentally hazardous, however, thanks to a stretch known as the **Three Gorges**, where the river squeezes between vertical limestone cliffs on the Chongqing – Hubei border. The gorges themselves are between 8km and 76km long, strung out over a 160km-long stretch between **Fengjie city** and the **Nanjin Pass**; as early as 220 BC, **plank roads** were morticed into cliff-faces here so that travellers could avoid the procession of shoals, rapids and vicious currents below. Shallow-draft vessels had to be hauled upstream by teams of **trackers**, and constantly fended away from rocks by boatmen armed with iron-tipped poles, in a journey that could take several weeks – if indeed the boat made it at all.

The modern river

Today, tales of the river's perilous past are academic. The completion in 2008 of the gargantuan **Three Gorges Dam** (see p.173) downstream in Hubei raised local water levels by up to 175m, effectively turning the Three Gorges section of the Yangzi into a vast lake. Hazards were submerged, but so too were landscapes, historic sights and entire communities, requiring the resettlement of millions of people.

Despite all this, spending a few days **cruising the Yangzi** between Chongqing and **Yichang** in Hubei offers a completely different take on travel in China. There are luxury "floating hotels", teeming public ferries serving riverside towns, hydrofoils that whisk past everything in a few hours, and even an opportunity for running rapids like in the old days. The scenery remains impressive, and key historic sights were saved from rising waters by physically shifting them to new locations. And note that, while the following account assumes you're travelling eastwards from Chongqing into Hubei, you can also **enter Southwest China** along the river, beginning the trip at Yichang.

To get the most from the trip, explore locally; some sights are right on the river, but others might need a bus journey to reach. Don't miss the humbling view into **Qutang**, the first of the Three Gorges; the limestone landscapes at **Tiankeng Difeng**; or the wild upper reaches of the **Daning River**, down which it's possible to make an exciting trip through the **Little Three Gorges**. Historic remains include **Baidi Cheng**, a military headquarters during the Three Kingdoms period, and a highly decorative pagoda at **Shibaozhai** – though **Ming Shan**'s entertaining dioramas of Chinese hell are also worth getting off the boat for. Functionally rebuilt above the rising waters, none of the regional **towns** are worth a specific look, though you might pass through some en route to outlying attractions.

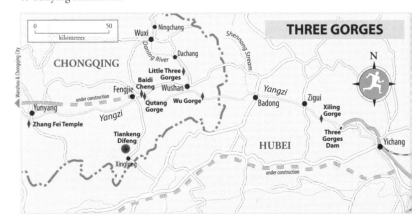

Fengdu

丰都, fēngdū

Set on the Yangzi's south bank among pleasantly hilly farmland 175km downstream from Chongqing, **FENGDU** is an entirely new town, built above its former, now submerged, site. It's a good place to catch a public ferry if you're coming up from Wulong (see p.160) – if so, you might have to spend a night in town – but otherwise can be safely skipped in favour of **Ming Shan**, directly opposite, where cruise boats will stop anyway.

Fengdu is a long grid of a place, 3km across and planted with ancient trees rescued from the old settlement. Main street **Pingdu Dadao**, parallel with the river and two blocks inland, runs west from Wenhua Park (文化公园, wénhuà gōngyuán), crossed by Mingshan Dadao, which descends north to the Yangzi ferry dock. There's nothing to do here, but Fengdu is a presentable example of a relocated riverside town; if you've time between connections, catch a cross-river ferry or taxi to Ming Shan.

2

ARRIVAL AND DEPARTURE
FENGDU

By bus Fengdu's bus station is down near the river on the west side of town along Binjiang Xi Lu; turn right out of the station, take the second main road on the right and you'll end up by Wenhua Park on Pingdu Dadao. For Wulong, catch a bus west to the Yangzi town of Fuling (涪陵, fúlíng) and change there.

Destinations Chongqing (3hr; ¥35); Fuling (1hr 30min; ¥23); Zhongxian (5 daily; 2hr; ¥25).

By boat The ferry dock (丰都港, fēngdū gǎng) is off riverside Binjiang Dong Lu, at the end of Mingshan Dadao. Ask at the dock about departure times for Yangzi vessels.

GETTING AROUND

By bus White minibuses to Ming Shan (15min; ¥3) can be flagged down along Pingdu Dadao, near the *Hongsheng* hotel. Be very clear about fixing the price before you get in; drivers have been known to demand ridiculous fares on arrival.

By boat Cross-river ferries to Ming Shan depart from Fengdu's docks at the end of Ming Shan Dadao (daily 6.30am–5.30pm; every 30min; 15min; ¥1). The last one back to Fengdu departs Ming Shan around 5pm.

ACCOMMODATION AND EATING

The *Hongsheng* and *Shiyou* have **restaurants**; otherwise the eastern end of Pingdu Dadao is lined with inexpensive hotpot, dumpling and stir-fry restaurants, whose owners – and customers – encourage you to stop as you walk past.

Hongsheng 宏声贵宾楼, hóngshēng guìbīn lóu. 88 Pingdu Dadao, close to Wenhua Park ☎ 023 7072 6666. Ludicrously grand for town, almost a resort, with a facade like a wedding cake, though the rooms are not especially expensive – the best have river views. Two restaurants, a Western-style canteen, bar and a night club. **¥260**, river view **¥480**

Jiangdong 江东宾馆, jiāngdōng bīnguǎn. Pingdu Dadao, cnr of Eryuan Lu, at the eastern end of town

☎ 023 7070 0999. Looks grotty from the outside, but it's actually a spotless, tiled, basic place; perhaps the cheapest deal in Fengdu. **¥70**

Shiyou 石油宾馆, shíyóu bīnguǎn. 28 Pingdu Dadao ☎ 023 7071 1111. Serviceable place on the third floor – look for the large illuminated sign at night – sandwiched between a popular nightclub and hotpot restaurant. **¥100**

DIRECTORY

Banks There's a large Bank of China with ATMs at the Pingdu Dadao – Ming Shan Dadao intersection.

Ming Shan

名山, míng shān • ¥80; chairlift ¥20 • Cruise boats stop here; otherwise, bus (15min; ¥3 – agree price before departure) or boat (every 30min; 15min; ¥1) from Fengdu

In Chinese lore, **Ming Shan** is the abode of **Tianzi**, King of the Dead, and the curvy hillside opposite Fengdu is covered in a mad array of temples, shrines and towers, one shaped as a giant head – very eerie seen from Fengdu if there's some low fog over the water. Ming Shan is something of a theme park to Chinese folk religion, and it's well worth getting off the boat for a couple of hours to explore.

From the entrance above the river, a chairlift or steps climb in a few minutes to a terrace full of little halls dedicated to a host of deities, including the gods of wealth, precious metals and health. The tiny, stone **Naihe Bridge** (奈何桥, nàihé qiáo) dates to the Ming dynasty; cross via the left arch for longevity and the right for riches, but watch out if you take the middle arch of judgement – sinners will fall through.

Press on upwards, through a stately 400-year-old temple complex, to **Ghosts' Pass** (鬼门关, guǐmén guān), guarded by stone demons, and along "Huangquan Lu", the road to the underworld. You end up outside **Tianzi's Palace** (天子殿, tiānzǐ diàn), a grim stone hall painted a dull blue instead of the usual cheerful red, guarded by lions with skull necklaces. Inside are colourful dioramas of hell, showing sinners being pummelled, boiled, bisected and strangled by animal-headed demons, while a grim-faced Tianzi, flanked by judges of the afterlife, looks on.

Shibaozhai

石宝寨, shíbǎozhài

Some 100km downstream from Fengdu, the river passes the busy but decrepit port of **Zhongxian** (忠县, zhōngxiàn), known for its fermented bean curd and memorial hall to the humanist poet **Bai Juyi**, before reaching **SHIBAOZHAI**, a small, rural marketplace comprising half a dozen streets on the north side of the Yangzi.

Lanruo Dian

兰若殿, lánruò diàn • ¥50

Just outside Shibaozhai, the stunning **Lanruo Dian** is an eleven-storey, 73m-high pagoda built into the face of an isolated riverside outcrop, its red wooden galleries pierced by portholes. It could not be shifted in the face of rising water levels, and a protective dyke now encircles its base.

Lanruo Dian's bright-yellow entrance is guarded by a statue of the unruly boy-god **Nezha**, who is subduing dragons with his trademark hoop. The wooden interior, dating to 1819, comprises successively smaller, lower-ceilinged halls stacked one on top of the other and linked by rickety staircases. Among dioramas and ancient stone engravings, one level is a shrine to **Ba Manzi** (see p.150), who was born nearby. The final three storeys, built in concrete, were added in the 1950s and an iron ladder gets you to the very top, for views of hilly country and barges dredging the river.

Guanyu Temple

关羽殿, guān yǔ diàn

Next door to Lanruo Dian, eighteenth-century **Guanyu Temple** is dedicated in part to **Qin Liangyu**, a female Ming-dynasty general who fought to keep the Manchus from invading China. At the rear, a sculpture of a guilty-looking Buddhist monk, hammer and chisel in hand, sits beside a **hole** in the floor. Legend has it that this hole once magically produced just enough rice to cater to the temple's needs, but after the monk greedily tried to enlarge it, the frugal supply dried up forever.

ARRIVAL AND DEPARTURE	SHIBAOZHAI

By bus There's a major bus station 20km from Shibaozhai at Zhongxian. Minibuses run on demand between Shibaozhai and Zhongxian (1hr; ¥10). Destinations from Zhongxian Chongqing (5hr; ¥55); Fengdu (2hr; ¥25); Shibaozhai (1hr; ¥10), Wanzhou (3hr; ¥32).

By boat Boats dock on the river near Lanruo Dian; approach crew directly about fares and destinations.

ACCOMMODATION AND EATING

There are a few places to **stay** in little Shibaozhai town, and plenty of plain, basic **restaurants** serving noodles, stir-fries and other staples along the two main streets.

Shibaozhai Lüyou Binguan 石宝旅游宾馆, shíbǎo lǚyóu bīnguǎn. In the street between Lanruo Dian and the town ☎023 5484 0758. A new, clean budget hotel, ordinary but with a friendly manageress. **¥80**

Wanzhou $\quad$ 2
万州, wànzhōu

The largest city between Chongqing and Yichang, and around 350km from either, **WANZHOU** sprawls over a terrace of steep hills on both sides of the Yangzi, though the main centre is on the north bank. Despite two-thirds of the old city having disappeared under water by 2008, Wanzhou feels unusually prosperous and cosmopolitan, a long-established economic hub and important port with a thick cluster of hospitals, banks and businesses along central **Tai Bai Lu** and its extension, **Baiyan Lu**. Having said this, you're only likely to alight at Wanzhou either to catch the **hydrofoil to Yichang**, or – having arrived from Yichang – to connect with high-speed buses heading west down the expressway to Chongqing.

ARRIVAL AND DEPARTURE $\quad$ WANZHOU

BY BUS

Wanzhou is connected to Chongqing by a fast expressway; slower roads head to Zhongxian and Fengjie. There are at least four bus stations; the most useful are covered below. Express coaches to Chongqing depart from outside the hydrofoil port.

Transit Centre (汽车客运中心, qìchē kèyùn zhōngxīn). On Guoben Lu, off the north end of Baiyan Lu. Destinations Chongqing (4hr; ¥100); Fengjie (4hr 30min; ¥69); Zhongxian (3hr; ¥32).

Xiamen Avenue station (厦门大道客运站, xiàmén dàdào kèyùnzhàn), 3km south of the centre on Xiamen Dadao. A taxi into the centre costs ¥7.

Destinations Chongqing (4hr; ¥100); Zhongxian (3hr; ¥32).

BY BOAT

Wanzhou's several ferry docks and the hydrofoil port (港口船客运中心, gǎngkǒu chuán kèyùn zhōngxīn) are on riverside Beibin Dadao, just downhill from the city centre. Express coaches to Chongqing depart from the hydrofoil port forecourt and connect with arriving services; buy tickets on board.

Hydrofoil Destinations Wushan (5 daily; 2–3hr; ¥110); Yichang (5 daily; 6–7hr; ¥300).

ACCOMMODATION AND EATING

For a formal **meal**, try the *Gloria Plaza* hotel's *Sampan* restaurant, which has Sichuanese and Cantonese menus plus waiter service. For a more "local" experience, head to central Baiyan Lu Yi Xiang (白岩路1巷, báiyán lù yī xiàng), an alley off Baiyan Lu which is packed with busy restaurants.

Dragon Boat Hotpot 龙船调火锅, lóng chuán diào huǒguō Baiyan Lu Yi Xiang. Somewhere to wolf down portions of fresh meat and vegetables, cooked by you at the table in an incandescent chilli stock. ¥40 a head.

Gloria Plaza 凯莱酒店, kǎilái jiǔdiàn. 91–97 Taibai Lu ☎023 5815 8855, ⓦgphwanzhou.com. Respectable business-class hotel, one of a national chain, right in the city's commercial heart; there's wi-fi throughout, several restaurants and a foreign currency exchange for guests. **¥352**

SPARERIBS AND PRINCESSES

If you stay long enough in Wanzhou to eat, make sure you try **gege** (格格, gégé), spicy spareribs coated in ground rice, steamed in tiny bamboo baskets, and served with lashings of coriander leaf. *Gege* are a popular snack throughout Chongqing and Sichuan, but locals claim the dish originated in Wanzhou; a similar banquet dish is made with chunks of rice-coated beef steamed inside a lotus leaf. The name *gege* (Manchu for "princess") has recently become slang in China to describe the materialistic, post-1985 generations.

2

Haixing 海星宾馆, hǎixīng bīnguǎn. 49 Baiyan Lu ☎023 8750 8877. This city-centre street has many big hotels but this isn't one of them; a bargain-basement option with hard beds, friendly staff and dated furnishings. **¥80**

Wanzhou 万州宾馆, wànzhōu bīnguǎn. 1 Gaosuntang Lu ☎023 8750 8888. Central older hotel in good condition, with bright, tidy rooms, a huge banqueting

hall and a vegetated rooftop terrace with views of the city and river. **¥220**

Xiao Taoyuan 小桃园, xiǎo táoyuán. 6 Baiyan Lu Yi Xiang. This popular, inexpensive restaurant is known for its *gege*, "soup dumplings" (汤包, tāng bāo; fun-but-messy steamed dumplings stuffed with a jellied stock that liquefies on cooking) and stir-fries. Two can eat well for ¥20.

Zhang Fei Temple

张飞庙, zhāng fēi miào • ¥40

Around 50km downstream from Wanzhou you pass **Yunyang** town, whose **Zhang Fei Temple**, across the river on the south bank, is dedicated to the fierce Three Kingdoms general of the state of Shu, killed in 221 AD at Langzhong in Sichuan (see p.92). His assassins fled with his head to rival warlord **Sun Quan**, who was then forced to ally with would-be-emperor **Cao Pi of Wei** to stave off the vengeful wrath of a 700,000-strong army sent against him by Shu. Zhang Fei's head was eventually buried near Yunyang, though the original site is now submerged and this nineteenth-century temple was moved brick by brick to its current location in 2006.

Vessels dock right below the temple, whose severe, fortress-like walls are outlined in red strip lighting at night. The inside is of most interest for history buffs, the half-dozen small halls filled with modern statues of Zhang Fei and dioramas featuring key scenes from his life.

Fengjie

奉节, fèngjié

FENGJIE has been around for millennia but has moved five times, settling in its current position, 90km from Wanzhou on the north side of the Yangzi, during the Song dynasty. As usual, the town itself holds little of interest – it's up on hills high above the river, with **Kuizhou Lu** as the 1500m-long main street, cut halfway along by a bridge – but you'll need to disembark here if you're planning to visit massive sinkholes at **Tiankeng Difeng** or head to **Wuxi**, home to some quirky history and start of an exciting trip down the **Daning River**. The **Three Gorges** themselves begin just downstream from Fengjie at the historic stronghold of **Baidi Cheng**, though you should see these close enough from cruise boats.

ARRIVAL AND DEPARTURE   FENGJIE

By bus Fengjie's main bus station (客运中心, kèyùn zhōngxīn) is at river level on the eastern outskirts of town; it's 3km uphill along a twisting road to central Kuizhou Lu, so catch bus #10 or #6, or a cab (¥7).

Destinations Wanzhou (4hr 30min; ¥69); Wuxi (3hr; ¥35). **By boat** The port office and dock (港务站, gǎng wù zhàn) is 250m from the bus station.

ACCOMMODATION AND EATING

Aside from the following central options, there are heaps of cheap places to **stay** around Fengjie's bus station and port, but it's a dusty, noisy area. Inexpensive **restaurants** and street stalls line Renhe Jie, north off Kuizhou Lu and next to the bridge.

Jindu 锦都宾馆, jǐndū bīnguǎn. Kuizhou Lu, near the bridge ☎023 8598 7856. Clean, tiled rooms come with computers with internet access. **¥100**

Shiyuan 诗苑大酒店, shīyuàn dàjiǔdiàn. 297 Kuizhou Lu ☎023 5685 5555. Smart, efficiently run place with large rooms, though a bit noisy, and a decent buffet

breakfast included in the price. **¥300**

★ **Taihe** 太和大酒店, tàihé dàjiǔdiàn. 460 Kuizhou Lu ☎023 5655 5188. Run by the mining company which seems to own half the town, this is an old, slightly shabby but well-maintained hotel, offering spacious, clean doubles. **¥140**

Baidi Cheng and Qutang Gorge

The Three Gorges begin 8km downstream from Fengjie (or 20km along winding roads), where the fortified islet of **Baidi Cheng** guards the spectacular entrance to 8km-long **Qutang Gorge**, whose cliffs drop sheer into the Yangzi from the hooked summit of Chijia Shan. Cruise boats should stop at Baidi Cheng for long enough to look around, before continuing east through the gorge; ferries probably won't, however, so you'll need to get out at Fengjie and bus to Baidi Cheng if you want to experience it close up.

Baidi Cheng

白帝城, báidì chéng • ¥70

Baidi Cheng is a little wooded hillock projecting out of the Yangzi, close enough to the north bank to be reached by a short bridge. Give yourself an hour to explore the tranquil complex of Ming-era buildings on top, commemorating **Liu Bei** (see p.69), the Three Kingdoms ruler of Shu. Liu died here in 223 AD, driven to his grave by the recent deaths of his dedicated oath-brothers Guan Yu and Zhang Fei; he left the kingdom of Shu to his sons, under the guidance of the wily strategist Zhuge Liang.

A small **bridge** crosses from the shore to the hillock, where steps ascend to a **hall** with a tableau of Liu Bei on his deathbed, surrounded by worried-looking ministers; his two young sons kneel to Zhuge, who holds a fan. Next door is a little **museum** of local archeological finds – a partial skeleton, tomb figurines, weapons and pots dating back to the Han era – and tiling depicting key scenes from the Three Kingdoms. Another hall contains three **hanging coffins** (悬棺, xuán guān; see p.98), once found in great numbers through the Three Gorges area; these were originally from Qutang Gorge. Note that you can enter Qutang Gorge **on foot** from Baidi Cheng (see below).

Qutang Gorge

瞿塘峡, qútáng xiá

The first of the Three Gorges, **Qutang** is also the shortest at 8km long, and the narrowest too – just 100m separates the huge, smooth cliffs through which an angry Yangzi once tore "like a thousand seas poured into one cup", according to the Song poet **Su Shi**. Today the river runs calm and smooth, but the sight of massive Yangzi ferries dwarfed by this enormous natural gateway and the peaks that rise behind it remains awe-inspiring.

You will, of course, get a view of all this from the bottom up as you cruise through the gorge, but you can also **walk in from Baidi Cheng** and see things from 100m above the river – give yourself an hour for the return trip. Once across the bridge and on Baidi Cheng islet, follow the path around to the left and down to the water, where a small **ferry** (free) carts you across the channel to Qutang's mouth. Steps ascend to a hall displaying a fossilized elephant, unearthed nearby in 1990; around to the side and overlooking Yangzi here are two tall, rusty iron poles, remains of a **cross-river barrage** erected in 1259 against an invading Mongol armada.

You can continue up from here to the **Ancient Battery** (古炮台, gǔ pàotái) – piracy was always an issue along the river, especially during the nineteenth century – or walk a short way into the gorge along a rapidly deteriorating hillside **track**. This is where to appreciate Qutang's scale; the opposite cliff looks almost close enough to touch, while a wicked set of knife-edged ridges spikes eastwards towards Chijia Shan's distant peak.

ARRIVAL AND DEPARTURE	BAIDI CHENG AND QUTANG GORGE
By bus Catch Fengjie city bus #5 (¥2) from the port area to the junction of the Baidi Cheng road at Bao Da Pin; then walk 2km along the main road to Baidi Cheng. Shared Fengjie–Baidi Cheng minibuses charge ¥6/person, but it's easier to find one returning than to catch one out.	**By taxi** Taxis from Fengjie charge ¥30 each way on the meter; they often ask double, pleading that they won't get a return fare. **By boat** Ferries dock below Baidi Cheng itself.

Tiankeng Difeng

天坑地缝, tiānkēng dìfèng • Daily 8am–6pm • ¥60 • From Fengjie, catch any bus to Xinglong (兴隆镇, xīnglóng zhèn; 2hr; ¥23) and ask the driver to set you down en route – last buses back to Fengjie pass by mid-afternoon; minibuses in Fengjie charge ¥400 for the return trip to Tiankeng Difeng, including waiting time

"Tiankeng" are giant sinkholes or dolines, a special feature of limestone **karst** formations (see p.318); they're found worldwide but most of them are in China, and the largest of them all lies 65km south of Fengjie at **Tiankeng Difeng**. This monstrous crack in the hills drops into a 662m-deep, vertical-sided pit over 250m across known as **Xiaozhai Tiankeng** (小寨天坑, xiǎozhài tiānkēng); the inside is covered in green vegetation and it's possible to zigzag down a narrow set of steps (2800 of them) to the cave passage at the bottom.

The Daning River

大宁河, dàníng hé

Fast-flowing and clear blue in its upper reaches, the **Daning River** runs south for over 100km from the Shaanxi border to the Yangzi, creating a useful water highway for this mountainous, remote region. Goods have long been shifted along this route, especially locally produced **salt**, which was mined along the river at **Ningchang** from as early as the Zhou dynasty (1100 BC) right into the 1960s. The Chinese god of salt is called **Wuwei**, and local names – Wuxi, Wu Gorge and Wushan – are possibly derivations.

Today, an overnight trip to the upper Daning gives you the chance to get a taste of the old days by running the rapids from **Wuxi** down the Daning. The best approach is to get a bus from Fengjie to Wuxi – where you can take a side-trip to some esoteric remains at Ningchang – before boarding a ferry back to the Yangzi at Wushan (see opposite).

Wuxi

巫溪, wūxī

WUXI is a small, tidy market town up in the jagged hills 70km northeast of Fengjie. There's not much to it, just the broad, 2km-long main road, **Binhe Lu**, hemmed in by a narrow valley; walk east along Binhe Lu, through a tunnel, and you're in a **market area** next to the **docks** (港口, gǎngkǒu). Wuxi marks the highest point that the Daning River is navigable, and ferries to Wushan depart at dawn, leaving you the afternoon free for a quick trip out to **Ningchang**, now virtually abandoned.

ARRIVAL AND DEPARTURE   **WUXI**

By bus Wuxi's bus station, with services to Fengjie (2–3hr; ¥35) is on Binhe Lu; turn left (east) out of the station and along Binhe Lu for accommodation and local transport. Ningchang transport (40min; ¥5) leaves from the road north – head across the short suspension bridge from the docks.
By boat See box, below.

THE DANING – WUSHAN FERRY

The long, low, flat-bottomed **Daning – Wushan ferries** seat around 50 people; they're like the river equivalent of a Chinese country bus, complete with wobbly seats and fractured perspex windows, which stop along the way to collect and set down passengers. Ferries are motorized, though the rougher upper sections of the river are navigated using a long, oar-like wooden rudder, which projects oddly out in front.

Ferries **depart** daily through the wetter summer months from Wuxi's docks at around 8am (5hr 30min; ¥53). **Buy tickets** at the *Xiajun* hotel opposite the docks at 6.30–7am on the day of departure. At other times of the year, call the *Xiajun* before heading to Wuxi, as water levels might be too low.

ACCOMMODATION AND EATING

Aside from the following, you might wrangle a **bed** at cheaper places surrounding the bus station. **Restaurants** and snack stalls surround the bus station and hotels; try *gege*, grilled fish and "dry wok" chicken.

Wuxi 巫溪大酒店, wūxī dàjiǔdiàn. Binhe Lu, up toward the tunnel ☎023 5153 3333. Wuxi's sole tourist hotel is a bland, under-used but well-maintained place with helpful staff. ¥150

Xiajun 峡郡宾馆, xiájùn bīnguǎn. 6 Zhenning He Jie, opposite the dock ☎023 5152 2638. Simple, clean hotel where passengers for the next-day ferry tend to spend the night. ¥80

2

Ningchang

宁厂古城, nìngchǎng gǔchéng • From Wuxi (40min; ¥5), cross the short suspension bridge above the docks to the road north, where vehicles congregate – ask around to find the right one; returning from Ningchang, wait for passing traffic – there's very little after 3pm

It's 12km up the Daning River gorge from Wuxi to the old salt-mining centre of **NINGCHANG**; keep your eyes peeled along the way for a dotted line of square holes neatly cut into the cliff above the river. These once supported a **galleried plank road** which ran right down along the Daning into the Three Gorges – all traces have been submerged lower down and Ningchang is one of the last places where evidence of this once-vital route survives.

Ningchang appears suddenly on the opposite bank, a thin 1500m-long ribbon, one house deep, strung out above the blue water beneath jagged mountains. The bus will set you down by the derelict **saltworks**, a collection of brick arches and wooden derricks, where artesian wells still gush brine into the river; cross the rickety wooden suspension bridge here into Ningchang. It's a ghost town really; most of the inhabitants left when the salt trade wound up decades ago, but some of the formerly grand houses are still lived in. Look for fragments of the **trade road**, flagged in ancient stones, which runs right through Ningchang and out to where the plank road once began.

Down the Daning

The ride down the **Daning River** from Wuxi to Wushan provides a thrilling run of rapids, shoals and stark scenery, your fellow passengers crammed shoulder to shoulder and trusting on the boat's crew to deliver them from evil. The river picks up speed immediately outside Wuxi, and within minutes the boatmen are fully occupied fending vessels off hazards with poles and shouting instructions to each other as they steer. Tall cliffs sprout up, the sun catching their upper heights and lighting the layered rocks yellow, grey and white; keep your eyes peeled for **birds**, especially kingfishers, egrets and mandarin ducks. A few lonely terraces and vegetable patches come into view as the river widens and calms down a little, passing a large old mansion with European flourishes at **Long Xi** (龙溪, lóngxī), the first likely stop.

By the time the rudder is shipped at the halfway point of **Shuikou** (水口, shuǐkǒu), the river has broadened into a placid lake and the most exciting part of the ride is over. On the far shore here, a major stop for locals is **Dachang** (大昌, dàchāng), an old town relocated here after the original site was flooded by dam waters; there's a big school and rows of Ming-style houses with grey-and-white brickwork.

Below Dachang, the scenery – if not the pace – returns as you enter the **Little Three Gorges** for the final hour down to where the Daning enters the Yangzi at Wushan.

Wushan and the Little Three Gorges

Tours are 2hr return; ¥240

Around 45km downstream from Fengjie at the mouth of the Daning River, **WUSHAN** (巫山, wūshān) is a charmless, cheaply built city on the Yangzi's north shore. Cruise boats pull in here to allow passengers to make sedate excursions up the Daning

2

through the **Little Three Gorges** (小三峡, xiǎo sān xiá) – the ferry ride downstream from Wuxi also takes in this stretch.

The low, glassed-in craft for Little Three Gorges cruises departs from the dock next to where ferries pull in. Passing under an arched road bridge you enter narrow **Longmen Gorge** (龙门峡, lóngmén xiá), whose splendid orange cliffs rise steeply out of the water to tower far above – look for macaque **monkeys**, which tear around the narrow ledges. About two-thirds of the way up the gorge, a 500m-long section of the ancient **plank road** is being reconstructed above the river, which will give a taster of what local travel was like before the waters rose. At the top of Longmen, before you reach Dachang, the boat turns around for the return trip.

Wu Gorge

巫峡, wūxiá

Just past Wushan, Yangzi cruises enter the mouth of the **Wu Gorge**, 45km of precipices where the goddess **Yao Ji** helped Yu the Great quell the river's terrible flooding, then turned herself and eleven handmaidens into mountain peaks, thoughtfully positioned to help guide ships downriver. The highest, **Shennu** (神女峰, shénnǚ fēng; "Goddess Peak") rises above a bend on the north bank, its jagged mass covered in vegetation and often hidden in cloud. A nearby rock face, now submerged, bore the inscription "Wu Gorge's Peaks Rise Ever Higher", ambiguous words attributed to the Three Kingdoms strategist Zhuge Liang which once so terrified an invading general that he turned tail and fled with his army.

Halfway through the gorge you cross into **Hubei province**, and at the far end the boat cruises safely over **Flint Rapids**, a once-dangerous shoal which was blown up in the 1950s and now lies deep beneath the new river levels.

Badong

巴东, bādōng

Out on the east side of Wu Gorge, vessels might pause at the new coal-mining town of **BADONG** for passengers to arrange side-trips north up an attractive 20km section of **Shennong Stream** (神农溪, shénnóng xī; 2hr; ¥240). While something of a re-run of the Daning River's Little Three Gorges (see above), it's a bit more romantic; the gorge isn't as tight but the boats are low wooden punts rowed with crossed oars by local **Tujia people**, and the bright green slopes dropping into the water look extremely atmospheric on a misty day.

Zigui

秭归, zǐguī

Continuing down the Yangzi from Badong, **ZIGUI** was the birthplace of the patriotic poet **Qu Yuan**, whose suicide in 278 BC as his beloved state of Chu was invaded by the conquering Qin armies is commemorated annually throughout China by dragonboat races. Zigui's **Qu Yuan Memorial Hall** (屈原祠, qū yuán cí; ¥90), full of calligraphy and scroll paintings extolling the writer, was founded in the ninth century and was recently shifted in its entirety above the rising waters.

Xiling Gorge

西陵峡, xīlíng xiá

Zigui marks the start of 76km-long **Xiling Gorge**, the longest of the Three Gorges and formerly the most feared, once a narrow, sunless chasm where boats ran a continual gauntlet of fierce rapids and treacherous whirlpools which spun vessels into submerged

2

THE THREE GORGES DAM

Completed in 2008 after almost a century of planning, the **Three Gorges Dam** is the largest of its kind in the world, a 1983m-long, 185m-high wall creating an artificial lake extending 670km through the Three Gorges to Chongqing. The project hopes to recoup its ¥205 billion cost through the dam's **hydroelectric output** – 32 generators will eventually produce 22,500 megawatts, almost five percent of China's needs – and the income that the region would receive from selling the generated power. Yet it's the dam's **flood-controlling** potential that really resonates in China; conquering the Yangzi's tendency to extravagantly burst its banks every few years, causing untold damage and often killing thousands of people, has long been the dream of China's leaders.

Naturally enough, the project has its detractors. The dam may actually do little to prevent flooding, which occurs along downstream tributaries as much as the Yangzi itself – a claim partially borne out during the disastrous "once-in-a-century" rains of 2010. In addition, increased water levels through the Three Gorges submerged countless communities and historical sites, forcing the **relocation** of two million people. **Ecologically**, the project is indefensible – Chongqing, one of China's most heavily industrial cities, pours its effluent directly into the new lake, while even the Chinese government admits that, at current rates of flow, siltation will make the dam unusable within seventy years.

rocks. The worst of the rapids, **Xin Tan**, was created by a landslide in 1524 which partially dammed the river; the only "safe" way through was to tackle one of the rock-lined channels either side of the obstruction. Today everything has gone: this close to the Three Gorges Dam, the waters have risen a full 175m, and Xiling is a broad, flooded valley.

The Three Gorges Dam

长江三峡大坝, chángjiāng sānxiá dàbà

At the far end of Xiling Gorge, cruise boats finally dock above the **Three Gorges Dam** (see box, above) at Sandouping, where passengers disembark. Fast buses from here make the hour-long run to Yichang; for a **tour** of the dam, head to the **Liuzhashou Reception Centre** (六闸首游客接待中心, liùzháshǒu yóukè jiēdài zhōngxīn; 1hr 30min; ¥105), from where you circuit the three viewing areas in a perspex-roofed bus offering vistas of the dam wall – during a wet summer, the amount of water exploding through the release gates is incredible.

Yichang

宜昌, yíchāng

Fresh off a cruise boat, there's no need to linger in **YICHANG**, 30km east of the Three Gorges Dam – though if you're after a good meal, a decent hotel or a cup of coffee (or indeed are starting your Yangzi trip here), it's an easy place to spend the night. Otherwise, there's plentiful transport into the rest of China.

Ringed by **car salerooms** – western Hubei is China's car manufacturing capital – Yichang stretches along the Yangzi's northern bank for around 5km, though the **centre** occupies a fairly compact spread either side of **Yunji Lu**. Yichang has no sights beyond the odd colonial relic hidden down the backstreets – such as the **St Francis Cathedral** (圣方济各堂, shèngfāng jǐgè táng) on Zili Lu – but early evening is a good time to head down to the river and watch crowds flying kites, gorging themselves on shellfish at nearby street restaurants, or just cooling off with an ice cream.

ARRIVAL AND DEPARTURE   YICHANG

There are plenty of options for onward travel. **Ferries** head up the Yangzi to Chongqing City, though the **hydrofoil** is much faster (see p.163). Heading east, Hubei's well-connected, powerhouse capital, **Wuhan** (武汉, wǔhàn), is down an

2

expressway by **bus** (5hr). Yichang's **train station** is on a spur to lines north–south through central China; heading west from here can mean a roundabout journey, though it's not too time-consuming to reach Chongqing City or Chengdu. Finally, you can **fly** to cities across China, including Chongqing and Kunming, though fares out of Yichang are about fifty percent higher than usual – you might save money by heading to Wuhan first. **Tickets** for everything except buses can be arranged through accommodation, the CITS, or relevant offices around town.

BY PLANE
Sanxia airport (三峡机场, sānxiá jīchǎng), 10km east of Yichang, a ¥60 taxi-ride away.
Destinations Beijing (2 daily; 2hr 10min); Chongqing City (1 daily; 1hr); Guangzhou (1 daily; 2hr); Kunming (1 daily; 3hr); Shanghai (4 daily; 1hr 45min); Shenzhen (1 daily; 1hr 30min).

BY BUS
A few buses terminate at a depot next to the Yiling Bridge, but Yichang's main long-distance bus station (长途汽车

客运站, chángtú qìchē kèyùnzhàn) is on Dongshan Dadao. You can get to places all over China from here, though the only destination visitors are likely to need is Wuhan (4–5hr; ¥120).

BY TRAIN
Main train station (宜昌火车西站, yíchāng huǒchē xīzhàn), centrally located above Yunji Lu atop a broad flight of steps.
Destinations Beijing (2 daily; 21hr); Chengdu (5 daily; 14hr); Chongqing (4 daily; 11hr); Shanghai (2 daily; 18–24hr); Wuhan (6 daily; 4hr 30min); Xi'an (1 daily; 15hr 30min).

East train station (宜昌火车东站, yíchāng huǒchē dōngzhàn), 15km east of town. This new station handles southbound traffic.
Destinations Guiyang (2 daily; 17–21hr); Huaihua (3 daily; 9hr 15min); Kunming (1 daily; 29hr); Zhangjiajie (3 daily; 5hr).

BY BOAT
Cruise boats, ferries and the hydrofoil tend to dock upstream from Yichang on the far side of the Three Gorges

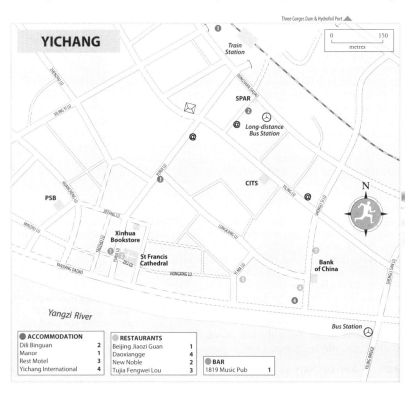

Dam. Ferry tickets are available from the bus station below the Yiling Bridge; use accommodation or the CITS for cruise boats or the hydrofoil. Ask how to reach the relevant dock when you buy your tickets, though a bus transfer from company offices in town is usually included. If you need an English speaker to explain things, try the CITS or staff at the *Yichang International* hotel.

Destinations by cruise boat and ferry See box, p.163.

Destinations by hydrofoil Five departures daily to: Fengjie (3hr; ¥220); Wanzhou (6hr; ¥300) ; Wushan (2hr; ¥190).

GETTING AROUND

By bus Yichang's public bus routes (¥1) were being reorganized at the time of writing – ask at accommodation for more information.

By taxi A fixed ¥6 within the city centre.

2

INFORMATION

Tourist information The CITS at 100 Yiling Lu (T 071 7625 3038, W yangtze.com) is a helpful, efficient office with English speakers, able to organize train, plane and ferry tickets.

ACCOMMODATION

Dili Binguan 帝丽宾馆, dìlì bīnguǎn. Tucked down an alley beside the SPAR supermarket at 135 Dongshan Dadao T 071 7605 4300. Close to the bus station, tired but clean, this is possibly the cheapest hotel in town for foreigners. **¥80**

★ **Manor** 山庄商务酒店, shānzhuāng shāngwù jiǔdiàn. 105 Dongshan Dadao T 071 7608 4500. Budget hotel comforts with smart new rooms, comfortable beds and modern en suites; a steal for the price (if you ignore the odd scuff mark). Up off the street behind a small terraced garden. **¥180**

Rest Motel 锐思特汽车连锁酒店, ruìsītè qìchēliánsuǒ jiǔdiàn. 31 Yunji Lu T 071 7623 6888. Similar to the *Manor* and even cheaper, though rooms are not as spacious. **¥160**

Yichang International 宜昌国际大酒店, yíchāng guójì dàjiǔdiàn. 121 Yanjiang Dadao T 071 7886 6999. This dated hotel is still one of Yichang's most upmarket options, featuring its own brewery, a revolving restaurant and 24hr café. **¥598**

EATING AND DRINKING

Cheap **Chinese staples** can be found at the handful of stir-fry places near the bridge along Yanjiang Dadao.

1819 Music Pub. Yunji Lu. Popular bar, packed out most nights with live bands or DJs.

Beijing Jiaozi Guan 北京饺子馆, běijīng jiǎozi guǎn. Shengli Si Lu. Informal northern-style dumpling restaurant, where you order lamb, beef, pork or vegetarian fillings by weight. A good place for an inexpensive, filling meal.

Daoxiangge 稻香阁, dào xiāng gé. 31 Shengli Si Lu. Moderately flash establishment, whose repertoire stretches from Chinese staples through to game meats. If you've spent four days eating plain food on public ferries, this will get you back on track. There's an English menu of sorts, but it's easier to use the Chinese photo-version. Mains around ¥40.

New Noble 新贵族, xīn guìzú. Yunji Lu. One of several English-signed cafés in the vicinity serving good coffee and Western-style pizza, pasta and steak. Around ¥35/head.

Tujia Fengwei Lou 土家风味楼, tǔjiā fēngwèi lóu. 33 Yi Ma Lu. Tujia home-style dishes, from an ethnic group spread through western Hubei and Hunan, into the Three Gorges area. Expect delicious, very spicy and sour flavours. Mains ¥15–40.

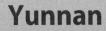

Yunnan

THE VIEW FROM FEILAI TEMPLE, PAST THE LANCANG
RIVER VALLEY TO MEILI XUE SHAN

Yunnan

Yunnan (云南, yúnnán) has always been remote from mainstream China, set high on the country's distant frontiers with Tibet, Burma, Vietnam and Laos, and shielded from the rest of the nation by the unruly, mountainous provinces of Sichuan and Guizhou. Ethnically diverse – Yunnan is home to half of China's 56 recognized minority nationalities – the province's terrain encompasses tropical jungle, deep river valleys, dry highlands and the magisterial mountains of the Tibetan plateau. The great events of China's history might not have been played out here, but Yunnan is crossed by ancient trade routes along which Chinese goods have been carried for millennia, bringing wealth to the nation – and which provided the earliest European visitors with their first impressions of the Chinese empire.

Yunnan's fairly flat, productive east is home to its easy-going capital, **Kunming**, whose mild climate earned the province its name ("Yunnan" means "South of the Clouds"). Spectacular rice terraces flanking the Hong He valley at **Yuanyang** are probably the best reason to linger in this side of the province, though it's hard to resist heading northwest towards Tibet via the famous old towns of **Dali**, **Lijiang** and **Shangri-La**, full of fairy lights, guides dolled up in ethnic costume and tour groups looking for "old China" among their narrow cobbled lanes and rustic wooden houses. If this fairground atmosphere grates at times, the surrounding countryside remains stunning, with Tibetan temples, rare animals and spellbinding scenery – not least the sight of a youthful Yangzi ripping through the chasm of **Tiger Leaping Gorge**, one of the deepest in the world.

Next to this, it's harder to justify the long trip west to **Tengchong** and the Burmese border, though volcanic remains and the border towns of **Wanding** and **Ruili** have an appealingly surreal edge to them. Southern **Xishuangbanna** is a more likely target, a wonderfully tropical pocket along the open border with Laos, whose forests, villages and cultures offer a complete break with the rest of China.

Yunnan is a major **hiking** destination, much of it fairly serious: there's an established, straightforward trail through Tiger Leaping Gorge, but die-hards will want to aim for **Meili Xue Shan**, right up on the Tibetan border, or the various routes over the extremely steep, high ranges of the **Three Parallel Rivers** – the Lancang (Mekong), Nu (Salween) and Jinsha (Yangzi) – which squeeze through adjacent valleys.

There are **international flights** into Kunming from Bangkok, Yangon, Singapore and Vientiane, and to Jinghong – near the border with Burma and Laos – from Chiang

Highlights

❶ **Rice terraces at Yuanyang** The Hong He valley's tall, sculpted flanks create a vivid backdrop to rural markets, Hani hamlets and easy country walks. **See p.199**

❷ **Market day at Shaxi** See the old Tea-Horse Road days return as this normally sleepy mud-brick village fills to bursting with Bai farmers, livestock and seasonal produce. **See p.216**

❸ **Tiger Leaping Gorge** Make a spectacular two-day trek between isolated villages, following a youthful Yangzi through one of the world's deepest gorges. **See p.233**

❹ **Meili Xue Shan** Enjoy stunning sunrises, glaciers, hot springs and tough trekking around

this row of thirteen icy mountain peaks, right on the edge of the Himalayan plateau. **See p.243**

❺ **Yunnan Snub-Nosed Monkey National Park** Track down one of the world's most endangered monkeys at this largely undeveloped spread of high-altitude cloud forest. **See p.231**

❻ **The Nu Jiang Valley** Yunnan's last undeveloped corner, up against the Tibetan and Burmese borders, offers scope for more cross-country exploration between isolated mountain villages. **See p.245**

❼ **Xishuangbanna** Tropical pocket of forest and farmland along the Burmese and Laoatian borders, home to the Dai and a dozen or more other ethnic groups. **See p.256**

HIGHLIGHTS ARE MARKED ON THE MAP ON P.180–181

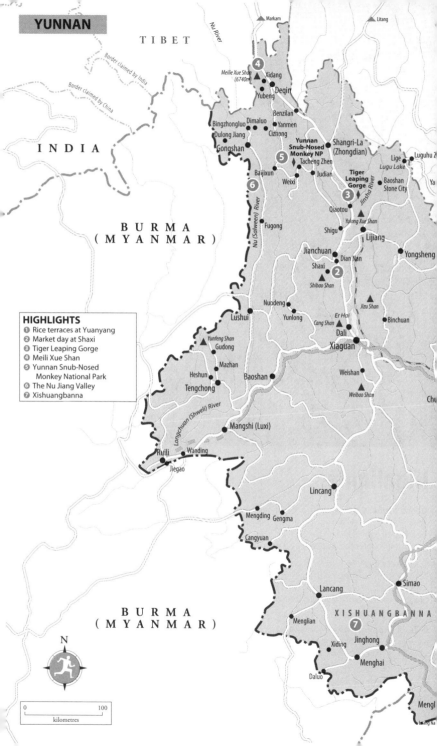

YUNNAN

T I B E T

Nu River

Markam

Litang

Meilie Xue Shan (6740m)

Xidang

Deqin

Yubeng

Benzilan

Bingzhongluo

Dimaluo

Yanmen

Dulong Jiang

Ciziiong

Gongshan

Yunnan Snub-Nosed Monkey NP

Tacheng Zhen

Shangri-La (Zhongdian)

Lige

Luguhu 2

Lugu Lake

Ya

Baijixun

Weixi

Judian

Tiger Leaping Gorge

Baoshan Stone City

Jinsha River

I N D I A

Border claimed by India

Border claimed by China

Qiaotou

Yulong Xue Shan

Fugong

Shigu

Lijiang

Yongsheng

Jianchuan

Dian Nan

Shaxi

Shibao Shan

Nuodeng

Yunlong

Jizu Shan

B U R M A
(M Y A N M A R)

Nu (Salween) River

Lushui

Er Hai

Cang Shan

Binchuan

Dali

Xiaguan

Weishan

Weibao Shan

HIGHLIGHTS
① Rice terraces at Yuanyang
② Market day at Shaxi
③ Tiger Leaping Gorge
④ Meili Xue Shan
⑤ Yunnan Snub-Nosed Monkey National Park
⑥ The Nu Jiang Valley
⑦ Xishuangbanna

Yunfeng Shan

Gudong

Mazhan

Heshun

Baoshan

Tengchong

Longchuan (Shweli) River

Mangshi (Luxi)

Ruili

Wanding

Jiegao

Lincang

Mengding

Gengma

Cangyuan

Lancang

Simao

B U R M A
(M Y A N M A R)

Menglian

X I S H U A N G B A N N A
⑦

Chu

N

Xiding

Jinghong

Menghai

Daluo

Mengl

0   100
kilometres

YUNNANESE FOOD

Yunnanese food is generally spicy and sour, and splits broadly into three cooking styles. In the north, the cold, pastoral lifestyle produces **dried meats** and – very unusually for China – **dairy products**, fused with Muslim cuisine, a vestige of the thirteenth-century Mongolian invasion. Typical dishes include **wind-cured ham** (火腿, huǒtuǐ), sweetened, steamed and served with slices of bread; dried cheese or yoghurt wafers (乳扇, rǔshàn or 乳饼, rǔbǐng); the local version of **crisp-skinned duck** (烧鸭, shāoyā), flavoured with Sichuan peppercorns – you'll see drum-shaped metal duck ovens outside many restaurants – and fish casseroles, served in an attractive clay pot (沙锅鱼, shāguō yú).

Eastern Yunnan produces the most recognizably "Chinese" food. From here comes **steam-pot chicken** (气锅鸡, qìguō jī) flavoured with medicinal herbs and stewed inside a specially shaped earthenware steamer, and **crossing-the-bridge noodles** (过桥米线, guòqiáo mǐxiàn), a sort of individualized hotpot eaten as a cheap snack all over the province; you pay by the size of the bowl. The curious name comes from a tale of a Qing scholar who retired every day to a lakeside pavilion to compose poetry. His wife, an understanding soul, used to cook him lunch, but the food always cooled as she carried it from their home over the bridge to where he studied – until she hit on the idea of keeping the heat in with a layer of oil on top of his soup.

Not surprisingly, Yunnan's south is strongly influenced by Burmese, Lao and, especially, **Thai cooking**, featuring such un-Chinese ingredients as lime juice, coconut, palm sugar, cloves and turmeric. Here you'll find a vast range of soups and stews, roughly recognizable as curries, displayed in aluminium pots outside fast-turnover restaurants, and oddities such as purple rice-flour pancakes sold at street markets. The south is also famous in China for producing good **coffee** and red **pu'er tea**, a favourite brew in Hong Kong and Tibet.

Mai and Bangkok. Getting around can be time-consuming, thanks to Yunnan's sheer scale, but **roads** are often surprisingly good, with new expressways springing up at a regular rate. Yunnan's limited **rail network** is expanding too, with recently completed services to Dali and Lijiang making these popular destinations more accessible than ever. You can also head into **western Sichuan** via Lijiang or Shangri-La (see p.141), although **traveling overland to Tibet** (see p.64) was not possible at the time of writing.

The **weather** is broadly warm and dry throughout the year, though northwestern Yunnan has extremely cold winters, and southern summers feature a torrential wet season. Roads in remoter areas are often closed, usually because of roadworks, but sometimes due to clampdowns on cross-border traffic in timber, gems and **opiates** – much of Asia's illegal drug production originates in Burma and is funnelled through China to overseas markets. The Yunnanese government is tough on the drugs trade, executing traffickers and forcibly rehabilitating addicts. All this means that there are military **checkpoints** on many rural roads, where you'll have to show passports.

Brief history

Yunnan's earliest history is murky, and its first known contact with the rest of the country was when the warrior-prince Zhuang Qiao broke away from central China's state of Chu and founded the pastoral **Dian Kingdom** near modern Kunming in 339 BC. The Dian were an aristocratic slave society, who vividly recorded their daily life in occasionally gruesome **bronze models** (see p.186); "Dian" is still a colloquial term for Yunnan. In 109 AD the kingdom was acknowledged by the Chinese emperor Wu, who funded the building of military **roads** through the province into neighbouring Burma, which were later incorporated into a wider web of trade routes. The Dian Kingdom ended up being propped up by the Chinese, and didn't survive the collapse of the Han empire in 220 AD, after which the region fragmented into competing statelets.

In the eighth century, an aspiring local prince named Piluoge invited all his rivals to dinner at Dali, set fire to the tent with them inside, took their lands, and founded the

Nanzhao Kingdom. His rule rapidly expanded to include much of modern Burma, Thailand and Vietnam, though in 937 the Bai warlord Duan Siping toppled the Nanzhao and set up a smaller **Dali Kingdom**, which in turn survived until Kublai Khan and his Mongolian hordes descended in 1252. Twenty years later the Mongols were ruling all China as the Yuan dynasty, and **Yunnan province** had been created to incorporate this distant territory. Directly governed by China for the first time, Yunnan served for a while as a remote dumping ground for political troublemakers, escaping the population explosions, wars and migrations that plagued the eastern provinces. However, the Mongol invasion had introduced a large **Muslim population** who, angered by their deteriorating status under the Chinese, staged a rebellion in 1856 (see box, below). Seventeen years of warfare ensued, and a wasted Yunnan was left to bandits and private armies for the next half-century.

Modern Yunnan

Strangely, it was the **Japanese invasion** of China during the 1930s that sparked a resurgence of Yunnan's fortunes. Blockaded into southwestern China, the **Guomindang government** initiated great programmes of rail and road building through the region – not least constructing the **Burma Road** to ferry supplies through Yunnan to Chongqing. After the war, the Maoist era didn't bring much joy, and it's only recently that Yunnan has finally benefited from its forced association with the rest of the country. Never agriculturally rich – only a tenth of the land is considered arable – the province looks to mineral resources, **tourism** and its potential as a future conduit between China and the much discussed, but as yet unformed, trading bloc of **Vietnam, Laos, Thailand** and **Burma**. Should these countries ever form an unrestricted economic alliance, the amount of trade passing through Yunnan would be immense, and highways, rail and air services have already been planned for the day the borders open freely.

3

THE MUSLIM UPRISING

Muslim **Hui** had first arrived in Yunnan with the Mongols in 1254, but there were few integration problems until Han migrants from eastern China begin to put pressure on resources during the eighteenth century. The Hui became targets for disaffection because, as shopkeepers, they controlled local economies, and because they ate lamb and beef, which disgusted the Chinese (lambs, which kneel to suckle, were seen as filial creatures; while cattle were companions in work, not food). After scuffles at a silver mine led to a village near Kunming being torched by Muslims in 1856, Kunming's governor issued a proclamation against rioting that was interpreted by local vigilantes as an official sanction to get rid of the Hui. On 19 May, 1856, the gates of Kunming were locked and the city's Muslim population slaughtered by the mob.

Once word got out, Yunnan's Muslim community rose in revolt, led at first by the charismatic **Ma Julong**. His army laid siege to Kunming the next year, and butchered all the Chinese who lived outside the city walls – some seventy percent of the capital's population. Meanwhile, Muslims in **Dali** kicked out the Chinese governor and set up an Islamic state, led by **Du Wenxiu**. The Qing government – already overstretched by the ongoing Taiping (see p.344) and Miao (see p.288) insurrections– was forced to negotiate. In return for ending his siege of Kunming, Ma Julong was given an official pardon, a government position and orders to pacify the rest of Yunnan.

It was not an easy task. His first attempts against Dali backfired, provoking Du Wenxiu to storm eastwards in retaliation and lay his own siege to Kunming in 1868, which was only defeated by the timely appointment of seasoned campaigner **Chen Yuying** as Yunnan's governor. Having chased Du back west, Chen posted Ma off to conquer southern Yunnan and sent his own forces to take Dali. Chinese troops stormed the city in 1873 and massacred over ten thousand Muslims, including Du Wenxiu, effectively ending the uprising.

Kunming

昆明, kūnmíng

Basking 2000m above sea level in the warm, fertile heart of the Yunnan plateau, **KUNMING** does its best to justify its traditional nickname, the City of Eternal Spring. A distinctly modern, well-organized and – above all – **unpolluted** city with an orderly traffic system (considering it has four million residents to shift around), Kunming's laidback population includes a large number of students and Western expats, the latter often deliberately fleeing eastern China's more crowded, hectic metropolises. Coupled with abundant restaurants and nightlife, Kunming is an enjoyable place to hang out for a few days while organizing international visas and planning your next move, though there are surprisingly few sights in the city itself – the **Yuantong Temple**, **Yunnan Museum** and shopping around central **Jingxing market** are the highlights. Once you've worked through these, good trips **around Kunming** (see p.193) can fill in a day or two, and then you'll be happy to move on.

Brief history

The domain of Yunnan's **Dian Kingdom** (see p.182), Kunming long profited from its position on the caravan roads through to Burma and Europe, though it remained a distant trade outpost for much of its history. It was visited in the thirteenth century by **Marco Polo**, who found the locals of Yachi Fu ("Duck Pond Town") using cowries for cash and eating their meat raw. Little of the city survived the 1856 **Muslim uprising** (see p.183), and forty years later the city was again destroyed during a revolt against working conditions on the French-owned Kunming–Haiphong rail line, when 300,000 labourers were executed.

In the 1930s, war with Japan brought a flock of wealthy east-coast refugees to the city, whose money helped establish Kunming as an industrial and manufacturing base for the wartime government in Chongqing. The allies provided essential support, importing materials along the **Burma Road** from British-held Burma and, when that was lost to the Japanese, with the help of the US-piloted **Flying Tigers** (see p.152), who escorted supply planes over the Himalayas from British bases in India. The city consolidated its position as a supply depot during the Vietnam War and subsequent border clashes and today is profiting from snowballing tourism and foreign investment. Neighbouring nations such as Thailand trace their ancestries back to Yunnan and have proved particularly willing to channel funds into the city, which has become ever more accessible as a result.

The city centre

Kunming's public focus lies west of the **Panlong River** in the crowded shopping district sandwiched between Renmin Zhong Lu and Jinbi Lu, where the **Nanping Jie** and **Zhengyi Lu** intersection marks a **pedestrianized** shopping precinct packed with modern clothing and department stores. Formerly at the heart of Kunming's Muslim community, there are echoes of former times here in **Jingxing market**, though the main sight is the **Yunnan Provincial Museum**, full of ancient bronzes. Zhengyi Lu runs south to **Jinbi Square** (金碧广场, jīnbì guǎngchǎng), whose huge ornamental stone gateways make it a distinctive landmark – they look great at night, lit up with coloured bulbs.

Jingxing Jie

京星街, jīngxīng jiē

West off Zhengyi Lu, narrow **Jingxing Jie** has long hosted Kunming's antique, flower and bird **market** (京星街花鸟珠宝世界, jīngxīng jiē huā niǎo zhūbǎo shìjiè), a great place to browse the jumble of streetside stalls. It's best at weekends, when bird dealers turn out en masse with their magpies, waxwings, cuckoos and hoopoes, along with dodgy

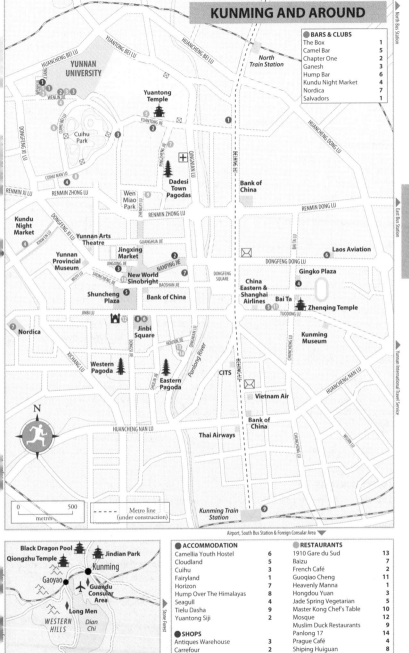

KUNMING AND AROUND

BARS & CLUBS

The Box	1
Camel Bar	5
Chapter One	2
Ganesh	3
Hump Bar	6
Kundu Night Market	4
Nordica	7
Salvadors	1

North Bus Station

East Bus Station

Yunnan International Travel Service

3

● ACCOMMODATION

Camellia Youth Hostel	6
Cloudland	5
Cuihu	3
Fairyland	1
Horizon	7
Hump Over The Himalayas	8
Seagull	4
Tielu Dasha	9
Yuantong Siji	2

● SHOPS

Antiques Warehouse	3
Carrefour	2
Gingko Shopping Plaza	4
Mandarin Books	1
Shuncheng Plaza	5

● RESTAURANTS

1910 Gare du Sud	13
Baizu	7
French Café	2
Guoqiao Cheng	11
Heavenly Manna	1
Hongdou Yuan	3
Jade Spring Vegetarian	5
Master Kong Chef's Table	10
Mosque	12
Muslim Duck Restaurants	9
Panlong 17	14
Prague Café	4
Shiping Huiguan	8
Yingjiang Daiwei Yuan	6

Airport, South Bus Station & Foreign Consular Area ▼

characters trying to unload lizards, monkeys, slow lorises and other oddities illegally collected from southern Yunnan's tropical forests. Other stalls sell jewellery and a generous cross section of generic souvenirs, brass-bound bamboo water pipes, swords, paintings and fishing gear; for **antiques** – or at least decent reproductions – head to the warehouse-sized indoor market between here and Guanghua Jie.

Jingxing Jie was once lined in old timber buildings, and while most have gone, the **Fulin Tang Pharmacy** (福林堂, fúlín táng), founded in 1857, survives on the corner with Sanshi Jie. The dusty interior, with its stuffed deer and ancient wooden cabinets, makes it look misleadingly like a period relic, but the company in fact runs a national chain with its own brand of medicines.

Wen Miao Park

文庙公园, wénmiào gōngyuán

Just north of Jingxing market over Renmin Zhong Lu, this tiny **garden** once attached to a vanished Confucian temple is one of the few places in Kunming that actually feels old. There's not much to it – an avenue of pines, an ancient pond and pavilion, and beds of bamboo, azaleas and potted palms – but the park is a calm spot, inhabited by elderly locals, who sit around in the shade drinking tea and playing chess.

Yunnan Provincial Museum

云南省博物馆, yúnnánshěng bówùguǎn • Dongfeng Xi Lu • Daily 9am–5pm • Free except special exhibitions

Not much was known about Yunnan's Dian Kingdom until 1955, when antiques being peddled at Kunming's Jingxing market led archeologists to 2000-year-old **grave sites** surrounding Dian Chi, south of the city. Hundreds of **bronzes** since unearthed are now on display at the **Yunnan Provincial Museum**, just west of the market; finds include weapons, sculptures of bulls and horses, an ornamental plate of a tiger attacking an ox, and a coffin in the shape of a bamboo house. Lids from cowrie **storage drums** (see p.350) are the most impressive, decorated with elaborate dioramas of battles and ceremonies, including a gory example of crowds attending what appears to be a human sacrifice – note the "king" up on the platform, surrounded by drums, his symbol of power. It's not all savagery; one of the liveliest pieces is a **belt buckle** in the shape of two dancing musicians. A replica of the Chinese imperial **gold seal** given to the Dian king early in the second century implies that his aristocratic slave society at least had the tacit approval of the Han emperor.

There's also a fine top-floor collection of ethnic **textiles** and **writing**, including Dongpa pictograms from Lijiang (see p.220) and Bai batik from the Dali area.

Two Pagodas

Two elegant **Tang-dynasty pagodas**, each a solid thirteen storeys of whitewashed brick crowned with four jolly iron cockerels, rise a short walk south of the city centre. Their square, layered, tapering design could almost be an emblem of the contemporary Nanzhao Kingdom (though the pattern survived well into the subsequent Dali Kingdom era), and you'll find similar ones throughout the Nanzhao's former territory, most notably at Dali (p.212) and atop Jizu Shan (p.204). The **Eastern Pagoda** (东寺塔, dōngsì tǎ) on Shulin Jie sits in a little garden, while the Western Pagoda (西寺塔, xīsì tǎ) is a few minutes' walk away at the back of a flagstoned square on Dongsi Jie. You can't enter either, but the sight of these 1300-year-old towers surrounded by modern office blocks is striking.

Cuihu Park

翠湖公园, cuìhú gōngyuán • Daily dawn–10pm • Free

Cuihu Park is essentially a small lake whose central islands, planted with plum, bamboo and magnolias, are interconnected by bridges and causeways. It's where people come to unwind, the haunt of amateur musicians and opera singers and full of crowds sauntering, exercising, or feeding wintering flocks of **black-headed gulls**. The main entrances are at the south, north and east of the park, and **Cuihu Lu** is lined with restaurants and bars, which spill into adjacent **Wenlin Jie**, the best place in the city to look for a drink and a feed (see p.190). Immediately north of the park, the **Yunnan University** campus offers a glimpse of old Kunming, its partially overgrown 1920s exterior reached via a wide flight of stone steps.

Yuantong Temple

圆通寺, yuántōng sì · Yuantong Jie · Daily 9am–5.30pm · ¥6

East from Cuihu Park along Yuantong Jie, **Yuantong Temple** was founded during the Tang dynasty, later expanded to become Kunming's main Chan (Zen) sect Buddhist monastery. You walk downhill into the complex, to where a green pond, inhabited by goldfish and turtles, is crossed by a bridge. In the middle there's a **pavilion** housing a Guanyin statue: the usually benevolent deity is portrayed in her warrior aspect, managing to look firm but fair. On the far side, the main hall's Buddhist trinity is completely overshadowed by two brilliant, 10m-high **dragons**, one blue, one red, claws bared as they coil around supporting pillars, facing off at each other.

South of the temple, there's a sad reminder of old times at the **Dadesi Twin Pagodas** (大德寺双塔, dàdésì shuāng tǎ), signed in Chinese at 43 Huashan Dong Lu. Surrounded by ugly concrete apartment blocks and in a bad state of repair, these 20m-high towers date to the sixteenth century and are all that's left of the Dade Temple; an ancient pine tree stands between them.

Zhenqing Temple

真庆观, zhēnqìng guàn · Free

East of the Panlong River on Tuodong Lu, **Zhenqing Temple** is an active Taoist complex founded in 1419 and recently rebuilt in traditional stone and red-lacquered timber. You're greeted by a golden statue of **Wang Lingguan**, a fierce protective deity with a severed demon's head as his belt buckle, wielding an iron pagoda and giving the finger to potential troublemakers. Inside, further statues from the Taoist pantheon sit below a ceiling made from intricately connected wooden brackets, while the cloisters are used for music recitals. The adjacent **Dulei Mansion** (都雷府, dūléi fǔ) houses a globe carried on the back of a turtle, covered in symbols illustrating the interactions between different directions, stars and zodiac animals.

Just north on Baita Lu, **Bai Ta** (白塔, bái tǎ) is a restored old stone gate tower and **Tibetan Buddhist stupa**, looking lost alongside one of Kunming's modern main roads. An attached photograph shows the same street in 1900.

Kunming Museum

昆明市博物馆, kūnmíngshì bówùguǎn · Tuodong Lu · Tues–Sun 9am–5pm · Free

Though there are more bronze drums and even some dinosaur fossils here, the highlight of the **Kunming Museum** is the **Dali Sutra Pillar**, an 8m-high, pagoda-like sculpture in pink sandstone, dating back to Yunnan's Dali Kingdom. Its octagonal base supports seven tiers covered in beatific Buddha images, statues of fierce guardian gods standing on subjugated demons, and a mix of Tibetan and Chinese **script**. Part is a religous mantra, the rest is a dedication, identifying the pillar as having been raised by the Dali regent, Yuan Douguang, in memory of an official named Gao Ming. The whole thing is topped by a ring of Buddhas carrying a ball – the universe – above them, and the pillar is full of a vitality and energy that later seeped out of the mainstream of Chinese sculpture.

Daguan Park

大观公园, dàguān gōngyuán • Daily 7am–8pm • Free • Bus #4 from Dongfeng Lu

Originally laid out during the Ming dynasty, Daguan Park is the largest in Kunming, set about 3km southwest of the centre on Daguan Stream, which flows south into Dian Chi (see p.194). There's a modern funfair here, but the park's original focal point is the square, three-storeyed **Daguan Tower** (大观楼, dàguān lóu), built to better enjoyment of the distant Western Hills and now a storehouse of calligraphy extolling the area's charms. The tower's most famous poem is a 118-character verse, carved into the gateposts by the Qing scholar **Sun Ran**; it's reputed to be the longest set of rhyming couplets in China.

ARRIVAL AND DEPARTURE
KUNMING

Aside from the train station, all **arrival points** are well outside the city centre – allow plenty of time to reach them. Departing to **Dali** (note that all "Dali" transport terminates at Xiaguan), express buses from the Western Bus Station are faster than rail; for **Lijiang**, the night train is perfectly timed, leaving late and arriving at dawn. Note too that "Shangri-La" also appears as "Zhongdian" on timetables.

BY PLANE
Kunming International Airport (昆明国际机场, kūnmíng guójì jīchǎng) is 15km southeast, with the international and domestic terminal buildings next to each other. Outside you'll find bus #A2, which runs through town via Tuodong Lu, Bai Ta Lu and Qingnian Lu; alternatively, bus #52 terminates at the Dongfeng Xi Lu–Renmin Zhong Lu intersection near Cuihu Park. A taxi into town costs ¥25–35 and can take 40min, depending on traffic. When opened after 2013, the metro should reach the airport too. For tickets, China Eastern and Shanghai Airlines headquarters share offices on Tuodong Lu (☎087 1316 4270, ⌨travelsky.com). Agents around town all offer the same fares.
International airline offices Laos Aviation, *Camellia Hotel*, 154 Dongfeng Dong Lu (☎087 1316 3000; daily 9.30am–5pm); Thai Airways, *Jinjiang Hotel*, 98 Beijing Lu (☎087 1351 1515, ✉reservation.kmg@thaiairways.com .cn; Mon–Fri 9am–5.30pm); Vietnam Air, near the Vietnamese consulate, 2F, Tower C, *Kai Wah Plaza Hotel*, 157 Beijing Lu (☎087 1351 5850).
Destinations Beijing (5 daily; 4hr 30min); Chengdu (8 daily; 1hr 10min); Chongqing (5 daily; 1hr 10min); Deqin ((for Shangri-La); 4 daily; 1hr); Guilin (1 daily; 1hr 20min); Guiyang (6 daily; 1hr 15min); Jinghong (8 daily; 1hr); Lijiang (8 daily; 50min); Mangshi (7 daily; 1hr); Nanning (4 daily; 1hr 10min); Shanghai (14 daily; 3hr); Shenzhen (4 daily; 2hr); Tengchong (4 daily; 1hr); Xi'an (7 daily; 2hr).

BY BUS
Buses leave from several stations (see box, opposite).
Destinations Baoshan (10hr; ¥198); Deqin (18hr; ¥240); Jianshui (3hr; ¥73); Jinghong (10hr; ¥180–260); Hekou (5hr; ¥83); Lijiang (9hr; ¥180); Shangri-La (13hr; ¥220); Tengchong (8hr; ¥170); Xiaguan (for Dali; 5hr; ¥138); Yuanyang (5hr; ¥128).

BY TRAIN
Kunming train station is down at the southern end of Beijing Lu. Departures are upstairs and the ticket office (daily 5am–11pm) downstairs. Aside from the metro up Beijing Lu, useful buses from here include #23 up Beijing Lu, and #59, which heads up Qingnian Lu to within striking distance of Yuantong Temple and Cuihu Park. If you're immediately heading onwards, there's also bus #C71 to the South Bus Station and buses #C72 or #80 to the Western Bus Station.
Destinations Anshun (12 daily; 10hr); Beijing (2 daily; 40hr); Chengdu (5 daily; 20hr); Chongqing (3 daily; 24hr); Dali (Xiaguan; 3 daily; 7hr); Emei Shan (3 daily; 16hr); Guilin (2 daily; 17hr); Guiyang (12 daily; 11hr); Lijiang (2 daily; 7hr 45min); Nanning (7 daily; 12hr); Panzhihua (5 daily; 5–11hr); Shanghai (3 daily; 38hr); Xichang (4 daily; 9hr).

GETTING AROUND
Kunming's rush hours, when roads become pretty clogged, are 7–9am and 5–7pm. Currently under construction, the city's first two metro lines – running north from the train station up Beijing Lu, and north up Chuncheng Lu – are due for completion in 2013. An east–west line is planned for 2016.
By bus Services operate from about 6pm until 9pm or later (¥1–2); they're very slow but useful for some sights.
By taxi Taxis ¥8 to hire; they're very cost-effective for outlying sights and transit points if you're in a group.
By bicycle The hostels all rent bikes for ¥3/hr, plus passport or ¥500 deposit.

INFORMATION

TOURIST INFORMATION
Aimed at foreign residents, GoKunming (⌨gokunming .com) is an excellent source of up-to-date listings, articles and general background information about all aspects of

KUNMING'S BUS STATIONS

Kunming's many **bus stations** are scattered around the city perimeter, generally at the point of the compass relevant to the destination. Allow plenty of transit time, even in a cab, especially during rush hours. Agents in town might be willing to buy tickets for a fee, otherwise you'll have to get out to the stations yourself.

The **Western Bus Station** (西部汽车客运站, xībù qìchē kèyùn zhàn), also known as **Majie Bus Station** (马街客运站, mǎjiē kèyùn zhàn), is 10km out towards the Western Hills. It deals with traffic to Xiaguan (Dali), Lijiang, Shangri-La (Zhongdian) and Deqin; and also Tengchong and Ruili. Arriving here, buses into Kunming include #82 to the western end of Nanping Jie and #C72 to Kunming train station; a taxi is ¥30.

The **South Bus Station** (南部汽车客运站, nánbù qìchē kèyùn zhàn) is 15km southeast, past the airport, serving Jianshui, Yuanyang, Hekou, Xishuangbanna, and Luang Prabang in Laos. Take bus #C71 to Kunming train station, or a taxi for ¥45.

The **East Bus Station** (东部汽车客运站, dōngbù qìchē kèyùn zhàn), 10km out, is for services to Shilin (for the Stone Forest) and points east, plus Hekou on the Vietnam border. Bus #60 runs to Kunming train station via Bailong Lu; a taxi costs ¥30.

Finally, unless arriving from Panzhihua in Sichuan, you're unlikely to find yourself at the **North Bus Station** (北部汽车客运站, běibù qìchē kèyùn zhàn), from where bus #23 heads through town to Kunming train station; or the **Northwest Bus Station** (西北部汽车客运站, xīběibù qìchē kèyùnzhàn), not linked to the city by any useful bus – catch a cab (¥35).

Note that in Kunming's listings and throughout the guide, where buses are **frequent** throughout the day (every 30min or more), we have not flagged departure frequencies.

3

the city and Yunnan. You can also read local news in English at ⓦen.kunming.cn.

AGENTS AND TOUR OPERATORS

These abound in Kunming, with accommodation travel services able to organize private tours around the city and to the Stone Forest (¥80/person), Dali (from ¥300/person), Lijiang (¥300) and Xishuangbanna (¥820), and to obtain visas and tickets for onwards travel. Expect to pay commissions of at least ¥20 for bus- or train-ticket reservations, though plane tickets shouldn't attract a mark-up.

CITS 328 Beijing Lu, Mon–Sat 9am–6pm ⓣ087 1315 7499, ⓦspringyunnan.com. Mostly concerned with organizing package tours to Lijiang, Xishuangbanna and Dali.

Mister Chen Rm 3116, *Camellia Hotel*, 154 Dongfeng Dong Lu ⓣ087 1318 8114. For flights and overland jeep trips to Lhasa in Tibet, if it becomes possible.

Yunnan International Travel Service (云南省国际旅行社, yúnnán shěng guójì lǚxíngshè) 111 Dongjiao Lu ⓣ087 1351 6008, ⓦfff33.com. Branches all over the city, offering the same as CITS.

ACCOMMODATION

There's a good range of **accommodation** in Kunming, fairly evenly spread around. Long Kunming's budget mainstay, the *Camellia* is in danger of being upstaged by newer, more centrally located hostels; if you've the money, the Cuihu Park area is the nicest place to stay.

BUDGET

Camellia Youth Hostel 茶花国际青年旅舍, cháhuā guójì qīngnián lǚshè. 96 Dongfeng Dong Lu ⓣ087 1837 4638, ⓦkmcamelliahotel.com. Skip the tired mid-range hotel out front for the youth hostel in a renovated rear wing, with a cheerful paint job, helpful staff and decent dorms. The tiny garden is a bonus. Take bus #2 or #23 from the main train station to Dongfeng Dong Lu, then any bus heading east for two stops. Dorms ¥35, doubles ¥120

Cloudland 大脚氏国际青年旅舍, dàjiǎoshì guójì qīngnián lǚshè. 23 Zhuantang Lu ⓣ087 1410 3777. Hard to find hostel, south off Xichang Lu near the Kundu Night Market, with the rooms in tiers around a

self-contained courtyard. Good café and hiking info for Tiger Leaping Gorge and Meili Xue Shan. Can be noisy, depending on who's staying, and the dorms are basic. Dorms ¥30, doubles ¥180

★ **Hump Over The Himalayas** 驼峰客栈, tuófēng kèzhàn. Jinbi Lu ⓣ087 1364 0359, ⓦthehumphostel.com. Three hundred police once raided this hostel but despite this wild reputation, today it's clean, organized and secure, with a comfy lounge-bar and rooftop terrace. The only downside is noise from surrounding nightclubs, but they'll give you earplugs if you ask. Dorms ¥35, double with en suite ¥150

Tielu Dasha 铁路大厦, tiělù dàshà. East side of Kunming train station square ☎ 087 1351 1996. Tidy, clean, faultless en-suite doubles in a standard budget hotel. The only reason this isn't the best deal for the price in the city is that it's a drab location and you're miles from anywhere interesting. **¥108**

HOTELS

★ **Cuihu** 翠湖宾馆, cuìhú bīnguǎn. Cuihu Nan Lu ☎ 087 1515 8888, ⊕ greenlakehotel.com. A long-established and good-value upmarket hotel in pleasant surroundings by Cuihu Park, with a fancy lobby complete with palm trees, and an excellent restaurant. Airport transfers can be arranged; all major credit cards are accepted. **¥1780**

Fairyland 四季酒店鼓楼店, sìjì jiǔdiàn gǔlóudiàn. 716 Beijing Lu ☎ 087 1628 5777. Budget business hotel, not in the smartest part of town but not far from Yuantong Temple and Cuihu Park either; cheaper rooms are tiny but pay a bit more and you get a

modern, comfortable place to stay. Bus #23 stops nearby. **¥198**

Horizon 天恒大酒店, tiānhéng dàjiǔdiàn. 432 Qingnian Lu ☎ 087 1318 6666, ⊕ horizonhotel.cn. A multi-starred place catering to conference delegates, with a mountain of marble in the lobby and an overflow of cafés and restaurants. Conveniently located in the town centre, though not as nicely sited as *Cuihu*. **¥1200**

Seagull 海鸥宾馆, hǎiōu bīnguǎn. 112 Cuihu Nan Lu ☎ 087 1531 5388. Set back off the south side of Cuihu Park, this budget business hotel has recently refurbished, plain but airy rooms, offering good value for the location. **¥200**

Yuantong Siji 圆通四季酒店, yuántōng sìjì jiǔdiàn. 88 Pingzhen Jie, diagonally across from Yuantong Temple ☎ 087 1515 0666. Spanking-new budget business hotel, stylish, smart and modern, with large rooms – hence a bit more expensive than usual for the type. **¥228**

EATING

Back lanes off Jinbi Lu host cheap **canteens** where you can battle with locals over grilled cheese, hotpots, casseroles, fried snacks rolled in chilli powder and loaves of meat-stuffed soda bread. There's a string of inexpensive **Muslim duck restaurants** on Huashan Nan Lu, southeast of Cuihu Park, but by far the best place to look for a feed is around **Cuihu Park** itself, especially along Wenlin Jie and its offshoot, Wenhua Xiang, home to scores of restaurants and foreigner-friendly bars.

THE CITY CENTRE

★ **1910 Gare du Sud** 1910火车南站, yījiǔyīlíng huǒchē nánzhàn. 8 Houxin Jie ☎ 087 1316 9486. Modern take on rural Yunnanese fare served in a former French colonial train station; there's a large balcony and courtyard and photos of colonial Kunming throughout. It's a popular place with trendy middle-class locals but not as expensive as service and decor would suggest, and two can eat very well for ¥100.

Guoqiao Cheng 过桥城, guòqiáo chéng. Tuodong Lu. An airy, busy food-court specializing in crossing-the-bridge noodles, *qiguo* and stir-fries. Not worth crossing town for, but useful for the museum and Zhenqing Temple. Dishes from ¥10.

Master Kong Chef's Table 康师傅私房牛肉面, kāng shīfu sīfáng niúròu miàn. Nanping Jie. Bright, clean and fairly smart Taiwan-style noodle bar specializing in beef noodle soups from about ¥25. Also juices, pearl milk drinks and sweet coconut desserts. An easy, convenient place for a light lunch.

Mosque 永宁清真寺餐厅, yǒngníng qīngzhēnsì cāntīng. Corner of Jinbi Lu and Dong Si Lu. Take the steps up from the shops at street level on Dong Si Lu to the mosque courtyard, where stalls serving all sorts of Chinese snacks for a few yuan each are arranged down one side. The restaurant beyond is more formal, with crisp-skinned chicken for ¥25.

Panlong 17 盘龙7号滇味家园, pánlóng qīhào

diānwèi jiāyuán. 17 Panlong Jie ☎ 087 1310 1817. Directly south of *1910 Gare du Sud*, and in a similarly stylish vintage building with courtyard garden and gallery bar. Menu is Yunnanese with an emphasis on cold-meat platters; the staff may be a little flustered with foreigners. ¥30/dish.

AROUND CUIHU PARK

Baizu 白族饭店, báizú fàndiàn. 68 Pingzheng Jie, not far from the Yuantong Temple. Looks like a standard stir-fry restaurant; in fact, serves hot-and-sour Bai food from the Dali area (see p.210). There's no English spoken or photo-menu, so bring some Chinese or point to what others are eating. Mains such as fish casserole from ¥18.

French Café 兰白红咖啡, lánbáihóng kāfēi. 70 Wenlin Jie. Rude staff but great pastries (especially the strawberry cheesecake) and first-rate arabica coffee at just ¥8 a cup. Upstairs gets a bit smoky.

★ **Heavenly Manna** 吗哪, manǎ. 74 Wenhua Xiang ☎ 087 1536 9399. Varied, interesting and very spicy home-style Yunnanese dishes. Setting is crowded, no-frills wooden tables and chairs; watch out for the low ceiling with protruding pipes upstairs. Try cumin beef, garlic duck, and a mint-leek salad. Mains around ¥20.

Hongdou Yuan 红豆圆餐厅, hóngdòuyuán cāntīng. 142 Wenlin Jie. A branch of the popular Sichuanese–Yunnanese chain, with an easy-to-follow

photo-menu. Not everything is spicy; they do excellent crisp-skinned duck with cut buns, cold-sliced pork, stewed spareribs and rice-coated pork slices. The deep-fried mandarin fish looks good too. Mains ¥25–45.

★**Jade Spring Vegetarian** 玉泉斋素食, yùquánzhāi sùshí. Near the Yuantong Temple, Yuantong Jie ☏087 1511 1809. An excellent place, reasonably priced and with a picture menu. It serves a mix of vegetable and imitation-meat dishes – the best of the latter are coconut-flavoured "spare ribs" (bamboo shoots, celery and fried bean-curd skin), "chicken" and fungus rolls (dried bean curd), and "fish" (deep-fried mashed potato served in a rich garlic and vinegar sauce). Mains ¥25.

Prague Café 布拉格咖啡馆, bùlāgé kāfēiguǎn. 40 Wenlin Jie. A good choice for whiling away a wet afternoon.

There's a big range of coffee and tea, and a small library; the downside is that tables are jammed in and it can feel cramped.

Shiping Huiguan 石屏会馆, shípíng huìguǎn. 24 Zhonghe Xiang, Cuihu Nan Lu ☏087 1362 7444. Tucked back off the street behind an ornamental archway and heavy stone wall (look for the name in Chinese on a blue background), this elegantly restored guildhall features a courtyard restaurant serving Yunnanese cuisine. Popular, so reservations are essential. ¥80/head should cover the bill.

Yingjiang Daiwei Yuan 盈江傣味园, yíngjiāng dǎiwèi yuán. 66 Cuihu Bei Lu, opposite the park entrance ☏087 1533 7889. Thai food modified for Chinese palates, though including tasty favourites such as *laab*, pineapple rice, sour bamboo shoots and whole spicy grilled fish. ¥30/dish.

DRINKING AND NIGHTLIFE

Kunming's population of expats, students and arty Chinese means it's a great place to go out, with plenty of reasonably priced **bars** and **clubs**. For information on the latest hot-spots and up-and-coming entertainment and cultural events, check out GoKunming (ⓦgokunming.com).

The Box 老夫子, lǎo fūzǐ. 69 Wenhua Xiang ⓦsaporeitalia.com.cn. Italian restaurant-bar popular with Chinese for its richly flavoured pizza, though Western regulars seem to favour the wine, ice cream and argumentative atmosphere.

Camel Bar 骆驼酒吧, luòtuo jiǔbā. 4 Tuodong Lu ⓦcamelbarkm.com. Relatively polished bar, with a lively, predominantly Chinese clientele. Downstairs there's a dancefloor, while the more laidback upstairs area is ideal for sitting over a coffee during the day.

Chapter One 146 Wenlin Jie ⓦchapteronekunming .com. Aussie-Brit pub with extensive beer and cocktail list, plus pub grub – shepherd's pie, pizza and steak. Cheap happy hour drinks daily 5–8pm.

Ganesh 印象阁, yìnxiàng gé. 156 Wenlin Jie. Sports bar with ice-cold imported beers, hefty wooden tables, big TV screens and terrible Indian food.

Hump Bar 驼峰酒吧, tuófēng jiǔbā. Jinbi Plaza, Jinbi Lu. Expats and backpackers from the hostel upstairs mix at this mellow, German-run venue, whose walls are

covered in Flying Tigers memorabilia (see p.152); there's a good range of domestic and imported beer, a small dance space and live rock and blues most weekends.

Kundu Night Market Off Xinwen Lu. A clutch of bars and discos with late-night restaurants and nail and tattoo parlours in between; stumble out of one venue and you fall straight into another. Everywhere's free to get in, but drinks cost at least ¥30.

Nordica 诺地卡, nuòdìkǎ. 101 Xiba Lu ☏087 1411 4692, ⓦtcgnordica.com. Gigs, club nights, theatre, art shows and talks inside an old factory converted into a complex of galleries, café and studio spaces. Kunming attracts a lot of artists, and *Nordica* is a good place to find them and their work.

Salvadors 沙尔瓦多咖啡馆, shāěrwǎduō kāfēiguǎn. 76 Wenhua Xiang ⓦsalvadors.cn. Expat-run and -populated, and somewhere to get information and conversation from slightly jaded, in-the-know foreign residents. Well-stocked bar with pavement taking overflow, plus good coffee and pub-style menu.

SHOPPING

Antiques There's a huge antiques warehouse between Guanghua Lu and the market on Jingxing Jie.

Books Mandarin Books at 52 Wenhua Xiang, near the university. Comprehensive English-language stock, including imported novels, obscure academic texts, translated Chinese novels, guidebooks and coffee-table works on China, all of it fairly pricey.

Department stores Gingko Shopping Plaza at 131 Baita Lu is full of international-brand clothing and accessory boutiques,

as is the Shuncheng Plaza on Nanping Jie, and the New World Sinobright on the Nanping Jie–Zhengyi Lu crossroads.

Supermarket Carrefour on Nanping Jie. A vast supermarket which includes a cache of imported Western foodstuffs, plus Yunnan ham sold in slices, chunks and entire hocks.

Tea Yunnan's famous *pu'er* tea, usually compressed into attractive "bricks" stamped with good-luck symbols, is sold almost everywhere – Carrefour has a decent range.

DIRECTORY

Banks The main branch of the Bank of China (Mon–Fri 9am–5.30pm) is at the corner of Beijing Lu and Renmin Dong Lu. There are smaller branches and ATMs all through the centre.

Cinema The Broadway Cinema (ⓦb-cinema.cn; ¥50–120), inside the Shuncheng Plaza between Shuncheng Jie and Jinbi Lu, shows some films in English. There's an IMAX screen here too for 3D releases.

Consulates A new Foreign Consular Area (官渡区外国领馆区, guāndùqū wàiguó lǐngguǎnqū) has opened 13km southeast of Kunming in Guandu District, and some of the following may relocate. Visas for these countries can also be obtained through travel agents. Burma (Myanmar), 99 Yingbin Lu, Foreign Consular Area, Mon–Fri 8.30am–noon & 1–4.30pm – closed during Burmese public holidays; Cambodia, Floor 20, *Jinquan Hotel*, 93 Renmin Dong Lu ☏087 1331 7320; Laos, Caiyuan Bei Lu, Foreign Consular Area ☏087 1733 5489, Mon–Fri 8.30–11.30am & 1.30–4.30pm – they take three working days to issue visas and charge according to the applicant's nationality; Thailand, in a building in front of the *Kunming* hotel on Dongfeng Dong Lu ☏087 1316 8916, Mon–Fri 9am–noon & 1–5pm; Vietnam, 507 Hongta Mansion, 155 Beijing Lu ☏087 1352 2669, ⓦvietnamconsulate-kunming.org,

Mon–Fri 9–11.30am, 30-day visas cost ¥400–600 depending on how quickly you want them.

Hospital The First People's Hospital of Yunnan Province, 172 Jinli Lu ☏087 1363 4031. For Traditional Chinese Medicine treatments, including acupuncture, visit the Sheng Ai Hospital (圣爱中医馆, shèng ài zhōngyī guǎn), opposite the Yuantong Temple.

Internet Most accommodation and foreign-friendly cafés have terminals and/or free wi-fi.

Left luggage If accommodation can't help, the train station left luggage office (6am–11pm) charges ¥3/item/day.

Mail The GPO is towards Kunming train station at 231 Beijing Lu (daily 8am–7pm).

Massage Blind masseur studios around town charge ¥35/hr for either feet or full body treatments – one is diagonally across from *The Box* bar on Wenhua Xiang.

PSB and Visa Extensions Exit and Entry Administration Service Centre (公安局西山分局出入境办证大厅, gōngānjú xīshānfēnjú chūrùjìng bànzhèng dàtīng) 123 Xingyuan Rd, Xishan District ☏087 1823 6900 (Mon–Fri 9–11.30am & 1–5pm). Well out towards the Western Bus Station, they speak good English but are fairly slow; the Dali office is faster.

Around Kunming

Black Dragon Pool and **Jindian Park**, two temples surrounded by greenery, are an easy ride north of Kunming on city buses – either makes for a pleasant morning's excursion. Off to the west and a little harder to reach, **Qiongzhu Temple**'s extraordinary sculptures provide unsurpassed atmosphere and could, as a long day-trip, be combined with a visit to the **Western Hills**, which offer brilliant views over **Dian Chi**, the lake south of Kunming. Further afield, every tour agent in Kunming offers day-trips to the much-touted **Stone Forest**, which tends to be overrun with tourists as a result.

Black Dragon Pool

黑龙潭, hēilóng tán • Daily 8am–6pm • ¥30 • Bus #9 from outside the defunct North Train Station, Beijing Lu

Ten kilometres north of the centre, **Black Dragon Pool** is surrounded by a garden of ancient trees, full of plum blossoms in spring. The two Ming temple buildings are bright but modest Taoist affairs dedicated to the Heavenly Emperor and other deities, while the pool itself is said to be inhabited by a dragon forced by the Immortal, Lu Dongbin, to provide a permanent source of water for the local people. It's apparently also haunted by a zealous Ming scholar who patriotically drowned himself and his family as invading Qing armies stormed Kunming in 1661; his tomb stands nearby.

Jindian Park

金殿公园, jīndiàn gōngyuán • Daily 7.30am–6pm • ¥30 • Bus #71 from Beijing Lu, north of Dongfeng Square, or bus #76 from Heilong Tan

Set in pleasant woodland 12km northeast of the city, the main feature of **Jindian Park** is a gilded **bronze temple** surrounded by hefty stone fortifications. The temple has a convoluted history: the original was built in 1602 as a copy of one that crowns Wudang Shan, a mountain in Hubei province famed for its martial arts and devotion to the Taoist mystic Zhen Wu. But thirty years later, the original was itself shifted from here to the summit of Jizu Shan (see p.204), and the current version – another exact copy, down to the life-sized bronze sculpture of Zhen Wu inside – was funded in 1671 by the traitorous general **Wu Sangui** (see p.306), who had been made governor of Yunnan by China's new Manchu rulers. Halls at the side contain Wu Sangui's long-handled broadsword and his "Big Dipper" sword, an enormous weapon needing two hands to heft. The woods here are full of fragrant camellias and weekend picnickers, and a tower on the hill behind encloses a large bronze bell from Kunming's demolished southern gates.

Avoid taking the cable car off the back of the park to the **1999 Horticultural Expo Site** – a monster scam at ¥100 for a walk through vast, drab squares of flowerbeds. The Chinese do excellent gardens, but this isn't one of them.

Qiongzhu Temple

筇竹寺, qióngzhú sì • ¥6 • Tour bus daily 8am (¥15 return) from outside the Yunnan Arts Institute, cnr of Longjing Jie and Dongfeng Xi Lu; otherwise, bus #82 (¥1) from the western end of Nanping Jie to the Western Bus Station, then bus #C61 (¥5) to the temple; return taxi from town ¥100 including waiting time

Up in the wooded hills 16km west of Kunming, **Qiongzhu Temple** is a tranquil complex of well-proportioned halls and stone courtyards, lovingly decorated with pot plants. What makes it worth the long bus ride from town are the temple's extraordinary statues of China's **500 luohans** (see p.78), created in 1883 by the famed Sichuanese sculptor **Li Guangxiu**. Halls either side of the entrance gate hold the bulk of them, about half life-sized and uncomfortably realistic despite the usual grotesque distortions; indeed, Li came under suspicion of having **caricatured** the temple's monks and was cast out, never to sculpt again. His masterwork, however, adorns the open-fronted **main hall**, where crews of devils, scribes, emperors and beggars are caught in holy contemplation, roaring with hysterical mirth or snarling grimly as they ride the foaming sea which comes crashing down off the walls. Photography is forbidden, but there are often painters and even sculptors about, busy recording Li's work.

Other courtyards at the temple are thick with **rhinoceros** motifs, ancient and modern – the exact meaning is ambiguous but the animal is always considered auspicious. There's also a good, if pricey, tearoom and **vegetarian restaurant** here open at lunchtime.

The Western Hills

西山, xī shān • Free – optional cable cars ¥25-40, entry fees for some sights • Bus #82 from the western end of Nanping Jie to the Western Bus Station, then bus #6 (daily 6.30am–8pm) from over the rail tracks to the park gates at Gaoyao (高峣, gāoyáo)

The forested **Western Hills**, 16km outside Kunming, are an easy place to spend a sunny day, with cable cars and walking trails ascending a 2500m-high ridge for views over **Dian Chi**, the 50km-wide lake southwest of town.

It's over an hour's walk uphill from the gate to the main sights, but take time to visit the atmospheric **Huating Temple** (华亭寺, huáting sì; ¥6) along the way, originally a country retreat for Gao Zhishen, Kunming's eleventh-century ruler. Converted to a monastery during the fourteenth century, it holds some fine **statues** – especially the two gate guardians inside the entrance hall. Further up and reached along a warped, flagstoned path through old-growth forest, **Taihua Temple** (太华寺, tàihuá sì; ¥6) is fronted by ancient **ginkgo** trees, and is best known for its slightly shambolic botanic gardens.

Past here you come to two **cable-car stations**: one descends towards Kunming's western suburbs (from where you could catch a cab back to town for ¥30), the other climbs to the Long Men area. You can walk to Long Men too: just carry straight on along the road and it's twenty minutes to the **ticket office** (¥40). Then head up the narrow flights of stone steps, past a group of minor temples, and into a series of chambers and narrow **tunnels**, all carved with Buddha figures, which exit at **Long Men** (龙门, lóng mén), the "Dragon Gate", a narrow balcony and ornamented grotto on a sheer cliff overlooking the lake. It took the eighteenth-century monk **Wu Laiqing** and his successors more than seventy years to excavate the tunnels and statuary, which continue up to where another flight of steps climbs to further lookouts. Dian Chi itself is flat and peaceful, though terribly **polluted**: the water below is livid green with algae.

The Stone Forest

石林, shílín • Daily 8.30am–6pm • ¥175 • Agents in Kunming offer return transfers from accommodation for ¥85; there are also public buses (¥35) from the East Bus Station – make sure you get one to the scenic area (石林景区, shílín jǐngqū), and not to Shilin town

Yunnan's renowned **Stone Forest** comprises an exposed bed of limestone spires weathered and split into intriguing clusters, 90km east of Kunming. While immensely photogenic, it has become a huge and over-touted tourist attraction, with large red characters incised into famous rocks, tour groups clogging the paths through the maze, and ethnic **Sani** in unnaturally clean dresses strategically placed for photographers.

It takes about an hour to slowly circuit the main trail through the pinnacles to **Sword Peak Pond**, a pool surrounded by particularly sharp ridges, which you can climb along a narrow track leading right up across the top of the forest. This is the most frequented part of the park, and if you're intimidated by the density of visitors, follow paths out towards the perimeter and smaller, separate stone groupings in the fields beyond where you could spend the whole day without seeing another visitor.

At the park gates, a mess of stalls and **restaurants** sell pretty good, reasonably priced food – roast duck, pheasant, pigeon or fish – as well as poor souvenir embroideries.

The southeast

Southeastern Yunnan is a nicely unpackaged corner of the province, stretching from Kunming to the Vietnamese border crossing at **Hekou**, though you might also be heading down this way on a roundabout route **to Xishuangbanna**. Closest to Kunming, **Jianshui** is an amiable old town worth an overnight stay for its traditional gardens, a few antique mementoes and nearby limestone caves, the source of an unusual Chinese delicacy. Further south, you could easily spend a few days in the **Yuanyang** region, where the **Hong He** valley's enormous, steep slopes have been sculpted into magnificent rice terraces dotted with villages of ethnic **Hani** – there's great hiking potential here.

Note that if you're ultimately aiming for **Vietnam**, it's best to tackle sights in the order given here; for Xishuangbanna, aim for Yuanyang first, then Jianshui, as Jinghong buses depart from here. Don't forget that, if planning to cross the border, you must obtain a Vietnamese visa in advance.

Jianshui

建水, jiànshuǐ

Around 220km south of Kunming, **JIANSHUI** was once a key trade and transport stop, reaching its heyday during the Qing dynasty, when the town was graced with elegant temples, gardens and family mansions. Battered by the twentieth century and now bypassed by major highways, a bland new settlement surrounds the rambling, unpretentious **old town**, a pleasant place to pull up for a day, stroll the streets and take in some unusual nearby sights – including the **Swallows' Caves** (see p.198).

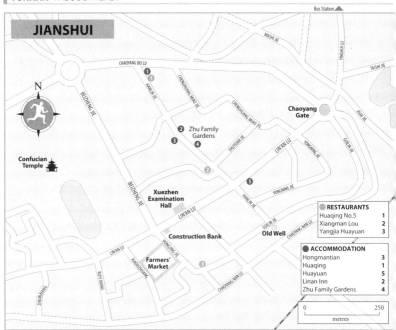

Chaoyang Gate and the backstreets

At the entrance to the old town, the large, russet stone **Chaoyang Gate** (朝阳楼, cháoyáng lóu) sits in the centre of a traffic circle, topped by a two-storey wooden pavilion; people come up here to lounge, fly kites and play cards. Partly pedestrianized **Lin'an Lu** runs southwest through the **old town**, flagstoned and lined with trees and tatty, old-style wooden buildings, but head instead down backstreet **Guilin Jie**, flagged by the thin spire of an ornamental pagoda. There are several old, unrestored buildings along Guilin Jie alongside **wells**, marked with multiple marble wellheads; many of Jianshui's older quarters still get all their water from them. After around 15 minutes, you'll find yourself on Hongjing Jie; there's a daily **farmers' market** down adjacent Xiaoxizhuang, or press on to Lin'an Lu.

The Zhu Family Gardens

朱家花园, zhūjiā huāyuán • Hanlin Jie • Daily 9am–10pm • ¥50 (combined ticket with Confucian Temple and Swallows' Caves ¥133)

The **Zhu Family Gardens** date from the 1880s, a series of interlocking stone courtyards, halls and ponds originally laid out on a grand scale after the family had made it big in trade and mining. The twentieth century didn't treat the family well, however, and the gardens only avoided complete destruction at the hands of Mao's Red Guards because the Zhus had fought both the Manchus in 1911 and the Nationalist army through the

---

CHINESE GARDENS

Chinese gardens are meant to be calming, contemplative places, which instead of trying to recreate nature, are all about the artful arrangement of limited space. Buildings, screens and water continually block, hint at and amplify what lies beyond, while natural elements – rocks, plants and trees – evoke scenery but leave the viewer's mind to fill in any gaps with their own ideas.

1930s. Reduced in scale, they were restored to their present condition in 1998, and a good amount of the original intent survives, the courtyards filled with bonsai and carefully placed screens. The finest buildings are the **Hua Ting**, a low, open-sided stone pavilion decorated with symbols of learning, wisdom and longevity, its timber roof brackets carved into dragon heads; and the beautifully proportioned **Ancestral Hall**, which overlooks a square pond and theatre stage.

The Xuezhen Examination Hall

学政考棚, xuézhèng kǎopéng • Free

Back on Lin'an Lu, Jianshui's seventeenth-century **Xuezhen Examination Hall**, currently under restoration, is where candidates from all over southern Yunnan sat the government tests which, if passed, were a path to a lifelong career in the service of the country. Based on the Confucian Classics, the examination system originated in 605 AD and survived for 1300 years, after which most examination halls were demolished; there's another example at Langzhong in Sichuan (see p.91).

The Confucian Temple

文庙, wén miào • Daily 9am–5pm • ¥60 (combined ticket with Zhu Family Gardens and Swallows' Caves ¥133)

Past the Beizheng Lu intersection on Lin'an Lu, the **Confucian Temple** was founded in 1285 and must once have been an imposing complex, though surviving buildings are few and mostly modern restorations. In early June, anxious parents bring their children here to pay their respects and ask for success in their National College Exams; they only get one chance to sit them, and the results determine their careers – much as the government tests used to do. A path circuits a large lotus pond, at the back of which is an ornamental **gateway** decorated with elephants, lions and mythical *qilin*. Just behind is a stone tablet showing Confucius strumming a *qin* beneath text outlining his opinions on music. A shrine loaded with marble statues of a pig, a bull and a ram fronts the **Hall of the First Teacher** (先师殿, xiānshī diàn); inside is a bearded statue of the sage, flanked by later Confucian scholars.

ARRIVAL AND DEPARTURE   JIANSHUI

By bus Jianshui's bus station is in the new town on main street Yinghui Lu; turn left out of the station and it's 1.5km to Chaoyang Gate, or catch bus #13 (¥1) to the Lin'an Lu–Hanlin Jie intersection in the old town. A taxi costs ¥5. Note that this is the most convenient place in the southeast to catch a Jinghong bus.

Destinations Hekou (3 daily; 3hr; ¥70); Jinghong (2 daily; 8hr; ¥170); Kunming (3hr; ¥73); Yuanyang Nansha (4hr; ¥33).

ACCOMMODATION

Hongmantian 红满天客栈, hóngmǎntiān kèzhàn. Hanlin Jie ☎ 087 3318 3818. Set back off the street, this formerly bland low-rise tourist hotel has been given a folksy makeover; the large rooms have modern en suites and small wooden balconies. **¥180**

Huaqing 华清酒店, huáqīng jiǔdiàn. 46 Hanlin Jie ☎ 087 3766 6166. Another hotel rebranding itself with local flavour, this time down to the staff's "ethnic" garb. Rooms are small and a little shabby around the edges, but some have balconies overlooking the street. **¥200**

Huayuan 花园宾馆, huāyuán bīnguǎn. Lin'an Lu, near Hanlin Jie intersection ☎ 087 3765 6285. One of several inexpensive places to stay nearby; you get a bed, a functioning bathroom and mosquito coils for the evening. **¥80**

★ **Linan Inn** 临安客栈, lín'ān kèzhàn. Hanlin Jie ☎ 087 3765 5866, ✉ linaninn@hotmail.com. Antique courtyard house with stone gateway, carved wooden trim and tasteful decoration; rooms are tidy and well maintained. Not much English is spoken, but they're a mine of useful local information. **¥120**

Zhu Family Gardens 朱家花园, zhūjiā huāyuán. Hanlin Jie ☎ 087 3766 7109. Atmospherically located inside the gardens, but the rooms – despite elegant antique wooden furniture and four-poster beds – are not quite up to the price. **¥480**

EATING AND DRINKING

Jianshui's culinary claim to fame is the **qiguo** (气锅, qìguō), an earthenware casserole with an inverted funnel which allows steam to enter and cook the contents, usually chicken and medicinal herbs. A few **restaurants** serve it, and you can buy the casserole pots from stalls along Hanlin Jie.

Huaqing No.5 华清5号, huáqīng wǔ hào. Hanlin Jie. Next to the *Huaqing* hotel, this dark, quiet place tries hard to be a foreign-style café-bar, serving beer, wine and Western food; the food is fine but a lack of customers deadens the atmosphere.

Xiangman Lou 香满楼, xiāngmǎn lóu. Hanlin Jie. A Qing-style teahouse-restaurant, with wooden shutters, heavy wooden tables and benches. The food – stir-fry staples and dumplings – is nothing special, but it's fun and suits the town. Mains ¥10.

★ **Yangjia Huayuan** 杨家花园, yángjiā huāyuán. 24 Hongjing Jie ☎ 087 3766 1777. Tucked away down a side-street south of the Beizheng Lu gateway, what remains of this old mansion and garden is now a restaurant overlooking an ornamental pond. The menu is Chinese only, and you're unlikely to make sense of the names of local dishes, but they're used to this and have all ingredients on display. Pricey but busy, with unbeatable character. Mains ¥30–80.

DIRECTORY

Banks There's a Construction Bank ATM, labelled for international cards, on Lin'an Lu.

Around Jianshui

As well as the popular **Swallows' Caves** (see below), a few sights around Jianshui could be bundled together into a half-day's outing by **hiring a minibus** – none are outstanding on their own, but together they emphasize Jianshui's local culture. Around 8km south of town in the middle of nowhere, the **Wenbi Tower** (文笔塔, wénbǐ tǎ) is a 31m-high brick construction shaped roughly like a writing brush; it dates to 1828 but nobody seems sure what it represents. The less ambiguous **Twin Dragon Bridge** (双龙桥, shuānglóng qiáo), 10km southwest, is a 148m-long, multi-arched stone span built in the eighteenth century; it was originally much shorter, but had to be extended after the river changed its course in 1839. For a miniature version of Jianshui, head 13km west to **Tuan Shan** (团山, tuán shān), a small town featuring largely unrestored old courtyard mansions with elaborately flared stone entranceways, and the **Zhang Family Gardens** (张家花园, zhāngjiā huāyuán).

The Swallows' Caves

燕子洞, yànzi dòng • Daily 9am–5pm • ¥80 (combined ticket with Zhu Family Gardens and Confucian Temple ¥133)

Some 28km east of Jianshui, the **Swallows' Caves** are named after the chattering swarms of swiftlets that breed here each year, their tiny cup-shaped **nests** collected for use in Chinese gastronomy. Made from dried saliva, the nests are tasteless but their unique gelatinous texture and supposed medicinal qualities have made them absurdly valuable – they sell in Hong Kong at HK$15,000 a kilo. If you can, catch the **Bird Nest Festival** on August 8, the only day of the year that collecting the then-vacant nests is allowed – a very profitable and dangerous task for local Yi men, who scale the cliffs as crowds look on.

From the park entrance, there's a short walk past wooded lawns (where you could picnic) to where a small river runs out of the 50m-high **cave mouth**. Thousands of screeching swiftlets arc around; the best place to watch them is the grotto opposite, inset with Buddhist statuary. An occasionally slippery **path** marked by low-wattage strip lighting follows the river into the cave (an umbrella is useful); the birds and smell thin out as you progress and around 700m along you reach a vast **cavern**. There's canteen-like seating here and various **snack stalls**, along with souvenir birds' nests for sale (¥220 each). Right at the back, coloured lighting picks out quirky rock formations; when you've finished exploring, catch a small **boat** back to the cave mouth.

GETTING AROUND | AROUND JIANSHUI

By minibus Minibuses from Jianshui cost around ¥150 for half a day, and are the only way to reach twin Dragon Bridge and the Wenbi Tower.

By bus Any bus heading west from Jianshui's bus station can drop you at Tuan Shan (¥7). Likewise, buses heading east pass the Swallows' Caves (¥10), though these drop you on the highway 2km short, from where minibuses (¥5) run to the caves.

The Hong He Valley and Yuanyang

Hong He (红河, hóng hé), the Red River, starts life near Weishan (see p.205) and runs southeast across Yunnan, entering Vietnam at Hekou and flowing through Hanoi before emptying its waters, laden with volcanic soil, into the Gulf of Tonkin. For much of its journey the river is straight, channelled by high mountain ranges into a series of fertile, steep-sided valleys. These have been terraced by resident **Hani**, whose adobe and thatch houses pepper the hills around the **Yuanyang** region and provide targets for local **hiking**. In spring and autumn thick mists blanket the area, muting the violent contrast between red soil and brilliant green fields; **photographers** flock here between March and May, when the flooded, silhouetted terraces reflect the sky at dawn and dusk.

The regional access point is **Yuanyang** (元阳, yuányáng), a district 80km south of Jianshui and 300km from Kunming. There are two settlements here: the humid hamlet of **Nansha** (元阳南沙, yuányáng nánshā), down at river level, little more than a transit point; and **Xinjie**, where you actually want to base yourself, 30km further south at the top of a high ridge. There are direct buses to Xinjie from Kunming and Hekou; coming from Jianshui, you'll have to change buses at Nansha.

3

Xinjie

元阳新街镇, yuányáng xīnjiē zhèn

The main base for exploring the Yuanyang area, **XINJIE** is an untidy, brick and concrete town with a broad **central square**, off which are fabulous views over the countryside. There's not much to the place: the road runs via a short tunnel to the bus station; accommodation and eating options surround the square; while take the steps down off the square and you're in the town's 500m-long shopping street. Xinjie is a hive of activity on **market days** (every five days), when brightly dressed Hani, Miao, Yi and Yao women pour in from surrounding villages.

ARRIVAL AND DEPARTURE

THE HONG HE VALLEY AND YUANYANG

BY BUS

Coming from Kunming or Hekou, there are direct buses to Xinjie; from Jianshui, you'll have to catch a bus to Nansha and then one of the regular shuttles uphill to Xinjie. Leaving Xinjie for Xishuangbanna, you'll need to travel via Nansha to Jianshui, then pick up a Jinghong bus there.

Destinations from Nansha Gejiu (3 daily; 2hr; ¥14); Jianshui (3hr; ¥33); Kunming (3 daily; 4hr; ¥118); Xinjie (1hr; ¥10).
Destinations from Xinjie Gejiu (3 daily; 2hr; ¥24); Hekou (4 daily; 3hr; ¥39); Kunming (3 daily; 5hr; ¥128); Nansha (1hr; ¥10).

INFORMATION

Tourist information Window of Yuanyang (元阳之窗, yuányáng zhī chuāng), signposted up steps from near the *Yunti* hotel in Xinjie; daily 11.30am–9pm ☎ 087 3562 3627, ⓦ yuanyangwindow.com. Supported by World Vision China, this helpful office promotes sustainable tourism, sells basic maps, and provides advice on the best places to visit and information about minibus rental, guides, hiking trails and market schedules. It also has internet and a simple café.

WALKS AROUND XINJIE

For an easy **walk** and a taste of local rural landscapes, follow the path beside the bus station (past the guesthouses) and, when it divides, take the downhill fork. This becomes a cobbled track and then a dirt road between fields; there are people planting, cutting or husking rice, depending on season, and water buffalo wallowing in mud or stoically pulling ploughs. You pass through a couple of poor, functional Hani villages but the scenery gets better the further you go, though there are no views of the famous terraces themselves. Around forty minutes along is **Longshuba** (龙树坝, lóngshùbà), a Yi settlement, beyond which the trail becomes a narrow footpath between the paddyfields, for which you'll need a **map**. Window of Yuanyang (see above) sells hand-drawn ones for a four-hour, cross-country circuit back to town via Longshuba, plus other local hikes.

ACCOMMODATION

Chen Family Guesthouse 陈家旅社, chénjiā lǚshè. Out of Xinjie bus station, turn hard left and you're there ☎ 087 3562 2343. A clean if basic option with excellent views off the rear terrace; doubles have large beds and en suites with squat toilets. Recent reports suggest the management try to push foreigners into taking their more expensive rooms. Dorms ¥25, doubles ¥65

Minzu 民族旅社, mínzú lǚshè. Just past Chen Family Guesthouse, Xinjie ☎ 087 3562 3618. One of several inexpensive guesthouses along this lane; a bit cleaner and newer than most, though without views. ¥50

Yunti 云梯大酒店, yúntī dàjiǔdiàn. Downhill from Xinjie bus station, through or around the tunnel, bear right, and it's ahead up a flight of steps where the road bends left ☎ 087 3562 4858, ⊛ yunti-hotel.cn. Xinjie's only place with pretensions to comfort, though these don't extend beyond the huge front desk and sofas in the lobby: rooms are tidy but threadbare. ¥150

Yunti Shunjie 云梯顺捷酒店, yúntī shùnjié jiǔdiàn. The big yellow pile across Xinjie's main square ☎ 087 3562 1588. Recently renovated and with splendid views, but some of the rooms are already mildewed; otherwise a good deal. ¥100

EATING

Lao Sichuan 老四川饭店, lǎo sìchuān fàndiàn. Xinjie's main square. The best of several inexpensive Sichuanese places around the square, all offering the same spicy dishes. The *Chuan Yu* (川渝饭店, chuān yú fàndiàn) is another decent option.

Yunti 云梯大酒店, yúntī dàjiǔdiàn. Downhill from Xinjie bus station, through or around the tunnel, bear right, and it's ahead up a flight of steps where the road bends left ⊛ yunti-hotel.cn. Decent restaurant in the hotel of the same name – it needs advance warning if you want a meal.

DIRECTORY

Banks There's a branch of the Agricultural Bank off the main square in Xinjie, whose ATM is labelled "Cash Disbursement of International Cards" – don't rely on it.

Around Xinjie

Villages and scenic lookouts surround Xinjie, with several roads heading out to them; accommodation and Window of Yuanyang provide **maps**, though none agree on exact names, distances or directions. Aside from landscape, don't miss **village markets**; alongside vegetables and fruit, you can buy honeycombs, complete with bees and their larvae, plastic utensils, clothes, chickens and buffalo. There's usually a spot of illegal gambling going on too, involving fairground-style dice games. Take a camera.

About 6km south of Xinjie, **Qingkou** (箐口, qīngkǒu; ¥30) is a "folk custom village" with traditionally thatched, mushroom-shaped Hani houses; tour groups get dances

HEKOU AND THE VIETNAM BORDER

HEKOU (河口, hékǒu), 360km southeast of Kunming, is only worth a visit if you're in transit between China and Vietnam. Exit the bus station, and the border post is a few minutes' walk away. Once out the other side and in Vietnam, **Lao Cai** has a huge market selling game meat, a few despondent hotels and a **train station** 3km south that offers two services daily for the ten-hour run to Hanoi. Most travellers take a bus or motorbike-taxi (US$5) to the hill resort town of **Sa Pa**.

  Arriving from Vietnam, keep this book buried in your bags, preferably with a false cover, because Chinese customs officials have been known to confiscate them. To change money, walk up the main street from the border, turn right after 200m, and you'll arrive at the **Bank of China** with an ATM (daily 8am–5.30pm; foreign exchange closed Sun).

ARRIVAL AND DEPARTURE

By bus Hekou's bus station is on the corner of Wenming Jie and Binhe Lu, about 50m from the border. There have been reports of some "baggage handlers" here harassing foreigners for outrageous fees – the only thing you have to buy here is a bus ticket.
Destinations Jianshui (3 daily; 3hr; ¥70); Kunming (10hr; ¥183); Xinjie (4 daily; 3hr; ¥39).

and ceremonies performed and there are some short walks out to lookout points. The **Panzhihua Road** (¥60 entry to the area) branches eastwards from here; the first stop is 16km from town at **Bada** (坝达, bàdá), where there's a short walk to two adjacent platforms offering expansive views across a deep valley to isolated hill villages, the terracing rising to 2000m.

Some 10km past Bada, another roadside platform – best for sunrises – overlooks the village of **DUOYISHU** (多依树, duōyīshù), whose houses are mostly concrete painted a sympathetic, earthy yellow; it's a lazy place whose muddy lanes are cruised by livestock, and the **hostel** makes it a good base for **hikes**.

The main destination southwest is **Laohuzui**, aka Mengpin (老虎嘴, lǎohǔzuǐ; 猛品, měngpǐn; ¥30), a fenced-off viewing area on the roadside 18km from Xinjie famous for its sunsets. It's the one place you'll get mobbed to buy souvenirs; note that similar views are available for free from the roadside nearby.

GETTING AROUND AND TOURS

On foot Window of Yuanyang sells hiking maps and can advise on good trails, from hour-long circuits to multi-day treks. A recommended hiking guide is English-speaking Jacky Wen (☏137 6938 5810, ✉haichao33@sohu.com), who charges ¥500/day and can also organize trips to minorities across Yunnan.

By minibus Local minibuses to villages display their destinations (in Chinese) on the windscreen and leave

AROUND XINJIE

when full from the road above Xinjie's bus station. There's most traffic on market days, though otherwise very little by mid-afternoon.

Minibus hire Window of Yuanyang negotiates private minibus hire for around ¥250/day, depending on how far you want to go. Five hours is enough time for a whip-round of key sights.

ACCOMMODATION

Sunny Guesthouse 阳光客栈, yángguāng kèzhàn. Duoyishu village ☏151 2639 9443, ✉guesthouse@163 .com. Contact in advance for directions because it's difficult to find, though worth a stay as the only formal accommodation in among the terraces. Hostel-like operation

with tiny, brightly coloured rooms, rattan mattresses and shared facilities. It's all pretty basic but the owner is helpful and speaks a little English, and there are great views from the guesthouse roof. You need to haggle over the doubles' rates. Meals available. Dorms ¥20, doubles ¥90

Northwest Yunnan

The 500km-long route through northwestern Yunnan begins west of Kunming among the subtropical hills and valleys surrounding the gateway city of **Xiaguan**, and steadily ascends onto the **Tibetan plateau**, a land of thin yak-grazed pasture, alpine lakes and shattered peaks painted crisply in blue, white and grey. The string of **old towns** marking the way were once capitals of local kingdoms, or staging posts on the *chama dao*, the centuries-old "**Tea-Horse Road**" caravan route between China and Tibet (see p.81). Some have become massive tourist draws while others are rarely visited; all offer romantically antique architecture, contact with the region's varied **ethnic groups**, and the chance to hike off into some superlative countryside.

Xiaguan itself has some underrated local attractions – best perhaps is the charismatic town of **Weishan** – though most visitors head straight to nearby **Dali**, drawn by its mix of Western-friendly cafés, lake-and-mountain setting and **Bai** population. Continuing northwest, tiny mud-brick **Shaxi** is another relic of the Tea-Horse days, and then you're at **Lijiang**, a picturesque collection of cobbles and wobbly wooden houses nestled at the base of snowcapped **Yulong Xue Shan**. Capital of the former **Naxi Kingdom**, Lijiang has been overexploited in the interests of tourism, but it's an attractive base to organize access to Yunnan's premier hiking destination, where the Yangzi cuts through **Tiger Leaping Gorge**; **Lugu Lake** up on the Sichuan border, home to the matrilineal **Mosuo**; or a trip to the **Lancang River Valley**, a remote region with rare monkeys and unexpected European connections.

VISITING NORTHWEST YUNNAN

Xiaguan is Northwest Yunnan's access point, from where there's at least regular, if not always speedy, services through the rest of the region. **Trains** link Kunming to Xiaguan (for Dali) and Lijiang, with talk of an extension to Shangri-La; and you can fly to Lijiang and Shangri-La. There are **bus** routes into Sichuan from Lijiang and Shangri-La too, but at the time of writing it was not possible to cross overland from Yunnan into Tibet. Ask agencies in Dali, Lijiang and Shangri-La about the latest situation.

Autumn is one of the best times to visit northwest Yunnan: winters are extremely cold, and while early spring is often sunny, summers – though fairly mild – can also be very wet, leading to landslides. Also be aware that the **Tibetan areas** around Shangri-La and Deqin (and including routes into Western Sichuan) might be closed off during March, historically a time of political unrest in Tibet (see p.64).

North of Lijiang, you enter Yunnan's Tibetan regions at **Shangri-La** (also known as Zhongdian), a nicely restored monastery town surrounded by yet more wild countryside and at one end of a popular backroads bus ride **to Daocheng** in Sichuan. By now you're barely in Yunnan, and a day's further travel will land you at **Deqin**, beyond which **Meili Xue Shan**'s spectacular string of peaks marks the Tibetan borderlands, and more well-established – but tough – hiking trails.

Xiaguan

下关, xiàguān, also known as Dali City (大理市, dàlǐ shì)

XIAGUAN is a transport hub 380km west of Kunming, its downtown overlooked by high ridges to the west, topped by a **wind farm**. The city is a gateway to the rest of Yunnan: north is the road to Dali, Lijiang, Shangri-La and Deqin; northwest lies the Nu Jiang Valley; west are Tengchong, Ruili and Burma; while Xishuangbanna is south via Route 214, designated a future Tibet – Laos Highway.

Dali, with all its attractions (see p.206) is just 18km north on local buses, and barely any visitors linger in Xiaguan except to get a **visa extension** from the efficient PSB. As a result, there are some overlooked attractions nearby, any one of which is well worth an overnight stay if you can pull yourself away from Dali's charms. Northeast of Xiaguan, there's a decent few hours' hike up to temples and pagodas atop of **Jizu Shan**; while if you like old towns but are finding Dali's streets too crowded for your tastes, aim south for **Weishan**, or northwest for the forgotten Bai village of **Nuodeng**.

ARRIVAL AND DEPARTURE   **XIAGUAN**

All "Dali" transport terminates at **Xiaguan**, not **Dali**. To get to Dali (大理, dàlǐ), catch local bus #4 or #8 (¥2) from Xiaguan (see below). A taxi between the two costs about ¥50. Note that agents in Dali sell tickets for onward travel, and long-distance buses heading north to Lijiang and beyond stop at Dali, so, despite Xiaguan's role as the local transit hub, if you're staying in Dali you can make arrangements there.

BY PLANE

The airport is 15km east, for which you'll need a taxi (¥60 to Dali). Planes head to Chengdu (3 weekly; 1hr 20min), Jinghong (2 daily; 50min) and Kunming (2 daily; 35min).

BY BUS

Dali bus station (大理汽车客运站, dàlǐ qìchē kèyùn zhàn), opposite the train station on Weishan Lu, is of most use for Kunming and Binchuan – for Jizu Shan (see p.204) – though there are also frequent buses to Wase (see p.215).

Catch city bus #8 to Dali from the train station forecourt. Destinations Binchuan (2hr; ¥25); Kunming (5hr; ¥138); Wase (40min; ¥10).

North bus station (客运北站, kèyùn běi zhàn) is 3km north of the centre on the Dali highway, with more buses to Kunming and regular departures for Lijiang and points north – again, the #8 bus for Dali stops right outside. Destinations Jianchuan (for Shaxi; 3hr; ¥27); Kunming (5hr; ¥138); Lijiang (3hr 30min; ¥46–66); Shangri-La (Zhongdian; 7hr; ¥120); Weixi (5 daily; 12hr; ¥89).

South bus station (客运南站, kèyùn nán zhàn) is on the south edge of town on Nanjian Lu and handles all Weishan buses. Catch bus #4 to Dali.
Destinations Weishan (1hr 30min; ¥13).

Xingcheng express bus station (兴盛高快客运站, xīngshèng gāokuài kèyùn zhàn), in town on Xingcheng Lu, handles fast traffic to Kunming and points west, such as Yunlong, Tengchong and Ruili, as well as Xizhou village on Er Hai (see p.214). For Dali, turn right out of the bus station, walk to the main intersection, then turn right again and it's 150m to the #8 bus stop.

Destinations Baoshan (9 daily; 3hr; ¥52); Jinghong (1 daily; 24hr; ¥195); Kunming (5hr; ¥138); Ruili (4 daily; 8hr; ¥128); Tengchong (6hr; ¥98); Xizhou (1hr 30min; ¥7); Yunlong (for Nuodeng; 3hr; ¥35).

BY TRAIN

The train station is in the east of town on Weishan Lu; city bus #8 to Dali stops right outside. A high-speed service to Kunming is due in 2013. Trains head to Kunming (3 daily; 6–8hr) and Lijiang (2 daily; 2hr).

DIRECTORY

PSB and visa extensions Mon–Fri 9–11.30am & 2–5pm ☏ 087 2214 2149. Located north of town on the Xiaguan–Dali highway; get off the #8 bus at the Century Middle School stop (世纪中学, shìjì zhōngxué) – it's the building with a radio tower on the roof. One of the most amenable police departments in Southwest China, and getting visa extensions here is straightforward.

Jizu Shan

鸡足山, jīzú shān • ¥60

Jizu Shan is a holy mountain 90km northeast of Xiaguan associated with Buddhism's Chan (Zen) sect, and especially the Indian monk **Jiaye**; Tibetans also consider it a major pilgrimage site. Today only a handful of temples remain from Jizu Shan's glory days under the Tang dynasty, though the scenery is splendid, especially views from the mountain's rounded, stony summit. You really only need a half-day on the mountain, but transport out dries up by mid-afternoon and you'll probably need to spend the night here. On the way up, you can ponder various unlikely explanations for Jizu Shan's odd name – it means "Chickenfoot Mountain".

The lower temples

The road here ends at a **minibus park** in woodland halfway up Jizu Shan; a nearby knot of cheap restaurants also offer accommodation. You're also within a few minutes' walk of the simple **Shizhong Temple** (石钟寺, shízhōng sì), fronted by sheds sheltering Buddha statues; **Wanshou Nunnery** (万寿庵, wànshòu ān), known for its old magnolia trees; and splendid Ming-dynasty **Zhusheng Temple** (祝圣寺, zhùshèng sì) whose halls are full of lively, naturalistically painted sculptures.

To the summit

Cable car ¥40 (single)

From the minibus park, follow the road uphill for 100m to a sharp kink, then take the unsigned path alongside the **horse pen** up the mountain. It's 3.5km on foot from here to the top, following steps through the forest and onto heathland; a kilometre along, there's also a cable car to just below the summit. Walking, give yourself at least two hours to complete the ascent; steps are not that steep, but there are plenty of them. Emerging through undergrowth, you'll find the rocky summit is marked by the ninth-century **Lengyan Pagoda** (楞严塔, léngyán tǎ) and accompanying **Jinding Temple** (金顶寺, jīndǐng sì), relocated here from Kunming in the 1630s (see p.193) and blindingly gilded in strong sunshine. People mass on the nearby terrace to watch the sunrise, but the broad views of slanting ridges rising out of the forest are good at any time of day.

ARRIVAL AND DEPARTURE   JIZU SHAN

By bus From Xiaguan's Dali bus station, aim first for Binchuan town (宾川, bīnchuān; 2hr 30min; ¥25). Minibuses to Jizu Shan depart from the back of Binchuan's station when they have eight passengers (daily 8am–4pm; 1hr 30min; ¥13); they return from the mountain on the same schedule.

ACCOMMODATION AND EATING

There are **restaurants** near the minibus park, and food shacks on the mountain path; check prices when ordering to avoid being overcharged.

Jizu Shan Binguan 鸡足山宾馆, jīzú shān bīnguǎn. Near Zhusheng Temple ☎087 2735 0478. Looks quite grand from the outside, but actually a disappointingly ordinary tourist hotel, with the usual slightly shabby decor. ¥180

Ye Caiguan 野菜馆, yě càiguǎn ☎087 2735 0018. One of many such establishments near the minibus park, providing basic rooms above a restaurant, with shared toilets and shower. ¥60

Weishan

巍山, wēishān

WEISHAN, 50km south of Xiaguan near the source of the **Hong He** (see p.199), was once the cradle of the Nanzhao kingdom and a prosperous stop on the old **Tea-Horse Road** between southern Yunnan and Tibet, which lasted from at least the Tang dynasty until modern roads and rail first put in an appearance during the mid-twentieth century. Today it's a laidback supply centre for local Bai, Muslim and Yi hamlets; Weishan's cobbled lanes are full of markets, wobbly adobe houses, temples and pagodas, and there's another holy mountain to hike up on its outskirts, but the town's biggest appeal is the way that nothing is geared to tourism, and people are just getting on with their lives.

Between the gates

There are few street signs in Weishan, so orient yourself at the **Gongchen Tower** (拱辰楼, gǒngchén lóu; ¥2), a huge tunnelled gateway built in 1390 which marks the town centre. At the top is a wooden pavilion, home to the **Weisha Nanzha Orchestra** (performances 8pm Sat and Sun); from here you'll see Weishan laid out in a 1.5km-long grid of little lanes, with the highway running down the west side and parallel **Huaxing Lu** to the east. The pedestrianized main street, lined with wooden shops, runs 500m south from Gongchen to the smaller **Xinggong Gate** (星拱楼, xīnggǒng lóu), once a bell tower. Past here, the street continues out of town through the cactus-encrusted **south gate**, beyond which is a daily **livestock market**.

The trade route days might be over but **horses** are still very much in use around Weishan: horse-cart "taxis" with shady awnings and padded benches ferry villagers in from the valley to two waiting areas on the highway side of town. Make sure you spend a half-day exploring Weishan's backstreets; there are old stables, a mosque, covered bridges and ruins. The **markets** seem to gather momentum through the day, peaking in early afternoon.

Weibao Shan

巍保山, wēibǎo shān • ¥50 • Minibuses to Weibao Shan (¥5/person; ¥40 for the vehicle) hang around on Huaxing Lu, the main road uphill from Weishan's Gongchen Tower

About 13km south of Weishan, **Weibao Shan** is a forested holy mountain dotted with layered, Nanzhao-era pagodas and Taoist temples known for their martial monks. There's a good deal of restoration in progress which promises to return the buildings here to their former glory after years of neglect following their closure during the 1960s. Minibuses run from town and you'll need about four hours for a return walk to the summit from the mountain's gates.

ARRIVAL AND DEPARTURE
WEISHAN

By bus Direct buses depart Kunming's West bus station and Xiaguan's South bus station. Weishan's bus station is on the main road through the valley; exit, turn left and turn left again for the old town.

Destinations Kunming (3 daily; 6hr; ¥110); Xiaguan (1hr 30min; ¥13).

ACCOMMODATION AND EATING

Near the Gongchen Tower, **Xiaochi Jie** (小吃街, xiǎochī jiē) or "Snack Street", is lined with inexpensive canteens selling spicy noodle soups and steamed beef buns; most are run by Muslims.

Gucheng Kezhan 古城客栈, gǔchéng kèzhàn. 59 Dongxin Jie, just east of the Gongchen Tower ☎ 087 2612 2341. Basic beds with shared showers and toilets in an old courtyard home; the closest you'll find to what would have been standard accommodation during Weishan's Tea-Horse Road days. ¥40

Lao Er Fanyuan 老二饭苑, lǎo èr fànyuàn. Similar outdoor courtyard setting to the nearby *Pinxiang*, but decorated with murals of the Yi Fire Festival and serving food with a definite hot-and-sour theme. Again, there's no menu, so just ask for a favourite or take pot luck. ¥20/head should cover a meal.

Mengshe Stagehouse 蒙舍驿站, mēngshě yìzhàn. 9 Nan Jie, 50m south of the old bell tower ☎ 087 2612 3338. Hotel set in a reconstructed old inn with spirit walls, little fish ponds and carved wooden furnishings, though rooms themselves are bland. ¥120

★ **Pinxiang Yuan** 品香苑, pǐnxiāng yuàn. 7 Xiaochi Jie. Courtyard house restaurant, where they set up low tables as customers arrive. No menu, so order dishes by name or go through to the kitchen and point. They serve home-style dishes such as stewed pork ribs with potatoes, nicely done; the setting makes it special. A meal for two costs ¥60.

Weishan Binguan 巍山宾馆, wēishān bīnguǎn. 52 Dongxin Jie ☎ 087 2612 2655. An old, rambling tourist hotel with renovated fringes and a huge range of rooms, from threadbare triples with shared bathrooms to large, en-suite doubles. ¥50–120

Nuodeng

诺邓, nuòdèng

This **Bai** village, 160km northwest of Xiaguan near **Yunlong town** (云龙, yúnlóng), is rather run-down nowadays, but until well into the twentieth century was another major station on local caravan trails and a producer of **salt**, dredged up as brine from artesian wells. Tucked into a fold on a steep hillside, the town is split into upper and lower sections by a small river. Some impressive buildings remain from better times: there are classic Bai **houses** with plaster-pink adobe walls; ornamental **gateways** over Nuodeng's rough, cobbled streets and stone steps; the two-storeyed **Yuhuang Pavilion** (玉皇阁, yùhuáng gé), whose curved roofline with exaggerated eaves is very much in the Bai style; the remains of a **guildhall** (古江西会馆, gǔ jiāngxī huìguǎn) for merchants from eastern China – sure proof of Nuodeng's former importance – and **temples** including the Dragon King's Hall (龙王庙, lóngwáng miào) and Longevity Palace (万寿宫, wànshòu gōng). This is definitely somewhere to stay the night and soak up some atmosphere and Bai culture (see opposite).

ARRIVAL AND DEPARTURE

NUODENG

By bus Get a bus from Xiaguan's Xingcheng express bus station to Yunlong (7 daily; 3hr; ¥35), then a minibus or motorcycle taxi 7km to the village (15min; ¥5).

ACCOMMODATION AND EATING

Fujia Liufangyuan 傅家六房院, fùjiā liùfángyuàn. There are several guesthouses in the village, all of which also provide meals, which you'll have to ask around to find. This is the nicest, a tidy courtyard home in the upper village. ¥60

Dali

大理, dàlǐ

Around 18km north of Xiaguan, **DALI** is the southernmost of the three large old towns – the other two are Lijiang and Shangri-La – lying along northwestern Yunnan's former trade routes to Tibet. Chinese holiday-makers flock here to see what Chinese towns used to look like before modernization stripped them of their character, while foreign backpackers drift through a Westerner-friendly theme park of beer gardens and cafés.

It's easy to enjoy Dali: despite tourist overkill, the town is pretty, interesting and relaxed, full of old houses and an indigenous **Bai** population; the area also marks the westernmost

THE BAI

Yunnan's two million **Bai** are concentrated in the Dali area, descendants of the peoples who lived here during the days of the Nanzhao and Dali kingdoms. **Traditional houses** are built around a courtyard, with a brightly painted gateway featuring huge, multi-layered flared eaves; there are plenty in Dali's backstreets, and country villages such as Xizhou and Nuodeng, but even modern buildings in Dali echo the design.

The Bai are nominally **Buddhist** – hence Dali's numerous pagodas – though their religion is strongly tinged with folk beliefs and every village has its own deity, or **benzhu**: these include Buddhist saints, legendary heroes or historic figures such as **Duan Siping**, founder of the Dali Kingdom. The Bai are famous for **tie-dyeing**, and dark-blue cloth patterned with flowers and fish is sold everywhere. **Bai cooking** includes country-style dishes such as fish casserole (沙锅鱼, **shāguō yú**); and dried cheese or yoghurt "fans", sometimes served as a relish or eaten on their own, deep-fried and sprinkled with sugar.

limit of **Yi** territory (see p.106). The grid-like **old town** covers around three square kilometres, contained within restored sections of its **Ming-dynasty walls**. The great long **Er Hai** lake, surrounded by Bai villages, is only 2km to the east, while the invitingly green valleys and clouded peaks of the **Cang Shan range** rear up behind the town, an obvious hiking target. Some visitors, seduced by Dali's charms (and occasionally the local **weed**) forget to leave, and Westerners run a good many businesses here.

If you can, visit during Dali's hectic **Spring Fair**, held for five days from the 15th of the third lunar month (April or May). Thousands of people from all over the region camp at the fairground just west of town to take part in horse trading, wrestling, racing, dancing and singing. The frankly scary **Bai torch festival** – held to commemorate the fiery foundation of the Nanzhao kingdom (see p.182) – is held on the 24th day of the sixth lunar month: expect extravagant fireworks, bonfires and torch parades, and people hurling gunpowder at each other.

Brief history

Dali sits astride a corridor between Tibet and Thailand, along which peoples have been migrating for millennia. Between the eighth and thirteenth centuries, Dali was at the centre of the **Nanzhao** and **Dali kingdoms**, which at their height encompassed Yunnan, Burma, Laos and Thailand, and even threatened Sichuan. In the mid-nineteenth century Dali became capital of the **Islamic state** declared by Du Wenxiu, during his Muslim Uprising (see p.183); millions died in the revolt's suppression and Dali was devastated, never to recover its former political position. The local Bai continued to trade, however, building up large fortunes and establishing mansions in villages around Er Hai; some Muslim Hui stayed on to become smiths, butchers and muleteers (and, more recently, truck drivers). An **earthquake** destroyed the town again in 1925, but after trade picked up through the 1930s it was rebuilt in its former style.

The South Gate

Start a tour of the town from Dali's monumental **South Gate** (南城门楼, nánchéng ménlóu; ¥20), a huge stone archway capped by a pavilion. Views south from the battlements take in **carpentry workshops** along Wenxian Lu and Xiaguan's suburbs, spreading irresistibly north towards Dali. About 500m southwest, the solitary Tang pagoda **Yi Ta** (一塔, yī tǎ) rises above the treetops, marking the site of a long-vanished temple.

South of Yu'er Lu

Once through the South Gate you're on pedestrianized **Fuxing Lu**, Dali's central cobbled axis. Its southern reaches are packed with tourists and souvenir stalls selling ethnic embroideries and silverware; push through them to the **Wuhua Tower** (五华楼, wǔhuá lóu). This was Dali's original south gate before the town expanded, stranding the

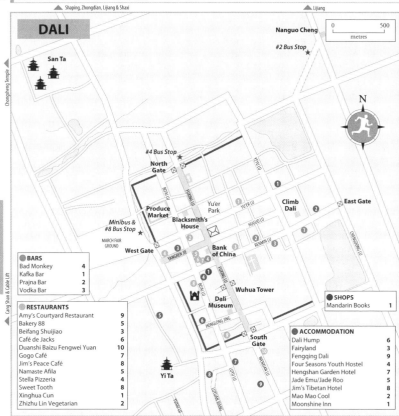

DALI

Nanguo Cheng

#2 Bus Stop ★

0		500
	metres	

San Ta

#4 Bus Stop
North Gate

Yu'er Park

Climb Dali

East Gate

Produce Market

Blacksmith's House

Minibus & #8 Bus Stop ★

MARCH FAIR GROUND

West Gate

Bank of China

Wuhua Tower

Dali Museum

South Gate

Yi Ta

Highway to Xiaguan

● BARS

Bad Monkey	4
Kafka Bar	1
Prajna Bar	2
Vodka Bar	3

● SHOPS

Mandarin Books	1

● RESTAURANTS

Amy's Courtyard Restaurant	9
Bakery 88	5
Beifang Shuijiao	3
Café de Jacks	6
Duanshi Baizu Fengwei Yuan	10
Gogo Café	7
Jim's Peace Café	8
Namaste Afila	5
Stella Pizzeria	4
Sweet Tooth	8
Xinghua Cun	1
Zhizhu Lin Vegetarian	2

● ACCOMMODATION

Dali Hump	6
Fairyland	3
Fengqing Dali	9
Four Seasons Youth Hostel	4
Hengshan Garden Hotel	7
Jade Emu/Jade Roo	5
Jim's Tibetan Hotel	8
Mao Mao Cool	2
Moonshine Inn	1

building inside the walls; after centuries serving as a bell tower, its lower floor has been converted to gift shops. East of Wuhua is a market square devoted to streaky-grey **Dali marble** from up in the hills, sculpted into all manner of trinkets.

Further along, Fuxing Lu is crossed by **Renmin Lu**; turn right, then right again for Dali's **Catholic Church** (天主教堂, tiānzhǔ jiàotáng). Built in 1927, the European arched windows and twisted columns are topped by an extravagantly Bai roof, all florid curves and points; the interior is painted a soothing blue.

Western extensions of Renmin Lu, parallel **Huguo Lu** and adjacent areas of **Bo'ai Lu** are crammed with cafés, bars and Bai ladies hissing "ganja, ganja, smoke?" at foreign tourists (Huguo Lu is also known as **Yangren Jie**, or "Foreigners' Street"). Hemp is grown for fibre all over the region; locals don't smoke dope, though plenty of Dali's foreign residents do. If you want to indulge, be discreet – recreational drugs are illegal in China and penalties can be severe (see p.46).

Dali Museum

大理市博物馆, dàlǐ shì bówùguǎn • Fuxing Lu • Daily 8.30am–5pm • Free

Guarded by stone lions and rusty cannons, **Dali Museum** occupies the site of the Qing governor's courthouse, which was appropriated as Du Wenxiu's "Forbidden City" during his insurrection. Only the layout has survived those times; the museum buildings are relatively new and showcase a Han-dynasty bronze "**money tree**" encircled by dragons, a few Buddhist figurines from the Nanzhao period and some lively statues of an orchestra and serving maids from a Ming noblewoman's tomb – a nice addition to the usual snarling gods and warrior busts.

The museum's pleasant rear courtyards are planted with camellias and bougainvillea, with a host of **steles** carved in what is possibly Bai writing; nobody understands this today, though the spoken language survives. A side-wing focuses on the Muslim Uprising, displaying rusty poleaxes, photographs of key sites and a copy of Du Wenxiu's seal stamp, in Arabic and Chinese script. Du is buried 4km southeast of Dali at **Qili Qiao** (七里桥, qīlǐ qiáo).

North of Yu'er Lu

North of **Yu'er Lu**, mass-market crowds suddenly thin among residential back lanes. **Yu'er Park** (玉洱公园, yù'ěr gōngyuán; daily 6am–8pm) is a pleasant, if small, patch of trees; and there's a **blacksmith's quarter** along Yincang Lu, stalls selling horse bells, hardware and cooking utensils – look for a house decorated with life-sized cranes, peacocks and monkeys, all made from scrap iron. Dali's northwesterly **produce market** is the usual spread of groceries and carcasses being hacked up with cleavers; it's busy daily but on the weekly main market day the chaos spreads into nearby streets.

Finally, the **North Gate** (北城门楼, běichéng ménlóu; ¥2) can be climbed for views, this time over grey rooftiles and solar hot water systems towards San Ta (see p.213); it's a quiet vantage point as few visitors bother with this end of town.

3

ARRIVAL AND DEPARTURE   DALI

Long-distance buses from **Lijiang and points north** drop off on the highways as they pass Dali, either near the West Gate – in which case, just walk through it – or outside Dali's northeast corner at the Nanguo Cheng building (南国城, nánguó chéng) – catch bus #2 via Yu'er Park and the Fuxing Lu crossroads to Bo'ai Lu. Otherwise, all "Dali"-bound buses, trains and flights actually terminate 18km south at **Xiaguan** (下关, xiàguān). To get to Dali (大理, dàlǐ), catch local bus #4 (which heads to Dali's North Gate; ¥2) or #8 (to Dali's West Gate; ¥2) – details of where to catch them are given in the relevant listings (see p.202). Buses cost ¥2 and run daily 6.30am–7pm. A taxi between Dali and Xiaguan costs about ¥50.
Onwards tickets (services all originate in Xiaguan) can be booked through accommodation or agents in Dali. Heading north by bus, agents should be able to arrange a pick-up from the highway as the bus goes past; for elsewhere, you'll have to go to the relevant transit point in Xiaguan – where you can, of course, also buy tickets yourself.
Transport schedules are given in our Xiaguan coverage (p.202).

GETTING AROUND

Dali is small enough to **walk** everywhere, but cycling and local buses come in handy for Xiaguan and nearby sights. Regular buses run to Xiaguan (see below).

By bus Xiaguan–Dali city buses run 6.30am–7pm. Of most use are bus #4 from Bo'ai Lu to Xiaguan's South bus station; and bus #8 from outside Dali's West Gate to Xiaguan's train station, via the PSB and north bus station. Other bus routes

are given in the text.
By bicycle You can rent bikes through accommodation for ¥10–20/day, depending on the bike's age and condition.

INFORMATION, AGENTS AND TOURS

Tourist information The cafés and bars clustered on Renmin Lu's western end, Yangren Jie and Bo'ai Lu make good places to meet other foreigners and swap travel news, and find martial art, language or painting courses. You'll find maps at stalls around town and at Mandarin Books on Renmin Lu – there are useful ones printed on heavy brown paper which include detailed spreads of Dali, Lijiang and Shangri-La .
Tour agents and bookings Accommodation tour desks, the Dali Tourist Distributing Center (26 Renmin Lu ☎087 2267 9116) and freelance agents, such as long-running Michael's Travel (68 Bo'ai Lu ☎8613 9885 54733) all arrange

transport bookings, tours to village markets (usually claiming special knowledge of smaller, less-visited affairs), Er Hai boat trips and cormorant fishing (¥100), Bai home visits (¥50), and discounts for the Cang Shan cable cars.
Tour companies As well as the agents listed (see above), try **Climb Dali** (393 Renmin Lu ☎087 2887 1230, ⊚climbdali .com). They're tucked back off the street – look for *Boulder Bar* signs – and offer climbing and kayaking trips and information, and general tourist advice for the Dali area. **Trekking AMIWA** (⊚amiwa-trek.com) advise on local routes through the Cang Shan and can provide English-speaking Bai guides.

ACCOMMODATION

Dali's **accommodation** rates can double during local festivals. There are also alternative places to stay **outside Dali** in the Cang Shan range and the lakeside village of Xizhou (see p.214). For **house rentals** – including double bedrooms, kitchen-diners, living rooms, bathroom, garden TV and internet from ¥2700/week – contact *Holiday Villas* ⓦ rentahouse-yunnan.com, ⓔ roland_hourcade@yahoo.fr.

Dali Hump 大理驼峰青年旅舍, dàlǐ tuófēng qīngnián lǚshè. Honglong Jing ☎087 2267 6933, ⓦ dalihump.com. Sister to the Kunming operation, and a major travellers' hangout. Rooms are arranged around a broad courtyard with a bar, a restaurant with communal seating and a laidback, hippyish vibe. There's lots of musical activity in the evenings. Dorms ¥30, doubles ¥100

Fairyland 连锁酒店, liánsuǒ jiǔdiàn. 31 Yangren Jie, west of Bo'ai Lu ☎087 2268 0999. Probably the smartest place in town for the price, with modern hotel rooms inside a restored old courtyard house set back from the street. ¥229

★ **Fengqing Dali** 风清大理客栈, fēngqīng dàlǐ kèzhàn. 150m south of the South Gate at 81 Wenxian Lu ☎087 2269 9761, ⓔ yipulaxin1116@hotmail.com. Two tiers of rooms around a central atrium, decked out in modern Chinese furnishings, with helpful, friendly staff. They put out tables and chairs among plants in the courtyard and serve free tea and nibbles. ¥140

Four Seasons Youth Hostel 春夏秋冬青年旅舍, chūnxiàqiūdōng qīngnián lǚshè. 46 Bo'ai Lu, at Renmin Lu ☎087 2267 7177, ⓔ yhafs@yahoo.com. Modern courtyard setting with pool table, free internet, amiable staff and the obligatory bar. Dorms and small doubles are pretty functional; larger doubles have Japanese-style beds and better furnishings. Dorms ¥25, doubles ¥120

Hengshan Garden Hotel 恒山升花园酒店, héngshān shēng huāyuán jiǔdiàn. Luyu Lu ☎087 2268 0288. Friendly, quiet Chinese-style hotel with basic doubles and larger – though slightly stuffy – ones with wooden four-poster beds. They give out good hiking info, but not much English spoken. ¥80, bigger doubles ¥160

★ **Jade Emu/Jade Roo** 金玉缘中澳国际青年旅舍, jīnyù yuán zhōng'ào guójì qīngnián lǚshè. West Gate Village ☎087 2267 7311, ⓦ jade-emu.com. Large, clean, institution-like hostel complexes, just 30m apart. There's a touch too much concrete around the place, though the exteriors are done out in Bai-style decorations; the manager is Australian, staff are all bilingual and everything is well geared to foreign needs. Dorms ¥30, doubles ¥150

Jim's Tibetan Hotel 吉姆藏式酒店, jímǔ zàngshì jiǔdiàn. 4 Luyuan Xiang ☎087 2267 7824, ⓔ jimstibetanhotel@gmail.com. Likeable Jim has been a Dali fixture for decades, and this colourful modern take on a traditional Tibetan home – with a rooftop terrace and multiple floors facing out into a rose garden – is a quiet, spacious option well geared to travellers' needs. There's an excellent restaurant and fair-value trips out of town. ¥280

★ **Mao Mao Cool** 猫猫果儿客栈, māomāo guǒ'ér kèzhàn. 419 Renmin Lu ☎087 2247 4653. Stylish, open-plan modern atrium building with goldfish pond; rooms have wooden floors and slick black furnishings – the larger ones are like studio apartments. Quiet location might be a plus. Café and small library too. ¥220

★ **Moonshine Inn** 苍岳别院, cāngyuè biéyuàn. 16 Yu'er Xiang, Yu'er Lu ☎087 2267 1319. Nicely restored old three-storey courtyard compound guesthouse where rooms are priced according to floor: the ones on the top, with access to a roof terrace, are the nicest and priciest. Note that all the loos are squat style. It's not easy to find at first, as it's 20m down a narrow alley off Yu'er Lu; look for the red sign. ¥100, top floor ¥150

EATING

The **restaurants** outside the South Gate and around the intersections of Fuxing Lu with Renmin Lu and Huguo Lu offer inexpensive steamers of dumplings and **Bai specialities**, including fish or tofu casseroles, snails and stir-fried mountain vegetables and fungi. Ingredients are fresh but cooks tend to go overboard with oil and salt. Muslim canteens display grilled kebabs and fresh bread, and are a sounder bet. **Tea** is popular, either *pu'er* from southern Yunnan or locally grown green; most restaurants also keep jars of **plum wine** (梅酒, méijiǔ) on the counter, sold by the glass. For **cafés and bars** serving a mix of Western and Chinese staples, head to Renmin Lu's western end, along with adjacent Yangren Jie and Bo'ai Lu.

Amy's Courtyard Restaurant 2 Bo'ai Lu, just past the gate. Excellent place to try Bai fish-head (or tofu) casseroles, cold cucumber salad and deep-fried goat's cheese with sugar. Around ¥25/person.

★ **Bakery 88** 88 Bo'ai Lu. German-run café with superb European cakes and breads to eat in or take away; it's also a deli selling bacon, artichokes and *baba ganoush*.

Beifang Shuijiao 北方水饺, běifāng shuǐjiǎo. Renmin Lu. Inexpensive hole in the wall specializing in northern Chinese boiled dumplings, with friendly, slow service.

★ **Café de Jacks** Bo'ai Lu. Large, comfortable place to spin out a wet afternoon over a coffee and chocolate cake, or dig into their selection of curries, pizzas and a few Bai dishes. The open fire makes it cosy on winter evenings. Their popular bar sometimes hosts live music events.

Duanshi Baizu Fengwei Yuan 段氏白族风味园

duànshì báizú fēngwèi yuán. Wenxian Lu, 100m outside the gate. Named after the founder of the Tang-dynasty Dali Kingdom, Duan Siping, this unpretentious, open-fronted Bai-style restaurant is one of the better cheaper places in town. A good meal for two costs under ¥60.

Gogo Café Renmin Lu. Popular for spaghetti, pizzas, large breakfasts, fruit juices and good coffee. They also have a book exchange, free internet and can burn CDs. Like most restaurant-bars in the street, they stick tables outside during the summer.

Jim's Peace Café Bo'ai Lu. Restaurant underneath *Jim's Peace Guesthouse*, with comfy sofas, a well-stocked bar and a fine yak stew. Get four people together for a Tibetan banquet (¥30/person), cooked by the owner's mother.

★ **Namaste Afila** 亚菲拉印度菜, yàfēilā yìndù cài. Tucked into a small courtyard off Bo'ai Lu. A Moorish mud-brick and tiled courtyard and a wide selection of mostly vegetarian Indian samosas, curries and *thalis* make this a very attractive place to dine. There's a huge fireplace indoors

for cooler weather. Stuff yourself for ¥50.

Stella Pizzeria Yangren Jie. The wood-fired clay oven delivers the best pizzas in town, and the laidback decor is appealing too, with lots of nooks and crannies for privacy.

Sweet Tooth 甜点屋, tiándiǎn wū. 52 Bo'ai Lu. A polished and pristine café run by deaf-and-dumb staff, firmly catering to Western tastes with great cheesecake and biscuits.

★ **Xinghua Cun** 杏花村饭店, xìnghuā cūn fàndiàn. 165 Yu'er Lu ☎087 2267 0087. Genuine Dai place that has been going for years, though it has yet to upgrade its bare furnishings. Tasty home-cooked fare – especially their fish casserole. Expect to spend ¥50 a head.

Zhizhu Lin Vegetarian 纸竹林素食苑, zhǐ zhúlín sùshí yuàn. Bo'ai Lu. Elegant courtyard teahouse and vegetarian restaurant, whose English menu explains the medicinal qualities of each dish. Imitation crispy duck and "boiled beef slices", along with aromatic lotus root, crunchy fungi and a good tea will set you back about ¥80.

DRINKING AND NIGHTLIFE

Dali's nightlife revolves around its **bars**, most of which are along Yangren Jie and Renmin Lu. There's no charge to get in, and drinks are fairly cheap; the entertainment is mostly you and fellow bar-flies. Alternatively, a stack of **music bars** flanks the recently installed stream on Honglong Jing, catering to a more Chinese crowd, with outdoor tables and lounge chairs – they're all identical, so suit yourself.

★ **Bad Monkey** Renmin Lu. Favourite hangout for long-term expat foreigners, run by a pair of English wide boys offering fish and chips, Lao and Belgian beer and droll chat.

Kafka Bar 210 Renmin Lu. Quiet early on, heats up through the night with frequent live bands and music events. Foreign and bohemian-Chinese crowd.

Prajna Bar 126 Renmin Lu. Friendly, hippified atmosphere with regular juggling and poi-twirling.

Vodka Bar 143 Renmin Lu. Popular speakeasy, typical of the lower-profile places down the eastern end of Renmin Lu, with a late-afternoon 2-for-1 happy hour.

SHOPPING

Fuxing Lu is a good place to pick up classic Dali **souvenirs**: a marble chess set or rolling pin, deep-blue Bai tie-dyes, and attractive silver jewellery – which is not made locally, even though there's always someone outside the shop hammering on a piece of metal (watch for a while and you'll notice they never get any further). For older **ethnic textiles** – many of them from Guizhou's Miao – check out the stalls along Yangren Jie, either side of Bo'ai Lu; unusual things also surface here, such as **Bai woodblocks** for making New Year good-luck prints to paste up outside the home.

Antiques A small antiques market is held next to the mosque on Saturday mornings.

Bookshop There's a branch of Kunming's Mandarin Books

on the western arm of Renmin Lu, with plenty of English and Chinese maps and works about the area.

DIRECTORY

Banks The Bank of China (foreign exchange daily 8am–7pm) is on Fuxing Lu, where you'll also find Dali's only ATMs.

Internet There's a 24hr internet café (¥3/hr) at the top of Renmin Lu, near Bo'ai Lu, though most accommodation and foreign-friendly cafés have terminals and free wi-fi.

Laundry The Shanghai Taijie Laundry Cleaning Chain Stores Bo'ai Lu, cnr of Honglong Jing, charge ¥20/kg for a

wash, ¥30/kg for dry-cleaning.

Mail The post office (daily 8am–9pm) is on Fuxing Lu, at Hugou Lu. Expect to have all parcels posted here thoroughly checked for drugs.

Martial arts training Contact Wuwei Si (see p.214).

PSB and visas In Xiaguan (see p.204).

Around Dali

Just a quick bus ride north of Dali, **San Ta** – the Three Pagodas – are proud relics of Dali's past, guarding the entrance to the far more modern **Chongsheng Temple**. It's definitely worth pausing outside San Ta, though the main attractions around Dali are the **Cang Shan** range – threaded with hiking trails – and **Er Hai**, though the lake itself is probably of less interest than the **villages** dotting its shore. Some of these also host markets full of activity and characters, where you can watch all manner of goods being traded. Both mountains and lake can be seen on day-trips, though there's also **accommodation** along the way, from upmarket boutiques to spartan temples. Aside from the local options listed in this section, **agents in Dali** (see p.209) can organize transport, activities, tours and discounted entry tickets.

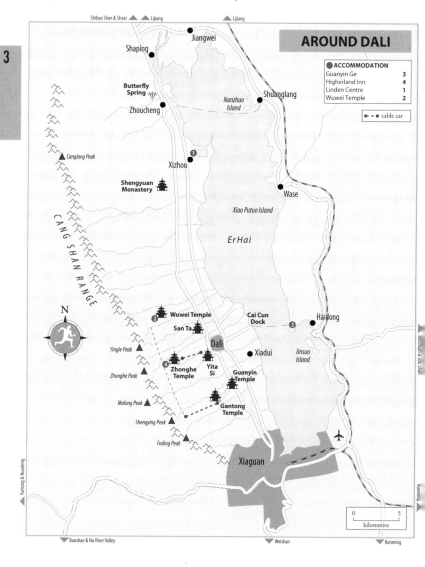

AROUND DALI

● ACCOMMODATION	
Guanyin Ge	3
Higherland Inn	4
Linden Centre	1
Wuwei Temple	2

● - ● cable car

San Ta and Chongsheng Temple

崇圣寺三塔, chóngshèng sì sān tǎ · San Ta ¥120, or ¥190 including temple complex · Bus #19 from Bo'ai Lu

Around 3km north of town, **San Ta** is Dali's most iconic landmark; three layered, cream-coloured pagodas gently tapering towards their summits, best seen at dawn as the sunlight picks them out against the dark green Cang Shan range. Built around 850 when the region was a major Buddhist centre, the 69m-tall, square-based **Qianxun Pagoda** is a century older than the two smaller octagonal towers which flank it, though all have survived a millennium of wars and earthquakes. Qianxun's design is classic Nanzhao, and other examples – in Kunming and Weishan, atop Jizu Shan, and outside Weixi and Dali's South Gate – stake out the boundaries of this former kingdom.

Having said all this, San Ta looks best at a distance; you can't climb the towers and the stiff entry fee only allows you to browse the souvenir stalls below. The adjoining **Chongsheng Temple** was founded in the ninth century, though the present oversized complex dates to 2005, an embarrassingly ostentatious example of a "build big" mentality, without the least hint of anything spiritual – save your money for other things.

Cang Shan

苍山, cāng shān · ¥30

Cang Shan, the Green Mountains, are just that: a 50km-long range peaking between 2100m and 4122m, cloaked in thick forest and cloud – and, often well into spring, snow. Exploring the heights is easy thanks to two **cableways**, accessible by bus or taxi from Dali, that take you part way up, their top stations linked by a level, 15km-long paved **walking trail** which passes lookouts, waterfalls, caves and shrines. In good weather, views off the mountain take in the whole Er Hai valley, with plenty of birdlife, the odd squirrel and colourful flowers alongside the path. Cang Shan's weather is very changeable, so take warm, weatherproof **clothing** whatever conditions are like when you start, and food and water.

To Zhonghe Temple

Taxi from Dali ¥10; cableway (25min) ¥35 single, ¥50 return

Cang Shan's **north entrance** (苍山北入口, cāngshān běi rùkǒu) is in the foothills behind San Ta, around 3km from Dali. The ski-lift-like **cableway** (苍山索道, cāngshān suǒdào) here doesn't operate in bad weather, or when not many tourists are expected, so check in town first – there's also an easy, two-hour hiking trail up.

The path and cable terminus meet at **Zhonghe Temple** (中和寺, zhōnghé sì), a bright place with a mix of Buddhist and Taoist iconography and a vegetarian restaurant; there are fantastic views out over the lake, and **accommodation** nearby at the *Higherland Inn* (see p.214). **Hikes** in the area include the easy, 15km-long trail south to the Gantong cable-car's upper station along a paved path, and a route up 4034m **Zhonghe Peak** (中和峰, zhōnghé fēng) – not something to be attempted without sound local advice on routes and conditions.

Southern Cang Shan

Bus #4 from outside Dali's North Gate (20min); cable car (25min) ¥50 single, ¥80 return

For Cang Shan's southern heights, take a bus 10km south of Dali to the roadside **Guanyin Temple** (观音寺, guānyīn sì), the focus for an important **festival** in late March, then walk or catch a cab (¥10) – it's a long, steep road – uphill to **Gantong Temple** (感通寺, gǎntōng sì). Once Dali's most celebrated Buddhist monastery, now reduced to two halls, Gantong is of most interest for its **cable car** (感通索道, gǎntōng suǒdào), whose gondolas traverse forested ridges with fantastic views over the town and lake as they climb to the upper station – note that there is **no walking trail** up the mountain from Gantong.

At the upper station, **Qingbi Stream** forms a kingfisher-blue pool as it cascades down a rockface, and it's a short walk to the **Grand Canyon**, a deep ravine with lookout platforms. From here, it's 15km along the main path to Zhonghe from where, if the cableway isn't working, you can walk back down to town.

3

Higherland Inn 高地宾馆, gāodì bīnguǎn. 10min walk up the stairs behind Zhonghe Temple ☎ 087 2266 1599, ⓦ higherland.com. A self-contained and well-equipped hostel with a garden; you need to book at least three days in advance, and can only get here on foot or via the cableway (see p.213). Dorms ¥30, doubles ¥120

Wuwei Temple 无为寺, wúwéi sì. In the hills 8km north of Dali – a cab costs ¥30. Not a hotel, but a working Buddhist temple whose monks run a martial arts school. There are strict rules for kung fu students: no meat, smoking or alcohol; separate dorms for men and women; and five hours training a day, six days a week. ¥300/week, all-inclusive.

Er Hai
洱海, ěr hǎi

Er Hai, the "Ear Lake", stretches 40km along the flat valley basin east of Dali, its shore fringed with Bai villages. The western side is well watered by streams descending the Cang Shan range, and the flat, 3km-broad belt between the mountains and water is coloured vivid green after rice planting in May. Er Hai's eastern shores are much drier, better suited to fruit; plenty of **garlic** is grown here too, and you can smell it in the air during harvest season.

Agents in Dali offer cormorant fishing trips (see p.209), but the only **cruises** available at present are on tourist ferries from Cai Cun dock, although there is also a ferry from **Zhoucheng**.

The lakeshore **villages** are perhaps more interesting – especially the Bai centre of **Xizhou** – and really fire up on **market days** (dates are given in specific accounts), when swarms of farmers, artisans and con-artists peddle their wares, from Bai textiles to huge bags of hemp seeds, trays of fermented "stinking tofu" and all manner of foods and spices (plus some grisly ad hoc dentistry). The Bai favour blue waistcoats, Yi women wear bright green smocks and Muslim Hui don't seem to favour any uniform. Tour agents run special market trips, or you can reach many of the villages easily enough by **cycling** or on **local buses** – though Er Hai's east shore is poorly served by public transport.

Xizhou
西洲, xīzhōu

About 20km north from Dali, right on the highway behind an ornamental lotus pond, **XIZHOU** is the single most important Bai town. Set in the middle of a prime agricultural area and well placed for supplying caravan routes, during the Qing dynasty its citizens were well travelled and wealthy, some trading down into Southeast Asia and even overseas. By the early twentieth century Xizhou was full of temples and ornate family mansions, though it fell into a decline after warlords, and then political turmoil, swept the region. The town survived, if not exactly in prime condition, and you can spend an enjoyable morning wandering around with a camera.

As you get off the bus, look for a lane heading lakewards beneath an enormous **banyan tree**, full of nesting egrets – it's hard to miss the smell and noisy croaking – and follow it down to Xizhou's slightly dishevelled **main square**; there are a few **snack stalls** here, some with English menus. On the square's south side, the large and ornate **Yan Family Mansion** (¥60; includes tea) is unusually well restored; the Yans are one of Xizhou's four Bai clans.

South of the square, Xizhou's **pedestrianized main street** is lined with small stores; side alleys are full of stone and brick Bai mansions, all cracked and patched, with their characteristic flared gateways and wooden doors. One lane leads to the **morning market**; another passes a busy **local deity temple** (本主庙, běnzhǔ miào) which generously gives space to Buddhist, Taoist and village spirits. Further down is the outer wall and **east gate**, just inside of which is the nineteenth-century "**General's House**" and its ancient caretaker, both in a bad state of repair.

Take the main lane out towards the lake and you'll soon pass the **Linden Centre** (喜林苑, xīlín yuàn), a 1940s mansion beautifully restored by an American art collector and now serving as a cultural centre and upmarket hotel (see p.216) – if you can't afford to stay here, at least call to see if you can drop in for a tour.

Zhoucheng

周城, zhōuchéng

ZHOUCHENG, a small and bland village another 10km up the highway from Xizhou, is a **tie-dyeing centre** where you'll see people sitting out on their front porches sewing designs into sheets prior to soaking them in indigo. There's a low-key market here to the south, under a shady fig tree; the more obvious **main marketplace** sells a mix of tourist tat, clothing and food every afternoon. Useful **ferries to Shuanglang** (see below) leave from the dock just north of town.

Behind Zhoucheng's main marketplace, the **Butterfly Spring** (蝴蝶泉, húdié quán; ¥80) is a deep, electric-blue pond haunted by clouds of butterflies when an overhanging acacia flowers in early summer. A pleasant place for a picnic, with stone tables and seats, it's also the focus for the **Butterfly festival** on the 15th of the fourth lunar month (late May or early June), where entry is free and crowds turn out to dance, sing and sacrifice pigs and chickens in front of the spring.

Shaping

Overlooking the northwest corner of the lake around 30km from Dali and 5km from Zhocheng, **SHAPING** (沙坪, shāpíng) is a timber depot and stonemasonry centre worth a visit for its all-day **Monday market**, when what seems like the entire regional population crowds onto the small hill behind town. Most people – traders and shoppers, laden down with wicker backpacks, almost always seem to be women, incidentally – deal in seasonal fruit, veg, fungi and lake fish, though a few stalls sell tie-dye cloths traditionally patterned with flowers and butterflies.

The east shore

From Shaping, public transport dries up as the road cuts around to Er Hai's east shore; there are further markets on Saturdays at **Jiangwei** (江尾, jiāng wěi), right at the top of the lake, and each Tuesday at **SHUANGLANG** (双廊, shuāngláng), on Er Hai's northeast shore. Once a sleepy Bai village, recent boutique redevelopment might see Shuanglang emerging as a slightly more traditional, lakeside version of Dali in coming years. Immediately offshore, **Nanzhao Island** is a tourist trap trading on regional history, whose unlikely "Summer Palace" – looking like a European castle – is visible from miles away.

A further 15km south and you're at **WASE** (挖色, wāsè), another small settlement of crumbling old houses and narrow back lanes, its waterfront thick with fishing gear and with another good market on dates ending in -5 or -0. Just south, **Xiao Putuo Island** (小普陀岛, xiǎo pǔtuó dǎo; ¥30) is a tiny rock completely occupied by a Ming-dynasty temple to Guanyin. From Wase, you might be able to wrangle a boat across to Dali; otherwise there are buses through the day to Xiaguan's Dali bus station.

GETTING AROUND   **ER HAI**

By bus Frequent buses from outside Dali's West Gate stop at Xizhou (30min; ¥7), Zhoucheng (40min; ¥9) and Shaping (50min; ¥12); there are also buses between Xiaguan and Wase (40min; ¥10).

By bicycle Quite a few people cycle around Er Hai, spending the night at villages such as Wase; you're looking at over 100km for a complete circuit via Xiaguan. The going is level throughout, but be aware that the highway between Xiaguan and Shaping is very busy with buses and trucks, and the east shore is drier and hotter. Rent bikes

through agents in Dali.

By boat Cai Cun Docks (才村码头, cái cūn mǎtóu), accessible via bus #2 from Dali's Bo'ai Lu, has tourist ferries (¥150 return) to Guanyin Ge, a flashy viewing pavilion next to an ugly cement factory on the east shore. You may also be able to wrangle a trip across to the east-coast villages from here. Ferries to Shuanglang depart from Zhoucheng's Taoyuan dock (桃源码头, táoyuán mǎtóu; 1hr; around ¥40), just down off the main road north of town; prices and schedules are by negotiation.

ACCOMMODATION

There are basic **guesthouses** in all the main villages around Er Hai, charging around ¥35/person/bed, with shared facilities.

★ **Linden Centre** 喜林苑, xǐlín yuàn. 5 Chengbei Xi, Xizhou village ☎ 087 2245 2988, ⓦ linden-centre.com. Very suave hotel and restaurant inside a beautifully restored Bai mansion, its rooms a mix of traditional and modern furnishings finished to the highest standards. They run various cultural workshops and tours; there's a three-night minimum stay. Contact them for prices, but you're looking at upwards of ¥800/night.

Shaxi and around

The attractive old mud-brick Bai town of **Shaxi** occupies a flat, heavily farmed valley 95km northwest of Dali. Shaxi's tiny size belies a long history as an important staging post at the foot of the Tibetan Plateau on the local **Tea-Horse Road** (see p.81), which flourished from the seventh century right up until modern times; **Buddhism** arrived along it early on, leaving temples along the valley and fabulous carved grottoes at nearby **Shibao Shan**.

The town is an easy detour off the Dali–Lijiang highway, via frequent minibuses from the tiny road junction of **Dian Nan** (甸南, diàn nán), known for its woodcarvers and a **Yi market** held on dates ending in a -0. Shaxi itself warrants an overnight stop, though you'll need a good half-day to visit Shibao Shan, and longer if you plan to trek the old trade routes up to the village of **Maping Guan**.

Shaxi

沙溪, shāxī • ¥30

After suffering neglect and desecration during the 1960s, **SHAXI** was sensitively restored in 2008 and makes an atmospheric place to spend a couple of nights; try and catch the exuberant **Friday market**, or the **Eryueba Buddhist Festival** in March, which inject a bit of life into this normally placid farming town. Everything revolves around Shaxi's pedestrianized old core, **Sideng** (寺登古村, sìdēng gǔ cūn), a network of tiny lanes clogged by livestock and seasonal threshing parties, which run between the patched, earth-brown adobe walls of Bai family compounds; look for the elaborately layered, flared eaves rising over doorways, some with carved reliefs of animals on their stone doorposts.

Sifang

四方街, sìfāng jiē

Shaxi's 50m-wide market square, **Sifang**, is overlooked by fierce guardian figures protecting westerly **Xingjiao Temple** (兴教寺, xīngjiāo sì), founded by the esoteric Azhali Buddhist sect in 1415. It's a small, calm place with a few courtyards and wooden-roofed hall housing ornately gilded Buddhist statuary; its famous Tibetan-style **murals**, as old as the temple itself, were being restored at the time of writing. Facing Xingjiao across the square, a **theatre stage** fronts a tiny museum, where locally excavated turquoise beads, cowrie shells and bronze weapons point to Shaxi being settled as early as 500 BC.

The gates and Yujin Bridge

South off Sifang, a 200m-long lane winds to the **south gate**, a two-storey mud-brick fortification bounded by wooden houses which is more of a boundary than any sort of serious defence. Many of the dwellings nearby have **twigs** stuck into the doorways, apparently to ward off snakes (not that these seem to be a problem in town).

Just east from Sifang, the **east gate** is even less imposing, and leads onto the banks of the **Heihui River**. About 200m downstream, the arched stone **Yujin Bridge** (玉津桥, yùjīn qiáo) marks the start of the old packhorse route north to Tibet; there are views from here out over the valley.

Shibao Shan

石宝山, shíbǎo shān • ¥50 • Minibus ¥160, including waiting time – find them on Shaxi's main road, or accommodation can organize

Shibao Shan, the "Stone Treasure Mountain", is a steep series of forested ridges in the hills 10km north of Shaxi; you can organize a minibus from town, or hike it cross-country in around three hours. A Buddhist site since the Tang dynasty, today the main target is **Shizhong Temple** (石种寺, shízhòng sì), perched on an outcrop and reached from the end of the access road along a short stepped path. Shizhong comprises two small complexes, piggy-backing each other among the pine forest; it's not the buildings that are of interest here but a series of life-sized, Nanzhao-era **sculptures** carved into a 100m-long sandstone grotto. The carvings' obvious **foreign influence** illustrates how cosmopolitan this now-remote spot once was, from a bearded, big-nosed camel handler to a curvy, Indian-style Guanyin and a very un-Chinese rendition of the sage Vimalakirti, cross-legged and turbaned. The **final niche** contains a sculpture of, as the caption tactfully puts it, "female reproductive organs", a popular destination for couples coming to pray for children, and which might predate Shibao Shan's Buddhist bias.

Down near the bottom of the mountain – you'll pass it on the access road, but it's too far for a day-hike from Shaxi – **Baoxiang Temple** (宝相寺, bǎoxiàng sì) was founded in 1291 but has recently been given an unflattering, over-large facelift, though there are hordes of **monkeys** here and paths scale the cliff behind to good viewpoints over the dense surrounding woodland.

Maping Guan
马坪关, mǎpíng guān

MAPING GUAN is an isolated village of about a dozen houses guarding a 3000m-high pass out of the valley above Shaxi; it was set up as a government inspection post to keep an eye on salt smugglers trying to poach from the brine wells at nearby **Dian Xi**. The main point in coming up here is simply to travel along the rugged old trade route, which is still used by locals and can be dusty or extremely muddy, depending on the weather; with an extra day you could push on west to **Mi Sha village** (弥沙, mí shā). Give yourself five hours on foot to reach Maping Guan, where it's possible to stay overnight with villagers – though you need to take food with you. Contact *Horse Pen 46* in Shaxi about arranging a trip.

ARRIVAL AND DEPARTURE   SHAXI AND AROUND

By bus Buses travelling the Dali–Lijiang highway can drop you off at Dian Nan (甸南, diàn nán); alternatively, get out at Jianchuan (剑川, jiànchuān), a highway town 10km further north. Jianchuan–Dian Nan–Shaxi minibuses (daily approx 8am–4pm) terminate on a modern street on Shaxi's west side; walk down the steps and you're on cobbles leading down through the old town

to Sideng. Heading back, Jianchuan has a proper bus terminal, while at Dian Nan you'll have to flag down passing traffic.
Destinations from Jianchuan Dali (1hr 30min; ¥27); Lijiang (2hr; ¥39); Shaxi (30min; ¥8).
Destinations from Dian Nan Dali (1hr 20min; ¥27); Lijiang (2hr; ¥39); Shaxi (20min; ¥8).

INFORMATION

Tourist information *Horse Pen 46* (see below) is a mine of information about the region, and can arrange minibus hire, mountain biking, abseiling and horse treks, plus

directions for hiking to Shibao Shan. A horse and guide for the overnight trek to Maping Guan costs ¥160.

ACCOMMODATION AND EATING

Shaxi's **accommodation** can be hard to locate despite bilingual signs. A couple of **teahouses** such as the *Old Tree Café* near Sideng offer snacks, with **stir-fry canteens** up on the main road where the minibuses stop. Some accommodation provides meals, coffee and drinks – *Laomadian's* **restaurant** is easily the best in town.

★ **Horse Pen 46** 马圈46客栈, mǎjuàn sìshíliù kèzhàn. Sifang ☎ 087 2472 2299, 🌐 horsepen46.com. On Shaxi's main square, opposite the temple to the right of the stage, this hostel surrounds a tiny atrium in a modernized old inn. Rooms are a bit rough around the edges, but this adds to the charm. The helpful staff speak

excellent English. Doubles with shared facilities **¥60**, en suite **¥100**
Jinshui Loutai 近水楼台客栈, jìnshuǐ lóutái kèzhàn. Between Sideng and the east gate ☎ 087 2472 1488. Flowery courtyard surrounded by tidy, clean, simple rooms; they also offer bar, internet and meals. **¥80**

3

★ **Laomadian Lodge** 老马店客栈, lǎomǎdiàn kèzhàn. On the north side of Sideng ☎ 087 2472 2666, ⓦ yourantai.com. Old stables and inn splendidly restored with wooden furnishings, all set around the inevitable flagstoned courtyard. Their restaurant serves excellent, rather spicy Yunnanese food, and they even have a wine list. **¥400**

Ou Yang Guesthouse 三家巷客栈, sān jiā xiàng kèzhàn. On the left as you walk downhill towards Sideng from the newer part of town ☎ 087 2472 2171. An old, unrestored Bai home with straightforward beds and shared facilities. Dorms **¥40**

Tea and Horse Caravan Trail Inn 古茶马客栈, gǔ chámǎ kèzhàn. Beigu Xiang, another backstreet alley north of Sideng ☎ 087 2472 1051. Twin courtyards, one with older, inexpensive dorms all with shared facilities; the other with neater, tidier en-suite doubles. Dorms **¥40**, doubles **¥120**

Lijiang

丽江, lìjiāng

LIJIANG nestles 150km north of Dali among green fields and pine forests, at the foot of the inspiringly spiky and icebound massif of **Yulong Xue Shan**. Surrounded by a modern city, Lijiang's **old town** is the capital for the **Naxi**, a Tibetan people who ruled this part of Yunnan from the thirteenth century onwards, and forms a maze of winding cobbled lanes lit by red lanterns and flanked by clean streams, weeping willows and rustic stone bridges. Lijiang has become a victim of its own success, and its pretty streets are now choked with visitors, with packhorses dutifully led up and down to add an "olde worlde" atmosphere and its traditional Naxi homes converted into ranks of quaint guesthouses and souvenir shops – mostly run by Han Chinese. Indeed, so popular is Lijiang that the "old town" grows bigger every year in order to accommodate the extra visitors.

Despite these dubious changes (which have become the model for the redevelopment of old towns right across China), it's easy to spend an enjoyable few days in Lijiang, especially if you've got children in tow or have been out in the wilds and need a good feed, a hot shower and somewhere to unwind. There's also genuine culture lurking around the town's fringes, and plenty of rewarding excursions into the **nearby countryside**. Note that, aside from onwards travel straight up the highway to Shangri-La, Lijiang is also the starting point for backroad trips northeast to Lugu Lake (p.229), on the Sichuan border, or northwest to a rare monkey reserve and a tough alternative trip to Deqin (see p.231).

The old town (Dayan)

大研古城, dàyán gǔchéng

Lijiang's old town – known locally as **DAYAN** – is completely pedestrianized and cobbled; take care on the slippery stones, worn smooth by centuries of use. **Streams** run all over the place – the town was laid out so that water passed by everyone's house – and there are said to be over three hundred **bridges** here. One of Dayan's charms is in the wobbly tiled rooflines and random angles of the many traditional wood-fronted houses; all have **fish** carvings under the eaves, as the sound in Chinese, *yu*, is auspiciously similar to the word for "surplus".

Along Dong Dajie

At the north of the old town, **Gucheng Kou** is a wedge-shaped square marking the boundary with the new town; city buses drop off either side, and there's a useful orientation point in the giant wooden **water wheel** to the west. Dayan's main street, **Dong**

LIJIANG FEES

While there is no charge to enter Lijiang itself, you do have to buy an **Old Town Maintenance Fee ticket** (¥80; valid for a month) before you can visit specific sights in Lijiang and the surrounding area – a few places have an additional entry fee on top of this.

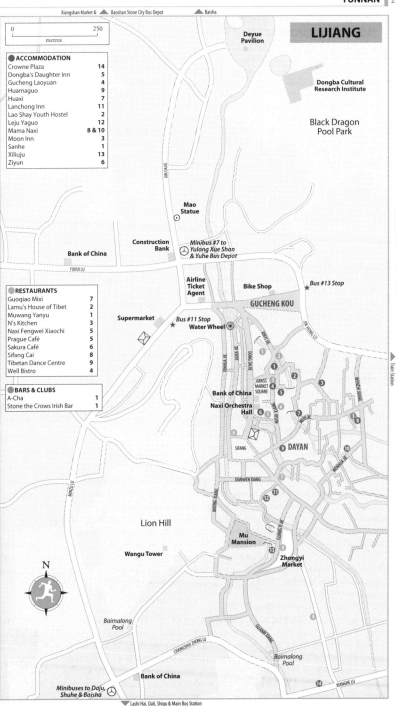

Xiangshan Market & Baoshan Stone City Bus Depot · Baisha

LIJIANG

0 — 250 metres

● ACCOMMODATION

Crowne Plaza	14
Dongba's Daughter Inn	5
Gucheng Laoyuan	4
Huamaguo	9
Huaxi	7
Lanchong Inn	11
Lao Shay Youth Hostel	2
Leju Yaguo	12
Mama Naxi	8 & 10
Moon Inn	3
Sanhe	1
Xiliuju	13
Ziyun	6

● RESTAURANTS

Guoqiao Mixi	7
Lamu's House of Tibet	2
Muwang Yanyu	1
N's Kitchen	3
Naxi Fengwei Xiaochi	5
Prague Café	5
Sakura Café	6
Sifang Cai	8
Tibetan Dance Centre	9
Well Bistro	4

● BARS & CLUBS

A-Cha	1
Stone the Crows Irish Bar	1

Deyue Pavilion

Dongba Cultural Research Institute

Black Dragon Pool Park

3

Mao Statue

Construction Bank

Bank of China

FUHUI LU

Minibus #7 to Yulong Xue Shan & Yuhe Bus Depot

Airline Ticket Agent

Bike Shop

Bus #13 Stop

GUCHENG KOU

Supermarket

Bus #11 Stop
Water Wheel

GRASS MARKET SQUARE

Bank of China

Naxi Orchestra Hall

SIFANG

DAYAN

XIANWEN XIANG

Lion Hill

Wangu Tower

Mu Mansion

Zhongyi Market

Baimalong Pool

CHANGSHUI ZHONG LU

Baimalong Pool

N

Bank of China

XIANGHE LU

Minibuses to Daju, Shuhe & Baisha

Lashi Hai, Dali, Shigu & Main Bus Station

Tram Station

3

NOMANDS AND MATRIARCHS: THE NAXI

The **Naxi** are descended from Tibetan nomads who settled the region before the tenth century, bringing with them a shamanistic religion known as **Dongba**. A blend of Tibetan Bon, animist and Taoist tendencies, Dongba's scriptures are written in the only hieroglyphic writing system still in use, with 1400 pictograms. The Naxi deity **Sanduo** is a warrior god, usually shown dressed in white, riding a white horse and wielding a white spear; murals depicting him and other deities still decorate many temples around Lijiang.

Strong **matriarchal** influences permeate Naxi society, particularly in the language. For example, nouns become weightier when the word female is added, so a female stone is a boulder, a male stone a pebble. Women inherit property, do most of the work, and own most of the businesses; accordingly, the Naxi women's costume of caps, shawls and aprons is sturdy and practical, while retaining its symbolic meaning; the upper blue segment of the shawl represents night, a lower sheepskin band represents daylight, and two circles around the shoulder depict the eyes of a frog deity. Naxi men often appear under-employed, though they have a reputation as good gardeners, musicians and falconers.

For an entertaining account of Lijiang and the Naxi during the 1930s, read Peter Goullart's *Forgotten Kingdom* (see p.395); it's sold at bookshops in town.

Dajie, runs south from here, lined with souvenir shops selling silver jewellery, hand-woven cloth, *pu'er* tea and bright baubles; look north to see Yulong Xue Shan's distant peaks. Dong Dajie terminates at **Sifang**, formerly Lijiang's main **marketplace**, a broad space still very much a social focus, especially fun at dusk, when Naxi women gather for surprisingly authentic-feeling group dances, in which everyone is welcome to join.

Backstreets

East from Dong Dajie and Sifang lies the intricate muddle of Dayan's old lanes, all great for a wander, though there are few actual sights. **Grass-market Square** (卖草场, màicǎo chǎng), where caravan owners would buy forage for their horses, is now a quiet, low-key place to sit out and watch the world go by. You'll probably also find yourself along **Wuyi Jie** at some point, a less cosmetic version of Dong Dajie with fewer souvenir shops and plenty of anonymous stir-fry joints, vaguely bohemian cafés and bars aimed at independent tourists.

Mu Mansion and around

Mu Mansion daily 8.30am–5.30pm • ¥60

South of Sifang behind a grand ornamental archway, the **Mu Mansion** (木府, mù fǔ) was home of the **Mu clan**, Lijiang's overlords for 470 years until the family fell into decline during the nineteenth century. The mansion was torched during an 1870 uprising, and what survived was destroyed in Lijiang's terrible **1995 earthquake**, but the grounds have been restored, containing ornamental halls and flower gardens. You can walk through them and up onto pretty **Lion Hill** (狮子山, shīzi shān; ¥15), site of some ancient cypress trees and the **Wangu Tower** (万古楼, wàngǔ lóu), the best place to look down over Dayan's ever-expanding mosaic of grey-tiled roofs. The lane leading down from Lion Hill to Sifang is lined with tiny cafés, several with more fine views.

Zhongyi Market and Baimalong Pool

Just east from the Mu Mansion, **Zhongyi Market** (忠义市场, zhōngyì shìchǎng) is where to glimpse a more "authentic" Lijiang, somewhere still patronized by resident Naxi. It's liveliest in the morning and, as usual with Chinese markets, is split into specialist sections. One corner is devoted to **metalwork** – the town is a marketplace for copper wares – including hand-beaten Mongolian hotpot cookers, basins, kettles, ladles, brass door decorations and **horse bells** (embossed with tiger heads to scare off bad luck). There are acres devoted to fruit and veg – fresh, pickled, dried and candied – not to mention tofu, preserved duck eggs, livestock and meat. There are tailors here too, all women of course, making traditional **Naxi capes** (¥300). **Tea** is also big business: not just in rough leaves and "bricks" of ubiquitous *pu'er*, but also medicinal additives such as rose buds, dried bitter gourd slices and wolfberries; there's even fresh **butter** for sale and little wooden churns for turning it into Tibetan butter tea.

Right down at Dayan's southern limit on Guanbi Xiang, **Baimalong Pool** (白马龙潭, báimǎlóng tán) is a spring split into three different ponds for drinking, rinsing food and washing clothes – the latter still very much in use.

Black Dragon Pool Park

黑龙潭公园, hēilóng tán gōngyuán • Daily 7am–9pm • Free on showing Old Town Maintenance ticket • Bus #8 from Minzhu Lu, or walk north along the stream from Gucheng Kou

Up on Lijiang's northern outskirts, **Black Dragon Pool Park** is a beautiful place to stroll, circuiting the central Yu Quan (Jade Spring): with the peaks of Yulong Xue Shan rising behind, the elegant mid-pool **Deyue Pavilion**, reached over a humpbacked bridge, is outrageously photogenic. In the early afternoon, you can watch traditionally garbed musicians performing **Naxi music** in the lakeside halls.

A path runs around the shore between a spread of trees and buildings, passing the cluster of compounds that comprise the **Dongba Cultural Research Institute** (东巴文化研究室, dōngbā wénhuà yánjiūshì). The word *dongba* relates to the Naxi shamans, about thirty of whom are kept busy here translating twenty thousand rolls of the old Naxi scriptures – *dongba jing* – for posterity. Further around the east shore are a group of halls, relocated from other sites: **Longshen Ancestral Hall** (龙神祠, lóngshén cí), dedicated to the pool's dragon deity; and the grand **Wufeng Palace** (五凤楼, wǔfèng lóu), a Ming-dynasty relic of the now-defunct Fuguo Temple, guarded by truly ancient stone lions and an equestrian sculpture of the Naxi god **Sanduo**.

ARRIVAL AND DEPARTURE   LIJIANG

Lijiang is a transport nexus for northwestern Yunnan, with abundant plane, train and bus connections. Accommodation and other agents can arrange **tickets** for a fee.

BY PLANE

Lijiang's airport is 20km southwest; airport buses (¥15) deliver to the airline ticket office (民航售票处, mínháng shòupiàochù ☎ 088 8539 9999), 1.5km west of the old town on Fuhui Lu – catch bus #11 from here to Minzhu Lu. A taxi from the airport costs ¥100. There's also a useful ticket agent at the western end of Gucheng Kou (☎ 088 8533 3333), charging the same prices.

Destinations Beijing (2 daily; 4hr 30min); Chengdu (4 daily; 1hr 10min); Chongqing (4 daily; 1hr 40min); Jinghong (4 daily; 1hr); Kunming (5 daily; 50min); Shanghai (3 daily; 4hr 30min); Shenzhen (1 daily; 4hr).

BY BUS

Long-distance buses from Lijiang head in all directions: south to Dali, north towards Tiger Leaping Gorge and Shangri-La, east to Panzhihua (which is on the Chengdu–Kunming rail line – probably the quickest overland route to Chengdu) and northeast into Sichuan via Lugu Lake. There's also a rough, unreliable route northwest to Deqin via Weixi and the remote Lancang River Valley. Note that Shangri-La is often called "Zhongdian" on bus timetables. Local buses head to sights closer to town (see p.225).

Main bus station (客运中心, kèyùn zhōngxīn) 3km south of Dayan on the edge of the new town; catch bus #11 from outside to the western end of Gucheng Kou on Minzhu Lu.

Destinations Dali (3hr 30min; ¥66); Deqin (8hr; ¥95); Kunming (9hr; ¥152); Lugu Lake (2 daily; 8hr; ¥60); Panzhihua (3 daily; 8hr; ¥87); Qiaotou (1hr 30min; ¥28); Shangri-La (3hr 30min; ¥65); Xiaguan (4hr; ¥40).

Express bus station (高快客运站, gāo kuài kèyùn zhàn), on the northeastern outskirts on Xiangelila Dadao; bus #8 passes the old town.

Destinations Dali (3hr 30min; ¥66); Kunming (9hr; ¥152); Shangri-La (3hr 30min; ¥65); Xiaguan (4hr; ¥40).

Yuhe bus depot (玉河停车场, yùhé tíngchēchǎng), just north of the old town off Xin Dajie.

Destinations Daju (2 daily; 2hr; ¥34).

Smaller stations such as the depot at the corner of Changshui Zhong Lu and Minzhu Lu deal with traffic to outlying destinations.

Destinations Baishui Tai (1 daily; 3hr; ¥40); Jiudian (4hr; ¥25); Shigu (1hr 30min; ¥10); Tacheng (1 daily; 4hr 30min; ¥45); Weixi (2 daily; 7hr; ¥83)

3

BY TRAIN

Lijiang's train station is 20min southeast of town on bus #13 from the east side of Gucheng Kou; the overnight service is the most convenient way to reach Kunming. The line is currently being extended north to Shangri-La (Zhongdian).

Destinations Kunming (2 daily; 7–9hr); Xiaguan (1 daily; 1hr 35min).

GETTING AROUND

By bus Buses through the new town to transit points run daily 6.30am–9pm and cost ¥1.

Bicycles Bikes can be rented through some accommodation, from *N's Kitchen* (see opposite), or from the shop on the north side of Gucheng Kou, for around ¥30/day plus your passport as deposit.

INFORMATION AND TOURS

Maps Lijiang maps are sold everywhere; bilingual ones printed on brown card called "Exploring Dali, Lijiang and Shangri-La" (¥6) have a detailed layout of the old town, along with an area map of all Northwestern Yunnan.

Tourist information The best source of information is your accommodation or one of the Western cafés such as *N's Kitchen* or *Lamu's House of Tibet*. Places calling themselves "Tourist Reception Centres" or similar only sell packaged tours; look instead for "Old Town Management Board Tourism Service Point" booths, which give neutral information about local buses and access details for outlying sights, though usually only Chinese is spoken.

Tours Trips are offered by accommodation and agencies around town; check what is included beyond transport as entry fees, English-speaking guide, meals and so on might be extra. Day-trips include excursions to Yulong Xue Shan (¥330) or Tiger Leaping Gorge (¥100); longer trips via Shangri-La cover Meili Xue Shan (¥550), or head to Yading and Daocheng (¥1560).

Websites Good resources include ⓦnorthwestyunnan .com, an ecotourism site with information and tours in the Lashi Hai and Wen Hai regions outside town.

ACCOMMODATION

Lijiang's old town is thick with **traditional Naxi homes**, featuring two tiers of wooden balconies around a central courtyard, that have been converted to guesthouses and hotels. Rooms on the ground floor are less private and sometimes cheaper. Though **addresses** are listed they aren't much help – many places are on side-alleys, off larger streets.

BUDGET

Dongba's Daughter Inn 东巴女客栈, dōngbā nǚ kèzhàn. 69 Wuyi Jie ☏088 8888 4066. Quiet and slightly out-of-the-way guesthouse, with friendly staff and inexpensive rooms; not the most modern, but feels far more like a genuine homestay than most. ¥120

Gucheng Laoyuan 古城老院客栈, gǔchéng lǎoyuàn kèzhàn. Xinyi Jie, off Mishi Xiang past the *Well Bistro* ☏088 8517 7853. Good-value modern take on the Naxi theme, with a cobbled courtyard and pleasant, though fairly small doubles. Don't take the room at the top of the stairs; they leave the safety light on all night. No English spoken. ¥130

Lanchong Inn 懒虫小住客栈, lǎnchóng xiǎozhù kèzhàn. 6 Xingwen Gang, Qiyi Jie ☏088 8511 6515. Laidback place popular with young middle-class Chinese backpackers, close to Sifang and the Mu Mansion, although the lane itself is fairly quiet. All rooms en suite. Lower floor ¥150, upper ¥170

Lao Shay Youth Hostel 老谢车马店, lǎoxiè chēmǎdiàn. 25 Jishan Xiang, Xinyi Jie ☏088 8511 6118, ⓦlaoshay.com. Located at the heart of the old town, with all the information you could ever need about the area; there's a wide range of rooms, though it's a little pricier than its competitors. Dorms ¥30, doubles ¥80

★ **Mama Naxi** 70 Wenhua Jie ☏088 85107713, ⓔzhao_gang1982@yahoo.com. Friendly, chaotic but ultimately well-run hostels – there are three branches in nearby lanes – though rooms can noisy and the garrulous owner is occasionally overbearing. This, the main branch, has an excellent restaurant offering communal, home-cooked meals. Dorms ¥20, doubles with en suite ¥150

Xiliuju 溪留居客栈, xīliújū kèzhàn. 120 Zhongyi Xiang, Guangyi Jie ☏088 8518 9667, ⓦlijtaiwan.com. Cool, quiet budget choice, even if furnishings are verging towards standard Chinese hotel quality (worn). There's an open-air lobby to laze around in and watch passing street life. ¥120

Ziyun 子云客栈, zīyún kèzhàn. Round the back of the Naxi Orchestra Hall, off Dong Dajie ☏088 8512 4559. Anonymous but decent place; the staff are genuinely friendly, the rooms are tidy and simple, and prices are low. Small doubles with shared bathroom ¥60, en-suite doubles ¥100

MID-RANGE AND UPMARKET

Crowne Plaza 丽江和府皇冠假日酒店, lìjiāng héfǔ huángguān jiàrì jiǔdiàn. 276 Xianghe Lu ☏088 8558 8888, ⓦichotelsgroup.com. International business hotel just south of the old town, modern but sympathetic with Naxi style, and colossally upmarket by local standards. There's plenty of timber and split stone, rooms are elegantly furnished, there's a spa and they organize golf packages. **¥2000**

Huamaguo 花马国客栈, huāmǎguó kèzhàn. Xingren Shangduan ☎088 8512 1688. Superb location right beside the main canal, which you can appreciate from a charming courtyard, but it's so open-plan that there's little privacy. A nearby bar gets noisy at night. **¥280**

Huaxi 桦溪文苑客栈, huàxī wényuàn kèzhàn. 19 Xingren Duan, Wuyi Jie ☎088 8511 2080, ✉huaxi828@163.com. Right on a stream, but tucked off the main drag. Very private, with a nice flower garden and large, well-appointed rooms; the manager is pretty helpful about local information, but doesn't speak English. **¥280**

★ **Leju Yaguo** 乐居雅国客栈, lèjū yǎguó kèzhàn. 13 Xinguan Xiang, Qiyi Jie ☎088 8888 2266, 🌐ljygkz

.com. A real beauty, friendly and with a courtyard garden full of flowers. Rooms are smart and modern with antique touches, and worth the higher-than-average price. Downstairs **¥200**, upstairs **¥230**

Moon Inn 新月阁, xīnyuè gé. 34 Xingren Xiang, Wuyi Jie ☎088 8518 0520, ✉mooninn@126.com. Large, quiet courtyard with chairs for lounging, and good-sized rooms hidden away in a quiet corner of the old town. Popular with independent travellers after some mid-range comforts. **¥220**

Sanhe 三合酒店, sānhé jiǔdiàn. 4 Jishan Xiang, Xinyi Jie ☎088 8512 0891, ✉sanhehotel@yahoo.com .cn. Comfortable, large but slightly tired courtyard hotel with spacious rooms, good service and English-speaking staff. Popular with small-scale foreign tour packages. **¥380**

3

EATING AND DRINKING

Lijiang's plentiful **restaurants** serve a good range of Western and Chinese dishes. Foreigner-oriented **cafés** around Sifang all have wi-fi, book exchanges, mellow music and set-price Western breakfasts.

Guoqiao Mixi 过桥米线, guòqiáo mǐxiàn. 47 Guangmen Kou, Qiyi Jie. Cheerful place hung with red lanterns, right on the stream overlooking a little cascade; the name means "Crossing the Bridge Noodles" and, sure enough, this is the house speciality – ¥30 will fill you up. Many similar places nearby serve pizzas, casseroles or hotpots.

★ **Lamu's House of Tibet** 56 Xinyi Jie. Restaurant-café serving Western and Chinese staples, open from 7am for huge breakfasts. The upstairs terrace gives good views over the street. The best place in town to pick up local cycling maps and the latest trekking information for Tiger Leaping Gorge.

Muwang Yanyu 木王宴语, mùwáng yànyǔ. Xinyi Jie. One of several local streamside restaurants serving Naxi-inspired food; camphor-smoked duck, medicinal herb soups, vegetable hotpots and roast meats, plus some Cantonese dishes. Not cheap – expect ¥100/person – but the setting and good service makes it worth a splash.

★ **N's Kitchen** On Grass Market Square. A tiny place upstairs in a rickety wooden house, with perhaps the best burgers you'll get in China – generously meaty but not greasy – plus pizzas and heaps of hiking and biking information, along with bike rental.

Naxi Fengwei Xiaochi 纳西风味小吃, nàxī fēngwèi xiǎochī. Tucked just off the street past the *Prague Café*. Small, inexpensive canteen with run of Yunnan staples and light meals. Steer clear of the yak stew though – too much stew and precious little yak. Mains ¥15–40.

Prague Café Xinyi Jie. Scores highly for its location just past the bridge, excellent coffee and blueberry cake; a good spot to people-watch through the windows. Some Chinese staples too. ¥50.

Sakura Café 樱花屋金酒吧, yīnghuā wūjīn jiǔba. 123 Cuiwen Xiang, Xinhua Jie. Actually there are about five adjacent places with this name, each claiming to be the first. All offer reasonably priced beers and coffees, Japanese and Korean food, and get lively in the evening. Count on ¥80/head for a full meal.

FOOD IN LIJIANG

Lijiang's most ubiquitous speciality is **baba**, a stodgy deep-fried flour patty stuffed with sweet or savoury fillings – it's no great delicacy, but a solid, tasty breakfast or on-the-go snack. Mongolian-style **hotpots**, where you boil thinly sliced meat and vegetables at the table in a distinctive copper funnel-pot, are also a staple of Naxi home cooking, though some restaurants serve them too; they're great fun in a group, and far lighter than the Sichuanese version (see p.61). More widespread restaurant items include roast and steamed pork dishes; Yunnan ham; *qiguo ji* (chicken steamed with medicinal herbs); crossing-the-bridge noodles; grilled fish; and unusual wild plants such as fern tips. Many shops sell small bottles of lightly sweetened yak-milk **yoghurt** (¥6). In winter, keep an eye open in the markets for the best **walnuts** in Yunnan, and bright orange **persimmons** growing on big, leafless trees around town – these have to be eaten very ripe and are an acquired taste.

NAXI MUSIC AND DANCING

Using antique instruments, Lijiang's celebrated **Naxi Orchestra** performs Song-dynasty tunes derived from the Taoist Dong Jin scriptures. It's a tradition said to have arrived in Lijiang with Kublai Khan, who donated half his court orchestra to the town after the Naxi chieftain helped his army cross the Yangzi. Banned from performing during the Cultural Revolution, the orchestra regrouped in the 1980s under the guidance of **Xuan Ke**, though the deaths of many older musicians have reduced their repertoire. To counter the dearth of material, the orchestra's scope has been broadened by including traditional **folk singing** in their performances.

The orchestra plays nightly in Lijiang in the well-marked hall on Dong Dajie (8pm; ¥120–160; some agents offer discounted tickets). The music is at once strident, discordant and haunting, but Xuan Ke's commentaries drag on a bit; try to catch the orchestra practising in the afternoon in Black Dragon Pool Park, for free.

A little further north on Dong Dajie, another hall called the "Inheritance and Research Base of China" hosts a **song-and-dance troupe** who put on spirited nightly performances to a small audience (8–9.30pm; ¥80). Expect to be dragged on stage at the end. Similar audience participation is encouraged in the **nightly dances**, led by Naxi matriarchs, that start around 7pm in Sifang Square.

Sifang Cai 私房菜, sīfáng cài. 84 Zhongyi Xiang, near the Mu Palace and market. Naxi-style hotpots cooked by you at the table in a copper funnel fondue pot; inexpensive and traditional local food. From about ¥30/head, depending on the quantity and type of ingredients you choose.

Tibetan Dance Centre 68–69 Guzuo Xiang, near the market ⓦ thetibetandancecentre.org. Tibetan and vegetarian food, plus a nightly floor show of Tibetan dancing, starting at 9.30pm.

Well Bistro 井卓, jǐng zhuó. 32 Mishi Xiang. This cosy place wins universal approval for its friendly manageress and tasty pasta, coffee, apple cake and chocolate brownies. Early opening too (around 8am).

NIGHTLIFE

Barn-sized copy-cat clubs line **Xinhua Jie** and narrow, parallel **Jiuba Jie** ("Bar Street"). Expect smoke machines, coloured spots and lasers, heavy "rustic" wooden furnishings and dancers in fake-ethnic garb doing routines to high-decibel pop; a beer costs ¥30.

A-Cha 阿茶酒吧, ā chá jiǔbā. 130 Wuyi Jie, at the intersection with Wenzhi Xiang. The most popular of several small bars along this street aimed at Western and Chinese backpackers; A-Cha is downstairs, Crows is up top. Both have beer, spirits and small-scale live music.

Stone the Crows Irish Bar 130 Wuyi Jie, at the intersection with Wenzhi Xiang, above A-Cha. More booze and live music, plus outstanding balcony views of the old town, lit up at night with red lamps and fairy lights.

SHOPPING

Books The small bookshop a few doors north of the Post Office on Dong Dajie sells works about the area in English and Chinese, including the classics Lost Horizon (see p.396)and Forgotten Kingdom (see p.395).

Markets Dong Dajie and Zhongyi Market are the best places to look for souvenirs such as silver jewellery, hand-woven shawls, hand-beaten copper pots and blocks of pu'er tea.

Supermarkets There's a supermarket near the bank on Dong Dajie, and another in the new town on Minzhu Lu.

DIRECTORY

Banks There's a Bank of China, with several ATMs, along Dong Dajie in the old town. There are also more ATMs in the new town.

Massage There's a hard-fingered blind masseur (¥50/hr) on Guangyi Jie: head down Dong Dajie into Sifang, and Guangyi Jie is ahead and slightly to the left; the masseur is 75m along, up a staircase on the left-hand side. Perfect for strained muscles after a day out exploring the sights around Lijiang.

Post Office Just north of Sifang on Dong Dajie (daily 8am–10pm).

PSB 110 Taihe Lu, 1km west of the old town down Fuhui Lu, behind the more obvious Government Offices ⓣ 088 8513 2266.

Around Lijiang

Lijiang's pretty countryside is dotted with small Naxi villages, mostly lying below the foothills of the looming, ever-present **Yulong Xue Shan**. The area north of town is the most accessible, with some rural temples, a rustic retreat at **Wen Hai** and attractive **Yuhu** village, the latter the home of a myth-making *National Geographic* journalist during the 1930s. Most distant is **Baoshan Stone City**, an isolated Naxi community built on a rocky outcrop, from where it's possible to hire guides for long hikes onward to Tiger Leaping Gorge (see p.233) or Lugu Lake (see p.229).

You could pack several nearby sights into a single day-trip by renting a **minibus** (some are accessible on local transport), and it's also a superlative area to **cycle** around, the summertime valleys brimming with wildflowers of all descriptions – pick up detailed **cycling maps** from *Lamu's House of Tibet* (see p.223). Wen Hai and Yulong Xue Shan need at least a day each; a return trip to Baoshan Stone City will realistically take at least three days. Note that you need to show an **Old Town Maintenance Fee** ticket for all sights in the area that also have an entry fee, including Yulong Xue Shan.

Lashi Hai

拉市海, lāshì hǎi • ¥30 • Boating and horseriding about ¥90 • Lijiang's official information booths can arrange shared taxis for ¥10/person each way

Lashi Hai is a seasonal wetlands area and lake out in the meadows 10km west of Lijiang, with the recently restored, elegant Tibetan Buddhist complex of **Zhiyun Temple** (指云寺, zhǐyún sì; ¥15), on the far shore. Chinese tour groups visit for short, easy horseriding excursions, or to take a boat out on the water for an hour or two. In winter, tens of thousands of migratory wildfowl – including rare **black-necked cranes** – pour in and can be stalked around the very muddy shoreline, though there are also a few boardwalks and observation hides among the reedbeds.

North of Lijiang

With a day to spare, it's hard to beat the attractions lying along the fairly flat, 17km-long road north from Lijiang to Yuhu – though if you've more time, consider detouring west to good hiking country around **Wen Hai**, or stop over at the hamlets of **Shuhe**, **Baisha** or **Yuhu** for a change of pace. If **cycling** from Lijiang, head west along Fuhui Lu for 1.5km, until you reach a major crossroads; turn north up Xianggelila Dadao and keep going to the end, then bear left for Shuhe and the Baisha–Yuhu road.

Shuhe

束河古镇, shùhé gǔzhèn

Just 3km northwest of Lijiang, **SHUHE** is a missed opportunity: instead of being maintained as the charming rural hamlet it was, this old town has been developed as a miniature Lijiang, with the same mix of cafés, shops and restaurants set around recently installed

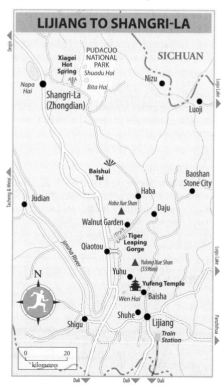

LIJIANG TO SHANGRI-LA

SICHUAN

Deqin

Xiagei Hot Spring

PUDACUO NATIONAL PARK

Shuodu Hai

Bita Hai

Nizu

Napa Hai

Shangri-La (Zhongdian)

Luoji

Lugu Lake

Tacheng & Weixi

Baishui Tai

Baoshan Stone City

Judian

Haba

Haba Xue Shan

Daju

Walnut Garden

Jinsha River

Qiaotou

Tiger Leaping Gorge

Yulong Xue Shan (5596m)

Yuhu

Yufeng Temple

Wen Hai

Baisha

Shuhe

Shigu

Lijiang

Train Station

Lugu Lake

Panzhihua

N

0   20
kilometres

Dali   Dali   Dali

streams and cobbles. It's definitely more laidback and rural than its larger neighbour – many houses here are still inhabited by farmers – and there's a vaguely arty, bohemian feel to the place, but not enough to make it noticeably different.

Baisha

白沙, báishā

BAISHA is a quiet three-street village 10km north of Lijiang, whose sprinkling of cafés and simple guesthouses make it an increasingly popular stopoff for independent tourists. It is one of the oldest Naxi settlements, predating the founding of Lijiang, and the main sight here is the **Dabaoji temple** (大宝积宫, dàbǎojī gōng; ¥30, plus the Lijiang Maintenance Fee ticket), a pleasantly proportioned complex of wooden halls and stone courtyards whose entrance is almost barred by the horizontal trunk of a 500-year-old tamarisk tree. Several of the halls are decorated with **fifteenth-century murals** (白沙壁画, báishā bìhuà), though surviving fragments are in a very sad state; one shows Buddha expounding his doctrines to the contemporary head of Lijiang's Mu clan.

Baisha's other claim to fame is **Doctor He Shixiu**, or "Doctor Ho", a traditional Chinese physician whose knowledge of local medicinal herbs is second to none. Those seeking miracle cures have been beating a path to his door since travel writer Bruce Chatwin profiled his skills during the 1980s; his surgery is amply signed in about ten languages. While the 80-year-old doctor quietly examines patients in a side-room, his son grabs sightseers, inundates them with piles of newspaper cuttings and harangues them with his father's life-story; it's overwhelming but if you can find a quiet moment and speak a little Chinese, the doctor is a fascinating man, who has led a tough but ultimately rewarding life.

Yufeng Temple

玉峰寺, yùfēng sì • ¥25, plus Old Town Maintenance Fee ticket

Around 4km up the road from Baisha, **Yufeng Temple** is a small, brightly coloured Tibetan affair in among pine forest; Naxi grannies perform a welcoming dance at the entrance and appreciate a small donation for their efforts. The temple halls, housing a statue of Tsongkhapa, founder of the dominant "Yellow Hat" lamaist sect, are not of great interest in themselves, but the pair of ancient, intertwined **camellia trees** (representing matrimonial harmony) on the top terrace produce huge magenta flowers in spring, when the courtyard with its mosaic floor is a nice spot for peaceful contemplation.

Yuhu

玉湖村, yùhú cūn

Four kilometres beyond Yufeng Temple, the tiny mud-brick settlement of **YUHU** is set in grassland on the lower slopes of Yulong Xue Shan. It's an oddly tidy, well-cared for place of perhaps thirty houses, where the eccentric explorer and botanist **Joseph Rock** based himself from 1921–49, and wrote articles on the Naxi that appeared in the *National Geographic* magazine, inspiring novelist James Hilton to pen his classic, *Lost Horizon* (see p.396).

WEN HAI

Wen Hai (文海, wén hǎi) is a beautiful alpine lake set 3000m up on Yulong Xue Shan's lower slopes, some 25km northwest of Lijiang; there's no road all the way, and it takes around four hours to walk in along signed paths from Shuhe, Baisha or Yuhu. The lake is a popular **hiking** destination, with small **Wenhai village** (文海村, wénhǎi cūn) acting as a base. Xintuo Ecotourism (☏ 1398 882 6672, ⊛ ecotourism.com.cn) charge ¥1000 for a five-day, four-night return trek to Wen Hai from Lijiang, including all transport, guides, accommodation and food; contact them in advance about accommodation if you plan to visit independently.

JOSEPH ROCK AND THE PLANT HUNTERS

Southwestern China's deep river valleys and tall, steep mountainsides nurture an incredible variety of **plant species**, from subtropical jasmines and hydrangeas to temperate wisterias, clematis, roses and azaleas, and alpine primulas, rhododendrons, gentians and saxifrages. Following up the findings of the French priests Delavey and David (see p.83), professional **plant hunters** from Europe and the US began to pour into the region during the early twentieth century, seeking new varieties of colourful blooms for gardens back home.

One of the first was **Ernest Wilson**, who tramped through Hubei and eastern Sichuan between 1902 and 1910, introducing Père David's **dove tree** to cultivation. He was followed by the phenomenally tough **George Forrest**, who narrowly escaped being murdered in an uprising along the Yunnan–Tibet border in 1905 (see p.233); undaunted, he returned to Yunnan seven times before dying in Tengchong in 1932. The prolific **Frank Kingdon Ward** collected seeds of the **blue poppy** in Yunnan's Lancang and Nu valleys in 1910, managing to get lost at every opportunity; while **Heinrich Handel-Mazzetti** circuited Yunnan and Sichuan during World War I, botanizing as he went. Thanks to his *National Geographic* articles, **Joseph Rock** is perhaps the most widely known of these collectors, and one of the last, being driven out of China by the Communists in 1949. He was equally expert on Hawaiian flora and spent much of his time in Yunnan researching his monumental anthropological work, *The Ancient Nakhi Kingdom of Southwest China*.

3

Rock's old home (洛克故居, luòkè gùjū; ¥15), an unpretentious courtyard house with grey-tiled roof and russet timber walls, is signed on the main street; inside is a collection of period photos (including a signed portrait of Rock dressed in furs) and mementoes of his stay – some household tools, pack-saddles and a gun. A steady trickle of foreigners turn up, but Yuhu is otherwise little visited and a **guesthouse** (see below) makes it an attractive place to stop over and do some **hiking** – Wen Hai makes a good target, or seasonal **Longnu Lake** (龙女湖, lóngnǚ hú), just 3km away – the guesthouse can provide directions.

GETTING AROUND   NORTH OF LIJIANG

Aside from the detour to Wen Hai, sights north of Lijiang are on, or near, the road running up to Yuhu. Shared **minibuses** shuttle from Lijiang to Shuhe and Baisha, though for the rest you'll need to rent a **minibus** or **cycle** your way around.

By shared minibus Shared minibuses to Shuhe (¥2) and Baisha (¥5–10) depart whenever full from a depot at the Minzhu Lu–Changshui Zhong Lu intersection in Lijiang. The depot is on the city bus #11 route between the old town and bus station; ask the driver to set you down at the Likelong Supermarket stop (丽客隆超市站, lìkèlōng chāoshì zhàn) and look for a cluster of vans.

By rented minibus Minibus rental touts gather at the western side of Lijiang's Gucheng Kou; a half-day whip around Shuhe, Baisha and Yushu costs ¥150 for a seven-seater vehicle. A recommended operator is 木愁 (mù chóu, ☎139 0888 3404), though she doesn't speak English.

ACCOMMODATION

Country Road Café 乡村路咖啡屋, xiāngcūn lù kāfēi wū. Baisha's main street ☎1528 448 0063. Supplies basic homestay accommodation out the back, plus Chinese and Western light meals, biking and hiking information and kung fu demonstrations. **¥60**

K2 Youth Hostel K2 国际青年旅社, K2 guójì qīngnián lǚshè. Shuhe's main street ☎088 8513 0110, ⓦk2yha.com. Tidy, friendly hostel in a modern wooden building; they've internet, 24hr hot water and

breakfast is included in the price. Dorms ¥25, doubles ¥128

Nguluko Guest House 雪嵩客栈, xuěsōng kèzhàn. Yuhu ☎088 8513 1616 or 139 8883 8431, ⓦsynotrip .com/yuhuhome. Hidden down a back lane in a courtyard house similar to Rock's old home, offering simple and clean accommodation with meals and shared facilities. They also arrange hiking and horseriding tours. Some English spoken. **¥100**

Yulong Xue Shan

玉龙雪山, yùlóng xuě shān • ¥80 • Minibus #7 (when full; 1hr; ¥15) from opposite the Construction Bank on the corner of Fuhui Lu and Xi Dajie

Legend has it that **Yulong Xue Shan**, the romantically named Jade Dragon Snow Mountain, is the abode of the protective Naxi deity Sanduo. The mountain's permanently icy 5596m summit has only been climbed once, but you can take in lower alpine meadows, glaciers and views of the peaks via three separate chairlifts. Minibuses run from town to each sight, though there isn't enough time to cover more than one in a single day.

Yunshan Ping (云杉坪, yúnshān píng; chairlift ¥50 one way) is a 3205m plateau with boardwalks leading out to grassland and gigantic fir trees, and views of the mountain's peaks rising above. Similar **Maoniu Ping** (牦牛坪, máoniú píng; ¥80) is higher at 3600m, with a temple; while the cable car at **Ganhaizi** (干海子, gànhǎizi; ¥160) is an impressive 3km long and climbs to 4506m, where a short trail leads over snowfields to a windswept viewing point across the **Yulong Glacier**. Ganhaizi is by far the most spectacular spot, and despite the altitude can get very crowded.

Baoshan Stone City

宝山石头城, bǎoshān shítou chéng

Around 110km northeast of Lijiang, **Baoshan Stone City** is more of a large village, built high on a rocky outcrop above the Yangzi, with views of tall mountains and steep, terraced slopes in all directions. Settled by the Naxi in the thirteenth century, before Lijiang was founded, it's still not easy to reach – a muddy, steep, hour-long footpath from the nearest road is the only way in – but the reward is immersion in village life and endless photo opportunities of this very uncosmetic, rural version of Lijiang.

Another good reason to visit is for local **hiking** opportunities – though you need a guide if you want to go far. The longest trail from Baoshan Stone City is a **four-day trek** to Lugu Lake (see opposite), through some remote Naxi and Mosuo territory. The route is unsigned and follows local footpaths, calling at the hamlets of Liuqin, Fengke, Gewa and Yongning, each of which offers simple guesthouse accommodation. There's also a two-day route to **Daju**, at the eastern end of Tiger Leaping Gorge (see p.233).

ARRIVAL AND DEPARTURE   BAOSHAN STONE CITY

Be aware that there are two places called **Baoshan** in Yunnan, with different Chinese characters but the same pronunciation: the Stone City Baoshan (宝山, bǎoshān), and Baoshan (保山, bǎoshān), over near Tengchong – "Baoshan" buses from Lijiang's main bus station are all heading to the wrong one. Note that the Stone City road passes through the Yulong Xue Shan park area, and that if park officials see you you'll be charged the ¥80 entry fee.

By bus For the Stone City bus station, catch Lijiang's bus #8 heading up Xin Dajie to Xiangshan Market (象山市场, xiàngshān shìchǎng), about 1.5km northwest of Lijiang old town. You'll need to ask around here about forthcoming departures a day in advance, but there's usually a morning bus to the Stone City (5hr; ¥40).

Similarly, ask at homestays in Baoshan Stone City for departures back to Lijiang.
By minibus In Lijiang, the *Mama Naxi* guesthouse can organize minibuses to Baoshan Stone City for around ¥150/ person. Groups should be able to charter an entire minibus for ¥500.

ACCOMMODATION AND EATING

Homestay **accommodation** is provided by Baoshan's hundred or so families. Meals can be arranged for around ¥10/ head; there are also a few simple stir-fry joints and a small general store selling basic necessities.

Youke Fumu Zhongxin 游客父母中心, yóukè fùmǔ zhōngxīn. Family-run homestay in an old courtyard building, at the upper end of many similar operations in the

village; basic but clean with squat toilet and solar hot water. Dorms **¥20**, doubles **¥60**

Lugu Lake

泸沽湖, lúgū hú · ¥80

Up on a 2500m-high plateau straddling the Yunnan–Sichuan border, 200km northeast of Lijiang, **Lugu Lake** is a beautiful, reed-fringed spread of blue hemmed in by low mountains. The people here are the matrilineal **Mosuo**, whose traditions include axia, or "Walking Marriage", where a woman changes partners as often as she likes. Women run the households and children are brought up by their mothers – men have no descendants or property rights, though they do govern village life. It's all glibly marketed as a "**Girl Kingdom**" to single Chinese men, though they quickly discover that Mosuo women are not casually promiscuous and are, in fact, the ones in control.

Some 10km across, and with small settlements such as attractive **Lige** dotted around its shore, the lake is increasingly touristed but remains a pleasant place to kick back for a couple of days. There's very little to actually do here though; once you've made a canoe trip onto the lake or cycled partway around the shore, you'll be ready to catch a bus eastwards **to Xichang** in Sichuan.

Luoshui

落水, luòshuǐ

The road from Lijiang descends through pine and rhododendron forests to west-coast **LUOSHUI**, the main tourist centre with gift shops, cobbles, a central square and scattering of facilities. It lacks character though, and you're better off carrying on clockwise around the shore.

Lige

里格, lǐgé

Around 6km from Luoshui at Lugu's northwestern corner, minute **LIGE** has become the destination of choice, its tiny bay and **Lige Bandao**, the short promontory to the east, packed solid with budget guesthouses. The main foreshore has been planted with willows, and traditional Mosuo **canoes** – called "pig-troughs" because of their dugout design – are usually drawn up on the sandy beach.

The great knuckle of a hill behind Lige, its grey cliff facing lakewards, is **Gemu Shan** (格姆女神山, gémǔnǚ shénshān), named after a female Mosuo deity who created the lake; there's a **cable car** (¥35) to the top, or you can walk up in around an hour – either way, the views over the shallow, tranquil waters are fantastic.

The east shore: Sichuan

East from Lige and you're in Sichuan, where **LUGUHU ZHEN** (泸沽湖镇, lúgūhú zhèn) is the small main town. There are stores, morning buses to Xichang and even a rustic **temple** here, but you're way back from the water and really need to head to **WUZHILUO** (五指落, wǔzhǐluò), a thin string of houses along the nearby shore. Wuzhiluo is a quiet place, far less commercialized than Lige, where you'll see men sitting about weaving baskets or doing household chores. Thick with reedbeds, this side of Lugu is called the **Grass Lake** (草海, cǎo hǎi), and canoes have to be poled, rather than rowed around.

ARRIVAL AND DEPARTURE
LUGU LAKE

By plane There's an airport under construction at Ninglang, due for completion in late 2012; initial flights are scheduled to Kunming and Guangzhou.

By bus Buses from Lijiang travel via Ninglang (宁蒗, Ninglàng), 60km south of Lugu, and then move up to lakeside Luoshui and Lige. Leaving, buses to Lijiang depart around 8am and you'll need to book your seat through accommodation the day before. For Sichuan, there's morning traffic from Luguhu Zhen to Xichang (see p.106), on the Kunming–Chengdu rail line.

Destinations Lijiang (9hr; ¥60); Xichang (1 daily; 9hr; ¥97).

3

GETTING AROUND

By minibus Minibuses shuttle between settlements through the day; your accommodation can tell you where to find them. Rides between Luoshui and Luguhu Zhen shouldn't exceed about ¥15 in total, though you might have to change vehicles en route.

By bicycle Accommodation and other places rent out bicycles at about ¥20/day, plus deposit.

By canoe There are wharves at Luoshui, Lige and Wuzhiluo for canoe rides out to islands in the lake, or between settlements. There's no protection from the elements, so choose your day carefully. Ask at accommodation about organizing, or with owners at the wharves.

Destinations Luoshui–Lige (2hr; ¥80); Luoshui–Wuzhiluo (2hr; ¥80); Lige–Wuzhiluo (4–5hr; ¥180).

ACCOMMODATION

Despite the venerable Mosuo grannies parked outside **guesthouses**, most places to stay are staffed and owned by Chinese. Accommodation can feed you, sort out local and long-range transport, and generally help out with anything else you need, though very little English is spoken. The settlements are so small that you won't have any trouble locating the following.

LIGE

Lake View Romance 印象传奇, yìnxiàng chuánqí. Lige Bandao, the little peninsula past Lige village ☎ 088 8588 1050. Cute, bright and cheerfully furnished rooms with waterside balconies; the problem is that a half-dozen more guesthouses are being built alongside, limiting privacy. Downstairs ¥160; larger rooms upstairs ¥240

Lao Shay Youth Hostel 老谢车马店, lǎoxiè chēmǎdiàn. Facing the water at Lige ☎ 088 8588 1555, ⓦ laoshay.com. Sister hostel to the one in Lijiang, with the usual perks – café-bar, internet, dorms and doubles, all in comfortable, casual surroundings. Dorms ¥35, doubles ¥128

Lige Wan 里格湾客栈, lǐgéwān kèzhàn. On the edge of Lige village, just before the short path to Lige Bandao ☎ 088 8582 3871. Locally owned guesthouse in wood and stone, all done up in Tibetan-Mosuo motifs. Rooms are a bit larger and more comfortable than most,

with beds facing lakewards through windows, though you're not quite on the waterside. ¥200

WUZHILUO

Muxi Zhijia 母系之家, mǔxì zhījiā. ☎ 1388 156 7535. Translating something like "Mum's Place", this Mosuo-run guesthouse is in a genuine two-storey family home. Rooms are fairly basic – tiled wet-rooms, hard beds and little furniture – but upstairs balconies give pleasant views over the quiet road to the reed-choked shore. Filling meals are included. ¥80

Wind's Guesthouse 湖畔青年旅舍, húpàn qīngnián lǔshè. ☎ 088 8582 4284, ⓔ wind77777@163.com. Built in three tiers around an open-sided courtyard, this clean place fills all the usual backpacker needs. With plenty of advance notice, they arrange ten-day horse treks to Yading in Sichuan (see p.140). Dorms ¥25, doubles ¥120

EATING

In the evening, accommodation and restaurants at Lige lay on alfresco **barbecues** of grilled lake fish, yak and whole suckling pigs for around ¥30 a head. Both *Lao Shay* and *Wind's Guesthouse* have cafés serving decent Chinese and Western staples – though come prepared for laidback service.

Up the Lancang River to Deqin

Northwest of Lijiang, the landscape compresses into deep, parallel valleys, where the upper reaches of three of Asia's greatest rivers – the **Yangzi**, **Lancang** (Mekong) and **Nu** (Salween) – run south side by side, separated by snowcapped mountain ranges. This narrow geographical band has been designated part of the protected **Three Parallel Rivers Reserve**, though development is making inroads and the first hydroelectric dams are being constructed.

Heading out this way from Lijiang takes you through the Yangzi and Lancang valleys, via a reserve for the rare **Yunnan snub-nosed monkey** and an intriguing European-founded community at **Cizhong**, but mostly you're doing this for the rough backroads journey **to Deqin** and **Meili Xue Shan** (see p.243), though this route skips Shangri-La – you'll also end up in the area if you've hiked over the mountains from Gongshan in the Nu River Valley (see p.245). **Buses** run from Lijiang to Weixi, where there's seasonal transport up the Lancang valley to Deqin; you can also hop through the region on local minibuses – stand by the roadside to flag them down. Note that there are **no foreign-friendly banks** or ATMs along the way.

Shigu

石鼓, shígǔ • Transport to and from Lijiang runs through the day

Just 70km west of Lijiang on the banks of the Yangzi – here called the Jinsha River
– is **SHIGU** (Stone Drum) is a small Naxi town named after a sixteenth-century drum-
shaped memorial tablet celebrating a particularly bloody victory by Lijiang's Mu clan
over an invading army – whether a Tibetan or a Chinese force depends on who is
telling the story.

The Yangzi makes its first major **bend** at Shigu, breaking out of alignment with the
Lancang and Nu rivers and deflecting sharply to the northeast towards Tiger Leaping
Gorge, having flowed uninterrupted in a 1000km arc from its source away on the
Tibet–Qinghai border. Shigu is really only somewhere to pull over for a couple of
minutes – there are waterfront viewpoints for photos of the river curving as it emerges
from its valley upstream.

The Yunnan Snub-Nosed Monkey National Park

滇金丝猴国家公园, diān jīnsīhóu guójiā gōngyuán • Daily 8am–5pm • ¥100, includes Chinese-speaking guide and
transport inside the park

From Shigu the road heads 140km northwest, leaving the riverbank and passing
Judian, where the Weixi road branches off to the west and, after another 10km, lands
you in **TACHENG ZHEN** (塔城镇, tǎchéng zhèn). Although this functional, one-street
trucking depot is charmless, the thick, cloud-swept pine forests above harbour the
Yunnan Snub-Nosed Monkey National Park, protecting a population of one of the
world's rarest simians, of which only 1700 survive. Also known as "golden monkeys"
the pot-bellied males actually sport thick grey fur, with massive lips and no visible nose
(females are slighter); they eat leaves and lichen, with some seasonal flowers and fruit,
and make a huge range of trills, quacks and barks while feeding. Around 80 live in
small groups inside the reserve, which they share with local **Lisu** people, who collect
wood and graze their cattle and pigs in the lower valleys; you'll need at least a half-day
here for the chance to locate a troop.

Around the national park

The **park entrance** is 4km from Tacheng along a sealed road, which degenerates into a
bumpy vehicle track inside the park. While staff radio field workers to locate a suitable
group of monkeys, you'll get a tour of the **museum**, which outlines the history of the
park – captions are all in Chinese. Then a bus will take you up the valley to the nearest
access point, from where you'll have to **walk** into the hills with a guide along steep,
slippery paths. It's worth persevering though: encountering such endangered creatures
is a magical experience, even if you have to shelter under a bush in the rain to do it.
While not tame, the monkeys seem unconcerned with being observed, and with luck
you won't need a zoom lens to get good pictures.

ARRIVAL AND DEPARTURE   TACHENG ZHEN

By bus Tacheng Zhen is the access point for the reserve. Lijiang–Weixi buses can drop you off (they pass by around 2pm), and there are also on-demand minibuses to Weixi and Judian (巨甸, jùdiàn), a kilometre-long market town back towards Shigu, from where you can find further minibuses to Lijiang.
Destinations Judian (2hr; ¥25); Lijiang (1 daily; 4hr 30min; ¥55); Weixi (2hr 30min; ¥30).

ACCOMMODATION AND EATING

In Tacheng, ask around for other places to **stay**; nowhere is signed. There's a small supermarket and some obvious stir-fry **restaurants**, and a proposed café at the national park might be operating by now.

National Park Yunnan Snub-Nosed Monkey National Park reserve entrance ☎ 088 7862 6704. Call ahead to check on plans to open a four-person bunkhouse at the reserve (see above), where facilities couldn't possibly be worse than in Tacheng. **¥180**
Shunda 顺达宾馆, shùndá bīnguǎn. Tacheng. The

best of Tacheng's decidedly average inns; if you're lucky the plumbing and power will be working and they'll have washed the sheets recently. **¥30**

Weixi

维西, wéixī

WEIXI occupies an elevated, heavily farmed valley some 250km by road from Lijiang, a Nanzhao-era **pagoda** on the southeastern fringes hinting at this small town's age. Not that anything else here is old; Weixi today mostly serves local logging and mining operations, its loop of shabby streets well stocked with stores selling practical items. The town is also central to the **Lisu**, an eastern Tibetan people who spread into Yunnan, Thailand and Burma – you'll meet plenty more if you're heading north up the Lancang valley to Deqin.

You'll be spending the night between buses in Weixi; there's plenty of accommodation, all of it inexpensive, and the town can be walked around in twenty minutes – **Xiaoping Jie** is the main shopping street.

ARRIVAL AND DEPARTURE   WEIXI

By bus Lijiang buses are a safe bet, but departures up the Lancang valley to Deqin are dependent on the road being open; in winter it can snow, and heavy summer rains cause landslides. Aside from scheduled buses, minibuses to the same destinations wait outside and go when – and if – they fill up. Destinations Deqin (1 daily; 7hr; ¥46); Lijiang (3 daily; 6hr; ¥65); Shangri-La (1 daily; 5hr 30min; ¥46); Yanmen (1 daily; 5hr; ¥40).

ACCOMMODATION

A-Keji 阿客吉商务酒店, ā kèjí shāngwù jiǔdiàn. Shuncheng Bei Lu ☎ 088 7862 8336. Exit the bus station, turn right and it's 100m uphill, across the road. Tatty but decent, and rooms have views over the encircling hills. **¥80**
Jindian 金点商业酒店, jīndiǎn shāngyè jiǔdiàn. Shuncheng Bei Lu ☎ 088 7862 9400. Just past A-Keji and much the same, if slightly newer. **¥80**
Prosperous 兴隆宾馆, xīnglóng bīnguǎn. Opposite the bus station, Shuncheng Bei Lu ☎ 088 7862 8960. Signed in English, this comfortably spartan place offers some of the cheapest rooms in town. Bed **¥30**

EATING

Cheap places to **snack**, all run by Sichuanese migrants, are dotted along the main streets. Several small **supermarkets** sell biscuits, instant noodles and fruit.

Sichuan Xiaochi 四川小吃, sìchuān xiǎochī. In the square at the junction of Shuncheng Bei Lu and Xiaoping Jie. Spicy stir-fries, noodle dishes and dumplings at this cheap representative of Weixi's restaurants.

DIRECTORY

Banks Weixi's branch of the Agricultural Bank on Shuncheng Nan Lu can't change foreign currency, and its ATM doesn't accept foreign cards.

The Lancang valley

Buses (1 daily) head from Weixi to Yanmen (5hr) and on to Deqin (7hr); minibuses take the same route, leaving when (if) they're full

Some 40km northwest of Weixi, the road slaloms down to the tiny town of **Baijixun** (白济汛, báijìxùn) and enters the deep and narrow **Lancang River Valley**, which runs 180km north from here to Deqin and Meili Xue Shan (see p.243) – and, in the other direction, all the way down to Thailand via Jinghong in Xishuangbanna (see p.256). There might not be many specific sights along the Deqin road, but it's a fabulously scenic drive, the dark green, subtropical mountain slopes punctuated by mud-brick Lisu hamlets and ugly, tiled villages, with a patchwork of fields on the western bank rising to the heights of the **Nu Shan range**, on the other side of which is the Nu Jiang valley and Gongshan (see p.246).

Cizhong Catholic Church

茨中教堂, cízhōng jiàotáng

Around 100km up the Lancang valley, **Cizhong Catholic Church** is an extraordinary sight in such a remote location, its angular European tower topped by a curvy Chinese-style tiled roof. Inside, bare grey stonework is offset by a brightly painted ceiling, divided into a grid of Western, Tibetan and Chinese religious motifs. A French mission was founded here in the 1880s, but was **torched** by a Tibetan war-party following the 1904 British invasion of Tibet; plant hunter **George Forrest** (see p.227) was staying here at the time and escaped thanks to friendly Lisu villagers, but the mission's two French priests and their entire Christian flock were slaughtered. The church was rebuilt in its current grand style around 1909; Cizhong's little community of a dozen houses grow grapes descended from French vines and produce their own **wine**.

Accommodation might be available here (see below), or head 10km further north to larger **YANMEN** (燕门, yànmén), from where there's also transport for the final 65km run to Deqin; the last half of the journey dominated to the east by the 5400m-high **Baima Snow Mountain** (白马雪山, báimǎ xuě shān).

ACCOMMODATION

Cizhong Catholic Church ☎088 7841 8022 or 135 0887 4738. There's a guesthouse at the church; contact them in advance to ask about availability.

Tiger Leaping Gorge

虎跳峡, hǔtiào xiá · ¥80

Around 70km north of Lijiang, the Yangzi channels violently through **Tiger Leaping Gorge**, the 3000m-deep rift between the line of ash-grey mountains marking the **Haba Xue Shan** range to the north and Yulong Xue Shan to the south. The **hiking trail** through the gorge is one of the most accessible and satisfying in Southwest China, somewhere to lose yourself among stark, grand scenery: there are no temples to see, the villages along the way are quaint but minute, and the pastoral residents have long since stripped the land of trees and shrubs. As to the gorge's romantic **name**, there's a place around the mid-point where the Yangzi is so narrow that a tiger once escaped hunters by leaping across – at least, that's the story trotted out for anyone who asks.

Through the Gorge

The Tiger Leaping Gorge trail is close on 40km long: it runs between westerly **Qiaotou**, on the Lijing–Shangri-La highway, via the mid-point hamlet of **Walnut Garden**, over the Yangzi and through to the eastern village of **Daju**, where you can pick up traffic back to Lijiang.

TIGER LEAPING GORGE: HIKING ESSENTIALS

Despite the 2500m-plus altitude, hiking Tiger Leaping Gorge is straightforward, though you'll need to be reasonably fit, carrying full weatherproof gear, a torch and a first-aid pack, and to be stocked up with snacks and a water bottle. Solid **boots** are a plus but, as long as your shoes have a firm grip, not essential. **Weather** can be warm enough in summer to hike in a T-shirt, but don't count on it; winters are cold. There's **accommodation** and **food** along the way – expect to pay ¥35 for a bed, ¥120 for a double (if available) and ¥25 per meal – so you won't need a tent or cooking gear. **Two days** is the minimum time needed for the full hike, though it's possible to spend just one day on the trail, or extend it far beyond the gorge.

The gorge trails are marked, but not always accurately, so before you arrive, pick up one of the detailed home-made **maps** that float around cafés in Lijiang and Shangri-La – ours (see p.234) will help, but it's only intended as a rough guide. **Landslides** are a potentially lethal hazard, so do not hike in bad weather or during the June–September rainy season; there have also been a couple of knifepoint **muggings** of solo travellers over the years. For current information, check Ⓦtigerleapinggorge.com, run by *Sean's Guesthouse* in Walnut Garden.

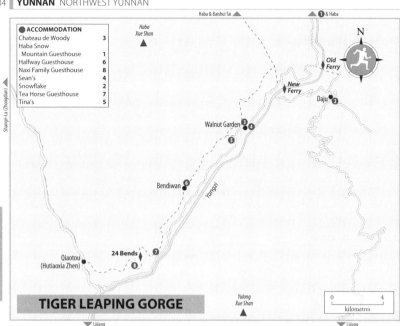

ACCOMMODATION

Chateau de Woody	3
Haba Snow Mountain Guesthouse	1
Halfway Guesthouse	6
Naxi Family Guesthouse	8
Sean's	4
Snowflake	2
Tea Horse Guesthouse	7
Tina's	5

TIGER LEAPING GORGE

Most people get an early bus to Qiaotou, leave anything heavy with a café (you might have to pay for this and it's worth checking their security arrangements), spend a day hiking to Walnut Garden along the scenically stunning **Upper Path**, and then arrange a ride back to Qiaotou along the former **Lower Path**, now a vehicle road. But it's worth at least exploring the gorge for a day around Walnut Garden, and completists might want to continue to Daju, though the scenery rapidly drops off. You could of course begin the hike at Daju so that you end at Qiaotou, with its transport to Lijiang or Shangri-La; it's also possible to hire guides in either Walnut Garden or Daju and hike far beyond the gorge (see p.237).

Qiaotou to the Twenty-four Bends

QIAOTOU, also known as **Hutiaoxia Zhen** (桥头, qiáotóu; 虎跳峡镇, hǔtiàoxiá zhèn) is a knot of cafés and shops on the highway at the western entrance to the gorge. Once across the bridge the vehicle road heads down along the river; hikers need to turn uphill onto the start of the **Upper Path** just past the school – you'll be followed by horse teams offering to carry your bags. It's steady going now, until you reach the *Naxi Family Guesthouse* (纳西雅阁, nàxī yǎgé) at the start of the steep, twisting **Twenty-four Bends**. At the top of this you're about five hours into the hike at 2670m, near the charming *Tea Horse Guesthouse* (茶马客栈, chámǎ kèzhàn), and gifted with superb views of Yulong Xue Shan's serrated, snowcapped summits.

To the Middle Gorge

From here the Upper Path levels out a bit before descending, via the stone *Halfway Guesthouse* at **Bendiwan village** (本地湾村, běndiwān cūn) and some waterfalls, down to the **Middle Gorge** and the vehicle road at *Tina's Guesthouse*. You've now been walking around nine hours, with a further thirty-minute level track to accommodation at **WALNUT GARDEN** (核桃园, hétáo yuán), a good base for exploring the local area. From either Walnut Garden or *Tina's*, there are trails down to where the Yangzi explodes through the narrowest part of the gorge, a splintered mass of rocks dropping into a sunless chasm.

3

Walnut Garden to Daju

The simplest option from Walnut Garden is to arrange a ride with minibuses back to Qiaotou along the vehicle road. Alternatively, continue the hike east to Daju: a couple of hours' walk, partly along the road, brings you to the **New Ferry** over the Yangzi. How much you'll pay depends on the whim of the ferryman, but don't expect to get off lightly – ¥40 or more per person is normal.

From here, you've another hour's walk to the vehicle roadhead at **Xiahu Tiao** (下虎跳, xiàhǔ tiào), 7km from laidback **DAJU village** (大具, dàjù), where there's more accommodation and transport back to Lijiang. You can also organize guides here for the two-day trip east to **Baoshan Stone City** (see p.228).

ARRIVAL AND DEPARTURE TIGER LEAPING GORGE

By bus Buses along the Lijiang–Shangri-La highway can drop you off or pick you up at Qiaotou. Buses to Daju depart Lijiang first thing in the morning from the depot at the corner of Changshui Zhong Lu and Minzhu Lu, just outside the old town's southwestern edge; the last bus to

Lijiang departs Daju around 1.30pm.
Daju destinations Lijiang (2 daily; 2hr; ¥34).
Qiaotou destinations Lijiang (several daily; 1hr 30min; ¥35); Shangri-La (several daily; 2hr; ¥30).

INFORMATION AND TOURS

Tours A horse and guide for the Baishui Tai or Haba Xue Shan treks costs around ¥100/day.

ACCOMMODATION AND EATING

You shouldn't need to **stay** at Qiaotou as it's not far to more scenic alternatives within the gorge, and buses continue both ways along the highway until late. Guesthouses named in the text along the Upper Path all offer beds for ¥35/person, with **meals** available for ¥25. There are no proper **stores** along the way, so bring all the snacks you'll need.

DAJU

★ **Snowflake** 雪花客栈, xuěhuā kèzhàn. ☎088 8532 6091. Charming, family-run guesthouse in an attractive old courtyard building; the owners cook up hearty, filling meals to order. Beds ¥35

HABA

Haba Snow Mountain Guesthouse 哈巴雪山客栈, hābā xuěshān kèzhàn. ☎087 1316 5661. Institution-like rooms, but the friendly owner serves coffee and has built a rudimentary shower – very welcome after the trek here. Beds ¥35

WALNUT GARDEN AND AROUND

Chateau de Woody 山白脸客栈, shānbáiliǎn kèzhàn. ☎130 8742 8371. On the outskirts of the little

hamlet, *Woody's* is similar to rival establishment *Sean's* and has been going nearly as long. Don't believe anything either says about the other. Beds ¥35

★ **Sean's** 山泉客栈, shānquán kèzhàn. ☎088 7820 2222, ⦿ tigerleapinggorge.com. A pleasantly low-key, friendly place with good meals, beer and warm beds; it was one of the first hikers' hostels in the gorge and the owner hands out heaps of useful information gleaned from over twenty years' experience. Beds ¥35

Tina's 中峡国际青年旅舍, zhōngxiá guójì qīngnián lǚshè. ☎088 7820 2258. Well-managed hostel 30min from Walnut Garden, and close to paths down into the most dramatic section of the Middle Gorge. Excellent viewing terrace looking south to the mountains. Dorms ¥35, doubles ¥100

Shangri-La (Zhongdian)

香格里拉, xiānggélǐlā (中甸, zhōngdiàn)

SHANGRI-LA sits on a high plateau in the borderland between Yunnan, Sichuan and Tibet, the surrounding alpine pastures grazed by shaggy yaks. When this former logging town – called **Gyalthang** in Tibetan – was hit by a 1998 ban on deforestation, the provincial government renamed it "Shangri-La" after the Buddhist paradise of James Hilton's 1930s novel, *Lost Horizon*, to try to stimulate a tourist boom. They also spent a fortune turning Zhongdian's dismally poor Tibetan quarter into what must be the newest "old town" in existence, complete with traditional houses, cobbled streets, religious monuments, cafés, guesthouses and bars. There's an excellent **monastery** just

WALNUT GARDEN TO HABA AND BAISHUI TAI

Accommodation in Tiger Leaping Gorge's Middle Gorge can arrange a guide – and horses if needed – for the popular and highly scenic **two-day trek** to the limestone terraces at **Baishui Tai** (see p.242). The first day is fairly tough going uphill to predominantly Muslim **Haba village** (哈巴村, **hābā cūn**), tucked into a fold on the slopes of 5396m-high **Haba Xue Shan**. There are several places to stay here, and – for the very fit, well equipped only – guides for a three-day return ascent of the mountain. Otherwise, it's another day's walk to Baishui Tai, along a level, steady path.

north of town and endless possibilities for local **hiking and horseriding** too, and you'll need several days to cover it all. The **altitude** here is over 3000m, so take it easy if you've arrived from the lowlands, and be aware that the climate is very cold between October and March.

The most obvious ports of call **after Shangri-La** are Lijiang and Tiger Leaping Gorge to the south, Deqin and Meili Xue Shan to the northwest, and Daocheng in Sichuan, via a rough bus ride northeast over the mountains. At the moment, the **Tibetan border** beyond Deqin is firmly shut, but check with Khampa Caravan (see p.238) to see if this situation has changed. Be aware too that there are **clampdowns** through all of China's Tibetan regions every **March**, when it will probably be impossible to travel into Sichuan from Shangri-La, or even to reach Deqin.

The old town (Dukezong)
古城, **gǔchéng**

Down at the south end of Shangri-La, the **old town** (which sports yet another name, **Dukezong**) is a tangle of unsigned lanes weaving off in all directions, but as the whole place is only a few hundred metres across you can't get seriously lost. The alleyways are lined with solid, two-storey wooden Tibetan homes which all look attractively dated, though they're only a decade or so old. The **main square** is full of souvenir stalls during the day, and locals gathering for social **dances** at dusk; up some slippery, uneven cobbles from here is **Turtle Hill** (龟山, **guī shān**), topped by a small temple and huge **golden prayer wheel**, apparently the largest in the world.

The new town
Despite its scruffy concrete-and-tile buildings, Shangri-La's **new town** is

RESTAURANTS
Arro Khampa	8
Bhaskar's Kitchen	2
Compass	5
Helen's Pizza	1
Karma Café	9
N's Kitchen	4
Potala Café	3
Raven	7
Rose's	6

SHOPS
| Inner Asia Rugs | 1 |
| The Thanka Academy | 2 |

ACCOMMODATION
Barley	4
Bright	8
Gyalthang Dzong	2
Harmony Guesthouse	7
Kersang's Relay Station	9
Kevin's Trekker Inn	3
Old Town Youth Hostel	6
Shangrila-Moon	5
Songtsam Retreat	1

SHANGRI-LA (ZHONGDIAN)

3

SHANGRI-LA'S TOURS AND AGENTS

There are many **expeditions** to be made from Shangri-La, and a number of **specialist agents** in town can help organize routes and guides. If you're planning anything major, contact them before you arrive – they'll need time to arrange things. **Cafés** (see p.240) and **hotels** (see below) also provide information and can book you on trips, including the three-day hike via Baishui to Tiger Leaping Gorge (see p.242).

Haiwei Trails Above the bar at the Raven ☎ 088 7828 9239, ⓦhaiweitrails.com. A range of imaginative treks, jeep tours and mountain-biking. They also put together tailor-made packages for Tibet, when it's open to visitors.

★ **Khampa Caravan** 207 Beimen Jie ☎ 088 7828 8648, ⓦkhampacaravan.com. This thoroughly professional and experienced company offers everything from easy day hikes and sorting out Tibet logistics to multi-day treks to Lijiang or into Sichuan;

one of their specialities is the demanding 14-day kora circuit around Meili Xue Shan (p.243). All their guides are local Tibetans, fluent in English.

Turtle Mountain Off Beimen Jie at 32 Gun Ma Lang ☎ 088 7823 3308, ⓦturtlemountaingear.com. The American manager, long resident in Shangri-La, has solid hiking and exploring information for all northwest Yunnan. They also stock a range of camping supplies and rent ski gear, snowboards, motorbikes (with breakdown support) and jeeps.

appealingly down to earth if you've come up via Dali and Lijiang and are growing tired of a street life comprising nothing but other tourists. Running north for 2km, **Changzheng Dadao** is lined with shops aimed at Tibetan customers, where you can buy everything from electric blenders for churning butter tea to carpets, horse saddles and bridles, copperware and fur-lined jackets and boots. The **Farmers' Market** (建塘农市场, jiàntáng nóng shìchǎng), about a block north of the main post office, has more of the same along with big blocks of yak butter and other foodstuffs; it's busiest before about 2pm.

Ganden Sumtseling Monastery

松赞林寺, sōngzànlín sì · ¥85 · Catch northbound bus #3 up Changzheng Dadao

The splendid **Ganden Sumtseling Monastery** sits 3km north of town, its rich-yellow walls and golden spires glowing against a backdrop of snowy peaks. Founded in the seventeenth century, it was almost destroyed during anti-Chinese uprisings during the 1950s, but is now home to around seven hundred monks and is said to be the largest Tibetan monastery in Yunnan. Among butter sculptures and a forest of pillars, the bright murals in the claustrophobic, windowless main hall are typically gruesome and colourful. Don't forget that, as in all Gelugpa-sect monasteries, you should walk **clockwise** around both the monastery and each hall. For a quick **hike** near Shangri-La, just head uphill from behind the monastery.

ARRIVAL AND DEPARTURE   SHANGRI-LA (ZHONGDIAN)

"Zhongdian" and "Xianggelila" are interchangeable on transport timetables for Shangri-La. There's talk of extending the Kunming–Dali–Lijiang **train line** to Shangri-La, but nobody can confirm likely dates. Aside from continuing your journey northwest to Deqin and Meili Xue Shan, don't forget that Shangri-La offers a back door into **Sichuan**, via the bumpy bus ride northeast to Daocheng (see p.139).

By plane Shangri-La Airport (香格里拉机场, xiānggélǐlā jīchǎng), also confusingly known as Deqing Airport, is 7km south; a taxi costs ¥25, or catch bus #6 to the bus station and then #1 to the old town. There's a convenient airline ticket office (☎088 7822 9555) just outside the old town at the small square on the junction of Changzheng Dadao and Tuanjie Lu.

Destinations Kunming (5 daily; 1hr); Lhasa (1 daily; 2hr); Shanghai (1 daily; 5hr).

By bus The bus station is in the far north of town, at the intersection of Xiangbala Lu and Kangding Lu; catch bus #1 south down Xiangbala for 2km to the old town's outskirts. Tickets are available from the station 36hr before departure.

Destinations Benzilan (2 daily; 2hr; ¥18); Dali (7hr; ¥105); Daocheng (1 daily; 12hr; ¥110); Deqin (3 daily; 5hr; ¥43); Haba (1 daily; 3hr 30min; ¥30); Lijiang (3hr 30min; ¥65); Weixi (3 daily; 6hr; ¥65).

GETTING AROUND

Shangri-La is small enough to **walk** around, though local buses, bikes, taxis and minibuses come in handy for arrival points and outlying sights.

By bicycle Some accommodation, plus *Compass Café*, *N's Kitchen* and Turtle Mountain, rent out bikes for ¥20 /day plus your passport. *N's Kitchen* also has cycling maps for Napa Hai.

By bus City buses run daily 6am–8pm and cost ¥1–2 a ride; catch them on Tuanjie Lu or Changzheng Dadao, just outside the old town. Minibuses hang around the car park lot outside the old town, at the bottom of Changzheng Dadao; expect to pay ¥300–500 a day for a seven-seat vehicle.

By taxi Fares are a fixed ¥6 within the town. Outside town, a half day costs ¥100–150, a full day twice this, depending on distance covered and bargaining skills.

ACCOMMODATION

Shangri-La's best **accommodation** options are down in the old town. Most have wi-fi (if not, head to cafés) and look, at least on the outside, as if they occupy traditional Tibetan houses. The Khampa Caravan tour company can organize **homestays** with Tibetan families outside town; ¥250/person for a guide, transport, beds and all meals.

★ **Barley** 青稞客栈, qīngkē kèzhàn. 76 Beimen Jie ☎ 088 78232100, ⓦ barley.hostel.com. Delightful courtyard guesthouse with a warm terrace run by a friendly Tibetan family, where they've taken some trouble to make the simple rooms attractive and comfortable. Dorms ¥30, doubles ¥120

Bright 鲁生追康客栈, lǔshēngzhuīkāng kèzhàn. 13 Dianlaka, next to the Raven ☎ 088 7828 8687. If you're after a straightforward, roomy en-suite double, this is your best bet – though, despite a "Tibetan" exterior, the hotel has little character. ¥70

Gyalthang Dzong 建塘宾馆, jiàntáng bīnguǎn. ☎ 088 7822 3646, ⓦ gyalthangdzong.com. A large boutique hotel 3km southeast of town, whose designer stonework and decor, all orange drapes, lacquer and longevity symbols, might best be described as Tibetan minimalist. There's a spa and a bar, but no TVs anywhere on site. ¥800

Harmony Guesthouse 融聚客栈, róngjù kèzhàn. 12 Dianlaka ☎ 1398 874 7739. Courtyard hotel with shared facilities and bare rooms that's a backpacker favourite, thanks to low prices and cheerful, can-do staff. Dorms ¥25, doubles ¥80

★ **Kersang's Relay Station** 格桑藏驿, gésāng zàngyì. 1 Yamenlang, Jinlong Jie, behind the *Arro Khampa* restaurant ☎ 088 7822 3118. Tibetan-run guesthouse decked in pine, Tibetan rugs and colourful furnishings. Rooms are small but all have balconies, making them feel more spacious. Rooftop terrace with views over town. ¥140

Kevin's Trekker Inn 龙门客栈, lóngmén kèzhàn. Just outside the town at 138 Dawa Lu ☎ 088 7822 8178, ⓦ kevintrekkerinn.com. Modern concrete buildings around a courtyard; the big lounge area, cheerful rooms and the manager's trekking and touring info make this a good choice. The only downside is a pair of over-friendly German Shepherd dogs. Dorms ¥30, doubles ¥120

Old Town Youth Hostel 古城国际青年旅馆, gǔchéng guójì qīngnián lǚguǎn. 4 Zoubarui, Jinlong Jie ☎ 088 7822 7505, ⓔ oldtowg_h@hotmail .com. Grand entrance but straightforward, slightly gloomy wood-panelled rooms, with a very helpful manager – not to mention a guardian husky. You can use the kitchen too. Dorms ¥25, doubles ¥80

Shangrila-Moon 月亮客栈, yuèliàng kèzhàn. 25 Beimen Jie ☎ 088 7822 5826, ⓦ shangrila-moon.com. Bare, large rooms in this basic guesthouse, whose hospitable owner will drag you into the kitchen for a tea and a chat. They run a range of local treks and tours. ¥120

★ **Songtsam Retreat** 松赞林卡酒店, sōngzànlínkǎ jiǔdiàn. Next to the Ganden Sumtseling Monastery, 3km north of town ☎ 088 7828 5566. The upmarket wing of the Ganden Sumtseling Monastery's accommodation; a very tasteful, atmospheric place to stay with views over the monastery building. The food in the restaurant is pretty inconsistent though. ¥900

EATING AND DRINKING

As with accommodation, the old town has the pick of the **eating** opportunities; the cafés also have booze and free wi-fi for customers. For cheap Chinese staples, there are a few hole-in-the-wall places on Tuanjie Lu, serving noodles and dumplings.

Arro Khampa 阿若康巴餐厅, āruò kāngbā cāntīng. Pijiang Alley ☎088 7822 6442. Excellent Nepali, Indian and Tibetan cuisine served up in a similar atmosphere to *Bhaskar's* – though without quite the panache. Expect to pay ¥60/person.

★ **Bhaskar's Kitchen** 巴斯卡厨房, bāsīkǎ chúfáng. Dawa Lu ☎088 7888 1213. With charismatic Nepali owner-chef Bhaskar in control, this comfortable restaurant lives up to its claim to produce the "best curry in Shangri-La". Chicken or vegetarian *thalis* (¥38) are the business too.

Compass 8 Dianlaka. Unashamedly Western food – pizza, burgers, spaghetti, sandwiches – served up in a sympathetic mock-Tibetan interior. Mains around ¥40.

Helen's Pizza Tuanjie Lu. Rated by nostalgic expats as whipping up the best pizza and calzone in all China – yours for only ¥38 – perhaps because they use imported olive oil, not yak butter.

★ **Karma Café** 66 Jinlong Jie ☎088 7822 4768. Almost unsigned behind an adobe wall in the back of town, at first sight the building looks run-down; inside, however, it's a beautifully restored old house serving outstanding yak steak and mashed potatoes for a bargain ¥48. Tibetan snacks and a set meal (¥60pp) will leave you bursting. Great place for quiet coffee too.

N's Kitchen 依若木廊, nóngruò mùláng. 33 Beimen Jie. This bright, modern and clean place is popular for Western breakfasts and great coffee, though it's just a little bit more expensive than its competitors.

Potala Café Tuanjie Lu. This upstairs Tibetan teahouse serves up huge portions of Western, Tibetan and Chinese food, and hot chocolate made with the real thing, not powder. The ambience is pleasant, attracting a mix of Chinese tourists, grizzly locals and foreigners. Fill up for ¥25.

★ **Raven** 乌鸦酒吧, wūyā jiǔbā. 19 Diankala ☎088 7828 9239. Friendly and atmospheric foreign-owned bar with pool table, beer and huge stock of spirits; cliquey but laidback and a good place to get the low-down on the local scene.

Rose's 15 Cuolang Jie. Tea, coffee and light meals served up by enthusiastic young couple in a pleasant café surroundings.

SHOPPING

Carpets Inner Asia Rugs, Jinlong Jie (🌐 innerasiarugs.com). The workshop and showroom here employs local women to hand-weave gorgeous, extremely expensive, woollen Tibetan rugs decorated with tigers and abstract motifs. You'll find far cheaper, factory-made versions in shops along southern Changzheng Dadao.

Souvenirs Stalls in the central square and shops through the old town sell Tibetan knives and swords in decorative scabbards, leather gloves and belts, ethnicky jewellery and hand-operated prayer-wheels. Pay less for a bigger choice of real Tibetan artefacts in shops along Changzheng Dadao; prices drop further you get from old town.

Thankas The Thanka Academy (唐卡学会, tángkǎ xuéhuì) 31 Jinlong Jie 🌐 thangkaacademy.com. Teaches the art of painting these intricate religious icons to local unemployed or underpriveleged Tibetans; each one takes months, if not years, to complete and a few are for sale. Profits fund a Khampa Tibetan cultural centre.

DIRECTORY

Banks There's a Construction Bank ATM which accepts foreign cards in the square just outside the old town, with main bank branches along Changzheng Dadao in the new town.

Post Office The main branch is in the new town on Changzheng Dadao.

Around Shangri-La

The area around Shangri-La is thick with attractions, from easily explored pasture surrounding **Napa Hai** and hot springs at **Xiagei** to **Pudacuo National Park**'s forests, lakes and hiking areas. Off to the southeast, picturesque limestone terraces at **Baishui Tai** are the biggest draw, from where you can also trek, via Haba village, into Tiger Leaping Gorge (see p.237). For somewhere truly remote, try to reach **Nizu**, an enigmatic community right on the Sichuan border. Most places are not served by public transport, so you'll need to hire a taxi or cycle.

Napa Hai

纳帕海, nàpà hǎi • ¥40 • Cycling maps from *N's Kitchen* in Shangri-La

Napa Hai is a shallow, seasonal lake 7km north of Shangri-La which attracts stately black-necked cranes and other migrant birds between November and April. Through the summer it's more of a pasture for yaks, with vivid green grass and wildflowers; there's a marked eco-trail at pretty **Hamugu Village**. Just outside the park, the **Botanic Gardens** (¥20) has a café, blue poppies and exotic orchids. There's a level, fairly decent

road around the lake, making it an easy drive or cycle, though there has been trouble with locals stopping vehicles and demanding their own fees for crossing their land.

Xiagei Hot Springs

下给温泉, xiàgěi wēnquán • ¥30

Ten kilometres east of Shangri-La, the **Xiagei Hot Springs** are attractively situated beside a river and below a cave. Skip the claustrophobic private rooms and swim in the small public pool; a shop on site sells swimming trunks (¥20).

Pudacuo National Park

普达措国家公园, pǔdácuò guójiā gōngyuán • Taxi from town ¥150–200, including waiting time

Pudacuo National Park covers a huge, largely inaccessible spread of lush alpine meadows and old-growth forests starting 25km east of Shangri-La, though the focus is on two well-touristed **lakes**, each with their own entrance. Note that the road past the park continues south to Baishui Tai.

Shudou Hai

属都海, shǔdōu hǎi • ¥160, including bus inside the park

Shudou Hai is a broad spread of deep blue amongst Pudacuo's forest; there's a restaurant and huge shop in the car park that sells traditional medicines such as ginseng and dried ants. Turn right and follow the lakeshore for a satisfying walk through the woods; you can circuit the lake in around four hours, or half this if you rent a **horse** (¥80). Ask at Turtle Mountain Gear (see p.238) about the tough **two-day hike** to Nizu from here.

Bita Hai

碧塔海, bitǎ hǎi • ¥30

Some way south of Shudou Hai at an altitude of 3500m, **Bita Hai** is less visited; the best way to explore the place is to ask to be dropped at either of its **two entrances**, south and west, and then picked up at the other. Most visitors arrive at the **south gate** (南门, nánmén), from where it's an easy walk down to the lake. Take a **rowboat** across (a negotiable ¥30/person) to the ferry quay, and then walk for around two hours along a well-marked trail to the west gate. **Horses** can be rented at either entrance for ¥50 or so.

Baishui Tai

白水台, báishuǐ tái • ¥80 • Bus from Shangri-La (2hr; ¥35)

Around 100km southeast from Shangri-La on the north side of Haba Xue Shan, **Baishui Tai** is a large, milky-white series of limestone terraces and pools, built up over thousands of years as pale blue, lime-rich water cascaded down a hillside. Wooden ladders allow in-depth exploration of the tiers, which look out over the valley and glow orange at sunset. It's a sacred spot for the Naxi, who celebrate the **Sanduo Festival** here on the eighth day of the second lunar month, in honour of their main deity.

The village at the foot of the site, **SANBA** (三坝, sānbà) is busily transforming itself into a tourist town of guesthouses, all of which offer basic and fairly unattractive rooms. Baishui Tai is also the start of a good two-day trek to Walnut Garden in Tiger Leaping Gorge via Haba village (see p.237).

Nizu

尼汝, nírǔ • For more information contact Turtle Mountain Gear (see p.238)

This remote river valley community, surrounded by mountains and old-growth forest way east of Shangri-La on the Sichuan border, is a **Bonpo** village, whose inhabitants follow Tibet's original religion (see p.118). At the moment, getting here is half the fun: you need to catch a bus to **Luoji** (洛吉乡, luòjíxiāng), around 70km from Shangri-La, and then hitch the last 37km. Surrounding forests are said to harbour

reclusive wildlife, and Nizu hosts a **horse festival** on the fifteenth day of the ninth
lunar month. It's also possible to hike here from Shudou Hai, and trek out with
horses to Yading (see p.140).

Benzilan

奔子栏, bēnzǐlán • Buses and minibuses run through the day along the highway to Shangri-La and Deqin (2hr; ¥18)

Heading northwest of Shangri-La up the Deqin highway, you pass **Nixi** (尼西, níxī),
famed for its black clay pots, then follow the **Yangzi** to the small Tibetan town of
BENZILAN. Surrounded by green fields in summer, Benzilan is an attractive place of
most note for the **Dondrupling Monastery** (东竹林寺, dōngzhúlín sì), 23km further
northwest, founded in 1667 and completely rebuilt in 1985. It's easy to get dropped off
here en route to Deqin and Meili Xue Shan; there's basic accommodation available and
spending the night gives you a glimpse of ordinary Tibetan life.

Meili Xue Shan and around

3

梅里雪山, méilǐ xuě shān

Some 170km northwest of Shangri-La via the transit hub of **Deqin**, magisterial **Meili
Xue Shan** sits astride the Tibetan border, its thirteen snowcapped summits a stunning
sight in the early-morning sun. The range is of immense significance to Tibetans: the
highest peak, unclimbed **Kawa Karpo** (6740m), is the site of an annual pilgrimage
circuit, the **Kawa Karpo kora**, three circumnavigations of which are said to guarantee a
beneficial reincarnation. The mountain range's lower reaches offer less extreme hiking
opportunities to the **Minyong Glacier** and isolated hamlets at **Yubeng**, and the region is
developing into a popular trekking destination, though excursions should be taken
seriously: always bring food, water, a torch, first-aid kit, full weatherproof gear and
good hiking shoes.

Deqin

德钦, déqīn

DEQIN lies 150km northwest of Shangri-La across the permanently snowy, 5400m-high
Baima Xue Shan range, and only 80km from the Tibetan border. A functional transit
town at the junctions of roads from Shangri-La and Weixi via Cizhong (see p.233), the
regional long-distance bus station is here, from where most people head straight to
better scenery at **Feilai Temple** or **Xidang** (see below).

Feilai Temple

飞来寺, fēilái sì • Bus (¥5) or shared cab (¥25) from Deqin

Some 15km from Deqin, the Feilai Temple area is a nicer place to spend the night,
despite increasing hotel and restaurant development. Perched high on the side of a
steep valley and looking west to Meili Xue Shan's icy peaks over the deep Lancang
River Valley, the **views** here are stunning – at least, they would be if the local
authorities, in a disgusting display of mean-spirited commercialism, hadn't built a
3m-high **wall**, forcing you to pay ¥60 to use an observation platform.

Xidang

西当, xīdāng • Bus (¥16) or taxi (¥250) from Deqin via Feilai Temple

From Feilai Temple, it's a further 1hr 30min drive to the **Meili Xue Shan reserve
entrance** at pretty **Xidang village**. The village sits above the Lancang River and *Nomad's
Guesthouse* here (see p.245) makes it a useful base for excursions into the rest of the
reserve, whether you're planning a hike to Yubeng or simply making the day-trip to
Mingyong Glacier. Guides can also be hired here, and the nearby **hot springs** (温泉,
wēnquán), could provide the last warm wash you'll have for a while.

Mingyong Glacier

明永冰川, míngyǒng bīngchuān • ¥83

The easiest trip from Xidang is the three-hour ascent to the **Mingyong Glacier**, one of the world's lowest at 2700m, and advancing quickly at 500m per year. The road is relatively good for the area, and you'll find a fair few souvenir shops and guesthouses at the glacier viewing point.

Yubeng

¥85

An excellent overnight trek west from Xidang lands you at **Yubeng**, a couple of isolated – and very poor – Tibetan hamlets, from where you can make further short trips. You shouldn't need a guide, but do discuss your plans with *Nomad's Guesthouse* (see opposite), who provide current information about the routes.

From Xidang, it's a tough four-hour ascent to the 3800m-high **Nazongla Pass**, followed by ninety minutes down a well-marked trail to **UPPER YUBENG** (雨崩上村, yǔbēng shàng cūn), a Tibetan settlement of considerable charm where you can stay with local families (expect to pay ¥10/night, plus ¥10 for a meal). There's a good day hike from here out to **Ice Lake** (冰湖, bīng hú) where you can steel yourself for a dip; the trail passes the **base camp site** from a fatal Japanese attempt to climb Kawa Karpo, and locals hire out tents here in summer, where you can spend the night and listen to avalanches thundering down the mountain.

Press on for another forty-five minutes past Upper Yubeng, over a stream and then a bridge, and you're at even prettier **LOWER YUBENG** (雨崩下村, yǔbēng xià cūn), completely surrounded by steep, forested peaks. There's further accommodation here, and a three-hour walk out to a dramatic **sacred waterfall** (雨崩神瀑, yǔbēng shénpù), with another icy pool.

ARRIVAL AND DEPARTURE

By bus The regional bus station is in Deqin, on the main road east of the centre. Note that foreigners are not allowed on buses through to Lhasa (¥500) at the moment. Destinations from Deqin Benzilan (frequent; 2hr; ¥25);

MEILI XUE SHAN AND AROUND

Dondruplin Monastery (frequent; 1hr 30min; ¥19); Lijiang (2 daily; 8hr; ¥96); Mingyong (1 daily; 2hr; ¥16); Shangri-La (frequent; 5hr; ¥43); Weixi (1 daily; 9hr; ¥67); Xidang (1 daily; 2hr; ¥16); Yanmen (1 daily; 3hr; ¥23).

ACCOMMODATION AND EATING

DEQIN

Caihong 彩虹大酒店, cǎihóng dàjiǔdiàn. 33 Chengnanping Jie ☎ 088 7841 4248. Standard Chinese affair covered in pink tiles, with KTV hall, restaurant and faded doubles in reasonably good order. **¥190**

Trekker's Home 旅行者之家, lǚxíngzhě zhījiā. Walk north from the bus station for 200m, turn left, and the hostel is on the right ☎ 088 7841 3966. Deqin's most useful accommodation option; the helpful owner has information on local treks. Dorms **¥25**

FEILAI TEMPLE

Meili Guesthouse 梅里客栈, méilǐ kèzhàn. ☎ 088 7841 6633. Cheerful Tibetan-style guesthouse, connected to the *Barley Hostel* in Shangri-La. Dorms **¥25**, doubles **¥120**, **¥140** with views.

Meili Shanzhuang 梅里山庄, méilǐ shānzhuāng. ☎ 1398 871 7636. Similar to the guesthouse of the same name, but not quite as comfortable. Dorms **¥30**, doubles **¥100**

Migrating Bird Café 季候鸟咖啡吧, jìhòuniǎo kāfēiba. The best place to eat, and also serves as an

---

THE KAWA KARPO KORA

If you're up for a tough trek, with the chance to visit a remote Tibetan area which sees few foreigners, consider making the Kawa Karpo *kora*, the pilgrimage circuit around Meili Xue Shan. The circuit takes **fourteen days** or so, beginning in Deqin and ending in the village of Meili. If you plan to attempt it, be aware that the route **crosses into Tibet** and you need permits, as the police keep an eye on this area. You also definitely need a **guide** – you're above 4000m most of the time and people have died attempting the trek solo. Travel agencies in Shangri-La (see p.238) can make all arrangements for you.

informal tourist agency and meeting point; good views from upstairs.

LOWER YUBENG
Aqinbu's Shenbu Lodge 神瀑客栈, shénpù kèzhàn. ☎088 7841 1082. Seven warm, dry, basic rooms, very welcome by the time you arrive here. Another handy base for local treks, which the helpful owner can advise on. Beds ¥20

XIDANG
★ **Nomad Tibetan Guesthouse**. ☎1518/499 0012, ✉nomad.china@hotmail.com. A friendly, family-run operation with views down over the Lancang River and endless sound advice on trekking in the region. They can also find you guides and packhorses. Beds ¥35

The Far West

Yunnan's far west, reaching south and west from Xiaguan to the Burmese border, offers two main destinations. First is the deep, straight **Nu River Valley**, part of the Three Parallel Rivers reserve (see p.178), whose upper reaches form a remote buffer between the Tibetan and Burmese borders. It's an area small in concrete sights – settlements such as **Gongshan** and **Dimaluo** provide only the basics – but rich in ethnic groups and (for the well-prepared) hiking potential. The other option out this way is to ride the highway southwest to the official Burmese border crossings at **Wanding** and **Ruili**, almost forgotten – and slightly bizarre – outposts of the Chinese empire. Along the way to Ruili, don't miss **Tengchong**, an attractive, low-key town whose nearby sights include extinct volcanoes and an antique village full of stately old houses.

Travel through the region is tedious rather than difficult, with regular buses from Xiaguan. Neither the Nu River Valley or routes to Ruili and the Burmese border offer any straightforward options for onwards travel, meaning that – unless you've previously organized **crossing into Burma** in Kunming, or are game for some tough hiking or long bus rides – you'll have to retrace your steps towards Xiaguan afterwards.

The Nu River Valley

Northwest from Xiaguan, on the far side of the huge wall of the **Gaoligong Mountains**, the **Nu River** (怒江, nùjiāng) runs south for 500km along China's border with Burma. Also known as the Salween, the Chinese name means the **Angry River**, and the spectacularly narrow, steep-sided valley has indeed created some especially raucous rapids – though these may soon be tamed by a **dam** (see p.246).

Cut off from the rest of Yunnan, the valley's only access is along a single road from **Lushui**, which passes the tiny settlements of **Fugong**, **Gongshan** and **Bingzhongluo** before degenerating into tracks, footpaths and then hard-to-follow trails up over the mountains into Tibet and adjacent valleys. It's a beautiful region, with old forest, waterfalls and poor, thatched-roofed villages; as the river narrows in its upper reaches, it's crossed by wobbly suspension bridges and downright scary **ropeways** (溜索, liù suǒ), where you sit in a sling and slide or haul yourself across on a wire cable. Most of the population are Tibetan, **Lisu** or **Drung** (Dulong), alongside a number of Catholics and **churches** – the result of French missionary work in the nineteenth century.

Buses from Xiaguan or Baoshan run to Lushui, from where you'll need at least two days to reach Bingzhongluo. After this, either retrace your route back south or put on your walking boots: a steady stream of hardy **hikers** trek out of the valley each year, but there are few facilities – don't expect anyone to speak English – and you'll need local **guides**. Autumn is the driest time of year, when **landslides** (a real hazard during the spring and midsummer) are less likely. There's **accommodation** in the towns and villages, but **no banks** capable of foreign currency transactions along the valley.

3

DAMMING THE NU RIVER

In 2011, the Chinese government approved plans to build a series of **hydroelectric dams** on the Nu River, the first of which is planned for the Lushui area. The Nu is within the nominally protected **Three Parallel Rivers** area, and damming it is certain to threaten the region's natural splendour and biological diversity – not to mention flooding out numerous communities. On the other hand, China desperately needs power and is the world's largest consumer of fossil fuels; hydroelectric dams are one way to reduce its carbon emissions. The Nu is the country's last major river yet undammed and could produce even more power than the Three Gorges Dam in Hubei (see p.173).

Lushui
泸水县, lúshuǐ xiàn

LUSHUI, also known as **Liuku** (六库, liùkù), is a drab administrative centre for the valley, straddling both sides of the river. There's little to do here except soak at **Mabu hot springs** (玛布温泉, mǎbù wēnquán; ¥50), a short ride north on bus #3, or cross the bridge and climb the western hillside for superb views of the valley – though the local tourist bureau (see opposite) can arrange trips to nearby villages. The town wakes up around December 20, when the Lisu hold their **Kuoshi festival**, at which, besides singing and dancing, you'll see local men showing off by climbing poles barefoot using swords as steps.

Fugong
福贡, fúgòng

North from Lushui, you pass through some very scenic Lisu villages that cling to the steep sides of the gorge, and the river begins to reveal its fierce character, so it's a shame that the next big town, **FUGONG**, 123km further on, is such a dump. Given its vistas of bleak concrete, it's basically a rest stop, though every five days there's a **market**, well attended by Lisu, Dulong and Nu people from nearby villages.

Gongshan
贡山, gòngshān

Around four hours' bus ride north of Fugong, tiny **GONGSHAN** marks the end of the main road, where there's a choice between continuing north to the Nu River's upper reaches, or heading northwest into the Drung Valley. Either way, you'll likely see **Drung** (Dulong) people here: older women have tattooed faces, supposedly for beautification, though the practice seems to have started as a way to dissuade Tibetan slave-traders from kidnapping them. A big **church** on the hill above town is where to get views of the area.

The Drung River Valley
独龙江, dúlóng jiāng

If you want to see more of the Drung, ask around in Gongshan for vehicles planning to tackle the 70km-long, four-wheel-drive road northwest to **DULONG JIANG** township (独龙江乡, dúlóng jiāng xiāng); it's a fabulous seven-hour ride over forested ridges. Dulong Jiang serves the beautiful **Drung River Valley**, which runs 80km north right up to the Tibetan border; there's a vehicle track to the halfway village of **Dizhengdang** (迪正挡, dízhèngdǎng), and experienced hikers have trekked over the mountains from here to **Xidang** (see p.243) in under two weeks, though you'll need a guide and plenty of stamina.

Dimaluo
迪麻洛, dímáluò

DIMALUO is a community of Nu, Lisu, Drung and Catholic Tibetans up in the hills off the Gongshan–Bingzhongluo road: from Gongshan, catch a Bingzhongluo bus and get out at **Pengdang** (捧当, pěngdāng), then cross the river and walk south until you reach a bridge and a dirt track, which you follow north for about two hours (5km). The attractive village is of most interest for *Alou's Tibetan Lodge*, whose owner has turned it into a base camp for two- or three-day treks along the "Weixi Road" (维西路, wéixī lù), which crosses east over the Nu Shan range via a 4000m-high pass and descends into the Lancang River Valley at **Yongzhi** (永芝, yǒngzhī) or **Cizhong** (see p.233).

Bingzhongluo

丙中洛, bǐngzhōngluò

The road from Gongshan judders to a close at **BINGZHONGLUO**, a one-street Tibetan and Nu township just 35km short of the Tibetan border and only 50km east of Burma. Don't expect anything romantic – it's another shabbily tiled place with a couple of basic guesthouses and stores – but there are plenty of less developed villages nearby.

Upstream are the pretty hamlets of **Wuli** (五里, wǔlǐ) and **Chala** (查腊, chálà); you can hike 5km uphill from the latter to **Xiao Chala** (小查腊, xiǎo chálà), a Drung village. South of Bingzhongluo, there's a large Catholic church at **Shuangla** (双拉, shuānglā); or catch a bus to Pengdang for the walk to Dimaluo.

ARRIVAL AND GETTING AROUND   NU RIVER VALLEY

By bus Starting from Xiaguan or Baoshan, your first stop is Lushui, from where you can reach Bingzhongluo via changes of buses at Fugong and Gongshan – you're unlikely to get further than Fugong on the first day. Destinations from Lushui Baoshan (5 daily; 5hr; ¥48); Fugong (8 daily; 6hr; ¥40); Xiaguan (2 daily; 6hr; ¥68).

Destinations from Fugong Gongshan (6 daily; 6hr; ¥68); Lushui (8 daily; 6hr; ¥40). Destinations from Gongshan Bingzhongluo (3 daily; 2hr; ¥20); Fugong (6 daily; 6hr; ¥68). Destinations from Bingzhongluo Gongshan (3 daily; 2hr; ¥20).

INFORMATION

Tourist information The Nujiang Travel Bureau (怒江旅游局, nùjiāng lǚyóu jú), is about 500m north out of Lushui towards Fugong, ☎ 088 6362 4247. The manageress doesn't speak much English, but they're extremely helpful, and run tours to outlying villages.

ACCOMMODATION AND EATING

BINGZHONGLUO

Chama Kezhan 茶马客栈, chámǎ kèzhàn. At the end of the road on the left; the only one of Bingzhongluo's places to stay with hot water. Beds ¥40

DIMALOU

Alou's Tibetan Lodge 阿洛客栈, āluò kèzhàn. ☎ 088 6356 6182, ⓦ angelfire.com/un/aloudekezhan, ⓔ aloudekezhan@yahoo.com. Guesthouse run by friendly and knowledgeable owner, who can also organize guides for treks into the Lancang River Valley or to Deqin. Beds ¥20

FUGONG

Fugong 福贡宾馆, fúgòng bīnguǎn. 8 Shiyue Jie, opposite the bus station ☎ 088 6341 2900. Totally unremarkable hotel that does the job. Beds ¥35, doubles ¥100

GONGSHAN

Bus Station Hostel 贡山客运旅社, gòngshān kèyùn lǚshè. At the bus station ☎ 088 6351 1496. The only real hotel in town, basic but not too noisy. ¥60

LUSHUI

For **food**, try the covered night market just south of the intersection of Renmin Lu and Zhenxing Lu, where you'll find game from the surrounding forests as well as Yunnanese staples.

Government Guesthouse 政府招待所, zhèngfǔ zhāodàisuǒ. Renmin Lu, north of the bus station ☎ 0886 362 2589. Dishevelled but cheap and close to the bus station. ¥80

Nujiang 怒江宾馆, nùjiāng bīnguǎn. 331 Chuancheng Lu, at the north end of town ☎ 0886 362 6888. One of the more aspirational hotels in town, trying to look smart but let down by average, worn rooms. ¥120

Post Office Hotel 邮电宾馆, yóudiàn bīnguǎn. Chuancheng Lu ☎ 0886 362 0500. Ordinary tower block concealing a splendid lobby, whose marble, gold and chrome elegance don't make it through to the rooms. A good deal, if you argue over the price. ¥120

3

3

> ## CROSSING TO BURMA
>
> You'll need to have arranged everything in advance if you're planning to cross overland from Wanding or Ruili **into Burma**. Visas are available through the Burmese consulate in Kunming (see p.193); they're expensive but can usually be obtained within a few days. You also need to organize a guide to meet you at the Burmese border in Ruili (see p.253); get their phone number and call them in advance to check they can speak English.

West to Burma

Southwest of Xiaguan, Yunnan's far west bumps up against the **Burmese border**, a tropical area of mountain forests and broad valleys planted with rice and sugar cane, cut by the deep watershed gorges of Southeast Asia's mighty **Mekong** and **Salween** rivers (in Chinese, the Lancang Jiang and Nu Jiang, respectively). Settlements have large populations of Dai, Burmese and Jingpo peoples, and until recently mainstream China never had a great presence here.

The regional artery between Xiaguan and the border roughly follows the route of the old **Burma Road**, built during World War II as a supply line between British-held Burma and Chinese railheads at Kunming. Something of the road's original purpose survives today, with towns along the way, especially ethnically mixed **Ruili**, right on the Burmese frontier, still benefiting from cross-border traffic. With the exception of **Tengchong**, however, sights out this way are few and – unless you're heading into Burma – the area's appeal is simply in experiencing an accessible but fairly untourist corner of Yunnan.

Aside from bussing through from Xiaguan, you can also fly into the regional capital, **Mangshi**, from Kunming. With the Burmese border so close, plus the area's perennial **drug-trafficking** problems, you might encounter **military checkpoints** where you have to show passports and wait while vehicles are checked for contraband. The **weather** is subtropically humid, especially during the wet season between May and October, when landslides frequently cut smaller roads.

Baoshan

保山, bǎoshān

BAOSHAN, 120km from Xiaguan, is a large, modern, bustling Muslim town on the edge of a broad plain, its stores well provisioned with locally grown coffee, smart suits and shoes. There's no reason to stop unless you're in transit to the Nu River Valley (see p.245); the nicest place to spend a couple of hours is **Taibao Shan Park** (太保山公园, tàibǎo shān gōngyuán), on the western outskirts of town at the end of Baoxiu Xi Lu, full of pine trees, butterflies and twittering birds.

ARRIVAL AND DEPARTURE   BAOSHAN

By plane Baoshan's airport is about 5km southwest of town; a taxi costs ¥10. Flights head to Kunming (3 daily; 1hr).

By bus The main bus station is 1.5km east of the centre, just off the Xiaguan–Ruili highway at the end of Baoxiu Dong Lu.

Destinations Jinghong (1 daily; 2 days; ¥200); Kunming (5 daily; 9hr; ¥178); Lushui (5 daily; 5hr; ¥48); Mangshi (frequent; 2hr; ¥45); Ruili (frequent; 4hr; ¥78); Tengchong (frequent; 3hr; ¥48); Xiaguan (9 daily; 3hr; ¥52).

ACCOMMODATION

Huatai 华泰宾馆, huátài bīnguǎn. 4 Lancheng Lu, just off Baoxiu Xi Lu ☏ 087 5216 0254. Inexpensive, adequate rooms just west of Baoshan's central roundabout. **¥100**

Landu 兰都大酒店, lándū dàjiǔdiàn. 46 Baoxiu Xi Lu ☏ 087 5212 1888. The best hotel in town, with clean,

modern rooms (some with views) and an excellent restaurant upstairs on the first floor. **¥220**

Longyang 隆阳大酒店, lóngyáng dàjiǔdiàn. 39 Jiulong Rd, just south of the central roundabout ☏ 087 5214 8888. Relatively new rooms in reasonable condition, though ageing fast. **¥100**

DIRECTORY

Banks The main Bank of China (Mon–Fri 8am–6pm) and ATM is at the Baoxiu Dong Lu – Zhengyang Lu intersection; other branches and ATMs are scattered along the main streets.

Tengchong

腾冲, téngchōng

Over the Nu River and off the main expressway 120km from Baoshan, **TENGCHONG** is a mix of newish main streets and shabby alleys dotted with small temples and rickety buildings which have somehow survived modernizations, carpet bombing during World War II and the **earthquakes** which frequently shake this area. A long-time staging post on overland routes between Burma, western China and Tibet, the British had a **consulate** in Tengchong until 1949 (they even planned to build a railway through from Burma), and the town became a base for Western travellers and explorers. Tengchong's streets are worth an aimless wander, though the real attractions lie outside.

Tengchong's kilometre-long central axes are **Fengshan Lu** and **Guanghua Lu**; a small produce **market** blocks the pedestrianized back lanes just east of here – some stalls specialize in wind-cured ham – while northeast, at the top of Fengshan Lu, **Wenxing Lou** (文星楼, wénxīng lóu) is a restored old gate tower, beyond which the cobbled road hosts a disappointingly bland new **jade market**.

Northwest up Guanghua Lu, where it crosses a canal onto Tengyue Lu, the old British Consulate, built in 1899, is now the **Tengchong Museum** (腾冲博物馆, téngchōng bówùguǎn), though it was closed at the time of writing. Turn right here, along Tengyue Lu, and it's 150m to **Yuquan Yuan jade market**, a tourist complex with gem shops inside old buildings, set around an ornamental pond.

Laifeng Shan Park

来凤山公园, láifèng shān gōngyuán

For fresh air and easy walks through thick woodland, head to **Laifeng Shan Park**, on Tengchong's western outskirts at the end of Fengshan Lu. Paths ascend to **Laifeng Temple**, a monastery-turned-museum, full of local historical items, with a thirteen-storey **pagoda** poking out of woodland at the park's summit. The renowned Scottish plant hunter **George Forrest** was buried at Laifeng Shan's **cemetery** in 1932, though the location of his grave has since been lost.

ARRIVAL AND DEPARTURE

TENGCHONG

By bus The main bus station (旅游客运站, lǚyóu kèyùnzhàn) is 1km south of the centre on Rehai Lu, handling traffic to Xiaguan and Baoshan; catch bus #2 into town. Services from Ruili use the old bus station (老客运

THE BURMA ROAD

When the Japanese invaded China in 1937 they drove the Guomindang government to Chongqing, isolating them from their eastern economic and industrial power base. Turning west for help, the Guomindang found the British, who then held Burma and were none too keen to see China's resources in Japanese hands. In fact, there had been plans for a link through to Burma for forty years, and Britain soon agreed to help build a supply line connecting Kunming with the Burmese rail head at **Lashio**.

What became the **Burma Road** was swiftly completed by 300,000 labourers in 1938, an incredible feat considering the basic tools available and the number of mountains along the way. After the Japanese stormed French Indochina in 1940 and halted rail traffic between Vietnam and Kunming, the road became China's only line of communication with the allies. Lashio fell a year later, however, and the road became redundant once more, remaining so after the war ended thanks to Burma's self-imposed isolation and the chaos of the Cultural Revolution. Now open again as the 910km-long **G56 Expressway**, the road remains – like the Great Wall – a triumph of stolid persistence over unfavourable logistics.

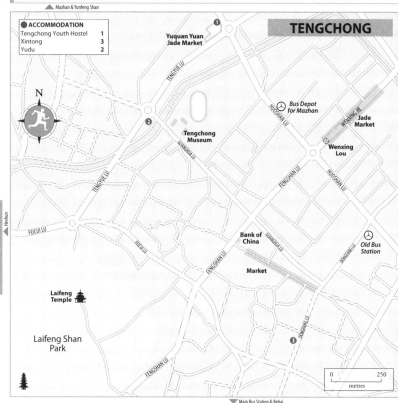

▲ Mazhan & Yunfeng Shan

ACCOMMODATION
Tengchong Youth Hostel	1
Xintong	3
Yudu	2

TENGCHONG

Yuquan Yuan
Jade Market

Bus Depot
for Mazhan

Jade
Market

Wenxing
Lou

Tengchong
Museum

Bank of
China

Old Bus
Station

Market

Laifeng
Temple

Laifeng Shan
Park

0   250
metres

▼ Main Bus Station & Rehai

站, lǎo kèyùn zhàn), on Dongfang Lu; you're just east of the centre here.

Destinations Baoshan (frequent; 3hr; ¥38); Mangshi (frequent; 2hr 30min; ¥35); Ruili (frequent; 6hr; ¥57); Xiaguan (frequent; 6hr; ¥98).

GETTING AROUND

By bus Tengchong's few buses charge ¥1; you might need them for arrival points and to reach some surrounding sights.

By taxi A flat ¥5 in town.
By bicycle *Tengchong Youth Hostel* rents out bikes for ¥20, plus deposit.

ACCOMMODATION AND EATING

There's more **accommodation** outside town at Heshun village (see opposite). Tengchong lacks any good **restaurants**; your best bet is along Guanghua Lu, where evening stalls also sell charcoal-grilled chicken and fish.

★ **Tengchong Youth Hostel** 玉泉园青年旅舍, yùquányuán qīngnián lǚshè. Yuquan Yuan jade market complex ☎ 087 5519 8677. It's a little overpriced, but this attractive wooden building is the nicest place to stay in town; English-speaking staff dispense local information, and the price includes breakfast. Dorms **¥40**, doubles **¥120**

Xintong 鑫通宾馆, xīntōng bīnguǎn. Dongfang Lu ☎ 087 5516 3199. Inexpensive, clean but basic Chinese option on five floors with no lifts. **¥80**
Yudu 玉都大酒店, yùdū dàjiǔdiàn. Near the jade market on Tengyue Lu ☎ 087 5513 8666. Tenchong's smartest venue has spacious modern rooms with computers and city views; unusually for China, it's in a relatively restrained, small-scaled building too. **¥380**

DIRECTORY

Banks There's a Bank of China, with foreign-friendly ATM, on central Fengshan Lu.

Around Tengchong

Heshun village provides an attractive alternative to staying in town, and nearby **hot springs**, plus extinct volcanoes and a mountain temple close to **Mazhan**, could hold you around Tengchong for a few days. The area is refreshingly uncommercialized for Yunnan, offering a rare chance to meet ordinary people doing ordinary things, in a region that doesn't yet depend on tourism for its income.

Heshun

和顺, héshùn • Free to enter village; ¥80 ticket for sights • Taxi from Tengchong ¥15, shared minibus from Feicui Lu ¥2

Five kilometres west of Tengchong among a spread of lush green paddyfields, **HESHUN** is a picturesque Qing-style village whose memorial gateways, lotus ponds, ornamental gardens and thousand or more stone houses are tightly packed within a whitewashed perimeter wall. Though garnering income as a staging post during the horse caravan days, the village owes its appearance to wealthy expatriates, who funded rebuilding in the early twentieth century; you could easily spend a pleasurable half-day here with a camera. Don't miss the **Horse Trail Museum** (古茶马道博物馆, gǔ chámǎ dào bówùguǎn) to the left of the entrance, which fills in on the old days with a wealth of paraphernalia; check out the cudgels and home-made pistols that muleteers carried as protection against bandits, and the gongs beaten to warn oncoming caravans on narrow mountain paths.

3

ACCOMMODATION   HENSHUN

Aside from the following, Heshun's many private **homestays** are signed "客栈" (kèzhàn) and charge around ¥50/person.

Lao Shay Youth Hostel 老谢青年旅舍, lǎoxiè qīngnián lǚshè. ☎ 087 5515 8398, ⓦ laoshay.com. Attractive modern wooden house built around a courtyard; rooms are youth-hostel-comfy and there's plenty of places to chill out. Dorms ¥30, doubles ¥120

★ **Zongbingfu** 总兵府客栈, zǒngbīngfǔ kèzhàn. Behind the museum ☎ 087 5515 0288. Another courtyard house, this time genuinely old though thoroughly renovated; it belonged to a local warlord. There's intricately carved woodwork everywhere, polished teak floors, and some of the pricier rooms are decked out in period furniture. ¥580

Rehai

热海, rèhǎi • Each pool ¥30; spa ¥168 • Minibuses (¥5) from near Tengchong's main bus station on Rehai Lu

Geological shuffles over the last fifty million years have opened up a couple of hotspots around Tengchong. The easiest to reach is **Rehai**, the "Hot Sea", 12km southwest along the Ruili road, where the scalding **Liuhuang** and **Dagungguo** pools steam and bubble away, contained by incongruously neat stone paving and ornamental borders. You can soak in cooler outdoor pools, or have a full spa treatment.

Mazhan

马站, mǎzhàn • Catch a minibus (45min; ¥10) from the small depot on Huoshan Lu in Tengchong

About 25km on the main road north of Tengchong, **MAZHAN** is a small town whose name – literally "Horse Depot" – is yet another reminder of the old days. A kilometre north, **Mazhan Volcano Park** (马站火山公园, mǎzhàn huǒshān gōngyuán; ¥40) encloses a cluster of low, overgrown rubble cones; over 3000 years old, they're not especially spectacular at around 100m high, but you get a good view from the top of other similar formations off towards the horizon.

Yunfeng Shan

云峰山, yúnfēng shān · ¥40 · Minibuses from small depot on Huoshan Lu in Tengchong via Mazhan to Gudong (固东, gùdōng; 1hr 30min; ¥10), then a taxi (¥30) to Yunfeng Shan

This 2445m-high granite mountain has a Ming-dynasty **Taoist temple** complex perched like a fortress right at the top; three thousand steps ascend to the summit or you can cheat and take the cable car (¥40). It's around 50km from Tengchong, and there's simple accommodation and food available at the temple, where people stay overnight hoping to catch sunrise over the "cloud sea" below.

Mangshi

芒市, mángshì

South of Baoshan, the highway makes a grand descent into the Nu Jiang Valley on the two-hour journey to **MANGSHI**, capital of Dehong Prefecture and also known as Luxi (潞西, lùxī). Set amid lush countryside, Mangshi is a small, tropical city with a reputation for excellent pineapples and silverwork, though the only reason you'd stop off here is to use the **airport**, 7km south, the closest one to the Burmese border at Ruili.

ARRIVAL AND DEPARTURE   MANGSHI

By plane Dehong Mangshi Airport (德宏芒市机场, déhóng mángshì jīchǎng) is 5km southwest of the city. Incoming flights are met by taxis and minibuses to town (¥5–15) and also to Ruili – the latter journey should take under three hours, and cost ¥35–50.
Destinations Kunming (5 daily; 55min); Guangzhou (1 daily; 4hr).

By bus There are lots of drop-off points and bus depots in Mangshi, and it's hard to know where you'll end up; the main station is at the south end of town on Tuanjie Dajie, though Ruili buses use a separate terminal nearby.
Destinations Baoshan (2hr; ¥45); Ruili (2hr; ¥25); Tengchong (2hr 30min; ¥35); Xiaguan (2 daily; 5hr; ¥70).

ACCOMMODATION AND EATING

Should you find yourself stuck in town for the night, there are numerous cheap **guesthouses** around the bus station, while countless **shacks** serve buns and curries in almost every lane through the town.

De'an Jiudian 德安酒店, dé ān jiūdiàn. 24 Kuoshi Lu ☎ 069 2221 1288. This clean, basic hotel at the north end of town near Dehong Square is functional enough. **¥120**

Wanding

畹町, wǎndīng · Buses from Tengchong, Baoshan and Xiaguan pass through; minibus shuttles to Ruli (30min; ¥10) run through the day

Some 225km down the expressway from Baoshan, or 150km along twisting back roads from Tengchong, sleepy **WANDING** faces the Burmese township of **Jiugu** over a shallow stream. Founded in 1938 as the customs post for the Burma Road, Wanding has today been totally upstaged by nearby Ruili; Jiugu looks almost totally abandoned, and with Ruili so close, there's no reason to stay here.

Not that Wanding is uninteresting. The **Wanding Bridge** crossing is decked in customs houses, smartly uniformed military, barriers, barbed wire, flags and signs everywhere prohibiting unauthorized passage. But it's all a sham; walk 500m downstream and there's a tiny roadside **park** (actually in Burma), where locals bypass all the official bother by rolling up their trousers and wading across a ford to where a border guard checks their identity cards.

Unfortunately, foreigners wanting to cross will find the situation very different. Westerners can only enter Burma either by flying to Yangon or, if wanting to cross the border overland at Ruili, by organizing permits and guides through agencies in Kunming (see p.193).

Ruili

瑞丽, ruìlì

Once the capital of the Mengmao Dai Kingdom, the frontier town of **RUILI** revels in the possibilities of its proximity to Burma, 5km south over the Shweli River; the borders here are so porous that locals quip, "Feed a chicken in China and you get an egg in Burma". It works the other way too: Burmese, Pakistani and Bangladeshi nationals wander around in sarongs and thongs, clocks are often set to Yangon time, the town's many **markets** are loaded with imported goods, and Ruili is reckoned to be the main conduit for Burmese **drugs** entering China.

Admittedly, Ruili's broad pavements and drab construction initially pin it down as a typical Chinese town, and a very long way from Yunnan's major attractions – without a Burmese visa, your onwards travel options are limited to retracing your steps or chancing an excruciating bus ride to Xishuangbanna. But this surreal outpost is worth a peek, and the surrounding countryside, studded with **Dai villages** and **temples**, is only a bike ride away.

The Jade and Gem Market

瑞丽珠宝街, ruìlì zhūbǎo jiē

The **Jade and Gem market** off northerly Bianmao Jie, has a "Disneyland Burma" look, but it's genuine enough to attract the odd ragged freelance miner touting little bags of stones to sell. Chinese dealers come to purchase ruinously expensive wafers of deep green jade, and – assuming you know what you're doing – there are some nice moonstones, sapphires and rubies available. For the newcomer it's probably safest to simply window-shop, watch the furtive huddles of serious merchants, or negotiate souvenir prices for coloured pieces of sparkling Russian glass "jewels".

Huafeng Market

华丰市场, huáfēng shìchǎng

Large **Huafeng Market**, off Jiegang Lu, is Ruili's most interesting quarter by far, especially in the evenings when food stalls fire up. Stallholders here can sell you everything from haberdashery and precious stones to birds, foul Burmese cigars, sarongs, enormous sculptures in teak, Mandalay rum, wooden lime-squeezers and

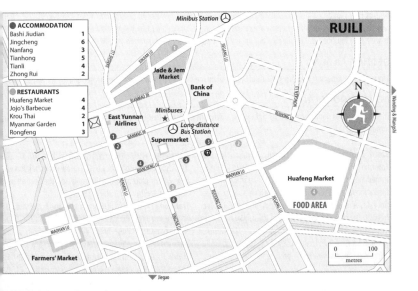

● ACCOMMODATION	
Bashi Jiudian	1
Jingcheng	6
Nanfang	3
Tianhong	5
Tianli	4
Zhong Rui	2

● RESTAURANTS	
Huafeng Market	4
Jojo's Barbecue	4
Krou Thai	2
Myanmar Garden	1
Rongfeng	3

RUILI

Minibus Station

Jade & Jem Market

Bank of China

Minibuses

East Yunnan Airlines

Long-distance Bus Station

Supermarket

Huafeng Market

FOOD AREA

Farmers' Market

Wanding & Mangshi

0 100 metres

Jiegao

Western-brand toiletries. Dai girls powder their faces with yellow talc, young men ask if you'd like to be shown to a backstreet casino, and street sellers skilfully assemble little pellets of stimulating **betel nut** dabbed in ash paste and wrapped in pepper-vine leaf, which stains lips red and teeth black. There are fruit and vegetable stalls too, and the northern side even has an ornamental pond to stroll around, or snack at in pavilions overlooking the water.

The farmers' market

综合农贸市场, zōnghé nóngmào shìchǎng

For a more rough-and-ready shopping experience, try the morning **farmers' market** at the western end of Maohan Lu, where you'll find not only meat, fish, fruit and vegetables, but also locally made wood and cane furniture as well as shoes, clothes and even roadside jewellers selling rings and bracelets by weight. You get some interesting characters turning up too, mouths full of gold and silver dentistry, and occasionally unusual game meats and even wildcat pelts, caught in the surrounding jungles.

Jiegao

姐告, jiěgào • Taxi from town ¥4

Just 5km south of town over the Shweli, **JIEGAO** is a bubble-shaped, free-market Chinese enclave within Burma – you don't need a permit or passport to enter. Taxis run right through to the **border crossing**, at the back of a huge square at the end of Guomen Dadao; the rest of Jiegao is a grid of broad, modern streets selling everything from nautical compasses to thermos flasks, solar panels, stationery, clothing and motorbikes. It's a startling contrast to Ruili's more mundane, practical markets, though a good deal less animated too; an hour here is plenty to get the feel of things and hail a taxi back.

ARRIVAL AND DEPARTURE   RUILI

By plane Flights depart Mangshi Airport (see p.252) for Kunming and Guangzhou. Buy tickets from East Yunnan Airlines, 15 Renmin Lu (☎ 069 2415 5700 or 2411 1111). A shared taxi or minibus to the airport (¥35–50) takes less than 3hr.

By bus Ruili's long-distance bus station is on Nanmao Jie, with departures to everywhere between here and Xiaguan, as well as to Jinghong in Xishuangbanna (see p.257) – an uncomfortable 36hr ride through spectacular countryside. Minibuses to Wanding and Mangshi depart the minibus station opposite the north end of Jiegang Lu, and also the small depot opposite the bus station on Nanmao Jie.

Destinations Baoshan (4hr; ¥78); Jinghong (1 daily; 36hr; ¥297); Mangshi (2hr 30min; ¥25); Nanshan (1 daily; 9hr; ¥98); Tengchong (6hr; ¥57); Wanding (30min; ¥10); Xiaguan (4 daily; 8hr; ¥128).

GETTING AROUND

Taxis charge ¥4/person, and run as a sort of unofficial bus service, often picking up other people going your way en route.

ACCOMMODATION

There's a choice of good-value **rooms** right in the town centre, though there are no real budget bargains. You need a/c in summer.

Bashi Jiudian 巴石酒店, bāshí jiǔdiàn. At the Nanmao Jie–Renmin Lu intersection ☎ 069 2412 9088. Immediately recognizable for the flame-like Thai/Burmese decorations around the entrance; inside it's a basic, spotless place favoured by gem dealers from over the border. Probably the cheapest proper hotel in town. **¥50**

Jingcheng 景成大酒店, jǐngchéng dàjiǔdiàn. Maohan Lu ☎ 069 2415 9666. A reliably comfortable pile with decent rooms, swimming pool, tennis court and gym. **¥280**

Nanfang 南方宾馆, nánfāng bīnguǎn. 42 Biancheng Lu ☎ 069 2415 6999. Another clean, laidback, inexpensive place, memorable only for the fact that it delivers a decent night's sleep. **¥90**

Tianhong 天宏宾馆, tiānhóng bīnguǎn. Behind the bus station at 83 Biancheng Lu ☎ 069 2410 1222. Cool, clean, ordinary Chinese hotel, with large tiled en suites. Some rooms come with computers and internet access. **¥100**

Tianli 天丽宾馆, tiānlì bīnguǎn. Biancheng Lu ☎ 069 2415 5188. Yet another simple, smart, clean option. **¥100**

Zhong Rui 钟瑞宾馆, zhōngruì bīnguǎn. 1 Nanmao Jie ☎ 069 2410 0556. Neat en-suite twins and doubles; as a comfortable budget option in the centre of town, it's more than adequate. **¥120**

EATING

The real treat in Ruili is heading to the covered food area in **Huafeng Market**, which has seating for several hundred diners and comes alive from about 8pm onwards, especially at weekends. The food is all laid out so ordering by pointing is simple, and you can wash it down with Myanmar beer. Places around town also sell refreshing, fresh tropical **fruit juices** – papaya, mango and others – for ¥5 a glass. For conventional **Chinese food**, head to restaurants on Ruijiang Lu, alongside the long-distance bus station.

★ **Jojo's Barbecue** Huafeng Market. Highly recommended, particularly the fish encrusted with bright-orange spices. There's an English sign, though not much English (or Chinese) is spoken.

★ **Krou Thai** 可泰饭店, kě tài fàndiàn. Biancheng Lu. Great Thai option with a photo-menu for easy ordering; their *tom yam* soup, grilled fish, curries and *laab* have just the right balance of sour and spicy flavours. Mains around ¥25.

Myanmar Garden At the Jade Market. Outdoor seating and good Thai and Burmese snacks at about ¥15 a plate. Good for a fill-up during the day, and will keep you going until the Huafeng market's stalls fire up.

Rongfeng 荣丰酒店, róngfēng jiǔdiàn. Maohan Lu. Western-style set meals plus brewed coffee at this cute place, with window tables on the second floor overlooking the street. Around ¥40/head.

DIRECTORY

Banks The main Bank of China, with ATMs, is on Nanmao Jie (foreign exchange Mon–Fri 9–11.30am & 2.30–4.30pm).

Internet The net bar on Biancheng Lu is modern and fast, charging ¥3/hour. They also serve snacks and drinks.

Around Ruili

Villages and Buddhist monuments dot the plains around Ruili, and are easy enough to explore either by asking your accommodation about renting a **bicycle**, or by **minibus** from the Nanmao Jie depot – just keep repeating the name of your destination and you'll be shepherded to the right vehicle. Most of the destinations below are only of mild interest in themselves, really just excuses to get out into Ruili's attractive countryside. For more about the **Dai**, see the Xishuangbanna section (p.256).

The Wanding road

About 5km east of Ruili along the Wanding road is the 200-year-old **Jiele Jin Ta** (姐勒金塔, jiělè jīn tǎ), a group of seventeen portly Dai pagodas painted gold and said to house several of Buddha's bones. In some open-air **hot springs** nearby, you can wash away various ailments. About halfway to Wanding, **Moli Rainforest Scenic Area** (莫里雨林风景区, mòlǐ yǔlín fēngjǐng qū; ¥50) lies 5km north of the main road, and features forest full of rasping cicadas and a big waterfall.

West of Ruili

Heading west, it's 5km to a small bridge near the region's largest Buddhist place of worship, the nicely decorated **Hansha Temple** (喊沙寺, hǎnshā sì). Ten kilometres further on, the town of **JIEXIANG** (姐相, jiěxiàng) boasts the splendid Tang-era **Leizhuang Nunnery** (雷奘相佛寺, léizhuǎngxiāng fósì), whose low square hall is dominated by a huge central pagoda and four corner towers, all in white. Another fine temple with typical Dai touches, such as "fiery" wooden eave decorations, **Denghannong Si** (等喊弄寺, děnghǎnnòng sì) is further west again. The current halls only date from the Qing dynasty, but Buddha is said to have stopped here once to preach.

Xishuangbanna

西双版纳, xīshuāngbǎnnà

A tropical spread of rainforests, plantations and paddy fields, nestled 750km southwest of Kunming along the Burmese and Laotian borders, **Xishuangbanna** owes little of its culture and history to China. Foremost of the region's many ethnic groups are the **Dai**, northern cousins to the Thais, whose distinctive temples, bulbous pagodas and saffron-robed clergy are a common sight down on the red-soil plains, particularly around **Jinghong**, Xishuangbanna's sleepy capital. The region's remaining 19,000 square kilometres are split between the administrative townships of **Mengla** in the east and **Menghai** in the west, peppered with villages of Hani, Bulang, Jinuo, Wa and Lahu; remoter tribes are still animist, and all have distinctive dress and customs. Cultural tourism aside, there are plenty of hiking trails and China's open **border with Laos** to explore.

Xishuangbanna's **tropical weather** divides into a dry stretch between November and May, when warm days, cool nights and dense morning mists are the norm; and the June–October wet season, featuring high heat and torrential daily rains. Given the climate, you'll need to take more than usual care of any cuts and abrasions, and to guard against mosquitoes (see p.40). The busiest time of the year here is mid-April, when thousands of tourists flood to Jinghong for the Dai **Water-Splashing Festival**; hotels and flights will be booked solid for a week beforehand.

Getting around Xishuangbanna is easy enough, with well-maintained roads connecting Jinghong to outlying districts. **Place names** can be confusing, though, as the words "meng-", designating a small town, or "man-", a village, prefix nearly every destination.

Brief history

There was already a Dai state in Xishuangbanna two thousand years ago, important enough to send ambassadors to the Han court in 69 AD; it was later incorporated into the Nanzhao and Dali kingdoms (see p.183). Following the Mongols' thirteenth-century conquest of Yunnan, the region was divided into **twelve rice-growing districts** or *sipsawng pa na* in Thai (rendered as "Xishuangbanna", or *pianling* in Chinese), and its peoples largely left to the pleasure of hereditary rulers, or *pianling*, until the early twentieth century, when warlords – including the tyrannical **Ke Shexun** – took over.

Xishuangbanna had a tough time during the Cultural Revolution, but there's been a steady flow of wealth through here since the Lao border opened up in the 1990s – though how much this has benefited locals is debatable. More contentious aspects of religion have been banned, extensive deforestation has occurred, and recent mass planting of **rubber** as a cash crop has permanently altered the landscape. Many

THE DAI

The **Dai** – or Thai – are found not only in Southwest China but also throughout Thailand, Laos and Vietnam. Considered skilful farmers, they have always flourished in fertile river basins, growing rice, sugar cane and bananas. Accordingly, Dai **cuisine** is characterized by sweet flavours not found elsewhere in China – you'll encounter rice steamed inside bamboo or pineapple, for instance. Oddities such as fried moss and ant eggs appear on special occasions.

Dai women wear a sarong or long skirt, a bodice and a jacket, and keep their hair tied up and fixed with a comb, and often decorated with flowers. Married women wear silver wristbands. Dai men sport plenty of **tattoos** across their chests and forearms, often featuring curly Dai script or tigers. Their homes are raised on stilts, with the livestock kept underneath. They're **Buddhists**, but like their compatriots in Southeast Asia follow the Thervada, or lesser wheel school, rather than the Mahayana school seen throughout the rest of China. When visiting Dai temples, it's important to **remove your shoes**, as the Dai consider feet to be the most unclean part of the body.

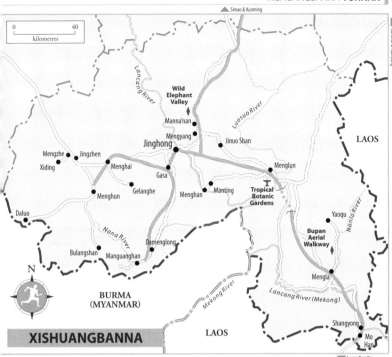

minority people feel the government would really like them to behave like Han Chinese, except in regard of dress – since colourful traditional clothing attracts tourists. While Xishuangbanna is an anaemic version of what lies across the border in Laos, probe around the border regions and you'll find people leading traditional lives, close to the forests and wildlife that surround them.

Jinghong

景洪, jǐnghóng

JINGHONG, Xishuangbanna's small and easy-going capital, first became a seat of power in 1180, when the Dai warlord **Bazhen** drove away Bulang and Hani tribes and founded his kingdom of Cheli on the fertile banks of the **Lancang River** (or Mekong). Jinghong has been maintained as an administrative centre ever since. There was a moment of excitement in the late nineteenth century when a battalion of British soldiers marched in during a foray from Burma, but they soon decided that Jinghong was too remote to be worth defending.

Today, Jinghong's contemporary Chinese architecture makes a drab backdrop for the Dai women in bright sarongs and straw hats who meander along the gently simmering, palm-lined streets, and for the most part the city is an undemanding place to spend a couple of days adjusting to the climate. Aside from energetic excesses during the water-splashing festivities, you'll find the pace of life is set by the tropical heat: nobody bothers rushing anywhere. Once you've tried the local food and poked around the temples that encroach on the suburbs, there's plenty of transport into the rest of the Xishuangbanna.

3

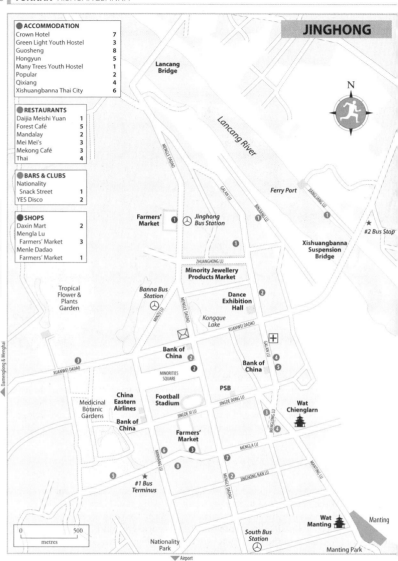

JINGHONG

ACCOMMODATION
Crown Hotel	7
Green Light Youth Hostel	3
Guosheng	8
Hongyun	5
Many Trees Youth Hostel	1
Popular	2
Qixiang	4
Xishuangbanna Thai City	6

RESTAURANTS
Daijia Meishi Yuan	1
Forest Café	5
Mandalay	2
Mei Mei's	3
Mekong Café	3
Thai	4

BARS & CLUBS
| Nationality Snack Street | 1 |
| YES Disco | 2 |

SHOPS
Daxin Mart	2
Mengla Lu Farmers' Market	3
Menle Dadao Farmers' Market	1

Squares and markets

Mengle Dadao is Jinghong's main street, running south through the city for a couple of kilometres. There's a big **farmers' market** (农贸市场, nóngmào shìchǎng) opposite the bus station, packed with Dai women picking over piles of tropical fruit and veg. A short way south, Zhuanghong Lu's "**Minority Jewellery Products Market**" is a 500m-long gauntlet of Burmese jade and jewellery shops with over-friendly staff, plus stalls selling clothes and ethnic textiles and trinkets; it's worth a half-hour browse.

Further down at the crossroads with Xuan Wei Dadao, **Kongque Lake** (孔雀湖, kǒngquè hú) is a pond really, the east side planted with trees, around which traditional

musicians gather in the evening. South again, **Minorities' Square** (民族文化广场, mínzú wénhuà guǎngchǎng) is a huge paved plaza, too hot during the day but popular with dancers after dark.

Tropical Flower and Plants Garden

热带花卉园, rèdài huāhuì yuán · Daily 7.30am–6.30pm · ¥40

Jinghong's **Tropical Flower and Plants Garden**, 500m west down Xuanwei Dadao, is a large sprawl of lawns, ponds, palms, bougainvillea beds and groves of frangipani. As is often the case with tropical species, however, there's a lot of leaf and precious little flower (though what there are tend to be highly scented). Turn up in the mid-afternoon to watch **Dai dances** put on for visiting tour groups.

Medicinal Botanic Gardens

药用植物园, yàoyòng zhíwùyuán · Daily 9am–6pm · ¥30

Opposite the Tropical Gardens, the **Medicinal Botanic Gardens** consist of quiet groves scattered among the shaded gloom of closely planted rainforest trees, all a source of traditional Bai, Tibetan and mainstream Chinese medicine. Signs are a bit scant, but there are lillies, gingers, trees bearing huge jackfruit and an **orchid house** full of colourful blooms. Shaded lawns here attract locals after an afternoon nap or a picnic.

Along the river

East off Xuanwei Dadao, riverside **Binjiang Lu** is a great place to stroll, shaded by fig and poincianas during the day, when you can watch children on the opposite bank cooling down by jumping off moored vessels and floating downstream in the current. At dusk, bars and food stalls along **Nationality Snack Street** (民族食尚街, mínzú shíshàng jiē) fire up, while locals fly kites on the shingle beach and drive down to wash their cars, trucks and motorbikes below the neon-striped **Xishuangbanna Suspension Bridge** (西双版纳大桥, xīshuāngbǎnnà dà qiáo).

Wat Manting

曼听佛寺, màntīng fósì

A kilometre southeast of the centre down Manting Lu, **Manting** (曼听, màntīng), once a separate village, has been absorbed into Jinghong's lazy spread. Near the end of the road, **Wat Manting** is Jinghong's main Buddhist monastery and the largest in all Xishuangbanna. The bright pink and red main hall is guarded by fierce golden lions, past which rises a **naga staircase**, flanked by giant snakes. The inside is cool and largely bare except for glossy **jinghua murals** and a placid, thin-faced Buddha statue, sitting in the lotus posture. Traditionally, all Dai boys spend three years at temples like Wat Manting getting a grounding in Buddhism and learning to read and write – skills therefore denied to Dai girls.

Manting Park

曼听公园, màntīng gōngyuán · Daily 7.30am–5.30pm · ¥40 · Evening Dai dance performances daily 7.40–9.40pm, ¥160–280

Next to Wat Manting is the more secular **Manting Park**, where royal slaves were formerly kept. A giant gold statue of former premier Zhou Enlai welcomes visitors, tour groups are treated to **water-splashing** displays every afternoon, and there's a large pen bursting with **peacocks**, which you can feed. Corners of the park are very pleasant, with paths crossing over one of the Lancang River's tiny tributaries to full-scale copies of Jingzhen's Bajiao Ting (see p.266) and a portly, Dai-style pagoda.

ARRIVAL AND DEPARTURE   **JINGHONG**

Confirm **visa requirements** for Laos and Thailand before booking transport to these countries; transit visas might be available at overland borders, but these won't allow you much time in the country. The nearest consulates are in Kunming (see p.193).

GETTING SLOSHED WITH THE DAI

Dai New Year celebrations, once set by the unpredictable Dai calendar, are now held annually, from **April 13–16**. The first day sees a **dragonboat race** on the river, held in honour of a good-natured dragon spirit who helped a local hero outwit an evil king. On the second day everybody in Jinghong gets a good soaking as **water-splashing** hysteria grips the town, and basinfuls are enthusiastically hurled over friends and strangers alike to wash away bad luck. Manting Park also hosts cockfighting and dancing all day. The finale includes **Diu Bao** (Throwing Pouches) games, where prospective couples fling small, triangular beanbags at each other to indicate their affection, and there's a mammoth **firework display**, when hundreds of bamboo tubes stuffed with gunpowder and good-luck gifts are rocketed out over the river.

Nightly carousing and dancing – during which generous quantities of *lajiu*, the local firewater, are consumed – take place in the parks and public spaces. Look out for the **peacock dance**, a fluid performance said to imitate the movements of the bird, bringer of good fortune in Dai lore, and the **elephant-drum dance**, named after the instrument used to thump out the rhythm.

3

BY PLANE

The **airport** is 10km southwest of Jinghong; catch bus #1 to its terminus at the western extension of Mengla Lu, or it's a ten-minute, ¥35 taxi ride into the centre. Aside from internal flights, there's a weekly departure to Bangkok and talk of a service starting up between Jinghong and Luang Prabang in northern Laos. Book **tickets** with China Eastern Airlines, 23 Minhang Lu ☎069 1212 6999, or agents around town.

Destinations Chengdu (2 daily; 2hr); Chongqing (4 daily; 1hr 30min); Kunming (6 daily; 55min); Lijiang (4 daily; 1hr), Shanghai (2 daily; 5hr 25min); Xiaguan (1 daily; 50min).

BY BUS

Jinghong bus station (景洪客运站, jǐnghóng kèyùn zhàn) on Mengle Dadao handles all long-distance traffic, including from Luang Namtha (南塔, nántǎ) in Laos, and some local services.

Destinations Baoshan (1 daily; 20hr; ¥220); Daluo (3 daily; 3hr; ¥45); Kunming (10hr; ¥180–260); Luang Namtha (1 daily; 8hr; equivalent of US$12); Menglong (2hr; ¥16); Menglun (3 daily; 2hr; ¥16); Ruili (1 daily; 32hr; ¥300);

Tengchong (1 daily; 20hr; ¥220); Xiaguan (2 daily; 18hr; ¥180).

Banna bus station (版纳客运服务站, bǎnnà kèyùn fúwù zhàn), right in the centre on Minzu Lu, deals with destinations within Xishuangbanna. Departures begin to dry up mid-afternoon.

Destinations Daluo (5 daily; 3hr; ¥45); Menghai (1hr; ¥15); Menghan/Ganlanba (1hr; ¥8.50); Menghun (1hr 30min; ¥16); Mengla (4hr; ¥48); Mengyang (1hr; ¥10).

South bus station (客运南站, kèyùn nán zhàn), 1km down Mengle Dadao on the #3 bus route

Destinations Damenglong (2hr; ¥16); Kunming (10hr; ¥180–260).

BY FERRY

The **ferry port** (景洪港, jǐnghóng gǎng) is across the river on Jingliang Lu; bus #2 runs over the bridge into town along Xuan Wei Dadao. Mekong ferries to Chiang Saen in northern Thailand depart 8am, more or less every other day (7hr; ¥650). There's a **ticket office** at the port (☎069 1221 1899; daily 8am–5.30pm), or Jinghong's cafés can make bookings.

GETTING AROUND

Bicycles can be rented from cafés and the *Green Light* and *Many Trees* hostels; expect ¥20/day plus around ¥300 deposit.

Buses (¥1) are useful for transit points: bus #3 also circuits the town via Mengle Dadao, Manting Lu, Galan Lu and the South bus station.

Taxis cost ¥7 to hire and shouldn't cost much more for anywhere central.

INFORMATION

Information and tours *Mei Mei* and *Forest* cafés arrange tours and provide up-to-date information about Xishuangbanna: festival and market dates, the latest jungle treks and the best spots for cultural tourism. Recommended, experienced tour guides include Sarah at the *Forest Café* (see p.262) and "Joe" Zhao Yao (☎137 6914 6987). Most trips include an overnight stay with a local host family and cost around ¥250/person; prices fall as the number of people in your group goes up.

ACCOMMODATION

All but the smallest **lodgings** have restaurants and tour agencies, and some offer computers in the room for an extra ¥20 or so. You'll need a/c in summer.

Crown Hotel 皇冠大酒店, huángguān dàjiǔdiàn. 70 Mengle Dadao ☎069 1219 9883, ⓦnewtgh.com. One of a number of upmarket places grouped around the Mengle/Mengla intersection, all aimed at wealthier Chinese tourists. Unmemorable but clean and comfortable. **¥300**

Green Light Youth Hostel 版纳绿光青年客栈, bǎnnà lǜguāng qīngnián kèzhàn. 93 Xuanwei Dadao ☎069 1213 8365. This popular budget guesthouse, close to the botanical gardens in the grounds of the university, has dorms and twin rooms with 24hr solar-powered hot water. The a/c is extra. Dorms **¥25**, doubles **¥60**

Guosheng 国盛大酒店, guóshèng dàjiǔdiàn. 14 Mengla Lu ☎069 1219 7088. Budget business place with modern, comfy doubles; their larger rooms are spacious enough to almost count as suites. **¥150**

Hongyun 鸿云酒店, hóngyún jiǔdiàn. 12 Galan Nan Lu ☎069 1216 5777. Older place but smart, with carpeted, quite spacious a/c rooms, and views towards the river (just). Cheaper rooms have squat toilets. **¥120**

Many Trees Youth Hostel 曼丽翠国际青年旅舍, mànlìcuì guójì qīngnián lǚshè. 5 Manyun Xiang, down a lane opposite the gymnasium on Galan Lu ☎069 1212 6210. Haphazardly brightened up Chinese hostel – hot water can be erratic – but a/c rooms are a fair deal for the money. Dorms **¥30**, doubles **¥85**

Popular 假日时尚酒店, jiàrì shíshàng jiǔdiàn. 104 Galan Zhong Lu ☎069 1213 9001. A decent, newish place with clean and tidy a/c doubles; the drawbacks are views over lacklustre rooftops and no lift. **¥100**

Qixiang 气象宾馆, qìxiàng bīnguǎn. 10 Galan Nan Lu ☎069 1213 0188. This place's small tiled rooms with a/c are a budget bargain. Squat toilets throughout. **¥60**

Xishuangbanna Thai City 西双版纳傣都大酒店, xīshuāngbǎnnà dǎi dū dàjiǔdiàn. 26 Minghang Lu ☎069 1213 7888. This low-key three-star establishment is about as upmarket as Jinghong gets, full of clean rooms, harassed staff and large Chinese tour groups. **¥280**

EATING

The knot of modern **tourist cafés** with outdoor tables on Menglong Lu have good, if pricey, Western-Dai-Chinese menus; locals eat at **barbecue stalls** in the small covered market on Manting Lu.

Daijia Meishi Yuan 傣家美食园, dǎijiā měishí yuán. Jiangliang Lu, near the port ☎069 1220 1499. Thai banquet with dance show at on open-air restaurant with bamboo buildings arranged around a tropical courtyard garden. It's a bit of a tour-group hangout but fun, and the food is good. Set meal for ten ¥300–400.

Forest Café Mengla Lu ☎069 18985122, ⓦforestcafe.org. Small café with a limited range of excellent Dai and Aini dishes, very different from the bright curries you find elsewhere. Contact Sarah here about local trekking. ¥35.

Mandalay 曼德勒餐厅, yēdénà měi cāntīng. North side of Renmin Square above the more visible Dico's. Inexpensive food court serving everything from fried chicken on rice to Burmese curries, kebabs and pizza. Great for cold fruit drinks and sweet desserts featuring coconut milk and sago too. Snacks under ¥10, meals around ¥25.

★ **Mei Mei's** Menglong Lu ☎069 12161221, ⓔzhanyanlan@hotmail.com. Popular, long-running café whose food is best if you ask them to hold the salt. Excellent coffee. Mains from ¥35.

Mekong Café Menglong Lu. Similar in decor and atmosphere to adjacent *Mei Mei's*, this friendly place serves French, Chinese and Dai food, doing well in all departments. ¥35.

Thai Opposite Mei Mei's on Menglong Lu. Bright, busy, open-sided eating hall serving inexpensive Thai meals, mostly one-plate curry and rice. Fork out a little for more substantial coconut and meat soups, or green papaya salad. It closes very early. Meals ¥15–35.

NIGHTLIFE AND DRINKING

Nationality Snack Street 民族食尚街, mínzú shíshàng jiē. Binjiang Lu. Jinghong's main after-dark entertainment is provided by this line of large, wooden riverside restaurant-bars with loud – sometimes live – music, decked out in coloured fairy lights. The establishments are all much the same; a drink costs at least ¥30.

YES Disco Jinghong Nan Lu. Packed until 3am every night with hard-drinking Dai kids; it's free to get in, and a beer costs ¥20.

SHOPPING

Markets For fresh fruit, including mangoes, coconuts, bananas, mangosteens and durian, head to either of the big produce markets on Mengle Dadao or Mengla Lu.

Supermarkets Jinghong's best is the Daxin Mart, underneath Renmin Square on Mengle Dadao; aside from daily necessities, you can buy *pu'er* tea, cheese and small packets of Yunnan ham.

DIRECTORY

Banks The main Bank of China (daily 8am–11.30am & 3–5.30pm), with ATM, is at 29 Minhang Lu, at the junction with Jingde Lu. There are ATMs all around the centre.

Internet There are plenty of internet cafés along Manting Lu; foreigner cafés and some hotels have wi-fi.

Laundry Foreigner cafés offer the least expensive laundry services in town.

Post The GPO (daily 8am–8pm), is on the corner of Xuanwei Dadao and Mengle Dadao.

Massage Taiji Blind Massage (太极宣人按摩中心, tàijí xuānrén ànmó zhōngxīn) is just north of the Jingde Dong Lu–Mengle Dadao intersection, on the east side of the road. Go through the arch marked "Blind Massage" then turn immediately left up the staircase to the second floor. Full body ¥40, feet ¥50.

PSB It's signed in English at 13 Jingde Dong Lu ☎069 1213 0366. Mon–Fri 8–11.30am & 3–5.30pm.

Eastern Xishuangbanna

There's a small knot of attractions **northeast of Jinghong**, but the most appealing sight lies east towards the Lao border at the Tropical Botanic Gardens outside **Menglun**, which are worth an overnight stay. Transport out this way departs from Jinghong's Banna bus station.

Huayao villages

MENGYANG (勐养, měngyǎng), 30km north of Jinghong, is a market and transport stop surrounded by a host of **Huayao** villages. The Huayao ("Flower Belt") form one of three Dai subgroups, though they differ greatly from the lowland "Water Dai", who scorn them for their overelaborate costumes – Huayao women wear turbans draped with thin silver chains – and the fact that they are not Buddhists. Though you'll see plenty of Huayao at Mengyang, the village considered most typical is about 10km further north along the main road at **MANNA'NAN** (曼那囡, mànnànān).

EXPLORING XISHUANGBANNA

The Lancang River neatly cuts Xishuangbanna into two regions on either side of Jinghong. To the east, there's a choice of roads through highland forests or more cultivated flatlands to the botanic gardens at **Menglun**, beyond which lies **Mengla** and the open **Laotian border**. Head **west** and your options are split between the **Damenglong** and **Menghai** regions – with a more varied bag of ethnic groups, better hiking and a closed border with **Burma**.

Larger places can be visited on day-trips from Jinghong, but you won't see much unless you stop overnight. Towns aren't so interesting in themselves – though some host good **markets** – so you'll need to get out to villages, small temples and the countryside to experience Xishuangbanna's better side. Be prepared for **basic accommodation** and bland, if plentiful, food. Some villagers may offer meals and a bed for the night in return for a small donation – or yank you enthusiastically into the middle of a festival, if you're lucky enough to stumble across one.

GETTING AROUND

Xishuangbanna's towns are connected to Jinghong by bus from about 7am until late afternoon. Once in the countryside, you'll be flagging down short-range minibuses between villages. Cycling is another possibility in the lowlands (Jinghong's cafés can rent you one) though Xishuangbanna's hill roads are steep, twisting and long. To get out to remoter villages, waterfalls and forest, it's best to take one of the guided treks offered by Jinghong's tourist cafés (see opposite).

Wild Elephant Valley

版纳野象谷, bǎnnà yěxiàng gǔ · Daily 8am–6.30pm; ¥80

A further 8km beyond Manna'nan, **Wild Elephant Valley** is a chunk of rainforest based around the Sancha Stream. The main attraction here is the slim chance of seeing wild elephants, though the jungle itself gets more interesting the further you get from the loud tour parties near the entrance. Give the captive monkeys and **elephant displays** a wide berth unless you enjoy watching animals perform circus tricks while a trainer jabs them with a spear.

Jinuo Shan

基诺山, jīnuò shān

Some 18km east of Mengyang, **JINUO SHAN** is home to the independently minded Jinuo, whose women wear a distinctive white-peaked hood – both sexes also pierce their ears and practise tattooing. The **Jinuo Folk Culture Village** (基诺山民族山寨, jīnuò shān mīnzú shān zhài; ¥50) here is touristy, but at any rate can give you a glimpse of Xishuangbanna's smallest ethnic group; the village is otherwise a fairly unwelcoming place.

Menghan

勐罕, měnghǎn · Menghan has a small bus station: services run to Menglun until 2pm, and Jinghong until 5pm

MENGHAN, or Ganlanba (橄榄坝, gǎnlǎnbà), is a small, quiet, palm-lined place a kilometre across, with a relatively modern centre and some traditional wooden houses on its outskirts. It sits some 30km southeast of Jinghong in the fertile "Olive-shaped Flatland", one of Xishuangbanna's three major **agricultural areas**, won by force of arms over the centuries and now vitally important to the Dai (the other two are west at Damenglong and Menghai). On the western outskirts, the **Dai Garden** (傣园, dǎi yuán; ¥100) offers another sanitized version of minority life to visiting tour groups.

The paddy fields and low hills that surround the town make a pleasant backdrop for plenty of day walks and cycle rides – any place you stay will be able to help you rent a bike. One popular trip is to take a bike across the nearby **Lancang River** via a local ferry, and then head left for Dai villages; alternatively, head a couple of kilometres east to **Manting village** (曼听, màntīng), where **Manting Buddhist Temple** (曼听佛寺, màntīng fósì) and **Dadu Pagoda** (大独塔, dàdú tǎ) are fine reconstructions of twelfth-century buildings destroyed during the 1960s.

Menglun

勐仑, měnglún · Buses pick up and drop off on the main road, usually among the restaurants on Menglun's eastern side

MENGLUN, 40km east of Menghan, comprises a dusty, busy grid of streets overlooking the broad flow of the **Luosuo River**. Take the side street downhill through the all-day **market**, and you'll find yourself by a large pedestrian **suspension bridge** crossing to Menglun's superb **Tropical Botanic Gardens** (热带植物园, rèdài zhíwùyuán; daily 7.30am–6.30pm; ¥80); you can also enter off the Menghan road. The gardens were carved out of the jungle in 1959, and are now divided up into shaded palm and bamboo groves, clusters of giant rainforest trees, lily ponds, vines and shrubs. There are plenty of birds and butterflies flitting about too – in all, an enjoyable mix of parkland and forgotten, overgrown corners. Look for Chinese visitors serenading (or simply screaming at) the undistinguished-looking "**Singing Plant**", which is supposed to nod in time to music.

Mengla

勐腊, měnglà · The bus station at the northern end of town has services to Menglun and Jinghong; border and Yaoqu buses head from the depot to the south

MENGLA, two hours southeast over the hills from Menglun, is a 1500m-long, functional town, the last major settlement before the Lao border (see opposite). There's the bronze-spired **Manbeng Pagoda** (曼崩塔, mànbēng tǎ), 3km south of town, but the only real reason to stop would be to try and explore jungle to the northeast, though it's fairly inaccessible – **Yaoqu** (see below) is as close as you're likely to get.

To Yaoqu

Buses run from Mengla each afternoon, returning in the morning

Transport to the small town of **Yaoqu** runs 40km north through the beautiful farmland and forest scenery that flanks the Nanla River. Not far off the road, just over halfway, look out for the **Bupan aerial walkway** (补蚌望天树空中索道, bǔbàng wàngtiānshù kōngzhōngsuǒdào; ¥50), a very insecure-looking metal "sky bridge" running across the forest canopy.

YAOQU (瑶区, yáoqū) itself is a roadhead for remote villages, with two hostels, and all sorts of people turning up to trade, including **Yao**, dressed in dark blue jackets and turbans, and **Kumu**, one of Xishuangbanna's several unrecognized ethnic groups.

The Lao border

The **Lao border** is 60km southeast of Mengla, via the small town of **SHANGYONG** (尚勇, shàngyǒng). This is home to Xishuangbanna's isolated **Miao** population (see p.284), who arrived here during the 1970s after being chased out of Vietnam and Laos following the Vietnam War. Not much further on, **MO HAN** township (边贸站, biānmào zhàn) is just 6km from the laidback border crossing (see below), which closes mid-afternoon.

3

GETTING AROUND   **EASTERN XINSHUANGBANNA**

Buses to everywhere in eastern Xishuangbanna as far as Mengla depart from Jinghong's Banna bus station (see p.261). Services thin out after lunch, so don't leave things too late. From Mengla, you'll have to catch local buses to the **border**, unless you're on a through-service into Laos from Jinghong.

ACCOMMODATION

You might well find yourself wanting to **stay** the night at the towns below, but all settlements have somewhere to stay if you ask around, typically charging around ¥35/person.

Chunlin Binguan 春林宾馆, chūnlín bīnguǎn. Xi Damen, by the suspension bridge, Menglun ☎ 069 1871 5681. Menglun's incumbent "cheap and cheerful" option, just outside the park. ¥50

Huaxin Binguan 华鑫宾馆, huáxīn bīnguǎn. The main road, Menghan ☎ 069 1241 1258. Just a cut above

other similar hotels on Menghan's main road, with clean, basic rooms plus a/c. ¥60

Post Office Hotel 邮电宾馆, yóudiàn bīnguǎn. 1 Mantala Lu, in the north of town, Mengla ☎ 069 1812 8888. Uninspiringly drab on the outside but actually clean and well maintained, and a decent deal for the price. ¥120

Western Xishuangbanna

Western Xishuangbanna has a few more towns than the east, and also a few more untrodden areas up against the Burmese border (many of the treks running out of

---

INTO LAOS

Assuming you've already obtained a visa from the Laotian consulate in Kunming (see p.193), the **border crossing**, either on foot having caught local transport from Mengla, or as part of the Jinghong–Luang Namtha bus ride, should be uncomplicated. On the opposite side lies **Ban Boten**, though this former boom-town is almost abandoned after its casinos hosted one too many gambling-related murders, and there's nowhere to stay or change currency for Laotian **kip**. The nearest **banks and beds** are a ¥10 truck ride away at the town of **Luang Namtha**, where the Jinghong bus terminates, from where you can hitch out to the early-morning markets at **Muong Sing** to see local people in full tribal regalia. Alternatively, there's transport from Luang Namtha to Nung Kie via Muong Tai, and thence by boat down the Mekong to Luang Prabang.

PU'ER TEA

Pu'er tea (普洱茶, pǔ'ěr chá) is a speciality of southern Yunnan, a red, musty brew named after a town which was once at the centre of the local trade. Dark, strong teas are not much appreciated within China, but the process used to create *pu'er* – fermenting, drying and then re-fermenting the leaves – helps **preserve** it, making the tea suitable for export north along **tea-horse roads** to Tibet (see p.81). The other main market is **Hong Kong**, where *pu'er*'s alleged fat-reducing properties make it the favoured drink to accompany a calorie-rich dim sum meal.

Very unusually for a Chinese tea, *pu'er*'s flavour actually **improves** with age, and vintage leaves cost a lot of money – the date of production is always stamped on packets. Indeed, when residents of Pu'er County became dissatisfied with bank interest rates in 2004, they began to **invest** heavily in tea instead, forcing prices of this formerly unappreciated brew to ridiculous levels, until the bubble burst four years later, leaving many bankrupt.

3

Jinghong's cafés come here) along with a handful of interesting **villages and markets**. Most traffic departs from Jinghong's Banna bus station.

Damenglong

大勐龙, dàměnglóng

DAMENGLONG – also known as **Menglong** – is an unprepossessing, busy crossroads town 55km south of Jinghong, with a vigorous all-day Sunday market. The disappointingly tatty **Black Pagoda** (黑塔, hēi tǎ) is just south of the central crossroads; much more appealing is the **North Pagoda** (北塔, běi tǎ; ¥5), 2km north of town above the village of **Manfeilong** (曼飞龙, mànfēilóng). Here, a long flight of stairs climbs a hillock planted with **rubber**, where you can see how the latex sap is tapped by deeply scoring the rubber tree's bark and then collecting the ooze in a strategically placed cup. At the top, the typically Dai-style pagoda is very different from Chinese versions, more like a Tibetan stupa in shape and adorned with fragments of evil-repelling mirrors and silver paint. It's also known as the **Bamboo Shoot Pagoda** (笋塔, sǔn tǎ), after its nine-spired design, which resembles an emerging cluster of bamboo tips. An alcove at the base reveals two depressions in the rock, said to be footprints left by Sakyamuni.

Menghai

勐海, měnghǎi • The bus station is on Fushuang Lu, where it intersects with Yanhe Lu, the road in from the highway

Western Xishuangbanna's principal town, **MENGHAI** is centrally placed on the highland plains 55km from Jinghong. An orderly assemblage of back lanes off the kilometre-long high street, **Fushuang Lu**, the town is a stop on the way towards outlying Dai and Hani settlements, and you might have to change buses here. Menghai was once a **Hani** (Aini) settlement until, as elsewhere, they were defeated in battle by the Dai and withdrew into the surrounding hills. The Hani remain there today as Xishuangbanna's second-largest ethnic group and long-time cultivators of **pu'er tea**; you can buy it in the town market, or from the factory display room out on the highway.

To Mengzhe

The road to Mengzhe town runs west from Menghai, covered by local minibuses. About 20km along, the bizarre **Jingzhen Octagonal Pavilion** (景真八角亭, jǐngzhēn bājiǎo tíng; ¥20) was built in the eighteenth century to quell an angry horde of wasps; as is often the case in Xishuangbanna, the building has been poorly rendered with concrete and then painted muted red, green and yellow. It's a further 10km to **MENGZHE** (勐遮, měngzhē), where the **Manlei Temple** (曼磊佛寺, mànlěi fósì; ¥20) is another underwhelming structure, but houses an important collection of Buddhist manuscripts written on fan-palm fibre.

Xiding
西定, xīdìng

Mengzhe is really just a stepping stone to the Hani village of **XIDING**, 15km southwest, whose busy **Thursday market** is one of the best in the region. You'll need to get here on Wednesday, as the market kicks off at dawn, and sleep over in one of Xiding's rudimentary **guesthouses**. Xiding sits at the edge of Xishuangbanna's least-developed corners, just 15km from the (closed) Burmese border: there's plenty of rainforest and villages nearby – **Manlai**, with its Akha population, or the Bulang village of **Zhanglang**, for example.

Menghun
勐混, měnghún

There are more ethnic minorities 25km southwest of Menghai at **MENGHUN**, whose excellent Sunday market starts at daybreak and continues until noon. **Akha** women arrive under their silver-beaded headdresses, **Bulang** wear heavy earrings and oversized black turbans and remote hill-dwellers come in plain dress, carrying ancient rifles. Most common of all are the Dai, who buy rolls of home-made paper and sarongs. Take a look around Menghun itself, too, as there's a dilapidated nineteenth-century monastery with a pavilion built in the style of Jingzhen's octagonal effort, and a pagoda hidden in the bamboo groves on the hills behind town.

As at Xiding, it's a good idea to get here the night before market day, to ensure you'll have caught the best of the action before tour buses from Jinghong descend around 9am.

Daluo and the Burmese border

At the end of the road 50km west of Menghun, **DALUO** (打落镇, dǎluò zhèn) is set just in from the Burmese border. Here there's a multi-trunked giant **fig tree** whose descending mass of aerial roots form a "forest", and a daily **border trade market**, timed for the arrival of Chinese package tours between 11am and 1pm. Foreigners can't cross, but Chinese nationals can also get a two-hour visa for Burma, ostensibly to shop for jade; in fact, many are really going over to catch **transvestite stage shows** held for their benefit.

GETTING AROUND   WESTERN XISHUANGBANNA

Most traffic departs from Jinghong's Banna bus station, with the **exception of buses to Damenglong**, which leave from the South bus station. **Menghai** is the transport hub for most of the region; aside from Jinghong and Menghun traffic, on-demand minibuses run out to villages all over western Xishuangbanna from here.

Destinations from Menghai Daluo (5 daily; 1hr 30min; ¥20); Jinghong (frequent; 1hr; ¥15); Menghun (frequent; 30min; ¥10); Mengzhe (frequent; 30min; ¥10).

ACCOMMODATION

In addition to the following, there's the usual collection of down-to-earth **accommodation** in all the local villages.

Dai Hotel 傣家宾馆, dǎijiā bīnguǎn. Signed in English near the post office, Menghun ☎069 1551 1209. The best of Menghun's rudimentary places to stay, and easily found. ¥50

Jintai 金泰宾馆, jīntài bīnguǎn. Damenglong ☎069 1274 0334. Look for a bright, eggshell-blue building down a backstreet towards the market. A great bargain, simple and spotless. ¥50

Guizhou

LONG-HORNED MIAO WOMEN DRESSING HAIR

Guizhou

According to a harsh Chinese saying, there's nothing to Guizhou (贵州, guizhōu) but rain, mountains and poverty. And to some extent it's true: this is China's wettest province, almost entirely covered by rough, thin-soiled limestone hills which limit agriculture and have blocked communications and trade. Still scarred by the aftermath of devastating nineteenth-century rebellions, Guizhou's towns are also visibly poor, often little more than shabby, shambolic shells, blighted by fallout from the province's two major industries, limestone quarrying and coal mining. At the same time, romantic landscapes and ethnic identity are marketable commodities in modern China, and Guizhou has these in abundance.

There are spectacular cave systems at Longgong and Zhijin in the province's west and impressive waterfalls at westerly Huangguoshu and at Chishui, right up on the Sichuanese border. For **wildlife**, head northwest to the Yunnan border at Cao Hai, a shallow lake where rare cranes flock every winter; or make the tough ascent of northeasterly Fanjing Shan, with its humid cloud forest and endangered golden monkeys.

But Guizhou's real draw are its **ethnic groups**, the province's isolation having helped them maintain their traditions; local festivals, featuring days of music, dancing, fireworks and alcohol, remain enthusiastically authentic affairs, worth whatever it takes you to reach them. The highest-profile group are the **Miao**, concentrated in villages surrounding Kaili, and also scattered through the hills above the unlovable industrial centres of Liuzhi and Liupanshui in western Guizhou. The rugged borders with Guangxi are the **Dong** heartlands (see p.293); **Bouyei** territory surrounds the provincial capital, **Guiyang**; while the **Anshun** area is home to descendants of Ming-dynasty Chinese migrants, who have clung to antique forms of dress and opera long after these have been forgotten by the rest of the country.

Guizhou's **weather** isn't as bad as its reputation suggests, though come prepared for sweltering, wet summers and winter snow. Rail lines run through the province into Chongqing, Hunan and Yunnan; there are also a surprising number of highways, and even minor sights are fairly accessible. The one major headache can be finding **accommodation** (especially at the budget end of things), as outside Guiyang relatively few hotels seem to have police permission to take foreigners. The situation is worst in western Guizhou, and is probably an attempt to shield Westerners from seeing the poorer side of Chinese life.

Brief history
Not much is known about Guizhou's earliest history except the names of some of the tribes that inhabited it, but by the Tang dynasty the region was known as **Qian** (still a

MIAO IN THE FESTIVAL SPIRIT, TAIJIANG

Highlights

❶ **Zunyi** Modern China was born in this town: visit the place where guerilla leader Mao Zedong took up the reins of power in 1935 during the Communists' incredible Long March. **p.279**

❷ **Sisters' Meal Festival** Join locals for three days of drinking, dancing, buffalo fights and general mayhem, as Miao women from the villages of Taijiang and Shidong choose husbands. **p.291**

❸ **Zhaoxing** Dong minority village with a gorgeous mix of vivid-green rice fields and creaky wooden buildings – including elaborately shaped drum towers and bridges. **p.297**

❹ **Zhenyuan** Old riverside garrison town away on the northeastern border, with intriguing stone temples and remains of China's mysterious "Southern Great Wall". **p.299**

❺ **Zhijin Caves** Guizhou is all limestone caverns and oddly shaped hills, but this massive cave system is the best of them all, with bizarre formations, bright lights and ceilings that stretch up to 60m. **p.308**

❻ **Cao Hai** This shallow lake forms an unexpected haven for wildfowl up on Guizhou's dry, remote western plateau – catch rare black-necked cranes here in winter. **p.310**

HIGHLIGHTS ARE MARKED ON THE MAP ON P.272–273

GUIZHOU

N

HIGHLIGHTS
1. Zunyi
2. Sisters' Meal Festival
3. Zhaoxing
4. Zhenyuan
5. Zhijin Caves
6. Cao Hai

Chongqing

Yangzi

Luzhou

Chisui

Sidonggou

S I C H U A N

Maotai

Zhaotong

Bijie

Cao Hai Weining
6

Nankai

Zhijin
5 ♨ **Zhijin
Caves**

Guiy

Liupanshui

Yachi River

Tianlong

Qing

Suoga

Liuzhi

Anshun

Zhenning

under construction

Guanling ♨ **Longgong
Caves**

**Huangguoshu
Falls**

Y U N N A N

Panxian

Beipan River

Qujing

Kunming

Anlong

Xingyi ♦ **Maling
Canyon**

Nanpan River

**Dashiwei
Tiankeng**

Baise & Nanning

0 ————— 50
kilometres

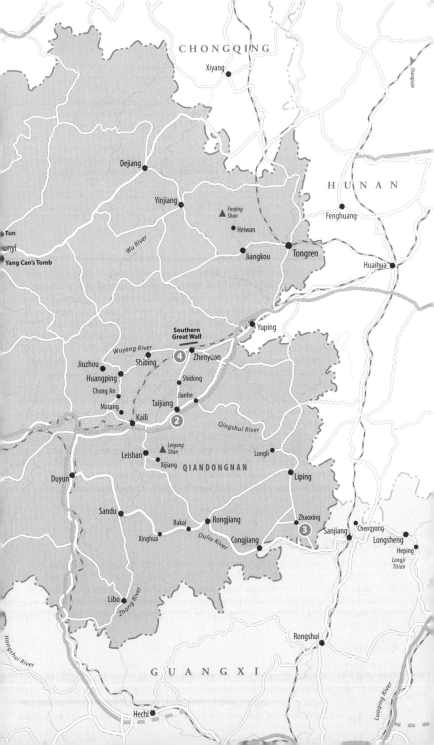

FOOD IN GUIZHOU

Guizhou doesn't really have its own **cuisine**, but it does have a typical taste: hot and sour, with plentiful chillies and pickles. In areas with large Han populations, you get generic Chinese food skewed to local palates, with occasional Muslim dishes like roast duck imported from neighbouring Yunnan. One fun Guizhou dish are the self-wrap **pancakes** known as "silk dolls" (丝娃娃, sī wáwa); you get a dozen little bowls of shredded pickles, cucumber, glass noodles, carrot, celery and bean sprouts along with a plate of small, elastic pancakes; wrap one in the other, dip in the spicy sauce, and eat.

In the countryside – especially the Miao and Dong areas – sour **hotpots** with either chicken or fish dominate, along with bowls of broad, flat rice noodles (河粉, hé fěn) in various soups. Villages also produce quite a bit of **sticky rice wine** (糯米酒, nuòmǐ jiǔ), consumed freely during festivals.

The other big culinary thing in Guizhou is **dog meat**, surreptitiously consumed all over China, but here served openly everywhere from rural street stalls to specialist restaurants. If you're worried about being served some by accident, say wǒ bù chī gǒuròu (我不吃狗肉) – "I don't eat dog".

colloquial name for the province). The Ming era saw some cautious probing by the Chinese – and the construction of **fortified garrison towns** to guard post roads and deal with the hostile local response – but it was a population explosion and land shortage in eastern China during the early Qing which caused the first major Han migrations into Guizhou, cementing the presence of trade, taxes and troops. There's no doubt local tribes felt imposed on: widespread anti-government rebellions smouldered from the 1720s onwards, culminating in the devastating **Miao Uprising** of 1854–73 (see p.288). Travelling through the province shortly afterwards, the British adventurer William Mesny described ruined towns, Miao hiding up in the hills, and a new wave of Chinese immigrants flooding into Guizhou's recently depopulated lowlands.

The situation stayed much the same into the 1930s, when Guizhou was awash with **opium-growing** Nationalist warlords – though there was a brief sign of things to come when **Mao Zedong** and his fellow Long Marchers spun through the northern town of **Zunyi** (see p.279). Left in limbo for decades afterwards, things began to improve only after the future Chinese leader **Hu Jintao** was posted here during the 1990s and experienced Guizhou's chronic underdevelopment first-hand. Since then, industry and infrastructure have been expanded considerably, though modernization seems paper-thin at times and the province still clearly lags far behind much of China's southwest.

Guiyang and around

Located pretty much in the centre of the province, Guizhou's capital, **Guiyang**, is something of a necessary pit stop, though it's also a friendly place, whose museum, few antique buildings and surprisingly wild **Qianling Shan Park** provide a bit of character. With a day to fill, consider a side-trip to the historic garrison town of **Qingyan** – one of many such towns in Guizhou, but also one of the best – easily reached by local buses.

Guiyang

贵阳, guìyáng

GUIYANG fills a valley basin along the **Nanming River**, hemmed in on all sides by constricting hills. Founded in the thirteenth century and provincial capital since the Ming dynasty, modern Guiyang is a patchwork of elderly concrete apartment blocks alongside glossy new offices and department stores, all intercut by a web of wide roads

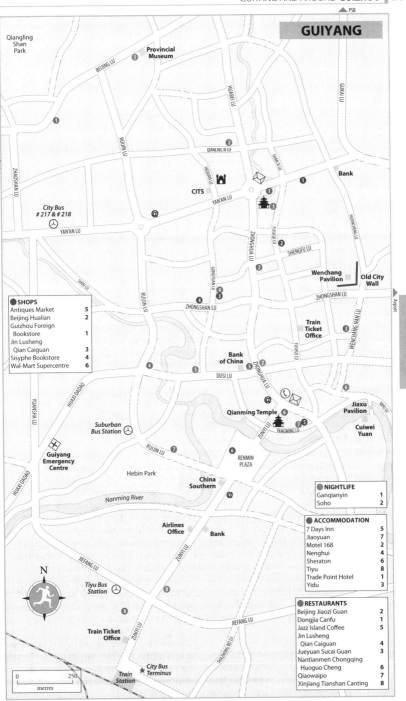

GUIYANG

Qiangling Shan Park

Provincial Museum

BEIJING LU

HUAIEI LU

GUKAI LU

QIANLING XI LU

ZHAOSHAN LU

RUIJIN LU

HEGUAN LU

SHAN XI LU

Bank

CITS

YAN'AN LU

ZHONGHUA LU

FUSHUI LU

HUICHENG LU

City Bus # 217 & # 218

YAN'AN LU

SHIU LU

SHENGFU LU

GONGYUAN LU

ZHONGSHAN LU

Wenchang Pavilion

Old City Wall

ZHONGSHAN LU

WENCHANG NAN LU

Train Ticket Office

RUIJIN LU

Bank of China

FUSHUI LU

ZHONGHUA LU

DUSI LU

Jiaxu Pavilion

SHIU LU

YUANSHA LU

HUAXI DADAO

HUAN DADAO

Qianming Temple

ZUNYI LU

YANGMING LU

Cuiwei Yuan

Suburban Bus Station

RUIJIN LU

RENMIN PLAZA

Guiyang Emergency Centre

HUAXI DADAO

Hebin Park

China Southern

NIGHTLIFE
Ganqianyin   1
Soho   2

Nanming River

JIEFANG LU

Airlines Office

Bank

ZUNYI LU

N

Tiyu Bus Station

JIEFANG LU

BI LU BINGUANG

Train Ticket Office

City Bus Terminus

Train Station

0 ——— 250
metres

PSB

Airport

4

SHOPS	
Antiques Market	5
Beijing Hualian	2
Guizhou Foreign	
Bookstore	1
Jin Lusheng	
Qian Caiguan	3
Sisyphe Bookstore	4
Wal-Mart Supercentre	6

ACCOMMODATION	
7 Days Inn	5
Jiaoyuan	7
Motel 168	2
Nenghui	4
Sheraton	6
Tiyu	8
Trade Point Hotel	1
Yidu	3

RESTAURANTS	
Beijing Jiaozi Guan	2
Dongjia Canfu	1
Jazz Island Coffee	5
Jin Lusheng	
Qian Caiguan	4
Jueyuan Sucai Guan	3
Nantianmen Chongqing	
Huoguo Cheng	6
Qiaowaipo	7
Xinjiang Tianshan Canting	8

and flyovers that seem to have been squeezed in wherever there was room. The central focus is paved **Renmin Plaza** (人民广场, rénmín guǎngchǎng), filled by early-morning crowds indulging in the local craze of spinning wooden tops, overlooked to the east by a large but inconspicuous statue of Chairman Mao. Just north over the bridge, recently renovated **Qianming Temple** (黔明寺, qiánmíng sì) is full of golden statues, surrounded by high-rises and a small park full of amateur folk musicians.

From here, a paved riverside promenade leads east to an arched stone bridge crossing to the mid-river **Jiaxiu Pavilion** (甲秀楼, jiǎxiù lóu; ¥10), a 29m-high, three-storey tower dating back to 1598. Built to inspire students taking imperial examinations, it now contains a teahouse and old photos. Continue on across the bridge to the far bank, and you're outside **Cuiwei Yuan** (梓惟园, cuìwéi yuán; ¥2), a Qing-dynasty ornamental garden whose buildings house more tearooms and souvenir shops.

Dashizi and Wenchang Pavilion

The bulk of Guiyang's department stores, businesses and services sit north of the river around the Zhongshan Lu–Zhonghua Lu intersection, known locally as **Dashizi** (大十字, dà shízi). East of here is a restored corner of Guiyang's **old city wall**, the 7m-high battlements capped by **Wenchang Pavilion** (文昌阁, wénchāng gé), a gate tower with flared eaves and wooden halls, built in 1596 and now yet another breezy teahouse.

The Provincial Museum

贵州省博物馆, guìzhōushěng bówùguǎn • 168 Beijing Lu, entrance on the left side of the main building • Tues–Sun 9am–5pm • Free • Buses #1 and #2 stop outside

This nicely presented collection covers most of Guizhou's history and culture without telling you too much about it. An elegant **bronze horse and carriage** with outsized wheels proves that Chinese metalworking skills and designs had trickled down to Guizhou as early as the Han dynasty, while space given over to the province's **ethnic groups** will whet your appetite for crashing a Miao festival: cases of colourful costumes, 4m-long lusheng gourd pipes, exquisite silver assemblages and a diorama of a dragonboat prow hung with geese. There's also a display of slightly nightmarish **ground opera masks** (see p.307), shamanistic accessories from around Anshun. The adjacent *Ganqianyin* teahouse hosts nightly folk music shows (see p.278).

Qianling Shan Park and Hongfu Temple

¥4 • Buses #1 & #2 stop close to the entrance on Beijing Lu

About 1km west of the Provincial Museum, **Qianling Shan Park** (黔灵山公园, qiánlíng shān gōngyuán) is a steep, jagged ridge right on the edge of town, thickly forested enough to harbour noisy groups of monkeys. Up on the ridge, **Hongfu Temple** (弘福寺, hóngfú sì) is an important Buddhist monastery housing a 32-armed Guanyin statue, each palm displaying an eye – follow steps uphill from the gates for thirty minutes. You exit the woods into a courtyard containing the ornamental, 4m-high **Fahua Pagoda** and a screen showing Buddha being washed at birth by nine dragons. On the right is a **bell tower** with a five-hundred-year-old bell, while bearing left brings you to a **luohan hall** inhabited by 500 glossy, chunky statues of Buddhist saints (see p.78).

ARRIVAL AND DEPARTURE
GUIYANG

Guiyang is a hub for transport through the province. **Buses** and **trains** run through the day to Zunyi, Kaili, Anshun and beyond, while Guiyang's **airport** connects with other Southwest China capitals, and cities nationwide.

BY PLANE

Longdongbao Airport (龙洞堡国际机场, lóngdòngbǎo guójìjīchǎng) is 11km southeast of Guiyang. An airport bus (daily every 30min 8.30am–10pm; 35min; ¥10) runs via the airline offices to the train station.

Buy plane tickets at China Southern (⊕ csair.com) or China Airways (☎ 0851 597 7777), both on Zunyi Lu. There's a tourist information booth just before the airport exit – the staff speak a little English and can advise about transport and accommodation.

Destinations Beijing (8 daily; 3hr); Chengdu (5 daily; 1hr); Chongqing (2 daily; 50min); Guangzhou (6 daily; 2hr); Guilin (1 daily; 45min); Kunming (6 daily; 1hr 5min); Nanning (3 daily; 55min); Shanghai (4 daily; 2hr 15min); Shenzhen (5 daily; 1hr 30min).

BY BUS

Jinyang bus station (金阳客车站, jīnyáng kèchēzhàn) is Guiyang's colossal main bus depot, 15km west of the centre, handling traffic to almost everywhere in Guizhou. But don't slog all the way out here without considering services from central Tiyu bus station first – or even a train for more distant destinations. If you wind up at Jinyang, catch bus #219 to the train station or #217 or #218 to Yan'an Lu (30min; ¥2).

Tiyu bus station (体育馆长途客运站, tǐyùguǎn chángtú kèyùnzhàn), about 250m from the train station, next to the gymnasium on Jiefang Lu.

Destinations Anshun (1hr 30min; ¥35); Congjiang (2 daily; 9hr; ¥110); Duyun (3hr; ¥50); Kaili (3hr; ¥55); Leishan (3 daily; 4hr 30min; ¥65); Liping (3 daily; 12hr; ¥148); Rongjiang (2 daily; 11hr; ¥135); Sandu (3 daily; 5hr; ¥68); Zhenyuan (1 daily; 6hr; ¥75); Zunyi (2hr 30min; ¥59).

BY MINIBUS

Freelance minibuses offering day-trips to Huangguoshu waterfall and Longgong caves congregate outside the gymnasium on Zunyi Lu; negotiate price and departure times but expect ¥350 for the vehicle for the day.

BY TRAIN

Tickets are available at the station itself, or at the advance purchase office 100m north of the station up Zunyi Lu. Buses #1 and #2 (see below) head into the centre from here.

Destinations Anshun (23 daily; 1hr 20min); Beijing (4 daily; 30–40hr); Chengdu (7 daily; 12–23hr); Chongqing (10 daily; 8–12hr); Dushan (8 daily; 2–4hr); Guangzhou (5 daily; 22hr); Huaihua (for Fenghuang; 23 daily; 7hr 30min); Kaili (24 daily; 2hr 45min); Kunming (12 daily; 10–13hr); Liupanshui (23 daily; 4–5hr); Liuzhi (21 daily; 2–3hr); Nanning (1 daily; 12hr 20min); Shanghai (5 daily; 30hr); Yuping (for Fanjing Shan; 20 daily; 5–6hr); Zhangjiajie (3 daily; 10–12hr); Zhenyuan (16 daily; 4hr 30min); Zunyi (16 daily; 2hr 30min–5hr).

GETTING AROUND

4

By bus Many city buses (¥1–2) terminate outside the train station. Two of the most useful are #1, which circuits Guiyang via Zunyi Lu, Zhonghua Lu, Beijing Lu and Ruijin Lu, passing through the city centre, the museum and Qianling Shan Park; and #2, which does the same route in reverse.

By taxi Surprisingly expensive at ¥10 to hire, though it shouldn't cost much more than this to reach anywhere central from the train station.

INFORMATION

Tourist information CITS (中国国际旅行社, zhōngguó guójì lǚxíngshè), Floor 7, Longquan Dasha, 1 Hequan Lu, near the corner with Yan'an Lu ☎0851 690 1575. Look for the tall yellow building, take the lane off Hequan Lu around to the police compound at the back, and head for the tiny lift lobby. Once there, the helpful staff are a mine of useful information about Guizhou and speak English, German and French – ask for Jessica Xiao or Arnaud Xie.

ACCOMMODATION

Guiyang's **accommodation** is mostly mid-range – the *Tiyu* is the only foreign-friendly cheapie, though you might be able to bargain the *Jiaoyuan* down a little.

7 Days Inn 7天连锁酒店, qītiān liánsuǒ jiǔdiàn. 149 Zhonghua Lu ☎0851 861 0088, ☎7daysinn.cn. Good central location at this budget hotel chain, though a bit noisy if you get a room overlooking the road. Rates rise slightly at weekends. **¥178**

Jiaoyuan 教苑宾馆, jiàoyuàn bīnguǎn. 130 Ruijin Nan Lu ☎0851 812 9519. Bright, ordinary budget hotel with slightly overpriced doubles, but it's convenient and friendly. More amenable to bargaining than *Motel 168* or *7 Days Inn*. **¥168**

Motel 168 莫泰连锁旅店, mòtài liánsuǒ lǚdiàn. 2 Shengfu Lu ☎0851 821 7692, ☎motel168.com. Not quite up to the usual budget-hotel standard – it looks like it was built in a rush – but still reasonable value if you avoid the cheapest, windowless rooms. Better rooms **¥198**

Nenghui 能辉酒店, nénghuī jiǔdiàn. 38 Ruijin Nan Lu ☎0851 589 8888. Four-star venture where all customers get free use of the gym, and executive suites garner many other discounts. **¥696**

Sheraton 喜来登贵航酒店, xǐláidēng guìháng jiǔdiàn. 49 Zhonghua Nan Lu ☎0851 588 8280, ☎sheraton.com/guiyang. Marble construction full of restaurants, where rooms are priced according to square metreage. You get use of the spa too. **¥970**

Tiyu 体育宾馆, tǐyù bīnguǎn. Behind the Tiyu bus station ☎0851 827 7808. Attached to the local gymnasium, this is one of the cheapest deals in town likely to accept foreigners, with blandly functional rooms. **¥100**

★ **Trade Point Hotel** 柏顿宾馆, bódùn bīnguǎn. Yan'an Dong Lu ☎ 0851 582 7888, ☮ trade-pointhotel .com. Sharp four-star option with local and Cantonese restaurants and all executive trimmings. They serve a great all-you-can-eat Western buffet breakfast at ¥81/person. **¥950**

Yidu 逸都酒店, yìdū jiǔdiàn. 63 Wenchang Nan Lu; reception is around the side ☎ 0851 864 9777. Tired mid-range hotel which allows single travellers to pay by the bed, rather than for a whole room. Beds **¥65**, doubles **¥138**

EATING

The best places for **snacks and street food** are the kebab and noodle canteens outisde the mosque on Hequan Lu, diagonally opposite the CITS, and the fried duck stalls on Fushui Lu, north of Zhongshan Lu.

Beijing Jiaozi Guan 北京饺子馆, běijīng jiǎozi guǎn. Qianling Xi Lu. Busy restaurant serving Beijing-style dumplings with a wide range of fillings, along with dry-fried spareribs, garlic cucumber and other northern favourites. ¥20/head with beer.

Dongjia Canfu 侗家餐府, dòngjiā cānfǔ. 242 Beijing Lu ☎ 0851 650 7186. Supposedly Dong-style food, though more a tourist vision of rural cooking than the real deal: bee larvae, grilled locusts, donkey kebabs and half buffalo heads. Softies can opt for stir-fries, veggies and Cantonese dishes. Expect ¥45/person in a group.

Jazz Island Coffee 爵士岛咖啡, juéshì dǎo kāfēi. Gongyuan Lu, cnr with Dusi Lu. Typical of the many Western-style cafés in town, serving drinks, snacks and light single-dish meals for around ¥35.

Jin Lusheng Qian Caiguan 金芦笙黔菜馆, jīn lúshēng qián càiguǎn. 18 Gongyuan Lu ☎ 0851 582 1388. Ethnic theme restaurant with a downstairs canteen serving Guizhou dumplings, jelly noodles, buns, sour hotpots, ice cream and fruit juices; upstairs is a smarter restaurant with staff dressed in colourful garb. Mains around ¥40.

★ **Jueyuan Sucai Guan** 觉园素菜馆, juéyuán sùcàiguǎn. 51 Fushui Bei Lu. Temple with a vegetarian restaurant at the front; peas with "sausage", eight treasures "chicken" with sticky rice (steamed in a lotus leaf) and "prawn" spring rolls are all made from vegetable substitutes. Portions are large and there's a photo-menu. Mains around ¥20.

Nantianmen Chongqing Huoguo Cheng 南天门重庆火锅城, nántiānmén chóngqìng huǒguó chéng. Wenchang Nan Lu ☎ 0851 587 7775. Bustling, cavernous Chongqing-style hotpot restaurant; you had better enjoy your chillies to eat here. ¥38/head.

★ **Qiaowaipo** 桥外婆, qiáo wàipó. 6 Yangming Lu ☎ 0851 586 0288. Smart setting and nicely presented Guizhou-style country dishes: crisp duck-skin slices, spicy jelly noodles, mushroom salads, squash with fried duck yolk and *baota rou*, a tower of stewed fatty pork belly. Stay off the pricey seafood and you'd expect to pay ¥35/main.

Xinjiang Tianshan Canting 新疆天山餐厅, xīnjiāng tiānshān cāntīng. Zunyi Lu. Uighur restaurant featuring grills, stews, noodle dishes and freshly made bread from China's Muslim northwest. Lots of meat, chillies, cumin and starch. ¥20–40/head.

DRINKING AND NIGHTLIFE

Ganqianyin 赶黔音, gǎnqiányīn. Guiyang Museum, 168 Beijing Lu; nightly 8–9.30pm; ¥180. Miao, Dong and Tujia folk music shows in an attractive "antique-teahouse" setting; performers are overloaded with silver and embroideries and the less choreographed pieces feel pretty authentic.

Soho 苏荷酒吧, sūhé jiǔbā. Kexue Lu, back from the Dusi Lu-Zhonghua Lu corner. Red brick fronts the exterior for this representative of a countrywide nightclub-bar chain. DJ and live-band venue packed nightly with a young crowd moving to dance music and rock in a mock-industrial setting; plenty of whisky at the bar. There's a knot of clones – *Brilliant, Pink, Mini* and *Band-On* – a short wobble away up Kexue Lu.

SHOPPING

Antiques There's a moribund indoor antique market near the *Qiaowaipo* restaurant, full of dusty piles of furniture, porcelain, paintings, books and junk.

Books Sisyphe Bookstore (西西弗文化, xīxīfú wénhuà) 38 Zhongshan Xi Lu, is by far the best in town, though fairly academic. The Guizhou Foreign Languages Bookstore on Yan'an Lu is of most use for maps.

Department stores Stores lie all along Zhonghua Lu between the river and Yan'an Lu.

Mobile phones There's a big emporium under the Dusi Lu–Zhonghua Lu intersection.

Souvenirs Anshun batiks, Miao-style silver and folk crafts, including clay zodiac figures from Huangping, are sold on the ground floor of the museum, and in the gift shop attached to the *Jin Lusheng* restaurant.

Supermarkets These include Beijing Hualian, up near the *Jueyuan* restaurant on Fushui Lu, and the crowded Wal-Mart Supercentre, beneath the glass pyramid in Renmin Plaza.

DIRECTORY

Banks The main Bank of China (Mon–Fri 9–11.30am & 1.30–5pm) with an ATM is just west off Zhonghua Lu on Dusi Lu. There are other branches with ATMs at the eastern end of Yan'an Lu, and opposite the airline offices on Zunyi Lu.
Internet Two convenient places charging ¥2/hr are on Yan'an Lu just east of Ruijin Lu, and opposite China

Southern on Zunyi Lu.
Post Office Cnr Huabei Lu and Yan'an Lu, daily 9am–6pm.
PSB The visa department (Mon–Fri 9am–noon and 1.30–5pm, ☎0851 679 7907) is northeast of the centre off Baoshan Bei Lu at 5 Da Ying Lu. Catch bus #20 heading north up Ruijin Lu.

Qingyan

青岩, qīngyán • Free entry, ¥2–5 to enter buildings

Some 30km south of Guiyang, **QINGYAN** was founded in 1373 as a walled military outpost to defend embryonic Ming-dynasty trade routes. Don't despair at the shabby main-road junction where the bus pulls up, but head west through the market into the kilometre-long **old town** (古镇, gǔzhèn), an oval maze of narrow lanes and stone walls, its flagstoned streets lined with low wooden shops, various small temples and pavilions and two **churches** – pioneering French missionaries introduced Catholicism in 1851.

The best area surrounds the **Baisui memorial arch** (百岁坊, bǎisuì fāng) at the southern end of town, decorated with crouching lions; past here the path leads through the town wall into the fields via the solid stone **south gate** (南城门, nánchéng mén). The Wanshou Palace (万寿宫, wànshòu gōng), an ornate nineteenth-century merchants' **guildhall** painted flamboyant yellow, is also worth seeking out, just west of the central crossroads. There are plenty of places to buy locally made silver jewellery and snack as you wander – deep-fried tofu balls are a speciality.

ARRIVAL AND DEPARTURE   QINGYAN

By bus From Guiyang's suburban bus station (郊区汽车站, jiāoqū qìchēzhàn) on Ruijin Lu, just west of the centre head to Huaxi (花溪, huāxī; 40min; ¥3), then cross

the road and pick up a minibus to Qingyan (20min; ¥4). Transport connections back run until late afternoon.

ACCOMMODATION

Guzhen Kezhan 古镇客栈, gǔzhèn kèzhàn ☎0851 320 0031. Simple en-suite rooms in an atmospheric

stone-and-wood courtyard building – once the Hunan merchants' guildhall – next to the market. **¥128**

Northern Guizhou

The main routes through northern Guizhou head up towards neighbouring Chongqing via Guizhou's heavily industrialized second city, **Zunyi**. Set near a strategic bottleneck 150km north of Guiyang, Zunyi has been fought over many times, most famously when the Red Army captured it in 1935 during the **Long March** (see box, p.280). The ensuing **Zunyi Conference** saw Mao elected as leader of the Communist Party, setting in motion their conquest of all China fifteen years later. The city's revolutionary monuments can be seen in half a day, though spending the night here will give you time to visit some older, quirkier **historical relics** outside of town.

The rail line and expressway run north of Zunyi to Chongqing, but there's also a 350km-long **road** northwest to the Sichuan border at **Chishui**, where you'll find red waterfalls and wild bamboo forests. You'll need a couple of days for this route, with onwards travel from Chishui towards Yibin and Zigong in Sichuan (see p.283).

Zunyi

遵义, zūnyì • Historic sites daily 8.30am–5.30pm

ZUNYI's crowded, messy city centre is awkwardly laid out around the triangular base of **Fenghuang Hill** (凤凰山, fènghuáng shān), with arrival points and all accommodation to

THE LONG MARCH

In 1927, Chiang Kaishek's Nationalist government ended a **general strike** in Shanghai by slaughtering the Chinese Communist Party leaders that had called it. The survivors fled to remote rural bases across China and fought back, using guerilla tactics championed by **Mao Zedong**. But, encouraged by their Russian advisers, they were drawn into several disastrous pitched battles, which saw them eventually blockaded into their main base in Jiangxi province. Facing defeat if they stayed, in October 1934 some eighty thousand Red soldiers retreated west to team up with sympathetic forces in Hunan – the beginning of the **Long March**.

But it soon became clear that the Long Marchers would never make it through to Hunan, which was thick with hostile warlords. Diverted into **Guizhou**, the Communists took Zunyi in January 1935 and convened the **Zunyi Conference**: the discredited Russian advisers were ousted and Mao, the seasoned guerilla fighter, elected as Communist Party head. Rejecting the Soviet model of an urban socialist uprising, Mao wanted to carry the revolution to the countryside – where most Chinese people actually lived – and decided that to achieve this they should base themselves at **Yan'an**, an isolated Red stronghold in northerly Shaanxi province.

Leaving Zunyi, the Long Marchers dodged into Yunnan, then suddenly cut up through western Sichuan and over the Yangzi via the **Luding Bridge** (see p.127), before tackling the snowbound mountains beyond. On the far side at Ma'erkang they found another branch of the Red Army under Zhang Guotao, who wanted to establish a Communist state at Ganzi in western Sichuan. Unable to convince Zhang otherwise, Mao and his followers battled north across the **Aba Grasslands**, where they somehow survived swamps, hostile nomads and starvation to reach Yan'an in October 1935. Only a few thousand of those who started from Jiangxi completed the 9500km journey.

Although romanticized by many historians, the Long March certainly succeeded in uniting the Communists under Mao, at the same time spreading the Red message throughout the rural areas that they tramped through. For a more critical appraisal of the story – or simply for an insightful travelogue about modern China – read *The Long March* by Ed Jocelyn and Andrew McEwen (see p.395).

the east, and the compact **old town** (老城, lǎo chéng) 4km away below Fenghuang's southwestern slopes, on the little **Xiang River**. The old town – containing all the revolutionary sites – is a pleasant, kilometre-wide collection of 1930s grey-brick buildings. Some of the genuine sites have closed, their elderly timbers unable to cope with the volume of tourists, and their contents have been collected in a large museum.

Zunyi Conference Museum

遵义会议博物馆, zūnyì huìyì bówùguǎn • Daily 8.30am–5.30pm • Free

The cavernous **Zunyi Conference Museum**, taken very seriously by Chinese visitors, is laid with red carpet and stuffed with old photos, maps charting complex battles, a few relics (including a machine-gun emplacement) and bronze dioramas of Red Army soldiers paying for food and helping the elderly. Incidentally, the original **Zunyi Conference Hall** (遵义会议遗址, zūnyì huìyì yízhǐ), the two-storey building with arched colonnades just inside the museum's gates, is now closed to the public; the conference took place upstairs in a room barely big enough for the twenty delegates, which included Mao, Zhou Enlai, Deng Xiaoping and the Russian-trained adviser "Li De", otherwise known as Otto Braun.

Yangliu Jie

Behind the Zunyi Conference Museum, **Yangliu Jie** is dotted with more revolutionary sites, though probably only the former **Red Army General Political Department** (红军总政治部旧址, hóngjūn zǒng zhèngzhì bùjiùzhǐ) is worth a special look, occupying a **Catholic church** built in 1866 in an interesting fusion of Chinese and European architectural styles.

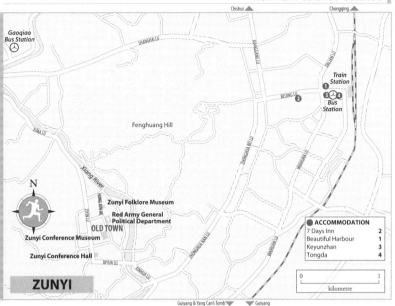

Hong Jun Jie

红军街, hóngjūn jiē

Hong Jun Jie – Red Army Street – is a cobbled, 500m-long affair running north from Yangliu Jie, with wooden shops selling snacks, crafts and alcohol to strolling tourists. Women dressed in Red Army uniforms perform patriotic dances in the street, and the **Zunyi Folklore Museum** (遵义民俗博物馆, zūnyì mínsú bówùguǎn; daily 9am–5pm; ¥20) includes a dry collection of period furniture, antique wooden printing blocks and locally unearthed archeological fragments spanning Chinese history. In all, it's a parade of everything the Communists were fighting against: veneration of the past, the idle bourgeoisie and capitalism.

ARRIVAL AND DEPARTURE   ZUNYI

Zunyi's **train** and **bus stations** are next to each other at the end of Beijing Lu, on the eastern side of the city.

By bus Anshun (10 daily; 4hr; ¥65); Chishui (5 daily; 7hr; ¥68); Chongqing (2 daily; 6hr; ¥130); Guiyang (2hr 30min; ¥59).

By train Anshun (2 daily; 5hr); Beijing (1 daily; 43hr); Chengdu (3 daily; 8–18hr); Chongqing (11 daily; 6–9hr); Guangzhou (2 daily; 25hr); Guiyang (16 daily; 2hr 30min–4hr); Kunming (2 daily; 13hr); Liupanshui (2 daily; 7hr 30min); Liuzhi (2 daily; 5hr 50min); Nanning (1 daily; 15hr 30min); Shanghai (2 daily; 30hr).

GETTING AROUND

By bus Bus #1 runs from outside the train station to the old town (20min; ¥1) – get off once you cross the river.

By taxi Taxis are ¥5 to hire; a ride across town costs ¥10.

ACCOMMODATION AND EATING

The **hotels** within 200m of the bus station on Beijing Lu are convenient, though the area is grotty. **Hostel** touts pester new arrivals, but these cheap places might not take foreigners. There's no accommodation in the nicer old town. There are plenty of **snack stalls** around; look for "Deng Xiaoping's carrypole noodles" (邓小平担担面, dèng xiǎopíng dāndān miàn), a local take on this spicy Sichuanese snack. **Restaurants** are scarce, though – try the *Beautiful Harbour* hotel for a proper meal.

7 Days Inn 7天连锁酒店, qītiān liánsuǒ jiǔdiàn. 36 Beijing Lu ☎0852 870 2888. The usual characterless, tidy rooms from this chain, a 5min walk from arrival points. ¥158

Beautiful Harbour 京腾丽湾酒店, jīngténg lìwān jiǔdiàn. Across from the bus station, cnr Dalian Lu and Beijing Lu ☎0852 864 9898. Despite the noisy, grubby location, this is a comfortable, well-run hotel with modern rooms offering a good level of service. ¥468

Keyunzhan 客运站宾馆, kèyùnzhàn bīnguǎn. At the bus station. Well-used, clean, basic rooms, fairly noisy thanks to the location on a busy road next to the bus station and the echoing, tiled halls. ¥80

Tongda 遵义通达大酒店, zūnyì tōngdá dàjiǔdiàn. Between the train and bus stations, 134 Beijing Lu ☎0852 319 1188. Tatty budget doubles with seriously soundproofed windows to help deaden all the traffic and market activity outside. Some rooms in much better condition than others. ¥108

Yang Can's tomb

杨粲墓, yáng càn mù • 10km southeast of Zunyi • Daily 9am–5pm • ¥20 • Hire a minibus (¥80 including waiting time) from Zunyi, or take city bus #5 from the train station to Zhoushui Qiao (舟水桥, zhōushuǐ qiáo), then a motorbike-taxi to the tomb (¥10)

Proving that Zunyi was an important town long before the Communists arrived, **Yang Can's tomb** dates to the last decades of the Song dynasty, built around 1252 for the military official Yang Can and his wife, whose family had ruled this area for four hundred years. The tomb was robbed in antiquity of everything but two bronze drums, but the 8m-long **burial chambers** sport elegant, accomplished relief carvings; dragon-wrapped columns, sprays of flowers and fruit, phoenixes and lions, a committee of fellow ministers and a portrait of Yang Can wearing a "winged" official's hat that must have given him trouble getting through doorways. Excavated in the 1950s, the site is isolated and sadly neglected, though there is talk of improving access.

Hailong Tun

海龙屯城堡, hǎilóng tún chéngbǎo • 30km northwest of Zunyi • Free

Hailong Tun is a stone fortress and defensive wall guarding a high mountain pass above the old Guizhou–Sichuan road. Established in the thirteenth century as the Mongols were massing to pour into southwestern China, it was later redeveloped under the Ming. Remains of the walls trail off for 10km along the ridges, with a far shorter set of paths connecting platforms, foundations, steep stone staircases and lookout posts that have survived among the encroaching vegetation. It's not easy to get here – you need at least a full half day for the return trip, plus a couple of hours on site – but the lack of crowds and, on a good day, spectacular views compensate.

ARRIVAL AND DEPARTURE   **HAILONG TUN**

Transport departs Gaoqiao bus station (高桥车站, gāoqiáo chēzhàn) on the west side of Zunyi; from the train or bus station, catch bus #1, #2, #3 or #4 (20min; ¥1) to Gaoqiao (高桥, gāoqiáo), cross the bridge and it's 100m – a cab costs ¥10. If the erratic direct bus (¥8) isn't running, either hire a minibus to Hailong Tun (1hr 30min; ¥150–200 return), or hop there in stages by local minibus for about ¥20 all up via Gaoping Zhen (高坪镇, gāopíng zhèn), Shawan Zhen (沙湾镇, shāwān zhèn) and Hunzi (混子, húnzǐ).

Chishui

赤水, chìshuǐ

CHISHUI is a kilometre-wide border town facing Sichuan across the broad **Chishui River**, 300km north of Zunyi. Geologically, the region belongs to Sichuan's red sandstone formations: *chishui* means "**red water**" and during the summer rains the river runs a vivid ochre with silt runoff from the surrounding hills. A substantial fragment of the **old city wall** still stands along Chishui's riverfront, but the town is best used as a stepping stone to nearby nature reserves – not to mention it being a little-used doorway into Sichuan itself.

THE SPIRITS OF MAOTAI

Maotai township (茅台, máotái), around 100km west of Zunyi on the Chishui road, has been nationally famous since travelling scholar Zheng Zhen declared it China's finest producer of **sorghum spirits** in 1704. There's nothing to see as such, but you'll know when you're close – roadside balustrades are shaped to resemble the Maotai brand's white porcelain bottle with its red diagonal stripe, and the air positively reeks of brewing, with scores of large ceramic wine jars outside homes and businesses, all sealed with red cloths and stamped with the character "酒" (alcohol).

Sidonggou

四洞沟, sìdònggōu • 14km south of Chishui • ¥40

The most accessible of the reserves around Chisui is **Sidonggou**, a verdant pocket of waterfalls and subtropical forest featuring bamboos, 3m-high spinulosa tree ferns, gingers, orchids and moss-covered rocks. Sidonggou's 6km of flagstoned paths follow a small, bright-red river through thick forest past three big **waterfalls** – including one 8m-high drop split neatly in two by a large boulder – to the trail's end where 30m-high **Bailong Falls** (白龙瀑布, báilóng pùbù) drops into a rough amphitheatre of shattered rocks. In addition to the lush scenery there's plenty of local life; everywhere people are harvesting **bamboo**, splitting it into lengths, weaving it into mats and digging up fresh shoots; you pass groups of farmers returning from market with pigs, their horses laden with daily necessities and jerrycans of wine. Also look for trackside stone **shrines**, eerie things carved with spirits' faces; take it easy and give yourself a good four hours for the return trip.

ARRIVAL AND DEPARTURE
CHISHUI

By bus Chishui bus station is uphill from the river on the corner of Xi Neihuan Lu and Renmin Lu. To head into Sichuan, walk across the river to tiny Jiuzhi (九支, jiǔzhī) and pick up one of the frequent minibuses to Luzhou (泸 州, lúzhōu; 3hr; ¥20), for connections to Yibin (see p.96). **Destinations** Guiyang (1 daily; 9hr; ¥98); Zunyi (5 daily; 7hr; ¥68).

GETTING AROUND

By minibus Shared minibuses from Chisui to Sidonggou (¥7/person) cruise Renmin Lu and Xi Neihuan Lu; they go when full. Transport back runs until late afternoon.

ACCOMMODATION AND EATING

The following **places to stay** are all in Chishui's small centre between the bus station and the river. Stalls and cheap diners along the old city wall are the best places to **eat**, serving "pressed bean duck" and "bamboo-fragrant chicken".

Chishui 赤水大酒店, chìshuǐ dàjiǔdiàn. Renmin Xi Lu ☎ 0852 282 1334. Aged, tiled building but decent-enough value once you argue the room rate down. **¥130**
Qianbei 黔北宾馆, qiánběi bīnguǎn. Wuxing Jie ☎ 0852 286 4508. Tidy, unassuming budget place with helpful manager. **¥110**

Zhongyue 中悦大酒店, zhōngyuè dàjiǔdiàn. 22 Nanzhen Jie ☎ 0852 282 3888. Chishui's best hotel is a well-maintained but soulless place; a bit pricey for what you get. **¥240**

Southeast Guizhou

About 170km east of Guiyang, **Kaili** is the gateway town for **Qiandongnan** (黔东南, qiándōngnán), the mountainous stronghold for the **Miao** and **Dong** peoples, which spreads southeast from here to the Guangxi border. It's somewhere to step back in time; there are hilltops covered in pine forests, buffalo ploughing the fields, wood and stone villages, lively markets and **festivals** where locals wear ornate silver jewellery and indigo-dyed jackets decorated with spectacular embroideries. With tourism increasing but yet to become mass-market, there's a feeling that you're really meeting local people on their own terms.

Transport through the southeast is on buses and minibuses; services aren't always reliable however, and – what with unexpected village activities to slow you down – you'll get the most out of the region with a flexible schedule. Note that Kaili is the only place with a **bank** capable of foreign currency dealings, though there are a few useable ATMs elsewhere in the region.

Kaili

凯里, kǎilǐ

KAILI is a small service centre with crowded, leafy streets and plenty of busy shops; Miao trade around the back lanes and there's a decent, if neglected, museum. Mostly, however, it's somewhere to seek information about forthcoming markets and festivals in outlying villages, and then plan a route through Qiandongnan – northeast towards **Zhenyuan** (see p.299), or southeast over the mountains to **Zhaoxing** (p.297) and the Dong heartlands along the Guangxi border.

The market

Kaili's main sight is its **market**, held along the cobbled eastern arm of Ximen Jie and especially busy on Sundays. There's a mix of town and country folk wandering around clutching chickens or carrying huge bags of goods on their backs, Miao women in blue jackets, their characteristically piled hair held in place by plastic combs and silver hairpins, and crowds huddled around cardsharps, tobacco sellers and folk-medicine hawkers. Each produce has its own section, though with embroideries here clearly machine-made, there's more appeal in the traditional farm gear, scythes and wooden packhorse saddles that you rarely see elsewhere nowadays.

Dage Park and the museum

Walk uphill from the market along little **Dage Xiang** – passing a rice-wine makers as you go – and it's five minutes to **Dage Park** (大阁公园, dàgé gōngyuán), a leafy hilltop with a five-storeyed stone pagoda offering views over the cobbled-together sprawl of houses,

---

THE MIAO

China's eight million **Miao** – also known as Hmong – are concentrated in Guizhou, though their population is spread through southwestern China and into Vietnam, Laos, Thailand and Burma. Tang-dynasty records suggest that Miao have occupied Guizhou for a very long time, though their history is tangled – "Miao" was previously a generic term for all the province's ethnic groups.

Miao generally live along river valleys, growing rice and corn and planting pine trees for much-needed timber. Their **wooden houses** have two or more storeys with a distinctive central balcony upstairs. Women take great pride in their skill at minutely decorating long-sleeved jackets, aprons, baby carriers and pleated skirts with embroidery and **batik**; many are machine-made nowadays, but once showcased a woman's talents at festivals and weddings. Designs and styles are specific to each village: Leishan's curly red and green designs, picked out with sequins; animals in brilliant red silk from Shidong and Taijiang; Chong An's dark, intricate geometric work; the panels of blue and white batik spirals worn by Matang's Geyi. Common motifs include plant designs, butterflies (bringers of spring and indicating hoped-for change), dragons, fish – a China-wide good luck symbol – and buffalo.

Miao **hairstyles** are equally unique – the strangest being the bulky bundles worn by western Guizhou's Changjiao Miao – as are the hairpins, combs and headwraps (often tea towels) that keep it all in place. At festivals you'll also see huge quantities of silver being worn by unmarried girls; braided necklaces, chunky bangles and multi-layered, horned tiaras covered in bells. At other times, some women wear a coin-sized stud through their ear.

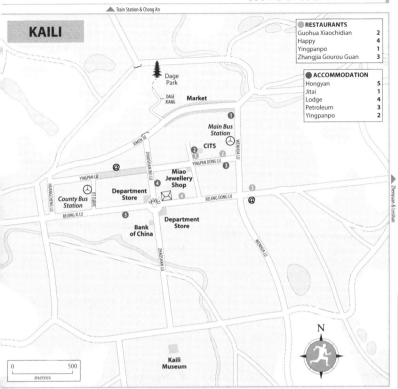

apartments and offices that fills the valley basin. There's an eerie little shrine at the gates to a red-capped god of wealth, who holds a peach and baby as he grins at you from his recess, the surrounding stonework smeared with soot, feathers and chickens' blood.

Down at the south end of town at the end of Zhongshan Lu, Kaili's **museum** (¥10) sits forlornly above a furniture emporium, though there's a thorough display over two floors of bright festival clothing and silver jewellery from local Miao groups.

ARRIVAL AND DEPARTURE   KAILI

BY BUS

Kaili's main bus station (长途汽车站, chángtú qìchēzhàn) on Wenhua Lu handles long-distance traffic plus some local destinations; it's busy but computerized and organized. Everywhere else is served by the little country bus station (老车站, lǎo chēzhàn) on Shifu Lu, which has been known to accidentally sell tickets for buses that have already left. Most services from either dry up by 5pm.

Main bus station destinations: Congjiang (6 daily, 7hr 30min; ¥90); Duyun (1hr; ¥32); Guiyang (3hr; ¥55); Huangping (4 daily; 1hr 30min; ¥24); Jianhe (1hr 15min; ¥28); Leishan (1hr 30min; ¥13.50); Liping (4 daily; 7hr; ¥88); Rongjiang (5hr; ¥65); Sandu (3hr; ¥35); Shidong (8 daily; 2hr 15min; ¥20); Taijing (1hr; ¥20); Xijiang (5 daily; 2hr; ¥40); Zhenyuan (6 daily; 3hr 30min; ¥25).

Country bus station destinations: ChongAn (1hr; ¥12); Guiyang (4hr; ¥45); Huangping (1hr 30min; ¥18); Jiuzhou (2hr 15min; ¥23); Shibing (2hr 30min; ¥28).

BY TRAIN

Kaili's train station is 3km north of town; catch buses #1 and #2 to the centre via the bus station on Wenhua Lu.

Destinations Anshun (8 daily; 4hr); Beijing (4 daily; 36hr); Chengdu (1 daily; 25hr); Chongqing (2 daily; 13hr 30min); Guangzhou (1 daily; 17hr 30min); Guiyang (24 daily; 2–3hr); Huaihua (22 daily; 4hr); Kunming (8 daily; 13–15hr); Liupanshui (9 daily; 7hr); Liuzhi (7 daily; 5hr); Shanghai (4 daily; 24hr); Yuping (for Fanjing Shan; 19 daily; 2–3hr); Zhangjiajie (3 daily; 7hr 30min–10hr); Zhenyuan (15 daily; 1hr 30min).

4

INFORMATION AND TOURS

Tourist information The CITS, in the grounds of the *Yingpanpo* hotel at 53 Yingpan Dong Lu (Mon–Fri 9am–5pm), is an invaluable source of festival, market and tour information; they speak good English too. The staff operate independently of one another; try Mr Wu Zeng Ou (☎ 0855 823 3487, ⓦ minority-tour.com), who comes from Zhaoxing and has years of experience guiding foreigners around; or the enthusiastic, if not as well-informed Billy Zhang (☎ 0855 381 8111, ⓦ toguizhou.com).

ACCOMMODATION

The concept of **hotel** maintainance seems alien to Kaili and standards tend to rapidly decline. The following were all sound at the time of writing.

Hongyan 鸿雁宾馆, hóngyàn bīnguǎn. 9 Beijing Xi Lu ☎ 0855 827 9088. Long-running hotel managed by the post office; you need to bargain hard to get a good deal for the tired but serviceable rooms. ¥138
Jitai 吉泰酒店, jítài jiǔdiàn. Wenhua Lu ☎ 0855 850 9999. New budget hotel with large, tiled en suites featuring big beds, trouble-free plumbing and computers with internet. ¥158
Lodge 百盛洛奇时尚酒店, bǎishèng luòqí shíshàng jiǔdiàn. Down a lane off Zhaoshan Bei Lu ☎ 0855 827 7000. Boutique hotel right in the town centre with spacious, bright, cute rooms, each done up in a different style. Some

seem to catch noise from the street worse than others. No restaurant but plenty of snack places nearby. ¥188
Petroleum 石油宾馆, shíyóu bīnguǎn. Yingpan Lu ☎ 0855 823 4331. It's old, basic and barely maintained – and unheated in winter – and the staff are the same. But until encroaching demolitions claim it, the *Petroleum* is the cheapest place in town. ¥80
★ **Yingpanpo** 营盘坡民族宾馆, yíngpánpō mínzú bīnguǎn. 53 Yingpan Dong Lu ☎ 0855 383 7918. This survivor has been Kaili's chief tourist hotel for decades; it's not upmarket but keeps up to scratch, with plain but tidy and comfortable en suites and helpful staff. ¥158

EATING

Kaili isn't overburdened with **restaurants**, though cheap dumpling and noodle houses fill the street between the bus station and Yingpan Lu.

Guohua Xiaochidian 国华小吃店, guóhuá xiǎochīdiàn. Opposite the Petroleum hotel on Yingpan Lu. Canteen-like affair where you get a huge plate of stir-fried rice, vegetables and meat for ¥8.
Happy Beijing Lu. Cheerful Taiwanese-style tearoom serving simple meals, including *si wawa* self-wrap pancakes (see p.274). There's wi-fi for customers.

★ **Yingpanpo** In the Yingpanpo hotel, 53 Yingpan Dong Lu. One of the best options in town; a tasty meal of white-cut chicken, dry-fried smoked beef, new bamboo shoots and a spicy mu'er salad comes to around ¥40 a head.
Zhangjia Gourou Guan (张家狗肉馆, zhāngjiā gǒuròu guǎn) Beijing Dong Lu. Kaili's main dog meat restaurant, with two adjacent branches.

WATCH THE RICE WINE: VISITING MIAO VILLAGES

You'll see most at the **Miao villages** around Kaili on market days or during one of the many festivals. **Markets** operate on a five-day cycle, with the busiest at Chong An and Shidong; **festivals** attract thousands of people for buffalo fights, dances, lusheng (a long-piped bamboo instrument) performances and horse or boat races. The biggest events of the year are the springtime Sisters' Meal (see p.291), Miao New Year around November, and the lusheng festival in October or November at Chong An, immediately followed by an even bigger affair at Gulong village near Huangping. Note that Chinese information sometimes confuses lunar and Gregorian dates – "9 February", for instance, might mean "the ninth day of the second lunar month".

Outside festival times, people are working in the fields and villages can be deserted, but you might be invited to lunch at a farmer's home (usually sour fish or chicken hotpot) and given impromptu performances by women in festival clothes – you'll have to pay, of course, but it's worth the price if you miss the real thing. Beware the hospitable Miao custom of encouraging guests to indulge in potent sticky rice wine.

All villages around Kaili are connected to the town by regular **buses**, though transport dries up by mid-afternoon, so be prepared to stay the night or hitch back if you leave things too late. There are no banks or ATMs in any of the villages.

DIRECTORY

Banks The Bank of China, just south of Kaili's central crossroads, has an ATM and is the only place in Qiandongnan that handles travellers' cheques (Mon–Fri 9am–5pm).

North of Kaili

The area north of Kaili hosts some pretty river gorges and farmland; **Chong An market** is the highlight, but you can easily make it up to the old trading town of **Jiuzhou** and back in a day. Don't bother with **Shibing** for its own sake, though it's just a short bus ride from here to the attractive, historic town of **Zhenyuan** (see p.299).

Services from Kaili's country bus station run until mid-afternoon to Huangping and Shibing. Shibing and Jiuzhou have their own proper bus stations; elsewhere, stand by the roadside and wave down passing traffic.

Matang

麻塘, mátáng

About 20km northwest of Kaili, a pink archway on the highway marks the start of a twenty-minute path across flat fields to **MATANG** (麻塘, mátáng). This wooden village is home to **Gejia**, famed for their cheerful orange embroidery and swirly **batik work**, otherwise unusual in this part of Guizhou. Though generally classified as Miao, the Gejia insist on their own identity and get pretty vocal if you bring the subject up. A steady trickle of visitors makes it here and they're familiar enough with tourists – you'll almost certainly be shown batik-making techniques, **weaving** using foot-looms, and plenty of souvenirs.

4

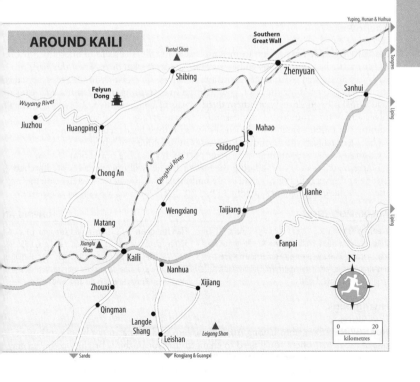

THE MIAO UPRISING

From 1855 to 1872, villages around Kaili were at the centre of the **Miao Uprising**, which rivalled the contemporary Taiping Rebellion (see p.344) in terms of chaos. New taxes and a famine inspired Miao at Taijiang to rebel, and soon the entire province was up in arms as local militia leaders – everyone from impoverished Han Chinese to Bouyei and Muslim Hui – followed their example. By the 1860s Guiyang was under attack and Kaili had been taken by rebels after a year-long **siege** in which the defenders had resorted to cannibalism to survive. It wasn't until imperial troops were freed up by the Taiping's defeat in 1868 that northern and western Guizhou were pacified, while the Miao held out in the southeast, trouncing troops sent against them at Huangping and Duyun after Chinese supply lines were cut. Finally, having recaptured Zhenyuan and Shibing, the Chinese stormed Taijiang in November 1870, slaughtering thousands; they took back Kaili the following year, and defeated the last Miao rebel leader, **Gao He**, on Leigong Shan in 1872.

Sadly, the Miao won nothing by their revolt: an estimated four million people were killed, whole towns were obliterated and a new wave of Chinese migrants later occupied their territory. Given the scale of the event, it's incredible that the uprising has been largely forgotten, though there are monuments to Miao heroes at Taijiang and Langde Shang.

Xianglu Shan

香炉山, xiānglú shān

Clearly visible 5km south of Matang, flat-topped **Xianglu Shan** is the mountain where rebel leader Zhang Xiumei met his end at the hands of imperial troops in 1872 (see above); a **hill-climbing festival** here on the nineteenth day of the sixth lunar month attracts tens of thousands of people to honour his memory.

Chong An

重安, chóng ān

A scruffy riverside town 35km from Kaili that at first doesn't seem to offer much reason to get off the bus, **CHONG AN** comes into its own on **market days**, when the place fills with sharp-elbowed Miao mothers pushing through the crowds with babies strapped to their backs; down along the river, people bring in everything from T-shirts and jeans to traditional pleated skirts to get them **dyed** in vats of boiling indigo. A few pedlars hawk silver – look for distinctive, "candle snuffer" Gejia earrings – and there are dwindling numbers of older women with blue tea towels on their heads selling home-made embroidery panels with asymmetric patterns in red, blue and white.

Chong An was once an important **river port** with a floating popuation of Han Chinese merchants, and wandering the few back lanes will uncover a restored **arched bridge** and several formerly grand stone buildings, now pretty well derelict, including the 1775 **Jiangxi merchant's guildhall** (万寿宫江西会馆, wànshòu gōng jiāngxī huìguǎn).

ACCOMMODATION · CHONG AN

Wenling Kezhan 文灵客栈, wénlíng kèzhàn. Off Nan Jie ☎ 1508 526 3831. Walk up along Nan Jie, the old Kaili road, and you'll see a wooden gate tower down a side-lane; this atmospheric, family-run courtyard building with basic facilities is just beyond. ¥80

Xiao Jiangnan 小江南宾馆, xiǎo jiāngnán bīnguǎn. 500m out of town along riverside Nan Jie ☎ 0855 235 1208. Another very simple place that has been putting up Chong An's occasional tourists for years and can advise on interesting villages to visit in the area. ¥80

Huangping

黄平, huángpíng

HUANGPING 15km from Chong An, is a modern grid of apartment blocks springing out of the fields, where you'll need to change buses for Jiuzhou. Brightly coloured **clay whistles** (黄平泥哨, huángpíng ní shào) in the shape of zodiac animals are produced here, and there's a **battlefield** (黄飘古战场遗址, huángpiāo gǔ zhànchǎng yízhǐ) 5km away in the hills where the Miao defeated Hunanese troops during their insurrection in 1869 – getting there is problematic, however.

About 12km from Huangping up the main road to Shibing, **Feiyun Dong** (飞云洞, fēiyún dòng; ¥8) is a quiet Taoist temple surrounded by trees and rocky outcrops. The moss-covered main hall houses a **museum** of Miao crafts, a dragonboat prow and a big bronze drum.

ARRIVAL AND DEPARTURE   HUANGPING

By bus Huangping sits about 500m off the Chong An–Shibing road; the bus shelter is by the town's fuel station. Services head to Chong An (30min; ¥5), Kaili (1hr 30min; ¥17) and Shibing (1hr; ¥10). Minibuses to Jiuzhou leave from the other side of the fuel station when full (40min; ¥5).

Jiuzhou

旧州, jiùzhōu

JIUZHOU stands 25km northwest of Huangping on a 10km-broad plateau. Comprising two parallel roads linked by small lanes, this was clearly once a cosmopolitan trading town, and a scattering of 300-year-old buildings survive behind its newer, nondescript facade. Several **guildhalls** – including the massive, defensively walled **Renshou Gong** (仁寿宫, rénshòu gōng) – point to a steady trickle of traders from Jiangxi and Hunan, while the remains of a **Tian Hou Temple** (天后宫, tiān hòu gōng) – built in 1901 and clearly converted to a factory at some stage – indicate the presence of southerners from Guangdong or Fujian provinces, where Tian Hou is a sea goddess. There's also a European-style **church** with Gothic windows; eighteen unassuming Qing-dynasty terrace houses separated by fire-baffle walls flanking cobbled **Xishang Jie** (西上街, xīshàng jiē); and a couple of mementoes of the **Red Army**, who passed through during the Long March. Another big **market** convenes here every four days – check dates with Kaili's CITS (see p.286).

ARRIVAL AND DEPARTURE   JIUZHOU

By bus Just off the main through road, the bus station has departures to Kaili (4 daily; 2hr 10min; ¥22), or catch a minibus to Huangping (40min; ¥5) and continue from there.

EATING

Yiguo Hong 一锅红, yīguō hóng. Opposite Renshou Gong on the rear street. Behind a mildewed 1930s facade and hardware shop, this family-run restaurant serves up hotpots and stir-fries among the remains of a once-grand courtyard house. The Long Marchers stayed here; there's a faded red star on the front of the building, and a pithy quotation from Mao above the courtyard door, comparing clearing away reactionaries to sweeping a room. Fill up on food and history for ¥20.

Shibing

施秉, shībǐng

Set in a wide, humid valley 35km from Huangping, **SHIBING** is a modern town laid out east–west along the south bank of the blue **Wuyang River** (舞阳江, wǔyáng jiāng). There's another market here, worth a look if you're passing through but fairly ordinary compared with other Miao efforts; the town's real attraction is the countryside surrounding **Yuntai Shan** (云台山, yúntái shān; ¥30), a tall, rugged peak 13km north across the river paved in walking tracks. Otherwise, you're here to catch a bus to Zhenyuan.

ARRIVAL AND DEPARTURE   SHIBING

By bus Shibing stretches east–west along the river for about a kilometre; the bus station is just off the main street at the west end of town.

Destinations Huangping (1hr; ¥10); Kaili (2hr 30min; ¥25); Yuntai Shan (infrequent, mostly weekends; 1hr; ¥15); Zhenyuan (1hr; ¥10).

ACCOMMODATION

Guangming 光明大酒店, guāngmíng dàjiǔdiàn. Yuntai Lu ☎ 0855 422 3031. Ordinary, tidy and forgettable place to crash. **¥120**

Shamu He 杉木河饭店, shāmùhé fàndiàn Shanmuhe Dadao ☎ 0855 422 2871. Another usefu friendly place, with standard comforts. **¥160**

Northeast of Kaili

Taijiang and Shidong, the main settlements northeast of Kaili, together host the springtime Miao **Sisters' Meal festival** (see opposite), the biggest event in all Guizhou. At other times, skip Taijiang in favour of **market day** at Shidong; there are direct roads from Kaili to both, and also a beautiful back road through wooded hills between Taijiang and Shidong. Extra transport is laid on throughout the region during Sisters' Meal.

Buses out this way depart from Kaili's main bus station – bear in mind too that you can continue from Shidong to Zhenyuan and onward to Fanjing Shan and Hunan province (see p.299).

Taijiang

台江, táijiāng

The famous Sisters' Meal Festival kicks off at the sports ground at **TAIJIANG**, 55km northeast of Kaili. That aside, this small collection of cheap tiled buildings, centred on a crossroads about 700m from the main road, doesn't have too much to offer; there's a mildly interesting daily market south of the crossroads and Wenchang Pavilion (文昌阁, wénchāng gé), a nineteenth-century Confucian hall at the northern end of town, though it's often locked.

The **Miao Uprising** began here, and rebels held Taijiang for fifteen years until imperial troops finally destroyed the town in 1870. Out on the highway is a rare monument to those events: a large bronze statue of **Zhang Xiumei** (or "Zangb Xongt Mil" as it's written in Hmong), who was born at the nearby village of Bading Zhai in 1823. Though his role in the uprising is murky, today he's widely believed to have been one o the ringleaders and is hailed as a hero for fighting against the Qing government.

ARRIVAL AND DEPARTURE   TAIJIANG

By bus Jianhe (30min; ¥5); Kaili (1hr; ¥20); Shidong (2 daily; 2hr; ¥18).

ACCOMMODATION

Lidu Lüguan 丽都旅馆, lìdū lǚguǎn. Near the crossroads. There's nothing much to choose between Taijiang's very basic places to stay – you'll probably only be looking for accommodation during the Sisters' Meal festival. There are simple tiled rooms here. **¥60**

Xingguang Gongguan 星光公馆, xīngguāng gōngguǎn. On the road between town and th highway ☎ 0855 532 8396. This place offers clean an basic accommodation. **¥110**

Jianhe and Fanpai

Minibuses (¥9) from Jianhe to Fanpai on demand

Around 15km up the highway from Taijiang, **JIANHE** (剑河, jiànhé) is somewhere to change buses; either for a rough, back-roads trip east **to Liping** (see p.295), or for a quicker sprint 10km uphill to **FANPAI** (方白寨, fāngbái zhài), an attractively dolled-up wooden Miao village surrounded by pine trees and terraced fields. Even Fanpai's men dress fairly traditionally in dark blue indigo jackets; the village is also known for its wooden drum dances.

Shidong

施洞, shīdòng

SHIDONG is a normally serene cluster of untidy wooden houses alongside the **Qingshui River**, 35km north of Taijiang, whose calm is shattered during Sisters' Meal and regular

THE SISTERS' MEAL FESTIVAL

The **Sisters' Meal festival**, where Miao teenagers meet to choose a partner, is held over three days from the fifteenth day of the third lunar month – confirm dates with CITS in Kaili (see p.286). Thousands of locals from surrounding villages turn up – alongside a fair few tourists – for what is the largest Miao festival of all. Everyone is dragged into the action at some point.

Taijiang hosts the first day, the town bursting with crowds jostling between lottery stalls and markets, where women peddle embroidery and silverwork. More of this is worn by teenage girls, who gamely tramp up and down the streets, sweltering under the weight of their decorated jackets and jewellery, jingling as they walk. By nine in the morning there's hardly standing room left in the sports ground, ready for the official opening; once speeches are out of the way, things kick off with two hours of energetic dancing and lusheng playing, after which the party breaks up and dancers and musicians practising for bigger things later on in the festivities.

At dusk the **dragon-lantern** dances get under way, a half-dozen teams carrying their wire-and-crepe, 20m-long hollow dragons and accompanying birds and butterflies into the main street. Candles are lit and placed inside the animals before things begin in earnest, the dragons animated into chasing swirls by the dancers, who charge up and down the street battling with each other; the mayhem is increased by drummers, whooping crowds and fireworks tossed into the throng.

Day two sees the action shifting to **Shidong**, the venue for mid-morning **buffalo fights**. These trials of strength between two bulls draw a good five thousand to see the competitors paraded up and down, decked out with plaited caps, coloured flags and pheasant tail-feathers. The fights begin with a skull-cracking charge ending in head-to-head wrestling with locked horns, bulls scrabbling for purchase; the crowds get as close as possible, scattering wildly when one bull suddenly turns tail and bolts. Back in town, the **Sisters' Meal** itself is under way, the young men handing parcels of multicoloured sticky rice to their prospective partner: a pair of chopsticks buried inside returned rice is an acceptance, a single chopstick or – even worse – a chilli, a firm refusal.

Day three is given over to **dragonboat races** on the Qingshui River. It's not long before everyone is drunk, thanks not least to the Miao habit of toasting guests with a buffalo horn of **rice wine**. The nattily dressed boat crews decorate their narrow, dragon-headed craft with dead chickens and practise for a couple of hours before the races warm up, begin and finish within a few minutes. Then dancing begins in earnest; first small groups, then livelier rings and finally everyone – absolutely everyone – joins in, until the crowds thin once again and couples drift off into the dark.

4

markets (check dates with Kaili's CITS). It's not a big place, just a short road with a post office at its southern end, and the bulk of the village filling the space between the road and river. It's also a **cockerel-fighting centre**, and you might see furtive clusters of men betting on their prize bruisers, great long-legged, muscular birds with pugnacious eyes, torn combs and patchy feathers.

The market

Shidong's **market** gets going after 10am on the riverside shingle, with a big area dealing in **livestock** in makeshift pens – principally ducks, chickens and pigs – and the rest given over to clothing, household goods and farm supplies. A string of stalls sell Shidong's distinctive **embroidery**, full of playful lions and mythical beasts picked out in crimson silk, often with smaller mice, butterflies and birds hiding around the fringes; most is machine-made but it's beautiful anyway. Some people with older handmade pieces track foreigners down, but these have become so collectable that either the quality is poor or prices are high, or both. There's a bit of **silver** too, from earrings and "writing-brush" hairpins at ¥50 to heavy bracelets costing over ¥1000.

ARRIVAL AND DEPARTURE · SHIDONG

By bus There's no station in Shidong. Buses heading south to Kaili via Taijiang assemble in the main street; traffic taking the faster Kaili–Zhenyuan road stops by the river bridge 2km north of town – this is where to catch Zhenyuan buses too.

Destinations Kaili (8 daily; 2hr 15min; ¥20); Taijiang (2 daily; 2hr; ¥18); Zhenyuan (1hr; ¥12).

ACCOMMODATION

Luoping 罗萍招待所, luópíng zhāodàisuǒ. Next to the post office ☏0855 535 9008. One of Shidong's two very down-to-earth inns with shared facilities. Beds **¥20**

Yingbin 迎宾招待所, yíngbīn zhāodàisuǒ. Next to the post office ☏0855 535 9174. Luoping's similarly basic neighbour. Beds **¥20**

South of Kaili

The 50km road south of Kaili to Leishan follows the narrow, steep-sided **Bala river valley** past some of the region's most picturesque villages, including **Langde Shang** and **Xijiang**, the largest Miao settlement of them all. It's the most commercially developed area around Kaili, but wait until the buses have gone and you'll find the villagers pretty friendly towards visitors who stay the night – and there are some good walks in the hills too. Note, however, that **Leishan**'s accommodation can be problematic, so if you plan to head to Rongjiang and Dong territory (see p.295) either catch a direct bus from Kaili or try to time things so you don't have to stay in Leishan.

There are **direct buses** between Kaili, Leishan and Xijiang; for anywhere else, catch a Kaili – Leishan bus and tell the driver where you're headed so they can put you off at the right spot.

Nanhua

南花, nánhuā • Buses stop on the main road; walk 500m up to the village

Around 13km from Kaili on the far side of the Bala River, **NANHUA** is an attractive spread of traditional homes with corncobs drying under the eaves, tucked into a fold in the steep hillside. As the official "Miao Customs Performance Village" things tend to feel a little artificial, with hornfuls of rice wine, dances, lusheng performances and souvenirs all laid on daily for tour buses; it's fun all the same, and the first place you'll see Leigong-style **Miao clothing**, all red and green embroideries, oversized silver headpieces, and long pleated skirts.

Langde Shang

郎德上, lángdé shàng • Buses stop on the main road; walk 1.5km up to the village

About 35km south of Kaili, **LANGDE SHANG** or "Upper Langde" is a tremendously photogenic collection of wooden houses, muddy lanes, fields and chickens set on terraced slopes capped in pine trees. The former home of **Yang Daliu** (杨大六故居, yáng dàliù gùjū), a rebel leader during the Miao Uprising, has been preserved; the entire conflict might have been sparked by a fight between a Langde man and an official from nearby Leishan. Festivals and performances focus on a circular cobbled square at the village centre; plenty of silverwork and embroidery is thrust at you as you wander, but get past this and the atmosphere is genuinely genuine.

There's a great 16km **hike** from Langde Shang, following gravel vehicle roads and walking tracks through outlying villages. Head first for Baode (报德, bàodé; 3.5km), then along a 5km footpath to Nanmeng (南猛, nánměng). You pick up a gravel road again here; it's 3.5km via Laomao (老猫, lǎomāo) to Jiaomeng (脚猛, jiǎo měng), where you can either continue along the track, or branch off along another footpath for the final 3.5km to the Kaili–Leishan road, about 3km south of Langde.

ACCOMMODATION AND EATING   **LANGDE SHANG**

Ask around and locals might offer a **bed** for the night for ¥15, plus ¥10 for simple meals.

Xijiang

西江, xījiāng • ¥60

XIJIANG is a picturesque mass of closely packed traditional dwellings ranged up the side of two adjacent hills, about 40km southeast of Kaili and 30km northeast of Leishan. Don't be too discouraged by the entry fee and the car park crowded with tour buses; wandering the narrow, stepped lanes through the village and onto the terraced fields above, where you could hike around for hours, is a great experience – and the views are tremendous.

The more you look around Xijiang, the more you find – you'll need to ask for directions at times. The grand wooden **Drum Treasure Hall** (鼓宝楼, gǔ bǎo lóu) conceals an enormous bronze drum hung above a water buffalo skull and there's a **museum** (西江博物馆, xījiāng bówùguǎn) displaying festival clothing, plus several traditional **sorcerers** (巫师, wūshī) – who act primarily as spiritual advisers rather than spell-casters. Incidentally, women pounding sticky rice with wooden mallets are preparing *baba*, the stodgy cakes that seem to be a major snack in town.

ARRIVAL AND DEPARTURE   XIJIANG

By bus On market days, transport out runs until dark; at other times, don't leave it this late, and confirm supposed departure times with bus drivers.

Destinations Kaili (5 daily; 1hr 30min; ¥15); Leishan (4 daily; 2hr; ¥15).

ACCOMMODATION AND EATING

Xijiang has many **guesthouses**, usually flagged by Chinese signs reading "农家乐" (nóngjiā lè; ¥20/person), which also offer communal evening meals at ¥15–30. A couple of early-closing **shops** around town serve boiled or fried rice noodles.

Leishan

雷山, léishān

Out on a plain at river level, 20km south of Langde Shang, **LEISHAN** housed a garrison during the Qing dynasty, but the kilometre-wide modern town is little more than a staging post for buses heading south over twisting mountain roads to Rongjiang. Overlooking the town, **Majia Shan** (马家山, mǎjiā shān) is the focus for a hill-climbing event on the first day of the Chinese New Year, similar to the one near Matang (see p.287).

Some 15km east of Leishan, **Leigong Shan** (雷公山, léigōng shān) is a forested, 2200m-high mountain where the rebels made their final stand during the **Miao Uprising**. Ask at Kaili's CITS (see p.286) about arranging overnight hikes to the top.

ARRIVAL AND DEPARTURE   LEISHAN

By bus Kaili (1hr 15min; ¥13.50); Rongjiang (4 daily, plus can flag down passing buses from Kaili; 4hr; ¥52); Xijiang (4 daily; 2hr; ¥15).

ACCOMMODATION

Leishan has plenty of **accommodation**, but little seems happy to take foreigners. If you're on a budget, allow plenty of time to try your luck at cheaper places, or head onwards.

Leigongshan International 雷公山双庆国际大酒店, léigōng shān shuāngqìng guójì dàjiǔdiàn. A kilometre out of town near the Kaili-Rongjiang junction ☎ 0855 333 6666. Foreign tour groups are about the only takers for this brashly upmarket option. ¥250

Dong country

Southeast of Leishan, you're heading into the territory of the **Dong** people (see p.340), a remote landscape of steep mountain terraces and dark wooden villages that spills into Guangxi province. Your first destination is the large town of **Rongjiang**, 130km

THE BACK ROAD FROM SANDU TO RONGJIANG

As an **alternative route** through Southeast Guizhou, consider the little-travelled back road from Sandu to Rongjiang (see opposite) along the deep Duliu river valley. Not as spectacular as the Kaili–Leishan–Rongjiang road, it's nonetheless a beautiful journey and not a difficult one, with the highlight being villages and people encountered along the way. The trip should take six to eight hours, including a few stops.

Aim first for **SANDU** (三都, sāndū), accessible directly from Guiyang or Kaili. Sandu is populated by the Shui minority, who settled here during the Tang dynasty – try to catch their autumn Duan festival, featuring bronze drums, horse races and ancestor sacrifices. Sandu itself is a shabby, part-modernized place full of phlegmatic ponies hauling cartloads of reinforcing rods and rice around; change buses here for Rongjiang. If you get stuck for the night, the *Haoyuan* (好园宾馆, hǎoyuán bīnguǎn; ☎0854 392 4358; ¥88) offers clean tiled floors, hard beds, air conditioning and working showers.

The next stage follows the increasingly substantial **Duliu River**, the bus wobbling along forested ridges or descending almost to water level, picking up passengers along the way: Shui in green, Miao wearing pleated skirts, blue embroidered smocks and puttees. About 50km along, **XINGHUA** (兴华, xīnghuá) has an incredible market (CITS in Guiyang and Kaili should know the dates), when the single street is jammed full of crowds and stalls selling everything from buckets to silver and livestock. There are more Shui and Miao in their holiday best, plus Dong wearing plain indigo turbans and jackets; many people are clearly spooked by foreign faces. About a kilometre upstream, **Bameng** is an attractive wooden village on the far bank (the ferry over costs ¥1), while **Baibei** sits high up on the hills above.

Wave down passing transport to continue you journey; it's another hour to **BAKAI** (八开寨, bākāi zhài), a large Miao village reached over a bridge with another fine market. From here, a final hour lands you at Rongjiang.

4

southeast of Leishan, from where there are two options for continuing to **Zhaoxing**, one of the most accessible – and picturesque – of all Dong villages. The longer route first detours to **Liping**, or you can follow a more direct route via **Congjiang**; either way, there are plenty of villages to explore, many capped by distinctive **drum towers**. After Zhaoxing, transport continues right through **to Sanjiang** in Guangxi (see p.339). Try not to rush things; you'll need to allow three days for the trip if you plan to see anything at all.

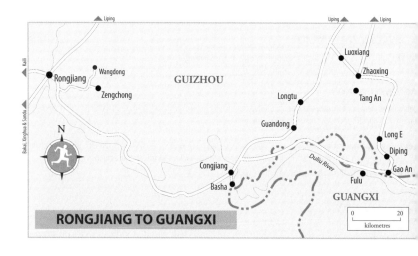

Rongjiang

榕江, róngjiāng

Reached from Leishan via a long, twisting road over thickly forested mountains, RONGJIANG reveals itself as a narrow mesh of dusty streets and the usual concrete-and-tile buildings in the flat of the **Duliu river valley**. You won't get lost: there's a sort of public space between the bus station and the bridge, with two parallel main streets running south from here, joined by lanes. The town is a busy **marketplace**, very lively on Sundays when hundreds of Miao and Dong descend for a bargaining frenzy in their finest indigo jackets; otherwise it's somewhere to organize side-trips to nearby **Bakai** (see opposite) and **Zengchong**.

ARRIVAL AND DEPARTURE   RONGJIANG

By bus Services run to Congjiang (2hr 30min; ¥25), Kaili (5hr; ¥65), Leishan (4hr; ¥52), Liping (2hr; ¥35), Sandu (5 daily; 5hr; ¥60) and Wangdong (2 daily; 1hr 30min; ¥16). For minibuses (useful for Zengchong and Bakai), turn right out of Rongjiang's bus station and look for a little pavilion with stone lions before the bridge, where vehicles wait to be hired out at ¥300/day.

ACCOMMODATION AND EATING

Rongjiang is full of good, clean, inexpensive **hotels** that wave foreigners away before you've even asked if rooms are available. Cheap places to **eat** surround the bus station.

Ronghe 榕和大酒店, rónghé dàjiǔdiàn. Xi Huan Lu ☎ 0855 662 6599. Turn left out of the bus station, take the first left (Xi Huan Lu) and it's a few minutes down on the right. Rongjiang's sole hotel that unquestionably accepts foreign custom, this well-maintained, tidy place is a relief if you've had a tough time reaching town. **¥160**

DIRECTORY

Banks There's a Construction Bank with an ATM in Xinglong Jie, near the *Ronghe* hotel.

Post Office Opposite the bus station.

Zengchong

增冲, zēngchōng • From Rongjiang, hire a minibus (¥300/day); alternatively, catch a bus to Wangdong (往洞, wǎngdòng; 2 daily; 1hr 30min; ¥16) and walk or hitch the final 6km – the bus leaves Rongjiang in the afternoon and returns in the morning, so you'll need to overnight

ZENGCHONG is an old, completely unrenovated Dong village up in the hills 30km east of Rongjiang. Once past the substantial **wind-and-rain bridge** on the village edge, you enter an unromantically medieval maze of lanes among the village's knot of rickety, multistorey wooden homes. Find your way through to the central square, above which rises a splendid, 400-year-old **drum tower** – apparently the oldest anywhere – where villagers gather for festivals and funerals. What with pigs, dogs and children in every direction, Zengchong is seriously rural, but it's also an appealing place **to stay** – ask around for a family to put you up.

Liping

黎平, lípíng

Around 100km northeast of Rongjiang on a good road, **LIPING** is where the Red Army made up its mind to storm Zunyi during the **Long March** (see p.280). A bright, moderately sized, partially modernized town, you can spend time between buses browsing old photos and admiring antique grey-brick courtyard architecture at either the **Site of the Liping Conference** (黎平会议会址, lípíng huìyì huìzhǐ) at 52 Dong Erlang Po, with its Communist Party slant, or the **Lianghu Guildhall** (两湖会馆, liǎnghú huìguǎn), built for travelling Hunan and Hubei merchants during the nineteenth century.

By bus Liping's bus station is 500m north of the centre on Kaitai Lu. Minibus drivers wait here too.

Destinations Congjiang (3hr; ¥30); Guiyang (3 daily; 12hr; ¥148); Kaili (4 daily; 7hr; ¥88); Rongjiang (2hr 30min; ¥25) Sanjiang (2 daily; 5hr; ¥38); Zhaoxing (2 daily; 2hr; ¥18).

ACCOMMODATION

Aside from the following, try your luck with inexpensive **hotels** around the bus station.

Gangsai 港赛大酒店, gǎngsài dàjiǔdiàn. 51 Ping Jie ☎ 0855 623 0888. This comfortable, central hotel, a 10min walk

south from the bus station, is a good deal for the price, though you might need to argue it down from the rack-rate. **¥168**

Longli

隆里古城, lónglǐ gǔchéng • Minibus from Liping around ¥200 for a half-day visit

LONGLI is a square-sided, medieval Han Chinese town, out on a plain about 45km by road north of Liping. Founded as a garrison in 1386 and still partially walled, there are gate towers at the main compass points, tidy paved streets, wood-fronted shops, public squares and ornamental stone gateways, all illustrating how Guizhou hasn't always been quite so remote, and that major trade routes – and armies – crossed the province in former times. It's a bit lifeless today, perked up slightly by people wandering around in period costume and performing martial arts displays in the main square.

Congjiang

从江, cóngjiāng

It's a bumpy few hours from Rongjiang, past logging depots and views of isolated wooden villages up on the hillsides, to the compact administrative centre of **CONGJIANG**. The town is thinly spread – just a couple of streets really – either side of the **Duliu River**, which continues its steady journey east from Sandu (see p.294) and Rongjiang into Guangxi. There's little to see in Congjiang itself (aside from a tourist-trade drum tower), but just up the hill is **Basha**, a large and unusual Miao village – you can stay there too, so won't need to linger in Congjiang unless you arrive late.

Basha

岜沙, bāshā

High up on a narrow, forested ridge 7.5km from town, **BASHA** is a rustic sprawl of five conjoined wooden hamlets dotted with satellite dishes, home to several thousand **Biasha Miao**, considered to be one of the oldest Miao groups in Guizhou. You'll appreciate this most if there are any TV documentary crews or anthropologists around, when men don crisp, shiny indigo jackets and trousers, and sport their distinctive **topknots** and brass-bound, home-made **guns**.

Basha is definitely somewhere to spend the night, soak up village life, and go for **walks**; paved paths lead between houses and rice-drying frames, through a woodland **lusheng ground** where festivals are held, and out into the rice terraces. If your Chinese is up to it, ask at the youth hostel for advice on longer hikes.

By bus Congjiang's bus station is east of the river on Jiangdong Nan Lu, the main road through town.

Destinations Kaili (1 daily; 8hr; ¥90); Liping (3hr; ¥30); Rongjiang (2hr 30min; ¥25); Sanjiang (1 daily; 7hr; ¥48); Zhaoxing (2 daily; 2hr; ¥18).

GETTING AROUND

By minibus or motorbike to Basha From Congjiang's bus station, turn left for 50m, cross the bridge and turn left again, and you'll find minibuses (¥10, though drivers often

ask far more) and motorbikes (¥5) for the 15min uphill run; heading back, flag down a minibus or walk (1hr).

ACCOMMODATION

Almost every building around Congjiang's bus station is a **hotel**, and for once nobody cares where you stay, though Basha is a more interesting spot to spend the night.

Congjiang Aoyue 从江奥悦酒店, cóngjiāng àoyuè jiǔdiàn. 9 Jiangdong Nan Lu, past the Wenguang hotel ☎ 0855 641 1808. Probably the most upmarket option in town, with a/c and clean rooms, though it's usually empty. **¥168**

★ **Gufengzhai** 古风寨青年旅社, gǔfēngzhài qīngnián lǚguǎn. Behind a fence on the outskirts of Basha ☎ 1388 554 9720. Youth hostel with tidy wooden rooms, a patio, a covered outside dining area and views

down off the escarpment from Basha village. Lots of hiking information, though no English is spoken. Beds **¥20**, doubles **¥60**

Wenguang 文广宾馆, wénguāng bīnguǎn. Jiangdong Nan Lu ☎ 0855 641 8316. Out of the bus station, turn right and it's 100m along on the far side of the road. Old and tired, but everything works and some rooms have computers. **¥80**

EATING

Aside from the *Chongqing*, **noodle houses** with piles of fresh ingredients laid out on the counters flank Congjiang's bus station; a large plate of stir-fried anything costs ¥15. At **Basha**, arrange meals through accommodation; a few shacks sell cold drinks, snacks and cooked noodles.

Chongqing Tese 重庆特色餐厅, chóngqìng tèsè cāntīng. Jiangdong Lu – turn left out of the bus station, walk past the bridge and it's 200m.

Chongqing-style hotpots, sour fish soup, rabbit and *gege* (steamed spareribs in ground rice). ¥20/head.

Zhaoxing
肇兴, zhàoxīng

ZHAOXING is a pretty Dong village some 80km northeast of Congjiang, set along a stream in a narrow, shallow valley. It's something of a museum piece: almost every house here is wooden (modern-looking buildings are banned) and there are no less than five **drum towers** and accompanying **wind-and-rain bridges**, each raised by separate clans and decorated with human and animal carvings. Everyone in town seems to be involved in making traditional **cloth**, soaking lengths in huge tubs of indigo pulp, hanging them up under eaves to dry, or pounding them smooth with heavy mallets. In summer, Zhaoxing's setting among brilliant-green rice paddies is gorgeous, though heavy traffic along the main street threatens the village's charm.

It's not hard to find your way around Zhaoxing; the main road follows the stream – though houses stop you seeing this – with most places to stay and eat in the 150m between the roadside **Xintuan Drum Tower** (信团鼓楼, xìntuán gǔlóu) and the little concrete road bridge.

Tang An
堂安, táng ān

If Zhaoxing feels too busy, set aside five hours for the return **hike** to hilltop **TANG AN**, a Dong settlement reached along flagstoned paths. From Zhaoxing's concrete road bridge, follow the stream alongside houses past the *Zhaoxing Binguan* hotel, then turn sharp right up steps to the start of the trail. There's a steep, sweaty stretch at first, then the going eases at **Xiage village** (厦格, xiàgé), where you'll find a pathside shrine and a small forest of tribute poles to local deity **Yang Gong**.

Weave through Xiage and continue uphill, passing four dumpy drum towers and a graveyard; there are fantastic views from the steep rice terraces above the village. **Tang An** itself is tiny, with old folk crashed out under its own central drum tower, and an ancient **stone drinking fountain** spilling water from a fresh mountain spring through three spouts.

ARRIVAL AND DEPARTURE

By bus There's no bus station in Zhaoxing; buses pick up along the main street. Ask drivers the night before about departure times. Sanjiang buses originate in Liping and, if full, don't stop in Zhaoxing. If this happens you'll need to hop to Sanjiang in stages: go to Diping, then take a minibus to the tiny intersection of Gao An (¥5/person), and wait there to flag down passing Sanjiang traffic.

Destinations Congjiang (2 daily; 2hr; ¥18); Diping (45min ¥10); Liping (2 daily; 2hr; ¥18); Sanjiang (2 daily; 3hr 30min; ¥30).

ACCOMMODATION

There are about a dozen places to **stay** in Zhaoxing, most of them basic but all with hot water and fans, if not en suite and a/c. Both the *Zhaoxing Binguan* and *Zhaoxing Fandian* use "Zhaoxing Hotel" on their English signs.

Dong Village 侗乡涉外旅馆, dòng xiāng shèwài lǚguǎn. Up a back lane away from the main road ☎ 0855 613 0188. This is a typical, family-run guesthouse in an old wooden building. **¥60**

Fuquan 福全旅馆, fúquán lǚguǎn. Just back from the main road ☎ 0855 613 0698. Friendly guesthouse, a little rusty around the edges. **¥60**

Zhaoxing Binguan 肇兴宾馆, zhàoxīng bīnguǎn. Older wing just off the main road, newer "VIP rooms"

streamside at the end of the village ☎ 0855 613 0800 The most modern, upmarket lodgings in town, though the wooden buildings look the part. The "VIP rooms" are more attractively rustic with balconies overlooking rice terraces Standard rooms **¥168**; VIP rooms **¥398**

★ **Zhaoxing Fandian** 肇兴饭店, zhàoxīng fàndiàn Next to the main-road drum tower ☎ 0855 613 0005. A spotless, tidy option with a welcoming manager and a good restaurant. **¥80**, with a/c **¥100**

EATING AND DRINKING

Food **stalls** serving Dong oil tea (see p.340) and noodle soups fire up around 8am; Zhaoxing's **restaurants** open only for lunch and dinner, and close by 8pm. Try local sticky rice wine, stored in clay jars and served in aluminium teapots.

A Mei 啊美餐馆, ā měi cānguǎn. Main street. Coffee, Western-style meals and Guizhou-Chinese staples in this friendly hole in the wall.

Happy Farmer On the main street. Their Chinese food is tasty, if a little expensive for the size of the portions, but what

sets this place apart is the a/c and closeable front doors keeping Zhaoxing's ubiquitous dust outside. ¥25 a dish.

Runrun 润润饭店, rùnrùn fàndiàn. On the main street. Inexpensive Chinese stir-fries, with a basic English menu.

SHOPPING

Souvenirs Zhaoxing's souvenir shops sell Miao and Dong crafts, including dark blue or green geometric embroidery and heavy silver jewellery with spiral designs. Asking prices are ludicrous; aim for a fifth of the opening offer.

Northeast Guizhou

Up beyond Kaili and the Miao regions near the **Hunan boder**, Northeast Guizhou has two main sights: the pleasant riverside town of **Zhenyuan**, the only one in all Guizhou worth a special effort to reach; and remote **Fanjing Shan**, a one-time holy mountain and monkey refuge, recently developed for tourism. It's easy to get up here – the northeast is traversed by the **Kaili–Hunan rail line**, with Zhenyuan actually on the line – though reaching Fanjing Shan requires a couple of bus rides. Note that you can continue eastwards by road and rail into **Hunan** (see p.341).

CROSSING INTO GUANGXI

The 40km road south from **Zhaoxing** to the **Guangxi border** is in poor condition and prone to landslides. Along the way, the scruffy villages of **Long E** (龙额, lóng é) and **Diping** (地坪, dìpíng) both offer basic accommodation, drum towers and bridges; then you reach the Guangxi border where tiny **Gao An** (高安, gāo ān) marks the T-intersection with the Congjiang-Sanjiang road. From here it's another 70km to **Sanjiang**, more Dong villages, and buses to Longji Titian (see p.337).

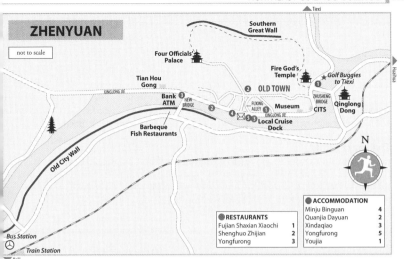

Zhenyuan

镇远, zhènyuǎn

ZHENYUAN was founded two thousand years ago, though today's town – occupying a straight, constricted valley 100km northeast of Kaili on the aquamarine **Wuyang River** – sprang up in the Ming dynasty to guard the trade route to central China. This is easily Guizhou's most attractive town: the river flows northeast, with Zhenyuan's tall, antique-style houses piled together along both banks, picked out at night in red lanterns and fairy lights. There's also a section of the long-forgotten **Southern Great Wall** guarding a high ridge to the north, and some watery parkland out at **Tiexi**, a refreshing place to cool off in summer.

The old town

古城, gǔ chéng

Zhenyuan's **old town** is a kilometre of Qing-style wood and stone buildings backed up against stony cliffs. The cobbled main street, **Xinglong Jie**, is almost entirely made up of restaurants and lodgings, many overlooking the river. **Fire-baffle walls** separating buildings are an eastern Chinese feature, their huge overhanging gables known as "horse heads" after their shape. Look for a small ornamental gateway marking **Fuxing Alley** (复兴巷, fùxīng xiàng), and follow it up between 5m-high stone walls to a clutch of **old courtyard homes**, some of the grander ones now smartened up as guesthouses. Steps climb from here to the Southern Great Wall (see p.300).

The museum

名城风貌殿, míngchéng fēngmào diàn • Daily 7.30am–5pm • ¥10

Back on Xinglong Jie, Zhenyuan's **museum** is full of old photos of the town, wall and thirteenth-century post road, but it's the traditional stone building itself – formerly a temple to the god of war, judging by the weighty cast-iron halberd and cannon out the front – which impresses most.

Qinglong Dong

青龙洞, qīnglóng dòng • Daily 7.30am–6pm • ¥30

Head east of the museum, and you'll cross the solid, Ming-dynasty **Zhusheng Bridge** (祝圣桥, zhùshèng qiáo), which spans the river via a central pavilion. On the far side is sixteenth-century **Qinglong Dong**, a sprawling complex of separate Taoist, Buddhist and Confucian halls growing out of a cliff face, all dripping wet and hung with vines.

Tian Hou Gong

天后宫, tiān hòu gōng • ¥2

On the north side of the river, **Tian Hou Gong** is a four-hundred-year-old complex of stone halls and ornate wooden screens. Founded by Fujianese merchants and dedicated to the southern Chinese protector of seafarers, it's one of a half-dozen such buildings in town raised by provincial trading guilds (see p.367) – the others are mostly in ruins.

The south bank

Across **New Bridge** (新大桥, xīn dà qiáo), you can duck west below a strip of the reconstructed **old city wall** (卫城垣, wèi chéng yuán), to walk west for a kilometre along the south riverfront to a small park and a fourteenth-century arched gateway. On summer nights half the town heads here for a stroll or a swim.

The Southern Great Wall

南长城, nán chángchéng • ¥30

A thirty-minute walk up steps from the top of Fuxing Alley, taking in forest and views over the town from little **Four Officials' Palace** (四官殿, sì guān diàn), brings you to a fragment of the sixteenth-century **Southern Great Wall**. The structure, built as protection against Guizhou's unruly tribes and running 300km eastwards to Fenghuang in Hunan (see p.341), was only identified in 2000. The unrestored section above Zhenyuan is worn down to only 3m at its highest point, and the impression you get is that the wall was less a defence and more of a road linking **lookout towers** together – there's one small blockhouse, buried in vegetation, just off the path.

Once you've taken in the scenery – you can see right into Hunan from here – follow another path down to town via the unassuming **Fire God's Temple** (火神殿, huǒshén diàn), which emerges next to Zhusheng Bridge.

Tiexi

铁溪, tiěxī • Entrance 5km from Zhenyuan • Catch golf buggies from Xinglong Jie, near the Zhusheng Bridge (¥3–6 depending on where you get off in the park)

Tiexi is a strip of wooded parkland along a few kilometres of tumbling stream that's packed during the sticky summers with people cooling down in the water; just stop the buggy when you see somewhere you like. Stalls sell snacks, ice cream and rubber rings, and the road continues through a beautiful valley to **Long Tan** (龙潭, lóng tán; ¥50), a scenic pool whose entry fee scares off everyone except locals, who get in for free.

ARRIVAL AND DEPARTURE	**ZHENYUAN**

Zhenyuan's **train and bus stations** are next to each other, about 3km west of town on the south side of the river – a taxi to the old town is ¥4. Unusually, train is your best bet, with plenty of departures to Kaili, Guiyang, Yuping (the jumping-off point for Fanjing Shan) and Huaihua in Hunan. Shidong is the one destination you can only reach by bus.

RIDING THE WUYANG

Zhenyuan's river setting can be explored on short **tours** through town and longer **cruises** taking in the dramatic local landscapes.

Local river cruises Buy tickets at the dock on Xinglong Jie for hour-long cruises through the town in three-person sampans (¥80), dragonboats (¥25/person), or sturdy craft with brightly decorated awnings and glassed-in viewing cabins (¥30–80).

Wuyang river trips Begin 17km from town towards Shibing, then cruise back past gorges, waterfalls and rock spires. Arrange them (¥160) through the CITS, 49 Shuncheng Jie (☎0855 572 6177), who speak a little English; you leave at 8.30am, and are back in time for lunch.

CLOCKWISE FROM TOP QINGLONG DONG , ZHENYUAN (P.299); HUANGGUOSHO FALLS (P.307); DONG DRUM TOWER NEAR CONGJIANG ›

By bus Kaili (6 daily; 3hr 30min; ¥25); Shidong (1hr; ¥12).
By train Anshun (3 daily; 5hr 30min); Beijing (1 daily; 36hr); Chengdu (1 daily; 27hr); Chongqing (1 daily; 15hr); Guangzhou (1 daily; 16hr); Guiyang (14 daily; 4hr); Huaihua (14 daily; 3hr); Kaili (14 daily; 1hr 30min); Kunming (2 daily; 16hr); Liupanshui (3 daily; 8hr); Liuzhi (3 daily; 6hr 30min); Shanghai (3 daily; 24hr); Yuping (16 daily; 50min–1hr 30min); Zhangjiajie (2 daily; 8hr).

ACCOMMODATION

Minju Binguan 民居宾馆, mínjū bīnguǎn. Xinglong Jie ☎ 0855 572 5488. The small, tidy, river-view doubles with balcony showers are good value, but would be better without the attached karaoke bar. **¥80**

★ **Quanjia Dayuan** 全家大院客栈, quánjiā dàyuàn kèzhàn. About 100m up Fuxing Alley on the way to the Southern Great Wall ☎ 0855 572 3999. A converted courtyard mansion, whose modern rooms are en suite with a/c; not on the river but very atmospheric. Twin **¥180**, doubles **¥200**

Xindaqiao 新大桥宾馆, xīn dàqiáo bīnguǎn. Right by the New Bridge ☎ 0855 387 8777. Basic standby just outside the old town with nice views of the walls and river at night. **¥80**

Yongfurong 永福荣客栈, yǒngfúróng kèzhàn. Xinglong Jie ☎ 0855 573 0888, ⊛ yongfurong.net Sitting over a popular restaurant, this is a comfortable river-view option, though you want to bargain the rate down or head up to the better *Quanjia*. **¥180**

★ **Youjia** 有家客栈, yǒujiā kèzhàn. On the corner of the Tiexi road and the Zhusheng Bridge ☎ 0855 572 6626. Smart, neat rooms, with balcony views over the old bridge to Qinglong Dong. **¥158**

EATING

The old town is full of **restaurants** serving hotpots, stewed tofu, red-cooked spareribs and Miao family-style dishes (苗家常, miáo jiācháng), with chilli and pickles added to Chinese stir-fries. In summer, it's more fun to cross the New Bridge and join locals tucking into hotpots and noodles at outdoor pavement tables, or at **barbecue fish restaurants** in the lane beside the old city wall.

Fujian Shaxian Xiaochi 福建沙县小吃, fújiàn shāxiàn xiǎochī. Xinglong Jie. Friendly canteen with unusually tasty rice noodles and steamed dumplings, one of many along the street.

Shenghuo Zhijian 生活之间, shēnghuó zhījiān. Xinglong Jie. Cold drinks, coffee and tea in this a/c Taiwanese-style café with plush seating.

Yongfurong 永福荣客栈, yǒngfúróng kèzhàn Xinglong Jie. Busy, comfortable restaurant with river views and comprehensive menu; ask them to hold the oil and the food is good. Mains from ¥25.

DIRECTORY

Banks The only foreign-exchange service in Zhenyuan is a Construction Bank ATM by the New Bridge.

Post Office Jinglong Jie.

Fanjing Shan

梵净山, fánjìng shān • ¥50

Hidden away in Guizhou's remote northeastern corner, 100km from Zhenyuan near the borders with Hunan and Chongqing, **Fanjing Shan** is a beautiful, thickly forested mountain, famed for its bizarre rock formations and critically endangered **golden monkeys** (金丝猴, jīnsī hóu) – though with the entire population numbering only 400 adults, you'll be lucky to see them. Until very recently the mountain was often isolated by landslides, and the ascent to the 2500m summit involved negotiating more than seven thousand steep steps, but modernizations have brought an all-weather road and a **cable car** to the top – though die-hards can still do it tough if they want. Little **temples** up here once brought in pilgrims, but most have been in ruins for centuries, and, despite increasing tourism, the atmosphere is occasionally spooky with dense summer fogs. Bring a torch and something warm for the top (it snows in winter).

The ascent

Taxis between Heiwan and the cable-car station/steps ¥10; cable car ¥90 each way

Fanjing Shan's entry point is tiny **HEIWAN** (黑湾, hēiwān), undergoing a hotel construction frenzy at the moment; shops here sell ponchos and walking sticks (both a good idea). You might be asked to register at the **police station**, before catching a taxi for the 9km run to the cable-car station (索道站, suǒdào zhàn), also where Fanjing Shan's steps begin. The cable car offers slow, grand views over the forest on its 3km cruise to the top; the steps rise with complete disregard for gradient beneath the vibrantly green canopy, a stiflingly humid trek in summer – allow five hours to reach the summit area.

Once at the top, you'll want about three hours to explore along flagstoned **paths**, through a mix of open heath, woodland, rhododendron thickets and strangely piled rock formations such as the **Mushroom Rocks** (蘑菇石, mógū shí). The **Golden Summit** (金顶, jīn dǐng) also has remains of temples and a 4m-long Ming-dynasty **bridge** linking two spires of rock together.

ARRIVAL AND DEPARTURE — FANJING SHAN

Fanjing Shan is reached via **Yuping** (玉屏, yùpíng), a stop on the Kaili–Zhenyuan–Hunan rail line. Exit the station and you'll find buses to the small town of **Jiangkou** (江口, jiāngkǒu; 2hr; ¥25), where you change again for buses to Heiwan (1hr; ¥10). Note that you can catch trains on from Yuping to Huaihua (for Fenghuang) and Zhangjiajie in **Hunan** (see box, p.341).

By train from Yuping Anshun (8 daily; 6hr 30min); Beijing (2 daily; 35hr); Chengdu (1 daily; 28hr); Chongqing (2 daily; 16hr); Guangzhou (1 daily; 15hr); Guiyang (25 daily; 5hr); Huaihua (19 daily; 1hr 30min); Kaili (19 daily; 2hr 30min); Kunming (8 daily; 17hr); Liupanshui (9 daily; 9hr); Liuzhi (7 daily; 7hr 30min); Shanghai (4 daily; 24hr); Zhangjiajie (2 daily; 7hr); Zhenyuan (14 daily; 1hr).

ACCOMMODATION AND EATING

Accommodation at Fanjing Shan was in complete disarray at the time of writing. **Hotels** are being built at Heiwan, but former bunkhouses on the mountain itself have all been closed down. There's also accommodation near the bus station at Jiangkou, charging ¥60 a double. Restaurant shacks at Heiwan provide inexpensive **stir-fry meals**; otherwise, bring snacks with you or eat at Jiangkou.

Western Guizhou

Just 100km west of Guiyang, shambolic **Anshun** guards the entrance to western Guizhou and routes to Yunnan, with enough nearby to occupy several days. The enormous **Longgong Caves** and spectacular **Huangguoshu Falls** make up for the town, though distant **Zhijin Caves** are even more impressive. For something lower-key, old stone villages feature ground opera (see p.307), ethnic Bouyei and, near **Tianlong**, a mountaintop stronghold linked to the most momentous love triangle in Chinese history.

Beyond Anshun, road and rail head towards Yunnan via remote Miao villages at **Suoga** and **Nankai**, most rewarding during periodic festivals, when thousands of locals dress in their finest and fill the hillsides for dancing, song and bullfights. Local powerhouse **Liupanshui** has few virtues, aside from buses up onto the Yunnan plateau at **Weining**, well worth a visit in winter to catch rare wildfowl at nearby **Cao Hai**. South of here, by the borders with Guangxi and Yunnan, the city of Xingyi offers access to the dramatic Maling Canyon.

Travel through the region is easy enough, but finding **accommodation** can be a nightmare. This is one of the last regions in all China where foreign-friendly options are strictly controlled by local authorities – though places occasionally bend the rules if they think they can get away with it.

Anshun

安顺, ānshùn

Like most of Guizhou's settlements, **ANSHUN** was originally a fortified outpost, its military here to enforce Han Chinese authority – ominously, its name means "Subjugated Peace". A friendly, lively market town for all that, Anshun's untidy modern veneer vanishes as soon as you leave the main streets for the muddy, rutted market lanes threading between tumbledown houses, though some surprisingly venerable buildings lurk around town.

Zhonghua Nan Lu

Just up from the bus station on **Zhonghua Nan Lu**, the **Small Traders' Market** covers an acre with wholesale stalls selling clothing, haberdashery, shoes and bedding, while out the back automatic looms churn out Miao and Bouyei embroideries. North of here, the seven-storey **White Pagoda** (白塔, bái tǎ), built of stone blocks, perches on a hillock above the roundabout; below is a nest of old buildings, including the bland **Yuantong Temple** (圆通寺, yuántōng sì) and a large, tottering **Catholic Church** with a Chinese-style tower and rose window. Up at the next intersection, the town's **Wu Miao** (武庙, wǔ miào), a temple to martial deity Guan Yu (see p.69), was being renovated on a grand scale at time of writing.

The Confucian Temple

文庙, wén miào • Daily 8am–5pm • ¥10 • Take the northern continuation of Gufu Jie, then turn right after about 100m

Anshun's **Confucian Temple** is a tranquil series of courtyards whose cracked flagstones, open beamwork, restrained decoration and comfortable proportions all point to a genuinely antique complex, dating in part to the fourteenth century. Cross over the stone bridge, with its fine latticework barriers, under a *pailou* arch – raised to record the donor's meritous deeds – and you'll find a handful of small halls, the last of which,

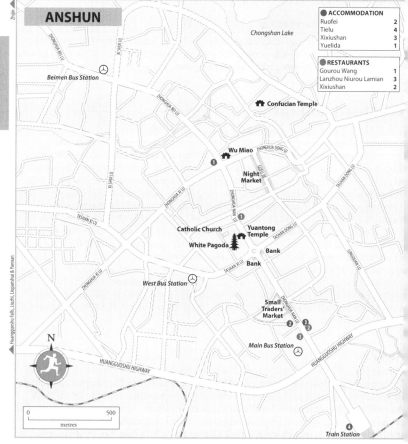

Dacheng Palace (大成殿, dàchéng diàn), sports dragon-wrapped pillars masterfully carved in deep relief, and a painted statue of the bearded sage flanked by his disciples.

ARRIVAL AND DEPARTURE   ANSHUN

Both local attractions and most of western Guizhou can be reached by **bus** from Anshun – the three stations are scattered around the town, all linked by buses #1 and #2 through the centre. Along with Liuzhi and Liupanshui, Anshun is a stop on the Guiyang–Kunming **rail line**. For Weining and Cao Hai, aim first for Liupanshui and pick up a local bus there.

BY BUS
Main bus station 750m south of the centre on Zhonghua Nan Lu.
Destinations Guiyang (1hr 30min; ¥35); Huangguoshu (1hr; ¥10); Liupanshui (3hr 30min; ¥55); Liuzhi (1hr 20min; ¥20); Xingyi (4hr 30min; ¥68).
West bus station 500m west of the centre on Tashan Xi Lu.
Destinations Longgong (1hr; ¥10).
Beimen bus station 1.5km northwest of th e centre on Zhonghua Bei Lu.

Destinations Zhijin (3hr; ¥40).

BY TRAIN
Anshun train station 1.5km south of the city centre at the end of Zhonghua Nan Lu.
Destinations Beijing (2 daily; 35hr); Chengdu (3 daily; 17hr); Chongqing (2 daily; 11hr); Guangzhou (2 daily; 24hr); Guiyang (23 daily; 1hr 30min); Kaili (9 daily; 4hr 30min); Kunming (11 daily; 9hr); Liupanshui (22 daily; 2hr 30min); Liuzhi (19 daily; 1hr); Shanghai (2 daily; 30hr); Zhenyuan (2 daily; 7hr).

GETTING AROUND

By city bus #1 and #2 run north from the train station up Zhonghua Nan Lu, pass the main bus station, turn west along Tashan Xi Lu via the west bus station, and continue north up Xi Shui Lu to the Beimen bus station.

ACCOMMODATION

Ruofei 若飞宾馆, ruòfēi bīnguǎn. 48 Zhonghua Nan Lu ☎0853 332 0228. An ordinary urban hotel with business pretensions, desperately overpricing their "standard single human life", as they bafflingly describe their double rooms. **¥300**
Tielu 铁路宾馆, tiělù bīnguǎn. On the left as you exit the train station ☎0853 329 0555. Clean, welcoming budget option, the cheapest deal for foreigners in town. **¥130**

Xixiushan 西秀山宾馆, xīxiùshān bīnguǎn. 63 Zhonghua Nan Lu ☎0853 221 1888. A variety of rooms in three buildings, from tatty old doubles to brighter, spick-and-span modern en suites. Cheap doubles **¥180**, en suite **¥300**
Yuelida 悦立达大酒店, yuèlìdá dàjiǔdiàn. On the Wu Miao crossroads ☎0853 333 5888. Plush tower block with all executive trimmings. Most rooms face away from the busy road. **¥618**

EATING

Anshun specializes in canine cuisine; if this isn't to your taste, inexpensive **canteens** surround the main bus station. For street snacks, try the **night market** after 7pm along Gufu Jie.

Gourou Wang 狗肉王, gǒuròu wáng. 5 Ruofei Nan Lu ☎0853 335 8991. Nationally famous dog restaurant, serving up every part of the animal in every conceivable way. Not for the faint-hearted. ¥50/person in a group.
Lanzhou Niurou Lamian 兰州牛肉拉面, lánzhōu niúròu lāmiàn. Zhonghua Nan Lu. This inexpensive Muslim place with slap-down service delivers signature spicy beef noodles, noodle soup, cumin-flavoured beef and a hundred other tasty variations on the theme. A photo -menu on the wall makes ordering easy. ¥15.
Xixiushan 63 Zhonghua Nan Lu. This hotel's competent restaurant offers dishes from around China, including juicy crisp-skinned chicken, dry-wok beef and cucumber with hoisin sauce. Slightly overpriced at around ¥ 30/dish.

SHOPPING

Batik Anshun is famous for its batik factory, begun in the 1950s to encourage local Bouyei (see p.307) to develop a commercial outlet for traditional crafts. Today it churns out decorative wall-hangings in blue, red and white; some of the designs, incorporating buffalo, tigers and dragons, are pretty lively. You'll find them in shops north of the main bus station on Zhonghua Nan Lu, outside the market.

4

DIRECTORY

Banks There's a Bank of China and a Construction Bank, both with ATMs, on the White Pagoda roundabout.

Tianlong and Tiantai Shan

天龙, tiānlóng • 30km northeast of Anshun • ¥30

TIANLONG is an old stone **Tunpu** village, good for a half-hour poke around narrow lanes to admire the skilful split-stone houses, walls and nineteenth-century **church school** built by French priests. The only major sight is the **Ground Opera Performance Hall** (地戏堂, dìxì táng), which is hung with masks and holds a couple of shows a day, or more if a big tour-group is visiting – incidentally, this is the only place anyone seems interested in seeing your entry ticket.

Tiantai Shan

天台山, tiāntái shān • ¥15

About 2km northeast of Tianlong via a concrete road into the fields, the fortified hilltop of **Tiantai Shan** was once home to the traitorous Ming-dynasty general **Wu Sangui**. Following the last Ming emperor's suicide in 1644, the warlord Li Zicheng kidnapped Wu's beautiful concubine, **Chen Yuanyuan**. Wu, until then staunchly patriotic, defected to the Manchus – who were laying siege to northern China – and let them through the Great Wall. Having stormed the country and founded the Qing dynasty, the Manchus rewarded Wu with kingship of Yunnan and Guizhou, though his conscience later got the better of him and he led an eight-year **anti-Manchu revolt** until his death in 1678.

From the road, steps ascend to the top of Tiantai Shan in fifteen minutes, where the tiny halls of **Wulong Temple** (伍龙寺, wǔlóng sì), a virtual castle, showcase relics of Wu Sangui – his water bucket, official's robe and sword covered in Taoist motifs – and photos of ground opera performances. There are also views over the valley from the uppermost terrace, and a plain room where Wu meditated on Buddhist texts.

ARRIVAL AND DEPARTURE **TIANLONG**

By bus From Anshun, catch a bus heading to Pingba (平坝, píngbà) and ask the driver to set you down at Tianlong (you're often left with a bit of a walk). From Guiyang, go to Pingba first and catch a Tianlong minibus from there. Destinations from Tianlong Anshun (40min; ¥8); Guiyang (1hr; ¥10); Pingba (20min; ¥4).

Longgong Caves

龙宫洞, lónggōng dòng • 28km from Anshun • ¥120

Way out in the countryside, **Longgong** features over 5km of fancifully lit caverns, rock formations, underground rivers and open fields to explore along well-trodden footpaths and, in a couple of places, by boat. Cumulatively, it's pretty spectacular, though the coloured lights have been overdone in places, and there are a few drab spots. The trail is fairly level, but boats are small so don't bring large bags. There's **nowhere to eat** on site.

From the western gate, you begin by being ferried down a river between willows and bamboo to a small knot of houses; walk through the arch, bear left, and it's 250m up some steps to **Guanyin Dong** (观音洞, guānyīn dòng), a cave filled with Buddhist statues. Follow the seemingly minor path around the entrance and through a short cavern lit by coloured lights, then out around a hillside to **Jiujiu Tun** – an old guard post – and **Yulong Dong** (玉龙洞, yùlóng dòng), a large and spectacular cave system through which a guide will lead you (for free). Out the other side, a small river enters **Long Gong** (Dragon's Palace) itself, a two-stage boat ride through tall, flooded caverns picked out with florid lighting, exiting the caves into a broad pool at Longgong's eastern entrance.

BLUE SMOCKS AND GROUND OPERA

A scattering of villages between **Anshun** and **Guiyang** are home to the so-called **Tunpu**, descendants of Ming-dynasty Chinese soldiers who have hung onto fourteenth-century traditions among their indigenous Bouyei neighbours. Aside from their dress – embroidered blue smocks with white or black turbans – and defensive stone architecture, a feature of Tunpu villages like Tianlong is **ground opera** (地戏, dìxì), where performers wear grotesque wooden masks as they act out episodes from the *Three Kingdoms* (see p.69). Similar opera styles from elsewhere in China are connected to a shamanistic ritual called *nuo*, from which Japanese *noh* theatre also derives.

ARRIVAL AND DEPARTURE   LONGGONG CAVES

By bus Minibuses from outside Guiyang's Tiyu bus station (2hr 30min; ¥45), or buses from Anshun's west bus station (1hr; ¥5–10), deliver to either end of Longgong. Transport runs until late afternoon from Longgong to Huangguoshu and, less frequently, to Anshun and Guiyang.

Shitou Zhai

石头寨, shítou zhài • 30km southwest of Anshun off the Huangguoshu road • ¥40

Six-hundred-year-old **SHITOU ZHAI** comprises forty or so houses grouped around a rocky hillock, all surrounded by vegetable plots. The people here are **Bouyei** (布依, bùyī), the main ethnic group around Anshun, best known for their split-stone houses with overlapping "fish-scale" roof tiles and **batik work**, all of which the village has in abundance. You'll be offered decorated jackets for sale, and might witness the entire batik process, from drawing the designs in wax to dyeing in indigo and boiling the garment to dissolve the wax, fix the colour and leave a white pattern on a blue background. The village itself shouldn't tie you up for more than an hour, though there's a good **guesthouse** here and many similar Bouyei hamlets to explore nearby, none of which charges admission.

ARRIVAL AND DEPARTURE   SHITOU ZHAI

By bus From Anshun, catch a Huangguoshu bus (40min; ¥8), ask the driver to put you off at the Shitou Zhai junction, and walk 2km to the village along the flat road. To return, retrace your steps and flag down passing buses to Huangguoshu, Anshun or Zhenning (镇宁, zhènníng), a town halfway back to Anshun where more Anshun traffic awaits.

ACCOMMODATION

Indigo Hotel 青定阁, qīngdìng gé. Not far inside the gate ☎ 0851 747 7033, ⌨ indigoculture.com. Attractive guesthouse with wi-fi, café-restaurant and comfortable, functional rooms. **¥180**

Huangguoshu Falls

黄果树瀑布, huángguǒshù pùbù • 65km southwest of Anshun • ¥180

At 74m high and 81m wide, **Huangguoshu Falls** may not quite rank as China's biggest cataract, but in full flood during the summer rains it's certainly among the loudest, the thunder rolling way off into the distance. Having said this, the Chinese hype far outstrips the reality – if you've seen a mid-sized waterfall before, don't fret if you miss this one. From the main entrance, a staircase descends past plagues of souvenir stalls to the blue-green river facing the falls; the most imposing view of Huangguoshu is off to the left where the full weight of its 81m span drops into the **Rhino Pool**. There's a path behind the water curtain too – prepare yourself for a good soaking from the spray.

Tianxing Bridge

天星桥, tiānxīng qiáo

Included on your Huanggoshu Falls ticket, **Tianxing Bridge** is about 6km away along a signposted path – you can also catch a minibus for a few yuan. The "bridge" is a natural stone arch spanning a narrow, fairly deep and rugged gorge; the river below barely flows nowadays, but it's a pleasant walk here through encroaching forest.

ARRIVAL AND DEPARTURE | HUANGGUOSHU FALLS

By bus Huangguoshu Falls are at little Huangguoshu township on the Guiyang–Yunnan highway. Buses from Anshun's main bus station (1hr; ¥12) and Guiyang (2hr 30min; ¥45) deliver to at the entrance. Buses return to Anshun and Guiyang through the day; if you're Yunnan bound, first catch a minibus 7km west to Guanling (关岭, guānlíng) and look for connections there.

Zhijin Caves

织金洞, zhījīn dòng • 100km from Anshun, 150km from Guiyang • Daily 9am–5pm • ¥120 • Compulsory 2hr guided tours need ten people, so you might be tacked onto a larger group

The immensely impressive **Zhijin Caves** lie hidden under a remote karst landscape northwest of Anshun. This is Bouyei territory, the winding country road passing their typical stone villages, some with intriguing flat-topped towers in them – perhaps lookout posts, perhaps grain stores. Eventually the bus arrives at **ZHIJIN** (织金, zhījīn), a dismal town in the throes of major renovation, but there's a lively **market** selling huge stoneware jars of rice wine, sackfuls of chillies and little brass **horse bells** stamped with protective tiger faces.

Minibuses for the 25km run from Zhijin to the caves depart when full – otherwise you'll need a taxi. You arrive at the **visitors' centre** and hook up with **tours** that wind through untold numbers of caverns, the largest of which is 240m long, 170m wide and 60m high. There are stone "waterfalls", eerie mists and huge stalagmites and stalactites looking like grotesquely melted wax candles; the inevitable names are more credible than usual, including Old Woman and Daughter-in-law, Puxian on his Elephant and Hermit on the Mountain. It's not cold, but come prepared for slippery stone steps.

ARRIVAL AND GETTING AROUND | ZHIJIN CAVES

By bus The last buses leave Zhijin town about 4pm. Anshun Beimen station (6 daily; 3hr; ¥40); Guiyang (4 daily; 4.5hr; ¥65).

By minibus Minibuses run from Zhijin to the caves (40min; ¥5).

By taxi Taxis between Zhijin and the caves are ¥80.

ACCOMMODATION AND EATING

There's **accommodation** at Zhijin town but if you get here early enough you might not need to stay, as buses out run until mid-afternoon. Dog meat is sold everywhere; the *Jinye*'s **restaurant** does tasty lotus-wrapped sticky rice with thinly sliced bacon and Chinese dates.

Jindu 金都大酒店, jīndū dàjiǔdiàn. 18–22 Bei Da Jie, Jinzhong Lu ☎ 0857 762 8111. Typical of the newer places emerging from the rubble around town, with bed, bathroom, phone and TV. ¥180

Jinye 金叶宾馆, jīnyè bīnguǎn. Downhill from the bus station near the market ☎ 0857 762 5327. Not very spruce, but the best choice close to the bus station. ¥68, en suites with a/c and heater ¥128

Liuzhi and around

LIUZHI (六枝, liùzhī), 70km west of Anshun, sits on the edge of a huge **coalfield** sprawling westwards into Yunnan. The town itself is a core of market streets attached to the grimy train and bus station area, but you might need to overnight here if you plan to visit surrounding villages of the **Changjiao Miao**, an isolated, 4000-strong ethnic group which takes its name – meaning "Longhorn Miao" – from the pointy projections women wear in order to support their vast, bundled hairpieces.

Up in the dry limestone hills 35km north of Liuzhi, the two-street township of **SUOGA** (梭嘎, suōgā) is central to China's twelve Changjiao Miao settlements. Motorbike-taxis await to cart you a final 5km up to the village of **LONGGA** (龙嘎, lónggā), where the joint Chinese – Norwegian **Ecological Museum** (生态博物馆, shēngtài bówùguǎn; daily 8am–6pm; ¥10) offers a small collection of photos, textiles and domestic utensils. They don't really expect independent travellers here, though the Chinese-speaking staff are helpful, and might offer to guide you around.

The rest of Longga comprises a loose grouping of houses – including just one old, traditional rammed-earth-and-thatch affair – and muddy paths, dogs and livestock; you really want to catch the **Tiaohuapo Festival** at Chinese New Year (in January or February), where thousands of women don their enormous piles of hair and wear jackets decorated with batik and orange-and-white embroidery.

ARRIVAL AND DEPARTURE — LIUZHI AND AROUND

Liuzhi's **bus** and **train** stations are within 500m on the western side of town. Buses to Anshun, Guiyang and Liupanshui leave almost continuously until 5pm, but trains are quicker.

By bus Anshun (1hr 20min; ¥20); Guiyang (3hr; ¥60); Liupanshui (3hr; ¥36).
By train Anshun (20 daily; 45min); Beijing (1 daily; 38hr); Chengdu (3 daily; 16hr); Chongqing (2 daily; 12hr); Guangzhou (2 daily; 25hr); Guiyang (21 daily; 2hr 30min); Kaili (7 daily; 5hr 30min); Kunming (9 daily; 8hr); Liupanshui (20 daily; 1hr 40min); Shanghai (1 daily; 32hr); Yuping (5 daily; 7hr 30min); Zhenyuan (3 daily; 7hr).

GETTING AROUND

By minibus Liuzhi–Suoga minibuses (1hr 30min; ¥12) leave when full from the van park out the back of the bus station; there's irregular traffic in both directions until mid-afternoon.
By motorbike-taxi Suoga to Longga (¥5).

ACCOMMODATION

Most **hotels** in Liuzhi won't take foreigners. There's no formal accommodation at Longga, but the Ecological Museum can arrange for you to stay with a Miao family.

Pujiang 浦江大酒店, pǔjiāng dàjiǔdiàn. 40 Pingzhai Jiaotong Lu, Liuzhi ☎ 0858 531 8888. Diagonally across from Liuzhi's bus station, and around the corner from the train station, this mid-range place doesn't even blink when foreigners walk in. Rooms are great right down to the carpets, which urgently need replacement. There's a good Chinese restaurant. **¥158**

Liupanshui

六盘水, liùpánshuǐ

The administrative hub for western Guizhou's mining operations, **LIUPANSHUI** (also known as Shuicheng) fills a narrow valley 150km northwest of Liuzhi with a 5km band of cracked paving, coal-streaked buildings, fume-belching trucks and shoddy architecture. Around 500 BC the county was home to Guizhou's earliest-known kingdom – the **Yelang** – but the only reason you'd visit Liupanshui today is to catch **onwards transport**: either to Miao festivals at nearby **Nankai**, or northeast again **to Weining** and Cao Hai (see p.310).

ARRIVAL AND DEPARTURE — LIUPANSHUI

Liupanshui is on rail and road routes into Yunnan. The main **bus station** (汽车站, qìchēzhàn) is on Renmin Lu in the central section of town; the **train station** is 500m north on parallel Xibei Lu. Buses to Nankai depart 3km east (see p.310).

By bus Liuzhi (3hr; ¥36); Nankai (1hr 10min; ¥15); Weining (3hr; ¥40).
By train Anshun (20 daily; 2hr 30min); Beijing (1 daily; 40hr); Chengdu (3 daily; 17hr 30min); Chongqing (2 daily; 13hr 30min); Guangzhou (2 daily; 27hr); Guiyang (21 daily; 4hr); Kaili (7 daily; 7hr 10min); Kunming (9 daily; 6hr 20min); Liuzhi (20 daily; 1hr 40min); Shanghai (1 daily; 33hr); Yuping (5 daily; 9hr); Zhenyuan (3 daily; 8hr 20min).

GETTING AROUND

By taxi ¥7 to hire; the ride from the centre to the Nankai bus stop costs about ¥10.

ACCOMMODATION AND EATING

Liupanshui is the worst place in all Guizhou for **accommodation** – at the time of writing there were no cheap options for foreigners. For cheap eats, lanes around the bus station are packed with **noodle stalls**.

Hai'an 六盘水海岸酒店, liùpánshuǐ hǎi'àn jiǔdiàn. 59 Zhongshan Dadao, Liupanshui ☎0858 612 8888. On Liupanshui's main street, one block south of the bus station, this opulent choice is smart, well run and comes with large rooms. **¥238**

Beijing Laopu Kaoya 北京老铺烤鸭, běijīng lǎopù kǎoyā. 5/F Taiyang Plaza, Zhongshan Dadao, above Wal-Mart. Beijing duck with all the trimmings, prepared by white-hatted chefs who carve and serve at the table. There are fabulous views out of scenery windows into the hills. Whole duck with pancakes, vegetables and soup. **¥118**

DIRECTORY

Banks There are branches of the Bank of China and Construction Bank with ATMs on a roundabout at the intersection of central Zhongshan Dadao and Shuixi Lu.

Nankai
南开, nánkāi

About 50km northeast of Liupanshui, **NANKAI** is home to **Xiaohua Miao**, named after their capes embroidered with abstract "small flower" designs in orange, red and yellow. As at Longga, Chinese New Year (known here as **Tiaohuapo**) is the best time to visit, when tens of thousands of locals crowd out nearby slopes to sing, dance, play lusheng pipes, watch buffalo fights and drink rice wine. At other times this is a bit of an anticlimax, a one-street township, though there are a few simple stores and places to stay.

ARRIVAL AND DEPARTURE   NANKAI

By bus Buses to Nankai from Liupanshui depart Taijin Lu in Changba district (场坝, chǎngbà), 3km east of arrival points; catch bus #6 (¥1) from the train or bus stations and tell the driver where you want to get off. Nankai buses or minibuses cluster on the roadside and go when full; there's no station as such. Buses return to Liupanshui through the day.

ACCOMMODATION

Chaoyang 朝阳旅舍, cháoyáng lǚshè. Nankai. Typical of the village's handful of no-frills inns. Beds **¥25**

Weining and Cao Hai

WEINING (威宁, wēiníng) sits above the clouds on a 2000m-high plateau, and enjoys a surprisingly mild microclimate. The town is another small, run-down shell of a place populated by a friendly mix of Muslim Hui and Dahua ("Big-flower") Miao, though it's the local **Yi** who have cornered the festival scene with their big **Torch Festival** (see p.106) on the 24th of the six lunar month, and masked Cuotaiji dance, performed 40km away at **Luoga village** (裸嘎寨, luǒgā zhài) during the first two weeks of the Chinese New Year. Wintering wildfowl also mass nearby on shallow **Cao Hai** – including rare **black-necked cranes** (黑颈鹤, hēijǐng hè), golden eagles, white-tailed sea eagles, black storks, Eurasian cranes, spoonbills and assorted ducks – and it's easy to make a boat trip onto the lake to find them.

Cao Hai
草海, cǎo hǎi • ¥1.5 motor-rickshaw ride or 30min walk from Weining • Four-person punt trip ¥200 for 3hr after negotiation

Immediately south of Weining, **Cao Hai** literally means "Grass Sea", although the Chinese word *hai* here is actually a corruption of the Mongolian for "lake"; the name is a souvenir of the thirteenth-century Mongolian invasion of southwestern China. Either translation fits: Cao Hai fills a shallow, twenty-five-square-kilometre lake basin with reed beds and blue water, the core of a regional nature reserve. On the lakeshore you'll be approached by touts wanting to take you out on a punt, and on a sunny day, Cao Hai's tranquillity is a complete break with daily life in China. Wintering cranes stalk around the shallows near the shore and are fairly easy to catch on camera.

ARRIVAL AND DEPARTURE   **WEINING AND CAO HAI**

By bus from Weining Kunming (1 daily; 12hr; ¥115); Liupanshui (3hr; ¥40).

ACCOMMODATION AND EATING

There's a clutch of **hostels** around Weining's bus station charging ¥60 a double, but they don't generally take foreigners. Weining is famous for **sheep** and **potatoes** – skewers of chilli-dusted kebabs made of mutton or spud are sold everywhere. A line of restaurants outside the *Heijing He* hotel serve up inexpensive stir-fries and hotpots.

Heijing He 黑颈鹤大酒店, hēijǐnghè dàjiǔdiàn. Jianshe Dong Lu ☎0857 623 6888. Exit the bus station, turn right, and it's the concrete-and-glass pile 100m beyond the crossroads on the left. There's a mix of older doubles and newer rooms; service is slow but otherwise it's a decent standby. Old doubles ¥120, new doubles ¥180
Mingzhu 明珠酒店, míngzhū jiǔdiàn. 99 Xiangyang Lu ☎0857 623 3088. Slightly shabby front but surprisingly clean and tidy interior; much the same as the *Heijing He*. ¥160

Xingyi and around

Right down in Guizhou's southwesternmost corner, squashed between the border with Guangxi and Yunnan, **XINGYI** (兴义, xīngyì) is a small, tidy city surrounded by occasionally dramatic limestone scenery. Around 250km from Anshun, it's a useful stop on the **Nanning–Kunming railway**, not far up the line from Baise in Guangxi (p.351). You might spot a few Dahua Miao with boldly patterned capes in Xingyi's back-lane markets, but the highlight here is the **Maling Canyon**, a tortuous river gorge featuring rapids, waterfalls, deep cliffs and hanging vegetation.

The Maling Canyon

马岭河峡谷, mǎlǐng hé xiágǔ • ¥50 • Maling Qingshuihe (马岭清水河生态旅游公司, mǎlǐng qīngshuǐhé shēngtài lǚyóu gōngsī; 7 Shifu Lu, Xingyi ☎0859 221 1488) run 3hr rafting trips for ¥180; accommodation can book you in too • Buses run from Xingyi's east bus station daily 7am–7pm (25min; ¥15)

East of Xingyi, the **Qingshui River** carves out the deep, 15km-long **Maling Canyon**, divided into upper and lower sections. The **lower section** is 15km away and makes for a good couple of hours' walking, with flagstoned paths leading down into the gorge and then heading upstream, and suspension bridges link tracks along both sides of the river. It's all pretty spectacular, with the ice-blue water twisting into ribbon falls and rapids, the high gorge walls green and dripping with moisture. The canyon's **upper** part is 25km from town, where you can arrange **whitewater rafting** trips.

ARRIVAL AND DEPARTURE   **XINGYI AND AROUND**

By bus Buses terminate at the long-distance bus station (长途汽车站, chángtú qìchēzhàn), just west of the centre on Xihu Lu or the east bus station (汽车东站, qìchē dōngzhàn), east on Hunan Jie. Services overlap, though the east bus station handles all local traffic, including to Maling Canyon.
Destinations Anshun (4hr 30min; ¥68); Baise (8 daily; 4hr 30min; ¥65); Guiyang (6hr; ¥95); Kunming (2 daily; 7hr;

¥160); Nanning (5 daily; 7hr 30min; ¥145).
By train Xingyi is on the Nanning–Kunming line; there's no rail link to Guiyang. The train station is 15km east of town, connected by minibuses.
Destinations Baise (7 daily; 3hr 30min); Guangzhou (3 daily; 20hr); Guilin (2 daily; 12hr 45min); Kunming (7 daily; 5hr); Nanning (7 daily; 7hr); Shanghai (1 daily; 37hr).

ACCOMMODATION AND EATING

The *Panjiang*'s **restaurant** is accomplished and even has a basic English menu, otherwise look for noodle-soup and dog-hotpot kitchens around town.

Panjiang 盘江宾馆, pánjiāng bīnguǎn. 4 Panjiang Xi Lu, 700m south of central Panjiang Square ☎0859 322 3456. Long-running hotel with broad range of rooms, from business luxury to three-person dorms, all in good condition though the cheaper end of things is the better deal. Three-bed dorms ¥160, doubles ¥380
Shuiwu Binguan 税务宾馆, shuìwù bīnguǎn. Dongfeng Lu, not far from the east bus station ☎0859 323 6262. Standard urban hotel, run by the Tax Office. ¥180

4

Guangxi

FISHING WITH CORMORANTS ON THE LI RIVER

5

Guangxi

Squashed between cool, forested plateaus to the north and a tropical southern coastline, Guangxi (广西, guǎngxī) is famous across China for the forest of contorted, cloud-swept karst peaks that sprouts from its mosaic of paddy fields, sugar cane and banana plantations. The most spectacular formations surround the northeasterly city of Guilin, from where you can cruise down the Li River through the heart of the scenery to the rustic tourist havens of Xingping and Yangshuo, and then cycle, climb or hike deeper into the landscape. Further afield, you'll find rice terraces and wooden villages north of Guilin around Longji Titian and Sanjiang, waterfalls, prehistoric cliff paintings and rare monkeys along the southwesterly border with Vietnam, and enormous, newly discovered sinkholes outside the northwestern town of Leye.

Most of Guangxi's cities – including the provincial capital, **Nanning** and the steamy port of **Beihai**, which boasts several beaches – are pleasant enough but serve more as staging posts than destinations in their own right. Sleepy **Huangyao**, a pretty collection of antique bridges and cobbled streets east of Yangshuo, is the least developed of Guangxi's handful of old towns, and retains much of its centuries-old ambience. On the whole though, it's Guangxi's **countryside** where you'll want to spend most time; it's easy to spend a week exploring around Guilin, Yangshuo and Xingping, or village-hopping on local buses from **Yao** hamlets at Longji Titian to wooden **Dong** villages such as **Chengyang** and **Gaoding** up along the Hunan – Guizhou borders.

Guangxi's decent infrastructure makes **getting around** straightforward, with Guilin and Nanning acting as road, rail and airline hubs for the north and south respectively. **Local transport** is mostly by bus and minibus, and it's only in remoter corners that you'll be pushed to find regular traffic, though roads become slower and rougher around the provincial fringes. Trains are useful between Guilin, Nanning, Beihai and, especially, for **crossing into Vietnam**.

Spring and autumn are pleasantly warm, though summers here are hot and wet, excessively so in the south, despite winters north of Guilin being cold enough for snow. Regional **cooking** mixes hearty country dishes with a Southwestern Chinese affection for chillies, though a Cantonese interest in lighter flavours (and dim sum breakfast sessions) occasionally seeps through from neighbouring Guangdong.

Brief history

Guangxi and adjacent areas of northern Vietnam were settled by the **Baiyue**, or "Hundred Southern Clans", as early as the Spring and Autumn Period (770–476 BC). These clans included the Xi'ou and Luoyue peoples, ancestors of today's seventeen-million-strong **Zhuang** nationality, now the largest ethnic group in China after the

Highlights

❶ Li River Spend half a day drifting between romantically contorted karst peaks and placid rural scenery between Guilin and Yangshuo, the landscape unrolling before you like a Chinese scroll painting. **See p.325**

❷ Huangyao Soulful old town over near the Guangdong border, whose twisting lanes, stone bridges and low-key shop-homes make for an atmospheric night's stay. **See p.335**

❸ Longji Rice Terraces Trek or relax among mountainsides of steeply terraced fields, coloured vivid green in summer and rich gold in autumn, spending the night in Yao and Zhuang hamlets. **See p.337**

❹ Dong villages Whole villages of wooden houses and cobbled streets populated by the Dong people, featuring richly decorated drum towers and wind-and-rain bridges and set among a stunning rustic countryside. **See p.341**

❺ Dashiwei Tiankeng An easy trip to this remote, almost unknown landscape of rugged, overgrown limestone peaks, pocked by crater-sized vertical shafts dropping straight down into the earth. **See p.352**

❻ Zuo River More riverside peaks and quiet farm scenery form the backdrop to a cliff-full of intriguing rock paintings left here by Guangxi's Zhuang ethnic group over 2000 years ago. **See p.356**

HIGHLIGHTS ARE MARKED ON THE MAP ON P.316–317

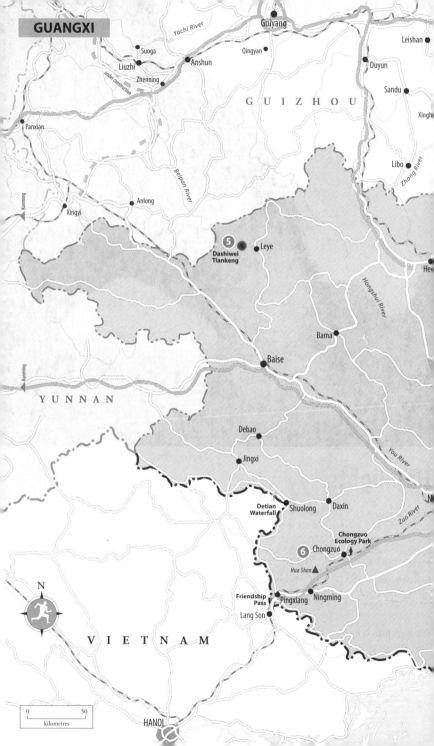

GUANGXI

Yachi River

Suoga
Liuzhi
Zhenning
under construction
Anshun

Guiyang

Qingyan

Leishan

Duyun

Sandu

Xingh

G U I Z H O U

Panxian

Beipan River

Anlong

Xingyi

Kunming

Libo

Zhang River

5 Dashiwei Tiankeng

Leye

Hongshui River

He

Bama

Baise

Kunming

Y U N N A N

Debao

Jingxi

You River

Detian Waterfall

Shuolong

Daxin

Zuo River

Chongzuo Ecology Park

6 Chongzuo

Hua Shan ▲

Friendship Pass

Pingxiang

Ningming

Lang Son

N

V I E T N A M

0 ____ 50
kilometres

HANOI

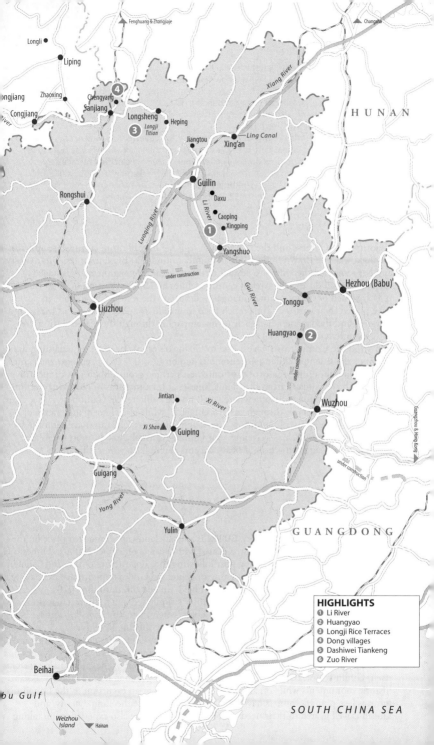

HUNAN

Changsha

Fenghuang & Zhangjiajie

Longli

Liping

Zhaoxing

ongjiang

Congjiang

River

Chengyang ④

Sanjiang

Longsheng ③

Heping

Longji
Titian

Jiangtou

Xiang River

Xing'an — Ling Canal

Rongshui

Luoqing River

GUILIN

Daxu

Li River

Caoping

Xingping ①

Yangshuo

under construction

Gui River

Hezhou (Babu)

Tonggu

Liuzhou

Huangyao ②

under construction

Jintian

Xi River

Wuzhou

under construction

Guangzhou & Hong Kong

Xi Shan ▲

Guiping

Guigang

Yong River

Yulin

GUANGDONG

Beihai

bu Gulf

Weizhou
Island ▲ Hainan

SOUTH CHINA SEA

HIGHLIGHTS
① Li River
② Huangyao
③ Longji Rice Terraces
④ Dong villages
⑤ Dashiwei Tiankeng
⑥ Zuo River

5

KARST

Southwest China's massive **karst** formations began life millions of years ago as a coral reef, which sprawled over much of what is now Southeast Asia. Geological shuffles compressed this into **limestone** and lifted it out of the sea, where the elements sculpted it into clusters of spiky peaks rising straight out of the surrounding plains. You'll find similar scenery to the Guilin area through parts of Guizhou and Yunnan, most famously in miniature at the **Shilin stone forest** outside Kunming (see p.195).

Limestone karst is also known for its vast subterranean **caverns**, hollowed out by underground rivers; China's best, lit by garish coloured lighting, are at Zhijin (see p.308) and Longgong (see p.306) in Guizhou. For kingfisher-blue water and **calcified terraces**, try Jiuzhaigou or Huanglong in Sichuan (see p.117), or Yunnan's Baishui Tai (p.242); while if you're after some of the world's largest **sinkholes** – formed when limestone caves collapse in on themselves – then visit Leye (see p.352) in northern Guangxi, or Wulong (see p.160) and Xiaozhai (see p.170) in Chongqing.

majority Han Chinese and then part of the regional bronze-drum cultures (see p.350). Guangxi was first drawn under China's thumb around 220 BC during the Qin dynasty, and has remained there despite periods of unrest – the Zhuang themselves staged a major rebellion during the twelfth century, while the **Taiping Uprising** of 1850 (see p.344) spilled out from central Guangxi to devastate the rest of China. Foreign powers have played their part too. The French tried to invade from Vietnam in the 1880s, and warlords and the Japanese had their turns rampaging through the region during the early twentieth century.

In 1958 the Communists gave a nod to Guangxi's ethnic heritage by renaming the province the **Guangxi Zhuang Autonomous Region** (广西壮族自治区, guǎngxī zhuàngzú zìzhìqū) though, unlike many of the Southwest's ethnic groups, there's not much to distinguish the Zhuang from the Han Chinese, at least in terms of colourful clothing and festivals. **Language** is somewhere you'll notice a difference: Cantonese rather than Mandarin is the default through eastern Guangxi, while elsewhere a huge range of local dialects are in use. In addition, street signs often use Zhuang transliterations instead of *pinyin* – such as "Gveilinz" for Guilin. As usual though, most locals are familiar with Mandarin – even if heavy accents can make answers difficult to understand.

Guilin

桂林, guìlín

Northeastern Guangxi's main city, **GUILIN** is a nicely landscaped, modern place on the west bank of the **Li River**, its suburbs dotted with clusters of iconic, 200m-tall limestone peaks. Having evolved as a trading post following the construction of the **Ling Canal** in 219 BC (see p.324), the first Ming emperor cemented Guilin's importance by making it the regional capital in 1372, a position it held, on and off, until the 1920s. Upheavals through the early twentieth century culminated in a million refugees pouring into Guilin during the war with Japan (when there was also a US airbase here), until the invaders finally captured the city after heavy shelling in 1944.

Today, largely low-rise and with little heavy industry, Guilin has dusted off its tourist credentials and bounced back as a busy hub for exploring northern Guangxi's limestone landscape, river scenery and ethnic groups. Though the pick of these lie outside the city itself, Guilin is a pleasant place to spend a day roaming among legend-laden peaks and historic monuments while organizing a **Li River cruise** or an excursion to the Longji rice terraces (see p.337). Tourists have been flocking here since the Tang dynasty, and Guilin is well geared to their needs: though some locals are also experienced in taking

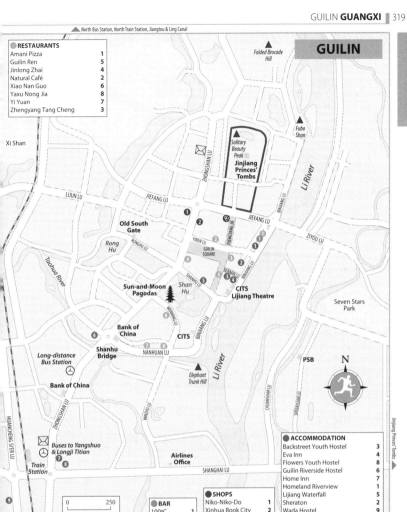

RESTAURANTS

Amani Pizza	1
Guilin Ren	5
Jinlong Zhai	4
Natural Café	2
Xiao Nan Guo	6
Yaxu Nong Jia	8
Yi Yuan	7
Zhengyang Tang Cheng	3

ACCOMMODATION

Backstreet Youth Hostel	3
Eva Inn	4
Flowers Youth Hostel	8
Guilin Riverside Hostel	6
Home Inn	7
Homeland Riverview	1
Lijiang Waterfall	5
Sheraton	2
Wada Hostel	9

SHOPS

Niko-Niko-Do	1
Xinhua Book City	2

BAR

100°C	1

advantage of the unwary. **Petty crime** – picking pockets and slashing backpacks – is a problem, as are relentless offers of "massages", and people posing as students trying to lure you into a restaurant or art gallery for various scams (see p.46).

The lakes

Rong Hu and Shan Hu, two stubby lakes on either side of central Zhongshan Lu, trace the lines of Guilin's Ming-dynasty defensive moats, now landscaped with trees and paving and turned into urban parks. There's a historical touch in the **old south gate** (古南门, gǔ nánmén) and a fragment of stone wall on westerly **Rong Hu** (榕湖, róng hú); **Shan Hu** (杉湖, shān hú) has more undergrowth, an antique-style humpbacked stone bridge, and the twin **Sun-and-Moon Pagodas** (日月双塔, rìyuè shuāng tǎ; ¥30), whose 30m-high towers are painted gold, red and green, and strikingly outlined in fairy lights after dark.

5

The Jingjiang Princes' Palace

靖江王城, jìngjiāng wáng chéng • Daily 8.30am–5pm • ¥70

Having conquered China in 1368 and become the first Ming emperor, the peasant-general **Hongwu** appointed his grandson Zhu Shouqian as the "**Jingjiang Prince**", and posted him off to govern southern China from Guilin. This was a backhanded compliment: it showed Zhu was trusted enough to run what amounted to his own kingdom; but it also removed a potential rival – and his loyal private army – a long way from the centre of real power.

Zhu Shouqian constructed the **Jingjiang Princes' Palace** as his own "Forbidden City" in 1372 – some 34 years before Beijing's more extensive version was completed. He eventually fell from favour, but the palace housed his thirteen successors before burning down in 1652 as the Ming dynasty collapsed in chaos. Today, Guangxi Normal University occupies the site, where a **museum** displays portraits of the Jingjiang Princes and hosts short performances of **ground opera** (see p.307). Restored original fragments include the 5m-high crenellated **outer walls**; and, at the yellow entrance gate, a **stone slab** carved with swirling clouds but missing the usual dragons – indicating the residence of royalty, but not of an emperor.

Solitary Beauty Peak

独秀峰, dúxiù fēng

At the back of the palace grounds, **Solitary Beauty Peak** is a short, sharp spire scaled by 306 steps, which protected the original palace from the "unlucky" northern direction. **Rock inscriptions** here include one by Song-dynasty official Wan Zhengong – 桂林山水甲天下 (guìlín shānshuǐ jiǎ tiānxià; "Guilin's scenery is the best under heaven") – which tourist authorities would have you believe is the sole reason for the city's fame. There are great views of the low-rise city centre from the summit, while the **cave** at the base – now full of modern Taoist sculptures – was opened up by the tenth prince, reputedly breaking the hill's protective power and dooming his dynasty.

Along the river

Three small **riverside peaks** linked by an hour-long walk provide a taster of local landscapes and legends, though don't feel you have to conquer them all – there are plenty more between here and Yangshuo. Most of the walk is pleasantly shaded by a mix of fig and sweet-scented **osmanthus trees** – "Guilin" means "Osmanthus Forest".

Elephant Trunk Hill

象鼻山, xiàngbí shān • Daily 6.30am–10pm • ¥40

Kick off southeast of the centre with **Elephant Trunk Hill** on Minzhu Lu, which really does look like an elephant taking a drink from the river (rather meanly, screens have been built on nearby Binjiang Lu to stop you admiring the view for free). The story goes that a passing emperor abandoned the animal in Guilin after it fell sick; the townspeople nursed it back to health but the emperor demanded its return, whereupon the elephant turned to stone in defiance. Paths climb to a dumpy brick pagoda on the top, and down to the "trunk" at river level.

Fubo Shan

伏波山, fúbō shān • Daily 7am–7pm • ¥15

From Elephant Trunk Hill, it's a kilometre north along **Binjiang Lu** to **Fubo Shan**, an isolated peak edging into the river. The name means "Quelling the Waves Hill", after a battle between the giant Jie Die and a river demon; thousands of weatherbeaten **Buddha carvings** lining the footpath to the top are also said to have protective power. At the base, the **sword-testing stone** is a large stalactite hanging within inches of the ground inside a grotto, and really does appear to have been hacked through.

Folded Brocade Hill

叠彩山, diécǎi shān • Daily 7am–7pm • ¥20

A final 500m up the Li River is **Folded Brocade Hill**, four undulating outcrops whose layered seams resemble an untidily stacked pile of fabric. There's a huge **tunnel** here with more Buddhist carvings and rock inscriptions dating back to the Tang and Song dynasties, and a path to the peak's 223m-high summit, with the best river views in town.

Seven Stars Park

七星公园, qīxīng gōngyuán • 500m east of the river at the end of Ziyou Lu • Daily 7am–7pm • ¥65 • Bus #11 from Zhongshan Lu and Jiefang Lu

Reached over a covered bridge, **Seven Stars Park** is a potted version of Guangxi: seven curiously shaped limestone hills arranged in the shape of the Big Dipper come complete with overgrown vegetation, a small cave system and even a few wild monkeys. Paths climb to pavilions dotting the peaks, the best of which is **Camel Hill** (骆驼山, luòtuo shān), which feasibly resembles a dromedary. The **caves** (七星洞, qīxīng dòng) have relatively few formations, but moody lighting and a small underground waterfall perk things up. The park is large enough to spend a couple of hours exploring and is popular with wedding photographers, so expect to see couples posing in their best among formal flowerbeds.

The Jingjiang Princes' Tombs

靖江王陵, jìngjiāng wánglíng • In the countryside 6km northeast of Guilin • Daily 9.30am–5.30pm • ¥50 • Bus #24 from Jiefang Lu or taxi

Set at the foot of rounded Yao Shan, the **Jingjiang Princes' Tombs** mark where eleven of the fourteen Jingjiang Princes were interred between 1408 and 1612. As such it's one of the most important collections of Ming tombs in China, though there's not so much to see – only the low, circular mound of the third prince, Zhuang Jian, has been tidied up to reveal an avenue of life-sized sculptures of zodiac animals, horses, grooms and eunuchs. These are carved in the blocky Song style: the early Ming dynasty shook off the recent humiliation of Mongol rule by looking back to the purely Chinese Song dynasty for artistic inspiration.

Incidentally, though two of the missing princes died in exile after stirring up trouble, the whereabouts of **Zhu Heng**, last of the line, is unknown – he vanished after fleeing Guilin in 1650.

Xi Shan

西山, xī shān • Northwest of the city centre • Daily 9am–5pm • ¥40 • Bus #3 from opposite the train station or taxi

Around 2km from the city centre, **Xi Shan** is similar in scale and scenery to Seven Stars Park, the bonus here being the city **museum** (free) – featuring antique porcelain and a collection of ethnic textiles – and **Xi Qinglin Temple** (西庆林寺, xī qìnglín sì), an important Buddhist monastery founded in the Tang dynasty. Nearby niches are filled with hundreds of exquisitely executed statues ranging from 10cm in height to more than life-sized.

Reed Flute Cave

芦笛岩, lúdí yán • Daily 8am–5.30pm • ¥60 • Northwest of the city centre on bus #3 from opposite the train station

Three kilometres north of Xi Shan, on the same bus route, **Reed Flute Cave** is a huge warren eaten into the south side of Guangming Shan which once provided a refuge from banditry and Japanese bombs. The caverns are not so extensive by regional standards, but there are some interesting formations and a small lake, which nicely

5

mirrors the wild, colourful lighting. You're meant to follow one of the tours that run every twenty minutes, but you can always linger inside and pick up a later group if you want to spend more time.

| ARRIVAL AND DEPARTURE | GUILIN |

BY PLANE

Liangjiang International Airport (桂林两江国际机场, guìlín liǎngjiāng guójì jīchǎng), 30km west of town. An airport bus (daily every 30min 6.30am–9pm; ¥20) runs to the airlines office on Shanghai Lu, just south of the city centre. Buy plane tickets from the airlines office (☎077 3389 0000 or ☎077 3384 7252) or Air China, beside the *Sheraton* at 15 Binjiang Lu (☎077 3286 6567, ⓦairchina.com).

Destinations Beihai (2 daily; 1hr); Beijing (6 daily; 3hr); Chengdu (1 daily; 1hr 30min); Chongqing (4 daily; 1hr); Guangzhou (5 daily; 50min); Guiyang (1 daily; 45min); Kunming (1 daily; 1hr 30min); Shanghai (3 daily; 2hr); Shenzhen (3 daily; 50min). Also several weekly each to Malaysia, Singapore and Hong Kong.

BY BUS

Long-distance bus station (桂林汽车总站, guìlín qìchē zǒngzhàn), Zhongshan Lu. Buses to almost everywhere, local and long-distance.

Destinations Beihai (5 daily; 8hr; ¥120); Guangzhou (8 daily; 12hr; ¥180); Guiping (1 daily; 6hr; ¥78); Heping (for Longji Titian; 2hr; ¥20); Hezhou (for connections to Huangyao; 3hr; ¥38); Longsheng (2hr; ¥32); Nanning (6hr; ¥110); Sanjiang (4hr; ¥48); Shenzhen (3 daily; 12hr; ¥180); Xing'an (90min; ¥15).

North bus station (客运总北车站, kèyùnzǒng běichēzhàn), 3km north of the downtown via bus #10

from Zhongshan Lu. Mostly local destinations, though long-distance services also wind up here.

Destinations Lingchuan (1hr; ¥5).

Train station forecourt Most use for the frequent departures to Yangshuo.

Destinations Beihai (6hr; ¥120); Dazhai (1 daily, 8.30am; 2hr 30min; ¥40); Ping An (1 daily, 10.30am; 2hr; ¥40); Yangshuo (1hr 20min; ¥18).

BY TRAIN

Guilin train station (桂林火车站, guìlín huǒchēzhàn) is just south of the centre on Zhongshan Lu. Buy advance tickets at the station ticket office (daily 7am–8pm) or the rail office at 241 Zhongshan Zhong Lu (daily 8am–8pm); Guilin's popularity makes it advisable to book sleepers at least three days in advance.

Destinations Beijing (4 daily; 28hr); Chengdu (1 daily; 26hr); Chongqing (1 daily; 19hr 30min); Guangzhou (2 daily; 11hr); Guiyang (1 daily; 12hr); Kunming (3 daily; 18hr); Nanning (16 daily; 6hr); Shanghai (4 daily; 24hr); Shenzhen (1 daily; 13hr).

Guilin North station is 3km north of the centre on Zhongshan Bei Lu; bus #18 from Jiefang Dong Lu. Most traffic from here also travels via the main station.

BY BOAT

Li River cruises (see p.325) leave from the docks 25km south of Guilin.

GETTING AROUND

By bus City buses (¥1.5 for normal buses, ¥2 for a/c) cover everywhere within a 3km radius of the centre between 6–7am and 8pm or later.

By taxi ¥7 to hire. They cruise the main streets, or find them outside the train station.

INFORMATION

Tourist information Accommodation tour desks book transport tickets and organize Li River cruises, trips to Crown Cave (¥180 including return bus, entry and Chinese-speaking tour guide) and day excursions to the Longji Rice Terraces

(¥180 including return bus, entry and guide). Alternatively book tours with the CITS (11 Binjiang Lu ☎077 3288 6393, ⓦguilincits.com). It's worth trying a couple of places to compare prices, though deals are broadly similar.

ACCOMMODATION

Guilin's **hotels** mainly cater to tour-groups, with a few **hostels** for the independent budget market. Riverside Binjiang Lu is close to central attractions, but trees effectively screen out river views except from the highest floors.

Backstreet Youth Hostel 后街国际青年旅馆, hòujiē guójì qīngnián lǚguǎn. 3 Renmin Lu ☎077 3281 9936, ✉guilinhostel@hotmail.com. Close to the river and pedestrian street, this hostel has ordinary rooms but comes with all the usual perks – café, internet, booking

desk. Dorms **¥30**, doubles **¥120**

Eva Inn 四季春天酒店, sìjì chūntiān jiǔdiàn. 6 Binjiang Lu, opposite the Sheraton ☎077 3283 0666, ⓦevainn.com. Popular, modern boutique-style affair near the river with smart rooms. **¥350**

★ **Flowers Youth Hostel** 花满国际青年旅馆, huāmǎn guójì qīngnián lǚguǎn. 6 Shangzhi Gang, Block 2, Zhongshan Lu ☎077 3383 9625, ⓦyhaguilin. com. Cross from the train station, walk through a dreary alley alongside the *Home Inn*, take the stairs up a flight and you'll find this bright, cheerful place, with a bar, café, internet, dorms and doubles. Dorms ¥30, doubles ¥120

★ **Guilin Riverside Hostel** 桂林九龙别墅酒店, guìlín jiǔlóng biéshù jiǔdiàn. 6 Zhumu Xiang, Danmen Qiao ☎077 3258 0215, ⓦguilin-hostel.com. Tucked down a quiet back lane, this friendly, central place is more like a smart guesthouse than a hostel. Wi-fi, bike rental and laundry available. Full breakfast ¥20 extra. Twin-bunk dorms ¥100, doubles ¥180

Home Inn 如家快捷酒店, rújiā kuàijié jiǔdiàn. Opposite the train station on Zhongshan Lu ☎077 3387 7666. Local representative of this budget hotel chain, offering value for money if you avoid the cheaper, windowless rooms. ¥199

Homeland Riverview 好地方江景酒店, hǎodìfang jiāngjǐng jiǔdiàn. 17 Binjiang Lu ☎077 3288 6611. Another urban budget hotel option with the usual comforts, though not worth the extra for a "riverview" room. ¥250

Lijiang Waterfall 漓江大瀑布饭店, líjiāng dàpùbù fàndiàn. 1 Shanhu Lu ☎077 3282 2881, ⓦwaterfallguilin.com. Huge tour-group and conference-delegate venue with all the high-end frills – and a waterfall in the lobby. ¥1550

Sheraton 喜来登大宇大饭店, xǐláidēng dàyǔ dàfàndiàn. 15 Binjiang Lu ☎077 3282 5588, ⓦsheraton.com/guilin. One of the nicest hotels in town, with pools, a gym, access to golf clubs and their priciest upper rooms just clearing the treetops for views across the river to Seven Stars Park. ¥1250

Wada Hostel 桂林瓦当旅舍, guìlín wǎdāng lǚshè. 212 Huangcheng Xi Yi Lu, about 300m south of the train station ☎077 3215 4888, ⓦwada-hostel.com. Unpretentious, helpful hostel with all the essential services – the popular *Bamboo Bar* is good for a couple of beers if you're in the area. Dorms ¥30, doubles ¥120

EATING

Guilin's restaurants are known for serving exotic game meats, with the menu often displayed alive in cages, tanks and buckets. There's also a taste for country-style **slow-simmered soups** serving 2–6 people, featuring duck, chicken or meatballs stewed with wild mushrooms, bamboo shoots and medicinal herbs. For **Western fare**, try the cafés along Zhengyang Jie and Binjiang Lu.

Amani Pizza 阿玛尼意式餐厅, āmǎní yìshì cāntīng. Binjiang Lu. Tiny place with a brick and wood interior, serving the best pizzas in town (from ¥35) – though their fruit juices are pretty bland.

Guilin Ren 桂林人聚福林美食苑, guìlín rén jùfúlín měishí yuàn. Zhengyang Jie. Local food and an easily navigated Chinese photo-menu. Everyone orders their excellent soups – the pork trotter with papaya, and meatballs with wild mushrooms are both popular.

Jinlong Zhai 金龙寨, jīnlóng zhài. 4/F, cnr of Zhongshan Lu and the adjacent plaza. Guangxi restaurant chain with typical country dishes featuring taro, huge soups, roast fowl and fatty pork. If this doesn't appeal, try their Sichuanese and Chinese staples, and less heavyweight cold snacks. Mains around ¥35.

Natural Café 闻莺阁, wényīng gé. Yiren Lu. Eclectic "foreign" menu including tasty (if not especially authentic) spaghetti, borscht, pizza and Southeast Asian coconut curries from ¥25, and steaks for around ¥65.

★ **Xiao Nan Guo** 小南国菜馆, xiǎo nán guó càiguǎn. 3 Wenming Lu. Lively local-style restaurant serving large portions, and always full of cheerful crowds.

Best deals are the crispy, juicy "barrel chicken" (木桶鸡, mùtǒng jī) and aromatic "pepper spare ribs" (黑椒牛仔骨, hēi jiāo niúzǎi gǔ). There's no English menu. Around ¥45/head.

Yaxu Nong Jia 雅叙农家菜馆, yǎxù nóngjiā càiguǎn. 159 Nanhuan Lu. Good choice for local rural cooking, with staff dressed in peasant garb and game choices on the menu including mallard, wild boar, sparrows, eels and mutjac deer. Pricey, with mains upwards of ¥50.

★ **Yi Yuan** 怡园饭店, yíyuán fàndiàn. 106 Nanhuan Lu. Sichuanese food served in comfortable surroundings, though quality varies depending on who is in the kitchen. There's an English menu; try the "mouth-watering" chicken, "crackling rice", garlic pork and dry-cooked aromatic beef. Mains ¥35/dish.

Zhengyang Tang Cheng 正阳汤城, zhèngyáng tāngchéng. Zhengyang Jie. The name (meaning "Soup City") and ceramic stockpots piled either side of the door give the game away. There's a perfunctory English menu; you're best off using the Chinese one or pointing to other diners' dishes. Their stewed pork, fried pigeon and slow-cooked medicinal soups are good. About ¥40 a head.

DRINKING AND NIGHTLIFE

In addition to the following, there are Western-style bars along pedestrianized Zhengyang Jie, serving imported beer in pub-like surroundings. The area gets very lively at night, when the action spreads out around central **Guilin Square** (桂林广场, guìlín guǎngchǎng).

5

100°C 百度酒吧, bǎidù jiǔbā. Binjiang Lu. Opened in 2004, this claims to be the longest-running Western-style club in town, with a restaurant-bar downstairs and regular live music and DJ sessions on the second floor. Their karaoke provides a very Chinese experience though.

Lijiang Theatre 漓江剧院, lijiāng jùyuàn. Binjiang Lu ☎ 077 3285 1280. Hosts the nightly song-and-dance spectacular "Fantastic Guilin", with simpering

performers draped in colourful ethnic garb dancing an singing against rear-screen projections of local scenery It's all very bright, gloriously cheesy and totally fake; you're after this sort of thing, "Liu Sanjie" at Yangshu (see p.333) goes even more overboard and uses the rea landscape. Tickets from the office out front cost ¥150- 220, with the upper end getting you larger seats closer t the stage.

SHOPPING

For **tourist souvenirs**, clothing and bright knick-knacks, head to pedestrianized Zhengyang Jie and its offshoots, or th nightly street market along Zhongshan Lu, a block either side of the Shanhu Bridge.

Niko-Niko-Do Cnr of Zhongshan and Jiefang Lu. Guilin's largest department store, with several floors of clothes and household appliances, and a supermarket in the basement.

Xinhua Book City 新华书城, xīnhuá shū chéng Diagonally across from Niko-Niko-Do, this has five levels o DVDs, music and books, with a good range of translate Chinese classics on Floor 3.

DIRECTORY

Banks Several of Guilin's larger Bank of China branches have ATMs and handle currency exchanges, with the most convenient at the Zhongshan Lu–Nanhuan Lu crossroads.
Left luggage The bus station's left luggage office is open daily 6.30am–11.30pm.

PSB and visa extensions The entry-exit departmen (公安局出入境管理处, gōng'ānjú chūrù jìngguǎn líchù) is east of the river at 16 Shijiayuan L (bus #25 eastbound along Jiefang Lu stops outside Mon–Fri 9am–1pm and 3–5pm; ☎ 077 3582 9930) Extensions usually take around 24hr.

Around Guilin

A couple of countryside sights are accessible by public bus from Guilin; each need a full day to explore properly. Closest to town, **Jiangtou** is worth a look if your itinerary in the Southwest doesn't include any other old villages; the **Ling Canal** is of mainly historical interest, though its great age might justify a visit.

Jiangtou

江头村, jiāngtóu cūn • Bus from Guilin's north bus station to Lingchuan (灵川, língchuān; ¥5), from there, get a bus to Jiuwu town (九屋, jiǔwū; ¥5) – about 90min in total; from Jiwu, it's a couple of kilometres to Jiangtou – walk or hire a three-wheeler for a couple of yuan

Some 30km north of Guilin, **JIANGTOU** is an attractive rural village whose residents claim descent from **Zhou Dunyi**, a Song-dynasty philosopher who espoused an influential version of Confucianism. Its narrow stone lanes are full of 300-year-old family compounds built in the local style – you can wander around some of them, though most are still lived in – with solid brick and stone outer walls, elaborate fire-baffle eaves and beautiful interior woodwork. There are also a few wells and ornamental stone lions dotted around, but once you get past its buildings Jiangtou feels pleasantly under-populated – making it a nicer prospect than many of China's more touristed antique villages. As yet there are no visitor facilities, so bring a packed lunch and spend a couple of hours wandering about with a camera.

The Ling Canal

灵渠, líng qú • Daily 8am–6pm • ¥50 • Buses run from Guilin's long-distance station to Xing'an (90min; ¥15)

In 214 BC China's first emperor, Qin Shi Huang, ordered the construction of the **Ling Canal** between the Xiang and Gui rivers, 80km northeast of Guilin. This linked together

5

ributaries of the Yangzi River (see p.162) and the Pearl River, allowing Qin Shi Huang to shift troops down to quell the troublesome south – and also creating a new trade route between central and southern China which remained in used for two thousand years.

No longer properly navigable, the canal is over 36km long, with some of the key structures preserved on the southeastern edge of the small town of **XING'AN** (兴安县, Xīng'ān xiàn). Alongside superfluous temples, pretty arched bridges and ornamental locks, you can see where the **Hua dyke** splits the Xiang into two, one part flowing northwards and the rest pooling behind the **Xiaotianping overflow dyke**, to be diverted again and flow down to Guilin as the Li River. As is sometimes the case in China, it's the site's associations, rather than tangible relics, which spark the imagination.

The Li River

漓江, lí jiāng

The **Li River** runs southeast for over 300km from Guilin down to join the **Xi River** (see p.344), its first 85km passing through a landscape of jutting, bizarrely shaped karst peaks, each with accompanying poetic name and apocryphal legend. A **cruise** down the Li allows a few hours' escape into a lush, rustic Chinese idyll: there's splendid scenery, a handful of old market towns such as **Daxu**, paddy fields and bamboo groves, placid water buffalo splashing about in the shallows and fishermen in conical hats poling around on nearly submerged bamboo rafts. About halfway along, the peaks reach a crescendo between **Yangdi** and the village of **Xingping**, where you could settle down for a few days' pleasant exploration or continue the cruise to touristy, foreigner-friendly **Yangshuo**, which offers more scope for an extended stay and intimate investigation of the scenery.

Daxu

大圩, dàxū • Buses run from Guilin's long-distance bus station (40min; ¥9)

During the Qing dynasty, flood-prone **DAXU**, 25km southeast of Guilin on the Li River, was a busy market port at the junction of now-defunct waterways into

---

CRUISING THE LI RIVER

Broad, flat-bottomed, single-storey **cruise boats to Yangshuo** – all of which have open-air observation decks up top – depart from wharfs about 25km southeast of Guilin near Daxu town. The cheapest deals are on **Chinese tours** (¥280), where you get transport to the wharf, lunch and a one-way, five-hour cruise to Yangshuo. **Foreign tours** (¥350–500, depending on the season and who you book with) offer the same deal plus an English-speaking guide, reportedly better food and a bus back from Yangshuo at the end of the trip. If you're taking more than a day-pack along, check in advance that there will be space. These cruises do not pull in anywhere along the river; if you want to visit the sights mentioned below, you'll have to backtrack from Yangshuo or Guilin. On-board tour guides often tout for an add-on excursion to the **Yulong river area** (see p.333) after arrival in Yangshuo – definitely worth considering if you're just day-tripping from Guilin.

Guilin's hostels can also arrange a six-person **bamboo raft** trip through the pick of the scenery between the halfway point at **Yangdi wharf** (杨堤码头, yángdī mǎtóu) and Xingping (¥100/person; 2hr); you'll get a bus to Yangdi, but there's no food, guide or storage space for large bags. Chinese speakers might be able to arrange a similar deal themselves from Caoping (see p.326).

Autumn is probably the best month to come, as water levels are high and the crowds are easing off – they get three million tourists a year here, and during the summer you can almost walk the length of the river on cruise boats. When the river's running low in **winter**, cruises sometimes only make hour-long circuits from Yangdi to the edge of the scenery, before returning to docks and bussing passengers to Yangshuo – though they won't mention this in advance and you'll get charged the same.

5

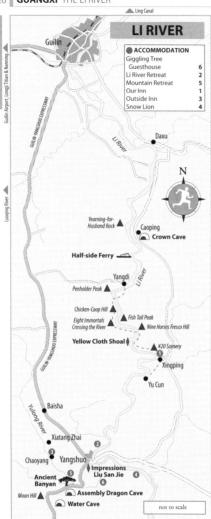

western Guangxi. Daxu is a bit dishevelled today, though its 2km-long flagstoned main street makes for an interesting few hours' excursion from Guilin, flanked by antique, wooden-fronted shops selling snacks and souvenir trinkets. Interesting structures include the arched, Ming-dynasty **Longevity Bridge** (万寿桥, wànshòu qiáo) and some of the smaller stores, which still carry on their traditional trades.

To Caoping and Crown Cave

Cruise boats (see p.325) kick off across the river from Daxu at Zhujiang Wharf, from where it's an uneventful ride to an isolated cluster of peaks capped by **Yearning-For-Husband Rock** (望夫石, wàngfū shí), said to be a woman who turned to stone waiting for her fisherman husband to return home.

Not far on, **CAOPING** (草坪, cǎopíng) is a small service town; cruise boats don't stop but buses run from Guilin (1hr; ¥12). Chinese speakers can organize small **sampans to Xingping** from here, though you'll need to be a tough negotiator – ¥150 per person is a fair deal. Caoping's main attraction – though not a stop for cruise boats – is **Crown Cave** (冠岩, guān yán; daily 8.30am–4.30pm; ¥70), a 3km-long system burrowing into a peak and full of the usual rock formations and coloured lights, which you travel through by light rail, elevators and a boat.

Caoping to Xingping

Downstream from Caoping, a cliff jutting into the river on the west bank obstructs footpaths, meaning local travellers have to get around it by boat (named the **half-side ferry**, as it stays on the same bank). After this comes the village wharf at **Yangdi** and then you're in among the best of the scenery, as the peaks suddenly mass along the riverside. Three-pronged **Penholder Peak** (神笔峰, shénbǐ fēng) drops down sheer into the water, followed by **Chicken-coop Hill** (鸡笼山, jīlóng shān), **Fish-tail Peak** (鱼尾岭, yúwěi lǐng) and **Eight Immortals Crossing the River** (八仙过江, bāxiān guòjiāng), before the river squeezes past **Nine Horses Fresco Hill** (九马画山, jiǔmǎhuà shān), a 100m-high cliff on whose weathered face you can pick out some horsey patterns. Look into the water past here for **Yellow Cloth Shoal** (黄布滩, huángbù tān), a flat, submerged rock at one of the shallowest spots on the river.

Xingping

兴坪, xīngpíng

Just downstream from Yellow Cloth Shoal, **XINGPING** sits on a sharp bend in the river about 70km from Guilin. Until recently an obscure market town, Xingping is gearing up to rival Yangshuo as a tourist destination: the first backpacker joints are already doing brisk trade, the best of the Li River's scenery is immediately upstream and news of an impending **rail line**, due to open around 2015, has seen property prices surge as developers move in.

At first glance the town, a dusty grid of concrete apartments connected to the river by 500m-long **Rongtan Lu**, isn't much to get excited about. But there's a busy **market** held on calendar dates ending in a 3, 6 and 9, full of hopeful dogs cruising the butchers stalls, stocky women lugging their purchases home on carrypoles, and ropy-muscled farmers with carelessly dangling cigarettes buying bamboo furniture and examining nasty bits of dried wild animals.

Walk back behind Rongtan Lu, and you're on atmospheric **Lao Jie**, a lane of shabby old teahouses and shops where men play cards, undisturbed – as yet – by the few tourist cafés and stalls. Down at the **docks**, a flotilla of bamboo rafts (often made from plastic piping nowadays), sampans and small **cruise boats** offer rides upstream to Yangdi, or down to Yu Cun and Yangshuo (see p.328).

Walks around Xingping

Walks head off in all directions, the easiest being fifteen minutes upstream from the docks to the **¥20 Scenery** (20元背景图, èrshí yuán bèijǐngtú) – the landscape on the back of a twenty yuan note. Paths continue for 17km from here **to Yangdi** via Nine Horses Fresco Hill, Chicken Coop Hill and the rest, though you'll need to use the cross-river ferries in several places – it's also cyclable. For the shorter hike to **Yu Cun**, see p.328.

ARRIVAL AND DEPARTURE
XINGPING

By bus Yangshuo buses arrive and depart from Rongtan Lu bus stop from dawn to dusk (50min; ¥7). There are no direct services to Guilin or Daxu.

By boat Negotiate with operators at the docks. Yangdi (2hr; ¥80/person); Yangshuo (2hr; ¥120/person); Yu Cun (40min; about ¥50/person).

ACCOMMODATION

Integrity Hotel 城信酒店, chéngxìn jiǔdiàn. Rongtan Lu ☎077 3870 3699. Right on the main street between the river and market, this is a basic, clean, tiled guesthouse, with a friendly manager. **¥60**

Old Place YHA 老地方国际青年旅舍, lǎo dìfang guójì qīngnián lǚshè. Near the docks on Rongtan Lu ☎077 3870 2887, ⓦtopxingping.com. One of the first hotels you'll see if arriving by water. The staff speak some English and are on a steep learning curve about Western backpackers' needs, and the restaurant is good, but the doubles are overpriced. Dorms **¥30**, doubles **¥180**

★ **Our Inn** 宝熊庄, bǎoxióng zhuāng. Over the river at Dahebei village ☎136 5963 8096, ⓦourinnxp .com. Smart rural tourist hotel, easily outpacing the competition in town. Contact them for details on how to get there. **¥180**

Xingpin Inn 兴坪客栈, xīngpíng kèzhàn. Rongtan Lu ☎077 3870 3089. An inexpensive option geared to Chinese visitors that's very similar to the nearby *Integrity*. **¥60**

EATING

All accommodation offers **meals**, with Western Chinese staples also on hand along Lao Jie. There's a **supermarket** on Rongtan Lu.

Hikers Home 熙绿庄, xīlǜ zhuāng. Lao Jie. Tasty, no-frills Cantonese meals and cold drinks served under a vine-shaded terrace outside a crumbling family house. Around ¥25/head.

Old Neighbour 老街坊餐吧, lǎo jiēfang cānbā, Lao Jie. Spectacular spring rolls and stuffed snails at this café-cum-restaurant. ¥25/head.

5

Yu Cun

鱼村, yú cūn • Negotiate at the village for rafts: Yangshuo (2hr; ¥120), Xingping (1hr; ¥50)

Around 10km downstream from Xingping, **YU CUN** is a tiny collection of old stone houses, principally famous for having been visited by former US president **Bill Clinton**. There's no road in; catch a raft or make the tiring ninety-minute **hike** over the hills from Xingping. A guide is useful, a sun hat and bottle of water essential, and the trail begins near the store on Rongtan Lu. After about fifteen minutes between groves of pomelo trees, it bends at a washing pool; bear left here, uphill, along a set of rough stone steps. Follow this track to some shady trees in a broad dip between the peaks, then cross between cattle pens to a second dip marked by a prominent lone pine. Bear **right** here around the overgrown bowl of a valley – the path becomes so rough that you'll think you've gone the wrong way – and then descend to the river and village.

Reaching Yu Cun is a mixed blessing; drink stalls are welcome, but you're seen as a giant wallet by people offering to guide you around, feed you and sell you trinkets. The best **views** are from the house the Clintons visited – you won't be allowed to miss it.

Yangshuo

阳朔, yángshuò

The celebrated terminus of Li River cruises, **YANGSHUO** sits among a romantic spread of gnarled, vegetated limestone peaks that rise sheer from surrounding fields. During the 1980s the village became China's first backpackers' hangout, after savvy locals provided cheap lodgings, Western-style cafés and tour guides for foreigners eager to extend their cruise by exploringYangshuo's superlative landscapes. Today, packed with souvenir shops, restaurants and nightclubs catering to escalating numbers of rowdy Chinese tourists, Yangshuo's original few streets are not so much booming as blowing apart at the seams. There's even talk of building a satellite town to take the overflow – though it looks like **Xingping** (see p.327) is shaping up to do this anyway.

But while no longer a quiet refuge, Yangshuo still has plenty to offer and it's not hard to spend a few days here shopping, exploring outlying hamlets by bike, kayaking or rock climbing around the landscape, or even taking courses in Chinese culture.

The market area

The **market** on Pantao Lu is by far the best local attraction, a vast covered affair divided into specific areas for birds, beasts and all manner of fresh, dried and pickled groceries; the main **market days** are on dates ending in a 3, 6 or 9. Despite the background cacophony of squawking roosters and thumping cleavers, it's less confrontational than many similar efforts in China, with seasonal specialities including a glut of pomelos from around November through into March.

Looming over everything, fang-shaped **Pantao Shan** (蟠桃山, pántáo shān) offers an easy scramble to the top for views down over the town – there's a path up the steep, overgrown slopes from behind the market. If this is too much, head to the easier small peak across the road inside **Yangshuo Park** (阳朔公园, yángshuò gōngyuán), ascended via a stone staircase.

Xi Jie

西街, xī jiē

Flanked with hard-sell souvenir shops and restaurants, **Xi Jie** (West Street) is busy all day and jammed every evening as people return from trips and head out for a feed. Browse here through piles of clothes, silver and jewellery, brand-name outdoor gear at suspiciously low prices, astronomically priced ethnic textiles, decorative scroll paintings and "new antiques", marbled or dusty with recently applied age. If you're looking for decent mementoes of your trip, it's a fun, rewarding place to browse, though firm, good-natured bargaining is essential – you also need to check everything thoroughly

5

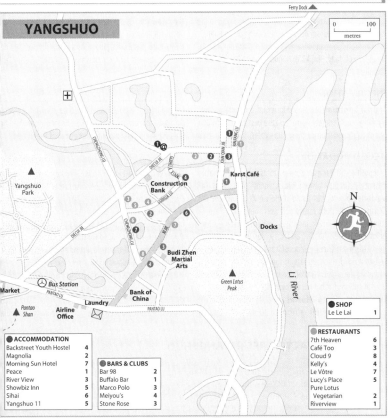

Ferry Dock ▲

YANGSHUO

Yangshuo Park

CHENGZHONG LU

DIECUI LU

DIECUI JIE

XIAN QIAN JIE

BINJIANG LU

①@

②
②
④

Karst Café
①

Construction Bank
③
⑤
④
②
⑥
⑤

GUIHUA LU

CHENGZHONG LU

BINJIANG LU

⑦
Budi Zhen Martial Arts
⑧
④

Docks

Li River

Green Lotus Peak

N

Bus Station

PANTAO LU

Market

Pantao Shan

Laundry

Airline Office

Bank of China

PANTAO LU

● **SHOP**
Le Le Lai 1

● ACCOMMODATION	
Backstreet Youth Hostel	4
Magnolia	2
Morning Sun Hotel	7
Peace	1
River View	3
Showbiz Inn	5
Sihai	6
Yangshuo 11	5

● BARS & CLUBS	
Bar 98	2
Buffalo Bar	1
Marco Polo	3
Meiyou's	4
Stone Rose	3

● RESTAURANTS	
7th Heaven	6
Café Too	3
Cloud 9	8
Kelly's	4
Le Vôtre	7
Lucy's Place	5
Pure Lotus Vegetarian	2
Riverview	1

▼ Moon Hill, Xingping & Yulong River

before handing over cash, and don't be swayed by any claims made about goods' quality, size or venerable origins.

Along the river

In summer, many people take to the river to **cool off**, paddling and floating around the shallows near the docks. There are a few shingle beaches upstream too, easily reached by following the riverside path for a few kilometres. To be safe, wait until the last tour boats have moored up around 4pm and watch the currents, which can run fast. Shops at the eastern end of Diecui Lu sell **beachware** and rubber rings.

Until recently, many local fisherman in Yangshuo used specially trained **cormorants** to catch fish from bamboo rafts; the birds were prevented from swallowing by a band around their throat and so brought their catches back to the boat (the fisherman let them eat every seventh fish). Though the practice has almost died out, you can still see the whole affair on an after-dark **cormorant fishing tour** (arrange through accommodation; 90min; ¥50/person), following a bamboo raft complete with fisherman and birds. In the daytime, fishermen and cormorants pose for photos down by the docks.

ARRIVAL AND DEPARTURE   YANGSHUO

By plane Agents in town can book train and plane tickets from Guilin for a mark-up; there's also an airline office on Pantao Lu (☎ 077 3882 2111, ⓦ cs-air.com). Taxis (around

90min; ¥300) run to Guilin airport.
By bus You can book long-distance buses from Yangshuo, though as these originate in Guilin, you tend to get stuck

5

with the worst seats if you board here (Huangyao is the exception). For local services, you generally pay on board. Destinations Gaotian (40min; ¥3); Guilin (1hr 20min; ¥18); Huangyao (1 daily; 3hr; ¥38); Nanning (6hr; ¥90); Xingping (50min; ¥7).

By boat The docks (see box, p.329) are about 500m upstream, leaving new arrivals with a gauntlet of souveni hawkers to push through before they reach town. Ferrie are not allowed to carry passengers on their return tri upstream.

INFORMATION

Tourist information Tours, bike rental, onward transport bookings and general information are best sorted through your accommodation or Yangshuo's cafés, some of which

cater to specific local activities (see box, below). The *Buffal Bar* (ⓦyangers.com), near the waterfront on Xian Qian Jie is an expat-run joint handing out plenty of useful tips.

ACCOMMODATION

Competition in Yangshuo keeps rates low and facilities decent – though always check rooms first. **Budget options** abound, but avoid those on Xi Jie, where the density of nightclubs means you won't get much sleep. In summer you'll need a/c; in winter – when room rates given below can halve – heating and hot water. The closest you'll get to **high-end** are the *Magnolia* and several good-value, self-contained rural retreats in the heart of the scenery, including the *Li River Retreat, Stone Bridge Country Villa* and several options further out of town (see p.335).

Backstreet Youth Hostel 桂花巷国际青年旅馆, guìhuā xiàng guójì qīngnián lǚguǎn. 60 Guihua

Xiang ⓣ077 3881 4077. This sister hostel to the one i Guilin is set down a quiet lane, with presentable dorms an doubles. Dorms **¥30**, doubles **¥120**

Li River Retreat About 1.5km upstream fror Yangshuo along the Li River ⓣ077 3882 895(ⓦli-river-retreat.com. Fairly standard Chinese hotel bu with attentive staff, riverside setting and rooms decked ou in antique chic. Doubles **¥360**, river view **¥590**

Magnolia 白玉兰酒店, báiyùlán jiǔdiàn. 7 Diecui L ⓣ077 3881 9288, ⓦmagnoliahotelyangshuo.com Mid-range, efficiently run place, smartly tiled throughou with minimalist wooden decor and large beds; a popula

---

TOURS AND ACTIVITIES IN YANGSHUO

Thanks to its spectacular natural location and popularity with foreign tourists, Yangshuo is one of the best places in China to find well-established guides for organized **activities**.

Freelance **guides** work Yangshuo's streets and cafés; all claim to have unique, untouristed places to take you for lunch with a farming family and offer insights into village life. Some have been doing this for years, including the English-speaking, cheery and helpful "Wendy" Li Yunzhao (ⓣ131 9763 8186, ⓔliyunzhaowendy@yahoo.com). Expect to pay about ¥50 per person per day.

The surrounding countryside (see p.333) offers some decent opportunities for cycling, and accommodation and operators at the western end of Xi Jie in Yangshuo **rent bicycles** for ¥300 deposit plus ¥10–30 a day, depending on whether the bike is an ordinary rattletrap or an off-roader with decent springs. The excellent **Bike Asia** (ⓦbikeasia.com) is based in town too, above *Bar 98* on Guihua Lu – they rent out bikes, and guide local and China-wide biking tours.

Yangshuo has become a **martial arts** hangout, with the long-established **Budi Zhen school** founded by the incredible, eighty-something Mr Gao and now run by his twin sons; their training hall (步地真功夫馆, bùdìzhēn gōngfuguǎn; ⓣ139 7735 0377, ⓦbudizhen.net) off Xi Jie, is open daily. Another good option is **Longtou Shan Taiji School** (龙头山太极拳学校, lóngtóu shān tàijíquán xuéxiào; ⓣ138 7837 6597, ⓦlongtoutaichi.com), based outside town on the Yulong River; call for a free pick-up.

For **cookery classes**, contact English-speaking Linda at *Cloud 9* restaurant, or the Yangshuo Cooking School (ⓣ137 8843 7286, ⓦyangshuocookingschool.com).

Yangshuo is also one of Asia's most accessible **rock-climbing centres** with over four hundred – mostly short but very tough – graded sports climbs on local peaks. New routes are being pioneered all the time though what is still perhaps the most respected – the inside of Moon Hill's hole (see p.334) – was first conquered in 1990. **China Climb** (ⓣ077 3881 1033, ⓦchinaclimb.com) is the main source of information; they also have a climbing wall and organize other outdoor activities, including **kayaking** (¥200/day).

If you're looking for something more sedate, explorations along the Yulong River (see p.333) and cormorant fishing tours (see p.333) are also on offer.

5

choice with small-group tours. **¥260**, king-size bed **¥380**

Morning Sun Hotel 晨光酒店, chéngguāng jiǔdiàn. 4 Chengzhong Lu ☎077 3881 3899, ⓦmorningsunhotel.com. Low-rise budget hotel with some "arty" Chinese flourishes, distant enough from Xi Jie's racket for sleeping, but close enough not to get lost on your way home from a club. Doubles **¥180**, with balcony **¥220**

Peace 和平假日酒店, hépíng jiàrì jiǔdiàn. Xian Qian Jie ☎077 3888 1289, ⓦyangshuo-hostel.com. Understated, family-run guesthouse offering large rooms with a/c, bathroom and balconies in a fairly quiet street. **¥130**

★ **River View** 望江楼酒店, wàngjiānglóu jiǔdiàn. Binjiang Lu between Xi Jie and Diecui Jie ☎077 3882 2688 (hotel) or ☎077 3882 9676 (hostel), ⓦriverview .com.cn. A touch above average with helpful staff and a riverside location (better once the tourist stalls have packed up after 4pm). Pricier rooms with balconies overlook the water across the road. Dorms **¥35**, hostel doubles **¥180**, hotel doubles **¥238**

★ **Showbiz Inn** 秀界青年旅舍, xiùjiè qīngnián lǚshè. 4 Lianfeng Xiang ☎077 3888 3123, ⓦshowbizinn.com. A bad name for one of Yangshuo's better hostels, well run and tidy, with reasonably sized dorms (though tiling means it gets a bit cold in winter).

Great views over the town from their rooftop bar, which ha a pool table too. Dorms **¥30**, doubles **¥120**

Sihai 四海饭店, sìhǎi fàndiàn. 73 Xi Jie ☎077 3882 2013, ⓦsihaihotel.com. The only accommodation worth considering along noisy Xi Jie, though it is a little tatt around the edges. Plump for the soundproofed rear rooms which are spacious if lacking much daylight. Dorms **¥30** doubles **¥130**

★ **Stone Bridge Country Villa** 石板桥山庄 shíbǎnqiáo shānzhuāng. Shi Ban Qiao village about 15min walk upstream from Yangshuo ☎13 3283 6162, ⓦthestonebridgeyangshuo.com. Eco friendly budget resort in a nearby village; the ordinary tile building offers bright, spotless en-suite rooms, some with small balconies overlooking the hills. There's a Western style café and evening country-Chinese meals by arrangement. Excellent martial art contacts too. Dorm **¥35**, doubles **¥128**

Yangshuo 11 阳朔11青年客栈, yángshuò shíy qīngnián kèzhàn. 11 Lianfeng Xiang ☎077 369 2228, ✉yangshuo11hostel@hotmail.com. Similar t nearby Showbiz with another roof bar, but a touch noisier staff are helpful with tour bookings and information Dorms **¥30**, doubles **¥120**

EATING

Yangshuo's **cafés** are scattered between Xi Jie and the foreigner-friendly Guihua Lu. All sport similar wooden decor, with graffitied walls and tie-dyed tablecloths, and open around 7am for set Western-style breakfasts and full meals – the similarl widespread **restaurants** have more extensive menus. The local cuisine includes snails, frogs, eels, cane rats and even dog avoid the unaccountably popular beer fish, which is mushy and unpleasantly sour. For inexpensive Chinese food look aroun the market and in the lane leading to the bus station. Yangshuo's cheapest **supermarket** is the Le Le Lai on Diecui Lu.

7th Heaven Chengzhong Lu. Good-quality Western and Chinese food served up in smarter surrounds than the average café – there's an outdoor terrace too, overlooking the bridge. A well-stocked bar completes the attractions. Around ¥40 a head.

Café Too Chengzhong Lu. Not such a great place to eat, but they do good coffee and have the largest English-language book exchange in town.

★ **Cloud 9** 聚福楼饭店, jùfúlóu fàndiàn. Upstairs, cnr of Chengzhong Lu and Xi Jie ☎077 3881 3686. Juicy and flavourful country-style food, including slow-simmered medicinal soups, heavy taro and pork stew, and dishes strewn with pumpkin flowers and pomelo. Everything is well presented, and they barely use salt or MSG. Around ¥40/head.

★ **Kelly's** 灯笼风味馆, dēnglóng fēngwèi guǎn. 43 Guihua Lu. Friendly foreigners' café-restaurant, with Western food alongside good home-style Sichuan cooking – try their fiery hot boiled beef slices or cooling chicken salad.

Le Vôtre Xi Jie. Set inside a Qing-era building with period furnishings, this accomplished, genuine French restaurant

serves croissants and coffee, entrées including foie gra pâté and mains such as provençal chicken and grilled duc breasts with orange. At least ¥50/head.

Lucy's Place Guihua Lu. Good atmosphere and slow service at this foreign-friendly establishment offering the usual mix of Chinese and Western meals, plus some of the best coffee in town.

★ **Pure Lotus Vegetarian** 暗香疏影素菜馆 ànxiāng shūyǐng sùcàiguǎn. 7 Diecui Lu ☎07 3881 8995. Elegant tea-shop decor with attractivel presented vegetarian food including stir-fried celery an cashews, "merit-and-virtue" tofu, green beans with bitte gourd and vegetarian medicinal soups. You could spend lot here, but don't have to – everything they do is tasty an well presented. From ¥25/dish.

Riverview 漓水一方, líshuǐ yīfāng. End of Diecu Lu ☎077 3882 0617. The café-style food here is fine but it's the romantic position as Yangshuo's onl waterfront restaurant, with views upstream to severa peaks, that is the real attraction. Two can eat well fo ¥90.

AN EPIC SONG AND DANCE

Impressions Liu Sanjie (印象刘三姐, yìnxiàng liú sānjiě) is a huge, open-air song-and-dance spectacular on the Li River, featuring a cast of 500 children, peasant women and boatmen, and full of flaming torches, wild costumes and coloured lights. It could be crass, if it wasn't all carried off with such verve, thanks to choreography by veteran film-maker **Zhang Yimou**, China's master of gorgeous visuals. Shops in Yangshuo sell DVDs of the original 1960s film *Liu Sanjie*, on which the show is based, about a local songstress who bested an evil landlord. Performances are held nightly at 8pm, with **tickets** arranged through accommodation; front row seats cost ¥188, rising to ¥680 for perches high up at the back with a better view.

DRINKING AND ENTERTAINMENT

Anywhere that serves food in Yangshuo also serves booze, although there are a couple of decent specialist **bars**. Xi Jie's **nightclubs**, all equipped with shades of black, dry ice, lasers and high-decibel music, include *Meiyou's*, *Stone Rose* and *Marco Polo*. They all get going after dark and entry is free. If you're after a glossy cultural evening, try Zhang Yimou's *Impressions Liu Sanjie* (see box, above).

Bar 98 Guihua Lu. Good place to warm up with a few drinks before moving on to a livelier venue. A gin here costs less than a coffee – and that's even before you factor in the 6–8pm happy hour. The part-outdoors streamside location is pleasant too.

Buffalo Bar Xian Qian Jie. If you just fancy a beer in a Brit-style pub, where conversation is possible, head to this expat-owned place.

DIRECTORY

Bank There's a Bank of China with an ATM on Xi Jie (foreign currency transactions daily 9am–noon & 1–5pm), plus a Construction Bank ATM on Diecui Lu.

Internet access Customers get free terminals and wi-fi at many cafés; otherwise, there's a net bar above the Xinhua Bookstore and Le Le Lai supermarket on Diecui Lu (¥3/hr).

Laundry The laundry service near the post office charges ¥10/kilo for same-day service (they use driers).

Medical 46 Guihua Lu. ☎1307 763 2299, ⊛dr-lily-li .com. For acupuncture or Chinese massage, contact Dr Lily Li. Treatments are fairly expensive – therapeutic massages from ¥80/hr, relaxation massage ¥70, foot ¥60 – but if you get the iron-fingered doctor herself, quite an experience.

Post Office On the highway, daily 9am–noon & 2–5pm.

Around Yangshuo

The countryside around Yangshuo is split into two main areas: rustic scenery on the Yulong River, just west; and a string of natural attractions – including **caves** and the unmissable **Moon Hill** – along the highway south of town. **Markets**, which rotate through villages on specific dates, make good excuses to drop in on otherwise torpid hamlets; those at Xingping (see p.327) or **Langzi** (see p.334) are recommended. All can be reached from Yangshuo by a combination of local transport, cycling and hiking, either on your own or with guides (see p.330). There's also a glut of comfortably rustic **places to stay** in the area, well worth considering if you feel Yangshuo is too commercial or noisy.

The Yulong River

玉龙河, yùlóng hé • Walk or cycle from Yangshuo, or organize a boat trip through accommodation, or with tour guides during a Li River cruise (2hr; ¥150/person)

Paralleling the highway to Guilin, a bike ride along the **Yulong River** west of Yangshuo, offers 12km of rural scenes, antique arched stone bridges and mud-brick farming hamlets – you could also walk the same route. There are no shops along the way, so take a packed lunch and some water.

The road from Yangshuo leaves the highway east of the bus station – you might have to ask for directions to **Chaoyang** (朝阳, cháoyáng), the first large settlement along the way – and follows the east side of the Yulong River via **Xiatang Zhai** (下堂寨, xiàtáng

5

zhài), the old villages of **Huangtu** (黄土, huángtǔ), **Jiuxian** (旧县, jiùxiàn) with its magnificent mansion, and **Gu Cheng** (古城, gǔ chéng), before rejoining the highway at **Baisha** (白沙, báishā), whose market runs on dates ending in a 1, 4 or 7. From here, either cycle or catch a bus back to Yangshuo.

Cruise-boat tours include a bus to an old village, a walk along the riverside and a short raft trip where women dressed in minority garb encourage you to sing along to saucy folk tunes.

South of Yangshuo

Of the many contrived tourist sights lining the highway south of Yangshuo, (such as the Totem Trail, where ¥50 buys access to a 20m-high statue of a "savage" in animal skins and a string of souvenir stalls), a handful justify their entrance fees. You can get within striking distance of them all by cycling, or catching one of the frequent buses to **Gaotian**, and asking to be set down along the way. Goatian itself is a small junction town, jumping-off point for the old village of **Langzi**, best seen on market days.

The Ancient Banyan

穿岩古榕, chuānyán gǔróng · ¥18

About 6km from Yangshuo, just past where the Gaotian road crosses the Yulong River, the 17m-high **Ancient Banyan Tree** casts a huge blob of green shade. The tourist industry dates it to the Sui dynasty (around 600 AD), which is perhaps a thousand years older than it really is, but it's beautiful anyway – though if you've seen one of these sprawling fig trees before, it's probably not worth your time.

Assembling Dragon Caves

聚龙洞, jùlóng dòng · Daily 8.30am–5.30pm · ¥45

On the main road around a kilometre past the Ancient Banyan, **Assembling Dragon Caves** is a fairly standard Chinese affair, with a short boat ride followed by an hour-long walk through underground caverns, where no expense has been spared to splash creative coloured lighting around the grotesque rock formations. Paths are wet in places but well formed.

Water Cave

龙门水岩, lóngmén shuǐ yán · Summer only · ¥150 · ⓦ watercave.net

Just short of Moon Hill, the bus passes the ticket office for **Water Cave**, a very different affair from Assembling Dragon. The caves themselves are 3km south of the road, and exploring them involves an exhilarating three-hour scramble through partially flooded tunnels, mud pools and hot springs; come prepared to get soaked and very, very dirty – a fun way to spend a hot summer afternoon.

Moon Hill

月亮山, yuèliàng shān · ¥15

Moon Hill is right on the highway, 10km from Yangshuo. An easy twenty-minute walk up stone steps from the road lands you beside the crescent-shaped hole in the summit, after which the peak is named; the view from here is stupendous, taking in a patchwork of brilliant green and gold fields far below, with karst spires rising all around. It's probably best in midsummer, as earlier on in the year the landscape can look a bit dry, and the colours less intense. The only downside are the persistent drink hawkers, who pursue you right to the top if you don't buy from them.

Langzi

郎梓, lángzǐ

LANGZI, 22km from Yangshuo, is a sleepy farming hamlet of cheap tiled buildings with a fortress-like, grey-brick clan mansion at its centre. The mansion's outer walls are stencilled with red **Mao-era slogans** which probably saved the building during the Cultural Revolution (see p.372). It's all fairly ruinous – though the square-sided lookout tower is intact – but sections remain lived in and you can spend an hour wandering courtyards and lanes embellished with carved wooden screens and doors, ornate roof baffles and ceramic tile ends moulded into auspicious designs. Unless period architecture is enough, combine your visit with **market day** (calendar dates ending in 2, 5 and 8); and note the *Qing Family* (see below), who can provide meals if contacted in advance.

GETTING AROUND   SOUTH OF YANGSHUO

By bus Minibuses to Gaotian (高田, gāotián), passing all the sights as far as Moon Hill, depart Yangshuo bus depot daily 8am–5pm; every 20min; ¥3) becoming increasingly scarce as the day goes on. For Langzi, catch a bus to Gaotian, then either wait for the Gaotian–Langzi shuttle (market days only; ¥2), or take a motorbike-taxi (¥5) the last 5km – the entire journey takes around 45min.
By bicycle You can explore the whole area on bikes (see p.330) from Yangshuo.

ACCOMMODATION AND EATING

The following **places to stay** offer a break from Yangshuo's bustle, with some gorgeous scenery thrown in too. Most will pick up from town, or take you in for the day if you want to visit; all provide **meals** – there are few other places to eat out this way.

Giggling Tree Guesthouse Aishanmen village, 5km from Yangshuo on the Yulong River (see p.333) ☏013 5678 66154, ⓦgigglingtree.com. Old farmhouse buildings converted to a rural hotel and restaurant by Dutch owners, with courtyard, tiled roofs and a viewing terrace for admiring the mountain backdrop. Dorms **¥50**, doubles **¥180**, family room **¥360**

Qing Family 卿家, qīng jiā. Langzi village ☏077 3877 6376. The family have restored an old stone house in the village and serve up full country-style meals if you call in advance; not much English is spoken, so you might have to get your accommodation service desk to phone for you.

Mountain Retreat 阳朔胜地, yángshuò shèngdì. 5km from Yangshuo on the Yulong River ☏077 3877 7091, ⓦyangshuomountainretreat.com. Airy suites and family rooms, most with river views, plus an excellent restaurant and good connections for arranging outdoor activities – biking, hiking, rock climbing and kayaking. Doubles **¥450**, river view **¥680**

Outside Inn 荷兰饭店, hélán fàndiàn. 4km from Yangshuo on the Yulong River ☏077 3881 7109, ⓦyangshuo-outside.com. Another former wood-and-adobe farmhouse with a range of accommodation available, including dorms, doubles and even your own farmhouse – check the website. Dorms **¥50**, doubles with fan **¥120**, with a/c **¥170**

★ **Snow Lion** 雪狮岭度假饭店, xuěshīlíng dùjià fàndiàn. Mushan village, about 2.5km downstream from Yangshuo ☏077 3882 6689, ⓦyangshuosnowlionresort.com. English-speaking staff, pleasant rooms enhanced by private balconies, rural views and – what really picks it out from the opposition – superb food (the hotel is run by *Cloud 9*'s owners). **¥298**

Huangyao

黄姚, huángyáo • ¥68

Surrounded by a pretty cluster of karst peaks 110km southeast of Yangshuo, HUANGYAO is a small but atmospheric jumble of rural Qing-dynasty buildings, cobbled streets and arched bridges. Though bypassed by modern highways, the town can trace its history back a thousand years and was once a major trading hub; today Huangyao's location, over near the Guangdong border, is inconvenient rather than truly remote. Chinese tour groups rock in on quick visits, and Huangyao has featured in period TV dramas, but stay the night and you'll probably have the place to yourself. Note that most people here are Cantonese-speaking and you might hear yourself called a *gweilo*, the local equivalent of *laowai*.

Huangyao is set around water, with a stream cutting a gorge through bedrock at one end of the village and a large pond, a reservoir really, at the other. In between are a

5

network of flagstoned lanes between the brick and granite houses which form the bulk of the old town; look for huge **fire-baffle** house ends, carved wooden gates and doors, **murals** – including a portrait of Chairman Mao and ancient adverts for cigarettes and eye-drops – and two-storey **gate towers**, complete with gun slots, which once guarded the main roads in and out.

Facing the pond is an **ancestral hall** built in the southern Chinese style, with a heavy granite entrance gate opening into a series of atriums, the ancestral tablet and shrine right at the rear. At the other end of the village, huge **fig trees** overhang the stream, which is spanned by the stone **Dailong bridge** (带龙桥, dàilóng qiáo).

Huangyao is a sleepy place – almost everybody here is either very young or very old – and on a hot day the town seems deserted except for artists painting street scenes and the odd brindle dog crashed out in a shady doorway. After dark, the streets are soulfully lit by red paper lanterns – bring a camera.

ARRIVAL AND DEPARTURE HUANGYAO

By far the best way to reach Huangyao is on the single daily **bus** from Guilin via Yangshuo. The nearest big town is **Hezhou** (贺州, hèzhōu; also known as 八步, bābù), which has a couple of daily services to Huangyao and buses onwards into adjacent Guangdong province.

By direct bus Huangyao has no bus station; buses terminate in the main street. Ask at accommodation in Huangyao about where to catch onwards services.
Destinations Guilin (1 daily; 3hr 40min; ¥38); Hezhou (2 daily; 1–2hr; ¥20); Yangshuo (1 daily; 3hr; ¥38).
By bus via Tonggu If you miss the direct bus, frequent

Guilin–Hezhou buses can set you down on the highway at Tonggu (同古, tónggǔ), from where you'll have to organize a taxi for the final 15km to Huangyao (¥30).
Destinations Guangzhou (5 daily; 6hr; ¥80); Guilin (4hr; ¥40); Huangyao (4 daily; 2hr; ¥20); Shenzhen (2 daily; 9hr; ¥120).

ACCOMMODATION

Aside from the following, some homes in the old town offer **beds**, though facilities are basic – look for Chinese signs outside houses.

Chance Family Lodge 偶然间客栈, ǒuránjiān kèzhàn ⊕077 4672 2046. Stone family mansion right by the Dailong bridge, modernized inside to comfortable hostel standard. Also has a small café and bar. **¥90**
Guzhen Renjia Kezhan 古镇人家客栈, gǔzhèn rénjiā kèzhàn. Inside the old town ⊕150 7814 1942. Ordinary, slightly cell-like rooms at the back of an old house, with ceiling fans but no a/c. **¥60**
Hongwei 宏炜旅馆, hóngwěi lǚguǎn. Zheng Da Jie

⊕077 4672 2208. Similar to the nearby *Jinlanju*, right down to the views, though they also have a computer room. **¥80**
★ **Jinlanju** 金兰居客栈, jīnlánjū kèzhàn. Xin Jie ⊕077 4672 2218. Clean and quiet rooms in a friendly family-run guesthouse on the main street through the newer part of town. Panoramas of the old town from the top floors. The Yangshuo bus delivers to the door. Doubles with a/c and shower **¥80**

EATING AND DRINKING

Huangyao is close enough to Guangdong province for **Cantonese food** to dominate, featuring light, chilli-free flavours and simply cooked dishes. Locally grown tamarinds and fermented black beans are sold from stalls around the old town.

Boke 泊客驿站, bókè yìzhàn. Just inside the old town off Xin Jie, the main road. Rather quiet café-bar, serving light Chinese meals and booze, which looks as if it has been transplanted from Yangshuo.
Dailong Qiao Nongjia Fan 带龙桥农家饭, dàilóngqiáo nóngjiā fàn. This inexpensive restaurant

serves country-style meals on a stone terrace next to the Dailong bridge. The menu depends on what was in the morning market but, if available, they do excellent stewed pumpkin, fried bamboo shoots and steamed spareribs with black beans. Around ¥25/head.

5

Longji Titian

龙脊梯田, lóngjǐ tītián・¥80

About 90km northwest of Guilin, **Longji Titian** – the Dragon's Backbone Rice Terraces – covers a huge swathe of steep mountainsides in contoured steps, brilliantly green, yellow, misty or silvered depending on the season. People up here are mostly Zhuang and Yao, and their dark wooden villages stand out against the paddy fields; more aspiring locals in the valleys below depict them as rustic savages, happy to own just a gun and a knife.

The area is just close enough to Guilin for a day-trip, but spend a night and make the most of the clean air, country walks and scenery – for once in Guangxi you're looking down from the mountain tops, instead of being surrounded by them. There are two places to base yourself, both featuring extensive wooden hamlets of attractive "ethnic" guesthouses: accessible **Ping An** and less touristed **Da Zhai**, linked to its near-neighbour by a road and an excellent, easy **hiking trail**. Longji gets very crowded in summer; winter is cold enough for snow and far quieter.

Ping An

平安, píng ān

Arrival in **PING AN** is not promising: facing the car park is a line of souvenir stalls, a crowd of hotel touts, and porters offering to carry your bags up the kilometre of stone steps leading to the village (¥10). Things get better as you head uphill to where Ping An, a "village" of hotels linked by narrow stone paths, spreads around a tight fold of hillside overlooking the famous terracing. Once you've found somewhere to stay there's not much to do here, but for most people, unwinding over a meal with the fantastic landscape spread out before you is enough.

Ping An's best views are from two **lookout points**, which you can circuit in about an hour along signposted paths: the Moon and Seven Stars (七星伴月, qīxīng bànyuè), whose descending bank of terraces is probably the most photographed scene in all

HIKING TO DA ZHAI

It's a five-hour **hike** to Da Zhai, along an easy – if not always easy to follow – path which weaves through villages, woodland and green terraces dotted with ancient, overgrown graves; you're doing this less for the views than simply getting stuck into the local landscape. Wear solid shoes for the muddy, rocky trail; some accommodation can assemble a packed lunch if you ask in advance. **Guides** can be hired through accommodation or along the way for about ¥50 – they're certainly helpful, but not essential if you speak some Chinese. At the far end, onward traffic is erratic, so plan to either spend a night in Da Zhai – where there are more hiking trails – to hire a minibus, or to trek back to Ping An.

From Ping An, you first follow the path towards Nine Dragons and Five Tigers lookout to a ridge just above the village, where Yao and Zhuang women wait in traditional pink and blue garb, offering to guide you. Take the dirt road uphill, then down past a small reservoir and over a concrete bridge, where the road degenerates into a track, occasionally flagstoned. This climbs through scrub to a pass, then undulates through boggy country between close, humid pockets and open hillsides, finally descending to the halfway point at the wooden Yao village of **ZHONGLIU** (中六, zhōngliù).

Zhongliu is beautifully located on a steep hillock among rugged, terraced ridges. If you haven't hired a guide, be warned that resentful locals will probably point you in the wrong direction. Head uphill through the village, following a silver water pipe; on the slope above, bear right and downhill along a small path for 200m, then turn left, uphill, at some isolated houses. Keep on this path as it climbs through a small hamlet, then follow it all the way to where signposts pop up for Da Zhai. At the angled intersection a short way on, turn left for five minutes to *Jinmei Ge* guesthouse (see p.338), or continue downhill to Tian Tou and Da Zhai.

5

Longji; and Nine Dragons and Five Tigers (九龙五虎, jiǔlóng wǔhǔ), which looks straight down to the village over tight bands of sharply stepped fields.

Da Zhai

大寨, dà zhài

DA ZHAI is smaller, quieter and less dependent on tourism than Ping An; away from the huge wooden hotels there's a chance to see people just getting on with life, farming their fields, cooking, chatting and portering huge loads up the steep, flagstoned paths. Views here are poor – Da Zhai sits at the bottom of a hill – but an extensive web of hiking trails climbs to superb scenery. You can stay higher up too; either a kilometre on at **TIAN TOU** (田头, tiántóu) – an even smaller version of Da Zhai – or various homestays dotted around the hilltop. It's a long walk up to them with luggage, however.

Da Zhai trails

The following paths are all clear and signposted to some extent, though hiring a **guide** will give you peace of mind on the longer trails.

Up above Tian Tou, paths climb to three **lookouts** offering classic terrace views, the fields looking like ribbed mirrors when they're flooded in spring. Give yourself a good four hours for the return trip up Xi Shan (西山韶乐, xīshān shàolè), with the steep, slippery path running right over Longji Titian's 1180m-high apex. In opposite directions, Qianceng Tianti (千层天梯, qiāncéng tiāntī) lies above the trail from Ping An; while Jinfo Ding (金佛顶, jīnfó dǐng) makes another good day-hike to some of the region's most extremely contoured slopes.

ARRIVAL AND GETTING AROUND

LONGJI TITIAN

Longji Titian sits west of the Guilin–Sanjiang highway near the town of **Longsheng** (龙胜, lóngshèng). From the tiny highway stop of **Heping** (和平, hépíng), about 20km south of Longsheng, separate roads head up to Ping An and Da Zhai. There is no regular transport between Ping An and Da Zhai. You can walk (see box, p.337), or minibuses charge ¥80–100 for the vehicle. Moving on to **Sanjiang**, flag down through-buses on the highway at Heping, or pick up services in Longsheng.

BY BUS

From Heping Guilin (2hr; ¥20); Longsheng (30min; ¥5).
From Longsheng Da Zhai (irregular; 1hr 40min; ¥12); Guilin (2hr; ¥20); Ping An (6 daily 7.30am–5pm; 1hr 20min; ¥8); Sanjiang (1hr 30min; ¥18).

BY MINIBUS

From Da Zhai Guilin (1 daily 4.30pm; 2hr 30min; ¥40);

Heping (irregular; 40min; ¥15); Longsheng (irregular; 1hr 40min; ¥12).
From Heping Da Zhai (irregular; 45min; ¥15); Ping An (15min; ¥5).
From Longsheng Da Zhai (irregular; 1hr 40min; ¥12); Ping An (6 daily 7.30am–5pm; 1hr 20min; ¥8).
From Ping An Guilin (1 daily 10am; 2hr; ¥40); Heping (15min; ¥5); Longsheng (6 daily 7.30am–5pm; 1hr 20min; ¥8).

ACCOMMODATION

Local **accommodation** is in boxy, three- or four-storey wooden hotels mimicking Zhuang and Yao designs. They all creak, but come with electricity and plumbing; pricier rooms have a/c and almost everywhere has views of some sort. Mosquitoes can be a problem in summer.

DA ZHAI

Jinmei Ge 金美阁, jīnměi gé. Above Tian Tou village on the Xi Shan path ☎ 077 3758 5638 or ☎ 137 3737 7986. Incredibly friendly, family-run guesthouse and restaurant with basic facilities on its own in the rice fields. At least an hour's uphill hike from the Da Zhai car park. ¥60

Jintian 金田酒店, jīntián jiǔdiàn. Tian Tou village ☎ 077 3758 5683. Typical of local options, though this one has the edge of views and food. ¥80
New Wisdom Inn 智者家园, zhìzhě jiāyuán. Da Zhai ☎ 077 3759 1660, ⓦ wisdom-inn.com. Smaller, more modern and more efficiently run than most; staff speak good English and there's wi-fi too. Price includes all meals, and they can pick up by arrangement from Guilin (for a fee). ¥280

5

MOUNTAIN FROGS AND BAMBOO CHICKEN

Western food is on offer in most hotel restaurants in Longji Titian, but you'll also find **local specialities**: bacon and bamboo shoots, sour fern fish, stewed mountain frogs and deliciously smoky bamboo chicken (竹筒鸡, **zhútǒng jī**) – virtually a whole chicken, salted, chopped, rammed into a bamboo tube and grilled over an open fire. Wash your meal down with sweet, locally made sticky rice wine (糯米酒, **nuòmǐ jiǔ**).

PING AN

Countryside Inn 乡村咖啡店, xiāngcūn kāfēidiàn ☎077 3758 3020, ✉liyue_lu@hotmail.com. Virtually the first place you come to if you follow the main path into Ping An village, with a great view from the restaurant. Rooms are carpeted and clean, but there's no a/c. Shared bathroom **¥60**, en suite **¥110**

Longying 龙颖饭店, lóngyǐng fàndiàn ☎077 3758 3059, ⑩longying88.com. In the left-hand side of the village, the best feature of this hotel is the small terrace, looking out over the fold in the valley. All rooms are a/c and en suite. **¥150**

Ping An Jiudian 平安酒店, píng ān jiǔdiàn ☎077 3758 3198. Clean, tiled lobby but rooms are a little faded; rates rise with floor and views. Good restaurant. **¥150**

EATING

Small **stores** in the villages sell snacks, ice cream, drinks and some seasonal fruit. All accommodation has **restaurants** serving backpacker staples as well as local dishes (see box, above). Food is good everywhere, but prices tourist-inflated; expect to pay around ¥80 a head in Ping An, less in Da Zhai's more rural homestays.

Sanjiang

三江, sānjiāng

Some 80km west of Longji Titian near the Guizhou and Hunan borders, **SANJIANG** is an untidy, partially modernized service town on the **Xun River**. It's not a big place overall, split in two by the 100m-wide Xun, with the older part of town on the west bank and an expanding, newer suburb to the east, linked by a single bridge. There are a few distractions, but Sanjiang is principally a stepping stone into the surrounding countryside, home to the **Dong** nationality: the appealing village of **Chengyang** provides a popular introduction to the area, and there's scope for some off-the-beaten-track wanderings along Guangxi's fringes, plus the chance to press deeper into Dong and Miao territory across provincial borders.

The drum tower

鼓楼, gǔlóu • Daily 8.30am–5pm • ¥5

Sanjiang's square-based **drum tower** overlooks town from the east bank. Built in 2003, this is the largest of its kind anywhere, 47m high and with eleven internal levels, all built from pegged cedar and supported by four mighty, centuries-old trunks – which, given their colossal size, took months to locate up in the hills before work could begin. Unusually for a drum tower, you can climb to the top for views; give the drum on the third level a good belt for luck.

5

THE DONG

The **Dong** have been living in the mountainous Guizhou-Hunan-Guangxi border region since at least the Tang dynasty, and call themselves **Gam**. Isolation has helped preserve their culture, and even relatively accessible villages such as Chengyang in Guangxi and Guizhou's **Zhaoxing** (see p.297) are still built almost entirely in pegged wood – Dong carpenters often boast that they never use nails. Fire is a major concern, though, and during the year each family takes turns to guard their village from this hazard.

Dong villages are dominated by tall **drum towers** with multistoreyed tiled roofs decorated in animal carvings, though as they seldom contain ladders (or even drums), they're more useful as a social focus than lookout posts. People gather underneath to lounge and celebrate festivals, such as those to the female deity **Sama** (held on the seventh day of the first, third and eighth lunar months). Different clans in a village sometimes build separate towers, as seen at Zhaoxing and **Gaoding** (see p.343). Most villages also sport covered **wind-and-rain bridges**, which again make sheltered places to sit and gossip. These too serve a religious purpose – many have statues grimed with incense smoke in their halfway alcoves.

The Dong favour sober, dark-blue clothing, though women also traditionally embroider their jackets with distinctive patterns and wear heavy silver jewellery, especially for festivals and big market days. Out in the villages you'll see lengths of home-made cotton being dyed in tubs of **indigo** and pig's blood, or being beaten with large wooden mallets prior to varnishing with egg-white as a protection against mosquitoes.

Dong **cuisine** revolves around sour hotpots, **oil tea** (侗族油茶, dòngzú yóuchá) – a bitter, salty soup made from fried tea leaves and puffed rice – and home-made rice wine.

Sanjiang Museum

三江博物馆, sānjiāng bówùguǎn • Daily 9am–4pm • ¥1

Sanjiang Museum is worth a look if you're interested in local history, though some Chinese is essential to get the most out of the enthusiastic and knowledgeable curator, Mr Wu. There are scale models of the area's main drum towers and bridges, alongside clothing, looms and musical and agricultural implements, and photos of local festival highlights – **bullfights** (see p.291), exploding firecrackers, and women wearing fantastically embroidered clothes. Maps and documents also explain that the Sanjiang area was a centre for guerilla action against the Japanese during the 1940s: the invaders captured Guilin but never managed to quell the Dong.

ARRIVAL AND DEPARTURE

SANJIANG

BY BUS

Bus stations on either side of the river handle local and long-distance traffic. Aside from traffic to Longsheng and Guilin, there are services northwest into Guizhou through Dong and Miao regions via Zhaoxing (see p.297). Be aware that the only people who have any idea about local departure times are the drivers themselves – if you're heading somewhere remote, track yours down to confirm return times or risk being stranded for a day.

Hedong bus station (河东车站, hédōng chēzhàn) is east of the river.

Destinations Guilin (6 daily; 4hr; ¥40); Longsheng (1hr 30min; ¥18).

Old bus station (汽车站, qìchē zhàn) is west of the river.

Destinations Baxie (several daily; 1hr; ¥10); Congjiang (several daily; 4hr 30min; ¥48); Dudong (several daily; 2hr 30min; ¥13); Hualian (several daily; 1hr 30min; ¥10); Liping (2 daily; 6hr; ¥40); Zhaoxing (2 daily; 3hr 30min; ¥30).

BY MINIBUS

Minibuses depart when full from outside the old bus station. You can also hire a minibus and driver for the day for about ¥350.

Destinations Chengyang (about 7am–6pm; 40min; ¥6); Mapang (about 7am to mid-afternoon; 50min; ¥6).

BY TRAIN

Sanjiang's train station is 10km by road northwest of town; a minibus taxi costs about ¥20. The line provides a route north into Hunan, plus west to Chengdu and south to Nanning. For Fenghuang in Hunan, first take the train to Huaihua and then catch a bus (2hr 30min).

Destinations Chengdu (2 daily; 18hr); Chongqing (1 daily; 13hr); Huaihua (4 daily; 4hr); Nanning (2 daily; 6hr 45min); Zhangjiajie (1 daily; 7hr 30min).

GETTING AROUND

By motorbike-taxi You can get around most places on foot, but yellow three-wheeler scooters are everywhere – between the two bus stations costs ¥2.

ACCOMMODATION AND EATING

Chengyang (see below) is a much better place to **stay the night**, but try the following, both near the old bus station north of the river, if you're stuck in Sanjiang. There are places to get a bowl of **noodles** or a stir-fry around both bus stations.

Baihuo Binguan 百货宾馆, bǎihuò bīnguǎn. Cnr across from the old bus station ☎ 1307 800 0219. Basic hostel above a department store, though comfortable enough. **¥78**

Sanjiang Binguan 三江宾馆, sānjiāng bīnguǎn. 15 Jiangfeng Jie, on the hill above the old bus station ☎ 077 2861 2228. Government-run pile, which means friendly but hopeless staff and minimal maintenance, though rooms are in fair condition. **¥150**

Chengyang

程阳, chéngyáng • ¥60

CHENGYANG is a pretty collection of Dong hamlets surrounded by streams and fields 25km northeast of Sanjiang. It's not exactly sanitized, but there's a distinct lack of the scummy ponds, grubby corners and hopeful dogs cruising roadside butcher stalls that characterize remoter Dong settlements. If you can, visit during Chengyang's **firecracker festival** on the fifth day of the first lunar month (Jan or Feb) – a no-holds-barred scrabble for possession of an iron hoop shot off into the fields on a rocket.

Minibuses deliver to Chengyang's **wind-and-rain bridge**, a 65m-long wooden affair dating to 1916 over a disproportionately tiny stream. Buy your ticket, drink a complimentary bowl of **oil tea**, browse the silver and embroideries being hawked by Dong women and cross into the main village. Turn right and you'll almost immediately stumble across steps up to the village square, overlooked by a stumpy, square-based **drum tower**, the space underneath full of elders sprawled in chairs, watching TV and smoking. The square itself hosts a couple of touristy, sociable and fun **dance sessions** daily, featuring men and women dressed in traditional clothing and playing **lusheng** gourd pipes.

TO WESTERN HUNAN: FENGHUANG AND ZHANGJIAJIE

The train makes rural Western Hunan accessible from Sanjiang, with the old town of Fenghuang and the gorges and cliffs of Zhangjiajie major targets. Despite relative isolation, both get packed out with tourists during the summer and national holidays.

FENGHUANG (凤凰, fènghuáng) is a charming, antique-style river town inhabited by Miao and Tujia people 200km north of Sanjiang on the Hunan–Guizhou border. Aside from wooden buildings, markets, stone bridges and traces of the "Southern Great Wall" (see p.300) about 13km from town, Fenghuang was also home to the twentieth-century Miao author Shen Congwen (see p.396).

Another 200km northeast of Fenghuang, **ZHANGJIAJIE** (张家界, zhāngjiājiè) is an awesome landscape of huge fractured sandstone cliffs and splintered limestone towers, all crammed into a gorge system and smothered in thick, subtropical vegetation. It covers a huge area, with flagstoned paths linking the sights – you'll need a few days to do it justice. The train station is 35km short of the scenery, with buses taking you to bases at Zhangjiajie village or Suoxi.

The Sanjing–Zhangjiajie **train** (see opposite) stops at **Huaihua** (怀化, huáihuà), from where buses run to Fenghuang; from Sanjiang allow seven hours to reach Fenghuang and eight hours to Zhangjiajie. Buses also link Fenghuang to Zhangjiajie via **Jishou** (吉首, jíshǒu), or west to Tongren in Guizhou (see p.273). There's a good number of well-priced **places to stay** in Fenghuang's old town. Zhangjiajie village's accommodation is more limited, but arrive before 7pm and you should have time to get a bus to the basic but appealing hotels in the reserve itself.

5

Don't leave without taking in the view over Chengyang and its rural patchwork of fields from the **pavilion** above the road by Chengyang's wind-and-rain bridge, a ten-minute ascent on steps.

Walking trails

Walk in any direction and you'll soon be out in the fields; a twenty-minute paved path crosses **Helong Bridge**, with its giant ceremonial drum and shrines to local deities, to another square-sided tower and guardian stone lion with lolling tongue just beyond at **Yan village**.

Accommodation can supply maps and advice for **longer trails** through successively poorer villages and off across the fields into the countryside. There's a good seven-hour circuit from Chengyang via Ping Tan, Gao Ma and Ji Chang; or you could hike in about six hours from Chengyang to the broad-based drum tower at **MAPANG** (马胖, mǎ pàng), and catch a bus to Sanjiang from there.

ARRIVAL AND DEPARTURE
CHENGYANG

By minibus There's no bus station at Chengyang; stand on the roadside by the bridge and flag down passing vehicles to Sanjiang (approximately 7am to late afternoon; 40min; ¥6). Mapang–Sanjiang minibuses (50min; ¥6) run on demand to Sanjiang's old bus station – they dry up by mid-afternoon.

By train Chengyang accommodation can advise about organizing transport to or from Sanjiang train station (see p.340).

ACCOMMODATION

Chengyang's **accommodation** is all in multistorey wooden houses, some of them genuine old homes, others built for tourism. Most rooms have en suite and fans or a/c; check for mosquito netting in summer or face an uncomfortable night. All offer meals and internet.

Chengyang International Hostel 程阳国际旅馆, chéngyáng guójì lǚguǎn. Just past Yang's ☎077 2858 2813, ⊛cyqtour.com. New operation aiming for the backpacker market, with comfortable rooms, lounge and bar. Dorms ¥30, doubles ¥110

Dong Village Hotel 侗家旅馆, dòngjiā lǚguǎn. Over the bridge and turn left ☎077 2858 2421, ⊛donghotel. com. Part-old, part-modern building with views of the bridge. A bit plusher than anywhere else, hence the higher prices. The owner speaks some English and knows the area well. ¥120

Grandma's Place 外婆家旅馆, wàipó jiā lǚguǎn. Near the Helong Bridge ☎077 2858 3303. Friendly, family-run place with a good restaurant and views over the bridge and paddy fields. ¥60

Yang's Wind & Rain Bridge Inn 程阳客栈, chéngyáng kèzhàn. Over the bridge, bear right and it's on the left ☎077 2858 3126, ✉xianhanqian@ hotmail.com. Especially helpful, long-running guesthouse; knowledgeable about walking routes and transport connections from Sanjiang. ¥60

Up the Meng Jiang

For a look at the untouristed side of Dong territory, head 60km northwest from Sanjiang to where the **Meng Jiang** – the "Miao River" – cuts a valley south through the steep, rounded hills below remote **Gaoding** village (though a planned highway might dispel this isolation). The scenery is beautiful, with pine forests and tea plantations, but – Gaoding aside – don't expect to see much traditional architecture, though there are some excellent bridges. Note that, if you're heading all the way to Gaoding, transport schedules will mean having to spend a night in Dudong.

Zhuolong and Mengzhai

About halfway between Sanjiang and Gaoding, the road runs into the Meng Jiang valley at **Zhuolong**, a dark-roofed village where Deng Xiaoping rested up during the Long March (see p.280). A few kilometres south, **MENGZHAI** (孟寨, mèngzhài) is half Dong, half Miao – the name means "Miao Stockade" – with each community settled on opposite banks. After generations of fighting over land, their leaders became reconciled in the 1940s, and together built the traditionally designed **Nationality Union Bridge** across the divide. Today it's hard to distinguish between the two communities, as both dress similarly – women wearing heavy metal earrings or a piece of white cord through their lobes – though the drum tower is, naturally enough, on the Dong side.

Baxie to Hualian

Continuing north up the Meng Jiang valley from Zhuolong, the next village is **BAXIE** (八协, bāxié), whose bright green and yellow wind-and-rain bridge was built in 1980 (purists might notice a few nails in the decking). The cobbled village square in front of Baxie's drum tower has a small stage carved with monkeys and lions for festival performances. Not far on, **PINGLIU** (平流, píngliú) has a buffalo-fighting ground (see p.291), and then comes **HUALIAN** (华联, huálián) and the oldest surviving wind-and-rain bridge anywhere, built in 1861.

Batuan

巴团, bātuán

Another few kilometres brings you to **BATUAN**, with a unique two-tier bridge – one lane for people and another for animals. This bridge still has its shrine, a cupboard with a bearded god on a stone slab, and, at the far end, a path leads along the riverbank to where tall trees shade a small temple.

Dudong and Gaoding

Some 5km north of Batuan, **DUDONG** (独峒, dúdòng) was a centre for guerrilla action against the Japanese during the 1940s. There's a rather shabby drum tower and bridge, but the real reason to come this far is to make out the **two-hour hike to Gaoding.**

For Gaoding, take the road uphill from town and keep going. After about ninety minutes there's a small stone bridge on the left (you might just be able to make the characters for "Gaoding" cut into the stonework); cross it and follow the unsealed, rocky road up to the village. **GAODING** (高定, gāodìng) is an attractive place of a hundred homes crammed into a deep fold in the hillside, with six drum towers, dogs and farm animals roaming the uneven, cobbled lanes, and nothing but wooden buildings (if you ignore the new school on the hill above).

ARRIVAL AND DEPARTURE	UP THE MENG JIANG
By bus Check all current schedules with drivers as departure times are extremely elastic. Services run from Sanjiang's old bus station to Dudong via Zhuolong, Baxie,	Hualian and Batuan (total 2hr 30min; ¥15). Separate services run to Mengzhai, usually via Tongle (同乐, tónglè); or get out at Zhuolong and walk or hitch south.

ACCOMMODATION AND EATING

Guesthouse By the marketplace, Dudong. Offers basic accommodation, and is the only place serving food – noodle	soups and stews – though not much of it, and only during daylight hours. There's also a small store selling necessities. **¥30**

5

Central Guangxi

Central Guangxi is dominated by the **Xi River**, part of a system that, under various names, flows east from Yunnan into Guangxi, Guangdong and finally down to Hong Kong. The landscape here, though hilly, lacks the scenic punch of Guilin's karst; the countryside is poor and overwhelmingly rural; and the cities – such as the rail nexus of **Liuzhou** (柳州, liǔzhōu), or **Wuzhou** (梧州, wúzhōu), over on the Guangdong border – hold little of interest to visitors. Yet during the 1850s, while the Qing dynasty was unravelling, this innocuous backdrop witnessed the beginnings of the **Taiping Uprising**, a movement which became the world's most appalling civil revolt, in which twenty million people lost their lives and China effectively lost its independence for a century (see box, below). Though out of the way, the village where it all started, **Jintian**, near the riverside town of **Guiping**, makes an interesting break in the journey between northeastern Guangxi and the south – you shouldn't need more than a day to see everything.

Guiping

桂平, guìpíng

GUIPING is busy, flood-prone town at the junction of the Xi and Yu rivers; its shabby, 1960s concrete facade was being given a comprehensive modern makeover at the time of writing. The town centres around **Guangchang**, a public square at the intersection of east–west-oriented Renmin Lu and south-pointing Guinan Lu.

Xi Shan

西山, xī shān • ¥35 • Public bus (daily 7am–4.30pm • ¥1) from Guangchang or walk west for 20min along Renmin Lu

Guiping's main sight is **Xi Shan** (西山, xī shān; ¥35), 2.5km west of town, a sacred mountain which provides an easy, enjoyable introduction to the Chinese passion for taming famous landscapes with paths and temples. Just inside the entrance, **Li Gong**

THE TAIPING UPRISING

The **Taiping Uprising** had its roots in the First Opium War of 1839–42 (see p.369), which left China militarily humiliated by Britain and beggared by taxes raised to pay off war indemnities. Popular resentment against the country's ineffectual, fossilized imperial house – who were themselves not Chinese but the hated Manchus – was crystallized by **Hong Xiuquan**, a failed civil-service candidate who believed himself to be the younger brother of Jesus Christ. In 1851 he assembled 20,000 armed supporters at **Jintian village** near Guiping and declared the formation of the **Taiping Tianguo**, the Kingdom of Heavenly Peace. Tearing up through central China, the Taipings routed imperial forces sent against them, devastating entire provinces and gathering followers as they went, and in 1853 capturing as their capital the great eastern metropolis of **Nanjing**.

From here on, however, the Taiping's cause lost momentum. Poorly planned expeditions failed to take Beijing or win over western China, though their efforts planted the seeds of Yunnan's **Muslim Uprising** (see p.183) and the **Miao Rebellion** (see p.288) in Guizhou), and Hong's leadership – originally based on the enfranchisement of the peasantry, sexual equality and the outlawing of opium and alcohol – descended into fanaticism. After the British sided with the Qing government (clearly preferring China to be ruled by an easily manipulated imperial court than a strong, popular leader, even if he was Christian), the Taipings were crushed with vast slaughter in 1864 and Hong committed suicide. Having again proved their military superiority over the Chinese – and other foreign powers – began to make even greater demands of the Qing government, a situation that persisted until well into the twentieth century.

In some ways the Taipings, influenced by a foreign faith and intent on overturning the old order, foreshadowed the arrival of Communism in China. Indeed, the enormous social devastation the Taipings left in their wake finds a curious echo in Mao Zedong's Cultural Revolution of a century later.

5

Memorial Hall (李公祠, lǐ gōng cí) is dedicated to a ninth-century official so taken with the local scenery that he resigned his post and lived here as a hermit. Adjacent **Xishi Nunnery** (洗石寺, xǐshí sì) sports a wealth of statuary and a **vegetarian restaurant** open for lunch. **Tea** has been grown on the mountain since the Tang dynasty; you can try the fragrant, pale yellow brew in the restaurant or buy the leaves in the temple shop – which locals claim are superior to those for sale in Guiping itself.

From the temples, a two-hour **hike** on paved paths climbs through a forest of fish-tailed palms and huge, ancient pines; there are the usual run of temples and pavilions too, but you're really here for the superb, hazy summit views of the two rivers snaking across a watery flatland to join at Guiping.

ARRIVAL AND DEPARTURE   GUIPING

By bus Guiping's long-distance bus station is near Guangchang on Guigui Bei Lu. If you're aiming for Guangzhou or Shenzhen, over near the Hong Kong border in neighbouring Guangdong province, you're best off first heading east to Wuzhou, a bigger city with more transport. Buses also run to Jintian (see below).
Destinations Guilin (8 daily; 6hr; ¥58); Nanning (3hr; ¥40); Wuzhou (3hr; ¥45); Yangshuo (8 daily; 4hr 30min; ¥35).

ACCOMMODATION AND EATING

All the following **hotels** are near the bus station and the central square. **Restaurants** are not Guiping's strong point; try the *Hualian* hotel, the Xishi Nunnery at Xi Shan or stalls around the bus station.

Changtai 长泰宾馆, chángtài bīnguǎn. Renmin Zhong Lu ☎077 5336 9988. This government-run hotel has been going forever, and features quiet, spacious rooms and a revolving restaurant on its roof, offering views of the river and Xi Shan. Service is slack, though. **¥210**
Dianzi 电子宾馆, diànzǐ bīnguǎn. On the west side of Guangchang square. Inexpensive, threadbare but clean rooms. **¥80**

Hualian Business Hotel 华联商务大酒店, huálián shāngwù dàjiǔdiàn. Shagang Lu ☎077 5336 9888. Standard business affair, comfortable but with indifferent staff. **¥200**
Ruquanjing 乳泉井酒店, rǔquánjǐng jiǔdiàn. Renmin Xi Lu ☎077 5336 9991. Well-run tourist hotel, clean and efficient with decent-sized rooms, which gets quite busy in the summer. One of the best restaurants in town, serving mostly Cantonese food. **¥280**

Jintian

金田, jīntián

About 25km north of Guiping, little **JINTIAN** town is where Hong Xiuquan's army first rallied. The original headquarters of the **Taiping Tianguo** (太平天国, tàipíng tiānguó; daily 9am–4.30pm; ¥15), the "Kingdom of Heavenly Peace", occupies a small wooded hill 4km west, where a heroic red sandstone statue of Hong greets you as you enter through the gates. To the right are the 3m-high, rammed-earth defensive walls of the **barracks**, now eroded and overgrown with pine trees. In the centre of this long rectangular enclosure is the "**pledge rock**", where Hong declared his insurrection under way on 11 January, 1851. There's also a **museum** here, to the left of the main entrance, though the blurred photos, old coins and rusty weapons throw little light on the ensuing chaos.

Frankly, though the site's associations are momentous, it's all very unpretentious – if not deliberately run-down. Hong's "revolutionary spirit" and anti-Manchu stance endeared him to China's first-generation Communists, but his example of a nearly successful popular uprising against the government probably worries the current authorities, as they grapple to hold the country together in the face of rapid modernization, emerging social divisions and endemic corruption.

ARRIVAL AND GETTING AROUND   JINTIAN

By bus Guiping–Jintian minibuses (¥4) depart whenever full from the western side of Guangchang square. Buses drop off in Jiantian's north-pointing main street. To get to the Taiping Tianguo, look for a concrete archway to the west and follow this road for 4km through fields; a motorcycle-taxi costs ¥5. Buses run back to Guiping at least until 5pm.

Nanning

南宁, nánníng

NANNING is a huge, sprawling, modern city on the **Yong River**, way down in southwestern Guangxi. Today it seems a little too isolated for a provincial capital, but the river – a western continuation of the Xi Jiang (see p.344) – formerly brought in trade, and Nanning's proximity to the **Vietnamese border**, just a few hours further to the southwest by road or rail, has made it something of an international hub. The city hosts the important annual **China-Asean Expo**, where the heads of Southeast Asian economies meet to discuss trade agreements, but essentially Nanning has the pace of a busy, tropical market town, somewhere to take stock before heading off to explore remoter landscapes along the border with Vietnam and Yunnan.

Downtown

Downtown Nanning occupies a few square kilometres between the train station and the river, with main-street **Chaoyang Lu** connecting the two. It's all about **shopping**: the area west of Chaoyang Lu between the train station and Renmin Xi Lu is a wholesale **hardware market**, with cleavers, duck-roasting ovens, strip lighting by the metre, bamboo steamers and mats spilling out of shops into the streets. Cramped,

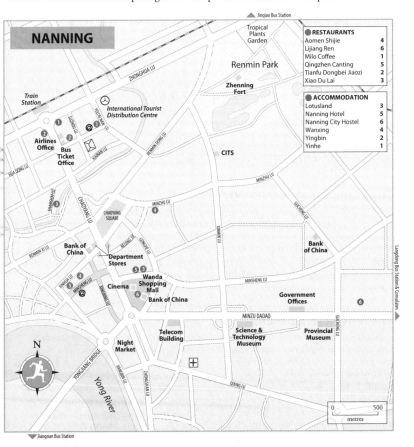

NANNING

Jinjiao Bus Station

Tropical Plants Garden

Renmin Park

Zhenning Fort

Train Station

International Tourist Distribution Centre

Airlines Office

Bus Ticket Office

CITS

RESTAURANTS
Aomen Shijie	4
Lijiang Ren	6
Milo Coffee	1
Qingzhen Canting	5
Tianfu Dongbei Jiaozi	2
Xiao Du Lai	3

ACCOMMODATION
Lotusland	3
Nanning Hotel	5
Nanning City Hostel	6
Wanxing	4
Yingbin	2
Yinhe	1

Chaoyang Square

Bank of China

Department Stores

Cinema

Wanda Shopping Mall

Bank of China

Bank of China

Government Offices

Telecom Building

Science & Technology Museum

Provincial Museum

Night Market

Langdong Bus Station & Consulates

Yong River

Yongjiang Bridge

Jiangnan Bus Station

N

0   500
metres

5

TO VIETNAM

Vietnamese visas, which are not available at the border, are issued by the Vietnamese Consulate, 1/F Investment Plaza, 109 Minzu Dadao (Mon–Fri 10am–3pm; ☎077 1551 0561). They cost ¥380–580 depending on whether you want same-day service (you need to apply at 10am for this) or can wait longer; take your passport and two photos. *Lotusland* and *Nanning City Hostel* can apply for you with no commission.

   Buses to Hanoi (8hr; ¥148), Haiphon (8hr; ¥158) and Yalong Bay (8hr; ¥168) depart several times daily from the **Nanning International Tourist Distribution Centre** (南宁国际旅游集散中心, nánníng guójì lǚyóu jísàn zhōngxīn), downtown on You'an Nan Lu. Hanoi buses also depart from Langdong station. The fare includes lunch along the way.

   The direct **train to Hanoi** departs at 6.45pm (12hr; sleeper ¥200–350); it stops on both sides of the border for passport checks and customs inspections, so you don't get much sleep. You can also cross the border **on foot** via the Friendship Pass (see p.356).

warehouse-sized **indoor markets** are full of the same, plus fishing rods, household electricals and everything cheap made in cardboard, plastic or china. Further south, pedestrianized **Minsheng Lu** and **Xingning Lu** are lined with restored colonial-era shophouses, mostly converted to clothing chain stores.

   Over the road, crowds lounge or exercise in paved **Chaoyang Square**, south of which the Xinhua Lu crossroads has **department stores** at three corners, with the modern **Wanda shopping mall** (万达大厦, wàndá dàshà) filling the next block down.

Renmin Park

Entrance on Renmin Dong Lu • Daily 6am–7pm • Free

Some 2km east of the train station, Renmin Park offers a bit of air and space during Nanning's sultry summers. Stone causeways zigzag across a goldfish-stuffed lake between islets inhabited by willows and chess players, while the western side is overlooked by **Zhenning Fort**, a gun emplacement built in 1917. The **tropical plants garden** (¥2) below has a medicinal herb plot and a carefully constructed undergrowth of philodendrons, palms, heliconias and giant "elephant-ear" taro, bird-nest ferns and cycads – its private recesses are popular with young couples.

The Science and Technology Museum

广西科技馆, guǎngxī kējì guǎn • Minzu Dadao • Tues–Sun 9am–5pm • ¥30 • Bus #6 from Chaoyang Lu

Four floors of interactive exhibits inhabit this space-age, mirrored-glass building full of rampaging children and exhausted parents. Displays probe the workings of everything from the human body to optical illusions, wind farms and global warming, but the biggest queues are for the **car driving simulator** and the giant, sparking Van de Graaf generator shows. Captions are in Chinese only, but if you're under ten this won't matter.

The Provincial Museum

广西省博物馆, guǎngxī shěng bówùguǎn • Minzu Dadao • Tues–Sun 9am–5pm • Free • Bus #6 from Chaoyang Lu

Once past the small but immaculate display of Ming and Qing porcelain on the ground floor, this museum concentrates on Guangxi's ancient history. A collection of enigmatic, spade-shaped tablets found arranged in rings prove that there were people here in Stone Age times, but it's the **bronzes** which really impress: **drums**, a cleverly designed lamp in the shape of a phoenix and two nightmarish, Western Han sculptures of snarling horses. A huge horde of Warring State swords, arrowheads and other weapons allows one caption to quote **Shang Yang**, the statesman whose reforms turned the state of Qin into the militaristic machine which conquered all China in 221BC : "A nation has only two concerns: farming and fighting". On a more peaceful note, the museum's rear gardens are full of Miao-, Zhuang- and Dong-style wooden buildings.

ARRIVAL AND DEPARTURE   NANNING

Vietnam is best reached by bus (see box, opposite).

BY PLANE

Nanning International airport is 35km southwest of Nanning; you can fly from here to Vietnam and most cities in China. The airlines office (domestic bookings ☎077 1241 6496, international bookings ☎077 1242 8418, ⓦtravelsky.com) is near the train station on Chaoyang Lu. The airport bus (hourly; 40min; ¥20) runs from outside the airlines office. Smaller private buses run from here for ¥15, while shared taxis cost ¥25/person.

BY BUS

Nanning has **bus stations** at every point of the compass, mostly off in the city's outskirts but all on convenient city bus routes. Langdong is the biggest, though services overlap. Aside from buying them at the relevant stations, **tickets** for buses from Langdong can be bought downtown from a booth on the corner of Chaoyang and Huadong Lu, just around from the airlines office, and also at the International Tourism Distribution Centre.

Bei Da Transit Centre (北大客运中心, běidà kèyùn zhōngxīn), 2km northwest of the train station on bus #31.

Destinations Baise (3hr; ¥80); Beihai (6 daily; 4hr; ¥35); Daxin (for Detian Waterfall; 3hr; ¥35).

International Tourism Distribution Centre 南宁国际旅游集散中心, nánníng guójì lǚyóu jísàn zhōngxīn. On central You'an Nan Lu.

Destinations Most use for Vietnam (see box, opposite), but also one bus daily direct to Detian (4hr; ¥50).

Jiangnan Bus Station 江南客运站, jiāngnán kèyùn zhàn. 7km south on the #31 bus from Chaoyang Lu.

Destinations Beihai (4hr; ¥50); Chongzuo (1hr 30min; ¥30); Ningming (3hr; ¥35); Pingxiang (4hr; ¥48).

Jinqiao Bus Station 金桥客运站, jīnqiáo kèyùn zhàn. 10km northeast; bus #66 or #202 passes the train station.

Destinations Guiping (3hr; ¥40).

Langdong Bus Station 琅东客运站, lángdōng kèyùn zhàn; 10km east; bus #6 to the train station via Minzu Dadao and Chaoyang Lu. Buses run daily from 7am–7pm or later.

Destinations Baise (4hr; ¥45); Beihai (4hr; ¥45); Chongzuo (1hr 30min; ¥35); Detian (2 daily; 4hr 30min; ¥55); Guilin (5hr; ¥90); Guiping (3hr; ¥30); Hezhou/Babu (11 daily; 8hr; ¥98); Ningming (5 daily; 3hr; ¥35); Pingxiang (4hr; ¥42); Wuzhou (6hr; ¥90).

BY TRAIN

Destinations Baise (4 daily; 3hr); Beihai (2 daily; 3hr); Chengdu (1 daily; 33hr); Guangzhou (4 daily; 14hr); Guilin (14 daily; 5hr 30min); Kunming (7 daily; 13hr); Sanjiang (2 daily; 6hr 45min); Wuzhou (2 daily; 6hr); Zhangjiajie (1 daily; 14hr 30min).

GETTING AROUND

By bus Local buses run between about 6.30am and 8pm and cost ¥1–2; they're of most use for reaching long-distance bus stations. It can take an hour to reach Langdong station in heavy traffic.

By metro A city subway and light rail network is under construction, due for completion around 2015. It will connect the train station to all major long-distance bus stations.

By taxi Starting charge is ¥7; it costs about ¥25 between Langdong bus station and the train station area.

ACCOMMODATION

Nanning is well provided with **hotels**, especially at the cheaper end of the market. Unusually, the train station area is by no means a seedy place, with plenty of decent options nearby.

★ **Lotusland** 荷逸居青年旅舍, héyìjū qīngnián lǚshè. 64 Shanghai Lu ☎077 1243 2592, ⓦlotuslandhostel.spaces.live.com, ⓔlotuslandhostel@163.com. Tidy, friendly and well-run hostel in a modern grey-brick building by a little park. Well located near to the train station, airport bus and market area. Dorms ¥50, doubles ¥120

Nanning City Hostel 南宁城市青年旅社, nánníng chéngshì qīngnián lǚshè. Apartment 1102, Building 12, Ou Jing Tingyuan, 63 Minzu Dadao ☎1527 771 7217, ⓦnanningcityhostel.com. Friendly homestay in a modern apartment block offering dorms, doubles and family rooms. They arrange Vietnamese visas too. Though close to the museum on a main road, it's difficult to find

5

THE BRONZE DRUMS OF POWER

A sophisticated **bronzeworking culture** flourished over two thousand years ago in Southwest China and Vietnam, manufacturing **bronze drums** which were traded as far afield as Burma, Thailand and Indonesia. The drums (also known as Dongson drums, after the place they were first discovered in Vietnam) vary a good deal in size – some are over a metre high and nearly as broad – but are typically narrow-waisted and decorated in stylized patterns depicting mythical animals, cattle, dancers, birds and rowers, with sun and **frog** designs on the top (frogs are the daughters of the thunder god in Zhuang mythology). Some examples from Yunnan (see p.186) also incorporate realistic **dioramas** on the lid of tigers, bulls and ceremonies involving human sacrifice.

The drums possibly originated as storage vessels for valuable **cowrie shells**, and show no sign of being played as musical instruments. According to a Ming historian, they were a symbol of power: "Those who possess bronze drums are chieftains, and the masses obey them; those who have two or three drums can style themselves king". Drums were cast locally up until modern times, and are still used in ceremonies and during **festivals** by Zhao, Yi, Miao and Yao peoples in China – and on the eastern Indonesian island of Alor.

– print out the map and Chinese name from their website. Dorms ¥70, doubles ¥150

Nanning Hotel 南宁饭店, nánníng fàndiàn. 38 Minsheng Lu ☎077 1210 3888. Smart, conference-delegate-style hotel inside a vast concrete-and-glass box of a building, with a gym and nine restaurants on hand. ¥350

Wanxing 万兴酒店, wànxīng jiǔdiàn. 47 Minzhu Lu ☎077 1210 2888. Bright budget business hotel in two separate buildings, a block apart; the newer and better one is on Minzhu Lu. ¥218

Yingbin 迎宾饭店, yíngbīn fàndiàn. 71 Chaoyang Lu ☎077 1211 6288. There are huge permutations of rooms in this basic but clean place. Singles are small and face the train station square over a busy road; doubles are a better deal. Some rooms come with computers and all have blackout curtains. ¥90

Yinhe 银河大酒店, yínhé dàjiǔdiàn. 84–86 Chaoyang Lu ☎077 1211 6688. Two buildings 50m apart: the northern wing has budget rooms, the southern one is more upmarket, showing signs of wear but good for the price. The fifth-floor restaurant serves Cantonese dim sum breakfasts. Dorms ¥30, doubles ¥168

EATING

The best places for snacks and light meals – buns, dumplings, noodles, grilled chicken wings, steamed rice packets and basic stir-fries – are along eastern Hua Dong Lu, or the Zhongshan Lu **night market** off the south end of Chaoyang Lu. **Fast-food chains** are grouped in and around the Wanda Mall. Stalls south of the station along Zhonghua Lu sell a wide range of fresh **tropical fruit**.

Aomen Shijie 澳门食街, àomén shíjiē. 19 Xinhua Lu. Popular place serving Cantonese-style dumplings, roast meats, quick-fried greens and single-plate meals. You get a card, which is marked by the waitress according to what you order from photographs at the counter. Dishes ¥5–25.

Lijiang Ren 漓江人, líjiāng rén. 2/F Gelan Yuntian Plaza, Chaoyang Lu. Yunnanese chain decked in heavy wooden "antique" furniture, offering chilli-rich stews and stir-fries. Mains ¥25–65.

Milo Coffee 米罗咖啡, mǐluó kāfēi. 7 You Ai Lu. Not cheap, but good if you're hankering after coffee, waffles and light Western-style meals. Opens around 9am. A pot of coffee costs ¥38.

Tianfu Dongbei Jiaozi 天宏东北饺子, tiānhóng dōngběi jiǎozi. Hua Dong Lu. Northeastern-style

dumplings with a big range of stuffings, ordered by the *liang* (50g), plus cold dishes such as spiced cucumber, spinach with peanuts, whole roasted aubergine, glass noodles, sliced beef with soy dressing and preserved eggs. A meal for two, with beer, costs around ¥35.

Qingzhen Canting 清真餐厅, qīngzhēn cāntīng. Xinhua Lu. Inexpensive Muslim restaurant on the ground floor of a pale-green mosque. It's best for big bowls of hand-made *lamian*, "pulled noodles" in soup, but can also whip up more complex dishes. Under ¥20/head.

Xiao Du Lai 小都来食街, xiǎo dū lái shíjiē. Western wing of the Nanning Hotel, Minsheng Lu. An upmarket version of *Aomen Shijie*, with a bigger selection of Chinese snacks and light meals from all over the country. You can stuff yourself for ¥35.

DIRECTORY

Banks The main Bank of China (foreign exchange Mon–Fri 8–11.30am & 2.30–5.30pm) is on Gucheng Lu, but there are smaller branches with foreign-friendly ATMs all over town.

Consulates Cambodia, Floor 2, Nanfeng Dasha, 85 Minzu Dadao ☎ 077 1588 9892; Thailand, 52-1 Jinhu Lu, off Mizu Dadao ☎ 077 1552 6945, visa section Mon–Fri 9–11.30am; Vietnam, 109 Miznu Dadao (see box, p.348).

Internet There are net bars all over town charging ¥2/hr.

Mail The most central post office is on Suzhou Lu (daily 8am–7pm).

PSB The visa department (Mon–Thurs 9am–4.30pm, Fri 9am–noon; ☎077 1289 1264 or ☎077 1289 1303) is 1.5km north of the train station, at 4 Xiuling Lu. Catch bus #14, #31, #71, #72, #84 or #85 and get off after the hospital.

Northwestern Guangxi

Northwestern Guangxi's settled river valleys, thick with sugar cane, cassava and banana plantations, don't prepare you for the rugged scenery beyond, especially the astounding giant **limestone sinkholes** outside the town of **Leye**. Despite being extremely isolated until recently, the area is now accessible via **Baise**, a stop on the Nanning–Kunming rail line, though you'll need a couple of days to see everything.

Baise

百色, bǎisè

BAISE, also written **Bose** after the local pronunciation, is a small, easy-going city with clean streets and busy shops some 220km up the Nanning–Yunnan rail line. The town sits almost entirely on the north bank of the **You River**, west of its junction with the much smaller **Dengbi River**, with main-road **Zhongshan Lu** running east–west through the centre. There's a big aluminium industry and a little history to the place – in 1929 the future Chinese leader **Deng Xiaoping** whipped up the abortive **Baise Uprising** here – but Baise is mostly just a springboard for heading northeast to Leye; you might need to spend a night here in transit.

You River Minorities Museum

右江民族博物馆, yòujiāng mínzú bówùguǎn • Chengdong Dadao • Daily 9am–5pm • Free • Over the small Dengbi River on the east side of town, climb the broad stairway to the sharp-tipped Baise Memorial and walk for 5min through the park; or take the bus – #1 drops you at the foot of the stairs

Despite an almost total lack of captions, the You River Minorities Museum gives some insight into the history of Baise's settlement, beginning with some heavy, wedge-shaped **Stone Age tools** unearthed from the river plain and believed to date back 700,000 years. Much more recent **bronzes** include drums (see opposite), an almost-comical equestrian statue and fragments of a nobleman's coffin. There's also a good display of **folk artefacts** – including a collection of colourful, brilliantly detailed Chinese opera puppets – and **Zhuang textiles**, with cases given over to loomed cloth, tie-dyed clothing and intricate, handmade embroideries.

The Uprising Memorial Hall

百色起义纪念馆, bǎisè qǐyì jìniànguǎn • Chengdong Dado, overlooking the You River east of town near the You River Minorities Museum • Daily 9am–5pm • ¥35 • Bus #1

The oversized **Uprising Memorial Hall** fills in the story of how Deng Xiaoping arrived in Baise in 1929 with a mandate to spread the Communist message, and on December 11 declared the formation of the **You Jiang Soviet** in town. This rash move drew overwhelming attention from Nationalist military forces, and Deng and his fellow survivors found themselves on the run for the next four years. Though there's a great diorama of the town as it was in 1929 and some heroic statuary capturing the historical drama, the rest forms a hopelessly unfocused collection of photos, weapons, documents and artefacts.

ARRIVAL AND DEPARTURE
BAISE

By bus Baise's bus station (百色客运站, bǎisè kèyùn zhàn), immediately north of the centre on Chengbei Lu.
Destinations Guilin (1 daily; 12hr; ¥120); Jingxi (for Detian Waterfall; 8 daily; 4hr; ¥38); Leye (every 30min 6.30am–5pm; 4hr; ¥40); Nanning (3–4hr; ¥98).

By train Baise train station is isolated 5km east of the centre, connected to town by bus #1 (¥1).
Destinations Kunming (7 daily; 9hr 45min); Nanning (9 daily; 3hr); Xingyi (7 daily; 4hr).

ACCOMMODATION AND EATING

There are the usual run of **cheap eats** at the bus station and backstreet canteens – *shuijiao* (Chinese ravioli) here come with plum sauce – otherwise dine at your **accommodation**.

Jindu 金都大酒店, jīndū dàjiǔdiàn. At the bus station, 29 Chengbei Lu ☎077 6288 1180. It's old and visibly patched up, but bargain hard and you can get a decent double here at far below the asking rate. ¥180
Jinpai 金牌大酒店, jīnpái dàjiǔdiàn. Cnr of Zhongshan Lu and Xinxing Lu, about 700m from the bus station ☎077 6288 9666. The best-value place in

town, with modern, smallish rooms and a variety of attached restaurants, including a Western-style café. ¥180
Shangwu Binguan 老区商务宾馆, lǎoqū shāngwù bīnguǎn. Diagonally across from the bus station, 32 Chengbi Lu ☎077 6288 8818. Chinese speakers should be able to wrangle a clean, ordinary double here. ¥100

DIRECTORY

Banks There's a Bank of China and Construction Bank with ATMs down Xiangyang Lu, 150m south of the bus station.

Leye

On a twisting, dusty road 180km north of Baise towards the border with Guizhou, **LEYE** (乐业, lèyè) is a small market town overlooked by a looming limestone plateau whose astonishing sinkholes, notably enormous **Dashiwei Tiankeng**, are the area's main attraction. There's a **climbing wall** across from the bus station on the outskirts of town, next to a free **geology museum** with a useful diorama of the region and the engagingly tacky **Luomei Lianhua Cave** (罗妹莲花洞, luómèi liánhuā dòng; ¥23), a small, garishly lit subterranean spread of "cave lotus" formations which resemble fossilized lily pads. Otherwise Leye is purely functional, and you're here to get up into the surrounding hills. Note that Leye has no foreign-friendly **banks** or **ATMs** – the closest are in Baise.

Dashiwei Tiankeng

大石围天坑, dàshíwéi tiānkēng • Daily 8am–5pm • ¥70 including transport within the park

A trove of some of the world's deepest sinkholes, also known as dolines or **tiankengs**, lies hidden up in the rough, green, scrub-tangled limestone mountains some 10km west of Leye, an area so remote that they were unknown to science until 1998. The sinkholes formed after groundwater gradually eroded huge subterranean caverns in the mountains' soluble bedrock, which have, in places, collapsed in on themselves to leave deep, sheer-sided pits ringed by the jagged remnants of peaks.

The bus from Leye drops you at the **Dashiwei Tiankeng park** gates, from where golf buggies and a Chinese-speaking tour guide cart you around a selection of the most impressive formations. A trail from one of the roadside viewing platforms climbs to a 1496m-high summit, from where grey-white cliffs drop sheer into **Dashiwei Tiankeng** itself – which, at 613m deep and 420m wide, is the second-largest such sinkhole in the world, only bettered by Xiaozhai Tiankeng in Chongqing (see p.170). You can't descend into the sinkhole's depths, which are choked with rank vegetation (though both the pit and 6km of its attached cave system were explored in 2001), but stone staircases partially circuit the rim above to another ridge, from where views extend out across a horizon filled with undulating karst hills. **Tour times** depend on the average walking speed of your party, but you could easily spend three hours up here.

5

ARRIVAL AND GETTING AROUND

By bus Leye's main bus station is about 1km south of town, with services to Baise (every 30min 6am–5.30pm; ¥40). The old bus station, for Dashiwei Tiankeng gate, is at the town's central crossroads (roughly 8am, 10am, noon, 2pm,

4pm; 30min; returning directly; ¥3).
By bicycle-rickshaw These head between Leye's main bus station and town for ¥2.

ACCOMMODATION AND EATING

The *Leye Fandian* is the only place officially allowed to take foreigners, but you might get into one of the many clean, basic and inexpensive backstreet **hotels** if you can persuade the management that they'll get away with it. The're just one dedicated **restaurant** in town, although you can also eat at the *Leye Fandian* and there are stalls at the central crossroads market selling grilled corn and steamed buns.

Jinniu Huoguo 金牛火锅, jīnniú huǒguō. Tucked down a side street off main Tongle Bei Lu. Sichuanese-style hotpots along with generic stir-fries; all inexpensive and tasty. Around ¥10 a dish.

Leye Fandian 乐业饭店, lèyè fàndiàn. 8 Chengnan Dadao ☎077 6792 8888. Decent modern hotel, empty, echoing and untarnished as staff wait for Leye to become a major tourist destination. **¥120**

To the Vietnamese border

Guangxi's southwestern corner bumps up against the **Vietnamese border**, with a slew of offbeat attractions drawing you into the Zhuang heartlands: a world of dark karst hills, grubby towns, water buffalo wallowing in green paddy fields and farmers in broad-sleeved pyjamas and conical hats. Though the area is a backwater today, the Zhuang hero **Nong Zhigao** led an uprising from here in 1052 which captured Nanning, until reprisals by Song troops the following year dispersed Nong and his followers into Yunnan, Vietnam, Laos and Thailand. Nong Zhigao is still worshipped in the region, especially around **Jingxi** town, which was his main base.

Detian waterfall, though isolated in itself, makes a fun return trip west from Nanning; otherwise, attractions are strung southwest along the road and rail between Nanning and the official crossing into Vietnam at the **Friendship Pass**. The pick of the sights are **Chongzuo Ecology Park**, home to critically endangered monkeys, and **Hua Shan** with its ancient rock art. Trains and buses head down to the border, and there's plenty of connecting transport if you want to get out and explore.

Detian waterfall

德天瀑布, détiān pùbù · ¥80

Detian waterfall forms a spectacular series of broad, 30m-high cataracts pouring over a remote stretch of the China – Vietnam border 150km west of Nanning. It's best seen in full flood during the summer rains, thundering away among the landscape, though the faintly surreal border market is worth a look even when the water slows to a trickle in winter.

From **DETIAN** (德天, détiān), the bus stop and tourist township at the entrance, paths lead out through fields to pavilions overlooking the falls, nestled in a hollow between dark grey mountains. The other side of the river is Vietnam; at the 200m-wide, deep-blue plunge pool below the falls, you can hire a **bamboo raft** and be punted over to straddle the mid-river divide.

The best part, however, is to follow the path along the top of the falls to its end in a field, where you'll find a **stone border market** proclaiming the Sino–Vietnamese frontier in French and Chinese, along with a bizarre **border market** – a clutch of trestle tables laden with Vietnamese sweets, cigarettes and stamps in the middle of nowhere.

Though locals wander back and forth over the border without harassment, try to cross into Vietnam yourself and police will spring out of nowhere to stop you.

ARRIVAL AND DEPARTURE   DETIAN WATERFALL

By bus Direct services to Detian are limited, and you might find yourself travelling in stages from Nanning or Baise to the nearest main-road village of Shuolong (硕龙, shuòlóng), and looking for a minibus-taxi to Detian (20min; ¥15) for the final 15km.
From Nanning Langdong station to Detian (2 daily; 4hr; ¥50). Alternatively, Beida Transit Centre to Daxin town (大

新, dàxīn; frequent; 2hr 30min; ¥40); then Daxin to Shuolong (frequent; 1hr; ¥12).
From Baise Baise to Jingxi town (靖西, jìngxī; 8 daily; 4hr; ¥40); then by village-hopping on minibuses which leave when full to Hurun (湖润, húrùn; 1hr 30; ¥10), then Xialei (下雷, xiàléi; 45min; ¥8), and finally Shuolong (30min; ¥4).

ACCOMMODATION AND EATING

There's no really cheap **accommodation** at the falls themselves; if you're on a tight budget, you'll need to spend the night 15km away at Shuolong, a rustic marketplace below cliffs on the main road. **Eat** at accommodation, though don't leave it too late – kitchens here have usually closed by 7pm.

Detian Binguan 德天宾馆, détiān bīnguǎn. Detian ☎ 077 1559 5608. Ordinary tourist affair offering clean, comfortable rooms. **¥130**
Detian Shanzhuang Dajiudian 德天山庄大酒店, détiān shānzhuāng dàjiǔdiàn. Detian ☎ 077 1377 3570. Perched on a slope above the falls, this

once-upmarket option has stunning views across the river into Vietnam, which compensate for the worn furnishings. **¥300**
Hongle 鸿乐旅馆, hónglè lǚguǎn. Shuolong. One of a handful of guesthouses in Shuolong township, offering beds in very basic rooms. Beds **¥30**

Chongzuo Ecology Park
崇左生态公园, chóngzuǒ shēngtài gōngyuán• ¥80

Chongzuo Ecology Park, a compact spread of limestone hills and flat valleys full of tall, scrubby grass, was established in 1996 by renowned panda specialist Professor Pan Wenshi to protect the endemic **white-headed langur** (白头叶猴, báitóu yèhóu), whose entire population numbers just 700 – making it one of China's rarest animals.

Some 250 monkeys live in the park, and there's a real thrill in seeing small groups of these endangered creatures fearlessly scampering across the cliff-faces. The adults have black bodies with white heads and tail tips, and live mostly on leaves (their Chinese name translates as "white-headed leaf monkey"); the golden-furred babies spend much of their childhood hanging on for dear life as mum hurls herself around the rocks.

Before turning up, note that this is a research base, not a zoo; visitors are welcome but the park is fairly wild (cobras are common) and summers are oppressively hot and wet. Staff act as **guides** to take you around the 5km or so of walking tracks, with best viewing times at dawn and dusk. Bring binoculars if possible; the monkeys stay high up on the cliffs.

ARRIVAL AND DEPARTURE   CHONGZUO ECOLOGY PARK

The park is 15km southeast of **Chongzuo** (崇左, chóngzuǒ), a small city halfway down the rail line between Nanning and the border. Aim for Chongzuo, then take a minibus to the park (¥7).

By train Nanning (3 daily; 1hr 30min–3hr); Ningming/Tuolong (2 daily; 1hr); Pingxiang (3 daily; 1hr 45–3hr 40).
By bus Nanning (1hr 30min; ¥35); Ningming (2hr; ¥36);

Pingxiang (2hr 30min; ¥35). Some buses from Nanning pass the park's gate, so ask the driver to let you off right outside.

ACCOMMODATION AND EATING

Former army barracks Right at the reserve gates. Basic doubles and ample Chinese meals (around ¥50/

person/day). Pack a torch as electricity can be erratic. **¥100**

5

Hua Shan

花山, huā shān · ¥50

Overlooking a remote stretch of the **Zuo River** (左江, zuǒ jiāng), which flows eastwards towards Nanning, **Hua Shan** is a tall, vertical cliff-face covered with enigmatic **rock art**, believed to have been painted over 2000 years ago by the ancestors of the Zhuang people. The paintings themselves, comprising 1900 stick-like figures daubed in ochre, are interesting mostly for their isolated setting and historic importance, but the added attraction is that you can only get here **by boat**, involving a relaxing five-hour return trip from the single-street rail junction of **TUOLONG** (驮龙, tuólóng).

Up the Zuo

It's a beautifully placid journey up the Zuo, past banks thick with spindly branched, red-flowering kapok trees. Buffalo wallow in the shallows and people fish from wooden rafts and tend family plots on the shores. Peaks begin to spring up after a while, flat-faced and sheer by the river, and it's here that you'll see the first symbols, many smeared and faded with age. The boat docks just short of Hua Shan, where a track leads to the main body of **paintings**, where you can clearly pick out drummers and dancers, dogs and cattle, a dragonboat race, men with arms bent upwards, a "king" with a sword and just two women, long-haired and pregnant. Some look suspiciously recent, although this might be due to restoration work. A few bronze weapons have also been found here.

ARRIVAL AND DEPARTURE   **HUA SHAN**

By train Tuolong (also known as Ningming station) is right next to the departure point for boats to Hua Shan. Destinations Chongzuo (2 daily; 50min–1hr 30min); Nanning (2 daily; 3hr–4hr 30min); Pingxiang (2 daily; 50min–1hr 20min).

By bus The nearest bus station is 5km south of Tuolong at Ningming (宁明, níngmíng), a nondescript concrete town choked in exhaust fumes. You'll need to get a motor-rickshaw (¥5) from here to the docks. Destinations Chongzuo (2hr; ¥36); Nanning (3hr; ¥38); Pingxiang (1hr; ¥15).

GETTING AROUND

By boat Tuolong Bridge Dock (驮龙桥码头, tuólóngqiáo mǎtóu) is 200m from the train station. Sampan owners here leave on demand and ask ¥100/boat for the return trip to Hua Shan. Bigger tourist boats charging about ¥120/person run if enough people show. Boats take around 2hr each way, and the amount of time spent on site is decided by negotiation.

ACCOMMODATION

Butterfly Valley 蝴蝶沟, húdié gōu. Near Hua Shan. Accommodation in riverside stilt houses for ¥150/person including meals. Note, though, that it only operates erratically – Chinese speakers should ask at Tuolong about the current situation. The nearest alternatives are at Ningming, where inexpensive hotels surround the bus station. **¥300**

Pingxiang and the Friendship Pass

PINGXIANG (凭祥, píngxiáng) is the last town before the Vietnam border at the Friendship Pass. It's a small marketplace of half a dozen streets, useful for transport, banks and accommodation; otherwise, head on.

The **Friendship Pass** (友谊关, yǒuyì guān), 15km southwest of Pingxiang, is marked by a huge stone **gate tower** and remnants of a Ming-dynasty **wall** running up into the hills, which you can follow for a short way before it deteriorates among the vegetation. The European-style **customs house** below dates from 1914, after the French had taken what was then **Tonkin**, northern Vietnam, from the Chinese during the 1880s. After an indecisive battle at the pass – the French were forced to retreat, but the Chinese suffered huge losses – France applied diplomatic pressure on the Qing court, forcing them to sign a treaty ceding this area to their control.

Assuming you already have a visa (see p.348), **crossing the border** is straightforward, though getting through Vietnamese customs can take a while. On the Vietnamese side, rickshaws and minibuses can take you the 4km to Dong Dang station, where trains run to Hanoi, or 18km on to Lang Son, the closest city to the border.

If arriving in China, you'll be besieged by touts wanting to take you to Pingxiang. Keep this guidebook buried deep in your bags – over-zealous customs officials sometimes confiscate them.

| ARRIVAL AND DEPARTURE | PINGXIANG AND THE FRIENDSHIP PASS |

Buses and trains run to Pingxiang. Three-wheeler **taxis** between Pingxiang and the Friendship Pass charge ¥10.

By bus Chongzuo (2hr 30min; ¥35); Nanning (4hr; ¥65); Ningming (1hr; ¥12).

By train Chongzuo (3 daily; 1hr 30min–2hr 30min); Nanning (3 daily; 3hr 30min–5hr 30min); Ningming (2 daily; 45min).

ACCOMMODATION

In Pingxiang, main street Bei Da Lu is packed with identical cheap **hotels** charging upwards of ¥30/person.

Jinxiangyu Dajiudian 金祥玉大酒店, jīnxiángyù dàjiǔdiàn. Bei Da Lu ☎077 1852 1303. A clean, quiet, tiled hotel, marginally more upmarket than other nearby options. **¥90**

Xigong 西贡大酒店, xīgòng dàjiǔdiàn. 99 Xinhua Lu ☎077 1509 5888. Friendly, modern hotel, one of the best deals in town, and especially welcome if you've had a long journey up from Vietnam. **¥180**

DIRECTORY

Banks There's a Bank of China and ATM close to Pingxiang's bus station on Bei Da Lu.

The tropical coast

Guangxi's **tropical coastline** is just a few hours south of Nanning, easily reached by train. The main city, **Beihai**, is nice enough and deserves a look as southwest China's only seaside resort; there's an old street or two, along with some pleasant but overhyped little **beaches** and nearby **Weizhou Island**. If you're serious about sun and sand, consider catching the **ferry to Hainan**, an island province 150km to the south.

Beihai

北海, běihǎi

BEIHAI is a languid, crowded port city with broad boulevards and widely spaced buildings. It was originally in Guangdong, but the border was shifted in the 1960s so that Guangxi would have a viable seaport; many people here still speak **Cantonese** as their first language The city centre is pretty functional, and you're really here for the beaches 5km south of town; Beihai's civic focus is **Beibuwan Square** (北部湾广场, běibùwān guǎngchǎng), a large paved area where Beibuwan Lu, running east–west across the city, crosses Sichuan Lu.

Zhuhai Lu

珠海路, zhūhǎi lù

Head a kilometre north up Sichuan Lu from the centre, and off to the east is **Zhuhai Lu**, a pedestrianized **historic quarter** built after Beihai was opened up to Western powers as a "Treaty Port" in 1876. There's a church or two, and some mouldering old warehouses, but most of the buildings are **shophouses**, whose colonnades provide an escape from the tropical heat and rain. This type of architecture, a sort of Chinese-European fusion, is found wherever the Chinese settled through Southeast Asia. There's

5

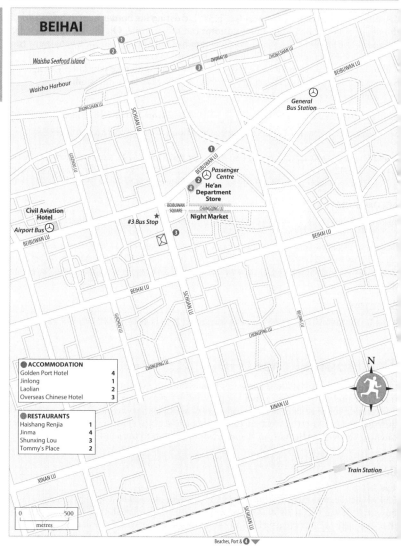

BEIHAI

Waisha Seafood Island

Waisha Harbour

ZHONGSHAN LU

ZHONGSHAN LU

ZIYOU LU

ZHONGSHAN LU

SICHUAN LU

BEIBUWAN LU

General
Bus Station

BEIBUWAN LU

Passenger
Centre

He'an
Department
Store

BEIBUWAN
SQUARE

CHANGQING LU

Night Market

Civil Aviation
Hotel

#3 Bus Stop

Airport Bus

BEIBUWAN LU

BEIHAI LU

GUIZHOU LU

BEIHAI LU

SICHUAN LU

BEIHAI LU

BEIHAI LU

BEIJING LU

CHONGQING LU

ACCOMMODATION

Golden Port Hotel	4
Jinlong	1
Laolian	2
Overseas Chinese Hotel	3

CHONGQING LU

GUIZHOU LU

XINAN LU

N

RESTAURANTS

Haishang Renjia	1
Jinma	4
Shunxing Lou	3
Tommy's Place	2

SICHUAN LU

Train Station

XINAN LU

0   500
metres

Beaches, Port & 4

also some low-key tourism – a couple of trendy boutiques, café-bars and souvenir shops selling pearls and seashells – and it's an atmospheric place to stroll, with a few buildings picked out with signs explaining their history.

Waisha harbour and Seafood Island

Back on Sichuan Lu, another 100m and you're on a bridge over the sheltered, canal-like **Waisha harbour**, packed with scruffy wooden junks and trawlers piled high with nets and fishing gear. On the other side is **Waisha Seafood Island** (外沙海鲜岛, wàishā hǎixiān dǎo), a seafront esplanade whose restaurants make it a good place to head in the evening.

HAINAN ISLAND

Floating in the South China Sea between Guangxi and Vietnam, **Hainan Island** (海南岛, hǎinán dǎo) is China's southernmost territory and major tropical beach resort. Originally inhabited by the indigenous **Li** ethnic group, Hainan was once a dustbin for political troublemakers such as the Sichuanese poet **Su Dongpo**, who died on his way back from exile here in 1101.

Today exiles have been replaced by holiday-makers, who arrive by ferry and plane at the north-coast capital, **Haikou** (海口, hǎikǒu) before tearing 300km south down the expressway to sprawl on the golden sands around **SANYA** (三亚, sānyà). Sanya has high-rise beachfront resorts and plenty of seafood restaurants, and there's even the chance for some halfway-decent scuba diving.

From Beihai, there are two ferries daily to Haikou; you can also buy all-inclusive tickets at the General Bus Station for a bus-ferry-bus combination into Haikou's downtown (see below).

Beaches

Beihai's **beaches** form a long strip of grey-white sand about 5km south of town; catch the **#3 bus** from just south of Beibuwan Square down Sichuan Lu via the **ferry port**. Hainan's beaches are in a different league altogether, so don't set aside a day here if you're heading that way.

Get off where you see a big silver globe and you're at **Haitan Park** (海滩公园, hǎitān gōngyuán), with a strip of lawn between you and the sand, and a row of alfresco seafood stalls opposite. Another kilometre along at the end of the bus route, **Yintan Park** (银滩公园, yíntān gōngyuán) is more popular and better organized; there are coconut palms, shaded seating and picnic tables, beachside barbecues, trinket stalls, showers, storage lockers and a safe swimming area marked by floating red buoys overlooked by lifeguard towers (though getting wet is perhaps not such a good idea, given that the city lacks a sewerage treatment plant). On the whole, the Chinese seem slightly bemused by beach life, sitting around and nervously eating or chatting as if they know it should be fun but are unsure of how to go about it.

ARRIVAL AND DEPARTURE   BEIHAI

BY PLANE

Beihai Airport is about 25km east of town. There's an airlines ticket office at the General Bus Station, and at the *Civil Aviation Hotel* (民航大酒店, mínháng dàjiǔdiàn; ☎0779 308 2099), 1.5km west from Beibuwan Square down Beibuwan Lu. The airport bus leaves from the *Civil Aviation Hotel* 2hr before each flight departs (30min; ¥10).
Destinations Beijing (2 daily; 3hr); Guangzhou (2 daily; 1hr); Guilin (2 daily; 1hr); Shanghai (4 weekly; 3hr); Shenzhen (1 daily; 50min).

BY BUS

Buses leave from two separate terminals.
Passenger Centre (客运中心, kèyùn zhōngxīn), Beibuwan Lu, about 700m east of Beibuwan Square on the #2 bus route between the square and the train station.
Destinations Guilin (1 daily; 9hr; ¥128); Nanning (4hr; ¥95); Shenzhen (6 daily; 13hr; ¥180).

General Bus Station (汽车总站, qìchē zǒngzhàn), Beibuwan Lu, about 1.5km east of Beibuwan Square on the #15 bus route.
Destinations Guilin (6 daily; 9hr; ¥125); Haikou (1 daily; 10hr; ¥120); Nanning (4hr; ¥95), Shenzhen (4 daily; 13hr; ¥180).

BY TRAIN

Beihai's train station is about 4km southwest of the centre on the #2 bus route (¥1) from Beibuwan Square.
Destinations Nanning (2 daily; 3hr; ¥38).

BY BOAT

All ferries depart from **Beihai International Port** (北海国际客运港, běihǎi guójì kèyùngǎng), 5km south of town down Sichuan Lu, on the #3 bus route (¥2) to the beaches.
Destinations Hainan (2 daily; 10hr; ¥120—360 depending on seat or cabin); Weizhou (4 daily; 1hr 30min; ¥180—240).

GETTING AROUND

By bus City buses connect all transit points except the airport with Beibuwan Square; they cost ¥1 a ride, ¥2 if a/c.

By taxi ¥7 to hire.

5

ACCOMMODATION

There are plenty of central **places to stay** within walking distance of Beibuwan Square, but the lack of decent hotels near the beaches is a seriously wasted opportunity.

Golden Port Hotel 金港酒店, jīngǎng jiǔdiàn. 8 Yingtan Dadao, Haitan Gongyuan ☎ 077 9389 7200. One of the few beach hotels that's well maintained and worth the price; moderately upmarket, large but low-rise, with several wings. Busy but feels a little isolated; town buses stop outside. ¥400

Jinlong 金龙宾馆, jīnlóng bīnguǎn. 40 Beibuwan Lu ☎ 077 9221 1777. No-frills but tidy hotel diagonally across from the Passenger Centre, a little off the road so quieter than other similar nearby operations. ¥110

Laolian 劳联宾馆, láolián bīnguǎn. 31 Beibuwan Lu near the Passenger Centre ☎ 077 9308 0088. Clean, large rooms with ADSL sockets, big TVs and not enough lighting. Useful for the bus station, and on the #2 and #3 bus routes. ¥120

Overseas Chinese Hotel 北海华侨宾馆, běihǎi huáqiáo bīnguǎn. 55 Sichuan Lu, just south of Beibuwan Square and more or less opposite the post office ☎ 077 9308 1588. The usual newish, comfortably bland low-end business hotel, with over-optimistic rack rates which you never end up paying. ¥388

EATING AND DRINKING

For cheap street food – kebabs, hotpots, stewed snails – head to the **night market**, which sets up after 7pm along Changqing Lu, east off Beibuwan Square.

Haishang Renjia 海上人家, hǎishàng rénjiā. Straight ahead off the end of Sichuan Lu, on the seafront, Waisha Seafood Island. One of several local restaurants with outdoor tables overlooking the water, serving consistently good Cantonese seafood. Order fish, prawns etc by weight from live tanks; fix prices when ordering to avoid unpleasant surprises. ¥40/head.

Jinma 金马美食城, jīnmǎ měishí chéng. Basement of the He'an department store, on Beibuwan Square. Clean, busy place serving tasty snacks from all over China; order from the surrounding food booths and your selection is delivered to your table. Dishes ¥5–30.

Shunxing Lou 顺兴楼, shùnxīng lóu. 1 Zhuhai Lu, on the pedestrianized old street. Period building serving good-value, tasty Cantonese snacks – prawn wonton soup, roast pork on rice, cold fruit juices and almond jellies. Nothing more than ¥10.

Tommy's Place 汤米西餐厅, tāngmǐ xī cāntīng. Waisha Seafood Island ⊛ tommysplace.org. Bear left before the seafront and look for the blue-and-white building. Australian-run restaurant-bar; excellent pizza, burgers and imported steak alongside filling Chinese and Southeast Asian staples – plus ice-cold beer. All-day breakfasts ¥30, mains from ¥35.

DIRECTORY

Banks There are several with ATMs around Beibuwan Square.

Maps Some Beihai city maps have inserts of Weizhou Island, if you're heading there.

Post Office 200m south of Beibuwan Square on Sichuan Lu.

Weizhou Island

涠洲岛, wéizhōu dǎo • ¥80

Another option for a seaside break, **Weizhou Island** is a 7km-wide oval of volcanic origins about 30km offshore from Beihai. Shamelessly promoted by the domestic tourist industry despite its underwhelming attractions, once you add up the cost of the ferry and the entry fee, you're looking at a decidedly expensive excursion. The island is largely flat and given over to banana cultivation, with a few tiny villages linked by concrete tracks. The **port** is on the northwest side, and the main settlement – just one street and a marketplace along the seafront – down on the south coast at **NANWAN** (南湾, nánwān).

Around Nanwan

Just west from Nanwan, the **Geology Park** (国家地质公园, guójiā dìzhì gōngyuán; ¥10) makes a big fuss over Weizhou's volcanic origins, though aside from some worn lava cliffs there's nothing to see. North of here, tiny **Shiluokou Beach** (石螺口, shíluókǒu) has white sand and casuarina trees, deckchairs and umbrellas for rent (¥10), basic seafood shacks and **introductory scuba dives** (¥100) on hand – the latter spent sitting on the sand in 10m of water.

The French Catholic Church

天主教堂, tiānzhǔjiào táng

The island's most unusual sight is the nineteenth-century **French Catholic Church** up at northeast **Shengtan village**, an extraordinary building of huge stone blocks with a square, Norman-style tower and Gothic arches which wouldn't look out of place in a rural European setting. It's the last indication that Weizhou was once under Vietnamese – and so, from the 1880s, French – control.

ARRIVAL AND DEPARTURE   WEIZHOU ISLAND

Ferries from Beihai dock at **Weizhou Port** (涠洲客运港, wéizhōu kèyùn gǎng) on the northwest side of the island, about 5km from Nanwan and the western beaches, and 6km from the church. Tractor taxis wait just outside the port.

By boat The ticket office and waiting hall is the large building on the right at the head of the jetty, and if you're only planning a day-trip, buy return tickets immediately on arrival.

Destinations Beihai (4 daily; 1hr 30min; ¥180–240 each way).

GETTING AROUND

At 7km across, exposed and very hot in summer, Weihai is a bit too large to **walk** everywhere.

By taxi Tractor taxis run to everywhere else on the island; you'll be lucky to get a ride across for under ¥15.

By bicycle Accommodation can sort bike rental at about ¥30 a day.

ACCOMMODATION AND EATING

Weizhou's **accommodation** is strung along the seafront at Nanwan; the only places to **eat** are at the hotels, though there's a market at the end of the bay if you're after fruit. Not much English is spoken anywhere.

Gangdao Jiudian 港岛酒店, gǎngdǎojiǔdiàn. Nanwan Jie, just as you reach Nanwan's main clutch of buildings ☎077 9601 3803, ⓦgangdaohotel.com. Also known as the *Kongtat*, after the local pronounciation, this is an unimaginative but modern and comfortable place facing the bay. **¥350**

Piggybar Hostel 猪仔吧青年旅舍, zhūzǎiba qīngnián lǚshè. Western end of seafront Nanwan Jie ☎077 9601 2804, ⓦpiggybar.com. A tropically shabby, pleasantly laidback hostel with a little too much concrete, but it's friendly, the cook knows what he's doing, and the staff can arrange bike rental. Dorms **¥30**

Weizhou Holiday Hotel 涠洲岛度假酒店, wéizhōu dǎo dùjià jiǔdiàn. Far end of Nanwan village, past the market ☎077 9601 3388. Similar to the *Gangdao*, though back from the sea. **¥350**

MIAO MUSICIANS IN BASHA, GUIZHOU

Contexts

History

For much of its history, Southwest China has lain well outside the national consciousness, but recent archeology indicates that sophisticated cultures have flourished here since antiquity. People were casting elaborate bronzes in Sichuan over three thousand years ago; new canals were linking major river systems together in the time of China's first emperor; while by 100 BC there were trade routes running through Yunnan and into Tibet, Burma and India. The Southwest later became known for rebellions and troublemakers – uprisings that began here during the nineteenth century caused the deaths of around thirty million people around China – but it was also famous for tea and silk, and as a refuge against hostile foreign powers. The following history focuses on the major national events occurring in eastern China – the "Middle Kingdom" between the Great Wall and the Yangzi River – and should also help set the context for Southwestern Chinese history covered in the guide.

Prehistory and the Three Dynasties

Chinese legends relate that the creator, Pan Ku, was born from the egg of chaos and grew to fill the space between Yin, the earth, and Yang, the heavens. When he died his body became the soil, rivers and rain, and his eyes became the sun and moon, while his parasites transformed into human beings. A pantheon of semi-divine rulers known as the **Five Sovereigns** followed, inventing fire, the calendar, agriculture, silk-breeding and marriage; later came **Yu the Great**, tamer of floods, who founded China's first dynasty, the **Xia**. The Xia lasted 439 years until its last degenerate and corrupt king was overthrown by the **Shang**, who were in turn succeeded by the **Zhou**, whose written court histories put an end to this legendary era. Together, the Xia, Shang and Zhou are generally known as the **Three Dynasties**.

As far as archeology is concerned, *homo erectus* remains – such as **Yuanmou Man**, unearthed in Yunnan – indicate that China was already occupied by human ancestors well before modern mankind began to emerge 200,000 years ago. Excavations of more recent Stone Age sites show that agricultural communities based between the fertile Yellow River and Yangzi basins in eastern China, were producing pottery and silk by 5000 BC.

It was along the Yellow River, too, that **bronze-working** emerged during the Three Dynasties – brought to a peak during the **Shang dynasty** (roughly1750 BC to 1040 BC), though recent discoveries at **Sanxingdui** in Sichuan show a parallel culture in the Southwest as early as 1600 BC.

4800 BC	2100 BC–771 BC	1600BC	770 BC–476 BC
First evidence of human settlement along the Yellow River basin in eastern China.	The Three Dynasties rule eastern China.	Bronze-working Shu culture appears at Sanxingdui, Chengdu	Spring and Autumn period. Jinsha replaces Sanxingdui; Ba appear at Chongqing; Dian Kingdom founded in Yunnan.

THE TORTOISE TEXTS

China's **earliest known writing** dates to the Shang dynasty and was used for divination. Questions were incised onto pieces of tortoiseshell or bone, which were then heated to study the way in which the material cracked around the words, indicating a positive or negative response to the questions posed. These **oracle bones**, while not describing events or people, cover topics as diverse as rainfall, dreams and ancestral curses. The characters used are ancestors of modern Chinese script, and in a few cases are recognizable when compared to modern forms.

From the Zhou to the Qin

Around 1040 BC the **Zhou** overthrew the Shang, expanded their kingdom west of the Yellow River and set up a capital near modern Xi'an. The Zhou ruled through a hierarchy of vassal lords, whose growing independence led to the gradual dissolution of the kingdom from around 600 BC, and drove freebooters to the edge of the empire to set up their own territories: the **Baiyue** peoples appeared in southern Guangxi, the **Dian Kingdom** was founded in Yunnan, and the **Jinsha culture** replaced Sanxingdui in Sichuan. Meanwhile, central China was fought over by some two hundred city states and kingdoms during the four centuries known as the **Spring and Autumn** and **Warring States** periods. This time of violence was also an era of vitality and change, with the rise of the ethics of Confucianism and Taoism, the first smelting of **iron** for weapons and tools and great developments in agriculture – such as the construction of eastern Sichuan's **Dujiangyan Irrigation Scheme** in 256 BC. By this point, only a handful of kingdoms were left, the others having been gobbled up by a new emerging power, the **Qin**.

The Qin dynasty

In 221 BC the Qin armies overran the last opposition and united China as a **single centralized state** for the first time, with a territory stretching from Sichuan to Mongolia and the eastern seaboard. The rule of China's first emperor, **Qin Shi Huang**, was absolute and harsh, his advisers favouring the philosophy of **legalism** – the idea that mankind is inherently bad, and needs to be kept in line by draconian punishments. Ancient literature and historical records were destroyed to wipe out any ideas that conflicted with his own, and peasants forcibly recruited to work as labourers on massive construction projects, including his tomb outside Xi'an (guarded by the famous **Terracotta Army**) and an early version of the **Great Wall**. Determined to rule the entire known world, he pushed his armies south, ordering the construction of the **Ling Canal** in Guangxi to create a waterway for moving troops between the Yangzi and southern China. When he died in 210 BC – ironically, during a search for mythical herbs of immortality – his heirs proved to lack the personal authority that had held his empire together, and the provinces rose in revolt.

The Han dynasty

In 206 BC the rebel warlord Liu Bang took Xi'an and founded the **Han dynasty**. Lasting some four hundred years and larger at its height than contemporary Rome, the Han was the first great Chinese empire, one that experienced a flowering of culture and a major

457 BC–221 BC	256 BC	221 BC	210 BC
Warring States Period. The Great Wall appears.	Li Bing and son build Dujiangyan Irrigation Scheme in Sichuan.	Qin Shi Huang unifies China – he later builds the Ling Canal to ferry troops through Guangxi.	Qin dies, leaving the Terracotta Army to guard his tomb.

THE MANDATE OF HEAVEN

The Zhou introduced the doctrine of the **Mandate of Heaven**, a belief justifying successful rebellion by declaring that heaven grants ruling authority to leaders who are strong and wise, and takes it from those who aren't – a concept that remains integral to the Chinese political perspective.

impetus to push out frontiers and open them to trade, people and new ideas. In doing so it defined the national identity to such an extent that the main body of the Chinese people – in contrast to the ethnic minority groups found throughout the Southwest – still style themselves "**Han Chinese**".

Liu Bang maintained the Qin model of local government, but to prevent others from repeating his own military takeover he strengthened his position by handing out large chunks of land to his relatives. This secured a period of stability, with effective taxation financing a growing civil service and the expansionist policies of a subsequent ruler, **Wu**, who from 135 to 90 BC **annexed Vietnam**, received tribute from Yunnan and established **trade routes** for tea, spices and silk through into Burma, India and Central Asia. At home, Wu stressed the Confucian model for his growing civil service, beginning a two-thousand-year institution of Confucianism in government offices.

Though power began once again devolving into the provinces after the formation of the **Eastern Han** in 25 AD, the period also saw the introduction of **Buddhism** into China from India, enriching thought, fine arts and literature, while itself being absorbed and changed by native beliefs. But eventually the central court lost authority, warlords saw their chance, and the Han dynasty ended as it had begun, in civil war.

The Three Kingdoms to the Sui

Between 200 and 280 AD the **Three Kingdoms period** (see box, p.69) saw the three states of **Wei** (in northern China), **Wu** (Southern China) and **Shu** (Sichuan) struggle for supremacy. During the following four centuries China was unified under a single government for only about fifty years, though there were periods of stability: in 386, northern China was taken by the Tobas, who established the northern **Wei dynasty** after their aristocracy adopted Chinese manners and customs – a pattern of assimilation that was to recur with other invaders – though their empire fell apart in 534.

After grabbing power from his regent in 581, General **Yang Jian** founded the short-lived **Sui dynasty**, with a capital again near today's Xi'an. As Emperor Wen, he simplified and strengthened the bureaucracy, brought in a new legal code, recentralized civil and military authority and made tax collection more efficient. Following Wen's death in 604, his successor **Yang Di** became a proverbially "Evil Emperor" thanks to his disastrous military campaigns against **Korea**, in which the Chinese armies were totally annihilated, and the use of forced labour to complete grandiose engineering projects. Half the total workforce of 5,500,000 died during the construction of the 2000km **Grand Canal**, built to transport produce from the southern Yangzi to his capital at Xi'an. Yang was assassinated in 618 during a military revolt led by General **Li Yuan**.

206 BC–220 AD	220–618	618–907	713
Han dynasty. Han emperors expand into Sichuan and Yunnan, and forge trade connections with the outside world.	Han disintegrates. China split into short-lived, regional kingdoms and dynasties.	Tang dynasty. Rise of Tibet, plus the Nanzhao and Dali kingdoms.	Work begins on the Great Buddha at Leshan – it takes 90 years to complete.

The Tang and Five Dynasties

Li Yuan spent only eight years in power, leaving his son **Tai Zong** to consolidate the new **Tang dynasty**. The Tang saw China opening up on an unparalleled scale to foreign traders and travellers, whose alien cultures influenced and enriched China's arts, cookery, fashion and entertainment, raising them to new heights. Chinese goods flowed out to India, Persia, the Middle East and beyond, and Chinese culture gained currency in Japan and Korea. At home, Buddhism remained the all-pervading foreign influence, with Chinese pilgrims travelling widely in India; the best known of these, **Xuan Zang** (see p.65), set off in 629 and returned after sixteen years with a mass of religious texts.

Meanwhile, the small, independent kingdoms which made up **Tibet** – including the Amdo and Kham areas of what is now northern Yunnan and western Sichuan – were coming under the sway of the aggressive ruler **Songtsen Gampo**. Though he never unified the country politically, his raiding parties proved so troublesome that he was able to demand tribute from his neighbours, including China. In 641, the Chinese **Princess Wencheng** was sent as a bride for Songtsen Gampo, with two mighty consequences: she converted him from Bon, Tibet's native religion (see p.118), to Buddhism; and her marriage was used in modern times to support China's annexation of Tibet. Songtsen's successors continued to champion the new faith, but lacked his military ambitions, and the country became insular and remote.

Back in China, the empress **Wu Zetian** – the daughter of a Sichuanese timber merchant – continued the patronage of Buddhism; monumental religious carvings such as Leshan's **Big Buddha** were started in the aftermath of her reign. Her successor, **Xuan Zong**, began well in 712, but his later infatuation with the beautiful concubine **Yang Guifei** saw the empire begin to fray. In 750, Yunnan's recently emerged **Nanzhao Kingdom** soundly defeated the Chinese armies sent against it, expanding unchecked into Burma, Thailand and Laos.

In Xi'an, the military defeat led to the **An Lushan rebellion** of 755, Emperor Xuan Zong's flight to Sichuan and Yang Guifei's death at the hands of his mutinying army – chaotic years recorded in verse by the poet **Du Fu** (see p.68). Xuan Zong's son, Su Zong, enlisted the help of Tibetan and Uigur forces (the latter a Turkic people from northwestern China), and in 763 recaptured Xi'an from the rebels; but though the court was re-established, it had lost its authority, and real power was once again shifting to the provinces.

The following centuries saw the country split into regional political and military alliances. From 907 to 960, central China's successive **Five Dynasties** were too short-lived to be effective, and the country was unable to hold onto its more distant territories. The overstretched Nanzhao Kingdom imploded in Yunnan, swiftly replaced in 937 by the smaller **Dali Kingdom**; and in 938 **Vietnam** gained independence by defeating China's Southern Han kingdom.

The Song and the Yuan

In 960, a disaffected army put General **Song Tai Zu** on the throne. His new ruling house, known as the **Northern Song**, made its capital at Kaifeng in the Yellow River basin, well placed at the head of the Grand Canal for transport to supply its million people with grain from the south. By skilled politicking rather than military might, the new dynasty consolidated authority over surrounding petty kingdoms and

907–1271	1271–1368	1273–92	1368–1644	1642
Five Dynasties and the Song. Buddhist sculptures carved at Dazu.	Mongols found the Yuan dynasty, ransacking Southwest China.	Marco Polo visits China.	Ming dynasty. Imperial fleet reaches Africa before China implements an isolationist policy.	Tibet unified under Song Gyatso, and the Yellow Ha (Gelugpa) school of Lama becomes dominant.

re-established civilian primacy. However, in 1115 northern China was occupied by the **Jin**, a nomadic group from beyond China's frontiers, who pushed the imperial court south to Hangzhou in 1126. Here, guarded by the Yangzi River, the **Southern Song** dynasty flourished for 150 years, inventing gunpowder, the magnetic compass, fine porcelain and movable type printing. In due course, however, the Song's preoccupation with art and sophistication saw their military might decline and led them to underrate their aggressive "barbarian" neighbours, whose own expansionist policies culminated in the thirteenth-century Mongol Invasion.

The Yuan dynasty

The **Mongols** were warring horsemen from the central Asian steppes whose raiding activities had been threatening China since the eleventh century. In 1206 the separate Mongol clans were unified by **Genghis Khan** into an immensely powerful army which swiftly embarked on conquest, spilling south and west towards China and Europe. **Tibet** capitulated without a fight a year later, introducing the Mongols to Buddhism, which later became their state religion. Sichuan's capital, **Chengdu**, was captured in 1236 and its entire population put to death, while the Dali Kingdom fell in 1253, and a large **Muslim population** – soldiers from central Asia who had fought for the Mongols – settled in Yunnan to guard this remote frontier.

Determined Chinese resistance at **Diaoyu Cheng** near Chongqing saw the Mongol leader **Mengge** killed in 1259 (see p.156), which halted the invasion of Europe. Instead, the Mongols' focus remained on Asia. In 1277, they conquered **Burma**, defeating King Narathihapade after the Khan's archers had stampeded Burmese war elephants back through their own lines, and by next year Ghengis Khan's grandson **Kublai Khan** was on the Chinese throne, first of the **Yuan dynasty**. The Yuan emperors' central control from their capital at Khanbalik – modern **Beijing** – once again threw China open to foreign emissaries, including the Venetian **Marco Polo**, who recorded his impressions of Yuan society after he'd served several years as a government official.

The Yuan only retained control over all China until 1368, their rapid demise a combination of spreading themselves too thin and losing the ruthless aggression which had gained them their empire in the first place. Famine and disastrous floods brought a series of uprisings in China, and a monk-turned-bandit leader from the south, **Zhu Yuanzhang**, seized the throne from the last boy emperor of the Yuan in 1368.

The Ming dynasty

Taking the name **Hong Wu**, Zhu Yuanzhang proclaimed himself the first emperor of the **Ming dynasty**. By the time of his death in 1398, all China, including Yunnan and Sichuan, was back in Chinese hands; southern China was being governed from **Guilin** by imperial relatives; and regions which had been depopulated under the Mongols – such as Sichuan – were resettled using migrants from eastern provinces (whose descendants built provincial **guildhalls** in Chengdu, Chongqing, Zigong and elsewhere). Later military campaigns saw Vietnam become a vassal state and a network of post-roads and garrison towns probing down through Guizhou. Hong Wu's reign was marred, however, by two appalling purges in which thousands of civil servants and literati died.

The Ming also produced fine artistic accomplishments, particularly **porcelain**,

1644	Late 18C	1839–62	1851–76
Qing dynasty begins. Manchu rule brings peace, prosperity, and a population boom.	Migrants flood into Southwest China, causing ethnic conflict. Emperor Qianlong rejects trade agreements with Britain.	Opium Wars. China bankrupted by indemnities levied by victorious Europeans; popular dissent against the Manchus swells.	Taiping Uprising devastates central China; Yunnan and Guizhou also laid waste by ethnic unrest.

which was exported via trade networks as far as Europe. During the reign of Yongle, Zhu's twenty-sixth son, the imperial navy (commanded by the Yunnanese Muslim eunuch, Admiral **Zheng He**) ranged right across the Indian Ocean as far as the east coast of Africa on a fact-finding mission. But after Yongle's death in 1424 the maritime missions were cancelled as being expensive, unproductive and incompatible with Confucian values, which held contempt for foreigners. China became **isolationist** and the initiative for **world trade and exploration** passed into the hands of the Europeans with the great period of voyages by Columbus, Magellan and Vasco da Gama. In 1514, **Portuguese** vessels appeared in the Pearl River at the southern port of Guangzhou (Canton), and in 1557 Portugal was allowed a trading post at nearby **Macau**. Although all dealings with foreigners were officially despised by the imperial court, trade flourished as Chinese merchants and officials were eager to milk the profits.

In later years, a succession of less able Ming rulers allowed power to slip into the hands of self-interested court officials, who wasted their energies on palace intrigues, rather than running the country. A series of peasant and military **uprisings** against the Ming began in 1627, and all China collapsed in chaos: Guilin was torched; "Yellow Tiger" Zhang Xianzhong ransacked Sichuan; and even the Mongols rose, invading Tibet in 1642 in the cause of the Fifth Dalai Lama, **Lobsang Gyatso**, who unified the disparate Tibetan kingdoms for the first time.

In 1644, the rebel warlord **Li Zicheng** captured Beijing to find that the last Ming emperor had hanged himself. Meanwhile, Chinese forces under **Wu Sangui** were trying to defend the country's northern borders against the **Manchus**, a clannish people from beyond the Great Wall in what is now northeastern China, who also had designs on the Chinese capital. But Li Zicheng made the mistake of kidnapping Wu Sangui's concubine, and Wu, enraged, let the Manchu armies through the Great Wall; they soon threw out Li, claimed Beijing as their own and founded the **Qing dynasty**.

The Qing dynasty

It took the Manchus a further twenty years to quell the south of the country, but on its capitulation China was once again under foreign rule. Manchu became the official language, the Chinese were obliged to wear the Manchu **pigtail**, and intermarriage between Manchu and Chinese was strictly forbidden.

Three outstanding early Qing emperors brought an infusion of new blood and vigour to government. **Kangxi**, who began his 61-year reign in 1654 at the age of six, was a great patron of the arts, and assiduously cultivated his image as the Son of Heaven by making royal progresses throughout the country. His fourth son, the emperor **Yungzheng** (1678–1735), ruled over what is considered one of the most efficient and least corrupt administrations ever enjoyed by China. This was inherited by **Qianlong** (1711–99), whose reign saw China's frontiers widely extended and the economy stimulated by peace and prosperity. In 1750 the nation was perhaps at its apex, one of the strongest, wealthiest and most powerful countries in the world.

During the latter half of the eighteenth century, however, problems arose. Peace and prosperity produced a **population explosion** in eastern China, putting pressure on food resources and causing a land shortage. This saw Chinese migrants moving in to settle

1899–1900	1904	1911	1921	1934-35
Anti-foreigner Boxer Rebellion; Christian missionaries slaughtered across the country, European officials besieged in Beijing.	Britain invades Tibet.	End of imperial China. Sun Yatsen becomes leader of the Republic.	Chinese Communist Party (CCP) founded in Beijing.	Communists make their Long March through Southwest China, via Guangxi, Guizhou and Sichuan.

the remoter western provinces, inevitably causing conflict as they dispossessed the original inhabitants.

Meanwhile, **European nations** were muscling into Asia, looking for financial opportunities. From around 1660, the southern port of Guangzhou (Canton) had been opened to British merchants shopping for tea, silk and porcelain, who were frustrated by the Chinese refusal to buy Western goods. Convinced of their own superiority, however, China's immensely rich and powerful rulers had no interest in bilateral trade: when **Lord Macartney** arrived in 1793 to propose a political and commercial treaty between Britain and China, the emperor bluntly rejected any idea of alliance with one who, according to Chinese ideas, was a subordinate.

The Opium Wars

Foiled in their attempts at official negotiations with the Qing court, the British East India Company decided to take matters into their own hands. Instead of silver, they began to pay for Chinese goods with **opium**, cheaply imported from their possessions in India. As demand escalated during the early nineteenth century, China's trade surplus became a deficit, as silver drained out of the country to pay for the drug. The emperor intervened in 1840 by ordering the confiscation and destruction of over twenty thousand chests of opium – the start of the **First Opium War**. After two years of British gunboats shelling coastal ports, the Chinese were forced to sign the **Treaty of Nanjing**, whose humiliating terms included a huge indemnity, the opening up of **Treaty Ports**, where foreigners could live and trade, and the cession of Hong Kong to Britain. The **Second Opium War** of 1856–60 forced further concessions, also opening up China to France, the US and Russia.

Uprisings

To be once more conquered by foreigners was a crushing blow for China, who now suffered major internal **uprisings** inspired by anti-Manchu feeling and economic hardship – themselves fuelled by rising taxes to pay off the massive **war indemnity** demanded by the victorious Europeans. The most widespread and devastating revolt was the **Taiping Uprising** (see p.344), which began in Guangxi and stormed through central China in the 1850s to occupy much of the rich Yangzi Valley. Having captured Nanjing as their "Heavenly Capital", the Taipings began to make military forays towards Beijing, and European powers decided to step in, worried that the Taipings' anti-foreign government might take control of the country. With their support, Qing troops defeated the Taipings in 1864, leaving twenty million people dead and five provinces in ruins.

At the same time, **Miao** in Guizhou – some of them battle-trained from fighting the Taipings – staged their own rebellion against the Chinese (see p.288), as did Yunnan's **Muslim** population (see p.183). Both uprisings lasted into the 1870s, and were only put down after further massive loss of life; estimates vary, but whole towns were reduced to rubble and it's likely that another six million people perished.

The Boxer Movement – the end of imperial China

By the 1890s, China was in tatters, with foreign powers getting ever bolder in their demands. France took the former vassal states of Laos, Cambodia and Vietnam in 1883–85; Britain gained Burma; Taiwan was ceded to Japan; while a Russian-built rail line into the northeast effectively gave Russia control of Manchuria. A final popular

1937–45	1945	1949	1950
War with Japan; China's government moves west to Chongqing.	Surrender of Japan. Civil war begins between the Guomindang and the People's Liberation Army.	Communist takeover and founding of the People's Republic of China.	Korean War. Chinese troops invade Tibet; Dalai Lama signs treaty of autonomy with the Beijing government.

uprising appeared in 1899 in the form of the **Boxer Rebellion**, a martial arts movement which turned itself loose to slaughter much-hated Western missionaries and Christian converts. During the summer of 1900 the Boxers took control of Beijing and besieged the foreign legations compound, though they were routed when an international relief force arrived on August 14.

Though they clung feebly on for another decade, this was the end of the Qing, and internal movements to dismantle the dynastic system and build a new China proliferated. The most influential of these was the Tong Meng Hui society, founded in 1905 in Japan by the exile **Sun Yatsen**, a doctor from a wealthy Guangdong family. In 1911, opposition to the construction of **foreign-funded rail lines** drew events to a head in Sichuan and Hubei province, igniting a popular uprising which finally toppled the dynasty. As two thousand years of dynastic succession ended, Sun Yatsen returned to China to take the lead in the provisional **Republican Government**.

From republic to communism

Unfortunately for the Republicans, China was already fragmenting. The former leader of the Imperial Army, **Yuan Shikai**, dismissed the government, forced Sun back into exile, and attempted to establish a new dynasty. But Yuan died suddenly in 1916, marking the last time in 34 years that China would be united under a single authority. **Warlords** turned Yunnan and western Sichuan – then known as **Xikang** (see p.80) – into private fiefs, funded largely by **opium** production. **Tibet**, which had been briefly invaded by Britain in 1904, asserted its independence. As civil war erupted, Sun Yatsen returned once more, this time to found the Nationalist **Guomindang** government in southern China.

Thus divided, China was unable to stem the increasingly bold territorial incursions made by Japan and other colonial powers as a result of World War I. Siding with the Allies, Japan had claimed the German port of Qingdao and all German shipping and industry in the Shangdong Peninsula on the outbreak of war, and in 1915 presented China with **Twenty-One Demands**, many of which Yuan Shikai, under threat of a Japanese invasion, was forced to accept. After the war, hopes that the 1919 Treaty of Versailles would end Japanese aggression (as well as the unequal treaties and foreign concessions) were dashed when the Western powers, who had already signed secret pacts with Japan, confirmed Japan's rights in China. This ignited what became known as the **May 4 Movement**, the first in a series of anti-foreign demonstrations and riots.

The CCP and Mao Zedong

Against this background, the **Chinese Communist Party** (CCP) formed in Shanghai in 1921, its leadership including the young **Mao Zedong** and **Zhou Enlai**, later Mao's closest confidant. Son of a well-off Hunanese farmer, Mao believed social reform lay in the hands of the peasants who, despite the overthrow of the emperors, still had few rights and no power base. Drawing upon the analyses of Karl Marx, Mao saw parallels between nineteenth-century Europe and twentieth-century China, and argued that a mass armed rising was the only way the old order could be replaced.

Even so, the CCP initially listened to its Russian advisers and supported the Guomindang in its military campaigns against the northern warlords, but this alliance began to look shaky after the relatively moderate Sun Yatsen died in 1925. He was

1956–58	1959	1966–8
The Hundred Flowers and Great Leap Forward attempt agricultural and social reform. Widespread famine ensues.	The Dalai Lama flees Lhasa during an anti-Chinese uprising; China annexes Tibet.	The Cultural Revolution: Red Guards desecrate temples, universities and old monuments, murdering monks, artisans and academics.

succeeded by his right-wing military chief **Chiang Kaishek**, who had no time for the
CCP's plans to end China's class divisions. In 1927, Chiang responded to a
CCP-inspired general strike in Shanghai by a massacre of five thousand Communists,
including much of the original CCP hierarchy. With opposition temporarily crushed,
Chiang was declared head of a national government in 1928.

The Red Army and the Long March
After events in Shanghai, the Communist **Red Army** of peasants, miners and
Guomindang deserters regrouped along the Hunan–Jiangxi border in southern China.
Using Mao's guerilla tactics, the Red Army did well until they over-reached themselves
in open assaults against the superior Guomindang forces. Chiang Kaishek mobilized
half a million troops, and encircled the Red stronghold with a ring of concrete
block-houses and barbed-wire entanglements.

Forced to choose between fight or flight, in October 1934 eighty thousand
Communist troops began the **Long March,** an epic 9500km retreat through
southwestern China. By the time it finished a year later, the Communists had lost
three-quarters of their followers to the rigours of the trip, but had also started their
path towards victory: Mao had become undisputed leader of the CCP at the **Zunyi
Conference** in northern Guizhou (see p.280), severing the Party from its Russian
advisers; and their journey had put the Red Army in touch with vast numbers of the
peasants whom they wanted to convert to the Communist cause.

Japanese invasion and the United Front
Meanwhile, **Japan** had taken over Chinese Manchuria in 1933 and installed **Pu Yi** (last
emperor of the Qing dynasty) as puppet leader. The Japanese were obviously preparing
to invade eastern China, and Mao wrote to Chiang Kaishek advocating an end to civil
war and a **United Front** against the threat. Chiang instead ordered his Manchurian
armies, under **Zhang Xueliang**, to finish off the Red Army. Zhang, however, wanted to
evict the Japanese from his homeland, and so secretly entered into an agreement with
the Communist forces. On December 12, 1936, Chiang Kaishek was kidnapped by
Zhang's troops and forced to sign his assent to the United Front – even if both sides
knew that the alliance would last only as long as the Japanese threat.

Full-scale **war with Japan** broke out in July 1937, and by the end of the year, the
Japanese had taken most of eastern China. The Chinese government were forced west
to their **wartime capital at Chongqing**, supported by British aid imported along the
Burma Road and, later, by the US-led **Flying Tigers** (see p.152).

The end of the war and the Guomindang
By the time the two atom bombs ended the Japanese empire and World War II in
1945, the Red Army was close on a million strong. The Communist position was not,
however, secure. During US-brokered negotiations in Chongqing, Chiang refused to
admit the CCP into government, knowing that its policies were uncontrollable while
the Red Army still existed. For their part, it was evident to the CCP that without an
army, they were nothing. The talks ended in stalemate.

However, buoyed by popular support, in 1948 the Communists' newly named
People's Liberation Army (PLA) rose against the Guomindang, decisively trouncing

1976	1980	1997	2000	2001
The Tian'anmen Incident reveals public support for moderate Deng Xiaoping. Mao Zedong dies.	Deng Xiaoping consolidates power; beginning of China's "open door" policy with the world.	Death of Deng Xiaoping.	Go West Campaign begins.	China admitted to the World Trade Organization.

PRESERVING HISTORY

While there's no doubt that a huge number of historic and religious monuments were vandalized or destroyed during the **Cultural Revolution**, others were saved by quick-thinking monks and locals, who daubed them with words like "Revolutionary Headquarters" or "Long Live Chairman Mao". Unwilling to deface these slogans – and so risk being branded as "counter-revolutionaries" – Red Guards on a rampage left the buildings alone; you can still see faded red characters on old rural mansions and temples in Sichuan, Guizhou and Guangxi.

It also has to be said that the structural damage wrought during the Cultural Revolution appears trivial next to the widespread **demolition** carried out nationwide since the 1990s – including historic districts in Chengdu and Kunming – in the name of modernization. At the same time, the current interest in preserving old villages and towns for tourism has seen previously dilapidated, forgotten wooden hamlets built up anew, and places like Lijiang in Yunnan actually expanding its "old quarter" to cope with demand.

them that winter at the massive battle of **Huai Hai** in Anhui province. With Shanghai about to fall before the PLA in early 1949, Chiang Kaishek packed the country's entire gold reserves into a plane and took off for **Taiwan** to form the Republic of China. Here he was to remain until his death in 1975, forlornly waiting to liberate the mainland with the two million troops and refugees who later joined him. Mopping-up operations against mainland pockets of Guomindang resistance would continue for several years, but in October 1949 Mao was able to proclaim the formation of the People's Republic of China in Beijing. The world's most populous nation was now Communist.

The People's Republic under Mao

With the country laid waste by over a century of social upheaval and war, massive problems faced the new republic. China's infrastructure, industries and agriculture were wrecked, and there were no monetary reserves. By the mid-1950s, however, all industry had been **nationalized** and output was back at prewar levels, while, for the first time in Chinese history, land was handed over to the peasants as their own. A million former landlords were executed, while others were enrolled in "criticism and self-criticism" classes, a traumatic re-education designed to prevent elitism or bourgeois deviancy from contaminating the revolutionary spirit.

With all the difficulties on the home front, the government could well have done without the distraction of the **Korean War**. After Communist North Korea invaded the south in 1950, US forces intervened on behalf of the south and, despite warnings from Zhou Enlai, continued through to Chinese territory. China declared war in June, and sent a million troops to push the Americans back to the **thirty-eighth parallel** and force peace negotiations. As a boost for the morale of the new nation, the campaign could not have been better timed.

China also turned its attention to **Tibet**, which had recovered from the 1904 British invasion and been effectively independent since 1912. The Kham and Amdo areas of western Sichuan and Qinghai had been a thorn in the side of the Communists during their Long March days, and warlords were still holding out in the region; lodged as it was between central Asia and a newly independent India, Tibet's potential future

2004	2006	2008	2010	2012
China's population reaches 1.3 billion.	Three Gorges Dam is finished, and the new railway line to Tibet opens.	The Beijing Olympic Games preceded by riots in Tibet and Sichuan. The Sichuan earthquake kills 80,000.	World Expo held In Shanghai; 73 million visitors attend.	New generation of leaders elected at the National People's Congress.

allegiances were a source of worry for the Chinese government. After negotiations with Lhasa broke down in 1950, PLA troops crossed the border and forced the Dalai Lama to cede to Chinese rule, though Tibet's religion, property and people were initially respected and the country left largely to its own devices. In 1956, however, unpopular land reforms in western Sichuan sparked an **uprising** against the Chinese; monastery towns such as **Litang** and **Aba** became centres of resistance and were bombed in air strikes by the PLA. In 1959 the fighting reached Lhasa and **in March** the Dalai Lama and his followers fled to Nepal, leaving Tibet in Chinese hands.

The Hundred Flowers campaign

By 1956 China's economy was healthy, but Mao – whose principles held that constant struggle was part of existence, and thus that acceptance of the status quo was in itself a bad thing – felt that both government and industry needed a shake-up. In 1957 he decided to loosen restrictions on public expression, and following the slogan "Let a hundred flowers bloom, and a hundred schools of thought contend", intellectuals were encouraged to voice their complaints. The plan backfired: instead of picking on inefficient officials as Mao had hoped, the **Hundred Flowers campaign** resulted in blistering criticisms of the Communist system itself. The campaign was quickly abandoned and the critics imprisoned and, from this point on, intellectuals as a group were mistrusted and scrutinized.

The Great Leap Forward

Agriculture and industry were next to be reformed. In August 1958 it was announced that all farmland was to be pooled into 24,000 self-governing communes, with the aim of turning small-scale farming units into hyper-efficient agricultural areas. Industry was to be fired into activity by the co-option of seasonally employed workers, who would

HOW CHINA IS GOVERNED

Since 1949 the Chinese state has been controlled by the **Communist Party** which, with 66 million members, is the biggest political party in the world. It has a pyramid structure resting on millions of local organizations, and whose apex is formed by a **Politburo** of 24 members controlled by a nine-man **standing committee**. The Party's workings are opaque; personal relations count more than job titles, and a leader's influence rests on the relations he builds with superiors and protégés, with retired party elders often retaining a great deal of influence. Towards the end of his life, for example, Deng Xiaoping was virtually running the country when his only official title was head of a bridge club. The country's head of state is its president, while the head of government is the premier. Politburo members are supposedly chosen by the three thousand delegates of the National People's Congress, officially a parliament though it in fact serves largely as a rubber stamp for Politburo decisions. All appointments at all levels come from within the party heirarchy; ordinary people have no say in who actually governs them.

The Party owes its success, of course, to the **military**, and links with the PLA remain close, though the army has lost power since its huge business empire was stripped in the 1990s. There is no PLA representative on the standing committee, but the military has a strong influence on policy issues, particularly over Taiwan and relations with the US, and generally maintains a hard line. There's much discussion at the moment as to what role the military will play in government after a new generation of leaders are promoted to the Politburo in 2012.

The **law** in China is a mix of legislation based on party priorities and new statutes to haul the economy into line with those of major foreign investors. The National People's Congress is responsible for drafting laws covering taxation and human rights, among other subjects. In other areas, the State Council and local governments can legislate. Even after laws have been passed there is no guarantee they will be respected; provincial governments and state-owned enterprises view court decisions as negotiable, and for the Party and the state, the rule of law is not allowed to supersede its own interests.

construct heavy industrial plants, dig canals and drain marshes. Propaganda campaigns promised eternal well-being in return for initial austerity; in a single **Great Leap Forward**, China would match British industrial output in ten years.

From the outset, the Great Leap Forward was a disaster. Having been given their land, the peasants now found themselves losing it once more, and were not eager to work in huge units. This, combined with the problem of ill-trained commune management, led to a slump in agricultural and industrial production. In the face of a stream of ridiculous quotas supplied by Beijing – one campaign required that all communes must produce certain quantities of steel, regardless of the availability of raw materials – no one had time to tend the fields. The 1959 and 1960 harvests both failed, and over fifteen million people starved to death across China.

The Cultural Revolution

The incident set members of the CCP Central Committee against Mao's policies for the first time, including the Sichuanese Long March veteran **Deng Xiaoping**, a moderate who favoured material incentives for workers. Mao sought to regain his authority, orchestrating the youth of China against his opponents in what became known as the **Great Proletarian Cultural Revolution**. Under Mao's guidance, the movement spread in 1966 to Beijing University, where the students organized themselves into a political militia – the **Red Guard** – and within weeks were moving out onto the streets.

The enemies of the Red Guard were the **Four Olds**: old ideas, old culture, old customs and old habits. Brandishing copies of the *Quotations from Chairman Mao Zedong* (the famous **Little Red Book**), the Red Guard attacked anything redolent of culture, capitalism or the West. Academics were assaulted, books were burned, temples and ancient monuments desecrated. As under the commune system, quotas were set, this time for unearthing and turning in the "Rightists", "Revisionists" and "Capitalist Roaders" corrupting Communist society. Officials who failed to fill their quotas were likely to fall victim themselves, as were those who failed to destroy property or denounce others enthusiastically enough. Offenders were paraded through the streets wearing placards carrying humiliating slogans; tens of thousands were ostracized, imprisoned, beaten to death or driven to suicide. On August 5, 1966, Mao proclaimed that reactionaries had reached the highest levels of the CCP: Deng Xiaoping and his followers were dismissed from their posts and imprisoned, condemned to wait on tables at a Party canteen, or given menial jobs.

Meanwhile, the violence was getting completely out of control, with Red Guard factions attacking foreign embassies and even turning on each other. In August 1967 Mao ordered the arrest of several Red Guard leaders and the surrender of all weapons to the army, but was too late to stop nationwide street fighting, which was halted only after the military stormed the Guard's university strongholds. To clear them out of the way, millions of Red Guards were rounded up and **sent down to the countryside**, ostensibly to reinforce the Communist message among the rural community.

Ping-pong diplomacy and the rise of the radicals

The US had continued to support Chiang Kaishek's Guomindang in Taiwan, while also stirring up paranoia over the possibility of a Sino–Soviet pact. After China exploded its first **atomic bomb** in 1964, however, the US began to tread a more pragmatic path. In 1970, envoy Henry Kissinger opened communications between the two countries, cultural and sporting links were formed (the latter gave rise to the phrase "**ping-pong diplomacy**"), and in 1971 the People's Republic became the official representative at the UN of the nation called China, replacing Taiwan. The following year US president Richard Nixon was walking on the Great Wall and holding talks with Mao, trade restrictions were lifted and China began commerce with the West.

GO WEST

Begun in 2000, the **Go West Campaign** has begun to narrow the gap between China's wealthy, rapidly modernizing eastern seaboard and its poorer, underdeveloped interior provinces. An estimated **3 trillion yuan** has been pumped into the region, both in infrastructure projects – including new airports, expressways, rail lines and high-speed trains – and direct investment by domestic and foreign companies. **Sichuan** and **Chongqing** have been the biggest beneficiaries, gearing up to become hubs for electronics and hi-tech companies who have been drawn inland from traditional centres like Shanghai and Shenzhen by cheaper operating costs and a huge local labour base. Intel's Chengdu testing facility inspects chips produced worldwide; Hewlett Packard and Acer have joined Chinese IT companies in Chongqing; while dedicated "Science Technology Industrial Parks" are opening across both provinces. According to government figures, the Go West Campaign has been a roaring success, with annual regional economic growth outstripping the national average at 12 percent, helping to double western China's GDP in less than a decade.

At times, however, aspects of the Go West Campaign pose negative **side effects**. Regional benefits have been uneven – Guizhou is still rated as China's poorest province – and there's still great discrepancies between the wealth and status of ethnic minorities and recent Han Chinese immigrants. Some of the colossal infrastructure projects are also questionable, not least the construction of major hydroelectric dams on the Chinese headwaters of the Lancang (Mekong) and Nu (Salween) rivers in Yunnan. These are causing international concern, with nations downstream experiencing declining water levels.

This new attitude of realistic reform derived from the moderate wing of the Communist Party, headed by Premier **Zhou Enlai** and his protégé Deng Xiaoping. But with Zhou's death early in 1976, the reform movement immediately succumbed to the **Gang of Four**, who, led by Mao's third wife **Jiang Qing**, had become the radical mouthpiece of an increasingly absent Mao. In early April, at the time of the Qing Ming festival commemorating the dead, the Heroes Monument in Beijing's Tian'anmen Square was filled with wreaths in memory of Zhou. On April 5 radical Communists removed the wreaths and moderate supporters flooded into the square in protest, causing a riot. Deng Xiaoping, who as leader of the moderates was the obvious scapegoat for what became known as the **Tian'anmen Incident**, was publicly discredited and thrown out of office for a second time.

The death of Mao

In July 1976 a catastrophic **earthquake** in northern China killed half a million people. The Chinese hold that natural disasters always foreshadow great events, and no one was too surprised when **Mao died** on September 9. Deprived of their figurehead, the Gang of Four were soon arrested and the radicals disbanded. Deng returned to the political scene for the third time and was granted a string of positions that included Vice-Chairman of the Communist Party, Vice-Premier and Chief of Staff to the PLA; titles aside, he was now running the country. The move away from Mao's policies was rapid: in 1978 anti-Maoist dissidents were allowed to speak out, and by 1980 Deng and the moderates were secure enough to sanction officially a cautious condemnation of Mao's actions. His ubiquitous portraits and statues began to come down, and his cult was gradually undermined.

Deng Xiaoping: "To Get Rich is Glorious"

Under Deng Xiaoping, China became unrecognizable from the days when the Red Guards enforced ideological purity and private wealth was anathema. Deng's legacy was the **open door policy**, which brought about new social freedoms as well as a huge rise in the trappings of Westernization, especially in the cities. The impetus for such sweeping changes was economic, not political, an approach that has guided policy ever since – best summed up by Deng's memorable statement "Poverty is not Socialism: to Get

HUMAN RIGHTS

Despite magnificent progress on the economic level, the Chinese state continues to be one of the world's worst regimes for **human rights abuses** – despite many of those rights being enshrined in its own constitution. China has no independent judiciary, rule of law or due process, and around half a million people are currently enduring detention without charge or trial. Torture and execution remain commonplace.

The **Communist Party** brooks no dissent or rival and locks up anyone perceived as a challenge, be they journalists, lawyers, bloggers, whistleblowers, petitioners or followers of religious cults such as Falun Gong. The most high profile incarcerated dissident is Nobel Prize winner Liu Xiaobo, whose crime was to write "Charter 08", a document calling for political reform; he is now serving an eleven-year sentence. Other activists currently in prison include Doctor Gao Yaojie, who exposed how blood collectors were spreading AIDS; Zhao Lianhai, who lobbied for compensation for the families of babies harmed by tainted baby milk; and Chen Guancheng, who campaigned against forced sterilizations. There are many more, and observers say that the situation for activists has worsened in recent years.

But the country's most serious human rights abuses are being perpetrated in **Tibet**, where dissent is ruthlessly suppressed and Tibetan culture is being swamped by Han migration. It is common for Tibetans to receive long sentences of hard labour not just for criticizing the regime (Dhondup Wangchen is serving six years for his short film, *Leaving Fear Behind*) but for singing songs about freedom or owning a picture of the Dalai Lama. March – the month the Dalia Lama fled to Nepal in 1959 – has become a fractious time in Tibet, when protests against the Chinese government are likely to break out. In the run-up to the Beijing Olympics in 2008, anti-Chinese riots in Lhasa spilled over into western Sichuan, notably at Aba (Ngawa). The situation in western Sichuan – home to the famously volatile Khampa nomads – has remained tense ever since, with the region frequently shut down to tourism.

The situation in Tibet is perhaps part of a wider problem in the way that the Chinese government views **ethnic minorities**. The general feeling is that they are ignorant and backward races, needing to be integrated into mainstream China for their own good; and that these minorities will be happy to ditch their traditions and culture – or dress them up as tourist attractions – if it brings them economic prosperity.

Rich is Glorious". Deng decentralized production, allowing more rational decision-making based on local conditions, and the production and allocation of goods according to market forces; factories now contracted with each other instead of with the state. In agriculture, the collective economy was replaced, and farming households, after meeting government targets, were allowed to sell their surpluses on the free market. On the coast, **Special Economic Zones** (SEZs) were set up, where foreign investment was encouraged and Western management practices, such as the firing of unsatisfactory workers, were cautiously introduced.

Tian'anmen Square

Economic reform did not precipitate political reform, and was really a way of staving it off, with the Party hoping that allowing the populace the right to get rich would halt demands for political rights. However, dissatisfaction with corruption, rising inflation, low wages and the lack of freedom was vividly expressed in the **Tian'anmen Square demonstrations** of 1989. These started in April as a mourning service for former Party General Secretary Hu Yaobang, who had been too liberal for Deng's liking and was dismissed in 1987; by mid-May there were nearly a million students, workers and even Party cadets around the square, demanding free speech and an end to corruption. On May 20, martial law was declared, and by the beginning of June, 350,000 troops were massed around Beijing. In the early hours of June 4 they moved in, crushing barriers with tanks and firing into the crowds, killing hundreds or possibly thousands of the demonstrators. Discussion of the event is still contentious in China – particularly as the issues the students identified have not been dealt with.

China in the twenty-first century

The **spectacular growth** of the Chinese economy was among the great success stories of the twentieth century and will be one of the most important factors in defining the character of the twenty-first. For a quarter of a century, China's GDP has grown at an average rate of nine percent per year, and it came quickly out of the global recession in 2010, overtaking Japan to become the **world's second largest economy**. China is now the world's main **producer** of coal and steel and, among other things, makes two-thirds of the world's shoes, DVD players and photocopiers. Chinese production and US consumption together form the engines for global growth. But China is also a massive **consumer**; in 2004, for instance, the nation bought almost half of the world's cement. Some predict that the Chinese economy will overtake that of the US by 2040.

The speed of this is astonishing: in the 1970s the **three big buys** – consumer goods to which families could realistically aspire– were a bicycle, a watch and a radio; in the 1980s they were a washing machine, a TV and a refrigerator; and today urban Chinese can aspire to the same material comforts as their Western counterparts. No wonder the country comes across as confident and ambitious.

Under Deng's successors – including **Hu Jintao**, who took over in 2002 – China continued its course of controlled liberalization. In its pursuit of a "socialist market economy with Chinese characteristics", the state continued to retreat from whole areas of life. The private sector now accounts for almost half of the economy, and foreign-funded ventures represent more than half the country's exports.

Today, "scientific development" and "harmonious society" are the catchphrases spouted by the Politburo technocrats. In practice that means both heavy-handed political control and a genuine effort to deal with social problems. Alarmed at growing income inequality, efforts have been made to shift society away from unbridled capitalism towards a more socially responsible model of development, exemplified by Chongqing Committee Secretary **Bo Xilai**, who has sought to encourage community values in the city (see p.148).

Stumbling blocks

Behind the talk of a wonder economy there are **problems**. Even now, more than half of China's citizens live on less than a dollar a day. Prosperity has been delivered unevenly – the east-coast cities have benefited most – and there's little in the way of medical care or subsidized education for either urban or rural poor. One of the more visible results of rising living costs (exacerbated by increased agricultural mechanization) has been the **mass migration** of the working class from the country to the cities, where most remain unemployed or are hired by the day as labourers.

Bubbles are forming in property and the steel market. Utilities such as **electricity and water** are running up against capacity constraints. China's **national debt** is estimated at 40 trillion yuan, over twenty percent of GDP, and annual **inflation** tops five percent, hitting poorer rural regions the worst – including much of Southwest China. **Short-term gain** has become the overriding factor in Chinese planning, with the result that the future is mortgaged for present wealth. Too little thought is given to the environmental effects of modernization, and China now boasts the most **polluted** cities in the world, with its citizens frequently exposed to **contaminated water and foodstuffs** – the latter problem often exacerbated by toxic additives deliberately used as preservatives, colouring or bulk by unscrupulous manufacturers. As success is largely dependent on *guanxi* (connections), the potential for **corruption** is enormous – indeed, graft is thought to be slicing at least a percentage point off growth figures. As in the past, a desperately poor peasantry is at the mercy of corrupt cadres who enrich themselves by setting and purloining local taxes.

Perhaps China's biggest problem is its massive **population** (1.3 billion in 2007), which could put unbearable pressure on resources if it continues to rise – fifteen million new jobs need to be created every year just to keep up with population growth.

Under the **one-child policy**, which began in 1979, couples who have a second child face a cut in wages and restricted access to health care and housing. The policy has been most successful in the cities, but given the heavy preference for male children, female infanticide, and the selling off of girls as brides, are not unusual, while there is a growing trend in the kidnapping of male children for ransom or sale.

Every year, there are **demonstrations** – and even public suicides – by villagers and homeowners protesting at **enforced land grabs and demolitions** by developers backed by local authorities. Promised **financial compensation** is frequently for a trivial amount, never paid at all, or stolen outright by corrupt officials. People who make a stand – including journalists brave enough to report such matters – are routinely beaten or even murdered by **chengguan**, thug-like law-enforcement squads employed by the government. Frustrations sometimes boil over: in 2010 at **Zhaotong**, northeastern Yunnan, protests against a new highway saw days of riots in which the local police were completely routed, and some 2000 troops were needed to quell the disturbance.

China and the world

Historically, being surrounded by "barbarians" and inhospitable terrain has led China towards insularity. Accordingly, the government's tactic during China's stellar period of economic development has been not to intervene on the world stage. But its explosive expansion is now forcing **international engagement** – and comment. As the world's biggest emitter of **greenhouse gases**, it is under increasing pressure to clean up its act. China's skewed **business environment** – lax enforcement of intellectual property and business laws, bullying of foreign companies in favour of local competition, unfair regulatory barriers and an artificially low currency – is now attracting plenty of criticism from its trading partners.

In order to fuel growth, China needs to look elsewhere for raw materials: in Africa, the Pacific and Southeast Asia, China has become the new resource colonizer, striking deals with all comers, including nations shunned by the West such as Zimbabwe and Sudan. China's willingness to bind itself to global rules, such as those of the **World Trade Organization**, has been a welcome way to assimilate it, but an authoritarian, anti-democratic China will never be easy for its neighbours to live with, and Chinese primacy in the Pacific is contested by both Japan and the US. The country is beginning to look for more amenable supporters, however; it regularly hosts meetings of **ASEAN**, the Southeast Asian trading bloc, and in 2011 held a convention of the emerging "**Bric**" economies – Brazil, Russia, India and China – who between them have 40 percent of the world's population, and a fifth of its economy.

China's **antipathy towards Japan** stems from Japan's perceived failure to be properly contrite over its crimes in World War II, and ongoing territorial disputes over some insignificant islands, and every year some trivial issue becomes a flashpoint for anti-Japanese demonstrations. These are awkward for the government: patriotic demonstrations in the last century were often the precursor to pro-democracy unrest, but at the same time the Party would rather not crack down on expressions of nationalism, as such fervour is whipped up by the Party to justify its existence and right to rule.

China today embraces the outside world as never before; witness the passion with which the English language is studied and the fascination with foreign mores, goods, even football teams. Both China and the world have much to gain from Chinese openness, and it would be a shame for both should political shakiness lead to a retreat from that.

Chinese beliefs

The resilience of ancient beliefs in China, and the ability of the Chinese people to absorb new streams of thought, has been demonstrated repeatedly over the centuries. Religious buildings litter the cities and the countryside, and while some seem more like cultural relics than places of worship, others are prosperous, busy places, teeming with monks and people who have come to ask for grandchildren – or simply for money. The atmosphere may not always seem devout or religious, but then perhaps it never did. Religious enthusiasm is a relatively new-found freedom: such "feudal beliefs" were derided by the Communists when they came to power in 1950, and during the 1960s thousands of temples, ancestral halls and religious objects were targeted for desecration. Monasteries were burnt to the ground, and their monks imprisoned; the classics of literature and philosophy – the "residue of the reactionary feudal past" – were burned. That Chinese beliefs survived such persecution – which was by no means the first during the country's long history – is because their outward manifestations are not essential: traditions are expressed more clearly in how the Chinese think and act than in the symbols and rituals of overt worship. This is especially true in Southwest China, where a large slice of the population follow minority or folk beliefs, and temples can be few and far between at times.

The Three Teachings

The product of the oldest continuous civilization on earth, Chinese religion actually comprises a number of disparate and sometimes contradictory elements. At the heart of it lie **three basic philosophies**: Confucianism, Taoism and Buddhism. The way in which a harmonious balance has been created among these three is expressed in the often quoted maxim *san jiao fa yi* – "Three Teachings Flow into One".

Confucianism

China's oldest and greatest philosopher, **Kong Fuzi**, known in the West by his Latinized name **Confucius**, was born during the Warring States Period in 551 BC, an age of petty kingdoms and constant conflict. Harking back to an earlier, mythic age of peace and social virtues, Confucius preached adherence to **ritual and propriety** as the supreme answer to the horrifying disorder of the world as he found it. No one paid much attention while he was alive; after his death, however, his writings were collected as the *Analects*, and this book became the most influential and fundamental of Chinese philosophies.

Never a religion postulating a higher deity, Confucianism is rather a set of **moral and social values** designed to bring the ways of citizens and governments into harmony with each other. A good ruler who exemplified the five Confucian virtues – benevolence, righteousness, propriety, wisdom and trustworthiness – would bring society naturally to order. Instead of God, five hierarchical relationships outline a structure of duty and obedience to authority: ruler to ruled, son to father, younger brother to older, wife to husband, and – the only relationship between equals – friend

GETTING AROUND A CHINESE TEMPLE

Whether Confucian, Buddhist or Taoist, **Chinese temples** share the same broad features. Like cities, they **face south** and are surrounded by **walls**. Gates are sealed by heavy doors, guarded by **paintings or statues** of warrior deities to chase away evil. Further protection is ensured by a **spirit wall** that blocks direct entry; although easy enough for the living to walk around, this foils spirits, who are unable to turn corners. Once inside, you'll find a succession of **halls** arranged in ornamental courtyards. In case evil influences should manage to get in, the area nearest the entrance contains the least important rooms or buildings, while those of greater significance – living quarters or main temple halls – are set deeper inside the complex.

There are other obvious differences too. **Confucian temples** – such as those at Anshun in Guizhou, or Jianshui in Yunnan – tend only to have statues of Confucius and his immediate followers. **Buddhist and Taoist temples**, however, can sometimes show a bewildering open-handedness about who they allow in: Guanyin, the multi-armed Buddhist incarnation of compassion, is often found inside Taoist temples too; and Taoism – which only became an organized religion after Buddhism arrived in China – seems at times to have evolved equivalents to the Buddhist pantheon. One way to tell Buddhist and Taoist temples apart is by the colour of the supporting **pillars** – Buddhists use bright red, while Taoists favour black. **Animal carvings** are also more popular with Taoists, who use decorative good-luck and longevity symbols such as bats and cranes.

to friend. The supreme Confucian virtue was always **obedience**, something used to justify totalitarian rule throughout Chinese history.

During the Han dynasty (206 BC–220 AD), Confucianism became institutionalized as a system of government that was to prevail for two thousand years. With it, and with the notion of the **scholar-official** as the ideal administrator, came the notorious Chinese bureaucracy. Men would study half their lives in order to pass **imperial examinations** based on Confucian thought, and so attain a government commission.

The ideal Confucian ruler never quite emerged (the emperor was not expected to sit the exams), and the scholar-officials often deteriorated into corrupt bureaucrats. The imperial examinations were abolished at the start of the twentieth century, and during the Cultural Revolution an **anti-Confucius campaign** was launched in an attempt to purge his memory from the national consciousness. Yet the very fact that Confucius could still be held up as an object for derision some 2500 years after his death reveals how deeply his philosophy has become embedded in the Chinese psyche. Today, many regard Confucianism, with its emphasis on order, harmony and cooperation, as providing the ideological foundations for the recent successes of Asian culture.

Taoism

Taoism is the study and pursuit of the ineffable **Way**, as outlined in the **Dao De Jing** (often written as Tao Te Ching). This obscure text comprises a compilation of the sayings of the semi-mythical hermit **Lao Zi**, held to be a contemporary of Confucius.

To the despair of the rationalist, the Tao is by its very nature **indefinable**. The first lines of the Dao De Jing read:

The Tao that can be told
is not the eternal Tao.
The name that can be named
is not the eternal name.

In essence, however, it might be thought of as the underlying principle and source of all being, the bond **uniting man and nature**. Its central principle, **Wu Wei**, can crudely be translated as "no action", though it is probably better understood as "no action which runs contrary to the natural order of existence".

Taoism's second major text is a book of parables written by one ideal practitioner of the Way, **Zhuang Zi**. In the famous butterfly parable, Zhuang Zi examines the many faces of reality:

Once upon a time Zhuang Zi dreamed he was a butterfly. A butterfly flying around and enjoying itself. It did not know it was Zhuang Zi. We do not know whether it was Zhuang Zi dreaming that he was a butterfly, or a butterfly dreaming he was Zhuang Zi.

In its affirmation of the irrational and natural sources of life, Taoism has provided Chinese culture with a **balance** to the rigid social mores of Confucianism. In traditional China it was said that the perfect lifestyle was to be Confucian during the day – a righteous and firm administrator, upholding the virtues of the gentleman/ruler – and a Taoist when relaxing. If Confucianism preaches duty to family and to society, Taoism champions the sublimity of withdrawal. The art and literature of China have been greatly enriched by Taoism's notions of contemplation, detachment and freedom from social entanglement, and the Tao has become embedded in the Chinese soul as a doctrine of yielding to the inevitable forces of nature.

Buddhism

Buddhism arrived from India around 65 AD, and enjoyed a glorious period of ascendancy under the Tang dynasty – during the eighth century there were over 300,000 Buddhist monks in China. But Chinese Buddhism became very different from the Indian model that spawned it. Most contemporary schools of Indian Buddhism taught that life on earth was essentially one of **suffering**, an endless cycle in which people were born, grew old and died, only to be born again in other bodies; the goal was to break out of this by attaining **nirvana**, which could be done by losing all desire for things of the world.

This doctrine was not likely to appeal to the regimented, materialistic Chinese, however and so it was the relatively small **Mahayana School** of Buddhism that came to dominate Chinese thinking (except in southern Yunnan, where the Dai people follow the more conservative **Theravada School**). The Mahayana taught that perfection for the individual was not possible without perfection for all – and that those who had already attained enlightenment would remain active in the world as **Bodhisattvas**, to help others along the path. In time Bodhisattvas came to be ascribed miraculous powers, and were prayed to in a manner remarkably similar to conventional Confucian ancestor-worship. The mainstream of Chinese Buddhism came to be more about maintaining harmonious relations with Bodhisattvas than about attaining nirvana.

Another entirely new sect of Buddhism also arose in China through contact with Taoism. Known in China as **Chan** (and in Japan as **Zen**) Buddhism, it offered a less extreme path to enlightenment. For a Chan Buddhist, it was not necessary to become a

FENG SHUI

Whatever the scale of a building project – from house to temple or even the traditional layout of a city – the Chinese consider **feng shui** an essential part of the initial preparations. Literally meaning "wind and water", *feng shui* is a form of **geomancy**, which assesses how buildings must be positioned so as not to disturb the spiritual aspects of the surrounding landscape. This reflects **Taoist cosmology**, which believes that disruption of a single harmonious element can cause potentially dangerous alterations to the whole. It's vital therefore that sites be **favourably oriented** according to points on the compass and protected from local "unlucky" directions by other buildings, walls, hills, mountain ranges or rivers. **North** is always unlucky: you can see this in the orientation of temples, whose main entrances always face south; Guilin's **Princes' Tombs**, which are protected from the north by Duxiu Feng peak; and at **Langzhong** in Sichuan, whose natural arrangement of rivers and hills is considered perfect *feng shui*.

monk or a recluse in order to achieve nirvana – instead this ultimate state of being could be reached through life in accord with, and in contemplation of, the Way.

In short, the Chinese managed to marry Buddhism to their pre-existing belief structures with very little difficulty. This was facilitated by the general absence of dogma within Buddhist thought. The **Tibetans**, too, found themselves able to adapt the new belief system to their old religion, Bon (see p.118), rather than simply replacing it. Over the centuries, Tibetans established their own schools of Buddhism, often referred to as Lamaist Buddhism or **Lamaism**, which differ from the Chinese versions in certain respects – Bon bequeathed the Tibetan version a far darker, fiercer iconography than the Chinese model. The now dominant **Gelugpa** (or Yellow Hat) school, of which the Dalai and Panchen Lamas are members, dates back to the teachings of Tsongkhapa (1357–1419).

Minority faiths and popular beliefs

Southwest China's **twenty-eight ethnic minorities** follow a vast range of animist customs, folk beliefs, and local versions of more widespread religions. It's hard to give even a partial assessment: you can travel through Guizhou and Guangxi without seeing a single recognizable religious monument, then stumble across a shrine smeared with blood and chickens' feathers; Yunnan's Bai have their own take on Buddhism, with Guanyin at its heart; strange things start to emerge during the Yi Fire Festival; while over on the Burmese border, the Wa still practised head-hunting within living memory. Two minority faiths here have become firmly entrenched, however; Islam and Christianity.

Islam

Merchants from the Arab world first brought in **Islam** to southern ports during the seventh or eighth centuries, with a second wave arriving **through Central Asia** with the Mongols – hence the large Muslim populations in parts of Yunnan and Sichuan. Islam is unusual in China in that, while widespread, it has never become integrated into the Chinese mainstream: unlike many Buddhist, Taoist and Confucian temples, where commercial interests are often obvious, mosques remain deeply spiritual places, usually closed to outsiders and having no truck with ethnic tourism. Muslims in general, though visually indistinguishable from other Chinese, have a reputation as tough customers – even more so in Yunnan, perhaps, given their nineteenth-century uprising against the Chinese (see p.183) – and this adds to their discernible separation from society.

SUPERSTITIONS

Though the Chinese are not generally religious in the conventional sense, they are often very **superstitious**. You'll see evidence of this everywhere you go, especially in the form of **wordplay**. Thus the Chinese expression for "let luck come", *fudao*, happens to sound similar to saying "upside-down luck"; hence the inverted *fu* character pasted up outside homes and businesses at Spring Festival, encouraging good fortune to arrive on the premises. Other **auspicious symbols** include bats (luck or prosperity), peaches, pine trees and cranes (longevity), fish (surplus), mandarin ducks (marital fidelity), bamboo (the Confucian virtues), dragons (male power), and phoenixes (female power).

Colours are also important. Red, the colour of fire, and gold, the colour of money, are auspicious, and used extensively for decorations, packaging, weddings and festive occasions. White traditionally represents death or mourning, though traditional Western wedding dresses are becoming increasingly popular. Yellow is the colour of heaven, hence the yellow roof tiles used on temples; yellow clothing was formerly reserved for the emperor alone.

Christianity

Christianity has come and gone several times in China: it first appeared at the Tang court in 635; rose again during the Mongol and early Ming periods; the Jesuits brought it back once more in 1582; and missionaries from Britain and Europe were active throughout the nineteenth century.

Until very recently, however, attempts to introduce this monotheistic religion were confounded by the Chinese **flexibility of belief**. One frustrated Jesuit put it thus: "In China, the educated believe in nothing and the uneducated believe in everything". In a country where a plethora of ghosts, spirits, gods and ancestors offered a buffer against the ills of the world, the Chinese were perfectly prepared to offer a nod to Christ as well – but not exclusively. Despite the construction of some spectacular **churches** – such as those in Cizhong in Yunnan and Guangxi's Weizhao Island – few real converts were made, and missionaries often risked violence from local communities.

In recent times, however, the numbers of **Christians in China** has boomed, with an estimated four million Catholics and ten million Protestants. The religion is monitored by the state, and some aspects are considered contentious (the Chinese Catholic Church, for example, does not recognize the Pope). It has become especially popular in certain cities, and also with minority groups including some Miao and remote Yi communities.

Traditional Chinese Medicine

As an agricultural society, the Chinese have long been aware of the importance of the balance of natural, elemental forces: too much heat causes drought; too much rain, floods; while the correct measure of both encourages farmers' crops to grow. The ancient Chinese saw heaven, earth and humankind existing as an integral whole, such that if people lived in harmony with heaven and earth, then their collective health would be good. The medical treatise Huang Di Neijing, attributed to the semi-mythical Yellow Emperor (2500 BC), mentions the importance of spiritual balance, acupuncture and herbal medicine in treating illnesses, and attests to the venerable age of China's medical beliefs – it may well be a compilation of even earlier texts. Acupuncture was certainly in use by the Han period, as tombs dated to 113 BC have yielded acupuncture needles made of gold and silver.

The belief in universal balance finds expression in **Taoism** (see p.380). As an extension of Taoist principles, life is seen as consisting of **opposites** – man and woman, sun and moon, right and left etc – whereby all things exist as a result of their interaction with their opposites. This is expressed in the black-and-white **Taoist diagram** which shows two interacting opposites, the **yin** ("female", passive energy) and the **yang** ("male", active energy). At the core of Traditional Chinese Medicine lies the belief that in order for a body to be healthy, its opposites must also be in a state of **dynamic balance**; for example, too much heat will cause a temperature, and too little cause chills. Chinese medicine therefore views the body as an integrated whole, so that in sickness, the whole body – rather than just the "ill" part of it – requires treatment.

Qi and acupuncture

An underlying feature of Chinese medical philosophy, **qi** is the energy of life: in the same way that electricity powers a light bulb, *qi*, so the theory goes, enables us to move, see and speak. *Qi* is said to flow along the body's network of **meridians**, or energy pathways, linking the surface tissues to specific internal organs that act as *qi* reservoirs; the twelve major meridians are named after the organ to which they are connected. The meridians are further classed as yin or yang depending on whether they are exposed or protected. In the limbs, for instance, the channels of the outer sides are yang, and important for resisting disease, while the channels of the inner sides are yin, and more involved with nourishing the body.

Mental and physical tensions, poor diet, anger or depression, even adverse weather, are said to inhibit *qi* flow, causing illness. **Needles** inserted in the body's **acupuncture points**, most of which lie on meridians and so are connected to internal organs, reinforce or reduce the *qi* flow along a meridian, in turn influencing the activities of the organs. When the *qi* is balanced and flowing smoothly once more, good health is regained; acupuncture is specifically used to combat inflammation, to regenerate damaged tissue, and to improve the functional power of internal organs.

That said, despite the growing acceptance of acupuncture in the West, there remains no good evidence for its efficacy. Studies have found that patients treated by acupuncturists had the same recovery rate as patients poked with needles at random positions. Sceptics argue that the act of sticking needles in the body produces pain-killing endorphins, which, combined with the placebo effect, aids recovery.

Herbal medicine

In the 2200 years since the semi-mythical Xia king **Shennong** compiled his classic work on **medicinal herbs**, a vast amount of experience has been gained to help perfect their clinical use. Approximately seven thousand herbs, derived from roots, leaves, twigs and fruit, are today commonly used in Chinese medicine, with another thousand or so of animal or mineral origin (still nonetheless classified as "herbs"). Each is first processed by cleaning, soaking, slicing, drying or roasting, or even stir-frying with wine, ginger or vinegar, to influence its effects; the brew is then boiled down and drunk as a tea (typically very bitter and earthy tasting).

Herbs are used to prevent or combat a wide variety of diseases. Some are used to treat the underlying cause of the complaint, others to treat symptoms and help strengthen the body's own immune system, in turn helping it to combat the problem. An everyday example is in the **treatment of flu**: the herbal formula would include a "cold action" herb to reduce the fever, a herb to induce sweating and thus clear the body-ache, a purgative to clear the virus from the system, and a tonic herb to replenish the immune system. In all treatments, the patient is re-examined each week, and as the condition improves the herbal formula is changed accordingly. Just as Western aspirin is derived from willow bark, many **Chinese drugs** have been developed from herbs. One example is the anti-malarial herb *qinghaosu*, or artemisinin, which has proved effective in treating chloroquine-resistant strains of malaria with minimal side effects.

Art

The Chinese have been producing, treasuring and collecting art objects for millennia, from prehistoric ceremonial bronze artefacts to ancient calligraphy and landscape paintings, through to a burgeoning modern art scene. Some of these have had a difficult history: in the nineteenth century many were acquired by Westerners; then the greatest collections were taken by the Nationalists to Taiwan, where they are now in the National Palace Museum; and many more art objects were destroyed during the Cultural Revolution. Yet an astonishing wealth of treasures still remains in China, mostly in local museum collections and a few monumental pieces still lie where they were created.

Pottery, bronzes and sculpture

The earliest Chinese objects – pottery vessels painted with geometric designs date back to the Neolithic farmers of the Yellow River's **Yangshao culture**. The decoration is from the shoulders of the pots upwards, as what has survived is mostly from graves and was designed to be seen from above when the pots were placed round the dead. From the same period come decorated clay heads, and pendants and ornaments of polished stone or jade. Rather later is the Neolithic **Longshan pottery** – black, thin and fine, wheel-turned and often highly polished, with elegant, sharply defined shapes.

The subsequent **Shang** era, from around 1500 BC, are dominated by **bronze** vessels that were used for preparing and serving food and wine, and for ceremonies and sacrifices. One of the most common shapes is the **ding**, a three- or four-legged vessel that harks back to the Neolithic pots used for cooking over open fires. **Casting methods** were highly sophisticated, using moulds, while design was firm and assured and decoration often stylized and linear, featuring geometric and animal motifs. Some of the most extraordinary designs belong to the otherwise undocumented **Shu culture** of Sanxingdui in Sichuan: colossal bronze masks with demented grins, "spirit trees" hung with coins, and a huge standing figure with oversized, clawing hands.

Later, under the **Zhou**, the style of the bronzes becomes more varied and rich: some animal vessels are fantastically shaped and extravagantly decorated; others are simplified natural forms; others again seem to be depicting not so much a fierce tiger, for example, as utter ferocity itself. Smaller contemporary objects – ornaments, ritual pieces and jewellery pendants – bear simplified but vivid forms of tortoises, salamanders and flying birds. In Guangxi, Yunnan and other remote corners of the Southwest, the local taste was for ever-larger **bronze drums**, a symbol of authority which persisted in these regions until modern times.

The next great flowering of art occurred during the **Han dynasty**, through a return to **pottery**, most of it as funerary gifts or decorating tombs. Far from being gloomy, they portray a lively, fun-loving people with sophisticated artistic values: there are scale models of houses, complete with dogs, pigs and other farm animals; miniatures of actors, acrobats and musicians; and finely carved reliefs with scenes of daily life and local industries, such as game hunting and mining salt.

Religious sculpture seems to have arrived from India in the third century alongside Buddhism – the friezes at **Shibao Shan** in Yunnan illustrate this early influence – but not until the Tang dynasty did a distinctly Chinese style evolve, reaching its peak in Southwest China with the monumental **Dafo** at Leshan. The Song dynasty continued o carve religious figures, and at **Dazu** in Sichuan, where the subject matter had broadened from the purely religious to include animals, ordinary people and scenes of everyday life, the treatment is down to earth, individual, even comic. As the Dazu carvings are well preserved, they can still be seen painted, as they were meant to be.

Ceramics

From Neolithic painted pottery onwards, China developed excellent **ceramics**, a pre-eminence recognized even in the English language, which took the word "china" to mean fine-quality ceramic ware. Shapes originally derived from bronzes, but soon the rise of regional potteries using different materials, and the development of special types for different uses, led to an enormous variety of shapes, textures and colours. This was really noticeable in the **Tang dynasty**, when an increase in the production of pottery for daily use was stimulated by the popularization of **tea drinking**, and by the restriction of the use of valuable copper and bronze to coinage. The Tang also saw major technical advances; the production of true **porcelain** was finally achieved, and Tang potters became skilled in the delicate art of polychrome glazing. You can see evidence of this in the *san cai* (three-colour) statuettes of horses and camels, jugglers, traders, polo players, grooms and court ladies, which have come in great numbers from imperial tombs, and which reflect in vivid, often humorous, detail and still-brilliant colours so many aspects of the life of the time.

The **Song** dynasty witnessed a refinement of ceramic techniques and of regional specialization. The keynote was **simplicity** and quiet elegance of colour and form. There was a preference for using single pure colours, such as the famous green **celadon** ware, the thin white porcelain ding ware and the pale grey-green ju ware reserved for imperial use. The Mongol Yuan dynasty, in the early fourteenth century, enriched Chinese tradition with outside influences – notably the introduction of **cobalt blue** underglaze.

The **Ming** saw the flowering of great potteries under imperial patronage, especially at **Jingdezhen** in southern China. Taste favoured increasingly elaborate shapes decorated with the now-famous **blue and white** pictorial designs, along with early experiments in bold colours. From the seventeenth century onwards, **Chinese export wares** flowed in great quantity and variety to the West, until Europeans learned the secrets of porcelain

ETHNIC TEXTILES AND SILVER

Southwest China's ethnic groups are especially renowned for their **textiles**. Often, skill at **silk embroidery** is a defining talent for young women hoping to find a good husband; both Guizhou's **Miao** and Yunnan's **Bai** and **Yi** people produce nit-pickingly embroidered jacket panels, baby carriers (long fabric slings tied across the back), children's "tiger hats", skirts and even shoes. **Designs** are rife in symbolism, either depicting recognizable plants and animals, or abstract patterns representing them, all of which are felt to protect and augment the wearer. Some styles – such as those by Guizhou's "Big-flower Miao" – are so specific you can trace them to particular villages; others are more generic. The Bai and Bouyei are also famous for their **tie-dye designs**, which, along with cloth manufactured by the **Dong** ethnic group in Guangxi, use natural **indigo** for the dark blue base colour.

Silverware is another ethnic speciality. Yunnan's Bai and **Naxi** have something of a reputation for good-quality pieces, though it's Guizhou's Miao that once more produce the finest – and most elaborate – designs, much of it for festive occasions. Miao headpieces, incredible confections decorated with embossed animals, bells, horns and flowers, have their roots In Ming dynasty bridal pieces once worn all over China.

Although textiles and silver are still easy to buy in villages throughout the Southwest, much of it is nowadays made by **machine**. Prices have risen dramatically in recent years for antique, handmade pieces, you'd be very lucky to find family heirlooms that other collectors have missed.

production themselves. The efforts of Chinese manufactures to follow what they saw as the tastes and techniques of the West in turn influenced Chinese designs, not always for the best. By the **nineteenth century**, form and colour was becoming overworked: bold palettes and complex designs were exquisite when handled with skill, but overbearing and ugly when used for their own sake. With the fall of the Chinese imperial house in 1911, the production of fine ceramics came to a close.

Painting and calligraphy

While China's ceramics were often mass-produced by highly skilled but anonymous craftsmen, **painting and calligraphy** were produced by famous scholars, officials and poets. It has been said that the **four great treasures** of Chinese painting are the brush, the ink, the inkstone and the paper or silk. The earliest **brush** to have been found dates from about 400 BC, and is made out of animal hairs glued to a hollow bamboo tube. **Ink** was made from pine soot, mixed with glue and hardened into a stick that would be rubbed with water on a slate inkstone. Traditionally, colour inks have been disdained in both painting and calligraphy as a distraction from the real intent: it is not realism or even the subject that make a masterpiece, but the **spirit** of the brush strokes – revealing the skill and soul of the artist.

Painting

The first known **painting** on silk was found in a Han tomb; records show that many such works were created, but in 190 AD the vast imperial collection was destroyed in a civil war, when soldiers used the silk to make tents and knapsacks. The British Museum holds a scroll in ink and colour on silk from around 400 AD, attributed to **Gu Kaizhi** and entitled *Admonitions of the Instructress to Court Ladies*, and it's known that the theory of painting was already being discussed by then, as the treatise *The Six Principles of Painting* dates from about 500 AD.

The **Tang period**, with a stable empire and a brilliant court, encouraged a great tradition of **figure painting**, especially of court subjects. **Wang Wei** in the mid-eighth century was an early exponent of monochrome landscape painting, but the great flowering of **landscape painting** came with the Song dynasty. An imperial academy was set up, and different schools emerged which analysed the natural world with great concentration and intensity; their style has set a mark on Chinese landscape painting ever since. But the period's most famous work is *Qingming Shang He* by **Zhang Zeduan**, a lively, lengthy scroll showing riverside town life during a festival.

Under the Mongols, many officials found themselves unwanted or unwilling to serve the alien Yuan dynasty, and preferred to retire and paint. This produced the "literati" school, in which many painters harked back to the styles of the tenth century. One great master, **Ni Can**, also devoted himself, among many others, to the **ink paintings of bamboo** that became important at this time. In this school, of which many examples remain, the highest skills of techniques and composition were applied to the simplest of subjects, such as plum flowers. Both ink painting as well as more conventional media continued to be employed by painters during the next three or more centuries. The **Ming dynasty** saw a great interest in collecting the works of previous ages, and a willingness by painters to be influenced by tradition. There are plenty of examples of **bamboo and plum blossom**, and bird and flower paintings being brought to a high decorative pitch, as well as schools of landscape painting firmly rooted in traditional techniques. The arrival of the Manchu Qing dynasty did not disrupt the continuity of Chinese painting, but the art became open to many influences. It included the Italian **Castiglione** (Lang Shi-ning in Chinese) who specialized in horses, dogs and flowers; the **Four Wangs** who reinterpreted Song and Yuan styles in an orthodox manner; and individualists such as the **Eight Eccentrics of Yangzhou** and certain Buddhist monks who objected to derivative art and sought a more distinctive approach to subject and style.

CONTEMPORARY ART

Contemporary art is flourishing in China, though not much has yet filtered through to the Southwest; you might see exhibitions at **Nordica** in Kunming (see p.192) or Chengdu's **Bookworm** (see p.74). Chinese art is seen as hot by **investors**, and there's plenty of money sloshing around the industry – and so, inevitably, a good amount of generic works churned out for foreign markets, and copying of commercially successful styles.

However, the first crop of modern Chinese artists, who emerged in the 1990s, initially worked in obscurity. They banded together for survival in artists' villages, their work expressing individualism and an ironic, jaundiced view of contemporary China; this was, of course, the generation that had seen its dreams of change shot down at Tian'anmen Square (see p.376). Nurtured by curator **Li Xianting**, as well as sympathetic foreign collectors, they built the foundations of the art scene as it is today. The most famous of these so-called "cynical realists" is **Fang Lijun**, whose paintings of disembodied bald heads against desolate landscapes are now some of the most characteristic images of modern Chinese art. Look out too for **Yue Minjun**'s paintings of the Tian'anmen massacre that reference Goya, **Yang Shaobin**'s slickly painted sinister figures, and the bitingly satirical caricatures of **Wang Yinsong** and **Song Yonghong**.

Artists such as **Wang Guangyi** developed another school of distinctly Chinese contemporary art, "political pop". Here, a mocking twist is given to the iconography of the Cultural Revolution in order to critique a society that has become brashly commercial; Red Guards are shown waving iPods instead of Little Red Books and so on. Of late this has become rather a hackneyed genre, though every artist seems to go through a phase of it, and it's enthusiastically collected in the West.

Although it's hard to pick out trends amid such a ferment of activity, artists these days are (not surprisingly) preoccupied with documenting the destruction of the Chinese urban landscape and the gut-wrenching changes that have accompanied modernization. As spaces for viewing art have grown, artists have diversified into new media such as **performance and video**; exciting new faces to look out for include **Cui Xiuwen**, whose videos of women in a toilet at a karaoke bar are shocking and memorable, and **Xu Zhen**, whose video *Rainbow* shows his back turning red from unseen slaps. **Documentary photography** is also popular; among its finest exponents is **Yang Fudong**, notable for his wistful images of city life. **Wu Gaozhong** first drew attention for a performance piece in which he climbed into the belly of a slaughtered cow, but his recent work, involving giant props implanted with boar hair, is more subtle, and has a creepy beauty. And it's always worth looking out for a show curated by *enfant terrible* **Gu Zhenqing**, who has a reputation for gleefully pushing the limits.

Calligraphy

Calligraphy was crystallized into a high art form in China, where the use of the brush saw the development of handwriting of various styles, valued on a par with painting. Of the various different scripts, the **seal script** is the archaic form found on oracle bones; the **lishu** is the clerical style and was used in inscriptions on stone; the **kaishu** is the regular style closest to the modern printed form; and the cursive **caoshu** (grass script) is the most individual handwritten style. Emperors, poets and scholars over centuries have left examples of their calligraphy cut into stone at beauty spots, on mountains and in grottoes, tombs and temples all over China. At one stage during the Tang dynasty, calligraphy was so highly prized that it was the yardstick for the selection of high officials.

Music

Visitors to China could be forgiven for thinking that the only traditional style of music to compete with bland pop is that of the kitsch folk troupes to be heard in hotels and concert halls. But an earthy traditional music still abounds throughout the countryside; it can be heard at weddings, funerals, temple fairs and New Year celebrations – and even downtown in teahouses. A very different, edgier sound can be heard in certain smoky city bars – the new Chinese rock, with its energetic expressions of urban angst.

Traditional music

Han music is **heterophonic** – the musicians play differently decorated versions of a single melodic line. **Percussion** plays a major role, both in instrumental ensembles and as accompaniment to opera, narrative-singing, ritual music and dance.

Chinese **musical roots** date back millennia – archeological finds include a magnificent set of 65 bronze bells from the fifth century BC – and its forms can be directly traced to the Tang dynasty. Descendants of these early tunes survive in Lijiang's **Naxi Orchestra** in Yunnan, which plays Taoist court music current during the Song and Yuan dynasties.

But in the turbulent years after 1911, some intriguing **urban forms** sprang up from the meeting of East and West, such as the wonderfully sleazy **Cantonese music** of the 1920s and 1930s. As the movie industry developed, people in Shanghai, colonial Canton (Guangzhou) and nearby Hong Kong threw themselves into the craze for **Western-style dance halls**, fusing the local traditional music with jazz, and adding saxophone, violin and xylophone to Chinese instruments such as the **gaohu** (high-pitched fiddle) and the **yangqin** (dulcimer). Composers **Lü Wencheng** and **Qiu Hechou** (Yau Hokchau), the violinist **Yin Zizhong** (Yi Tzuchung), and **He Dasha** ("Thicko He"), guitarist and singer of clown roles in Cantonese opera, made many wonderful commercial 78s during this period. While these musicians kept their roots in Cantonese music, the more Westernized (and even more popular) compositions of **Li Jinhui** and his star singer **Zhou Xuan** subsequently earned severe disapproval from Maoist critics as decadent and pornographic.

"**Revolutionary music**", composed from the 1930s onwards, was generally march-like and optimistic, while in the wake of the Communist victory of 1949, the whole ethos of traditional music was challenged. Anything "feudal" or "superstitious" – which included a lot of traditional folk customs and music – was severely restricted, while Chinese melodies were "cleaned up" with the addition of rudimentary harmonies and bass lines. The Communist anthem "**The East is Red**", which began life as a folksong from the northern Shaanxi province (from where Mao's revolution also sprang), is symptomatic. Its local colour was ironed out as it was turned into a conventionally harmonized hymn-like tune. It was later adopted as the unofficial anthem of the Cultural Revolution, during which time musical life was driven underground, with only eight model operas and ballets permitted on stage.

The conservatoire style of **guoyue** (national music) was an artificial attempt to create a pan-Chinese style for the concert hall, with composed arrangements in a style akin to Western light music. There are still many conservatoire-style chamber groups – typically including **erhu** (fiddle), **dizi** (flute), **pipa** (lute) and **zheng** (zither) – playing evocatively titled pieces, some of which are newly composed. While the plaintive pieces for solo *erhu* by musicians such as **Liu Tianhua** and the blind beggar **Abing** (also a Daoist priest) have been much recorded by *guoyue* virtuosos, there is much more to Chinese music

than this. Folk music has a life of its own, and tends to follow the Confucian ideals of moderation and harmony, in which showy virtuosity is out of place.

The North: Blowers and Drummers

Classical traditions derived from the elite of imperial times live on today in **folk ensembles**, which are generally found in the north of the country, though you can see many of their instruments played at festivals everywhere. The most exciting examples are to be heard at **weddings and funerals**.

These occasions usually feature raucous **shawm** (a ubiquitous instrument in China, rather like a crude clarinet) and percussion groups called **chuigushou** – "blowers and drummers". While wedding bands naturally tend to use more jolly music, funerals may also feature lively pieces to entertain the guests. The "blowers and drummers" play not only lengthy and solemn suites but also the latest pop hits and theme tunes from TV and films. They milk the audience by sustaining notes, using circular breathing, playing even while dismantling and reassembling their shawms, or by balancing plates on sticks on the end of their instruments while playing.

Mentioned as far back as the tenth century BC, the **sheng** ranks among the oldest Chinese instruments. It comprises a group of bamboo pipes of different lengths bound in a circle and set in a wooden or metal base into which the player blows; similar gourd versions (called **lusheng**) are still used by Guizhou's **Dong and Miao** ethnic groups. Frequently played for ceremonial and festival music, it adds an incisive rhythmic bite. Long and deafening strings of **firecrackers** are another inescapable part of village ceremony.

The South: Silk and Bamboo

In southeast China, the best-known instrumental music is that of **sizhu** ("silk and bamboo") ensembles, using flutes (of bamboo) and plucked and bowed strings (until recently of silk). More mellifluous than the outdoor wind bands of the north, these provide perhaps the most accessible Chinese folk music.

The most famous of the many regional styles is that of **Shanghai**, where enthusiasts get together in the afternoons, sit round a table and take it in turns to play a set with Chinese fiddles, flutes and banjos. You can't help thinking of an Irish session, with Chinese tea replacing Guinness. The contrasting textures of plucked, bowed and blown sounds are part of the attraction of this music, each offering individual decorations to the gradually unfolding melody. Many pieces consist of successive decorations of a theme, beginning with the most ornate and accelerating as the decorations are gradually stripped down to a fast and bare final statement of the theme itself.

Although *sizhu* music is secular and recreational in its urban form, the instrumentation originated in ritual ensembles. In fact, amateur ritual associations exist all over southern China, as far afield as **Yunnan**, punctuating their ceremonies with sedate music reminiscent of the Shanghai teahouses, albeit often featuring the *yunluo* gong-frame of northern China.

THE TEMPLES

All over China, particularly on the great religious mountains, **temples** are not just historical monuments but living sites of worship. Morning and evening services are held daily, and larger rituals on special occasions. The priests mainly perform vocal liturgy accompanied by percussion. They intone sung hymns with long **melismas**, alternating with chanted sections accompanied by the relentless and hypnotic beat of the woodblock.

Melodic instrumental music tends to be added when priests perform rituals outside the temples. These styles are more earthy and accessible even to ears unaccustomed to Chinese music, featuring wonderfully mellifluous pieces for silk-and-bamboo instruments, gutsy blasts on the **shawm**, music for spectacularly long trumpets, and a whole battery of percussion.

Opera and other vocal music

Classical Chinese musical drama became popular with both the elite and common people from the Yuan dynasty onwards. Of the several hundred types of regional opera, **Beijing Opera**, a late hybrid form dating from the eighteenth century, is the most widely known – now heard throughout China, it's the closest thing to a "national" theatre. The rigorous training – and the heavy hand of ideology that saw it as the most important of "the people's arts" – is graphically displayed in Chen Kaige's film *Farewell My Concubine*. Many librettos now performed date back to the seventeenth century and describe the intrigues of emperors and gods, as well as love stories and comedy. **Sichuan opera** (see p.74) is remarkable for its female chorus, and its recently added stunts of fire breathing and rapid-face-changing. **Ritual masked opera** or *Nuo*, a blend of animist ceremony and episodes from the *Three Kingdoms* handed down from Ming times, are performed in the countryside of Yunnan, Anhui and Guizhou. Southern China also has beautiful ancient styles of opera: **Pingju** and **Huangmei Xi** are genteel in style, while **Cantonese opera** is funkier. If you're looking for more music and less acrobatics, try to seek out the classical but now rare **Kunqu**, often accompanied by the sweet-toned *qudi* flute. There are also some beautiful **shadow-puppet operas**, often performed for ritual events; you might catch a show in rural Sichuan where the tradition persists.

While Chinese opera makes a great visual spectacle, **musically** it is frankly an acquired taste, resembling to the uninitiated the din of cats fighting in a blazing firework factory. The **singing style** is tense, guttural and high-pitched, while the music is dominated by the bowed string accompaniment of the *jinghu*, a sort of sawn-off *erhu*. It also features plucked lutes, flutes and – for transitional points – a piercing shawm. The action is driven by **percussion**, with drum and clappers leading an ensemble of gongs and cymbals in an assortment of set patterns. Professional opera troupes exist in the major towns, but **rural opera performances**, which are given for temple fairs and even weddings, tend to be livelier. Even in cities you'll come across groups of old folk meeting in **parks**, often first thing in the morning or at dusk, to go through their favourite opera excerpts.

Narrative-singing also features long classical stories. You may find a teahouse full of old people following these story-songs avidly, particularly in Sichuan – try **Qingyang Temple** (see p.67) in Chengdu, where one popular style is accompanied by the *yangqin* (dulcimer). Elsewhere, amateurs sing through traditional *jingyun dagu* ballads, accompanied by drum and *sanxian* banjo; *pingtan*, also accompanied by a plucked lute, is a beautiful genre.

Chinese rock

Although often connected to the Hong Kong/Taiwanese entertainment industry, China's indigenous **rock** is a different beast, one which has its traditions in passionate and fiery protest, and which still possesses a cultural and political self-awareness. The rock scene was nonexistent in China until the mid-1980s, when foreign students on cultural exchange brought tapes of their favourite rock and pop music (and their own electric guitars) to the Chinese mainland, and shared them with their fellow students. Their music quickly caught the imagination of Chinese university youth and the urban vanguard.

Chinese protest-rock strangely has its roots with the Taiwanese pop singer **Teresa Teng** (known to the Chinese by her original name, Deng Lijun; 1953–95). Probably the most popular Chinese singer of her time, her recordings were circulated in China on the black market from the late 1970s onwards, when such music was officially banned. **Cui Jian**, a young, classically trained trumpet player with the Beijing Symphony Orchestra, was greatly influenced by her music, which he fused with Anglo-American protest rock in the mid-1980s. His love song "**Nothing To My Name**" became an anthem of the democracy movement, evoking a memorable complaint from General Wang Zhen, a veteran of the Long March: "What do you mean, you have nothing to your name? You've got the Communist Party, haven't you?"

Notable 1980s bands that followed in Cui Jian's wake include **Black Panther** (Hei Bao) and **Tang Dynasty**, though their long hair and leathers were perhaps more influential than their soft rock. They were followed by **Cobra**, China's first all-female rock band, folk-rocker **Zhang Chu**, bad boy **He Yong**, **Compass**, **Overload** and **Breathing**, among others. Unsigned, these bands would perform for very little money as part of vaudeville shows, until 1990, when China's first domestic full-scale **rock concert** took place. Six bands, including Tang Dynasty and Cobra, played at the Beijing Exhibition Centre Arena and were immediately signed by Japanese and Taiwanese labels, who then brought their music to the mainstream. They paved the way for **homegrown labels** such as Modern Sky, Scream, New Bees Records and Badhead, which now specialize in Chinese rock, hip-hop and alternative music.

The **rock scene** these days is healthy, with hundreds of bands orbiting the Beijing clubs – and often getting out to hip provincial capitals such as Chengdu, whose springtime **Zebra Music Festival** premiered in 2009.

For visitors, it's well worth exploring, and surprisingly accessible, as most bands sing at least half of their songs in English. Sex Pistols wannabes **Joyside** split in 2009 but live on in the rockumentary "Wasted Orient", but current acts to watch for include folk-punk showmen **Top Floor Circus**, long running ska punk outfit **Brain Failure** and Joy Divisionistas the **Retros**. For dance and electronica you can't beat **Queen Sea Big Shark**, while **Car Sick Cars** are the indie shoegazers to catch.

Stephen Jones & Joanna Lee,
with additional contributions from Simon Lewis

Books

Books specific to Southwest China are thin on the ground, but there's some excellent writing about the country as a whole, from republished travel classics to Western commentators' views on current economic and social upheavals, translated journalism and popular novels, and often eccentric expat memoirs. Classics aside, few of the titles below are available in China, so it's best to locate them before your trip; the publishers are listed throughout. Titles marked ★ are particularly recommended; o/p means "out of print".

CULTURE

Catherine Bourzat and Philippe Fatin *Undiscovered China* (Hachette, UK). Beautiful coffee-table work on the Miao and Dong peoples of Guizhou; intimate photos of villagers, festivals, markets, textiles and landscapes, with unusually in-depth text.

C.P. Fitzgerald *The Tower of Five Glories* (Caravan Press, China). Academic in tone but often a fascinating insight into the traditional lives of the Bai people, descendants of the Nanzhao Kingdom, who live around Dali in Yunnan.

Lin Yutang *My Country and My People* (Benediction Classics). An expatriate Chinese scholar writes for Western audiences in the 1930s about what it means to be Chinese. Dated in parts, but overall remarkably accessible.

Robert Temple *The Genius of China* (Andre Deutsch, UK; Inner Traditions, US). Derived from Joseph Needham's epic work *Science and Civilization in China*, this thoroughly illustrated compendium covers hundreds of important Chinese inventions through the ages – though the text overstates how little credit the West gives China's creative talent.

Alan Winnington *Slaves of the Cool Mountains* (Birlinn, UK). Following the founding of the People's Republic of China in 1949, Chinese re-education groups moved into the Sichuan–Yunnan border regions to dismantle the caste systems and religions of local Yi, Wa and Jingpo peoples. Winnington gives a surprisingly objective account of the original cultures, given that he was a journalist writing for the British Communist Party, and supported what the Chinese were doing.

HISTORY

Asiapac *Wu Zetian: The Mighty Woman Sovereign of China* (Asiapac Books, Singapore). Witty cartoon history of China's sole recognized empress, born in Sichuan, a controversial character who executed half the court and founded her own, short-lived, dynasty.

Edmund Candler *The Unveiling of Lhasa* (Earnshaw Books, China). China was not the first country to barge into Tibet: in 1903, the British marched on Lhasa, using modern machine guns against the peasant armies sent to stop them. Candler, a journalist embedded with the expedition, paints an ultimately disillusioned picture of the events, which were to open the country up to colonization.

Jung Chang *Wild Swans* (Perennial, UK; Touchstone, US). Set partly in Sichuan, this three-generation family saga was banned in China for its honest account of the horrors of life in turbulent twentieth-century China. A good read and an excellent introduction to modern Chinese history.

Patricia Buckley Ebrey *Cambridge Illustrated History of China* (Cambridge University Press, UK). Readable, profusely illustrated outline of China's development, from prehistory up to the 1990s.

Ann Paludan *Chronicle of the Chinese Emperors* (Thames & Hudson, UK). China's Dynastic history told through sketches of every one of its rulers – the great, the incompetent and the ugly – beginning with Qin Shi Huang and ending with Puyi.

Sima Qian *Records of the Historian* (Columbia University Press, US). An entertaining masterpiece of Chinese history up until the Han dynasty, focusing on characters as much as events: court jesters, the despotic first emperor of Qin, military strategist Sun Wu, and brave members of the public.

MODERN CHINA

Tim Clissold *Mr China* (Constable and Robinson, UK). The eye-opening story of how the author went to China to make a fortune and lost $400 million. A great first-person account of the eccentric Chinese business environment, and a must for anyone thinking of investing there.

Chen Guidi and **Wu Chuntao** *Will the Boat Sink the Water?* (Public Affairs, UK). Modern China was founded to improve the lot of its peasant majority, but the journalist authors show how – and how badly – the country's officials are failing them. Banned in China, it has since sold ten million copies on the black market.

Fuchsia Dunlop *Shark's Fin & Sichuan Pepper* (Ebury Press, UK; W.W. Norton, US). Beautifully written account of the author's love affair with Sichuanese food, leading her to spend three years honing her skills at a Chengdu cookery school. Slightly romantic, but also sharp and entertaining.

Peter Hessler *River Town: Three Years on the Yangzi* (John Murray, UK; Perennial, US). How the American author handled teaching English in a provincial industrial town outside Chongqing during the 1990s. Alternately naive and literary, it avoids cynicism when portraying China's social problems and contradictions.

Duncan Hewitt *Getting Rich First* (Chatto & Windus, UK). A foreign journalist with long involvement in China moves beyond the commonplace Western views – all dynastic history, Cultural Revolution and economic boom – with an informed look at the major social themes shaping the nation.

★ **Ma Jian** *Red Dust* (Vintage, UK; Anchor, US). Facing arrest for spiritual pollution in the 1980s, writer Ma Jian travelled to China's remotest corners – including Guizhou, Sichuan and Yunnan – often living in extreme poverty. This tale of China in the first phase of its opening up is told in lively prose and offers the kind of insights only an alienated insider could garner.

Matthew Polly *American Shaolin* (Abacus). A stereotypical weakling, Polly dropped out of a US college to spend two years studying kung fu at the legendary Shaolin Temple. Not just the vain macho romp you'd expect, the book is also self-deprecating and steers clear of cultural cringe.

Zhang Xinxin and **Sang Ye** *Chinese Profiles* (Panda, China). First published in national newspapers during the 1980s, these short interviews reveal the aspirations and lives of all manner of Chinese people, from hairdressers to military officials, street urchins and even a man who hunted tigers with his bare hands.

TRAVEL

Carl Crow *Long Road Back to China* (Earnshaw Books, China). After the Japanese invaded eastern China in World War II, the perilous Burma Road between Kunming and Rangoon became the country's lifeline with the rest of the world, and Crow wrote this melodramatic first-hand account of its dangers following a trip in 1939.

★ **Freeman and Ahmed** *The Tea Horse Road* (River Books, Bangkok). Gorgeous photography and engaging text, as the authors follow the ancient trade routes through Sichuan and Yunnan, and into Tibet. Resurrecting the roads and old villages along them is an emerging theme in Southwest China's tourist industry, and this book takes you straight to the paved trails and old marketplaces along the way.

★ **Peter Goullart** *Forgotten Kingdom* (Yunnan Publishing, China). Sent to Lijiang by chance during the 1930s, Peter Goullart found himself among the remnants of a people who had once ruled half of Yunnan. This is an affectionate, insightful portrait of his nine-year stay in what was then an idyllic, busy trading town, far removed from the conflicts afflicting the rest of the world – and unrecognizable from the tourist trap Lijiang has become today.

Alexander Hosie *Three Years in Western China* (Kessinger Publishing, US). A rare snapshot of Southwestern China in the 1880s, written by a British consular official whose work investigating the opium trade took him through Sichuan, Guizhou and Yunnan. There are great accounts of meeting Miao, Tibetans and Yi – even if laced with inevitable Victorian-era superiority – plus the rigours of descending Emei Shan.

Robert Logan Jack *Back Blocks of China* (o/p). A Scottish-Australian geologist's cross-country expedition in 1900, tackling the frightful Three Gorges, observing Sichuan's cormorant fishing, traders' guildhalls and spindly rope bridges, and making it through Yi territory to Lijiang and the Yunnan-Tibet border – all as the anti-foreigner Boxer Rebellion was breaking out. Exciting stuff.

★ **Ed Jocelyn and Andrew McEwen** *The Long March* (Constable). Two Westerners footstep Mao's Communist guerillas in 2004, following the route of their mammoth 1930s retreat through Guizhou, Guangxi and Sichuan. Explodes some of the myths surrounding the march, while doing nothing to lessen the achievement of those who completed the gruelling journey – and reveals much about life in the modern Chinese countryside.

Frank Kingdon-Ward *The Land of the Blue Poppy* (Merchant Books, UK). An entertaining account of the prolific Kingdon-Ward's first plant-hunting expedition, to the Sichuan-Yunnan-Tibet regions in 1911. Vivid descriptions of the journey, landscape and flowers – and Ward's innate ability to lose a trail – carry the story, even if he seems to have been unable to get on with locals.

William Mesny *Chinese Miscellany* (o/p). Incredible tale of how a young adventurer from the Channel Islands arrived in Shanghai in 1860, and spent the next fifty-nine years smuggling arms along the Yangzi, fighting in the Chinese army against the Miao, running an iron foundry, travelling to Guangxi, Vietnam and northwestern China for the government, and writing his memoirs. Originals are rare collectors' items but you can read extracts at ⓦ mesny.org.

André Migot *Tibetan Marches* (o/p). Deeply sympathetic portrait of western Sichuan's Kham Tibetan regions, based on the author's experiences while investigating Buddhism there in 1947 – barely three years before the Chinese annexation.

G. E. Morrison *An Australian in China* (o/p). In 1894, George Morrison – later famous as China correspondent for the *London Times* – set out to travel overland from Beijing to Burma. This informed, highly opinionated and vivid account of his journey is all the more extraordinary, given that Morrison spoke virtually no Chinese.

Marco Polo *The Travels* (Penguin, UK & US). Said to have inspired Columbus, *The Travels* is a fantastic read, full of amazing details picked up during Polo's 26 years of wandering in Asia between Venice and the court of Kublai

Khan. There's some juicy gossip about the customs of rural Yunnan too.

Joseph Rock *China on the Wild Side* (Caravan Press, China). Collected reprints of *National Geographic* articles by this Austrian-American botanist, anthropologist and explorer, who lived and roamed all over Southwest China from 1925 until 1949.

E. H. Wilson *A Naturalist in Western China* (o/p). Dry, factual but nonetheless engrossing account of the author's eleven-year search for new plants in the backblocks of Hubei, Sichuan, Yunnan and Tibet, right at the start of the twentieth century. Unlike Kingdon-Ward, Wilson was clearly cool, professional and had good rapport with his Chinese assistants.

GUIDES

★ **BBC** *Wild China* (BBC, UK). Bright and beautiful book and DVD of the TV series on China's extraordinary wildlife, much of it filmed in the Southwest. Will get you out into the mountains looking for pandas, golden monkeys and Temminck's tragopan.

★ **Fuchsia Dunlop** *Sichuan Cookery* (Penguin, UK; W.W. Norton, US). The best available English-language cookbook on Chinese cuisine, from this talented writer and experienced Chinese cook. Dishes smell, look and taste exactly as you find them in Sichuan.

★ **Hope Justman** *Guide to Hiking China's Old Road to Shu* (iUniverse, US). Informative manual for following one of

Southwest China's most intact historic trade routes, full of detailed maps, photos and useful background information.

John MacKinnon *A Field Guide to the Birds of China* (Oxford University Press, UK). By far the best book on the subject, with over 1300 species illustrated (mostly in colour), plus outline text descriptions and distribution maps.

Yukiyasu Osada *Mapping the Tibetan World* (Kotan, Japan). Much more than a detailed, practical guidebook, this is a great introduction to Tibetan history and culture. Covers not only Tibet and the Kham-Amdo regions of Sichuan, Yunnan and Qinghai provinces, but also Nepal and Sikkim.

LITERATURE

★ **Pearl S. Buck** *The Good Earth* (Simon & Schuster, UK; Washington Square Press, US). The best story from a writer who grew up in China during the early twentieth century, *The Good Earth* follows the fortunes of the peasant Wang Lung from his wedding day to his dotage, as he struggles to hold onto his land for his family through a series of political upheavals.

Louis Cha *The Book & the Sword* (Oxford, UK). Northwestern China becomes a battleground for secret societies, evil henchmen, Muslim warlords and sword-wielding Taoists as a quest to save a valuable copy of the Koran uncovers a secret that threatens to topple the Qing emperor. Written in the 1950s by China's foremost martial-arts novelist – and the most-read author in the Chinese world.

★ **James Hilton** *Lost Horizon* (Summersdale, UK; Pocket, US). The classic 1930s novel of longevity in a secret Tibetan valley, which gave the world – and the Chinese tourist industry – the myth of Shangri-La.

Jiang Rong *Wolf Totem* (Penguin, UK). Set in Mongolia during the 1960s, and contrasting the purity of a wild rural idyll with the corruption polluting mainstream Chinese society, you'll either love this tale's romantic imagery, or

loathe it for the same reason. A good illustration of how "primitive" ethnic groups are seen (and used) in modern China.

Lao She *Rickshaw Boy* (Foreign Languages Press). Lao She was driven to suicide during the Cultural Revolution for his belief that all politics were inherently unjust. The story is a haunting account of a young rickshaw-puller in pre-1949 Beijing.

Lu Xun *The True Story of Ah Q* (Foreign Languages Press). Widely read in China today, Lu Xun is regarded as the father of modern Chinese writing. *Ah Q* is one of his best tales, short, allegorical and ironic, about a simpleton who is swept up in the 1911 revolution.

Mian Mian *Candy* (Back Bay Books, USA). This trashy tale of self-destruction, drugs, sex and navel-gazing garnered its colourful Shanghai authoress a reputation as China's foremost literary wild child – it helped, of course, that it was banned.

Shen Congwen *Recollections of West Hunan* (Panda Books, China). The author, a Miao from the Hunan-Guizhou borders, writes about growing up in his native village during the early twentieth century. Steeped in local folklore, Shen's tales are tinged with a sadness reflecting his own life – he was persecuted by both the Nationalist and Communist governments.

Chris Taylor *Harvest Season* (Earnshaw Books, China). Loosely based on Taylor's experiences as a travel writer, *Harvest Season* depicts a group of dormant expats, living in an idyllic corner of rural Yunnan, who find their peace shattered by an aggressive newcomer determined to open the place up to mass tourism.

Robert Van Gulik *The Judge Dee Mysteries* (Perennial, UK; University of Chicago Press, US). Crime stories set in the Tang dynasty and starring the wily Judge Dee, who gets tough on criminals as detective, judge and jury. There are a lot of them; recommended are *The Chinese Bell Murders*, *Celebrated Cases of Judge Dee* and *The Chinese Nail Murders*. Fun, informative and unusual.

CLASSICS

⭐ **Li Bai and Du Fu** *Li Po & Tu Fu* (Penguin, UK & US). Fine translations of China's greatest Tang-dynasty poets, with a detailed introduction that puts them in context. Li Bai was a drunken spiritualist, Du Fu a sharp-eyed realist, and their surprisingly accessible and complementary works form an apex of Chinese literature.

⭐ **Luo Guanzhong** *Romance of the Three Kingdoms* (Foreign Languages Press). An electrifying retelling of the battles, political schemings and myths surrounding China's turbulent Three Kingdoms Period, much of it set in Sichuan. One of the world's great historical novels.

Pu Songling *Tales from a Chinese Studio* (Penguin, UK). Born during the early Qing dynasty, Pu Songling spent his life amassing these contemporary folk tales, which range from the almost believable to downright weird stories of spirits, ghosts and demons.

Shi Nai'an and **Luo Guanzhong** *Outlaws of the Marsh*, aka *The Water Margin* (Foreign Languages Press). A heavy dose of popular legend as a group of Robin Hood-like outlaws takes on the government in feudal times. Wildly uneven, and hard to read right through, but some amazing characters and set pieces.

⭐ **Wu Cheng'en** *Journey to the West* (Foreign Languages Press). Absurd, lively rendering of the Buddhist monk Xuanzang's pilgrimage to India to collect sacred scriptures, aided by Sandy, Pigsy and the irrepressible Sun Wu Kong, the monkey king. Arthur Waley's abridgement, *Monkey* (Penguin), retains the spirit of the tale while shortening the hundred-chapter opus to paperback length.

RELIGION AND PHILOSOPHY

Chuang Tzu *The Book of Chuang Tzu* (Penguin, UK & US). Wonderful Taoist parables, written in antiquity by a philosopher who clearly had a keen sense of humour and a delight in life's very inexplicability.

Confucius *Analects* (Penguin, UK & US). Good modern translation of this classic text, a collection of Confucius's teachings focusing on morality and the state.

Lao Zi *Tao Te Jing* (Penguin, UK & US). The collection of mystical thoughts and philosophical speculation that form the basis of Taoist philosophy.

Mao Zedong *Quotations from Chairman Mao Tse-Tung* (Foreign Languages Press). The famous "Little Red Book" of the 1960s, filled with catchy one-liners ("Political power grows out of the barrel of a gun") and numbingly pedantic homilies.

Sun Zi *The Art of War* (Penguin, UK; Running Press, US). "Lure them with the prospect of gain, then take them by confusion". This classic on strategy and warfare, told in pithy maxims, is as relevant today as when it was written around 500 BC. A favourite with the modern business community.

398 CONTEXTSLANGUAGE

Language

Used by over a billion people, China's national language, Mandarin, has more native speakers than English and Spanish combined. While Southwest China is also rife with heavy accents and regional dialects, Mandarin, the language of education, is the default everywhere – indeed, its Chinese name, putonghua, translates as "common language" – and a grasp of even the basics will massively enhance your trip. Be aware, however, that some Chinese peoples, such as Miao, Yi and Tibetans, speak their own entirely different languages, though you'd be very unlucky to wind up somewhere Mandarin isn't understood at all. Foreign languages – primarily English – are spoken to some extent by many students, and at upmarket hotels and places where Western tourists are common; elsewhere you'll need at least a phrasebook.

Speaking Mandarin

Despite Chinese being seen as difficult for Western students to learn, in many ways spoken Mandarin is relatively easy, as **grammatical rules** are straightforward: there are no plurals, no agreements, no declensions, no genders and no tenses. Instead, **context** and fairly rigid rules about **word order** are key, along with words such as "some", "many", "yesterday" or "tomorrow".

For English-speakers, Chinese word order follows the familiar subject-verb-object pattern, and you'll find that by simply stringing words together you'll be producing comprehensible basic Chinese. Just note that adjectives, as well as all qualifying and describing phrases, **precede nouns**.

Pinyin

Because Chinese characters have no inherent pronunciation (see p.401), it is impossible – even for a native speaker – to know how to pronounce a character they have never seen before. To get around this issue, in the 1950s the Chinese government devised the **pinyin** system, which uses the Roman alphabet (except the letter "v") to spell out the sounds of Mandarin Chinese, with Mandarin's four tones represented by **accents** above each syllable. Although pinyin has in no way replaced Chinese characters, it's now the standard way of transliterating Chinese in mainland China, and is used throughout this guide.

On the ground in China, you'll see unaccented pinyin spellings on street signs, which is useful for finding your way around cities, but otherwise only Chinese university students are likely to be familiar with the system – don't expect a taxi driver to be able to read it. Occasionally, you might encounter **archaic systems** of rendering Mandarin into Roman letters, such as Wade-Giles, which has no accents and writes Mao Zedong as Mao Tse-tung. Also note that **other dialects of Chinese** – such as Cantonese, or Zhuang in Guangxi – cannot be written in pinyin, and use their own system of transliteration.

Pronunciation

Pinyin letters do not all have the sounds you would expect, so make sure you spend an hour or two learning them. Bear in mind too that each syllable in pinyin represents a single Chinese character, and you need to pronounce each **syllable** separately: for example, women, (us, we), is pronounced "wo men" and not as in the English word "women". The only exception are dipthongs such as shuang (twin), which is pronounced "shuang" and not "shu ang".

The tones

There are **four tones** in Mandarin, and almost every syllable is characterized by one of them. While often seen as a major issue, actually pronouncing these tones is not difficult, as they are also used in English. The difference is that English uses tone for **effect** – emphasis, questioning, listing, rebuking - while in Mandarin, using a different tone changes the word's actual **meaning**, rather like vowels in English (think of saying "wall" instead of "well"). The wrong tone used with *ma*, for example, can turn "mother" into "horse" or "hemp".

Conversely, many Mandarin words – though written using completely different characters – have identical **pronunciation**. *Shi* pronounced with a falling tone can mean "is", "business", "market", "look" and many other things – one reason that context is so important in spoken Chinese.

Having said all this, don't get overly paranoid about your tones: with the help of context, intelligent listeners should be able to work out what you are trying to say. If you're just uttering a single word, however, for example a place name – without a context – you need to hit exactly the right tone, otherwise don't be surprised if nobody understands you.

First or "High" ā ē ī ō ū. In English this level tone is used when mimicking robotic or very boring, flat voices.

Second or "Rising" á é í ó ú. Used in English when asking a question showing surprise, for example "eh?"

Third or "Falling-rising" ǎ ě ǐ ǒ ǔ . Used in English when echoing someone's words with a measure of incredulity. For example, "John's dead." "De-ad?!"

Fourth or "Falling" à è ì ò ù. Often used in English when counting in a brusque manner – "One! Two! Three! Four!"

Toneless A few syllables do not have a tone accent. These are pronounced without emphasis, such as in the English **u**pon.

Note that if there are two consecutive characters with the third tone, the first character is pronounced as though it carries the second tone.

Consonants

Most **consonants** are pronounced in a similar way to their English equivalents, with the following exceptions:

c as in ha**ts**

g is hard as in **g**od (except when preceded by "n" when it sounds like sa**ng**)

h in Southwest China, an initial "h" can be either very guttural or pronounced more like "f"

n in Southwest China, an initial "n" is often pronounced somewhere between "n" and "l"

q as in **ch**eese

r as in g**rrrr**

x has no direct equivalent in English, but you can make the sound by sliding from an "s" sound to a "sh" sound and stopping midway between the two

z as in su**ds**

zh as in fud**ge**

Vowels and diphthongs

As in most languages, the **vowel sounds** are rather harder to quantify than the consonants. The examples here give a rough description of the sound of each vowel followed by related combination sounds.

a usually somewhere between f**a**r and m**a**n

ai as in **eye**

ao as in c**ow**

e usually as in f**ur**

TRAVELLERS' TIBETAN

Most rural **Tibetans** speak only their native tongue, with perhaps a smattering of Mandarin, so the following few phrases might be useful – and should at least get you a friendly smile – if you're planning to spend much time in the Tibetan regions of Yunnan and Sichuan.

Tibetan has no similarity at all to Mandarin; the language is not tonal and has its own alphabetic writing script containing thirty consonants and five vowels, which are placed either beside, above or below other letters when written down. There are many dialects across the region; the useful **Lhasa dialect** is used in the vocabulary below. Word order is back to front relative to English, and verbs are placed at the ends of sentences – "this noodle soup is delicious" becomes "tukpa dee shimbo doo", literally "noodle soup this delicious is". The only sound you are likely to have trouble with is "ng" at the beginning of words – it is pronounced as in "sa**ng**".

BASIC PHRASES

Hello	tashi delay	I'm going to …	nga … la drogee yin
Goodbye, to	kalay shu	Where is the …?	… kaba doo?
someone staying		Hospital	menkang
Goodbye, to	kalay pay	Monastery	gompa
someone going		Temple/chapel	lhakhang
Thank you	tuk too jay	Restaurant	sakang
Sorry	gonda	Is there … ?	… doo gay?
Please	coochee	Hot water	chu tsa-bo
How are you?	kusu debo yinbay? **or** kam	A candle	yangla
	sangbo dugay?	I don't have …	nga … mindoo
I'm …	nga …	Is this OK/ Can I do this?	deegee rebay?
Fine	debo yin	It's (not) OK	deegee (ma)ray
Cold	kya	(Not) Good	yaggo (min)doo
Hungry	throko-doe	This is delicious	dee shimbo doo
Thirsty	ka gom	Do you want … ?	kayrang …
Tired	galay ka		gobay?
I don't understand	nga ha ko ma-song	I want tea	nga cha go
What is your name?	kayranggi mingla karay ray?	I don't want this	dee me-go
My name is …	ngeye mingla… sa	What is this/that?	dee/day karray
Where are you from?	kayrang kanay ray?		ray?
I'm from …	nga … nay yin	When?	kadoo?
Britain	Injee	Now	danta
Australia	Otaleeya	Today	dering
America	Amerika	Yesterday	kezang
How old are you?	kayrang lo katsay ray?	Tomorrow	sangnyee
I'm …	nga lo … yin	How much is this?	gong kadso ray?
Where are you going?	kaba drogee yin?		

NUMBERS

1	chee	10	chew
2	nyee	11	chew chee
3	soom	12	chew nyee
4	zhee	20	nyee shoo
5	nga	21	nyee shoo chee **etc**
6	droo	100	gya
7	doon	200	nyee gya
8	gyay	1000	dong
9	goo		

ei as in g**ay**

en is an unstressed sound as at the end of hyph**en**

eng as in s**ung**

er as in f**ur** (ie with a stressed "r")

i usually as in t**ea**, except in *zi, ci, si, ri, zhi, chi* and *shi*, when it is a short clipped sound like the American military "s**ir**"

ia as in **ya**k

ian as in **yen**

ie as in **yeah**

o as in b**ore**

ou as in sh**ow**

ü as in the German **ü** (make an "ee" sound and glide slowly into an "oo"; at the mid-point between the two sounds you should hit the "ü"-sound)

u usually as in f**oo**l except where *u* follows *j, q, x* or *y*, when it is always pronounced **ü**

ua as in s**ua**ve

uai as in **why**

ue as though contracting "you" and "air" together, **you'air**

ui as in **way**

uo as in **wo**re

Chinese characters

There are tens of thousands of **Chinese characters**, though many are redundant and 2500 is enough to read a newspaper. While learning anything like this number is beyond the scope of a short stay, characters can be fun to memorize and with a bit of effort you may well pick up enough to get the gist of a menu.

Originating several thousand years ago as **pictograms**, each character represents a **concept** rather than a specific pronunciation, exactly like Arabic numerals in the West: for example, the symbol "2" means the same thing whether pronounced "two", "dos" or "tveir". This is how people speaking different Chinese dialects, which might sound mutually incomprehensible, can understand each other once things are written down. The downside is that, with no system of spelling apart from *pinyin* (see p.398), Chinese speakers have to **memorize** the exact sounds of every character they learn.

Although Chinese characters might seem impossibly complex, there is a logic behind their **structure**. They can very broadly be broken up into two **components**, which often also exist as characters in their own right: a **main** part, which frequently gives a clue as to the pronunciation; and a **radical**, which usually appears on the left side of the character and which vaguely categorizes the meaning. As an example, the character for "mother" (妈, mā) is made up of the character for "horse" (马, mǎ; note the similar sound), combined with the radical 女, which means "female". In some cases, the connection between the pictogram and its meaning is obvious – the character 木, "wood", resembles a tree – though others require some lateral thinking or have become so abstract or complex that the meaning is hidden.

In an attempt to increase levels of literacy, the Chinese government has **simplified** several thousand common characters since the 1950s, making them easier to learn and quicker to write. For example, the character for dragon is traditionally written 龍, which becomes 龙 in the simplified form. These simplified characters have been adopted in mainland China and Singapore; but Hong Kong and Taiwan continue to use the older, traditional forms. They have also made a recent comeback on business signs on the mainland, where they are seen as being both quaint and sophisticated.

Useful words and phrases

The Chinese terms in this book have been given both in **characters** and in **pinyin**; the pronunciation guide below is your first step to making yourself comprehensible.

LANGUAGE COURSES AND RESOURCES

The following **Mandarin language courses** come as textbook-plus-recordings packs. The emphasis is on learning spoken Chinese using pinyin; some also include introductions to Chinese characters.

Colloquial Chinese (Kan Qian; Routledge) Benchmark course whose several different packs can take you from absolute beginner through to technical level. Very thorough in teaching grammar but also straightforward and easy to use.

Teach Yourself Chinese (Elizabeth Scurfield; Teach Yourself) Similar to *Colloquial Chinese*, if perhaps a bit more lively; little to choose between the two.

Fun with Chinese Characters (Straits Times, Singapore). Brilliant series of picture books, which use cartoons and folktales to help memorize characters.

DICTIONARIES

Dorling Kindersley *Chinese–English Visual Bilingual Dictionary* Has useful, clear photos, though there are too many irrelevant spreads dealing with non-Chinese topics such as cream cakes, American football and garden tools.

Langenscheidt *Pocket Dictionary* Excellent portable dictionary for day-to-day or travel use, with enough colloquial and technical terms to be useful without becoming obscure.

APPS

There are a growing number of excellent Chinese **language apps** available – many free – handy for when you want to decipher a menu or a street sign.

Dian Hua A free Chinese dictionary where you can search using English, pinyin or characters. For a fee you can update it to include audio.

eStroke Useful for those who want to learn to write Chinese characters. This app has a huge dictionary of characters and will teach you the exact stroke order using animations.

iCED Another free and comprehensive dictionary; there's a pay-to-use version too, with more features.

Pleco A great dictionary that includes example sentences as well. The basic package is free (and more than enough for the short-term traveller).

Chinese put their **family names** first followed by their given names, the reverse of Western convention. The vast majority of Chinese family names comprise a single character, while given names are either one or two characters long. So a man known as Zhang Dawei has the family name of Zhang, and the given name of Dawei.

When asked for their name, the Chinese tend to provide either just their family name, or their whole name. In formal situations, you might come across the terms "Mr" (xiānsheng), "Mrs" (tàitai, though this is rarely used and married women often are known simply by their name) or "Miss" (xiǎojie or gūniang), which are attached after the family name: for example, Mr Zhang is zhāng xiānsheng. In more casual encounters, friends might use familiar terms such as "old" (lǎo) or "young" (xiǎo) attached in front of the family name, though "old" or "young" are more relative terms of status than indications of actual age in this case: Mr Zhang's friend might call him "lǎo zhāng", for instance.

BASICS

I	我	wǒ
You (singular)	你	nǐ
He	他	tā
She	她	tā
We	我们	wǒmén
You (plural)	你们	nǐmén
They	他们	tāmén
That	那个	nà ge
This	这个	zhè ge
I want...	我要	wǒ yào...

No, I don't want...	我不要 ...	wǒ bú yào...
Is it possible...?	可不可以...?	kěbùkěyǐ...?
It is (not) possible	(不)可以	(bú) kěyǐ
Is there any/Have you got any...?	有没有...?	yǒuméi yǒu...?
There is/I have	有	yǒu
There isn't/I haven't	没有	méiyǒu
Please help me	请帮我忙	qǐng bāng wǒ máng
Mr...	.....先生	xiānshēng
Mrs...	.....太太	tàitai
Miss...	.....小姐	xiǎojiě

COMMUNICATING

I don't speak Chinese	我不会说中文	wǒ bú huì shuō zhōngwén
My Chinese is terrible	我的中文很差	wǒ de zhōngwén hěn chà
Can you speak English?	你会说英语吗?	nǐ huì shuō yīngyǔ ma?
Can you get someone who speaks English?	请给我找一个会说英语的人	qǐng gěi wǒ zhǎo yí ge huì shuō yīngyǔ de rén?
Please speak slowly	请说得慢一点	qǐng shuōde màn yìdiǎn
Please say that again	请再说一遍	qǐng zài shuō yí biàn
I understand	我听得懂	wǒ tīngdedǒng
I don't understand	我听不懂	wǒ tīngbùdǒng
I can't read Chinese characters	我看不懂汉字	wǒ kànbùdǒng hànzì
What does this mean?	这是什么意思?	zhè shì shénme yìsi?
How do you pronounce this character?	这个字怎么念?	zhè ge zì zěnme niàn?

GREETINGS AND BASIC COURTESIES

Hello/How do you do?	你好?	nǐ hǎo?
How are you?	你好吗?	nǐ hǎo ma?
I'm fine	我很好	wǒ hěn hǎo
Thank you	谢谢	xièxie
Don't mention it/You're welcome	不客气	búkèqi
Sorry to bother you...	麻烦你	máfan nǐ
Sorry/I apologize	对不起	duìbùqǐ
It's not important/No problem	没关系	méi guānxi
Goodbye	再见	zài jiàn
Chitchat	聊天	liáotiān
What country are you from?	你是哪个国家的?	nǐ shì nǎ ge guójiā de?
Britain	英国	yīngguó
Ireland	爱尔兰	ài'ér lán
America	美国	měiguó
Canada	加拿大	jiā'nádà
Australia	澳大利亚	àodàlìyà
New Zealand	新西兰	xīnxīlán
China	中国	zhōngguó
Outside China	外国	wàiguó
What's your name?	你叫什么名字?	nǐ jiào shénme míngzi?
My name is...	我叫...	wǒ jiào...
Are you married?	你结婚了吗?	nǐ jiéhūn le ma?
I am married	我结婚了	wǒ jiéhūn le
I am not married	我没有结婚	wǒ méiyǒu jiéhūn
Have you got (children)?	你有没有（孩子?	nǐ yǒu méiyǒu (háizi)?
Do you like...?	你喜不喜欢...?	nǐ xǐ bùxǐhuān....?
I (don't) like...	我不喜欢...	wǒ (bù) xǐhuān...

What's your job?	你干什么工作?	nǐ gàn shénme gōngzuò?
I'm a foreign student	我是留学生	wǒ shì liúxuéshēng
I'm a teacher	我是老师	wǒ shì lǎoshī
I work in a company	我在一个公司工作	wǒ zài yí ge gōngsī gōngzuò
I don't work	我不工作	wǒ bù gōngzuò
Clean/dirty	干净/脏	gānjìng/zāng
Hot/cold	热/冷	rè/lěng
Fast/slow	快/慢	kuài/màn
Pretty	漂亮	piàoliàng
Interesting	有意思	yǒuyìsi
That's great	好极了	hǎo jí le
I (don't) like...	我(不)喜欢...	wǒ (bù) xǐhuān ...
Too...	太...了	tài ...le

NUMBERS

To state fractions such as ¥1.5, follow the pattern "one (yuan, or whatever you are measuring) five", 一元五, yī yuán wǔ.

Zero	零	líng
One	一	yī
Two	二/两	èr/liǎng*
Three	三	sān
Four	四	sì
Five	五	wǔ
Six	六	liù
Seven	七	qī
Eight	八	bā
Nine	九	jiǔ
Ten	十	shí
Eleven	十一	shíyī
Twelve	十二	shíèr
Twenty	二十	èrshí
Twenty-one	二十一	èrshí yī
One hundred	一百	yībǎi
Two hundred	二百	èrbǎi
One thousand	一千	yīqiān
Ten thousand	一万	yīwàn
One hundred thousand	十万	shíwàn
One million	一百万	yībǎiwàn

*liǎng is used when enumerating, for example "two people" liǎng ge rén. èr is used when counting.

TIME

Now	现在	xiànzài
Today	今天	jīntiān
(In the) morning	早上	zǎoshàng
(In the) afternoon	下午	xiàwǔ
(In the) evening	晚上	wǎnshàng
Tomorrow	明天	míngtiān
The day after tomorrow	后天	hòutiān
Yesterday	昨天	zuótiān
Week/month/year	星期/月/年	xīngqī/yuè/nián
Monday	星期一	xīngqī yī
Tuesday	星期二	xīngqī èr
Wednesday	星期三	xīngqī sān
Thursday	星期四	xīngqī sì
Friday	星期五	xīngqī wǔ

Saturday	星期六	xīngqī liù
Sunday	星期天	xīngqī tiān
What's the time?	几点了?	jǐdiǎn le?
10 o'clock	十点钟	shídiǎn zhōng
10.20	十点二十	shídiǎn èrshí
10.30	十点半	shídiǎn bàn

TRANSPORT

North	北	běi
South	南	nán
East	东	dōng
West	西	xī
CAAC	中国民航	zhōngguó mínháng
CITS	中国国际旅行社	zhōngguó guójì lǚxíngshè
Airport	机场	jīchǎng
Ferry dock	船码头	chuánmǎtóu
Train	火车	huǒchē
(Main) Train station	主要火车站	(zhǔyào) huǒchēzhàn
Bus	公共汽车	gōnggòng qìchē
Bus station	汽车站	qìchēzhàn
Long-distance bus station	长途汽车站	chángtú qìchē zhàn
Express train/bus	特快车	tèkuài chē
Fast train/bus	快车	kuài chē
Ordinary train/bus	普通车	pǔtōng chē
Minibus	小车	xiǎo chē
Sleeper bus	卧铺车	wòpù chē
Lower bunk	下铺	xiàpù
Middle bunk	中铺	zhōngpù
Upper bunk	上铺	shàngpù
Hard seat	硬座	yìngzuò
Soft seat	软座	ruǎnzuò
Hard sleeper	硬卧	yìngwò
Soft sleeper	软卧	ruǎnwò
Soft-seat waiting room	软卧候车室	ruǎnwò hòuchēshì
Timetable	时间表	shíjiān biǎo
Left-luggage office	寄存处	jìcún chù
Ticket office	售票处	shòupiào chù
Ticket	票	piào
Can you buy me a ticket to…?	可不可以给我买到 … …的票?	kěbùkěyǐ gěi wǒ mǎi dào… de piào?
I want to go to…	我想到… …去	wǒ xiǎng dào… qù
I want to leave at (8 o'clock)	我想(八点钟)离开	wǒ xiǎng (bā diǎn zhōng) líkāi
When does it leave?	什么时候出发?	shénme shíhòu chūfā?
When does it arrive?	什么时候到?	shénme shíhòu dào?
How long does it take?	路上得多长时间?	lùshàng děi duōcháng shíjiān?
Upgrade ticket	提高票等级	tígāo piào děngjí
Unreserved ticket	无座	wúzuò
Returned ticket window	退票窗口	tuìpiào chuāngkǒu
Platform	站台	zhàntái

GETTING ABOUT TOWN

Map	地图	dìtú
Where is…?	….在哪里?	…zài nǎlǐ?
Go straight on	往前走	wǎng qián zǒu

Turn right	往右拐	wǎng yòu guǎi
Turn left	往左拐	wǎng zuǒ guǎi
Taxi	出租车	chūzū chē
Please use the meter	请打表	qǐng dǎbiǎo
Underground/Subway station	地铁站	dìtiě zhàn
Bicycle	自行车	zìxíngchē
I want to rent a bicycle	我想租自行车	wǒ xiǎng zū zìxíngchē
How much is it per hour?	一个小时得多少钱?	yí gè xiǎoshí děi duōshǎo qián?
Bus	公共汽车	gōnggòngqìchē
Which bus goes to…?	几路车到…去?	jǐ lù chē dào…qù?
Number (10) bus	(十)路车	(shí) lù chē
Does this bus go to…?	这车到…去吗?	zhè chē dào…qù ma?
What time is the next bus?	下一班车几点开?	xià yì bān chē jǐ diǎn kāi?
The first bus	头班车	tóubān chē
The last bus	末班车	mòbān chē
Please tell me where to get off	请告诉我在哪里下车	qǐng gàosù wǒ zài nǎlǐ xià chē
Museum	博物馆	bówùguǎn
Temple	寺院	sìyuàn
Church	教堂	jiàotáng
Mosque	清真寺	qīngzhēn sì
Toilet (men's)	男厕所	nán cèsuǒ
Toilet (women's)	女厕所	nǚ cèsuǒ

ACCOMMODATION

Accommodation	住宿	zhùsù
Hotel	宾馆	bīnguǎn
Hotel (downmarket)	招待所，旅馆	zhāodàisuǒ, lǚguǎn
Hostel	旅社	lǚshè
Is it possible to stay here?	能不能住在这里?	néng bù néng zhù zài zhèlǐ?
Can I have a look at the room?	能不能看一下房间 ?	néng bù néng kàn yíxià fángjiān?
I want the cheapest bed you've got	我要你最便宜的床位	wǒ yào nǐ zuì piányi de chuángwèi
Single room	单人房	dānrénfáng
Twin room	双人房	shuāngrénfáng
Three-bed room	三人房	sānrénfáng
Dormitory	多人房	duōrénfáng
Suite	套房	tàofáng
(Large) bed	（大）床	(dà) chuáng
Passport	护照	hùzhào
Deposit	押金	yājīn
Key	钥匙	yàoshi
I want to change my room	我想换一个房间	wǒ xiǎng huàn yí ge fángjiān
Laundry (the action)	洗衣服	xǐyīfu
Laundry (the place)	洗衣店	xǐyīdiàn
Washing powder	洗衣粉	xǐyīfěn

SHOPPING, MONEY AND THE POLICE

How much is it?	这是多少钱?	zhè shì duōshǎo qián?
That's too expensive	太贵了	tài guì le
Have you got anything cheaper?	有没有便宜一点的?	yǒu méiyǒu piányi yìdiǎn de?
Department store	百货商店	bǎihuò shāngdiàn
Market	市场	shìchǎng
¥1 (RMB)	一块(人民币)	yí kuài (rénmínbì)

US$1	一块美金	yí kuài měijīn
£1	一块英镑	yí kuài yīngbàng
Change money	换钱	huàn qián
Bank of China	中国银行	zhōngguó yínháng
Travellers' cheques	旅行支票	lǚxíngzhīpiào
ATM	提款机	tíkuǎn jī
Credit card	信用卡	xìnyòng kǎ
PSB	公安局	gōng'ān jú

COMMUNICATIONS

Internet café	网吧	wǎngbā
Do you have internet?	有没有因特网?	yǒu méiyǒu yīntèwǎng?
Post office	邮电局	yóudiànjú
Envelope	信封	xìnfēng
Stamp	邮票	yóupiào
Airmail	航空信	hángkōngxìn
Surface mail	平信	píngxìn
Telephone	电话	diànhuà
Mobile phone	手机	shǒujī
Sim card	SIM卡	sim kǎ
Mobile top-up card	充值卡	chōngzhí kǎ
International telephone call	国际电话	guójí diànhuà
Reverse charges/collect call	对方付钱电话	duìfāngfùqián diànhuà
Fax	传真	chuánzhēn
Telephone card	电话卡	diànhuàkǎ
I want to make a telephone call to (Britain)	我想给(英国)打电话	wǒ xiǎng gěi (yīngguó) dǎ diànhuà

HEALTH

Hospital	医院	yīyuàn
Pharmacy	药店	yàodiàn
Doctor	医生	yīshēng
Medicine	药	yào
Chinese medicine	中药	zhōngyào
Diarrhoea	腹泻	fùxiè
Vomit	呕吐	ǒutù
Fever	发烧	fāshāo
I'm ill	我生病了	wǒ shēngbìng le
I've got flu	我感冒了	wǒ gānmào le
I'm (not) allergic to	我对…(不)过敏	wǒ duì…(bù) guòmǐn
Antibiotics	抗生素	kàngshēngsù
Condom	避孕套	bìyùntào
Mosquito coil	蚊香	wénxiāng
Mosquito netting	蚊帐	wénzhàng

A food and drink glossary

The following lists should help out in deciphering the characters on a **Chinese menu** – if they're written clearly. If you know what you're after, try sifting through the staples and cooking methods to create your order, or sample one of the everyday or regional suggestions, many of which are available all over the country. Don't forget to tailor your demands to the capabilities of where you're ordering, however – a street cook with a wok isn't going to be able to whip up anything more complicated than a basic stir-fry. Note that some items, such as seafood and *jiaozi*, are ordered by weight.

GENERAL

Restaurant	餐厅	cāntīng
Bar	酒吧	jiǔbā
House speciality	拿手好菜	náshǒuhaǒcài
How much is that?	多少钱?	duōshǎo qián?
I don't eat (meat)	我不吃(肉)	wǒ bù chi (ròu)
I'm Buddhist/I'm vegetarian	我是佛教徒/我只吃素	wǒ shì fójiàotú/wǒ zhǐ chī sù
I would like...	我想要	wǒ xiǎng yào...
Local dishes	地方菜	dìfāng cài
Snacks	小吃	xiǎochī
Menu/set menu/English menu	菜单/套餐/英文菜单	càidān/tàocān/yīngwén càidān
Small portion	少量	shǎoliàng
Chopsticks	筷子	kuàizi
Knife and fork	刀叉	dāochā
Spoon	勺子	sháozi
Waiter/waitress	服务员/小姐	fúwùyuán/xiǎojiě
Bill/cheque	买单	mǎidān
Cook these ingredients together	一块儿做	yíkuàir zuò
Not spicy/no chilli please	请不要辣椒	qǐng búyào làjiāo
Only a little spice/chilli	微辣	wēilà
500 grams	1斤	yī jīn
1 kilo	1公斤	yī gōngjīn

DRINKS

Beer	啤酒	píjiǔ
Sweet fizzy drink	汽水	qìshuǐ
Coffee	咖啡	kāfēi
Milk	牛奶	niúnǎi
(Mineral) water	(矿泉)水	(kuàngquán) shuǐ
Wine	葡萄酒	pútáojiǔ
Spirits	白酒	báijiǔ
Soya milk	豆浆	dòujiāng
Yoghurt	酸奶	suānnǎi
A bottle (of beer)	一瓶 (啤酒)	yī píng (píjiǔ)
A glass (of water)	一杯 (水)	yī bēi (shuǐ)

TEAS

Tea	茶	chá
Black tea	红茶	hóng chá
Chrysanthemum	菊花茶	júhuā chá
Green tea	绿茶	lǜchá
Iron Buddha	铁观音	tiěguānyīn
Jasmine	茉莉花茶	mòlìhuā chá
Pu'er	普洱茶	pǔ'ěr chá

STAPLE FOODS

Aubergine	茄子	qiézi
Bamboo shoots	笋尖	sǔnjiān
Bean sprouts	豆芽	dòuyá
Beans	豆	dòu
Beef	牛肉	niúròu
Bitter gourd	苦瓜	kǔguā
Black bean sauce	黑豆豉	hēidòuchǐ
Bread	面包	miànbāo

Buns (filled)	包子	bāozi
Buns (plain)	馒头	mántou
Carrot	胡萝卜	húluóbo
Cashew nuts	腰果	yāoguǒ
Cauliflower	菜花	càihuā
Chicken	鸡	jī
Chilli	辣椒	làjiāo
Chocolate	巧克力	qiǎokèlì
Coriander (leaves)	香菜	xiāngcài
Crab	蟹	xiè
Cucumber	黄瓜	huángguā
Duck	鸭	yā
Eel	鳝鱼	shànyú
Eggs (fried)	(煎)鸡蛋	(jiān)jīdàn
Fish	鱼	yú
Fried dough stick	油条	yóutiáo
Garlic	大蒜	dàsuàn
Ginger	姜	jiāng
Green pepper (capsicum)	青椒	qīngjiāo
Jiaozi (ravioli, steamed or boiled)	(意式，蒸，煮) 饺子	(yìshì, zhēng, zhǔ) jiǎozi
Lamb	羊肉	yángròu
Lotus root	莲藕	lián' ǒu
MSG	味精	wèijīng
Mushrooms	蘑菇	mógu
Noodles	面条	miàntiáo
Omelette	摊鸡蛋	tānjīdàn
Onions	洋葱	yángcōng
Oyster sauce	蚝油	háoyóu
Pancake	摊饼	tānbǐng
Peanut	花生	huāshēng
Pork	猪肉	zhūròu
Potato (stir-fried)	(炒)土豆	(chǎo) tǔdòu
Prawns	虾	xiā
Preserved egg	皮蛋	pídàn
Rice, boiled	白饭	báifàn
Rice, fried	炒饭	chǎofàn
Rice noodles	河粉	héfěn
Rice porridge (aka "congee")	粥	zhōu
Salt	盐	yán
Sesame oil	芝麻油	zhīma yóu
Sichuan pepper	四川花椒	sìchuān huājiāo
Snails	蜗牛	wōniú
Snake	蛇肉	shéròu
Soup	汤	tāng
Soy sauce	酱油	jiàngyóu
Squid	鱿鱼	yóuyú
Sugar	糖	táng
Tofu	豆腐	dòufu
Tomato	蕃茄	fānqié
Vinegar	醋	cù
Water chestnuts	马蹄	mǎtí
White radish	白萝卜	báiluóbo
Yam	山药	shānyào

COOKING METHODS

Boiled	煮	zhǔ
Casseroled	焙	bèi
(see also "Claypot")		
Deep-fried	油煎	yóujiān
Fried	炒	chǎo
Poached	白煮	báizhǔ
Red-cooked	红烧	hóngshāo
(stewed in soy sauce)		
Roast	烤	kǎo
Steamed	蒸	zhēng
Stir-fried	清炒	qīngchǎo

EVERYDAY DISHES

Braised duck with vegetables	炖鸭素菜	dùnyā sùcài
Cabbage rolls (stuffed with meat or vegetables)	菜卷儿（肉馅 或 菜馅）	càijuǎn'er (ròuxiàn huò càixiàn)
Chicken and sweetcorn soup	玉米鸡丝汤	yùmǐ jīsī tāng
Chicken with bamboo shoots and babycorn	笋尖嫩玉米炒鸡片	sǔnjiān nènyùmǐ chǎojīpiàn
Chicken with cashew nuts	腰果鸡片	yāoguǒ jīpiàn
Claypot/sandpot (casserole)	沙锅	shāguō
Crispy aromatic duck	香酥鸭	xiāngsūyā
Egg flower soup with tomato	蕃茄蛋汤	fānqié dàn tāng
Egg-fried rice	蛋炒饭	dànchǎofàn
Fish-ball soup with white radish	萝卜鱼蛋汤	luóbo yúdàn tāng
Fish casserole	焙鱼	bèiyú
Fried shredded pork with garlic and chilli	大蒜辣椒炒肉片	dàsuàn làjiāo chǎoròupiàn
Hotpot	火锅	huǒguō
Kebab	烤串肉	kào chuànròu
Noodle soup	汤面	tāngmiàn
Pork and mustard greens	芥末肉片	jièmò ròupiàn
Pork and water chestnut	马蹄猪肉	mǎtí zhūròu
Pork and white radish pie	白萝卜肉馅饼	báiluóbo ròuxiànbǐng
Prawn with garlic sauce	大蒜炒虾	dàsuàn chǎoxiā
"Pulled" noodles	拉面	lāmiàn
Roast duck	烤鸭	kǎoyā
Scrambled egg with pork on rice	滑蛋猪盖饭	huádàn zhūrougàifàn
Sliced pork with yellow bean sauce	黄豆肉片	huángdòu ròupiàn
Squid with green pepper and black beans	豆豉青椒炒鱿鱼	dòuchǐ qīngjiāo chǎoyóuyú
Steamed eel with black beans	豆豉蒸鳝	dòuchǐ zhēngshàn
Steamed rice packets wrapped in lotus leaves	荷叶蒸饭	héyè zhēngfàn
Stewed pork belly with vegetables	青菜烧肉	qīngcàishāoròu
Stir-fried chicken and bamboo shoots	笋尖炒鸡片	sǔnjiān chǎojīpiàn
Stuffed bean-curd soup	原爆瓤豆腐	yuánbào ràng dòufu
Stuffed bean curd with aubergine and green pepper	茄子青椒瓤豆腐	qiézi qīngjiāo ràng dòufu
Sweet-and-sour spareribs	糖醋排骨	tángcù páigǔ

Sweet bean paste pancakes	赤豆摊饼	chìdòu tānbǐng
White radish soup	白萝卜汤	báiluóbo tāng
Wonton soup	馄饨汤	húntun tāng

VEGETABLES AND EGGS

Aubergine with chilli and garlic sauce	大蒜辣椒炒茄子	dàsuàn làjiāo chǎoqiézi
Aubergine with sesame sauce	拌茄泥	bàn qiéní
Bean curd and spinach soup	菠菜豆腐汤	bōcài dòufu tāng
Bean-curd slivers	豆腐花	dòufuhuā
Bean curd with chestnuts	马蹄豆腐	mǎtí dòufu
Braised mountain fungus	炖香菇	dùnxiānggū
Egg fried with tomatoes	蕃茄炒蛋	fānqié chǎodàn
Fried bean curd with vegetables	豆腐素菜	dòufu sùcài
Fried bean sprouts	炒豆芽	chǎodòuyá
Monks' vegetarian dish (stir-fry of mixed vegetables and fungi)	罗汉斋	luóhànzhāi
Pressed bean curd with cabbage	卷心菜豆腐	juǎnxīncài dòufu
Spicy braised aubergine	家常茄子	jiācháng qiézi
Stir-fried bamboo shoots	炒冬笋	chǎodōngsǔn
Stir-fried mushrooms	炒鲜菇	chǎoxiān'gū
Vegetable soup	素菜汤	sùcài tāng

REGIONAL DISHES

NORTHERN

Beijing (Peking) duck	北京烤鸭	běijīng kǎoyā
Fried prawn balls	炒虾球	chǎoxiāqiú
Lion's head (pork rissoles casseroled with greens)	狮子头	shīzitóu
Mongolian hotpot	蒙古火锅	ménggǔ huǒguō
Red-cooked lamb	红烧羊肉	hóngshāo yángròu

EASTERN

Beggars' chicken (baked)	叫花鸡	jiàohuājī
Dongpo pork casserole (steamed in wine)	东坡肉	dōngpō ròu
Five flower pork (steamed in lotus leaves)	(荷叶蒸)五花肉	(héyè zhēng) wǔhuāròu
Soup dumplings (steamed, containing jellied stock)	汤包	tāngbāo
Steamed sea bass	清蒸鲈鱼	qīngzhēnglúyú
Stuffed green peppers	瓤青椒	ràng qīngjiāo
West Lake fish (braised in a sour sauce)	西湖醋鱼	xīhúcùyú
"White-cut" beef (spiced and steamed)	白切牛肉	báiqiē niúròu
Yangzhou fried rice	扬州炒饭	yángzhōu chǎofàn

SICHUAN AND WESTERN CHINA

Boiled beef slices (spicy)	水煮牛肉	shuǐzhǔ niúròu
Carry-pole noodles (with a chilli-vinegar-sesame sauce)	担担面	dàndànmiàn
Chaoshou (Sichuanese wonton)	抄手	chāoshǒu
Crackling rice with pork	锅巴肉片	guōbā ròupiàn

Crossing-the-bridge noodles	过桥面	guòqiáo miàn
Dry-fried green beans with garlic	干煸四季豆	gānbiān sìjìdòu
Dong'an chicken (poached in spicy sauce)	东安子鸡	dōng'ān zǐjī
Twice-cooked pork	回锅肉	huíguōròu
Dried yoghurt wafers	乳饼	rǔbǐng
Dry-fried pork shreds	油炸肉丝	yóuzhá ròusī
Fish-flavoured pork	鱼香肉丝	yúxiāng ròusī
Gongbao chicken (with chillies and peanuts)	宫保鸡丁	gōngbǎo jīdīng
Green pepper with spring onion and black bean sauce	豆豉青椒	dòuchǐ qīngjiāo
Hot and sour soup (flavoured with vinegar and white pepper)	酸辣汤	suānlà tāng
Hot-spiced bean curd	麻婆豆腐	mápó dòufu
Rice-flour balls, stuffed with sweet paste	汤圆	tāngyuán
Smoked duck	熏鸭	xūnyā
Strange flavoured chicken (with sesame-garlic-chilli)	怪味鸡	guàiwèijī
Stuffed aubergine slices	瓤茄子	ràng qiézi
Tangerine chicken	陈皮鸡	chēnpí jī
"Tiger-skin" peppers (pan-fried with salt)	虎皮尖椒	hǔpí jiānjiāo
Wind-cured ham	火腿	huǒtuǐ
Zhong dumplings	钟水饺	zhōng shuǐjiǎo

SOUTHERN CHINESE/CANTONESE

Casseroled bean curd stuffed with pork mince	瓤豆腐煲	ràng dòufu bǎo
Claypot rice with sweet sausage	香肠煲仔饭	xiāngcháng bāozǎi fàn
Crisp-skinned pork on rice	脆皮乳猪盖饭	cuìpí rǔzhū gàifàn
Fish-head casserole	砂锅鱼头	shāguō yútóu
Fish steamed with ginger and spring onion	清蒸鱼	qīngzhēngyú
Fried chicken with yam	芋头炒鸡片	yùtóu chǎojīpiàn
Honey-roast pork	叉烧	chāshāo
Kale in oyster sauce	蚝油生菜	háoyóu shēngcài
Lemon chicken	柠檬鸡	níngméngjī

DIM SUM

Dim sum	点心	diǎnxīn
Barbecued pork bun	叉烧包	chāshāo bāo
Crab and prawn dumpling	蟹肉虾饺	xièròu xiājiǎo
Fried taro and mince dumpling	芋头饺	yùtou jiāo
Lotus paste bun	莲蓉包	liánróngbāo
Moon cake (sweet bean paste in flaky pastry)	月饼	yuèbǐng
Pork and prawn dumpling	烧麦	shāomài
Prawn dumpling	虾饺	xiājiǎo
Spring roll	春卷	chūnjuǎn
Stuffed rice-flour roll	肠粉	chángfěn

Stuffed green peppers with black bean sauce	豆豉馅青椒	dòuchǐ xiànqīngjiāo
Sweet sesame balls	麻团	mátuān
Turnip-paste patty	萝卜糕	luóbo gāo

FRUIT

Fruit	水果	shuǐguǒ
Apple	苹果	píngguǒ
Banana	香蕉	xiāngjiāo
Durian	榴莲	liúlián
Grape	葡萄	pútáo
Honeydew melon	哈密瓜	hāmì guā
Longan	龙眼	lóngyǎn
Lychee	荔枝	lìzhī
Mandarin orange	橘子	júzi
Mango	芒果	mángguǒ
Orange	橙子	chéngzi
Peach	桃子	táozi
Pear	梨	lí
Persimmon	柿子	shìzi
Plum	李子	lǐzi
Pomegranate	石榴	shíliu
Pomelo	柚子	yòuzi
Watermelon	西瓜	xīguā

Glossary

Arhat Buddhist saint.

Baozi Steamed bun, usually filled with mincemeat.

Bei North.

Bodhisattva Buddhists who have attained enlightenment but remain in the world to help humanity.

Bon Tibet's original religion, fused with Buddhism to create Lamaism.

Buddhism Indian religion imported into China during the first century AD.

Butter tea A blend of tea leaves, salt, water and yak butter, churned into a thin soup and consumed in huge quantities in the Tibetan regions.

Chiang Kaishek Leader of China's Nationalist Guomindang (or Kuomintang) party from the 1920s. Beaten by Mao's forces, Chiang and the Guomindang fled to Taiwan in 1949.

Chorten See Stupa.

Confucius Moralist whose philosophy of hierarchies, descending from the emperor at the head of the country down to a household's daughter-in-law (at the bottom of everything), so perfectly encapsulated the Chinese psyche that he's still held in high regard, 2500 years after his death.

CITS China International Travel Service. Tourist organization primarily interested in selling tours, though they can help with obtaining train tickets.

CTS China Travel Service. Tourist organization similar to CITS.

Cultural Revolution Ten-year period beginning in 1966 and characterized by destruction, persecution and fanatical devotion to Mao (see p.374).

Dadao Avenue, boulevard, main road.

Dong East.

Duomu Taoist version of Guanyin.

Feng Peak.

Feng shui A system of geomancy used to determine the positioning of buildings.

Fire-baffle walls Large brick dividers between separate houses in joined buildings, designed to stop the spread of flames in the event of a fire. Often decoratively shaped into high curves above rooftops.

Ge Pavilion.

Gelugpa "Yellow-Hat Sect", the dominant strain of Lamaism in Western Sichuan.

Gompa Tibetan monastery.

Gong Palace; usually indicates a Taoist temple.

Guan Pass; in temple names, usually denotes a Taoist shrine.

Guanxi Literally "connections": the reciprocal favours inherent in the process of official appointments and transactions.

Guanyin The ubiquitous Buddhist Goddess of Mercy, the most popular Bodhisattva in China, who postponed her entry into paradise in order to help ease human misery. Derived from the Indian deity Avalokiteshvara, she is often depicted with up to a thousand arms.

Guan Yu, aka Guan Gong. Hero of the Three Kingdoms period, now the red-faced god of war and healing.

Gulou Drum tower; traditionally marking the centre of a town, this was where a drum was beaten at nightfall and in times of need.

Guomindang (GMD) The Nationalist People's Party. Under Chiang Kaishek, the GMD fought Communist forces for 25 years before being defeated and moving to Taiwan in 1949, where it remains a major political party.

Hai Chinese for "sea" but also the Mongolian term for lake, used widely in Southwest China.

Han Chinese The main body of the Chinese people, as distinct from other ethnic groups such as Miao, Hui, Yi or Tibetan.

He River.

Hu Lake.

Hui Ethnic Muslim. Visually they are often indistinguishable from Han Chinese.

Hutong A narrow alleyway.

Jiang River.

Jiaozi Crescent-shaped, ravioli-like dumplings, originally from northeastern China but now found country-wide; it's good luck to eat them at Chinese New Year. Served steamed, boiled or fried, with a variety of fillings, and ordered by the liang (50g).

Jie Street.

Kham Once a the eastern Tibetan region, now incorporated into the fringes of Sichuan, Yunnan, Gansu and Qinghai provinces. The Khampa people here are tough cowboy nomads, very different from Tibetans further west.

Lajiao Chilli pepper, occasionally known in Sichuan as *haijiao* or "overseas pepper".

Lamian "Pulled noodles", a Muslim speciality usually served in a spicy soup.

Legalism In the Chinese context, a belief that humans are intrinsically bad and that strict laws are need to rein in their behaviour.

Ling Tomb.

Little Red Book A selection of "Quotations from Chairman Mao Zedong", produced in 1966 as a philosophical treatise for Red Guards during the Cultural Revolution.

Liu Bei Ruler of the state of Shu (Sichuan) during the Three Kingdoms period; buried in Chengdu.

Long March The Communists' 9500km tactical retreat in

1934–35 from Guomindang troops.

Lu Road.

Luohan Buddhist saint.

Lusheng Bamboo and gourd woodwind instruments found in rural districts, especially in Guizhou's Miao and Dong villages.

Mao Zedong Head of the CCP and Chairman of China's first Communist government from 1949 until his death in 1976. A great guerilla leader, but his adherence to dogma saw millions die of starvation during the 1950s "Great Leap Forward", and the country thrown into destructive, anarchic violence during the Cultural Revolution of 1964–72.

Men Gate/door.

Miao Temple, usually Confucian.

Middle Kingdom A literal translation of the Chinese words for China.

Nan South.

PLA The People's Liberation Army, the official name of the Communist military.

Prayer wheels Cylindrical metal drums full of paper prayers which are "activated" when the drums are rotated; Tibetans believe they bring merit to the person turning them. They vary from pocket-sized, to be carried on pilgrimages, to the metre-high colonnades of drums flanking courtyards in Tibetan temples.

PSB Public Security Bureau, the branch of China's police force which deals directly with foreigners.

Pagoda Tower with distinctively tapering structure.

Pailou Ornamental stone memorial arch, usually commemorating people whose lives reflected the Confucian virtues of female chastity and parental respect.

Pinyin The official system of transliterating Chinese script into Roman characters.

Pu'er tea Famous dark tea from southern Yunnan, packed into compressed "bricks" and drunk mostly in Hong Kong and Tibet.

Puxian Buddhist incarnation of wisdom.

Qiao Bridge.

Qilin Mythical guardian animal looking like a cross between a dragon and a lion.

Qin Stringed musical instrument, played like a zither by plucking the strings.

RMB Renminbi. Another name for Chinese currency literally meaning "the people's money".

Red Guards The unruly factional forces unleashed by Mao during the Cultural Revolution to find and brutalize any "reactionaries" among the populace.

Red-Hat Sect The old Nyingma school of Tibetan Buddhism, largely replaced by the Gelugpa (see opposite).

Renmin The people.

Sakyamuni Name given to future incarnation of Buddha.

Shan Mountain.

Shi Market, city or municipality.

Shui Water.

Shuijiao Similar to *jiaozi* but boiled or served in a thin soup.

Si Temple, usually Buddhist.

Siheyuan Traditional courtyard house.

Spirit wall Wall behind the main gateway to a house or temple, designed to thwart evil spirits, which, it was believed, could move only in straight lines.

Stele Freestanding stone tablet carved with text.

Stupa Multi-tiered tower associated with Buddhist temples that usually contains sacred objects.

Sutra Buddhist texts, often illustrative doctrines arranged in prayer form.

Ta Tower or pagoda.

Taiping Uprising Peasant rebellion against Qing rule during the mid-nineteenth century, which saw over a million troops led by the Christian fanatic Hong Xiuquan establish a capital at Nanjing before their later annihilation at the hands of imperial forces.

Taoism Tao (or Dao), literally "The Way", is a philosophy of observing and following the natural order of things; attributed to the mythical Lao Zi, supposed author of the Taoist canon Tao Te Jing. It became organized as a religion only after Buddhism arrived in China, and has absorbed many local deities and folk beliefs.

Tea-Horse Road Old trade routes stretching from southern Yunnan, through Sichuan and into Tibet, along which tea, salt and horses were traded until recent times.

Three Kingdoms The period following the break-up of the Han dynasty, approximately 220–280 AD.

Tian Heaven or the sky.

Treaty port A port in which foreigners were permitted to set up residence, for the purpose of trade, under nineteenth-century agreements between China and foreign powers.

Waiguoren Foreigner.

Wenshu Buddhist incarnation of wisdom.

Xi West.

Yellow-Hat Sect See "Gelugpa".

Yamen Local government headquarters and courthouse in ancient China.

Yuan China's unit of currency. Also a courtyard or garden (and the name of the Mongol dynasty).

Zhang Fei Fierce Three Kingdoms hero, buried at Langzhong, Sichuan.

Zhan Station.

Zhong Middle; China is referred to as *zhongguo*, the Middle Kingdom.

Zhuge Liang Master strategist during the Three Kingdoms; Chengdu's Wuhou Ci is dedicated to him.

Index and small print

A ROUGH GUIDE TO ROUGH GUIDES

Published in 1982, the first Rough Guide – to Greece – was a student scheme that became a publishing phenomenon. Mark Ellingham, a recent graduate in English from Bristol University, had been travelling in Greece the previous summer and couldn't find the right guidebook. With a small group of friends he wrote his own guide, combining a highly contemporary, journalistic style with a thoroughly practical approach to travellers' needs.

The immediate success of the book spawned a series that rapidly covered dozens of destinations. And, in addition to impecunious backpackers, Rough Guides soon acquired a much broader readership that relished the guides' wit and inquisitiveness as much as their enthusiastic, critical approach and value-for-money ethos.

These days, Rough Guides include recommendations from budget to luxury and cover more than 200 destinations around the globe, as well as producing an ever-growing range of eBooks and apps.

Visit **roughguides.com** to see our latest publications.

Rough Guide credits

Editor: James Smart
Layout: Dan May
Cartography: Katie Lloyd-Jones and Ed Wright
Picture editor: Nicole Newman
Proofreaders: Karen Parker (English), Sandra He (Chinese)
Managing editors: Kathryn Lane and Keith Drew
Assistant editor: Dipika Dasgupta
Editorial assistant: Lorna North
Production: Rebecca Short
Cover design: Nicole Newman
Senior pre-press designer: Dan May

Marketing, Publicity & roughguides.com: Liz Statham
Design director: Scott Stickland
Travel publisher: Joanna Kirby
Digital travel publisher: Peter Buckley
Reference director: Andrew Lockett
Operations coordinator: Becky Doyle
Operations assistant: Johanna Wurm
Publishing director (Travel): Clare Currie
Commercial manager: Gino Magnotta
Managing director: John Duhigg

Publishing information

This first edition published January 2012 by
Rough Guides Ltd,
80 Strand, London WC2R 0RL
11, Community Centre, Panchsheel Park,
New Delhi 110017, India
Distributed by the Penguin Group
Penguin Books Ltd,
80 Strand, London WC2R 0RL
Penguin Group (USA)
375 Hudson Street, NY 10014, USA
Penguin Group (Australia)
250 Camberwell Road, Camberwell,
Victoria 3124, Australia
Penguin Group (NZ)
67 Apollo Drive, Mairangi Bay, Auckland 1310, New
Zealand
Rough Guides is represented in Canada by Tourmaline
Editions Inc. 662 King Street West, Suite 304, Toronto,
Ontario M5V 1M7
Printed in Singapore by Toppan Security Printing Pte. Ltd.

© David Leffman 2012
Maps © Rough Guides
No part of this book may be reproduced in any form
without permission from the publisher except for the
quotation of brief passages in reviews.
432pp includes index
A catalogue record for this book is available from the
British Library
ISBN: 978-1-84836-482-0
The publishers and authors have done their best to ensure
the accuracy and currency of all the information in **The
Rough Guide to Southwest China**, however, they can accept no responsibility for any loss, injury, or inconvenience
sustained by any traveller as a result of information or
advice contained in the guide.
11 12 13 14 8 7 6 5 4 3 2 1

Help us update

We've gone to a lot of effort to ensure that the first edition
of **The Rough Guide to Southwest China** is accurate and
up-to-date. However, things change – places get "discovered", opening hours are notoriously fickle, restaurants
and rooms raise prices or lower standards. If you feel we've
got it wrong or left something out, we'd like to know, and
if you can remember the address, the price, the hours, the
phone number, so much the better.

Please send your comments with the subject line
"**Rough Guide Southwest China Update**" to ✉mail
@uk.roughguides.com. We'll credit all contributions and
send a copy of the next edition (or any other Rough Guide
if you prefer) for the very best emails.
   Find more travel information, connect with fellow travellers and book your trip on ⓦroughguides.com

ABOUT THE AUTHOR

David Leffman first visited China in 1985 and seems to have spent most of his life since contributing to books on the place, struggling with Mandarin and getting beaten around by martial artists. If he had spare time he'd go scuba diving.

Acknowledgements

David Leffman For Narrell, with love. Immense thanks to the following for information, company, conversation and hand-to-hand combat: Kirsten Allen, Heather Bacon, Dr Sarah Bexell, Terry Bolger and Noi, Kim Dallas, Lobsang Dolma, Dwight, Kieran Fitzgerald, John Gardener, Peter Goff, Michelle Haynes, Chris Horton and Matthew, Jay, Mr Jiang, Joe and Jo, Hope Justman, Kevin, Emily King, Li Guirong, Li Laoshi, Jacob Lotinga, Faraz Maani, Daniel Mc-Crohan, Darren Novac, Corey Peatey, Catherine Platt, Rui Xi, Damien Ryan, Amanda Schmidt, Christine Shives, Xiao Shusheng, CS Tang, "Rainbow" Zhu. And not forgetting the two officials who gave us a lift back from Ningchang, the police who forced hotel staff to let us stay in Liupanshui,

and the driver of the black Audi who stopped at Ming Shan – thus preventing bloodshed. Also special thanks to Ed Wright and Katie Lloyd-Jones for great maps, Simon Lewis for his excellent Contexts text and my editor, James Smart, for knocking everything into shape.

The editor would also like to thank Dipika Dasgupta (late checks), Danielle Haughan (language advice), Kathryn Lane (guidance and liquorice), Dan May (moustachioed multi-tasking), Nicole Newman (smashing pics) and Lorna North (extra edits). Plus, of course, David Leffman – an all-round good egg.

Photo credits

All photos © Rough Guides except the following:
(Key: t-top; b-bottom; c-centre; l-left; r-right;)

p.1 National Geographic/Getty, Michael S. Yamashita
p.2 AWL, James Montgomery
p.4 Superstock , Tao Images
p.5 Victor Borg
p.9 Victor Borg (t); JTB Photo Superstock (b)
p.10 NaturePL, Grus Nigricollis
p.11 Victor Borg
p.12 Superstock
p.13 Getty, Jochen Schlenker (b); Alamy, dbimages (t)
p.14 Getty, James Balog (t); Superstock, Yoshio Tomii (c); Superstock, SEUX Paule (b)
p.15 Superstock (t); Victor Borg (l); Alamy, dbimages (r); Bjorn Svensson Photolibrary (b)
p.16 Photolibrary (t); Axiom, Eitan Simanor (c); Photolibrary (b)
p.17 Photolibrary, Dennis Cox (t); David Leffman (b)
p.18 Victor Borg (t); Superstock (c); Superstock (b)
p.19 Victor Borg (tl); Corbis, Frank Lukasseck (tr); Photolibrary, Thomas Boehm (b)
p.20 Photolibrary (l); Superstock (r)
p.22 Getty, Gallo Images
p.54 Superstock, Luong Quang-Tuan
p.57 Photolibrary, Bjorn Svensson
p.75 Victor Borg (t); Getty, Ed Freeman (b)
p.103 John Henshall Alamy (t); Cornelia Doerr Getty (b)
p.131 Getty, Jochen Schlenker (t); Getty (bl); Superstock (br)
p.142 Superstock, Tao Images
p.145 Alamy, John Henshall

p.161 Alamy, Robert Harding (t) ; Superstock, Christian Kober (b)
p.176 Superstock, Angelo Cavalli
p.179 Corbis, Keren Su
p.191 4Corners, Huber (t); Superstock (b)
p.203 SuperStock (bl); Getty, Redlink (br)
p.235 Superstock (t); Photolibrary (b)
p.245 Superstock
p.259 Superstock, Guiziou Franck (t); Corbis, Redlink (c); Getty, Guang Niu (b)
p.268 Corbis, Qiao Qiming
p.271 Getty, ChinaFotoPress
p.301 Corbis, Wu Dongjun (t); Alamy, Danita Delimont (bl); Bruno Morandi, SIME, 4Corners (br)
p.312 Corbis, Frans Lanting
p.315 Superstock
p.331 Superstock, Tao Images (t); AWL, Michele Falzone (b)
p.353 Corbis, XinHua
p.345 Superstock, Seux Paule (t); Corbis, Sheng Jiuyong (b)
p.362 Superstock, Christian Kober

Front cover Longsheng County, Guangxi © Corbis, Keren Su
Back cover Songzhanling Monastery, Zhongdian © AWL, Danita Delimont (t); Giant panda feeding, Qionglai mountains, Sichuan © SuperStock (bl); Xiaruoduojio mountain and horse, Yading Nature Reserve © Getty, Robert Harding (br)

Index

Maps are marked in **grey**.

Map symbols

The symbols below are used on maps throughout the book

✈	Airport	☪	Mosque	⊠	Gate		Building
★	Transport stop	⛩	Temple	⚶	Viewpoint		Market
Ⓐ	Bus station	⛩	Temple	⛰	Mountain range		Church
Ⓜ	Subway station	⛩	Pagoda	▲	Mountain peak		Stadium
✉	Post office	⊙	Statue	◓	Cave		Park
@	Internet access	♜	Fortress	♨	Hot spring	▬	Wall
Ⓒ	Telephone office	♦	Place of interest	⚮	Waterfall	― ―	Ferry
⊞	Hospital	⊤	Garden	●	Sinkhole	●–––●	Cable car
♛	Museum	🌳	Banyan tree				Monorail

Listings key

● Accommodation
● Restaurant/café
● Bar/club
● Shop

ROUGH GUIDES

WE GET AROUND

ONLINE start your journey at roughguides.com

EBOOKS & MOBILE APPS

GUIDEBOOKS from Amsterdam to Zanzibar

PHRASEBOOKS learn the lingo

MAPS so you don't get lost

GIFTBOOKS inspiration is our middle name

LIFESTYLE from iPads to climate change

...SO YOU CAN TOO

BOOKS | EBOOKS | APPS